The Economics of
Industrial Organization

Fifth Edition

The Economics of Industrial Organization

Fifth Edition

William G. Shepherd
University of Massachusetts

Joanna M. Shepherd
Emory University

WAVELAND

PRESS, INC.

Long Grove, Illinois

For information about this book, contact:
Waveland Press, Inc.
4180 IL Route 83, Suite 101
Long Grove, IL 60047-9580
(847) 634-0081
info@waveland.com
www.waveland.com

For Theo, in everything

Kim, in medicine

Ed, in medicine

Helen, in law

Tim, in law

Lorri, in marketing

Fred, in political science

George, in economics and law

CONTENTS

Preface x

PART 1: BASIC CONCEPTS 1

1 Basic Concepts and Debates 3
 I. Concepts and Trends 6
 II. Real-world Markets and Trends 10
 III. Competition's Nature and Paradoxes 16
 IV. The Field Evolves 18
 V. The Sequence of Topics 26

2 Theories of Competition and Monopoly 31
 I. Performance Values 31
 II. Competition and Performance 36
 III. Effects of Monopoly Power 39
 Appendix: Topics, Methods, and Sources
  for Student Research Papers 51

PART 2:   MARKET STRUCTURE 59

3 Market Definition, Market Imperfections, and Degrees of Competition 61

   I.   Defining the Market 62
   II.   Market Imperfections 68
   III.   The Elements of Market Structure 70
   IV.   Degrees and Concepts of Partial Competition 75
   V.   Degrees of Competition in Real Markets 83

PART 3:   PERFORMANCE 91

4 Market Power's Effects on Prices, Profits, and Efficiency 93

   I.   Effects on Prices and Profits 93
   II.   Effects on Efficiency 96

5 Innovation, Fairness, and Other Values 109

   I.   Innovation 109
   II.   Empirical Analysis of R & D and Innovation 116
   III.   Fairness 120
   IV.   Competition Itself: Benefits and Costs 123
   V.   Other Values 126

PART 4:   DETERMINANTS OF MARKET STRUCTURE 133

6 Capital Markets, Mergers, and Other Influences on Structure 135

   I.   Capital Markets 135
   II.   Mergers 139
   III.   Other Determinants of Structure 145

7 Economies and Diseconomies of Scale 151

   I.   Historical Shifts in Technology Trends 152
   II.   Basic Concepts 154
   III.   Plant-Level Economies and Diseconomies 157
   IV.   Multiplant Economies and Diseconomies 160
   V.   Methods of Research 161
   VI.   Empirical Findings 162

PART 5:   BEHAVIOR AND RELATED TOPICS 169

8 The Firm: Concepts and Conditions 171
   I.   Concepts of the Firm 171
   II. Motivation 177
   III. Real Firms 181

9 Monopoly, Dominance, and Entry 185
   I.   Leading Cases and Trends of Dominance 186
   II. Sources and Sustaining Factors of Monopoly
      and Dominance 187
   III. Models of Dominant Firms 188
   IV. Concepts of Entry and Limit Pricing 190
   V.   Firms' Choices in Light of Potential Entry 196
   VI. The Special Case of Ultrafree Entry
      (Contestability) 200

10 Price Discrimination and Predatory Actions 205
   I.   The Nature of Price Discrimination 206
   II. Price Discrimination's Effects 210
   III. "Predatory" Actions, Including Pricing 215
   IV   Cases of Price Discrimination 219

11 Tight Oligopoly: Theories and Real-world Patterns 225
   I.   Conflicting Incentives: Cooperation Versus
      Cheating 226
   II. Basic Theories of Interdependence 227
   III. Game Theory: Models of Noncollusive Duopoly 228
   IV. Tacit Collusion and Price Leadership 241
   V.   Conditions Favoring or Discouraging Collusion 243
   VI. Collusion in Real Markets 244
  VII. Types of Collusion 244

12 Vertical Conditions, Size and Diversification, and Advertising 253
   I.   Monopsony and Bilateral Monopoly 253
   II. Vertical Integration 255
   III. Vertical Market Power and Restrictions 257
   IV. The Effects of Bigness 260
   V.   Diversification 261
   VI. Product Differentiation, Especially Advertising 263

PART 6:   INDUSTRY CASE STUDIES 271

13 Case Studies of Dominant Firms: Microsoft, Newspapers, Baby Bells, Computers, Beer, Electricity, and Others 273

I.   Microsoft 274
II.   Newspapers in Local Markets 275
III.   Local Telephone-Service Markets (The Baby Bells) 278
IV.   Mainframe Computers (IBM) 281
V.   Beer (Anheuser-Busch) 283
VI.   Electricity 286
VII.   Capsule Studies 289

14 Case Studies of Tight Oligopolies: Passenger Aircraft, Airlines, Sports, Ready-to-Eat Cereals, and Trash Removal 295

I.   Passenger Aircraft (Boeing and Airbus) 295
II.   Airlines 298
III.   Sports 302
IV.   Breakfast Cereals 307
V.   Trash Removal 310

PART 7:   PUBLIC POLICIES TOWARD MONOPOLY 317

15 Antitrust Policies: Standards and Methods 319

I.   Origins and Standards of U.S. Antitrust and Regulation Policies 320
II.   U.S. Antitrust Policies: Forms and Coverage 330
III.   Antitrust in Other Countries 340

16 Antitrust Applied toward Dominance, Mergers, and Conduct 345

I.   Toward Existing Dominance: Section 2 Cases 345
II.   Toward Mergers 360
III.   Toward Price Fixing and Other Actions 364
IV.   Policy Imbalance? 368

17 Regulation, Deregulation, Public Enterprise, and Privatization 375

I.   Regulation of Natural Monopoly 376
II.   Partial Deregulation and Price Caps 387
III.   Full Deregulation 388
IV.   Public Enterprise 391
V.   The Privatization of Public Firms 393

18 Further Study 403

Name Index 405

Subject Index 413

PREFACE

The issues reach into the most important conditions of economic life. Who will control markets and gain riches? Is the playing field level or slanted? Is there open, effective, creative competition, or instead monopoly with its controls and exclusions?

These are deeply embedded human conditions, at the heart of economic striving and progress. They were decisive in primitive times, well before Pharaonic Egypt and classical Greece (note Aristotle's example in chapter 1), in all intervening cultures, and on down to the modern industrial era.

There is still great depth and human drama, even though it now often arises in impersonal, complex corporate settings. Under the cool concepts of market shares, innovation, and profit rates lie hot practical issues of power and human conflict.

These issues remain fractious partly because they involve the very largest commercial interests. Students are usually amazed and delighted with this big-league subject, where a gigantic IBM, General Motors, or Microsoft becomes just another big company, whose conditions and officials' assertions are to be assessed skeptically.

Moreover, the field itself has undergone strenuous and dramatic changes. Various post-1970 "new" schools have cropped up to challenge mainstream concepts, and after 1990 conflicts in real markets became even starker. In just one example, AT&T announced in 1995 and in 2001 that it would break itself up *again*, these times voluntarily! And yet an enormous flood of other mergers put together more large dominant firms, many seeking to diversify rather than have a single focus.

In dealing with clashing views and actions like these, readers need a balanced coverage of the topics and viewpoints. They must also learn, above all, to think independently in judging complex issues that do not have definitive research answers. Mastering the concepts and techniques—and unruly facts—is task 1; applying them skillfully to form independent judgments is the mature task 2.

This book lays out the core topics in their natural order, in a format tested over many years of teaching at the University of Michigan, the University of Massachusetts, Yale University, Williams College, Emory University, Georgia State University, and Clemson University. The coverage of the differing schools of thought has benefited from the senior author's serving during 1990–2001 as the General Editor of the *Review of Industrial Organization*, a professional research journal; that position required him to know all points of view and to deal fairly with authors on all sides.

The book's emphasis on independent judgment is one special feature; it is extended in chapter 2's appendix on student research papers. Another feature is the basic format, which presents the forms of competition and monopoly in chapters 1 through 3 and then moves immediately to monopoly's effects on performance in chapters 4 and 5. Still another special feature is the many compact case studies, grouped in chapters 13 and 14.

This edition is even more concise than the fourth edition, while enlarging the necessary technical detail. Policy coverage (of antitrust and regulation) has been enlarged, both in chapters 15 through 17 and in examples throughout the earlier chapters. As before, this book can be used in many course settings, from basic coverage in sophomore courses up to senior-level and graduate courses.

Teachers still have much choice in topic emphasis, order of subjects, and depth of detail. For example, chapters 6 and 8 can be covered early in the course to stress the role of capital markets and the enterprise. For a behavioralist emphasis, chapters 9 through 12 can be covered earlier and in more detail. The case study chapters (13 and 14) can even be assigned from the outset of the course to give students a practical focus from the start. As before, the sequence spotlights the structure-performance issue, letting the reader think carefully about the basic question of causation. The debates between the mainstream, the free-market school, and other points of view are posed squarely. The policy chapters also encourage the student to consider a variety of points of view.

In citing the literature, we have tried to include many landmark sources and cases that have shaped the ongoing debates. We have also tried to include some of the latest writings, even though their eventual roles are less sure.

Material that used to be in appendixes has been absorbed elsewhere or pruned out. The historical review is consolidated into chapter 1. Many of the review questions at the ends of the chapters have also been adjusted, and a separate Instructor's Manual discusses possible answers. The manual also provides a variety of assistance for teachers.

Now, a word to students: we always insist that the goal of education is to learn to think skillfully and maturely, but also **independently.** Every single issue in these pages is still open and debatable, even though some partisans may declare many to be closed. This openness applies even (or especially) for the most basic questions of causation and the nature of effective competition. The recent discord and debates among competing schools can be seen as healthy ferment, as long as you think for yourself in evaluating them.

We continue to benefit from the help of many people in the evolution of this book. First are many hundreds of students at the University of Michigan, the University of Massachusetts, Yale University, Williams College, Emory University, Georgia State University, and Clemson University.

Over the years, we have learned much from such gifted colleagues as James R. Nelson, Shorey Peterson, Henry W. de Jong, Harry M. Trebing, Richard E. Caves, Walter Adams, Donald J. Dewey, Leonard W. Weiss, William J. Adams, Alexander Cairncross, Kenneth D. Boyer, Donald F. Turner, William S. Comanor, Oliver E. Williamson, Takao Nakao, Alfred E. Kahn, George J. Stigler, Frederic M. Scherer, John S. Heywood, Eleanor M. Fox, and many others. We are also indebted to Don Rosso for excellent editing.

Our Shepherd spouses have provided wise and patient advice on many points. It may seem stereotypical to thank them, but that's what we need to do.

The gaps and limits in the book, despite all this help, are our responsibility. If readers will be kind enough to let us know where changes are most needed, we will endeavor to make the next edition more useful. Your advice has been helpful with earlier editions, and it will continue to be warmly received.

William G. Shepherd   Joanna Mehlhop Shepherd
Amherst, Massachusetts   Clemson, South Carolina

Part

1

Basic Concepts

Chapter

1

Basic Concepts and Debates

> Com-pe-ti-tion: . . . 1: the act or action of seeking to gain what another is seeking to gain at the same time and usually *under or as if under fair or equitable rules and circumstances:* a common struggle for the same object especially *among individuals of relatively equal standing* . . . 4b: a market condition in which *a large number of independent buyers and sellers* compete for identical commodities, deal freely with each other, and retain *the right of entry and exit from the market.* . . .
>
> —*Merriam-Webster Dictionary of the English Language*

This book is about **effective competition**: what it means, how to measure it and its effects, and how to promote it with good antitrust policies. The opposite of competition is **monopoly power**, and we describe that too, in detail. In most markets in the United States and elsewhere, competition is fully effective. The resulting struggles play out endlessly in gleaming skyscrapers from New York to London and other cities in the European Union, to Tokyo, the Pacific Rim, and Australia, on down to gritty factories and shops just about everywhere.

Competition drives market action as companies scramble to survive in the marketplace. Hopes, greed, creativity, hard work, cruelty, egotism—competition harnesses all these human emotions and others into struggles to produce and sell in the world's marketplaces. The results can be very positive indeed: efficient operations, a flow of innovations, fairness, and wider values of free choice and cultural health.

But things become difficult when one or several firms actually "win," by fair means or foul. When that happens, the winner holds much or most of the market, and it can reap excess profits by raising its prices, limiting consumers' choices, and even manipulating the entire market's nature. These payoffs can be huge; indeed, many famous family fortunes throughout history have come from them. Their size explains why every market is a tense arena filled with unending efforts by everyone to "win"—and get rich.

Monopoly power (or market power) is significant in perhaps a fifth of the U.S. economy and in important parts of other nations. We will meet many of these famous cases in these pages: Microsoft, Boeing Aircraft, IBM, General Motors before 1980, the old Standard Oil monopoly, most city newspapers, and many drug-industry monopolies (you can look ahead at tables 3.4, 3.6, and 3.7 to see others).

In many other markets, there is risk that a new monopolist will somehow "win," become dominant, and become entrenched enough to suppress further competition. And in all economies, new industries often emerge that are quickly monopolized at the start. Recent U.S. examples are the Internet sector (Microsoft in software, Intel in chips) and the health-care sector (many hospitals, some insurers). Encouraging competition is an unending challenge; would-be monopolists are always planning and taking actions to defeat the rest.

Competition is not only fascinating, it is ingrained in much of modern Western society. During the 1980s and 1990s, it became a reigning icon, particularly in the U.S. Free-market zealots worshipped competition as an overpowering process that gave magically perfect results. Whatever occurred in a "competitive" market was declared to be superb and immune to criticism. Even entrenched monopolists asserted that they faced severe competition.

But the magic had always been overstated, and doubts were strong even during competition's 1980–1999 golden era. The immense merger boom of the 1990s raised severe questions, and then the business scandals of Enron and others after 1999 poisoned the free-market ideology further. Free-market fundamentalism is well past its crest.[1]

Real competition has always been much more interesting than purists' extremes of perfect competition. Competition comes in many types and degrees, some weak, some strong. What's needed for a healthy market is robust **effective competition**, where competitors are numerous enough and reasonably well-matched. It results in "competitive balance" because nobody captures lasting control and gets entrenched in dominance. Effective, balanced competition delivers the innovation, efficiency, and fairness that make modern economies so powerful. It also delivers larger, non-economic values, such as freedom of choice, healthy democracy, and cultural variety.

But in some cases competition is unstable and degenerates into dominance. One or several firms subdue other competitors, take control, and inflict the various harms of monopoly.

Competition may be as familiar as water and air, but the word *competition* is often abused, bandied about like a bumper-sticker slogan.[2] The confusion is often worsened by companies that hold great monopoly power but flatly deny it.

Competition is a complicated process that plays out within distinct markets, and it comes in many types and degrees. It and monopoly are usually sophisticated conditions that are subject to change. There is no simple yes-no contrast.

Competition and monopoly are more than academic subjects that often baffle even the most astute experts and citizens. They are big-league topics, embodying the largest corporate interests with global impacts. With so many billions of dollars and millions of jobs at stake, the debates are hot and rugged. Language itself gets twisted into a weapon and used to blast opponents.

But the concepts themselves are neutral, and they apply to all markets and companies alike, from the biggest to the smallest. You will soon come to regard Microsoft, Intel, IBM, and Boeing as just ordinary companies among all the others operating in thousands of markets.

Amid all the controversy, some of the intellectual issues in this field of "industrial organization" are stark and divisive.[3] The mainstream research indicates (as we will see) that monopoly usually inflicts large economic harms. Yet some schools of theorists have argued the opposite: that monopoly is often—or even usually—a good thing.

Competition and monopoly are ancient, timeless, and universal issues with their roots deep in human history and human nature. From the earliest eras of tribal life, people have competed to survive. They have also sought to prevail over others by gaining control over parts of the economy. Wielding market power, the winners have captured the spoils of riches and power.

But the conditions are not just ancient; they occupy center stage right now. Leading U.S. examples include John D. Rockefeller's billions from the 1870s on, and William Gates's $50 billion and more from the Microsoft monopoly in the 1980s and 1990s. They and thousands of others with industrial wealth have defined and controlled much of American society. Often the winners have come to dominate even government and culture.

But much market power is prosaic and small. As an early example, Aristotle mentions an instance in 347 B.C.:

> There was a man of Sicily who, having money deposited with him, bought up all the iron from the iron mines; afterwards, when the merchants from the various markets came to buy, he was the only seller, and without much increasing the price he gained 200 percent.[4]

That kind of behavior has continued down the ages, nowadays often in billion-dollar, complicated corporate versions. From the earliest eras on to the endless future, competition and monopoly are timeless and immense topics.

This book is your map through the minefields of these heavy debates. Your task is to learn the ideas and to **think for yourself in judging them.**

Effective competition has three core elements. They ensure reasonable parity among numerous competitors, who subsequently are able to apply strong pressure on each other. That usually requires:

1. **At least 5 comparable competitors.** That is enough to prevent collusion to raise prices or control the market.

2. **No firm is dominant.** For true competitive balance, no one firm should have more than a 40 percent market share, and all five should have at least 10 percent each.

3. **Easy entry into the market.** That reinforces competitive pressure.[5] When these conditions aren't met, competition is usually **ineffective.**

We present not only the mainstream research since the 1890s but also other schools and views, including several that have emerged since 1970. "New IO theory" is now in fact a distinct, parallel field, exploring pure theoretical cases of two-firm game situations.

For more than a century, scholars have been developing and debating the field of industrial organization, which covers the core of modern capitalism. We will review that history later, in section 4 of this chapter, showing how ideas have changed and defenses of monopoly have come in waves.

The field of industrial organization, like other scientific fields, exists on two planes:

1. **Pure logic.** Concepts and analytical methods may clarify markets. These tools involve theory, with relatively few but powerful ideas.

2. **Facts and matters of degree.** Scholars assess the data about actual markets, which teem with the drama and follies of real, struggling firms. These matters of degree require mature judgments about complex magnitudes.

You need both an abstract ability to grasp logical concepts and mature skills in assessing complex matters of amounts and effects to fully understand industrial organization.

Not only are the patterns complicated, the stakes are often immense and affect society deeply. Leading American families such as the Astors, Vanderbilts, Rockefellers, Mellons, and Du Ponts drew much of their wealth from monopolies.[6] Monopoly also has harmed efficiency, even (or especially) in giant firms like General Motors and IBM.[7] Other cases of market power will be noted in these pages, along with other examples where effective competition has yielded gains.

This chapter presents the basic concepts of the field in section 1. Section 2 summarizes the real markets and trends of competition in the U.S. economy. Section 3 presents effective competition in more detail, and it considers why the Internet has not spread perfect competition everywhere, nor even very far at all. Section 4 reviews the history of the field and its schools. Section 5 explains the format of the book.

I.   CONCEPTS AND TRENDS

The core issues of competition and monopoly, in concise form, are the following:

1. All firms seek higher market shares in order to gain higher profits.

2. When these firms' struggles hold each other in check, effective competition exists. It yields low costs, low prices, rapid innovation, and various wider benefits.

3. If one or several firms come to dominate, competition is usually ineffective. Their market power causes higher prices and restricted output, and it imposes social costs: inefficiency, slower innovation, unfair shifts of income and wealth, reduced freedom of choice, and others.

4. These monopoly costs may be offset by large-scale economies or superior performance by the dominant firms.

1. THE DEGREE OF MONOPOLY

The **degree of monopoly** is critical. It is embodied in the demand for the firm's product, as illustrated for a simple case in figure 1.1. A highly **elastic** demand curve means that the firm has little scope for raising its price, as shown by curve 1; with even a small price rise, the firm will sell nothing at all. If demand is highly **inelastic**, as shown by curve 3, the firm can raise its price sharply and still sell large amounts. Its profit-maximizing price will be well above the competitive level.

Demand elasticity can be of any degree between infinity and zero, so the effectiveness of competition is a matter of degree, not either-or or yes-no. But elasticities are hard to measure, and in most situations they are simply unknown. Instead economists usually rely on indirect evidence, such as market shares, concentration, and barriers to entry.

2. STRUCTURE, BEHAVIOR, AND PERFORMANCE

Each market has three main categories of conditions that indicate competition and monopoly: the market's structure, behavior, and performance. They encompass most of the concepts and facts of the field, and each can vary with the degree of monopoly.

The Mainstream Hypothesis: Structure Generally Affects Performance.   As the field of industrial organization developed and matured in the decades from 1890 to 1970, mainstream scholars reflected theory, common sense, and business experience. They assumed that each market's structure influences how its firms behave and how efficient and innovative they are.

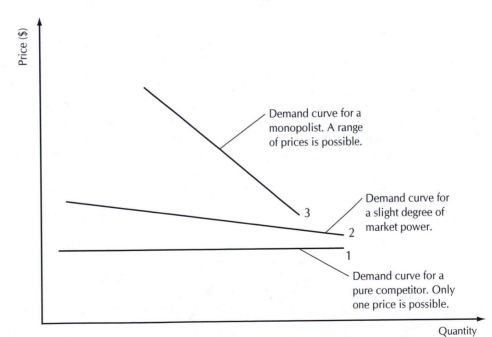

Figure 1.1   The monopolist's demand curve slopes down.

Industrial Organization   Public Policies

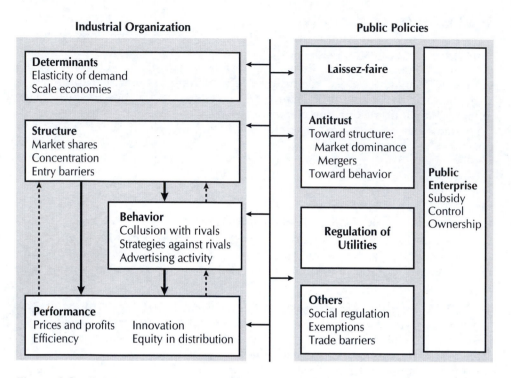

Figure 1.2 Policies act upon markets (but are also acted upon).

This main pattern of cause and effect is illustrated on the left side of figure 1.2. (The right side shows the main U.S. public policies that are used to prevent or control market power, which are summarized in chapters 15, 16, and 17.) Causation flows mainly downward, as illustrated by the thick arrows.

Suppose that the "structure" of a market involves a dominant firm with a 70-percent market share and high entry barriers. The "behavior" of the dominant firm might include higher prices, price discrimination, and tactics to intimidate smaller rivals. The resulting "performance" might involve raised prices, excess profits, inefficiency, and slower innovation.

If structure instead involves just three leading firms, they may compete strongly. Or instead they might collude with each other some or much of the time. A more concentrated structure therefore tends to encourage market power and its effects.

Of course, causation can run the other way, as free-market advocates have urged. This is illustrated by the dotted lines pointing up. For example, a firm may create fine new products so rapidly that it "wins" in the market. It raises its market share to 70 percent or 80 percent, and it reaps high profits. Its excellent performance will affect the market's future structure. Mainstream researchers have always recognized this alternative causation, but it requires splendid performance that is rarely found or sustained in real companies. So both logic and wide business experience have indicated that causation usually flows downward, in the mainstream direction.

Possible Determinants. Underlying this triad of conditions (structure, behavior, and performance) are some possible determinants that may shape structure. There are two main types: imperfections and economies of scale.

Any **market imperfections** reduce the chances that competition will be effective. The many types of imperfections are covered in chapter 3. They are a contentious topic; the mainstream has recognized since the 1880s that imperfections can be large, whereas free-market writers deny their importance.

Economies and diseconomies of scale may range in size from nil to large. At one extreme is "natural competition," in which the economies of scale are small, so that firms can be (or must be) small. Competition will be intense. At the other pole is "natural monopoly," with very large economies of scale. In markets in which technology causes large economies of scale (for instance, in electric power systems and water service), there may be room for only one firm, which will be a monopoly. Obviously economies of scale can shape structure. But whether they do, and in which directions, are factual questions, which chapter 7 will assess.

The mainstream premise regarding causation is often called *structuralist* because it regards structure as influential in many cases. But structuralists (who include a wide variety of scholars with a range of views) have regarded structure as only an influence, never as a tight determinant of performance. Firms are organizations of humans with much room for variety, historical change, and contrasting motives.

One Alternative: Free-Market Advocates. A self-consciously anti-structuralist view came to prominence during the 1970s, as we see in more detail in section 4. It is a radical mutation—in fact, the opposite—of the original Chicago School of the 1930s to 1950s, which thought monopoly to be a major threat.[8]

The new school reverses the direction of causation. Each firm's own relative efficiency is said to be the real determinant of its position in the market's structure and behavior. If monopoly exists, that firm must have been superior. Therefore, by assumption, monopoly conveys only benefits, not harms. To believe that, one must contend that: all markets have no significant imperfections; and capital markets in particular are close to perfect.

Another Alternative: Free Entry by Potential Competitors. In another variant point of view, entry from outside the market may be seen as so powerful and decisive that it renders the market's internal structure irrelevant. Scholars espousing this view are called free-entry or "contestability" economists (see section 4 and chapter 9).

A Third Alternative: New Industrial-Organization Theory. A third school called new-IO developed after 1970 and gave enormous attention to game theory, focusing on the abstract modelling of two-firm situations.

All three schools are summarized in section 4. Each school's views are valid as pure logic, and each may be relevant for at least one market. The main disputes concern amounts and facts: What share of actual markets really fits each of these competing theories? Are the theories useful or just fun for seminar chat? The answers cannot be deduced by pure logic, no matter how brilliant the theorist.

The resolution of this discord hinges on real conditions and evidence from real industries. Which way does causation mainly run? Which elements of structure are usually the most important? Later chapters will summarize the research results that bear on these questions.

Your own judgment will develop as you learn, and you may adopt any position among these alternatives. Your specific views are likely to change and mature as you continue studying. What matters most is the degree of skill with which you think and study.

3. THE MEANING OF STRUCTURE

Now consider structure. It is embodied in the **size distribution of firms**. Imagine that the extent of a market can be exactly defined (a key problem: see chapter 3), and that each firm's share of the market can be precisely measured. You array the firms in order of their market shares, as figure 1.3 illustrates.

Market Share.   As every business executive knows, the main feature of each firm's market position is its own market share. Firm 1, with a 50-percent share, is in a radically different market situation from firm 4 with 6 percent, firm 10 with 2 percent, and so on. Though they may be in the same market, all of the smaller firms are under more severe competitive stress than the dominant firm.

Concentration.   Concentration in the market is often indicated by summing up the shares of the largest four firms. Such concentration ratios help to describe the degree of horizontal market power held by the leading firms in the market.[9] The shares within any given four-firm concentration ratio range between roughly equal and sharply unequal.

Barriers to Entry.   At the outside edge of the market, there may be barriers to entry that keep out whatever potential competitors might be waiting outside the market. The height of the barriers may range from nil to extremely high. The higher the barrier, the larger a new firm needs to be in order to get firmly established. The group of most likely potential entrants poised outside the market may range anywhere from large and strong down to small and weak.

4. ALTERNATIVE SOURCES OF MONOPOLY

Monopoly and dominance may arise from good causes such as economies of scale and superior performance. Or they may come instead from neutral or anti-competitive causes, which exploit or even magnify market imperfections. Competitors may simply merge to capture more of the market. Or a firm may take strategic actions that prevent other firms from competing fairly.

From 1880 to 1970, researchers emphasized imperfections and anti-competitive causes. But after 1970, free-market and other theorists said that imperfections are insignificant and that only good causes are at work.

Assessing the various sources of monopoly, as they are reviewed in chapters 6 and 9 through 12, will be your challenge. That task tests the skills of every specialist in the field.

II. REAL-WORLD MARKETS AND TRENDS

These concepts are not mere theories. Their forms can be observed in real markets.

1. INDUSTRIES AND SECTORS

The economy's array of individual markets are divided into a number of major sectors, as suggested by figure 1.4. They are arranged in larger patterns of production and flows.

Farming and natural-resource industries feed their products mostly into manufacturing industries. In turn, manufactured products flow to still other industries or out through distribution sectors to final consumers. The utilities and construction sectors provide basic services such as electricity, transport, and communications. The Internet has since 1990 vastly increased the scope of communications.

Labor markets absorb the great variety of workers' skills and efforts into firms. Service markets cover a wide range of activities, from serving hamburgers to providing health care or a college education. Over all of these industries are the financial sectors, which provide funds, monitor activity, and exert control.

Services now provide over half the economy, while manufacturing has dwindled to only about one-fourth of economic activity. Yet many cases of market power continue to occur in manufacturing industries, from computers and newspapers to film and cereals. Others are in former utilities, including various communications markets.

For further perspective, consider the following major industries: steel, automobiles, publishing (newspapers, books, and magazines), computers, communications, banking, airlines, broadcasting, motion pictures, and sports (amusement

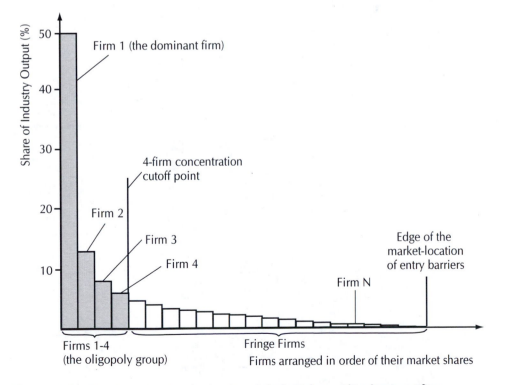

Figure 1.3   The firm-size distribution in a typical market with a dominant firm.

and recreation services). These industries are very prominent, and they will be discussed frequently throughout this book. Yet their total contribution to the gross national product (GNP) is only about 6 percent.

In short, the economy contains a vast array of ordinary industries that draw little attention because they function reasonably well under effective competition. Those with market power are important, but only a small fraction of the total economy.

2. LEADING FIRMS

It is natural to focus attention on larger, leading firms, such as the U.S. corporations in the annual Largest 500 listings. Review them carefully to develop a sense of the names and industries that matter. Many are familiar to readers from personal use of their products. Others are important in U.S. industrial history, or they simply bulk large in the economy.

Some of these firms have substantial market power, some have only a little or none at all. Study large-firm lists carefully from the start, refer to them as you proceed, and scout out stories about these firms in the business press.[10] This approach will help you to grasp the ideas and their uses more readily.

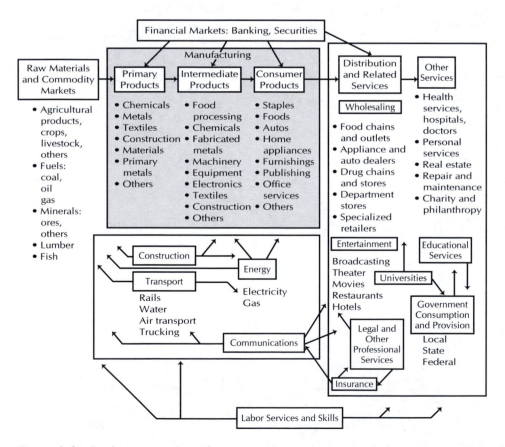

Figure I.4   A schematic outline of sectors in the modern economy.

3. CATEGORIES OF MARKETS

Each sector contains many industries, and each industry usually embraces many individual markets, as defined in two dimensions: by **their specific product types** and **their geographical areas** (chapter 3 explains how to define actual markets). Each of these thousands of U.S. markets has its own structure, behavior, and performance, ranging from pure competition to pure monopoly, with infinite gradations and variations in between.

The research field has defined four main categories of markets, which embody the various degrees of competition and monopoly. They are summarized in table 1.1, with recent examples of each kind. These categories are useful for concepts, but actual markets exist along a continuum, of course, and so they often do not fit neatly into these boxes.

Pure monopoly is one extreme; just one firm (local electricity and local water service, for example) has a 100-percent market share, usually with inelastic demand and high entry barriers. The next category is the **dominant firm** type, where one firm has at least 40 percent of the market and no close rival (Kodak and Campbell Soup are instances). That category shades into **tight oligopoly**, in which the leading four firms have a combined market share of over 60 percent. They, too, enjoy some inelasticity of demand, and are often able to cooperate in setting prices.

Market power is usually large in these three types, and competition will commonly be ineffective, resulting in the various costs of monopoly. The remaining varieties all have effective competition. **Loose oligopoly** occurs with many firms, a combined four-firm share below 40 percent, easy entry, and little real chance to hold prices high by means of price fixing. Each firm's relatively elastic demand

Table 1.1 The Main Types of Markets, from Pure Monopoly to Effective Competition

Market Type	Familiar Examples
Pure Monopoly One firm has 100 percent	Patented goods (e.g., pharmaceuticals), local electric supply, water, transit
Dominant Firm One firm has over 40 percent	Microsoft, many newspapers, Gatorade, Campbell Soup, Yellow Pages, Baby Bells, Anheuser-Busch, Boeing, De Beers, Gerber, Frito-Lay, Hallmark Greetings
Tight Oligopoly Four firms hold over 60 percent	Nike and Adidas, cigarettes, ready-to-eat cereals, Coca-Cola and Pepsi, video games, Boeing and Airbus, jet aircraft engines, disposable diapers, FedEx and UPS, toys, garbage disposal
Effective Competition Four firms hold less than 40 percent. Entry is free. (includes Loose Oligopoly, Monopolistic Competition, and Perfect Competition)	Everything else; over 70 percent of the U.S. economy

tempts it to cut prices, so prices are pressed down close to the level of cost. Moving further down in the degree of monopoly, many competitors, each with a slight degree of market power, results in **monopolistic competition**. Then comes the extreme case of **pure competition** with scores or hundreds of competitors, none of which influences the market at all.

4.   THE EXTENT AND TREND OF COMPETITION

These market categories help to estimate the relative extent of competition and monopoly in the U.S. economy. The larger picture is shown in figure 1.5, covering the U.S. economy since 1940. There are three main lessons to be drawn, as follows:

1. **Variation.**   The degree of competition varies widely among markets, from about 2 percent of national income in pure monopolies to the roughly 75 percent in effectively competitive markets.

2. **Competition Generally Prevails.**   The U.S. economy has become pre-dominantly competitive. Since the 1980s, only about 25 to 30 percent of total production has been in the ineffective-competition categories.

3. **Rise in Competition.**   Competition rose slowly from 1940 to 1960, but then it climbed sharply between 1960 and 1980. The rise occurred in scores of markets, including automobiles, steel, cameras, aircraft, banking, telephones, legal services, and even professional sports. After 1980 utilities continued shifting toward competition, but other sectors probably saw rises in market power.

By coincidence, free-market views became more influential in the 1970s just as competition in many real markets was already rising. The 1980s were an era of ideological worship of competition, with claims that monopoly had become rare and weak. The 1990s brought even more iconic worship of competition, invoking it to legitimize every result of competitive markets, no matter how bad. But major new problems arose in many markets, including electricity, telecommunications, accounting, and finance, and 1992–1999 brought the wild merger boom. All this forced more realism about market deviances.

Yet since 1990 the Internet has developed and spread. Along with its role in the stock-market bubble, it stimulated the euphoric idea that the Internet might automatically create perfect competition throughout the economy. In particular, the Internet was hypothesized to have a profound pro-competitive effect on market structure in most or all markets and sectors. The Internet is a vast system of instant access to information. Therefore it may allow even the smallest, newest firms to immediately enter into markets and then to compete head-on with even the most deeply entrenched dominant firms.

It is true that the Internet may increase price competition by lowering the costs of distribution. Often Internet retailers do not have any physical store or an inventory of the products they sell. As was frequently boasted during 1998–2000, clicks might wholly supersede bricks. Eliminating these distribution costs could allow Internet retailers to charge lower prices for their products.

Also, the Internet can lower consumers' search costs by making it easier to locate and compare products. Before the Internet existed, consumers often would buy the most conveniently located product to decrease the large costs of searching for cheaper products. You probably experience this in supermarket shopping: Why shop around for the cheapest loaf of bread or gallon of milk when you can buy them all at one easy location?

In contrast, consumers can use the Internet to roam widely and instantly. They can quickly compare the prices of similar products from different retailers and buy the cheapest product. Because retailers know that Internet consumers are more sensitive to price, they are likely to keep their prices down close to the level of their competitors' prices, which can intensify price competition down to the penny.

Yet there are many obstacles to competition that the Internet cannot overcome. First, the dominant firm in retail stores is also likely to be the dominant firm on the Internet. When consumers search for products, they naturally search the Web sites of familiar companies. Often, the companies are familiar because they are the dominant retail supplier of the product.

Furthermore, even though some consumers may shift from shopping at the major seller's physical retail stores to shopping at the major sellers' Web site, many other consumers may shift instead from shopping at small sellers' physical retail stores to shopping at the major seller's Web site. In this way, the Internet may actually strengthen the market position of the dominant firm.

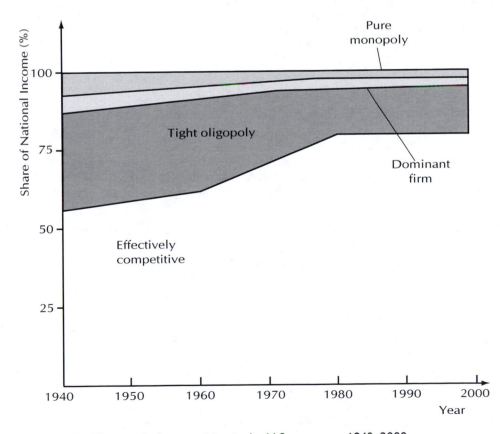

Figure 1.5   The trend of competition in the U.S. economy, 1940–2000.

Also, for many products, Internet shopping is not a good substitute for retail shopping. Consumers will probably never view on-line grocery shopping as a substitute for feeling the produce at the local grocery store. Similarly, many consumers will never be happy buying clothing without trying on selections. On top of that, getting the physical products to customers (by mail, delivery vans, etc.) can create big problems and costs. Altogether, in many industries the Internet will probably have little impact on the market structure.

So it seems that the Internet will probably increase price competition in some markets. But the Internet should not be expected to reduce very much dominance, nor spread perfect competition widely.

III. COMPETITION'S NATURE AND PARADOXES

1. UNITY AMONG MODELS OF COMPETITION

Whatever the specific conditions may be, the essence of competition is always the same: the mutual exertion of pressure to perform well. Even when models of competition seem to differ sharply, they share this meaning.

Two centuries ago, Adam Smith noted in *The Wealth of Nations* that competition spurs efficiency by preventing complacency and that competitors are always tempted to collude: "People of the same trade seldom gather together, whether for merriment or diversion, but the conversation ends in a conspiracy against the public or some contrivance to raise prices." For a century after Smith, classical economists argued against monopoly and state controls.

The Neoclassical Equilibrium Model. As neoclassical analysis developed after 1870, economists began to carry the concept of competition to an extreme in order to derive precise abstract conclusions about efficiency (see chapter 2).[11] Perfect competition was eventually defined as an extreme caricature to require numberless competitors, each with its horizontal demand curve. Their choices yielded an equilibrium state of strictly efficient allocation. It was a pure theoretical state, not a real interactive process.

A Realistic Process of Rivalry. This pure, abstract model gave precise results, but economists and business managers rightly pointed out that it was extreme. The mainstream concept of competition is quite robust even when there are large departures from perfect conditions.

Markets with relatively few rivals can sometimes be intensely competitive in a dynamic process of struggle over time. Schumpeter's process of "creative destruction" was the most colorful of these images of rivalry (see chapter 2), but they all suggested that the pure neoclassical model of atomistic competition was too extreme.[12]

In fact, all versions of competition share a basic unity: competition applies mutual pressure and prevents dominance. It narrows a firm's choice over price by lowering its demand curve, forcing costs down, and inducing innovation.

A Robust Concept. Competition is robust; it applies over a wide range of market conditions. Competition is usually effective even when there are some imperfections and significant concentration in a market. Only when conditions approach high degrees of monopoly does competition lose much of its force.

A Test of Excellence.   Competition can also play an important cultural role. The United States, especially, relies on it as a fair and efficient process, with a Darwinian effect of letting the best competitors win "on their merits." This reliance derives from a number of roots, such as the cultural fluidity caused by large-scale immigration into the U.S. during 1880–1910, the rigors of frontier life, and the Protestant ethic of effort and reward. Competition commonly permits superior talents to prevail and to gain appropriate rewards. Competition does have certain costs, which chapter 2 will note, but it is a sound general basis for inducing good performance.

2. A PARADOX: IF WINNING CAUSES DOMINANCE, THEN COMPETITION IS NO LONGER EFFECTIVE

The competitive process can pose a dilemma. Each competitor strives to win so as to gain higher rewards. But if one wins big, then competition can be replaced by monopoly or dominance.

In such cases, competition seems to be self-destructive, leading to monopoly with its lack of parity and small number of firms. Yet to restore parity by limiting the new monopolist is often criticized severely; that "penalizes superior efficiency." Indeed, officials of monopolistic firms say just that; they denounce any resistance to their market dominance, saying that it "destroys the incentive to succeed."

This problem has arisen frequently in real markets. Standard Oil, IBM, and Eastman Kodak have attained dominant market positions, exerted control to extract monopoly profits, and created imperfections to sustain dominance. But critics of these harms are denounced for "seeking to punish success" and for being anti-competitive by rejecting the outcome of a healthy competitive struggle.

The sports world solves this paradox by firm divisions; it divides competitors carefully into leagues on the basis of age, size, sex, and so on. The vital parity is carefully preserved. Moreover, sports competition recurs in ongoing series of games, seasons, and yearly championships. No loss is permanent; play begins anew at each new tourney or season, with every person or team given a fresh start on an equal footing. Also, players age, and as leading athletes grow older and decline, the way is opened for others. Competition is continually renewed and is usually effective, but only because there are elaborate rules and a remorseless aging process.

In industrial markets, of course, there are no such careful divisions, processes, and balancing factors, nor any aging process. Once competition becomes lopsided and ineffective, there are no league rules or aging to restore effective competition. Moreover, dominance may arise from non-efficient causes. When dominant firms gain high profits, they can use those extra resources to create imperfections, reinforce their position, and suppress effective competition. In fact, once a firm *begins* to attain dominance, it naturally accumulates greater profits, which often enables it to grow even larger and maintain its dominance.

Genuinely superior firms need to be sufficiently rewarded, of course, but the termination of effective competition is harmful. Also, imperfections may create dominance and entrench it. How to distinguish and guard against these cases while renewing the competitive process is a central problem posed by market dominance.

Fortunately competition remains effective and balanced in most actual markets. Even so, it can be an unstable and fragile condition, hard to revive once it's gone.

IV. THE FIELD EVOLVES

Like every field of study, industrial organization evolves and changes. You are studying it at a time when certain concepts and research results happen to be prominent. But as in earlier decades, some of these popular ideas will fade quickly. By reviewing the history of this subject up to now, you will better understand how to evaluate the field's current content and anticipate future changes.

1. THE LITERATURE

Every discipline is created by the thinking and writing of specialists, especially professors at research universities. The journal articles and books that they write become the literature of the field, some of which is cited in the footnotes of this book. Professional journals and book-length monographs form the core of this literature.[13] Far from being dry articles and dusty tomes, many of these writings are weapons used against opposing sides in ongoing debates. Authors seek to disprove earlier ideas or results, establish their own points, and promote their own careers.

2. DEBATES

Debates among the leading researchers as published in the literature are how conflicting ideas and evidence get resolved and refined. Scholars are influenced by what happens in the economy—for example, the Internet, merger waves, or a trend to higher competition—and so the changing reality shapes research. Public policies toward industry also have influence. If, for instance, public officials permit an immense merger boom, as occurred in the 1980s, that will stimulate research into the effects of mergers (see chapter 6). Airline deregulation in 1978 spawned a wave of 1980s research into that experiment (see chapter 14).

The process of debate is intensely human, with clashes among schools, ideologies, and vested interests as well as dedicated scholars. With luck, the best ideas endure, and the literature evolves toward a core of sound concepts and methods for testing them. But remember, these are merely people's ideas, not engraved laws or truths. They often lag long behind events, and some topics are neglected for decades. Moreover, dubious new ideas often crowd out solid older concepts as fads come and go. Aggressive scholars often use glib claims to create their reputations. In addition, vested industrial interests pour money into sponsored "research" that is not neutral, but intended to advance their chances for control and profits.

Amid all these pressures and funds, the best specialists are rather few. Perhaps fifteen or twenty scholars are most influential in each decade, and they are frequently engaged in controversy with each other. All writers, both leading and lesser, are fallible, often making errors of logic and facts or pressing ideas that are empty or irrelevant.

Consequently, industrial organization is a lively, contentious, and changing discipline that continues to be hammered out amid powerful vested interests. Today's ideas will change; a textbook in the year 2020 may differ sharply from this book. Each student must think the issues through independently, developing a good sense for what is mainly valid, possibly biased, or just plain wrong.

3.   MAIN LINES AND PERIODS OF THE DEBATES

Understanding this field's long, rich, and distinguished history is necessary to evaluate the merits of current ideas.

Origins.   The problems we have discussed were as urgent in ancient times as they are now. Their true beginnings are lost in antiquity. Through many centuries, members of early tribes surely struggled over who would control their meager weapons, tools, and land. With the growth of settled cultivation, clever members would have gained larger holdings. Trade in grains and implements also would have provided large gains from fixing prices by collusion or by outright monopoly.

As ancient towns and then cities grew in the Middle East and elsewhere, the problem of monopoly probably was chronic. When the Code of Hammurabi, king of Babylon, included references to monopolistic practices in about 2100 B.C., these practices were already many centuries old. State and religious controls often gave the ultimate economic power to exploit to the ruling hierarchy.

The pre-Classical Greek city-states began to develop true entrepreneurial ventures, and they also bristled with private and city-based efforts to seize control of markets. By 480 to 420 B.C., when Athens reached its zenith, the operations of banking, industry, and public utilities were well advanced. There were also elaborate rules to prevent monopoly exploitation, as frequent judicial hearings and penalties attest.

The Romans developed all this on larger scales, and for centuries they faced routine serious problems of monopoly. Later, in A.D. 483, the edict of Emperor Xeno prohibited all monopolies, combinations, and price agreements. The Code of Justinian in 533 attempted much the same, perhaps with no more success. Competition was as vital, and monopoly was as stubborn, as they are today.

The Dark Ages were marked by a descent into localism, the eclipse of large-scale production and markets, and a decline in entrepreneurship. Market controls were embedded throughout feudal and religious systems of power. The early Renaissance after 1000 featured trading among areas and merchant guilds and crafts. Though it was 1600 before coal and iron works in Britain brought early industrial growth, monopoly and collusion were chronic. "Forestalling, engrossing and regrating" (holding supply back, monopolizing, and raising price, especially by grain owners exploiting townspeople) had long been crimes under common law when a statute of Edward I in 1285 formally prohibited them.

Rising monarchies in western Europe often replaced guilds by means of direct monopoly grants to nobles and court favorites as well as to inventors.[14] Queen Elizabeth did this frequently from 1560 to 1603. In a reversal of the tide, Parliament in 1623 enacted a Statute of Monopolies forbidding most such grants.

Still, the period from 1500 to 1770 was mercantilist, with a range of policies by which monarchs sought to control or alter markets. Gold was to be amassed by the king and the state, even at the expense of production and trade. Yet by 1700, the essential rudiments of modern markets were widespread in western Europe and its colonies. Massachusetts, among others, in 1641 and 1779 formally opposed monopoly, and the common law firmly recognized and prohibited it.

Events in the 1770s upset the mercantilist orthodoxy favoring restrictions on markets. The British industrial revolution began, and Adam Smith's *Wealth of Nations* in 1776 at one stroke established classical economics, with its stress on free trade in free markets.[15] Smith extended the doctrine of the invisible hand, a metaphor for the organizing force of a market system. If each person sought personal gain, the economy would tend to reach the best economic outcome for society as a whole.

Yet this approach would work only if markets were genuinely competitive and free from harmful political controls. Effective competition was therefore a critical part of classical economic doctrine about the value of free markets.

By 1850, industrialization was stirring in the United States, France, and Germany. The railway booms of 1840 to 1890 were the mainspring of U.S. industrial growth, breeding heavy-metals and engineering industries. Railroads also widened local markets into national ones. Capital markets also developed rapidly. Though suffused with trickery and instability, they made possible the financing of large-scale industrial firms. Certain utilities were already long standing—gas, water, postal service, canals—but the modern electricity and telephone utilities burst on the scene during 1876–1879.

The widening of markets from 1865 to 1900 increased competition, often radically. Western railroads themselves posed classic monopoly problems, however, with extremes of price discrimination, excess profits, and degrees of internal inefficiency. The main evils of monopoly were displayed on full view and became familiar to the public and to the handful of economists in the fledgling economics profession.

Other monopolies soon emerged, with Standard Oil being the most notorious. Indeed, railroad rebates helped to breed Standard Oil's vastly profitable monopoly. The struggle between Main Street and Wall Street—small business versus high finance and large industry—intensified across the country. Each financial panic or genuine depression mowed down thousands of small companies, and large firms used increasingly unfair tactics to increase their power. Tariffs and other political actions seemed also to be applied mainly for the benefit of large finance and industry.

The 1880s saw the rapid evolution of industry along with the parallel growth of neoclassical economics. Marginal productivity, utility, and costs were the new analytical language, and the competitive conditions of markets began to be worked out in detail. This strengthened some economists' belief that market processes were beneficial and should not be restrained. Conservative economists like Jeremiah Jenks lauded the new dominant-firm trusts for being modern and efficient, blessed by natural selection. Other economists saw monopolies as harmful and cruel.

More than a century ago, therefore, economists were debating monopoly with most of the same ideas now seen in the mainstream/new-Chicago-school/free-entry debates of today. Since then a few new ideas have been added, but readers should realize that most "new" ideas are really old and that most of the current debates simply repeat earlier debates almost word for word.[16]

1880–1910.   The 1880–1910 period was crucial in three ways:

1. The emerging competitive conditions of industry shifted sharply toward monopoly, especially in the United States.

2. The study of industrial organization advanced quickly.

3. Public policies in the United States crystallized in antitrust and utility regulation along lines sharply different from those in other countries.

Table 1.2 (see pages 24 and 25) indicates how changes in the economy related to research ideas and public policies.

During 1894–1901, an extraordinary wave of mergers created near-monopolies in hundreds of U.S. industries.[17] Many mergers were arranged by large-scale financiers such as J. P. Morgan and the Rockefeller brothers. A crisis of public anxiety quickly erupted. The trusts' defenders declared that consolidation was necessary, even inevitable, to achieve modern efficiency.[18] But the populace feared that the new monopolists would simply exploit the public (as many of them candidly admitted they aimed to do). Above the individual market monopolies there was fear of a new Morgan-Rockefeller money trust engulfing and controlling the whole economy.

The Sherman Act, passed in 1890, was applied in 1899 to outlaw most price fixing and in 1911, after spectacular legal battles, to dismantle Standard Oil and the American Tobacco monopoly. Other trustbusting actions advanced during 1910–1917, but World War I intercepted them, leading to lax antitrust activities during the Roaring Twenties. Though the regulation of utilities spread in many states, antitrust activity against normal industries virtually stopped until 1937.

Modern Debates.   The modern study of competition and monopoly began in the 1880s.[19] Some of its concepts were deeply and firmly set by 1901 through the scholarly work of John Bates Clark, Henry Carter Adams, Richard T. Ely, and Charles J. Bullock, among many others.[20] The spectacular wave of monopoly-enhancing mergers from 1897 to 1901 merely intensified the debates and gave them major industrial applications. The Bureau of Corporations was created to support and inform the antitrust effort, and it made a series of massive factual studies of the leading trusts.

Most of the current ideas at the center of the field—degrees of monopoly, actual and potential competition, efficiency and other effects of monopoly, economies and diseconomies of scale, oligopoly, price discrimination, first-mover advantages, the importance of innovation, dynamic processes, overhead costs, risk and uncertainty—were already fully recognized and discussed extensively by 1925.[21] Not only Alfred Marshall in England but also J. B. Clark, Ely, Adams, Bullock, Knight, J. M. Clark, and other economists in the United States had advanced the literature considerably, and the concepts had been applied to a large number of major industries.[22]

Most observers took it for granted that market share was the key element of monopoly. The concept of economies of scale was prominent, and many writers soon recognized the difference between technical and pecuniary economies. The danger of collusion among tight oligopolists was recognized, as had occurred in the steel, meat-packing, pipe, and many other industries. The understanding of "utilities" was also quite thorough and sophisticated by 1925.

In economics, two strands of thought had emerged. One was **neoclassical**, stressing the invisible hand's efficiency with increasingly abstract analysis. The other was more realistic. It embraced the variety of conditions actually posed by market power and the mass of new information about its real-world roles. Neoclassicals were increasingly complacent, while realists were critical.

The 1930s.   The modern study of market power is often dated to the 1930s. The field grew more technical in the 1930s, with more complex theoretical study of the oligopoly problem (e.g., Chamberlin and Robinson). The realists performed extensive statistical research on concentration, costs, and profits and led the Temporary National Economic Committee (TNEC) investigations of 1939 to 1941. Also, the original Chicago school voiced deep concern about the rise of monopoly power.

The 1930s also formed the field's basic conceptual design involving structure, behavior, and performance.[23] Structure was seen as influencing behavior and performance, though not rigidly or tightly. There was also a strong anxiety that corporate power was increasing and causing higher economic instability, as Karl Marx had predicted in *Das Kapital*.

The 1940s and 1950s.   Research increased rapidly, generally showing the serious dimensions, anti-competitive sources, and harmful effects of monopoly power.[24] George Stocking and Myron Watkins assembled detailed assessments of cartels and monopoly conditions, both in foreign and domestic markets. Fritz Machlup published comprehensive and sophisticated books assessing monopoly, price discrimination of all kinds, strategic actions, and public policies.[25] By 1955, George J. Stigler assembled a wide range of scholarship on major branches of the field.[26]

Joe S. Bain's work on barriers emerged in 1956, Simon Whitney thoroughly analyzed twenty industries in 1958, and Carl Kaysen and Donald F. Turner provided a comprehensive, subtle analysis of the tight-oligopoly problem in 1959.[27] Many case studies of important industries were developed, both in scholarly treatises and antitrust cases.

The 1960s.   Next came many broad cross-section econometric studies of structure and performance by Leonard W. Weiss, F. M. Scherer, William S. Comanor and Thomas Wilson, William G. Shepherd, and others. Oliver E. Williamson developed further the study of internal complexities of firm behavior.[28] Harvey J. Leibenstein's X-efficiency concept originated in 1966.[29] Edwin Mansfield and his associates prepared extensive studies of innovation, and Scherer's work in the mid-1960s was important.[30] Scherer's survey treatise on the entire field appeared in 1970.[31]

Moreover, public-utility economics, with its lengthy studies of profit and price-cost criteria, underwent sharp changes in the 1960s, as Alfred E. Kahn explored in his major survey of the subject in 1971.[32] George J. Stigler fostered a series of studies seeking to show that regulation had few good effects, and the free-market challenge to mainstream ideas began to develop.[33]

In short, the field was rich and diverse, with an accumulation of knowledge and technical skills that combined theory, econometrics, cases, and policy issues. No orthodoxy prevailed amid vigorous debates among many schools and research methodologies. Meanwhile, antitrust and regulatory policies were distinctly moderate—the prospect of breaking up AT&T was scarcely conceivable, and the removal of railroad and airline regulation was only a faint hope among a few specialists. Yet that and more had actually happened by 1984 and are now regarded in retrospect as high successes.[34]

1970 to 1990.   After 1970 the mainstream continued to develop, including a renewed focus on market share as a main element of market power. Other important research studies include Scherer and associates on economies of scale, Williamson on transactions costs, Michael Porter on enterprises' competitive strategies, many econometric studies of profitability and structure, Mueller, Ravenscraft, and Scherer on mergers, William Shepherd's assessment of the trend of competition, and scores of case studies.

Parallel to this research-rich mainstream, three other schools emerged and gained importance:

- pure theoretical modeling, especially with game theory, in what was called "new IO theory"
- pure free-market theories stressing the benefits of monopoly
- pure theories of perfect contestability

New IO Theory.   Rising numbers of younger theorists began to develop pure theoretical models, exploring various propositions about duopolies. Analyses usually were based on abstract short-run, Cournot-Nash assumptions (see chapter 11), with static consumer surplus as the criterion for assessing the benefits of competition.[35]

Some of this work clarified real markets, but most of it really is part of a new, parallel field—a branch of microeconomic theory—separate from the mainstream of this field. Although (and because) the game-theory models are rigorous, they often have limited relevance for real competitive processes in real markets.

New-Chicago-School Free-Market Analysis.   Meanwhile, free-market writers emphasized the positive aspects of monopoly.[36] They advanced the following four main hypotheses:

1. All monopoly merely reflects superior efficiency.

2. Therefore, all monopoly is virtuous and only collusion creates real market power.

3. Collusion always collapses quickly.

4. The costs of attaining monopoly commonly use up any possible monopoly profits in advance.[37]

These ideas were usually offered as theories, with little supporting evidence. Meanwhile, the IBM and AT&T companies, defendants in two major antitrust cases in the 1970s, employed many leading economists as expert witnesses. Some of the resulting arguments were published, further advancing free-market positions.[38] In 1981, the new Reagan administration quickly adopted these doctrines as a rationale for eliminating most antitrust enforcement and for further deregulating many sectors.

Table 1.2   Time Line of Industrial Organization, the Economy, and Policies

1880	1890	1900	1910	1920	1930	1940 →

The Industrial Organization Field

Early economists denounce monopoly, favor regulation.	Conservative economists defend the trusts.	Intense debate ensues over monopoly, scale economies, and the trust question. Extensive studies are done on actual industries.		Factual studies of trusts and industries continue.	Chamberlin and Robinson launch the study of oligopoly. Berle and Means say large firms have uncontrolled power. Quantitative studies begin, showing the prevalence of oligopoly.	Game theory raises interest in oligopoly as the central topic.

The U.S. Economy

Railroad and oil monopolies are formed. Telephone and electric utilities begin.	Industrial merger wave, 1897–1901, forms hundreds of dominant firms.			World War I. Merger boom occurs, peaking in 1929. Economy collapses. There is apparent rise of market power in industry. Scandals occur in utility sectors and banking.		World War II causes boom, followed by long postwar growth. Confidence in private industry revives.

Policies toward Market Power

Supreme Court approves regulation in the public interest.	Sherman Antitrust Law is enacted, 1890.	Price fixing is flatly prohibited, 1899.	Roosevelt-Taft trust-busting wave affects Standard Oil, American Tobacco, and many others. States begin forming commissions to regulate utilities.	World War I cuts off antitrust. Clayton Act (1914) imposes limits on market power. Federal Trade Commission is formed as the second antitrust agency (1914).	Antitrust lapses during 1920–37.	Strict banking laws and regulations applied. Regulation spreads to electric, telephone, trucking, and airline sectors. NRA briefly supports price fixing.	Antitrust is revived 1937–52. Major cases are brought to court and won.

Public enterprise is largely rejected in favor of regulated private utilities.

continued

Table 1.2   *(continued)*

1950	1960	1970	1980	1990	2000

The Industrial Organization Field (cont.)

1950 / 1960	1970	1980	1990
Many industry studies are done. Bain develops study of entry barriers. Chicago-UCLA-school economists assert the prevalence of competition and futility of regulation, gain rising acceptance.	Large-scale econometric studies of concentration, innovation, economies of scale, advertising, and profits are done. Mathematical modeling gains popularity.	The field contains great variety among theorists, statistical studies, industry experts, conservatives, and the mainstream.	Free-market theory recedes. More research on real-market conditions.

The U.S. Economy (cont.)

1950	1960	1970	1980	1990
Concentration rises both in industries and in total shares of large firms.	Economies of scale begin substantial shrinkage, with new technology replacing smoke-stack industries.	A general rise in competition occurs, caused by imports, antitrust, and deregulation.		Massive 1990s merger boom, often creating dominance. Internet growth. The dot com rise and crash. Chaos in some electricity markets. Accounting scandals.
		Vietnam War stirs attacks on corporate power. Merger boom occurs, peaking in 1969.	A merger boom occurs in 1981–89.	

Policies toward Market Power (cont.)

1950	1960	1970	1980	1990
New public enterprises are developed in electric sector: TVA, New York, Nebraska, the West	Antitrust recedes, 1952–60.	Several big antitrust cases go to court: IBM, AT&T, Xerox, cereals.	The AT&T case brings large changes, 1984.	Deregulation troubles. Microsoft antitrust case. Weak merger policies.
	Merger rules are tightened: New law is passed in 1950; first cases brought to court in 1950; tightest landmark case occurs in 1966.	Deregulation begins in stock markets, airlines, railroads, banking, telephones, broadcasting, trucking, etc.	Further deregulation. Reagan officials sharply reduce antitrust actions. They also extend deregulation fur-ther.	

Contestability Theory.   From 1975 to 1982, a third school developed, the Baumol-Bailey-Willig "contestability" school, which focused on an arcane theory of perfectly free entry.[39] These theorists argued that entry conditions could entirely nullify existing pure monopoly. The condition of contestability should, they said, displace competition itself in economic theory.

Altogether, the period from 1970 to 1985 brought marked changes. As the economy grew more competitive, many economists embraced pure theory modeling, the free-market view that monopoly was beneficial, and the assumption that entry would nullify monopoly power. Imperfections ceased to be discussed, and the anti-competitive ways to gain monopoly power were denied or neglected, as if the field's core research had somehow vanished.

The 1990s and Early 2000s.   By 1990 the free-market approach had crested and was receding; contestability had largely been rejected as irrelevant; a new empirical industrial-organization approach had spread; and the mainstream reasserted itself. Although the field regained balance, in many departments the topic was taught as virtually pure new-IO theory. Rising international competition—plus the creation of the Internet—gave reason to regard market power and market imperfections as slight.

In short, the field continues as a scene of colorful struggles, with some tendency toward balance among the divergent views and methods. The U.S. economy continues as a great practical experiment in competition. The 1980s brought extreme doctrines that denied the importance of market realities and monopoly power. The field continues in interesting turbulence, with no clear outcome. As always, you need to apply careful judgment, using logic and weighing complex facts.

The 1990s brought enormous booms in mergers and the stock market, more deregulation, and a few efforts by antitrust officials to seem more strict. Very few mergers were seriously screened, while many mergers that enhanced dominant positions were permitted. After the FTC failed to take action against Microsoft, the Antitrust Division mounted an ambitious case. But the case was largely symbolic, as we note in chapter 16. In short, policies since 1980 have done little to deal with monopoly power and turbulence in markets.

V. THE SEQUENCE OF TOPICS

This book presents the concepts and details in a logical sequence, showing how they relate to one another. First come the basic theories of competition and monopoly in chapter 2. An appendix offers some methods, topics, and sources that help students to prepare valuable research papers. Then come the four major topic areas: part 2, Market Structure; part 3, Performance; part 4, Determinants of Market Structure; and part 5, Behavior and Related Topics. That leads to case studies in part 6 and the main public policies in part 7.[40]

Chapter 3 presents the all-important topic of defining markets, surveys the categories of partial competition, and suggests how to assess the evidence about actual markets. Part 3, Performance, considers the effects of monopoly on prices, profits, and efficiency (chapter 4), and on innovation, fairness, and other elements (chapter 5).

In part 4, on determinants, chapter 6 covers all influences on structure other than economies of scale. Chapter 7 then covers research on scale economies and diseconomies.

Part 5, Behavior and Related Topics, covers a wide variety of subjects. First is the nature of the firm as the building block of the economy in chapter 8. Monopoly and dominant firms are covered in chapter 9, along with barriers to entry and "contestability." The related topics of price discrimination and predatory (that is, anti-competitive) actions are treated in chapter 10.

Chapter 11 presents theories of oligopoly. The chapter also gives evidence about oligopoly collusion and action in real markets. Chapter 12 moves to quite different topics: vertical ties between stages of production, conglomerate ties linking unrelated types of production, and advertising.

Next, in part 6, chapter 13 presents leading dominant firms, and chapter 14 gives leading tight oligopolies. These chapters demonstrate how the elements of the analysis fit together in real cases.

Three chapters on U.S. public policies round out the text. Chapters 15 and 16 summarize U.S. antitrust policies, and chapter 17 covers (very briefly) the regulation of utilities, deregulation, public enterprise, and privatization.

So, welcome to the dramatic and intriguing world of industrial organization! It involves fateful matters, as well as many strange and amusing ones. Its ideas clarify the modern free-market system, from the arcane realms of high finance and great corporate power on down to the modest shops along thousands of Main Streets. It also tests and develops your skills in complex evaluation.

QUESTIONS FOR REVIEW

1. Explain how the inelasticity of demand for a firm governs the degree of monopoly by controlling the range for raising price.

2. Explain how parity and sufficient competitors are crucial to effective competition.

3. Explain the basic logic of causation in the triad of structure, behavior, and performance.

4. Explain how the new-Chicago view reverses the logic of the structure-behavior-performance triad. Show how it makes monopoly appear to be valuable and desirable.

5. Explain the recent evolution of research ideas in the field, with examples from several schools of thought.

ENDNOTES

[1] "In short, the pendulum has swung. For 25 years, the reach of market principles grew steadily, penetrating every aspect of our lives and every corner of the globe ..." bringing "... marketization, deregulation and privatization. ... But now the long fingers of the market are pulling back, as people focus more on its shortcomings." Alan Murray, "No Longer Business as Usual for Forces of U.S. Capitalism," *Wall Street Journal* (October 1, 2002): p. A4.

[2] For example, a politician may assert that workers "should be more competitive," but that means only that they should try harder or accept a cut in wages. The "competitiveness" of the U.S. economy in world markets often means only that its prices may be lower than others.

Monopoly firms often claim that they face a lot of competition. Learn instead to apply *competitive* to the conditions inside markets, where firms may interact as they try to win.

[3] "Industrial organization" is a branch on the main stem of microeconomics: it is the applied economics of supply. In popular terms, it covers big business, corporate power, and the monopoly problem. Often it is presented as "the case for competition," or "antitrust economics."

[4] Aristotle, *Politics*, book 1, chapter 12.

[5] Under an extreme theoretical assumption of absolutely, instantly free entry, the simple price result could be the same as competition, even if there is monopoly inside the market. But no "perfectly contestable" market is known to exist, as chapter 9 notes.

[6] Even some leading universities' names reflect monopoly wealth: Vanderbilt University (railroads), the Rockefeller Institute (oil), Carnegie-Mellon University (steel and aluminum), Duke University (cigarettes), and Stanford University (western railroads).

[7] General Motors was dominant in the automobile industry from the 1930s to the 1970s, and IBM dominated computers from the 1950s to the 1980s. Both became inefficient and stagnant, because market power permitted it. During 1980–92, their stock prices dived as the companies foundered, causing over a $60 billion decline in asset values for the investors in each company. By 1995 both companies were on the mend, but only after convulsive changes in management and deep cuts in employment. See William G. Shepherd, "Antitrust Repelled, Inefficiency Endured: Lessons of IBM and General Motors for Future Antitrust Policies," *Antitrust Bulletin* 39 (Spring 1994): pp. 203–34.

[8] The history of this school has two remarkably contrasting phases. Leaders of the original Chicago school in the 1920s and 1930s—Frank H. Knight, Henry C. Simons, and Jacob Viner— were deeply opposed to monopoly of every kind. See especially Simons' *Economic Policy for a Free Society* (Chicago: University of Chicago Press, 1949).

Then in the 1950s the school's viewpoint was reversed to rosy optimism by Aaron Director (a law professor) and George Stigler (who arrived in 1957). Competition was suddenly seen to be everywhere, while monopoly was said to be limited, brief, and weak. Only the state could cause harmful monopoly by its bad policies. In the 1960s and 1970s their followers pressed the concepts further, led by Harold Demsetz and J. Fred Weston at UCLA, John McGee at the University of Washington, Richard A. Posner and Sam Peltzman at Chicago, and Robert H. Bork at Yale.

[9] Other measures of concentration can also be used, as chapter 3 discusses.

[10] The best sources covering ongoing developments include the *Wall Street Journal*, the business pages of the *New York Times* and *BusinessWeek* magazine. We use them liberally in these pages. For added coverage, the common stock handbooks issued by Moody's and by Standard and Poor's are often useful.

[11] See George J. Stigler, "Perfect Competition, Historically Contemplated," *Journal of Political Economy* 65 (February 1957): pp. 1–17, reprinted in Stigler's *Organization of Industry* (Homewood, IL: Irwin, 1968).

[12] See Joseph A. Schumpeter, *Capitalism, Socialism and Democracy* (New York: Harper, 1942); chapter 3 presents the process in more detail. See also John Vickers, "Concepts of Competition," *Oxford Economic Papers* 47 (January 1995): pp. 1–23; and John M. Clark, *Competition as a Dynamic Process* (Washington, DC: Brookings Institution, 1962).
Mainstream scholars generally adhered to realistic ideas about degrees of competition. They treated the pure atomistic model as a mere theoretical ideal.

[13] Current literature is summarized in the *Journal of Economic Literature*. Mainstream journals (in the U.S., the *American Economic Review–Review of Economics and Statistics*, the *Quarterly Journal of Economics*, and the *Journal of Political Economy*) contain a scattering of articles in this field.
For more concentrated coverage, see the field's specific leading journals. The *Journal of Industrial Economics*, the *International Journal of Industrial Organization*, and the *RAND Journal of Economics* tend toward high technical content and methods. The *Journal of Law and Economics* and the *Review of Industrial Organization* focus more on factual research and policy debates. The *Antitrust Bulletin* focuses on antitrust economics and policies, and regulation-oriented journals include the *Yale Journal on Regulation*, the *Journal of Regulatory Economics*, and the *Journal of Regulation*.

[14] See Charles W. Cole, *Colbert and a Century of French Mercantilism* (New York: Columbia University Press, 1939); and William H. Price, *The English Patents of Monopoly* (Boston: Houghton Mifflin, 1906).

[15] Adam Smith, *The Wealth of Nations* (New York: Random House, Modern Library, 1776).

[16] For detailed coverage of the debates over the meaning of competition during recent centuries, see Kenneth G. Dennis, *Competition in the History of Economic Thought* (New York: Arno Press, 1977).

[17] See especially John Moody, *The Truth about the Trusts* (Chicago: Moody Publishing, 1904); William Z. Ripley, ed., *Trusts, Pools and Corporations* (Boston: Ginn, 1916); and Anthony P. O'Brien, "Factory Size, Economies of Scale, and the Great Merger Wave of 1898–1902," *Journal of Economic History* 48 (1988).

[18] The best known of the academic apologists were William Graham Sumner and Jeremiah Jenks. See Almarin Phillips and Rodney E. Stevenson, "The Historical Development of Industrial Organization," *History of Political Economy* 6 (Fall 1974): pp. 324–42.

[19] See John Bates Clark, "The Limits of Competition," *Political Science Quarterly* 2 (1887): pp. 45–61; Henry C. Adams, "Trusts," in American Economic Association, *Papers and Proceedings* 5 (December 1903): pp. 91–107; Richard T. Ely, *Monopolies and Trusts* (New York: Macmillan, 1900); and the important survey in Charles J. Bullock, "Trust Literature: A Survey and Criticism," *Quarterly Journal of Economics* 15 (February 1901): pp. 167–217.

[20] For a masterly summary of the weaknesses of the merger apologetics, see Bullock's "Trust Literature: A Survey and Criticism," (1901).

[21] See Alfred Marshall, *Industry and Trade* (London: Macmillan, 1920); Frank H. Knight, *Risk, Uncertainty and Profit* (New York: Harper & Row, 1921); and John M. Clark's masterful coverage of multiproduct costs and price discrimination in his *Studies in the Economics of Overhead Costs* (New York: Macmillan, 1922).

[22] Major studies and antitrust actions occurred in the first wave of Sherman Act Section 2 cases against Standard Oil, American Tobacco, U.S. Steel, Du Pont gunpowder, International Harvester, the meatpackers' oligopoly, Alcoa, and even AT&T. See Philip Areeda and Donald F. Turner, *Antitrust Law*, 7 vols. (Boston: Little, Brown, 1978); Hans B. Thorelli, *The Federal Antitrust Policy* (Chicago: University of Chicago Press, 1954); and William Letwin, *Law and Economic Policy in America* (New York: Random House, 1965).

[23] Edward H. Chamberlin, *The Theory of Monopolistic Competition*, 8th ed. (Cambridge: Harvard University Press, 1960); and Joan Robinson, *Economics of Imperfect Competition* (London: Macmillan, 1933). Another influential book was Adolph A. Berle and Gardiner C. Means, *The Modern Corporation and Private Property* (New York: Macmillan, 1932). In 1940 there were twenty-one TNEC reports and extensive hearings, in which Congress explored the dimensions of corporate power and its effects. They include two superb volumes: Walton Hamilton and Irene Till, *Antitrust in Action*, vol. 16, and Clair Wilcox, *Competition and Monopoly in the American Economy*, vol. 21, Temporary National Economic Committee (Washington, DC: U.S. Government Printing Office, 1940).

[24] See William J. Fellner, *Competition Among the Few* (New York: Knopf, 1949) for a major formulation of the oligopoly problem; and George W. Stocking and Myron W. Watkins, *Monopoly and Free Enterprise* (New York: Twentieth Century Fund, 1951). Morris A. Adelman denied that concentration was rising in his "Measurement of Industrial Concentration," *Review of Economics and Statistics* 33 (November 1951): pp. 269–96.

[25] See Fritz Machlup, *The Political Economy of Monopoly* (Baltimore: Johns Hopkins University Press, 1952) and *The Economics of Sellers' Competition* (Baltimore: Johns Hopkins University Press, 1952).

[26] Stigler, ed., *Business Concentration and Price Policy* (Princeton: Princeton University Press, 1955).

[27] Joe S. Bain, *Barriers to New Competition* (Cambridge: Harvard University Press, 1956) started the systematic study of entry barriers; Simon N. Whitney, *Antitrust Policies: American Experience in Twenty Industries*, 2 vols. (New York: Twentieth Century Fund, 1958); Carl Kaysen and Donald F. Turner, Jr., *Antitrust Policy: An Economic and Legal Analysis* (Cambridge: Harvard University Press, 1959).

Other influential works in the 1950s include Edward S. Mason, *Economic Concentration and the Monopoly Problem* (Cambridge: Harvard University Press, 1957); Morris A. Adelman, *A & P: A Study in Price-Cost Behavior and Public Policy* (Cambridge: Harvard University Press, 1959); Martin Shubik, *Strategy and Market Structure* (New York: Wiley, 1959); and Walter Adams and Horace Gray, *Monopoly in America: The Government as Promoter* (New York: Macmillan, 1955).

[28] See Williamson, *The Economics of Discretionary Behavior* (Chicago: Markham, 1967); and Richard M. Cyert and James G. March, *A Behavioral Theory of the Firm* (Upper Saddle River, NJ: Prentice Hall, 1963).

[29] Leibenstein, "Allocative Efficiency vs. 'X-Efficiency'," *American Economic Review* 56 (June 1966): pp. 392–415; and his *Beyond Economic Man* (Cambridge: Harvard University Press, 1976).

[30] See Mansfield, *Industrial Research and Technological Innovation* (New York: Norton 1968); Mansfield et al., *Research and Innovation in the Modern Corporation* (New York: Norton, 1971); and the papers by F. M. Scherer gathered in his *Innovation and Growth* (Cambridge: MIT Press, 1986).

[31] Scherer, *Industrial Market Structure and Economic Performance* (Skokie, IL: Rand McNally, 1980 and 1991 editions by Houghton Mifflin).

[32] Kahn, *The Economics of Regulation*, 2 vols. (New York: Wiley, 1970).

[33] See papers collected by Stigler in his *Organization of Industry* (Homewood, IL: Irwin, 1968).

[34] Indeed, AT&T voluntarily and eagerly divided itself up again in 1995–96 and again in 2001–2002!

[35] For a major survey of new IO theory, see Richard Schmalensee and Robert D. Willig, *Handbook of Industrial Organization* (Cambridge: MIT Press, 1989); for critical judgments about that survey by six leading scholars, see *Brookings Papers on Economic Activity*, Special Issue (1991): pp. 201–76. Major textbooks and surveys include Jean Tirole, *The Theory of Industrial Organization*, 2nd ed. (Cambridge: MIT Press, 1993); Stephen Martin, *Advanced Industrial Economics* (Oxford: Basil Blackwell, 1993); John Sutton, *Sunk Costs and Market Structure* (Cambridge: MIT Press, 1991); and John Cable, ed., *Current Issues in Industrial Economics* (New York: St. Martin's Press, 1994).

[36] Leading writings include Stigler, *The Organization of Industry*; Richard A. Posner, *Antitrust Law* (Chicago: University of Chicago Press, 1976), and "The Social Costs of Monopoly and Regulation," *Journal of Political Economy* (August 1976): pp. 807–27; and Fred S. McChesney and William F. Shughart, eds., *The Causes and Consequences of Antitrust* (Chicago: University of Chicago Press, 1995). Most free-market-oriented papers have appeared in the *Journal of Law and Economics* and the *Journal of Political Economy*, both located at the University of Chicago and edited by University of Chicago economists, rather than in leading mainstream journals. A number of the new-Chicago writers are legal scholars, not trained economists. Most notable is Robert H. Bork, *The Antitrust Dilemma: A Policy at War with Itself* (New York: Basic Books, 1978). His discussion of economics is at a beginner's level.

[37] See Posner, *Antitrust Law* (1976) and "Social Costs of Monopoly and Regulation" (1976). For a summary and evaluation, see William G. Shepherd, "Three 'Efficiency School' Hypotheses about Market Power," *Antitrust Bulletin* 33 (Summer 1988): pp. 395–415.

[38] See, for example, Franklin M. Fisher, John C. McGowan, and Joen E. Greenwood, *Folded, Spindled and Mutilated: Economic Analysis and U.S. v. IBM* (Cambridge: MIT Press, 1983).

[39] See especially William J. Baumol, John C. Panzar, and Robert D. Willig, *Contestable Markets and the Theory of Industrial Structure* (San Diego: Harcourt Brace Jovanovich, 1982); and Baumol and Willig, "Contestability: Developments Since the Book," *Oxford Economic Papers*, Special Supplement (November 1986).
For critical reviews, see W. G. Shepherd, "'Contestability' versus Competition," *American Economic Review* 74 (September 1984): pp. 572–87; and William G. Shepherd, "Contestability vs. Competition—Once More," *Land Economics* 71 (August 1995): pp. 299–309; also Marius Schwartz, "The Nature and Scope of Contestability Theory," *Oxford Economic Papers*, Special Supplement (November 1986).

[40] After much experimenting, we find that putting structure and performance in direct sequence is the best way to show their connection. Readers see clearly the probable effects of structure. The issue of causation is squarely posed, so that students can assess the mainstream, free-market, and contestability evidence clearly.

Chapter

2

THEORIES OF COMPETITION AND MONOPOLY

Here you'll meet some old friends: the happy theory of how competition delivers efficiency, and the bleak analysis of how monopoly usually distorts that cheerful result. You've already met these theories in beginning economics; now we refine them. You'll come out of this chapter ready to begin the more advanced study of markets in chapter 3 and to absorb the details in the rest of the book.

We begin in section 1 with the economic criteria for good performance. Then section 2 presents competition's role as an "invisible hand," guiding the market system toward static efficiency. But this hand does not reach everywhere; section 2 shows its sharp limits. Section 3 introduces monopoly power, shows its several effects, and compares monopoly's costs to its possible benefits using scale economies. It also notes the opposite free-market point of view.

This chapter also has an appendix about research to help you design, find sources for, and finish a research paper.

1. PERFORMANCE VALUES

Economic performance has many dimensions, as table 2.1 summarizes. Some economists (usually free-market economists) only consider efficiency. Others have focused on three main elements: efficiency, innovation, and fairness in distribution.[1] But the competitive process itself provides even more values. They include competition itself, freedom of choice for consumers and other groups, avoidance of severe risk, basis for healthy democracy, and social diversity.

31

Table 2.1   Performance Values

1. Efficiency in Resource Allocation.
    a. Internal efficiency (also called X-efficiency or business efficiency).
    b. Allocative efficiency. Resources are allocated among markets and firms in patterns that maximize the value of total output. Prices equal long-run marginal cost and minimum average cost.
    c. Avoiding simple resource wastes.

2. Technical Progress
New products and production methods are adopted rapidly.

3. Equity in Distribution
There is a fair distribution (in line with the society's standards of fairness) of
    a. Wealth,
    b. Income, and
    c. Opportunity.

4. The Competitive Process
Competition itself provides social values of open opportunity and rewards to effort and skill.

5. Other Dimensions
Including
    a. Individual freedom of choice,
    b. Security from extreme economic risks of financial and job losses,
    c. Support for healthy democratic processes, and
    d. Cultural diversity.

---

1.   EFFICIENCY

Microeconomics has traditionally turned first to efficiency, even though other values may actually be larger. Efficiency's basic meaning is simple: a maximum total value of outputs from any given set of inputs. This is **static efficiency** when using a current set of resources. There are two main categories: internal efficiency and allocative efficiency. Also, any simple waste of inputs is to be avoided.

Internal Efficiency.   Good management keeps cost low at each level of output, reaching "X-efficiency." [2] Though this goal is obvious, companies often deviate from it (chapter 4 will give some examples). As normal human beings, managers tend to perform better under some pressure and relax when pressures are reduced. In very large companies, which often have large profit flows as a cushion, it is often easy for internal efficiency to slacken without being detected and corrected. X-inefficiency occurs in two main forms: (1) when a firm buys more inputs than are necessary and (2) when employees don't work at maximum levels. The resulting X-inefficiency is the excess of actual costs over minimum possible costs. As shown in figure 2.1 by points A and B for output Q_1 and C and D for output Q_2, it means being above the lowest possible average cost curve. Its amount is:

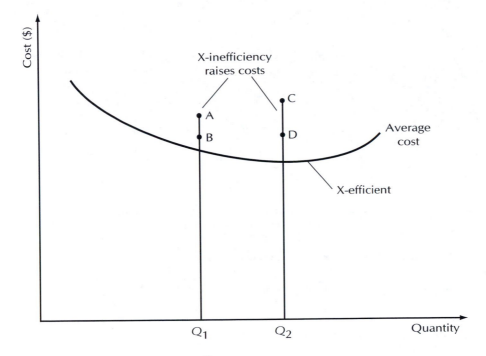

Figure 2.1   Illustrations of X-inefficiency.

$$\text{Degree of X-inefficiency} = \frac{\text{excess cost}}{\text{minimum cost}}$$

X-inefficiency is common, and many actual cases of inefficient firms are candidly discussed in the business press. Though measuring the size of excess costs is difficult, most cases probably fall in the range of 1 to 10 percent of costs (see chapter 4).

Allocative Efficiency.   In an efficient general equilibrium, each output of each firm is at the level where marginal cost equals price. Price also will equal the minimum level of long-run average cost. These and related conditions apply throughout the economy. Even if they are reached only approximately, the result can be close to maximum efficiency.

As a result, consumer surplus is maximized, and the net total value of production cannot be increased by any further change. Consumer surplus is the excess of value that consumers receive over what they must pay for a good. It is shown by the area *under* the demand curve but *above* the price paid for the good, as illustrated in figure 2.2.

The size of the consumer surplus depends on the elasticity of demand. Low elasticity means that consumer surplus is large (panel 1 of figure 2.2); this applies to goods that are urgently wanted, like life-giving drugs and other broadly defined necessities such as water, food, and housing. With high elasticity (when there are close substitutes), consumer surplus is small (panel 2 of figure 2.2).[3]

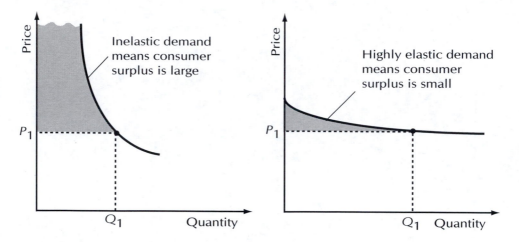

Figure 2.2   The amount of consumer surplus depends on elasticity of demand.

An efficient outcome will maximize consumer surplus by forcing prices down to costs. The total of all shaded areas under all demand curves in the economy—total consumer surplus—is then as large as possible. Even if this result is reached only approximately, it is powerful.

2.   Technological Progress

Efficiency is *static*; it occurs only within a given state of technology and a specific set of resources. Innovation is *dynamic*, occurring over time. It raises the state of the art, so that more and better outputs can be achieved from the same inputs.

Innovation is glamorous because it creates new products and processes. Furthermore, its yields can be high. The rate of innovation tends to build on itself, growing geometrically over the years like compound interest. A sustained high rate of innovation can accumulate to extremely high gains over a series of years.

But innovation is seldom free; usually it requires resources to accomplish it, often called R & D (research and development). Therefore the proper goal in each market is a rapid rate of innovation with only the minimum amount of R & D spending to achieve efficiency for each period.

Innovation also involves uncertainty since it explores the unknown and the untried. For example, nuclear power seemed to hold high promise in the 1950s, but it developed severe problems; miniaturization in computer technology, on the other hand, has yielded undreamed-of returns. Moreover, even defining and measuring innovation are difficult, as chapter 5 will show.

3.   Equity

Equity means fairness in the distribution of wealth and income among rich and poor. Wealth is perhaps the most important dimension. Fairness can be a separate force from efficiency and innovation. An efficient and innovative economy is sometimes reasonably fair, but it may instead be mildly or radically unfair. Because competition and monopoly can deeply affect distribution, fairness is an appropriate goal to consider.[4]

Fairness cannot be defined simply. It involves ethics as well as economics, and there are differing ethical criteria of what is fair.

1. **Equality**, which is rooted in Western values of sharing and social justice.

2. **Effort.**

3. **Contribution** (or productivity); this criterion often relates a person's affluence to effort, but the affluence may instead come from talent and training (i.e., in a lazy genius).

4. **Need.**

There are still others, but these four are enough to indicate how diverse and often conflicting the criteria of fairness may be.

A tentative summary of traditional standards of fairness in the United States might be stated as a broad preference for equality, modified for clear differences in effort and contribution, with an avoidance of severe extremes of wealth and poverty. Opportunity especially is to be made equal.

4. COMPETITION AS A VALUE

The competitive process itself provides a performance value. When competition is fair and effective, it provides a wide array of opportunities, freedom of choice, an outlet for talent, and incentives for superior performance. In most types of human endeavor—at work, in the arts, in inventing, and in setting personal ambitions—competition can be a strong stimulus toward excellence and diversity.

Competition among people can impose important costs, especially for the majority of the population who are not hyper-active competitive types. Many highly creative people actually avoid the competitive grind. More generally, competition in the workplace often sets people against each other. Personal competition can be divisive and generate too much stress. No normal person wants to strain to the max all the time in work, in sports, or in anything.

But in the *industrial* arena, maximal competition among companies is unambiguously favorable. It generates high levels of corporate performance.

5. OTHER VALUES

Other values include

Freedom of choice, which is a particularly strong American value. Some economies and societies provide their members with much wider freedoms than others. Competition enhances such freedoms.[5]

Security from extreme economic risks is another value. Risks include personal injury, loss of job, and financial ruin from sickness and other random events.

Good content of jobs is another goal. Jobs define much of our personal identity, and they occupy most of our waking hours. Unpleasant or degrading jobs are a deviation from good performance.

Prospects for healthy democracy. Leading economists ranging from Adam Smith, John Stuart Mill, and Alfred Marshall to Henry Simons, Paul Samuelson, and many others consider competition in political markets to be a leading value.

Democracy works better when economic power and wealth are widely spread throughout competitive markets.

Finally, cultural richness and diversity are important values. People have enormously diverse interests. A well-performing economy responds to those interests with a rich variety of goods and services. The opposite, negative extreme is quite possible—a wasteland, with deadening uniformity.

II. COMPETITION AND PERFORMANCE

Under certain conditions, competition is likely to achieve many or most of these goals. Efficiency will be shown first with the metaphor of the invisible hand. But innovation or some of the other goals may often provide the larger actual yield.

1. AN INVISIBLE HAND?

Perfect Competition. We begin with the abstract case of perfect competition, which is a theoretical caricature of real-world effective competition.[6] The perfect-competition theory involves **pure competition** in every market (with hundreds of tiny competitors), plus certain other strict assumptions, as follows:

1. perfect knowledge by all participants of all relevant present and future conditions in the market;

2. perfect mobility of resources and participants;

3. rational behavior by all participants (all consumers maximize utility, all producers maximize profits);

4. all of the underlying preferences, technology, and surroundings are stable and unchanging during the period, so that an equilibrium can be reached;

5. there are no interdependencies among consumers or producers.

Assumptions 1 and 2 are extreme, and the others are often violated. Therefore most analysis relies instead on pure competition. It too is an extreme case, but its assumptions may be reasonably approximated in many markets that have large numbers of sellers and buyers. Each firm operates independently, as one tiny participant, and it has no market influence. The resulting process adjusts toward efficient allocation.

Each firm's choices are simple, as is shown in panel 1 of figure 2.3. Technology determines the average and marginal cost curves in panel 1. In figure 2.3, by assumption, the average cost curve has a definite U-shape at a small size, so that the firm must remain small in its market.

The firm maximizes its profits (that's a purely commercial, private goal, which is much narrower than the many social goals reviewed earlier). Under competitive pressure, the firm has to set output at the level where

$$price = marginal\ cost = minimum\ average\ cost$$

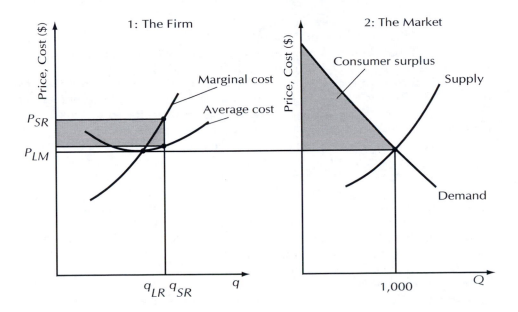

Figure 2.3   Conditions reached under competition.

in order to survive in the long run, when price is forced down to P_{LR} in panel 1. If price instead briefly rises, for example to P_{SR}, excess profits will be briefly available. They are shown by the shaded rectangle.

The firm's demand curve is a horizontal line at the going market price, because this pure competitor has no discretion over price.[7] It is a "price taker," not a "price maker." To maximize profits, the firm (like all firms) sets its output where marginal revenue equals marginal cost. When the demand curve is flat, **marginal revenue equals average revenue** (which is price itself, by definition), and therefore **price equals marginal cost**. In the long run, the choice lies at the low point of the average cost curve, where price equals both long-run marginal cost and the minimum level of average cost.

Managers of firms do not make these choices explicitly using these diagrams. But that does not matter. Rational action, plus the need to survive, drives them to behave usually *as if* they did make these choices. The end results, in inputs, outputs, and marginal conditions, are the same. The "as if" assumption is extremely important.

Under these conditions, there is no X-inefficiency, because inefficient firms cannot survive. Also, the firms use inputs up to the point where each input's marginal contribution to the value of production just equals its price. All elements of the producer's choices are efficient. Consumer choices also are efficient. Each good is consumed to the point where its marginal utility is in line with its price. Under competition in every market, the system is efficient throughout, since no marginal shift could improve allocation. Any gain from increasing output of one kind would be less than the sum of losses caused by reductions in other outputs.

When price equals marginal cost, there is a surprisingly deep and meaningful situation. Consider price: it is the degree of value or esteem that people feel for a good as shown by what they are willing to pay for it out of their own pockets and in free choices between this and other goods. From Adam Smith, David Ricardo, John Stuart Mill, and Alfred Marshall on, price in free markets has held center stage as the basic measure of true economic value.

Marginal cost is an equally profound index of the true sacrifice made to produce the efficient level of the good. Work is onerous. Tangible resources are scarce, as their prices show. Marginal cost precisely reflects the summed sacrifice made by everybody who participates in producing the good.

Logic and good sense require that value and sacrifice ought to be in line with each other at the margin; price = marginal cost does just that. All resources are used efficiently throughout the economy, without any central direction or plan.

To put Adam Smith's idea into more technical prose, the invisible hand of the competitive market system guides allocation in line with marginal conditions throughout the economy. Self-interested people striving to maximize their own good may be unconcerned with any social goals, but their actions bring about efficiency and other benefits throughout the economy.

Moreover, the efficient competitive result is robust. Even if outcomes happen to pull away from the pure conditions, the system pulls them back toward the efficient conditions. Price is still brought toward marginal cost. Consumer surplus is still virtually maximized, consistent with covering the costs of production. Other goals also are reached.

2. But There Are Limits on the Benefits of Competition

Paradise is not assured, however. There are limits to the reach of the invisible hand. The process may create a universal optimum or, instead, only a small domain of efficiency within a wider realm of gaps and distortions. At least five types of gaps may be important, as discussed in the paragraphs that follow.

External Effects.   Because of external costs or benefits, private prices and costs may diverge from their true social levels. An external cost occurs when a private activity imposes costs on people not directly engaged in the activity. For example, air pollution is an external cost inflicted by chimneys spewing smoke and cars emitting fumes. Those owning the chimneys and cars are concerned only with their own private costs and benefits, and they choose a level of activity based on those private costs.

Because they don't have to pay for harming others, they underestimate the true social costs of the activity and they exercise too little self-restraint. In this way, the invisible hand does not make people consider the external costs that they impose on others.[8]

Public Goods.   The invisible hand fails to provide public goods, which involve an enormous variety of crucial services and systems. For example, public goods include all streets and highways, national defense, police activities of all kinds, the courts, all public schools, public health protections, local and national parks (e.g., the invisible hand would spread cities, suburbs, and malls throughout the Grand Canyon and Yosemite National Park), and many others.

A public good is "non-excludable"; no one can be excluded from using it. One person's consumption of the good does not affect another person's consumption. If a private party attempted to supply public goods, consumers would try to be "free riders" by benefiting from the good without paying for it. Therefore, public goods must be produced by governments.

Inequity. Efficient allocation does not guarantee a fair outcome. Open competition usually spreads opportunities and wealth widely. But the efficient conditions may instead coexist with preexisting inequity in the distributions of wealth, income, and opportunity.

For example, an unjust feudal society may develop into a competitive free-market industrial economy. Yet it may retain all its old structure of wealth and privilege, and factory hands may be exploited as ruthlessly by wealthy owners as the peasants were. Or it may shift to a new structure that is even more unjust; or possibly instead it may develop a much fairer set of distributions.

Insecurity and Risk. Each firm is tiny and vulnerable in its market. Competition can ruthlessly mow down these little firms, and workers have little protection against being let go. Relentless competition therefore breeds insecurity with no safety net.

Other Criteria. Competition does tend to maximize freedom, but job satisfaction and culture are outside the competitive system and may be hurt. There is considerable literature on the desolation that remorseless competitive market processes may cause in actual societies, such as Great Britain during the nineteenth century.

These limits are all matters of degree. There could be a little of each defect around the edges of a largely efficient economy, or instead the defects could be so large as to dwarf the gains from efficient allocation. In any event, the invisible hand remains powerful as far as it reaches, but it has limits.

III. EFFECTS OF MONOPOLY POWER

We now return to the case of efficient outcomes, but here we examine what happens if one market becomes a monopoly. As simple theory and personal experience attest, the main effects are to cut output, raise price, and create excess profits. Yet the act and its effects can be complex, and some of the effects are not obvious. We evaluate them step by step.

1. THE MONOPOLIST'S CHOICES

Pure monopoly exists when one seller controls all sales in a market. The market demand curve then becomes the monopoly firm's own demand curve, with whatever inelasticity exists for that product. Inelasticity gives the seller some ability to choose the level of price as well as output.

Marginal Revenue. As shown in figure 2.4, a marginal revenue curve now appears, located below the demand curve. Marginal revenue is now less than price, because the firm must cut its price in order to sell a higher quantity. It therefore loses some of the revenue that it would have drawn from the inframarginal units. So its net money yield from selling an added unit (that is, the marginal revenue) is that unit's price, but **minus** the revenue lost by cutting price on all the previous units. Therefore the marginal revenue curve always lies below a down-sloping demand curve.

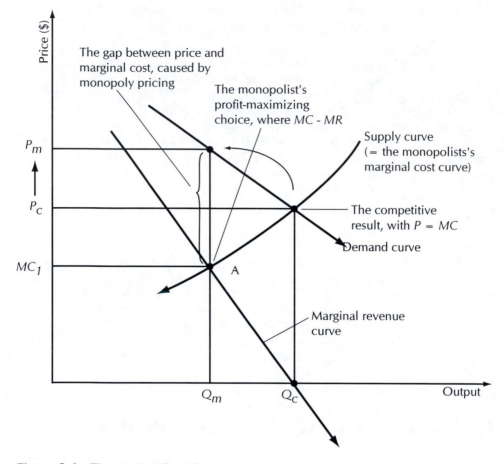

Figure 2.4   The simple effect of monopoly.

As a practical matter, the marginal revenue curve is easy to locate. It lies halfway between the demand curve and the vertical axis. Practice this, so that you can place it correctly.

Marginal Cost.   The monopolist's marginal cost schedule is now the supply curve of the entire market, which previously equaled the sum of all the competitive firms' marginal cost curves. Since the single monopolist now includes all those firms, its marginal cost curve is the summation of all the little firms' marginal cost curves.

The monopolist's two crucial curves, marginal revenue and marginal cost, cross at point A in figure 2.4, which is the profit-maximizing output. As always, the firm produces only up to the level at which the extra unit is just worthwhile, that is, that extra unit adds as much to revenue as it adds to costs.

Effects on Price and Output.   The monopolist violates the efficient price = marginal cost outcome by cutting output, which means that price is above marginal cost at that reduced output level. There is economic harm in that disparity. In figure 2.4, people are willing to pay—when they're forced to—a price more than twice as high as the marginal cost of the good. At the margin, the value they place on the good is twice as high as the cost of the resources used to produce that last unit. This condition is a clear signal that more of the good should be produced, generating more value than the cost. Evidently, monopoly's impact is strong.

Decades ago, this effect was labeled the *Lerner index of monopoly.*[9] It is the following ratio:

$$\text{Lerner index} = \text{price} - \frac{\text{marginal cost}}{\text{price}}$$

This ratio can be restated using the elasticity of demand, as follows:[10]

$$\text{Lerner index} = \frac{P - MC}{P} = \frac{1}{\text{elasticity of demand}}$$

The lesson to be learned is that greater elasticity yields a smaller monopoly distortion, which precisely fits the visual lesson of figure 1.1.

Remember from chapter 1 that monopoly power exists in the inelasticity of the firm's demand curve. We have now seen more formally how inelastic demand involves monopoly power as a matter of degree. But the Lerner index is more a conceptual insight than a practical indicator, because elasticity is usually impossible to measure reliably.

In real cases, the impacts of monopoly may be large or small. Case 1 in figure 2.5 shows an urgently needed good with inelastic demand; also, marginal cost is relatively flat. Accordingly, monopoly drastically changes both output and price. The price is four times the original price and five times marginal cost, and output is only half of the competitive level.[11] In contrast, the good may have close substitutes and a rising marginal cost curve, as in case 2. Then the effect is mild; price is only nudged up (and output down) by a little.

2.   MONOPOLY'S EFFECTS ON ECONOMIC PERFORMANCE

Other effects flow from these effects on price and output.

X-Inefficiency.   Freed from competitive pressures, the monopoly firm's management may slacken its efforts. Cost controls may loosen and effort may decline, because everyone working for the firm knows that there is a cushion of excess profits. The slack may absorb some of the monopoly profits; the reduced accounting profits would then hide some of the actual monopoly impact.

Misallocation.   Monopoly distorts the allocation of resources by (1) cutting output from the most efficient level and (2) driving a wedge between price and marginal cost. The cutback in output forces some of the inputs into other markets where their economic value is less. These distortions ripple through adjacent markets into the whole economy. Monopoly in one part of the economy warps allocation in the whole system. The larger the monopolized industry and the more severe the direct effects are, the greater the economic harm.

Misallocation is defined as a reduction in consumers' surplus. Recall that pure competition maximizes that surplus (consistent with covering costs). Monop-

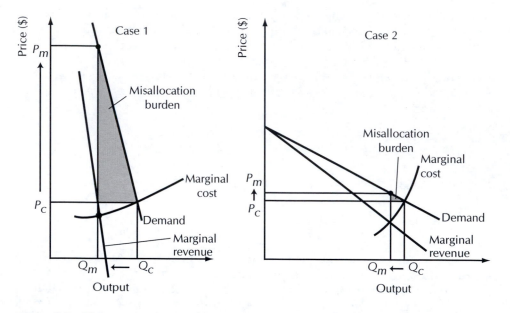

Figure 2.5   The severity of monopoly's effects depends on demand and cost conditions.

oly's effect stands in contrast. By raising the price, as in figure 2.6, the monopolist eliminates some of this consumer surplus, which shrinks from ABC to ADE.

Now suppose for simplicity that average costs are constant (and therefore equal to marginal cost). Then the loss of consumer surplus has two components:

1. The rectangle EDFC in figure 2.6 represents the increased dollar payments by consumers because the price to them has been raised. These dollars are taken by the firm as its monopoly profits, transferred from the pockets of customers.

2. The triangle DBF represents the welfare loss to society resulting from the resource misallocation caused by the monopoly power. This surplus value, previously enjoyed by consumers, now simply disappears.

The loss, often called the "**welfare triangle**," may range from small to large. Again, the slopes of the demand and cost curves influence that amount. In case 1 in figure 2.5, the burden is large—as much as 40 percent of the monopolist's total sales revenue. In case 2, the burden is a mere sliver—perhaps only 1 percent of sales revenue.

Redistribution.   The monopoly profit shifts income and wealth from consumers to the monopoly's owners. The amounts are illustrated in figure 2.7; total monopoly profits are calculated by multiplying the profit per unit times the number of units sold: $(P_m - AC) \times Q_m$. The magnitude of excess profits depends on the positions and shapes of the demand and cost curves. In case 1 in figure 2.7, because the steep demand curve is well above average cost, the excess profits are large. In case 2, where demand is more elastic and is close to average cost, the excess profit is small.

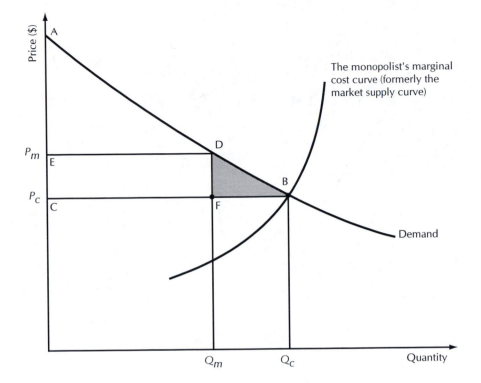

Figure 2.6   Monopoly reduces consumer surplus.

The excess profit usually represents a degree of unfairness. Many consumers suffer a reduction in their purchasing power, while the few owners of the monopoly rake in a lot of money.[12] This sharpens inequality, because consumers usually have lower incomes than the monopoly's owners (think of dollars going from working buyers to investor owners). And this **income shift** quickly becomes an even steeper **wealth shift**. The monopoly's stock price rises to reflect the increase of current and future monopoly profits, so the owners can sell out now and put their wealth into other investments. Thus monopoly often creates family fortunes for a few at the expense of the many.

Free-market economists do not regard this result as a negative; to them, any shift of income and wealth is only an ethical matter that cannot be said a priori to be bad or good. But most economists do regard the shift toward more inequality as a social burden, at least in part.

Invention and Innovation. Monopoly retards progress. A monopoly feels less pressure to invent new products or methods, so the inventing process becomes largely voluntary. And for any new invention, there is less pressure to convert new inventions into practical innovations. In fact, the pace of innovation will slow down, because innovations destroy the value of the monopolist's existing products and processes. By reducing incentives, monopoly discourages innovation.

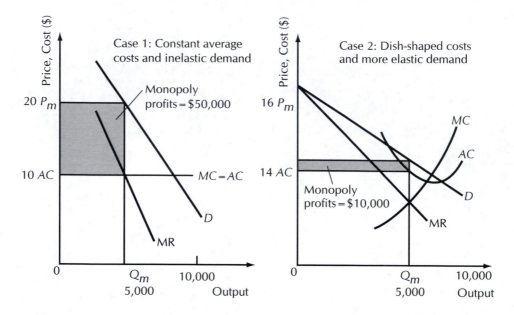

Figure 2.7 The monopoly's profits may be large or small.

Other Effects of Monopoly. Monopoly also eliminates the competitive process itself, with the resulting loss of social value.

Freedom of choice is reduced for everyone except the monopolist. Consumers cannot switch to other suppliers, for there are none. Only the monopolist's goods are available, and they now carry higher prices. **Suppliers** also have less choice. Their sales are restricted to what the single monopolist will buy. **Workers** also have fewer choices, because the monopolist is now the only employer in the industry. The monopolist will cut employment, drive wages down, and become more arbitrary in dealing with workers. **Economic insecurity** is raised as workers lose their jobs.

Democracy may also be hurt by monopoly power. As Henry Simons noted, "Political liberty can survive only within an effectively competitive economic system. Thus, *the great enemy of democracy is monopoly, in all its forms:* gigantic corporations, trade associations and other agencies for price control, trade unions. . . ."[13] When there are fewer firms with less diversity of interests, the monopolist becomes a bigger political force, with its excess profits and market power to protect. It is in a position to use and abuse the political process to preserve and enlarge its economic advantage.

Culture and society can also be affected. Diversity is reduced, and when markets are monopolized, society becomes more stratified and rigid.

Altogether, there are many monopoly impacts, not just the loss of static efficiency.

3. An Example: Local Student Housing

These ideas may become clearer with a numerical example that shows the large financial rewards of monopoly.

Consider a college town that has 10,000 private student apartments. Competition is effective, driving rents down to the actual level of average cost, namely, $300 per month per person (which includes the cost of the invested capital). At an investment value of $20,000 for each student living unit, this stock of housing is worth $200 million.

Now a group of ten clever economics students sees the opportunity and seizes it. They pool a mere $10,000 in cash, form a company (naming it the Student Benevolent Housing Society), and issue one share to each member at a value of $1,000 per share. They secretly tell a local bank of their plan, get a bank loan of $200 million, and very quietly buy up all of the 10,000 apartments currently used by students. Then, with a little bribery or blackmail, the society persuades the city council to declare all other buildings unsafe and illegal for use as student housing. That political step blocks any future entry of new housing capacity, thereby protecting the new monopoly from competition.

This new student housing monopoly has the curves shown in figure 2.8. The flat marginal cost curve reflects the constant-cost conditions; each housing unit has the same cost of supply, at $300 per month.

Benevolent Housing now acts on figure 2.8's facts: it closes 5,000 of the apartments and raises the rent of the remaining 5,000 units a "mere" 8.5 percent, to $325 per month. Half of the people who operate, maintain, and rebuild apartments—the managers, janitors, painters, plumbers—are fired and have to seek work in other industries. The use of paint, furniture, lumber, and other apartment supplies is also cut in half, so that the resources in those supplying industries become partly unemployed. The closed apartment buildings are sold for other uses, such as offices or warehouses, perhaps recouping approximately all of their

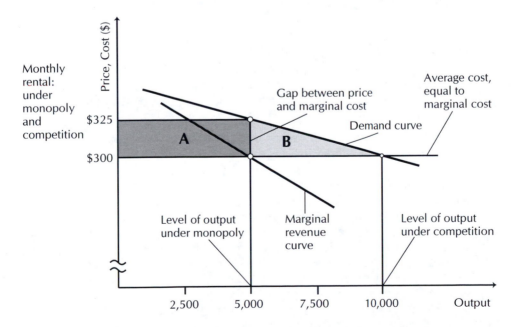

Figure 2.8   The simple monopoly effect.

investment cost. With those proceeds, the society can pay off up to half of its $200 million loan immediately. The rest of the loan continues, routinely covered as part of normal economic costs.

The new monopoly will make $25 per month in excess profit on each of the 5,000 housing units that remain open. That profit equals $300 in each twelve-month year. The total excess profits are therefore $300/year × 5,000 = $1.5 million per year. Those hefty profits occur even though the rents were raised by only 8.5 percent, from $300 to $325.

The future flow of $1.5 million yearly in excess profits may well have a capitalized present value in the range of $15 million.[14] (That is, the profits are about equivalent to the interest at a 10 percent rate on $15 million in bonds.) That amount of new wealth equals $1.5 million for *each* of the original ten owners, who can now sell out immediately and hold a tidy fortune. Nothing can then be done to recoup this skimming of monopoly wealth from students.

If the monopolists invest their money in 6 percent tax-exempt municipal bonds, they will each collect about $90,000 per year in income, for no further effort. They can then live on $50,000 a year, invest the other $40,000, and watch their fortunes grow, without ever having to work again. They, and perhaps their children, are now in the leisure class, independently wealthy (that is, independent of the need to work).

All this from monopolizing just one modest local market in one town! Comparable family fortunes have been created thousands of times in the United States in small local and regional markets. Generalize this effect to all markets and you see starkly why the struggle to monopolize continues—the rewards are large, immediate, and lasting. To put it in clear prose: Only effective competition protects the hard working populace from the creation of a class of idle, monopoly-enriched drones.

4. ECONOMIES AND DISECONOMIES OF SCALE

Scale economies may justify a monopoly. When an industry has large economies of scale, that may make a dominant firm or even a full monopoly the "natural" result. Larger size results in lower average costs. Here we summarize the concept; chapter 7 covers it in detail.

Economies of scale.   Economies of scale may arise in any of a firm's activities, such as production, marketing, or innovation. Figure 2.9 illustrates four alternative shapes for cost curves, among many other variations.

Each curve has two technical features: minimum efficient scale, and the cost gradient. Together they define how large the economies are.

Minimum efficient scale (MES) occurs where average cost stops declining and the average cost curve reaches its lowest level. Think of MES as the "capacity" level of the firm, which is the best size for production. Beyond the MES level, there may be diseconomies of scale that tip the curve up, or there may be constant costs with the flat range illustrated by curve A.

The cost gradient is the steepness of the curve's down-slope. It shows how strong the economies are. The gradient can be any degree between steep and nearly flat. Steeper means that economies are larger. At outputs above MES, the gradient of **diseconomies** may be small or large, with important consequences.

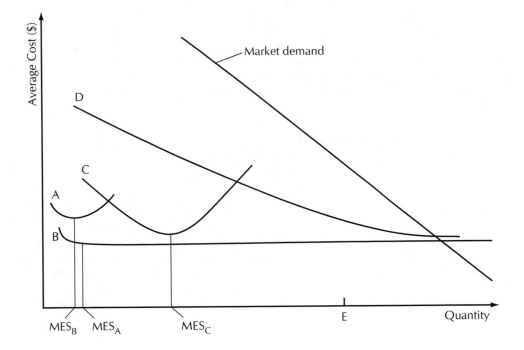

Figure 2.9   Differing overage cost curves, with differing room for competition.

In each market, the scale economies influence the "room for competition" and "excess market share."

Room for Competition.   Economies range between small (as in curves A and B) and large (curves C and D). Very large-scale economies (curve D) cause **natural monopoly,** with room for only one efficient firm. Curve A is the opposite extreme: **natural competition**. Curve C may be a **natural oligopoly,** with room for only two or three firms. Curve B's flat range of lowest cost leaves the outcome indeterminate; firms may be as small as MES or instead much larger.

Economies of scale can make it efficient to have some degree of market power. Effective competition is impossible in case D and unlikely in case C; there is not enough "room." Even in case B, firms may capture sales levels (and market shares) that are much larger than MES. Then they may be able to exert a degree of monopoly power.

Excess Market Share.   If a firm holds a market share greater than MES, that extra amount gives no efficiency gains. It is **excess market share**. In figure 2.9, the excess is illustrated by the interval MES_A to E. The firm's size (which also determines its market share) exceeds the level needed to obtain minimum costs at MES_A, and the excess market share may add to the firm's market power.

If economies of scale justify some portion of monopoly positions by lowering costs, that depends critically on both the size of MES and the cost gradient. chapter 7 will examine these magnitudes.

Two Basic Cost Curves. In any event, two kinds of cost diagrams should be kept in mind.[15] One reflects the industry's underlying long-run cost conditions (figure 2.9). The other shows the current cost curves of an ongoing firm (figure 2.10). In both cases, there is a level of capacity, where average costs are lowest and equal to marginal cost. Below that capacity, marginal costs are well below average costs; above that level of capacity, marginal costs may rise sharply (or gently, or remain flat).

5. GRADATIONS OF MARKET POWER

Between pure monopoly and pure competition lie infinitely many grada-tions and varieties of markets. The literature has settled on six main categories of markets: monopoly, dominant firm, tight oligopoly, loose oligopoly, monopolist competition, and pure competition. But how do economists assign markets to one of these categories?

Combining Market Share and Other Elements. Fundamentally, a firm's market power varies mainly with its market share. Intermediate market shares cause gradations of intermediate monopoly effects. Figure 2.11 illustrates the basic function relating market share and profitability (explained in chapter 4).

Of course, variations around this central tendency may occur, as follows:

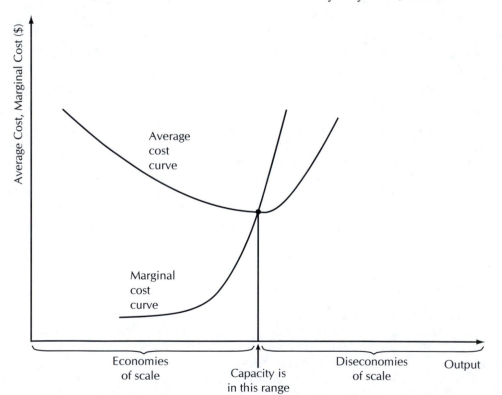

Figure 2.10 Present cost curves of an ongoing firm.

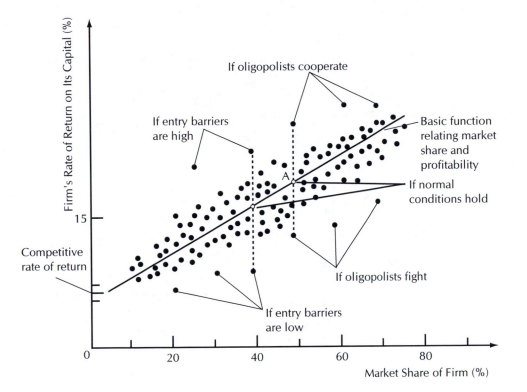

Figure 2.11   The basic relationship between market share and profit rate.

1. Interactions among oligopolists may push the outcome up or down. For example, a 50 percent market share may yield a profit rate of 15 percent on average (at point A). But the profit rate may go up to, say, 20 percent if the firm cooperates with the other oligopolists; or instead it may drop to only the competitive rate of 10 percent if the oligopolists fight one another.

2. Entry barriers may also affect the outcome, as illustrated in figure 2.11 for a firm with a 40 percent market share. High barriers enable the oligopolist to obtain high profits; low barriers (with the threat of new competitors coming in) force profits down.

Generally, a firm with a low market share (below 10 percent) has no market power, regardless of the structure of the whole market. Such a low share limits the firm to a (nearly) flat demand curve. Higher market shares usually give more steeply sloped demand curves with greater degrees of control over price and quantity.

Rate of Decline of Market Share over Time.   The last basic issue is simple but important: the rate at which monopoly power declines over time. Any high market share may decline swiftly or slowly, or it may persist or even increase, as figure 2.12 illustrates. Monopoly power that declines rapidly is much less serious than monopoly power that endures over time.

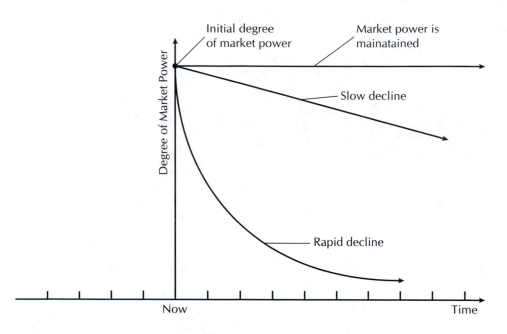

Figure 2.12   Three alternative time paths of market power.

This simple matter holds important practical lessons about which there is much dispute. The more hard-line free-market analysts assert that the rate of decline is rapid. Monopoly is not only rare, weak, and justified by efficiency, they say, but it is also quick to evaporate unless: (1) the firm continues to attain superior efficiency or (2) government interferes to help the firm.

Other economists are more realistic and skeptical. They expect that market dominance often persists, even when the monopoly is not more efficient or the state is not interfering to prop it up. The market may have imperfections that let the monopoly arise, and the monopoly may possibly create still more imperfections.

Chapter 3 will present evidence on this point.

Questions for Review

1. Show in diagrams that the less elastic the demand, the sharper the monopoly effect will be.

2. Show in diagrams the net effect of monopoly on price when X-inefficiency is roughly: (1) 10 percent and (2) 25 percent; and when economies of scale cut costs by: (3) 5 percent, (4) 15 percent, and (5) 30 percent.

3. Explain why X-inefficiency is likely to be larger than allocative inefficiency.

4. "By allocating resources so that price equals marginal cost for every firm and every good, the invisible hand achieves a deeply meaningful result." Explain why that equality is so meaningful.

5. Explain the main limits on the invisible hand.

6. A monopolist company uses its marginal revenue curve to reach the monopoly result. Where was that marginal revenue curve before? Why wasn't it used?

7. Explain how minimum efficient scale can determine the structure of a market, making it naturally competitive, a natural oligopoly, or a natural monopoly.

APPENDIX: TOPICS, METHODS, AND SOURCES FOR STUDENT RESEARCH PAPERS

When writing a research paper, you practice the same steps that professionals do in their research; they assess the best literature on a topic, frame the issue using their independent judgment, try to solve the issue with new hypotheses or evidence, and then write up the results. In effect, **you pose an issue and take a stand on it, presenting your reasons and evidence and arguing persuasively for your conclusions.** That is what economists do in their research papers and monographs.

If you start the process early with an outline and write a first draft about two-thirds of the way through the course, the teacher can then give suggestions for revision or added work. This sequence of framing the issue, drafting, comments, and revision is exactly what professional economists do for their research articles and books. What matters is that you treat the issues carefully with a professional degree of skill, and that your final paper makes the best case for your approach and interpretations.

In research and writing projects, the most direct approach is to reexamine a point from one of the chapters. For example, you can

1. treat a specific issue as a matter of theory, using abstract reasoning to derive new results

2. perform an applied industry study (on a small scale) about a real firm or market

3. try to show how data could test a general hypothesis about competition, economies of scale, price discrimination

Suggestions for these approaches are given in the following four sections. For some topics, I provide specific references as a starting point. Read them and use their endnote citations to track down other references. For other topics, the passages in this book cite various sources in the endnotes. Usually your teacher can also suggest references or entirely new and timely topics to work on. In fact, a research paper is a fine vehicle for teachers to convey their research skills and attitudes to their students, and for the students to observe a professional specialist (their teacher) at work.

I stress that you should pose an issue and take a stand on it. Otherwise the project can be a dull and lifeless chore.

1. ISSUES

Nearly every issue in this book is eligible for critical rethinking and new evidence, either as it stands now or by reviewing past debates that have led to the current views. A selection of good topics might begin with the following (which may be supplemented by your teacher):

1. What are the best methods and types of evidence to use when defining markets?

2. Does a firm's market share usually show its degree of monopoly?

3. Are price-fixing agreements really unstable? What conditions influence the degree of stability?

4. Estimate the height of entry barriers and the amount of actual entry in three different industries.

5. Can vertical integration increase market power? Start with Spengler, Bork, and Scherer and perhaps analyze a specific vertical merger.

6. What is the true scope of natural monopoly in electricity, telephone service, or postal service? Start with references in chapters 3 and 9.

7. Trace the economic effects of a specific antitrust action, such as Standard Oil (1911), American Tobacco (1911), Alcoa (1945), or the electrical equipment price-fixing cases (1960).

8. Is Schumpeterian competition relevant to specific parts or all of the economy? Which parts especially?

9. Do dominant firms decline? Trace three dominant firms from 1950 to the present. Analyze the factors that influence the rate of decline.

Some leading book-length sources on these and other issues are as follows:

Walter Adams and James W. Brock, *The Bigness Complex* (New York: Pantheon Books, 1986).

Joe S. Bain, *Barriers to New Competition* (Cambridge: Harvard University Press, 1956).

Robert H. Bork, *The Antitrust Paradox: A Policy at War with Itself* (New York: Basic Books, 1978).

Avinash K. Dixit and Barry J. Nalebuff, *Thinking Strategically: The Competitive Edge in Business, Politics and Everyday Life* (New York: Norton, 1991).

Kenneth G. Elzinga and Robert A. Rogowsky, eds., "Relevant Markets in Antitrust," special issue of *Journal of Reprints for Antitrust Law and Economics* (New York: Federal Legal Publications, 1984).

Walton Hamilton and Irene Till, *Antitrust in Action*, Monograph no. 16, Temporary National Economic Committee, Investigation of Economic Power (Washington, DC: U.S. Government Printing Office, 1940).

John Jewkes et al., *The Sources of Invention*, 2nd ed. (New York: Norton, 1969).

John Moody, *The Truth About the Trusts* (Chicago: Moody Publishing, 1904).

Dennis C. Mueller, ed., *The Determinants of Mergers* (Boston: Oelgeschlager, Gunn & Hain, 1980).

Michael E. Porter, *Competitive Advantage: Creating and Sustaining Superior Performance* (New York: Free Press, 1985).

David J. Ravenscraft and F. M. Scherer, *Mergers, Sell-offs and Economic Efficiency* (Washington, DC: Brookings Institution, 1987).

Stephen A. Rhoades, *Power, Empire Building, and Mergers* (Lexington, MA: D. C. Heath Lexington Books, 1983).

F. M. Scherer et al., *The Economics of Multiplant Operation* (Cambridge: Harvard University Press, 1975).

William G. Shepherd, *The Treatment of Market Power* (New York: Columbia University Press, 1975).

John Sutton, *Sunk Costs and Market Structure: Price Competition, Advertising, and the Evolution of Concentration* (Cambridge: MIT Press, 1991).

M. A. Utton, *Profits and Stability of Monopoly* (Cambridge: Cambridge University Press, 1986).

Leonard W. Weiss and Michael W. Klass, eds., *Regulatory Reform: What Really Happened* (Boston: Little, Brown, 1986).

Oliver E. Williamson, *Antitrust Economics* (Oxford: Basil Blackwell, 1987).

2. TOPICS IN THEORY AND RESEARCH METHODS

Some students thrive on abstract analysis and technical points. For them, many theoretical topics are excellent term-paper subjects. You may try new variations on oligopoly models, analyze some aspect of strategic pricing, assess free-rider topics, or restate the efficiency properties of competition, etc. The theory of contestability is also an interesting area to explore (see chapter 9).

Theoretical papers can be much shorter and more concise than those on empirical topics because you do not need to assemble evidence. Begin with the sources cited in the endnotes, and consult the *Journal of Industrial Economics, International Journal of Industrial Organization*, and *RAND Journal of Economics* for interesting papers. The leading, comprehensive source in book form is Richard Schmalensee and Robert D. Willig, eds., *Handbook of Industrial Organization*, 2 vols. (Cambridge: MIT Press, 1989). It has extensive chapters on all major topics in the field.

Among other interesting books on recent new-IO theory are the following:

William J. Baumol, John C. Panzar, and Robert D. Willig, *Contestable Markets and the Theory of Industry Structure* (San Diego: Harcourt Brace Jovanovich, 1982).

Timothy F. Bresnahan and Richard Schmalensee, eds., *The Empirical Renaissance in Industrial Economics* (Oxford: Basil Blackwell, 1987).

Oz Shy, *Industrial Organization: Theory and Applications* (Cambridge: MIT Press, 1996).

Joseph E. Stiglitz and C. Frank Mathewson, *New Developments in the Analysis of Market Structure* (Cambridge: MIT Press, 1986).

Lester Telser, *Theories of Competition* (Amsterdam: North Holland, 1988).

Jean Tirole, *The Theory of Industrial Organization*, 2nd ed. (Cambridge: MIT Press, 1993).

Michael Waterson, *Economic Theory of Industry* (Cambridge: Cambridge University Press, 1984).

3. INDUSTRY STUDIES

Choose an interesting industry. Study its structure and/or behavior and/or performance; emphasize one part or cover all three. Then

1. judge how competitive it is. (You may wish to draw contrasting estimates of high and low market power in the industry.)

2. bring an earlier industry study up-to-date, trying to explain recent changes.

3. compare a leading firm and a lesser firm in the industry, showing which is more profitable, efficient, innovative, etc. Try to explain the difference.

Each industry usually presents one or two leading questions, which your paper can focus on. For example, in computers, it is the near-collapse of IBM in the early 1990s and the new dominance of Microsoft. Telecommunications poses the complex impacts of the new procompetition law in 1996. In beer, it might be the real cause of rising concentration in the industry. In health care, it might be the impact of health maintenance organizations: Do they provide for effective competition, and are they efficient? In electricity, will competition become effective? In cereals, was the FTC shared-monopoly case in the 1970s a sound one?

The capsule industry studies in chapters 13 and 14 of this book offer good starting points. As a next step, three recent books offer excellent concise industry studies as starting points for some twenty different industries; they overlap on many industries, giving alternative viewpoints.

Walter Adams, ed., *The Structure of American Industry*, 9th ed. (New York, Macmillan, 1994), 11 industries.

Larry L. Duetsch, ed., *Industry Studies* (Upper Saddle River, NJ: Prentice Hall, 1993), 15 industries.

John E. Kwoka, Jr. and Lawrence J. White, eds., *The Antitrust Revolution: The Role of Economics*, 2nd ed. (New York: HarperCollins, 1994), 15 chapter-length studies of industries or antitrust cases.

George Symeonidis, *The Effects of Competition: Cartel Policy and the Evolution of Strategy and Structure in British Industry* (Cambridge, MA: MIT Press, 2002).

For comparison with Europe, see Peter Johnson, ed., *European Industries: Structure, Conduct and Performance* (Aldershot, UK: Elgar Publishing, 1993), 11 industry case studies.

The business press can be extremely helpful, with occasional major articles on companies, industries, merger trends, foreign comparisons, etc. Get familiar with the *Wall Street Journal*, *Fortune* magazine, and *BusinessWeek*. Also, the investors' services Moody and Standard & Poor have useful periodical and annual compendiums of company and industry reports.

Some article-length industry studies are cited in the endnotes of this book. Most full industry studies are in book-length monographs. Some leading examples follow:

Richard F. Hirsh, *Power Loss: The Origins of Deregulation and Restructuring in the American Electric Utility System* (Cambridge, MA: MIT Press, 1999).

Alfred E. Kahn, *Letting Go: Deregulating the Process of Deregulation* (East Lansing: Michigan State University, 1998).

Marc Allen Eisner, *Regulatory Politics in Transition*, rev. ed. (Baltimore: Johns Hopkins University Press, 2000), a broad review of regulation history and trends.

Bill Bradshaw and Helen Lawton Smith, eds., *Privatization and Deregulation of Transport* (London: St. Martin's Press, 2000).

David M. Newbery, *Privatization, Restructuring and Regulation of Network Utilities* (Cambridge, MA: MIT Press, 1999).

William L. Megginson and Jeffrey M. Netter, "From State to Market: A Survey of Empirical Studies on Privatization," *Journal of Economic Literature, 39*, June 2001, pp. 321–389.

Elliott D. Sclar, *You Don't Always Get What You Pay For: The Economics of Privatization* (Ithaca, NY: Cornell University Press, 2000).

Mitsuhiro Kagami and Masatsugu Tsuji, eds., *Privatization, Deregulation and Economic Efficiency:*

A Comparative Analysis of Asia, Europe and the Americas (Northampton, MA: Elgar, 2000).

Paul L. Jowkow, ed., *Economic Regulation* (Northampton, MA: Elgar, 2000).

Robert B. Ekelund, Jr., ed., *The Foundations of Regulatory Economics*, 3 vols. (Northampton, MA: Elgar, 1998). 76 significant papers in regulation: origins, Modern approaches, and deregulation.

Zoltan Acs, *The Changing Structure of the U.S. Economy: Lessons from the Steel Industry* (New York: Praeger, 1984).

Elizabeth E. Bailey, David R. Graham, and Daniel P. Kaplan, *Deregulating the Airlines* (Cambridge, MA: MIT Press, 1985).

Gerald W. Brock, *The U.S. Computer Industry* (Cambridge, MA: Ballinger, 1975).

Kerry Cooper and Donald Fraser, *Banking Deregulation and the New Competition in Financial Services* (Cambridge, MA: Ballinger, 1984).

Robert Crandall, *The U.S. Steel Industry in Recurrent Crisis* (Washington, DC: Brookings Institute, 1982).

Robert W. Crandall, *After the Breakup: U.S. Telecommunications in a More Competitive Era* (Washington, DC: Brookings Institute, 1991).

Andrew F. Daughety, ed., *Analytical Studies in Transport Economics* (Cambridge: Cambridge University Press, 1985).

Richard Thomas DeLamarter, *Big Blue: IBM's Use and Abuse of Power* (New York: Dodd, Mead, 1986).

Edward J. Epstein, *The Rise and Fall of Diamonds* (New York: Simon & Schuster, 1982).

David S. Evans, ed., *Breaking Up Bell* (Amsterdam: North Holland, 1983).

Paul J. Feldstein, *Health Care Economics*, 2nd ed. (New York: Wiley, 1983).

Franklin M. Fisher et al., *Folded, Spindled, and Mutilated: Economic Analysis and U.S. v. IBM* (Cambridge, MA: MIT Press, 1983).

James Frey and Arthur Johnson, *Government and Sport* (New York: Rowman and Allanheld, 1985).

Timothy Green, *The World of Diamonds* (New York: William Morrow, 1981).

James M. Griffin and David J. Teece, *OPEC Behavior and World Oil Prices* (London: Allen & Unwin, 1982).

J. A. Hunker, *Structural Change in the U.S. Automobile Industry* (Lexington, MA: D. C. Heath, 1983).

Paul L. Joskow and Richard Schmalensee, *Markets for Power* (Cambridge, MA: MIT Press, 1986).

Gorham Kindem, *The American Movie Industry* (Carbondale: Southern Illinois University Press, 1982).

Paul W. MacAvoy, *Crude Oil Prices* (Cambridge, MA: Ballinger, 1982).

John R. Meyer and Clinton V. Oster, *Deregulation and the New Airline Entrepreneurs* (Cambridge: MIT Press, 1984).

Roger G. Noll, ed., *Government and the Sports Business*, rev. ed. (Washington, DC: Brookings Institute, 1985).

Emmanuel N. Roussakis, *Commercial Banking in an Era of Deregulation* (New York: Praeger, 1984).

Anthony Saunders and Lawrence J. White, *Technology and the Regulation of Financial Markets* (Lexington, MA: Lexington Books, 1986).

Steven A. Schneider, *The Oil Price Revolution* (Baltimore: Johns Hopkins University Press, 1983).

Harry M. Shooshan, ed., *Disconnecting Bell: The Impact of AT&T Divestiture* (New York: Pergamon Press, 1984).

Andrew Zimbalist, *Baseball and Billions* (New York: HarperCollins, 1992).

4.   EMPIRICAL STUDIES

Students often prefer to explore basic sources of empirical evidence, using them to practice quantitative research. This gives students a better feel for the meaning of empirical research results. Here I list several sources and suggest simple questions to try to answer.

Concentration Ratios and HHI. The basic source is in the U.S. *Census of Manufactures* for 1947, 1954, 1958, 1963, 1968, 1972, 1977, and 1982. The 1982 report is Bureau of the Census, *Concentration Ratios in Manufacturing* 1982, MC82-S-7 (Washington, DC: U.S. Government Printing Office, 1985). Topics are in chapters 3 and 4.

1. Adjust ratios to reflect true concentration in properly defined markets (examples: drugs, milk, bricks, newspapers, automobiles, computers, sports equipment).

2. Calculate the average degree of concentration.

3. List the twenty most concentrated and twenty least concentrated industries. What factors explain their differences?

4. Which industries have changed concentration most sharply over time? Analyze the causes.

Profits. Use the *Fortune Directory of the 500 Largest U.S. Industrial Corporations* (issued yearly in April) and the directories for other groups (banks, utilities, foreign firms), which are published yearly in the summer months. See *Moody's Industrial Manual* (yearly) for more detailed data, and use references in chapter 5.

1. Evaluate the most profitable companies. Do they hold market power? Are there economies of scale?

2. What is the normal or competitive rate of return?

Company Divisions. On the so-called Form 10-K used to report to the Securities and Exchange Commission, firms disaggregate their total sales figures. Use these forms to judge market structure and company positions in more detail.

Mergers. Until 1981, the FTC published yearly a complete listing of mergers involving over $10 million in assets since 1948 (FTC Bureau of Economics, *Statistical Report on Mergers and Acquisitions*). See also *Mergers & Acquisitions* magazine.

1. Evaluate the trends and volume of mergers.

2. Check the classification of horizontal, vertical, and conglomerate types, using five selected mergers.

3. Trace mergers in one industry, appraising their impact on structure.

Advertising. Use *Advertising Age* magazine's summary (yearly in August) of the 100 firms that spend the most on advertising. See other sources in chapter 12.

1. Calculate advertising intensity for firms in three industries.

2. Analyze why the firms differ in advertising intensity.

3. Is advertising intensity related to the firms' profitability?

X-Efficiency. The *Wall Street Journal* and *BusinessWeek* frequently discuss the efficiency of firms. *Moody's Handbook of Common Stocks* (quarterly) gives brief descriptions and performance data for nearly 1,000 firms.

1. Find ten efficient firms and ten inefficient firms.
2. Compare these firms' profit rates and stock price movements.
3. Is market power present?
4. Try to trace whether management undergoes changes in the inefficient firms.

ENDNOTES

[1] Which values to include and how to weight them are old and important issues lying at the heart of economic science. Important earlier discussions are Alfred Marshall, *Principles of Economics*, 8th ed. (London: Macmillan, 1920); and Joe S. Bain, *Industrial Organization*, rev. ed. (New York: Wiley, 1968).

For two contrasting views, see John M. Blair, *Economic Concentration* (New York: Harcourt Brace Jovanovich, 1972); and Fred S. McChesney and William F. Shughart, eds., *The Causes and Consequences of Antitrust* (Chicago: University of Chicago Press, 1995). Blair's expansive view embraces broad values, including social impacts. McChesney and Shughart present the free-market view, discussing only static efficiency.

[2] The expression was coined by Harvey J. Leibenstein in 1966; see his *Beyond Economic Man* (Cambridge: Harvard University Press, 1976). See also Richard E. Caves and David R. Barton, *Technical Efficiency in U.S. Manufacturing Industries* (Cambridge: MIT Press, 1990).

[3] Generally, broad categories and short-run time periods make demand *inelastic*. For example, the short-run demand for all food is highly inelastic.

In contrast, narrow categories and long-run time periods make demand *elastic*. For example, the long-run demand for green cotton blouses is highly elastic.

[4] Some economists take a narrow view that distribution is strictly an ethical matter, outside the competence of economists to analyze; see the discussion and sources in McChesney and Shughart, *The Causes and Consequences of Antitrust*. In this view, all distributions are ethically neutral; none (even if one person owns everything) can be said to be better or worse than any other, except by mere personal opinion. There are complex elements to this debate, but in any event the field overall has not adopted this position.

[5] See especially Henry C. Simons, *Economic Policy for a Free Society* (Chicago: University of Chicago Press, 1948); and Walter Adams, ed., *The Structure of American Industry*, 9th ed. (New York: Macmillan, 1995), pp. 299–318.

[6] See George J. Stigler, "Perfect Competition, Historically Contemplated," *Journal of Political Economy* 65(1): pp. 1–17: and Louis Makowski and Joseph M. Ostroy, "Perfect Competition and the Creativity of the Market," *Journal of Economic Literature* 39 (June 2001): pp. 479–535.

[7] In practice, effective competition in real markets makes the firm's demand curve reasonably close to being flat, enough to give the same result as strictly pure competition.

[8] The Coase theorem notes that some external effects will be prevented by negotiations between their victims and the firms that cause them. In practice, that would reduce the severity of some bad effects. See Ronald H. Coase, "The Problem of Social Cost," *Journal of Law and Economics* 3 (1960): pp. 1–44.

[9] After Abba P. Lerner's early discussion of it in "The Concept of Monopoly and the Measurement of Monopoly Powers," *Review of Economic Studies* (June 1934): pp. 157–75.

[10] Because marginal revenue equals marginal cost at the profit-maximizing price, MR can be substituted for MC in the first Lerner index equation. After rearranging terms and changing the value of elasticity to positive, the result is as shown in the second equation, incorporating the elasticity of demand.

[11] The flat marginal cost curve means that the cut in output will be by 50 percent; remember, the marginal cost curve is always halfway between the demand curve and the vertical axis.

[12] As the great Chicago-school economist Henry Simons put it, "the gains from monopoly organization in general are likely, of course, to accrue predominantly to the strong and to be derived at the expense of the weak." Henry C. Simons, *Economic Policy for a Free Society* (Chicago: University of Chicago Press, 1948), p. 49.

[13] Simons, *Economic Policy for a Free Society*, p. 43.

[14] Generally, any income flow is capitalized into an asset value, depending on the expected size and duration of the flow and the rate of time discount. If the flow is expected to be constant and long-lasting (over twenty years, say), then the asset value is approximated by the equation

$$\text{capitalized value} = \frac{\text{yearly income}}{\text{interest rate}}$$

where the interest rate is the time discount rate applied by investors. In asset markets, the valuation is commonly about ten times the income flow, though it often varies between five and fifteen or even higher.

[15] For clarity the curves are drawn as precise lines, as is customary in all textbooks; lawyers call them "bright lines." In practice, the cost curves for firms are not known so precisely, and they may usually instead be blurred bands or ranges of costs (see the detailed coverage in chapter 7)

Part

2

Market Structure

Chapter

3

MARKET DEFINITION, MARKET IMPERFECTIONS, AND DEGREES OF COMPETITION

There are many thousands, perhaps millions, of actual markets in the U.S. economy, and far more in the rest of world. They range from restaurants, bulldozers, and broadband services nation-wide, to real estate in Ames, Iowa and obstetrical services in Columbus, Ohio, over to banking in Japan and guided tours in Moscow. Moreover, each of us makes decisions in hundreds of those markets each week, as we buy routine items, consider future trips or household changes, and go out for meals.

In all cases, defining the market is the essential first step toward judging the degree of competition. For example, is Microsoft (or Kodak, or AT&T, or the *Wall Street Journal*, or Anheuser-Busch, or Nike, or Velcro, or the local hospital) really dominant in one or more markets?

Only when you've defined the market can you then assess how effective the competition is. Section 1 presents the core logic and details of market definition.

Then we turn to the conditions inside the market, especially the many kinds of **market imperfections** (in section 2), and the main **categories of partial competition** (in section 3). From these concepts, we then turn in section 4 to facts: the main patterns of competition in **real markets**, especially in the United States.

I. DEFINING THE MARKET

Defining the market means drawing a market's edges. All closely substitutable goods are included in a market, whereas all goods that are not substitutable are outside it.

The exercise often stirs controversy because **the size of the market determines the apparent degree of monopoly that exists inside it.** Firms said to have monopoly power (such as Microsoft, the *Washington Post*, or Ticketmaster) will usually argue that their market is extremely large and that their own share of it is small. The opposite side (such as a little firm suing a dominant firm) usually makes the opposite claim, that the market is small and the defendant has a high share of it.

In research, too, the debate can be sharp. Bias always is a possibility because researchers often have general beliefs about the extent of monopoly power, and that shapes their views about individual markets. Free-market economists, for example, usually see markets as exceedingly wide.

A market is a group of buyers and sellers, exchanging goods that are highly substitutable for one another. Markets are defined mainly by demand conditions; they embody **the zone of consumer choice** for the good.

Markets exist in two main dimensions: the **product type** and the **geographic area**. In the simple, ideal case, there is one distinct product that is sold in a distinct geographic area, such as restaurants in an isolated town. That market's extent is clear and sharp in both the product-type and the geographic-area dimensions, with what lawyers call a "bright-line" edge around the market. The market's scope reflects precisely the true zone of consumer choice for that good.

But most cases involve fuzzy edges between adjacent markets, as illustrated in figure 3.1. Suppose that all forms of fresh milk are closely substitutable for each other. Everybody decides how much milk to drink with no thought of the other drinks they use. In that situation, a genuine market for milk exists alongside adjacent markets for soft drinks, fruit juices, beer, wine, and liquor, shown by panel A. If each drink is chosen without considering the others, then all of these markets are real and distinct.

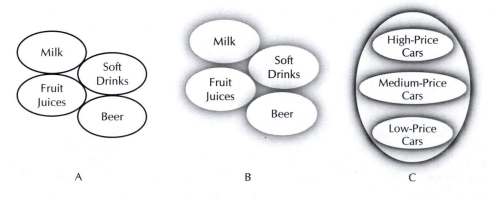

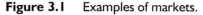

Figure 3.1   Examples of markets.

But if the other drinks are all regarded by many buyers as good substitutes for milk, then the milk market's edges will blur and overlap with the others. And if many or most buyers regard all these drinks as close substitutes for one another, then there may exist just one larger market embracing all drinks, as in panel B of figure 3.1.

Now consider panel C of figure 3.1, a market with segments or **submarkets**. The larger market is the US market for new automobiles, and within it are sub-markets for low-priced, medium-priced, and high-priced automobiles.[1] The larger market is meaningful in assessing broad patterns of choice, since there is substantial substitution among these groups as well as within them. But the submarkets also may be relevant in defining the main range of choices made by many consumers, who tend to focus their choices within one group of cars.

Substitutability by buyers is the key condition for defining markets. Close substitutes are in the market together; other goods are outside it. Each market exists like a single cell within the great honeycomb of the whole economy.

1. CROSS-ELASTICITY OF DEMAND

The correct technical definition of substitutability begins with cross-elasticity of demand. It shows how sharply a price change for one product will cause the quantity sold of another—possibly substitutable—product to change. The formula is as follows:

$$\text{Cross-elasticity of demand between goods 1 and 2} = \frac{\%\ \text{change in quantity of good 2}}{\%\ \text{change in price of good 1}}$$

Cross-elasticities apply both to the product-type and geographic-area market dimensions.

Product Types. For example, suppose that goods 1 and 2 are red apples and green apples. A 10-percent rise in the price of red apples might cause a 50-percent rise in the quantity of green apples sold as most buyers switch away from the now-more-expensive red apples. The two goods are therefore close substitutes with a **high positive cross-elasticity of demand**, and so they can be considered to be in the same market.

Comparable other pairs would be Coke and Pepsi, Fords and Chevrolets, and different brands of gasoline. By contrast, shoes and ice cream aren't substitutable for each other, and so they are clearly in separate markets. If shoe prices rise, that won't induce people to shift to ice cream. Similarly with houses and pencils, or tractors and popcorn. Their sales quantities do not respond to each other's prices. They are all in separate markets.

Geographic Market Areas. Think of goods 1 and 2 as being the same physical good, but sold in different locations. For example, let good 1 be fresh bread sold in Chicago and good 2 be fresh bread sold in Denver. If the price of fresh bread in Chicago rises by 20 percent, will people switch to fresh bread in Denver? No, they just can't make that change. Substitutability is zero, and so those two cities are in distinct geographic markets for fresh bread.[2]

Substitutability for some products may extend around the world. For example, stock markets, diamond markets, and gold markets seem to be fully global, because buyers can and do communicate worldwide and can easily shift purchases from one area to another. At the opposite extreme are tightly limited local markets. For example, the markets for restaurant meals, newspapers, and ready-mix concrete are mainly local, because substitutability among areas is slight. Also, shipping costs are high relative to the value of the products. Most buyers do not shift their purchases beyond those areas.

Cross-Elasticities Are Impractical. Though cross-elasticities are clear and logical in concept, they have not been of much practical use in defining markets, because they are virtually impossible to measure accurately.[3] Markets are not laboratories in which neat price-quantity experiments can be performed. Moreover, the critical variables exist along the following continuums, not in categorical boxes:

1. **Time Periods.** Responsiveness exists in time—the length of the response period between goods or areas is infinitely variable. And (recall from chapter 2) the shorter the period chosen, the less responsiveness there will be. The choice of time period to examine is therefore important, but it is also usually arbitrary: a day, 16 days, 7 months, 4.5 years, etc.? Moreover, the practical effects of time intervals vary among industries; compare strawberries and lumber, fast-food meals and steel-mill equipment.

2. **Gradations of Product Characteristics.** Goods usually have a range of attributes that vary by degrees. This means there are gradations of cross-elasticities, rather than a distinct break between close mutual substitutes and all other goods. The same is true for geographic ranges.

So even if cross-elasticity values could be measured, they would reflect at least two continuums: (1) time and (2) product and geographic features. Therefore cross-elasticities vary continuously (*if* they could be measured at all!). There are seldom jumps or gaps in cross-elasticities that clearly show where a market's edges are.

Even when gaps might occur, there are no fundamental criteria for deciding which level of cross-elasticity (.4?, .63?, .77?) is the "correct" threshold level for setting market's edges.

2. Traditional Practical Evidence for Defining Markets

Because cross-elasticities are almost always impractical, economists (and judges in antitrust cases) have long resorted to a variety of other evidence to define markets. The main conditions are summarized in table 3.1.

Product Types. Four criteria can define product-type markets. First is the general character of the goods, as tested against experience. Do they have the same features and provide for the same uses for most buyers? Can they be interchanged easily by most buyers? Caviar and hamburgers, for example, can conceivably be used in place of each other occasionally, but not by most users under normal conditions. The same is true for cotton shirts and down parkas. In contrast, many types of small cars, orange juice, or blankets are close substitutes for each other.

Second is the judgment of participants in the market, especially the officials of companies that produce and sell. They know from their close daily experience exactly which firms and goods actually compete in the market. They study the matter continuously and thoroughly because their own personal success depends

Table 3.1   Specific Conditions Defining "the" Market

Substitutability
Cross-elasticity of demand
The general character and uses of the goods
Judgments of knowledgeable participants

Product Dimensions
Distinct groups of buyers and sellers
Price gaps among buyers
Independence of the good's price moves over time

Geographic Area (Local, National, International)
The area within which buyers choose
Actual buying patterns
The area within which sellers ship
Actual shipping costs relative to production costs
Actual distances that products are normally shipped
Ratios of goods shipped into and out of actual areas

precisely on knowing the extent of interactions among the firms and goods. Their views will often add up to a solid consensus, especially when, as in antitrust cases, they testify under oath.

Third, if goods are sold by separate and different groups of **sellers**, they may not be substitutable. For example, loans by established banks may differ sharply from loans by local loan sharks. The differing sellers may be able to set different prices without causing substitution by their customers. The same is true if **buyers** are in distinct groups; again, sellers may be able to charge them different prices without triggering substitution. To continue the banking example, small personal loans ($10,000–$50,000) are distinct from large wholesale loans to businesses ($500,000 to $20,000,000).

Fourth is an assessment of whether the goods' prices are close together, and whether they move in parallel or independently.

1. **Similar Prices.**   Equal prices often indicate close substitutability, for the substitution among like goods naturally forces their prices into line with each other. Sharply divergent prices suggest that the goods are sold to different buyers for different purposes. A $29.95 motel room on the edge of New York City, for example, and a $370 room at the Waldorf-Astoria in midtown Manhattan may both be the same physical size, but the radical price contrast suggests that they are in different true product markets.

2. **Price Movements.**   If the two goods' prices move independently of each other, that suggests that the goods are not closely substitutable. Truly substitutable goods' prices usually interact and move in parallel.[4]

Learn to handle "uniform" products cautiously. Usually they are less uniform than they seem. An example is electricity. Though kilowatt-hours are technically uniform, their cost and demand conditions differ sharply by time of day, time of week, and time of year, as well as by the type of user—residence, factory, etc.

Geographic Extent.   The geographic extent of markets can be delineated using other kinds of evidence. First, if transport costs are high relative to the goods' value, then geographic markets are likely to be small. For example, bricks are a high-weight item, with high shipping costs compared to their value. That alone suggests that market size is limited.

Shipping distances, the actual miles that the product is shipped, provide a second kind of evidence. If ready-mix concrete in trucks, for example, is rarely driven more than 40 miles for delivery, then that is a good indicator of the maximum radius of most cement markets.

A third kind of evidence is the amount shipped into and out of a given region. Ten percent is a common rule of thumb. For example, when testing if Ohio is a geographic beer market, one asks if more than 10 percent of its local production is shipped out of the state and more than 10 percent of its consumption is shipped in from outside. If both figures were 50 or 70 percent, then Ohio would be merely part of a multiple-state regional beer market.

The criteria in table 3.1 are commonly used, but others have been employed from time to time. All require care and judgment, and none give simple, definitive answers. Market definition is complex because most markets are complex.

Subdivided Industries and Multiple Levels of Markets.   Within many industries there are a large number of true markets. For example, the drug industry sells at least eight distinct categories of drugs, and each type is comprised of specialized subtypes. The chemicals industry includes hundreds of distinct product markets, from sulfuric acid to plastics. McDonald's and Wendy's compete within literally thousands of geographic markets in the U.S. and abroad.

Moreover, an industry may have several tiers of product and geographic markets (from local to international), with the same firms operating at all levels. For example, banks in large cities usually compete for business clients in local, regional, national, and even international markets. They also compete for personal customers in local "retail banking." These banks are operating in several levels of markets at the same time.

3.   An Alternative Method for Estimating Markets

In 1982, Reagan administration officials at the antitrust division of the Justice Department adopted a different technique for defining markets in antitrust cases as part of their *Merger Guidelines.*[5] The method was said to be more scientific and reliable than traditional methods. Yet it is actually based mainly on speculation and arbitrary criteria, and so it is often less practical and less reliable than the conventional approach. Its users usually rely on traditional evidence to apply and confirm its findings.

Its stated aim is to define a market as **the area within which price could be profitably raised**, given market power in it. To use the method, one begins by selecting the narrowest plausible version of the market in question. An example might be summer-weight wool skirts. One then hypothesizes:

1. a **significant price rise** (usually assumed to be 5 percent) for this good and asks whether within

2. a **reasonable time period** (usually assumed to be exactly one year) there will occur

3. a **significant shift of buyers** (usually taken to be 5 percent) to specific substitute goods, so that the price rise would not be profitable.[6]

If so, then the market is redefined as larger to include these substitutes. (In our example, if buyers shifted to polyester and cotton skirts and/or to winter-weight skirts, then these goods would be added to the market.)

The speculation is then repeated, product by product (in the example, perhaps to consider sportswear dresses, then suit dresses, and then slacks), until there is no further significant substitution into the market as defined. Whenever the substitution is not significant, the exercise stops and the market is considered to be correctly defined.

If the data were accurate and complete, this method might rival or surpass the conventional methods. But the technique has two major defects:

1. **Speculation.** The estimates are speculative, not genuinely scientific. Meaningful tests, using objective data, can rarely be done. If the data actually are available, then they could be used to assess cross-elasticities directly.

2. **Arbitrariness.** All three of the new method's crucial benchmarks (size of price changes, time periods, and quantity response) are arbitrary and debatable; they have no particular justification either in theory or in practice. Adjusting the benchmarks to other plausible values can make the defined markets much larger or smaller. That too is either arbitrary or an exercise of judgment.

In any event, the assumed benchmark values need to be different for each different industry case (e.g., fresh lettuce versus oil-refining equipment), but there is no scientific basis for guiding the selection of "correct" benchmark values. Moreover, the responses may show no sharp break or gap among the products in question that could be used for drawing the market boundary.

As has frequently been the case with new-industrial-organization ideas since 1970, this new "scientific" technique is much less valuable than its authors have claimed. Moreover, these estimates are usually presented with extensive use of the traditional evidence to confirm them.

In short, the standard methods and criteria, when used with cautious judgment, are still the most general and effective way to try to define actual markets.

4. SUPPLY CONDITIONS

Markets are defined by the zone of choice that **consumers** have, but certain conditions of **supply** can also be relevant. Some analysts suggest relying heavily on the **cross-elasticity of supply**.

Cross-elasticity of supply reflects the ability of outside producers to switch their productive capacity from other goods and enter a market. For example, producers of men's shirts might easily shift to producing women's blouses if the price of women's blouses goes up. If they are hovering at the edges of the market, their quick entry when prices rise can affect the degree of monopoly. Obviously, the quicker and bigger the entry, the less the market power in this market will be.

Cross-elasticity of supply relates goods adjacent to the market for good 1 to the prices of goods in this market, as follows:

$$\begin{array}{c}\text{Cross-elasticity of supply}\\\text{between good 1 inside the}\\\text{market and adjacent goods}\end{array} = \frac{\text{\% change in quantity of adjacent goods}}{\text{\% change in price of good 1}}$$

Some analysts have gone so far as to say that these supply conditions play the major role in defining markets. They even label these outside firms as "uncommitted entrants," as if they were somehow already in the markets![7]

But that is dubious. Supply conditions deal with entry **into the market**. It is confusing to mix the definition of the market with the **possible** entry of firms into the market. Instead, it is logical to define the market first on the basis of demand conditions of consumer choice. Then any relevant entry conditions can be clarified.

A technical definition of a market can be arduous, especially in high-stakes antitrust cases (see chapters 15 and 16). But it usually just begins with good sense and intuition, and then allows for distinctive conditions. You will encounter many market definitions in this book, especially in chapters 13 and 14, and that should develop your skill.

II.   MARKET IMPERFECTIONS

Market power is related closely to **imperfections** in the market. Firms often capture dominance by exploiting imperfections such as consumer ignorance or brand loyalties. And dominance itself usually creates more imperfections. Economists in this field studied imperfections thoroughly in the decades before the 1960s. Since the 1970s, though, free-market advocates have minimized or denied the importance of imperfections.

Many of the most important imperfections are summarized in table 3.2. Many of them relate to the entry barriers listed in table 9.1, in chapter 9.

Imperfections' actual extent varies from case to case. Many markets are essentially free of them, while others have strong elements of one or several. Still other markets are extensively afflicted with many imperfections. Free-market advocates argue that these imperfections are negligible in virtually all markets. You will judge that from the following chapters and the business press.

Table 3.2   Nineteen Categories of Market Imperfections

1. ***Pecuniary Gains May Be Obtained By Some Firms.***   They occur when a firm is able to buy its inputs at cheaper prices than its competitors can. The firm can then obtain high profits based on something other than superior performance.

2. ***Consumers May Exhibit Irrational Behavior.***   Some or many consumer preferences may be carelessly formed, unstable, or inconsistent. They may pursue goals other than maximizing utility in the neoclassical manner. They may let elements other than self-interest (e.g., copying other people or complying with advertising) interfere with their decisions.

3. ***Producers May Exhibit Irrational Behavior.***   Some or many of them may have limited or inconsistent decision-making abilities. They may distort their accounts or pursue goals other than pure profit maximizing.

4. ***There May Be Large Uncertainties Which Interfere With Decisions Made By Consumers and/or Producers.***   The main criteria for decision making may be unknown, or may change unpredictably, so that consumers or producers cannot make properly informed or consistent decisions.

5. ***Lags May Occur In The Decisions and/or Actions of Consumers or Producers.***   Actions may not be timely, permitting firms to take strategic actions that prevent competition and/or beneficial outcomes. The firms may gain advantages that don't reflect economic efficiency.

6. ***Consumer Loyalties May Be Strong.***   They may be instilled or intensified by advertising and other marketing activities. The loyalties make them willing to pay higher prices, like captive customers.

7. ***Some Firm Managers Also May Hold Irrational Loyalties.***   They will remain with the firm throughout their careers rather than moving freely to other employers for better pay. The loyalties may permit the firms to pay abnormally low salaries and rewards.

8. ***The Segmenting of Markets May Be Accentuated and Exploited.***   If producers can segregate customers on the basis of their demand attributes, then the producers may be able to use price discrimination strategically so as to raise their monopoly power.

9. ***Differences In Access To Information, Including Secrecy.***   If some firms have more information than their rivals and/or consumers, then these firms may gain excess profits without having superior efficiency. The patterns of innovation also may be distorted.

10. ***Controls Over Key Inputs and Technology.***   Firms may obtain specific controls over crucial inputs, such as superior ores, specific talents of expert personnel, favorable geographic or urban locations, and patents or other access to critical technology. These controls may permit the direct exclusion of competitors and exploitation of consumers.

(continued)

Table 3.2 Nineteen Categories of Market Imperfections (continued)

11. ***Barriers Against New Competition*** (see chapter 9). New entry may be blocked or hampered by a variety of conditions that raise entry barriers. Some twenty sources of barriers are known to be significant in real markets.

12. ***Risk Aversion.*** Some consumers and/or producers may be strongly risk averse, which may make them unwilling to take the normal range of competitive actions.

13. ***Transaction Costs and Excess Capacity May Be Significant.*** They may occur naturally or be increased by firms' deliberate actions. These costs and rigidities may cause the market to deviate from instant and complete adjustments in line with true costs.

14. ***Firms May Have Sunk Costs, Including Excess Capacity and Switching Costs That Arise From Past Commitments.*** These sunk costs may prevent the firms from making free and rapid adjustments. They may also curtail or prevent new entry.

15. ***Because of "Principal-Agent" Problems, Firms May Deviate From Profit Maximizing.*** Managers may seek their own personal gains, which may conflict with shareholders' interests. The business-fraud scandals of 2000-2002 illustrate these.

16. ***Internal Distortions in Information, Decision Making, and Incentives May Cause High Costs and Distorted Decisions.*** There may be misperceptions and conflicts of interest between shareowners and managers, and between upper and lower management groups. Especially in large, complex companies, there may be bureaucracy, excess layers of management, and distorted information and incentives.

17. ***Owners of a Firm's Securities May Be Unable To Coordinate Their Interests and Actions Perfectly.*** The owners may be unable to organize among themselves with perfect information and efficiency. That reduces their ability to enforce efficient behavior by managers.

18. ***In International Markets, There May Be Artificial Exclusionary Conditions, Including Barriers at Borders.*** Attempts by firms to operate freely across borders may be impeded by customs, levies, taxes, required permissions, formalities, and other artificial burdens. Also, cultural and social differences may prevent the free exchange of standardized goods among global markets.

19. ***In International Markets, Firms May Often Have Differences In Information Due To Languages and Cross-Cultural Differences.*** That may give advantages to some firms and prevent the perfect-market outcomes that could occur in cross-national firms and markets. Some firms may ignore real opportunities or problems, make inefficient mergers, or incur added costs and inefficiencies.

III. THE ELEMENTS OF MARKET STRUCTURE

Once you've defined a market, you can assess how competitive it is. The internal structure of a market is embodied mainly in the **size distribution** of its competing firms.

Recall that the three main elements of structure are:

1. Market share, especially of the leading firm

2. Concentration of the leading rivals

3. Entry barriers

Next we consider each of these elements in detail. Market share is the leading element, but concentration and entry barriers also can be significant.

1. MARKET SHARE

A firm's own market share is a simple concept. It is the firm's percentage share of the market's total sales revenue, and it can range from virtually zero up to 100 percent.[8]

Market share is the most important single indicator of a firm's degree of monopoly power. Higher market shares almost always provide higher monopoly power, whereas low shares involve little or none. Within a market, monopoly power will usually vary in line with market shares.[9]

As a firm's market share rises to about 15 percent, market power begins to have significant effects. At higher shares such as 25 to 30 percent, the effects of market power become even more substantial. Market shares over 40 to 50 percent—that is, market dominance—usually give high market power and large effects, as illustrated in figure 2.11.

The economic literature has long recognized the crucial role of market share, and business practice is often rightly fixated on raising market shares. A company's successes are commonly reported in terms of its market shares as well as profits and stock prices.

Market share is important because it generates higher profits. There is a general relationship between each firm's market share and its degree of profitability (recall figure 2.12). This relationship often fits a simple formula:

$$\text{Rate of return} = a + b \text{ market share}$$

where a is the competitive rate of return, and b is the slope of the line.

The a value is actually the cost of capital to the firm. The firm must earn the rate a (which may be in the range of, say, 10 percent on investment) just to pay its investors their opportunity cost—the return they would have received on their best alternative investment. Profit rates above a represent excess returns. If the b slope is high, then market share is particularly rewarding, and it will be sought more fiercely.

2. CONCENTRATION

Concentration is the combined market share of the leading firms in a market. In a tight oligopoly, the concentration ratio for the largest four firms is over 70 percent.

Concentration directly shows the degree of tight oligopoly. Oligopolists may occasionally coordinate their actions nearly as tightly as if they were a genuine monopoly. Or they may compete fiercely or fluctuate in the middle range. Their combined market power is simply a diluted version of the dominance that a single firm with that market share can exert.

Oligopolists have mixed motives, as chapter 11 explores; monopoly instead exerts its own unified control. The degree of oligopoly dilution depends on many things due to the complexity of oligopoly. The complexity has three main causes.

1. **Gradations in Concentration.** There are infinite gradations in the degree of oligopoly. Economists simplify by focusing on "tight" and "loose" oligopoly, but some real markets lie between those categories. Often, too, the oligopoly group is not distinct from the rest of the market.

2. **Variations in Interdependence.** The degree and effect of interdependence between oligopoly firms can vary. Oligopolists may fight, coordinate, or simply ignore one another and pursue independent policies.

3. **Variations in Market Shares.** The group's internal structure may influence the outcome. A symmetrical group (all members equal) may behave differently from an asymmetrical group (dominated by one firm). There are infinite varieties of such internal structures.

Accordingly, the measured relationship of actual concentration ratios to actual profitability is likely to be loose or nonexistent. Any given concentration ratio may cover a variety of internal structures and degrees of interdependence.[10] This point is important because the weak pattern actually found by decades of research was often said to prove that market power has no effects. Instead, tight oligopoly concentration is simply too complicated a matter.

Oligopoly widens the variation of outcomes around the market-share relationship, as shown in figure 2.12 (page 50). That is because tight oligopoly veers between high profits for a cohesive group and low profits for a contentious group of oligopolists. Even if concentration is too loose causally to be an important element of market structure, it remains useful as a descriptive statistic, for it conveys the main shape of an industry reasonably well in one ratio.[11]

The HHI. Other indexes of concentration have been developed in the hope of showing the entire size distribution of firms in just one number. Since 1980, the two U.S. antitrust agencies have adopted one variant of such a "comprehensive" index, the so-called "Hirschman-Herfindahl Index" ("HHI" for short).[12] Like other comprehensive indexes, it uses the market shares of all firms. That is a defect: the HHI requires much more detailed information than does the standard concentration ratio, which is based on just the largest four firms.

The HHI was obscure and largely ignored until the U.S. Antitrust Division adopted it in 1982 in place of concentration ratios. This experiment has had only mediocre success at best, even though it continues to have official approval. The index is a pure-ratio number with virtually no real-world meaning, so it is hard to interpret in any clear way. The user typically refers immediately to the "real" concentration-ratio level, so as to give the HHI number some genuine meaning. Moreover, officials can only guess at the right threshold values for judging when an HHI is "too high."[13] Therefore, we present the HHI here because it is used officially, even though on most points it is inferior to standard 4-firm concentration ratios.

The HHI is quite simple, as shown in table 3.3; it equals the sum of the squared market shares of all firms in the market. It is 10,000 for a pure monopoly, and below 100 for atomistic competition. To illustrate, consider a tight oligopoly

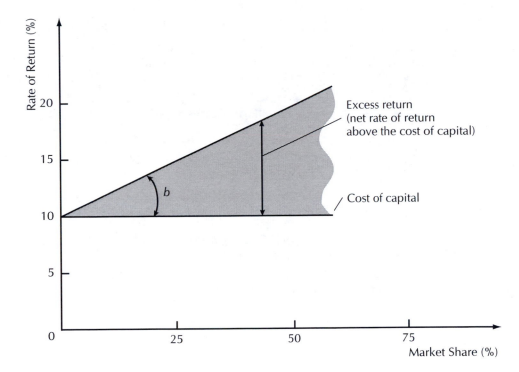

Figure 3.2 The basic relationship between market share and profitability

with market shares of 30, 25, 20, 15, and 10. The HHI would be as follows:

$$\text{HHI} = (30)(30) + (25)(25) + (20)(20) + (15)(15) + (10)(10)$$
$$= 900 + 625 + 400 + 225 + 100 = 2{,}250$$

Sample HHI values for middle ranges of concentration are given in table 3.3. They correspond roughly to standard concentration ratios, as the table shows, but only loosely.

Officials say that HHI values below 1,000 involve no significant monopoly power, whereas those over 1,800 clearly do. But that judgment has little real content. It simply refers to loose oligopoly (concentration below 40 percent, and HHIs roughly below 1,000) and tight oligopoly (concentration above 70 percent, and HHIs roughly above 1,800).

The HHI is therefore one of several recent tools that remove real content from the monopoly problem.[14]

The HHI does have a strong point: it reflects single-firm market dominance with very high HHI values, as it should. Thus a market share of 60 percent has an HHI of 3,600, which is much higher than the tight-oligopoly threshold value of 1,800 for substantial market power. Microsoft's 90-percent share in operating software, for example, and typical city-newspaper shares over 70 percent, show up—correctly—as very high HHI levels. This reflects the fact that dominance is a much more serious problem than even tight oligopoly.

Table 3.3   Sample HHI Calculations

The HHI is the sum of the squared market shares. For example, the HHI for four 25 percent oligopolists is $625 + 625 + 625 + 625 = 2,500$; for ten 10 percent firms, 100 times $10 = 1,000$. Rough equivalents with four-firm concentration ratios are as follows:

Firms' Market Shares	Four-Firm Concentration	HHI
Ten 10 percent firms	40	1,000
Six 16 percent firms	64	1,536
Five 20 percent firms	80	2,000
Four 25 percent firms	100	2,500
Three 33 percent firms	100	3,300

Roughly, an HHI below 1,000 is loose oligopoly, while an HHI above 1,800 is tight oligopoly.

To measure the rise in the HHI when two firms merge, multiply the two market shares together and then double that number. Examples are as follow:

Firm A	Firm B	Multiplied	Rise in HHI
5 percent	5 percent	25 X 2	= 50
7 percent	7 percent	49 X 2	= 98
10 percent	10 percent	100 X 2	= 200
8 percent	4 percent	32 X 2	= 64
15 percent	4 percent	60 X 2	= 120

3.   BARRIERS TO ENTRY

At the edge of the market there may be barriers to entry that impede potential competitors from entering. Anything that decreases the likelihood, scope, or speed of their entry is a barrier.

The idea of entry barriers is intuitively simple and has been common since John Bates Clark first mentioned them in 1887, followed by Schumpeter's 1940s idea of an entry process that quickly ousts dominant firms, and Joe S. Bain's work on barriers in the 1950s (recall chapter 1). Barriers include all manner of legal devices (e.g., patents, mineral rights, franchises; see chapter 9), as well as more general economic impediments *and* the strategic actions that firms can voluntarily choose to repel entry.

Bain stressed that barriers rest on fundamental features of the market, especially large size, large economies of scale, and heavy advertising, all of which make it expensive to establish a viable new company. These are **exogenous conditions of entry;** they are inherent, outside the control of the incumbent firms. At least twelve categories of such exogenous barrier conditions have been discussed in the literature. They are listed in table 9.1, where there is a detailed analysis.

Endogenous conditions, which are under the control of the incumbent firms, also can deter entry. Table 9.1 lists ten categories of endogenous conditions, including a variety of strategic actions and retaliations that firms can choose to take. These actions are discretionary, chosen freely by the incumbent firms to suit their interests.

Since there are many sources of barriers, it is virtually impossible to estimate reliably the "height" of actual barriers, as chapter 9 notes. But rough-and-ready estimates made for some industries show a range from no barrier at all ("free entry") to very high barriers that exclude all entry. Since precise measurements are impossible, Bain resorted to rough guesswork; he started the custom of classifying barriers by three categories of height (low, medium, and high), even though the actual variation is continuous.

Entry and Exit.   Equally unclear is the meaning of entry and exit. The idea seems simple enough; outside firms merely jump in, creating new competition for incumbent firms. Yet close inspection (see chapter 9) shows that entry is a complicated matter that is difficult to define and study. It turns out to involve the extent and speed of net entry (after deducting exit). It is probably best measured by the loss of market share by the leading firms, after allowing for changes by the small firms already in the market.

In short, the seemingly simple ideas of barriers and entry turn out to involve very complex and obscure conditions, which are nearly impossible to estimate or verify. A prudent view is that barriers and potential entry usually don't matter very much, compared to the market's internal conditions. Potential entry is usually (and literally) a peripheral matter.

IV. DEGREES AND CONCEPTS OF PARTIAL COMPETITION

The elements of market structure (along with some behavior and results) are combined when judging the degree of competition in a market. Recall that effective, balanced competition usually requires at least five strong competitors, no dominance, and reasonably free entry.

There are three main categories of competition: dominant firm, tight oligopoly, and loose oligopoly (including monopolistic competition). These categories were noted briefly in chapter 1. Although they shade into one another, each has distinctive features.

1.   MARKETS WITH A SINGLE DOMINANT FIRM

A firm is dominant when it has over 40 percent of the sales in its market and has no close rivals. The higher the dominant firm's market share, the closer it comes to being a pure monopoly.

The dominant firm can act unilaterally, much like a pure monopoly, even though its power over the market is not complete. There is some competition from small competitors, but it often is minor.[15]

Persistent Dominance.   Dominant firms are unusual because a high market share is hard to capture and maintain. Yet those firms that do attain market dom-

Table 3.4 A Selection of Leading Dominant Firms as of 2002

Dominant Firm Name	Market	Approximate Market Shares of the Leaders[1] (% of Revenue)
Bell operating companies	Local telephone service	85–100
Newspapers *Los Angeles Times New York Times Chicago Tribune Washington Post Wall Street Journal*	Local and specialty newspapers	60–95
Microsoft	Operating software in the U.S.	90
Intel	Computer chips	80
IBM	Mainframe computers in the U.S.	85
Electric utilities	Local electric distribution in the U.S.	85–100
Eastman Kodak Fuji Film	Amateur film in the U.S.	75 15
Anheuser-Busch Miller Coors	Beer in the U.S.	50 22 12
Gatorade	Sport drinks in the U.S.	85
Gillette Schick Bic	Wet-shaving products in the U.S.	70 20 5
Yellow pages	Local classified directories	90–100
Ticketmaster	Ticket services in the U.S.	70
De Beers	Diamonds in the world	70
Campbell Soup	Canned soup in the U.S.	75
A.C. Nielsen	TV ratings in the U.S.	90–100
Frito-Lay	Snack foods in the U.S.	45–65
Gerber	Baby food in the U.S.	70
Zildjian	Cymbals in the U.S.	60

[1] A range of estimated values indicates that the firm holds varying shares in specific products and geographic markets.

inance often persist for decades and become household names. Notice the familiar company names in table 3.4—Microsoft, Kodak, Intel, and IBM. Many local markets also contain dominant firms. Your local newspaper is probably one, and so perhaps are the biggest local bank and hospital.

Dominant firms usually impose the two standard monopoly effects on prices: (1) they raise the **level of price**, and (2) they create a **discriminatory structure of prices,** with some high and some low. Those two strategies yield excess profits. The relationship between market share and profit rate (noted in chapter 2) is a relatively close one, rising toward monopoly levels as market shares rise above 60 percent.

Price discrimination is common because dominant firms cover most of the market, which includes widely differing consumers with varying elasticities of demand. Dominant firms can often segment their markets and set varying price-cost ratios for different customer groups in line with their differing inelasticities of demand.[16] They also use discrimination as a weapon to beat back individual competitors.

Dominance prevents competitive parity and strong mutual pressure among numerous rivals, and a dominant firm can often prevent entry by threats and actual retaliation. **Dominance is usually ineffective competition**, and it imposes the standard monopoly harms on innovation, efficiency, and fairness.

Schumpeter's Competitive Process: Brief Dominance?   An alternative view toward dominant firms, often called the "Schumpeterian process," is more optimistic. Joseph A. Schumpeter (rhymes with 'zoom-greater') was a deeply learned and conservative theorist who was distressed in the 1930s by criticism against big businesses such as General Motors and DuPont. He argued that giant enterprises, even those that hold monopolies, would give even better results than the neoclassical competitive outcome. His concept of "creative destruction" is an interesting dissent from the prevailing neoclassical view.[17]

It posits competition as an exciting process of **dynamic disequilibrium**, rather than a set of equilibrium conditions reached at one time. Competition and progress occur together, he said, but in a series of brief and ill-fated monopolies. **The Schumpeterian process is the exact reverse, point by point, of the neoclassical analysis of monopoly.**

In each time period, each market may be dominated by one firm that raises prices, earns monopoly profits, and holds back innovation. The profits attract other firms, one of which soon innovates a better product and pushes out the first dominant firm. The new dominant firm then has its chance to set monopoly prices, causing the usual distortions and monopoly burdens. But soon it, too, is ousted by the next newcomer, and so on.

This cycle of creative destruction continues—innovation creates dominance, which gains monopoly profits, which stimulate new innovation, which creates new dominance, and on and on. As time passes, the average degree of monopoly profits in each period may be very high. Indeed profits, disequilibrium, distortions, and market dominance may all be large at each point of time. Yet the process of innovation-by-the-entrant is rapid, and it is the prominent feature of the model. It may generate benefits of technical progress that easily exceed any costs of static misallocation caused as market power is created and destroyed.

The Schumpeterian process is exciting, and some specialists are proud Schumpeterians who favor rugged, progressive processes, even at the expense of some monopoly harms. Moreover, the concept is a refreshing contrast to dry neoclassical theory. And it is logically valid.

Yet it requires some dubious assumptions. The dominance is quite harmful; it is only the entrant's push that brings innovation. So the critical question is how quickly the ouster happens. Dominant firms must be vulnerable and toppled easily and quickly.

But that speed rarely occurs because dominant firms are usually fierce and resourceful in beating back small competitors. Entry barriers must be low or weak enough to permit rapid entry on a scale large enough to displace the dominant firm quickly. Such overwhelming, rapid entry is rare.

In fact, the main task for any entrenched dominant firm is to harden and extend its dominance. And there are a great many dominant firms that have had market shares above 50 percent lasting 40, 50, and even more years. Some are listed in tables 3.4, 3.6, and 3.7.

In any event, a Schumpeterian entrant must attack only by launching major innovations, rather than by resorting to other less glamorous (but common) tactics such as pricing, heavy advertising, etc. Finally, the dominant firm retards its own innovations while it's on top, so the new entrants' innovations must be very large indeed in order to offset that retardation.

Seen in perspective, Schumpeter's contrast with neoclassical analysis is not really so stark. Effective competition also envisions a process of adjustment. It too can involve some significant market shares, rather than just swarms of atomistic firms. And monopolies can set prices high enough to attract new competition. Therefore there is a good deal of common ground between the Schumpeterian and neoclassical concepts of competition and monopoly.

Does Dominance Persist or Fade Rapidly?   The general evidence is quite clear: the natural rate of erosion has been slow. The decline of dominant-firm market shares in U.S. industries from 1910 to 1935 was about one percentage point per year.[18] And some of those declines didn't just happen; they reflected antitrust cases (e.g., Standard Oil, American Tobacco) that directly reduced market shares.

Later, for the 1950–1975 period, Pascoe and Weiss observed only a 7-point average decline (only 0.3 point per year) in a panel of twenty-three large U.S. firms with initial market shares above 40 percent. During 1960 to 1969, another panel of large U.S. firms displayed a slightly higher rate of decline: just over 1 point per year. During the 1970s, the rate of decline may have risen, but since then it has probably been lower. A panel of forty-seven U.K. firms studied by Shaw and Simpson showed declines averaging 0.3 to 0.8 point per year. In Japanese dominant-firm industries from 1952 to 1966, the leading firms' shares declined by an average of 1 to 1.5 points per year.[19]

Geroski concludes that shares do decline, "but only at a glacial pace," possibly 0.3 point per year. Our own estimate is closer to 1 point per year. A consensus estimate for general purposes might be 0.5 point per year, subject to wide variations in some individual cases. Altogether, dominance lasts for 10 or 20 years, even when average decline occurs. Moreover, further rises in market share often occur (e.g., in 32 of the 108 firms surveyed by Geroski). On average, a 70-percent market share would take twenty years to decline to 60 percent, which is still quite dominant.

Geroski also concludes that declines occur primarily because of "sleepiness" in dominant firms, not because they are overwhelmed by market forces. Dominance can usually be sustained by firms that do not succumb to X-inefficiency and retardation of innovation.

Many dominant market shares manage to avoid declining, some (such as General Motors, Eastman Kodak, Gillette, IBM, and Campbell Soup) for at least several decades, sometimes even six or seven decades. Chapters 4, 5, 9, and 13 note that many dominant firms are able to retain their positions for long periods. For a further example, the ten most valuable brands in the world in 2002 were Coca-Cola, Microsoft, IBM, GE, Intel, Nokia, Disney, McDonald's,

Marlboro, and Mercedes.[20] All except Nokia, Intel, and Microsoft had been dominant for at least 40 years and are not fading. As for the three exceptions, they have dominated since their young industries began, and they show no signs of fading.

Also, the "big three" U.S. automobile companies dominated from the 1930s to the 1980s, even though they were inefficient from at least the 1950s.[21] Still another example is the U.S. drug industry, where patent monopolies have yielded very high profits since the 1940s. Competition from generic-drug makers finally rose in 2001 to 50 percent of the prescription-drug market. But generics were negligible from the 1950s on, only reaching 20 percent in 1986.

Altogether, the averages and the important examples show extremely slow erosion of dominance. The Schumpeterian model may have only a limited relevance as an occasional exception.

2. TIGHT OLIGOPOLY

The critical distinction is between **tight** oligopoly, where collusion is likely, and **loose** oligopoly, where it is not. Tight oligopoly does not usually result in effective competition, whereas loose oligopoly does.

Despite much theorizing about oligopoly since the 1930s, there is no single solution or model, and the phenomenon remains largely a riddle. Game theorists have attempted explanations, but their main focus is the two-firm situation, which is rare in actual markets. Table 3.5 presents some of the most interesting and significant tight oligopolies in the U.S. economy. Chapter 11 presents some of the theoretical models of oligopoly behavior, and chapter 16 gives case studies of some of the industries in table 3.5.

Table 3.5 A Selection of Leading Tight Oligopolies as of 2002

Leading Firms	Market	Estimated Market Share of the Leaders (% of Revenue)[1]
Boeing Airbus	Passenger aircraft in the world	55 45
Coca-Cola Pepsi Cola	Carbonated drinks in the U.S.	45 35
Federal Express United Parcel Service Airborne Freight	Rapid package delivery in the U.S.	40 35 15
Nike Adidas New Balance	Athletic shoes	45 30 20
Kimberly-Clark Procter & Gamble	Disposable diapers in the U.S.	40 35
Kellogg General Mills General Foods	Ready-to-eat cereals in the U.S.	33 25 20
Mattel Hasbro	Toys in the U.S.	30-60 20-50

(continued)

Table 3.5   A Selection of Leading Tight Oligopolies as of 2002 (continued)

Leading Firms	Market	Estimated Market Share of the Leaders[1] (% of Revenue)
Procter & Gamble Colgate Lever	Soaps and detergents in the U.S.	30-55 20-25 10-25
Fire departments Private firms	Ambulance services in U.S. locales	30-80 0-40
Sega Nintendo	Video games in the U.S.	60 40
General Electric United Technologies Rolls Royce	Jet aircraft engines in the world	40 35 25
Bertelsmann Music EMI Music Distribution Warner-Elektra-Atlantic Sony Music Entertainment Universal Music Group	Audio music CDs	(100 total)
Hallmark American Greetings Gibson Greetings	Greeting cards in the U.S.	45 35 8
General Electric	Locomotives in the U.S.	40
American Airlines United Airlines Northwest Delta US Airways Southwest Airways	Airlines in the U.S., including major airport hubs	25-60 23-65 15-70 15-70 10-45 8-35
EchoStar Hughes Electronics	Satellite TV services in the U.S.	50 40
WMX (Waste Management) BFI	Garbage disposal in the U.S. and 100s of locales	30-50 30-50
Leading hospitals	Hospital services in small and large cities	40-100
Intelsat SES Global Panamsat Eutelsat	Global satellite operators	30 27 24 19

[1] A range of estimated values indicates that the firm holds varying shares in specific products and geographic markets.

Sources: various business press accounts, including Stephanie Fitch, "Reengineering 101," *Forbes* (May 13, 2002): pp. 82–88 (about Boeing), and Jerry Useem, "Boeing vs. Boeing," *Fortune* (October 2000): pp. 148–160.

The main ideas of the topic are as follows:

1. Oligopoly is about **fewness** and **interdependence**. It embraces a wide variety of forms, ranging from pure duopoly with just two firms, down to loose oligopolies with eight to fifteen substantial firms.

2. There is **indeterminacy**. Actions cannot be simple unilateral steps, as they are in pure competition, pure monopoly, and dominance. In those cases, each firm's demand is set and known. In contrast, under oligopoly, each firm's demand depends on its rivals' reactions to its actions.

3. Therefore **strategy** is required. Like chess players, each firm must think ahead strategically over a wide range of actions and possible reactions.

4. Oligopoly also means **a wide range of outcomes**, varying from pure cooperation all the way over to pure conflict. At one extreme, a set of oligopolists may cooperate so fully that they attain a pure monopoly, with a joint maximizing of their shared profits. At the other extreme, they may act with strict independence and hostility, forcing each other down to the purely competitive result. More usually, they will settle somewhere in the middle range, or they may veer between extremes and middle outcomes as their perceptions and behavior shift.

5. Perhaps most fundamentally, **oligopolists always have mixed, conflicting incentives between competing and colluding.** Each firm could compete intensely, seeking every way to maximize its own profits. But collusion is also attractive. Each oligopolist knows that if they all cooperate, then they can attain higher joint profits, just as a monopoly brings higher profits than does competition.

Yet all firms also know that cheating may occur, which will weaken or destroy any collusion. Each firm can gain by cutting its price while all the others cooperate to keep the collusive price up. Each firm would like to be in a market that is rigged collusively, but to be **outside** that price-fixing ring. All firms share the temptation to cheat, and so their collusion is always prey to cheating and collapse. Yet all oligopolists also know that if only they can make the collusion stick, the joint rewards will be high.

Actual markets reflect the intricate mingling and conflicts among these incentives. One oligopoly may settle into snug cooperation, behaving like a total monopoly, while another may be the scene of endless warfare, with low prices and frantic innovation. Free-market advocates assert that collusion tends to collapse quickly from its inner conflicts. Others are less optimistic, noting that many important cartels have lasted for ten, twenty, or more years.

Yet even with all this complexity, some general patterns emerge. First, **the higher the concentration, the greater the likelihood that collusion will succeed and persist.** There are two reasons for this. First, high concentration means that there are fewer firms with which to organize and enforce mutual agreements. Second, price-cutting by any renegade is easier to discover and penalize. If there are only three firms, the other two will quickly know if the first firm cheats. But if ten or fifteen firms are involved, then any one of them will be more strongly tempted to chisel, since it can expect to succeed for a longer time before being discovered.

Accordingly, **collusion is likely to crystallize and persist in tight oligopoly, whereas it is likely to fail in loose oligopoly.** Tight oligopoly often tends to act like a "shared monopoly," as the rewards for collusion prevail over independent action. Loose oligopoly tends instead toward effective competition, with uncontrollable price cutting.

The second pattern of oligopoly is that tight-oligopoly cooperation is strengthened if the firms have similar demand and/or cost conditions. Because their interests coincide, they can be more confident that the cooperation will last.

Finally, as time passes, the firm's managers learn about each other and find it easier to predict each other's behavior more accurately. Misunderstandings become less likely, and mutual confidence grows. Thus, oligopolies in older industries tend to have tighter cooperation.

Types of Coordination.   Oligopolies may range from tight, explicit collusion to informal parallel behavior. If price fixing is legal, the price fixing can become so complete that it approaches the level a pure monopoly would achieve. A **cartel** (an organization created by companies to manage their cooperation) may fix prices and enforce penalties against members who violate the agreement. Cartel managers may also set output quotas, control investments, and pool profits. Most cartels exist in Western European countries and in certain international markets, such as OPEC in the world oil market.

Price fixing has been against the law since 1899 in most U.S. industries, under Section 1 of the Sherman Act (see chapters 15 and 16). Antitrust policy therefore shifts many oligopolists' margin of choice away from collusion and toward competition. Nonetheless, some secret price fixing does occur.

Does Collusion Usually Fall Apart or Last?   Though collusion is theoretically under pressure to collapse, actual conditions may instead help it to last, perhaps for long periods. A recent survey of U.S. and European price fixing cases finds that some price fixing has lasted for many years, even where it is illegal.[22] Therefore the free-market claim that price-fixing is always fragile is wrong.

Tacit Coordination.   Price fixing can also occur in a milder form, variously called tacit collusion, indirect collusion, parallel pricing, or price signaling. The oligopolistic firms do not conspire directly or sign binding agreements for fear of being caught. But a firm can give indirect hints and signals of its preferred price levels. The other leading firms may then simply go along with the same price changes. Under tight oligopoly, tacit collusion may sometimes result in control that is almost as complete as a full-blown cartel (or even a pure monopoly).

3.   EFFECTIVE COMPETITION, INCLUDING LOOSE OLIGOPOLY, MONOPOLISTIC COMPETITION, AND PURE COMPETITION

Now we come to the categories of effective competition. The realm of loose oligopoly ranges widely, from moderate concentration to nearly pure competition. There is little distinctive theory for this category because it generally fits the competitive model, with prices forced down near cost, costs forced down toward minimum levels, rapid innovation, and so on.

V.   DEGREES OF COMPETITION IN REAL MARKETS

With the concepts of structure in mind, we now turn to real markets in the United States. The appraisal here will serve as the basis for chapters 4 and 5, in which we assess how structure affects performance in real markets.

U.S. markets range from pure monopoly (say in local transit systems and water supply) to intensive competition (among thousands of wheat farmers in the Grain Belt). In this chapter, we review all sizes and sectors of markets, showing how degrees of competition and monopoly are appraised.

But first we review the main types of industries, as determined by their technology, age, and geographic scope. Next we see how the elements of structure fit together. Then we assess the economy-wide rise in competition from 1960 to 1980, and finally we conclude with dominant firms and their rate of decay, with utility sectors and foreign comparisons.

1.   VARIETIES OF MARKETS

First consider three basic conditions of industries.

Technology and Capital Intensity: Heavy Industry and Others.   Technology varies widely, from capital-intensive industries like oil refining and steel to light industries such as retailing and personal services. High capital intensity usually imposes a higher degree of risk, for large volumes of assets are frozen in specific long-lived forms (e.g., machines, buildings) that cannot easily be sold off.

Age and Growth Phase.   Quite a few industries are old, with origins antedating even the nineteenth century; examples include farming, forestry, weaving, and printing. Others are new, with a history of years rather than decades; instances include the Internet and cell phones.

The normal life cycle of industry involves slow early growth, explosive expansion as the product spreads toward saturating the market, and then normal growth, possibly followed by stability, displacement, and eventual decline.[23] Structure tends to grow rigid in such cases. By contrast, new industries tend to be formative, flexible, and technically changing.

The economy is an evolving array of such old and new industries with the new displacing the old. Firms in older industries often try to diversify into new ones. The normal life cycle can be broken if new conditions rejuvenate a mature industry. Still, age often explains much of an industry's structure, behavior, and degree of flexibility.

Geographic Scope, from Local to International.   A large share of services and trade is local, and so are many industrial markets (bread, milk, bricks, ready-mixed cement, etc.). Transportation costs and distinctive local demand are the two main reasons for such localism. In some cases, raw materials are focused in small areas, and the transport cost of raw materials is high relative to costs of shipping the final products. Such industries are therefore tied to the area of their resource base. Thus the textile industry was concentrated in New England, the steel industry in Pennsylvania, meatpacking in Chicago, and automobile making in Michigan.

All of these industries became more widespread after 1930. Regional concentration now includes oil in Texas and California, steel in the Chicago-to-Pennsylvania area, furniture in the Southeast, and food processing in the Midwest. Nowadays the cutting-edge information-technology industries have spread much more evenly and randomly among regions and countries.

2.   Composite Structure

A variety of statistical tests have been applied to U.S. firms to see which elements—market share, concentration, or entry barriers—correlate most closely with profit rates. All of the elements are significantly correlated with profitability, but **market share emerges as the central element of structure.**[24] That result fits reality; firms are often obsessed with gaining and protecting high market shares.

Oligopoly concentration appears to be a relatively minor causative factor once market share is allowed for. Apparently, U.S. firms do not gain very much by indirect collusion, compared to their ability to exert straight market power based on their individual market shares. As for entry conditions, they seem to have only a limited importance in most markets. That too fits experience; the same managers who fixate on their market shares often have much less concern about entry barriers and possible new competitors.

Of course, the idea of reversed causation—from performance to structure—might instead play a role. High profit rates might reflect efficiency or innovativeness instead of market power, as we have noted. The next chapter will address this issue in detail. In either case market share is still the main profit-enhancing element of structure.

3.   Patterns of Structure

Now we turn to the actual patterns of structure in real markets. We look at both average conditions and the range of variation.

Market Shares and Dominance.   Market shares span the entire range from 100 percent to trivial. Unfortunately, no comprehensive set of market shares is published by any official or private source, mainly because firms naturally go to great lengths to keep such sensitive information secret. Instead, leading-firm shares must be sifted out and estimated from a variety of sources, and in many cases the estimates are debatable.[25]

Reasonably reliable estimates are possible, however. Tables 3.6 and 3.7 list some of the leading dominant firms during the 1910–1973 period, including famous corporate names from different periods in twentieth-century American corporate history. Note that some of these firms persisted for decades, whereas others receded or abruptly disappeared.

By 1980–1985, most of these older dominant firms had yielded to the corrosive forces of competition or to direct antitrust attacks. Yet many dominant posi-

Table 3.6   Instances of Dominant Firms in Major U.S. Industrial Markets, 1910 and 1935

Company	Estimates of 1910			Estimates of 1935	
	Market Share (%)	Entry Barriers	Assets ($ million)	Market Share (%)	Entry Barriers
U.S. Steel	60	Medium	1804	40	Medium
Standard Oil	80	Medium	800	35	Medium
American Tobacco	80	Medium	286	25	Medium
International Harvester	70	High	166	33	Medium
Central Leather	60	Low	138	—	—
Pullman	85	High	131	80	Medium
American Sugar Refining	60	Low	124	35	Low
Singer Manufacturing	75	Medium	113	55	Low
General Electric	60	High	102	55	High
Corn Products	60	Low	97	45	Low
American Can	60	Medium	90	51	Medium
Westinghouse Electric	50	High	84	45	High
E. I. du Pont de Nemours	90	Medium	75	30	Low
International Paper	50	Low	71	20	Low
National Biscuit	50	Low	65	20	Low
Western Electric	100	High	43	100	High
United Fruit	80	Medium	41	80	Medium
United Shoe Machinery	95	High	40	90	High
Eastman Kodak	90	Medium	35	90	Medium
Aluminum Company of America	99	High	35	90	Medium

tions remain hidden within conglomerates, which do not report detailed conditions of their individual divisions or products. Also, new dominant positions are emerging in some markets.

All told, dominant firms probably account for less than 3 percent of GNP in the United States. The problem is sharp but limited. These cases involve much of the large-scale monopoly problem that remains in the U.S. economy. A skeptic might say that only the top few cases represent a high degree of market power; some new-Chicago observers would say that none of them holds any market power at all. Others would say that all of these cases plus many lesser ones might represent high market power.

Concentration. Concentration data are more abundant, but they raise long-standing problems of **market definition**. There is no official comprehensive source for correctly defined markets, but the U.S. Census Bureau prepares concentration data for manufacturing industries and product groups every four years or so when there is a census of manufacturers.

The census industry categories are based mainly on the selling companies' conditions: technology, groups of firms selling similar products, and common production features of products. These conditions can deviate substantially from the true basis of **markets**, which is the zone of **consumer choice** among substitutable products. Because census staff members ignore much of the consumer-choice side, their industry and product-group categories often stray far from true market edges.

Table 3.7   Instances of Dominant Firms in Major U.S. Industrial Markets, 1948 and 1973

Company	Estimates of 1948			Estimates of 1973	
	Market Share (%)	Entry Barriers	Assets ($ million)	Market Share (%)	Entry Barriers
General Motors	60	Medium	2958	55	High
General Electric	50	High	1177	50	High
Western Electric	100	High	650	98	High
Alcoa	80	High	650	40	Medium
Eastman Kodak	80	Medium	412	70	Medium
Procter & Gamble	50	Medium	356	50	Medium
United Fruit	80	Medium	320	60	Medium
American Can	52	Medium	276	35	Low
IBM	90	Medium	242	70	High
Coca-Cola	60	Medium	222	50	Medium
Campbell Soup	85	Medium	149	85	Medium
Caterpillar Tractor	50	Medium	147	50	Medium
United Shoe Machinery	85	High	104	50	Low
Kellogg	50	Medium	41	45	Medium
Gillette	70	Medium	78	60	Medium
Babcock & Wilcox	60	Medium	79	40	Medium
Du Pont (cellophane)	90	High	65	50	Medium
Hershey	75	Medium	62	70	Low

Adjusting the census ratios to reflect true markets requires care and judgment. There is no simple, mechanical method. Notice, too, that any econometric research that simply uses unadjusted concentration ratios is almost certain to contain gross errors and to give meaningless results. Unfortunately, there have been many such incautious studies. Moreover, the census concentration data cover only the manufacturing sector, which accounts for just about one-quarter of total U.S. economic activity.

The HHI.   HHI ratios are distorted by wrong market definitions just as much as are the four-firm concentration ratios. And although they are provided by the census for most industries, they are withheld for many important dominant-firm industries.

The Range of Concentration.   Actual concentration ratios in U.S. industries range from 100 percent down to a mere few percent. A maximum, 100-percent ratio usually does not mean maximum market power; it might indicate four 25-percent market share firms rather than one 100-percent firm.[26] Maximum concentration, therefore, may mask widely differing degrees of monopoly. The same is true of lesser ratios. A 60-percent ratio may include four 15-percent firms or one 57-percent firm holding genuine dominance.[27]

Gradations of Market Shares.   The typical market structure includes a gradation among market shares. Usually there is not a distinct oligopoly group;

instead, the market shares taper down from the largest firms to a fringe of small ones. In the average case each firm has about twice the market share of the next.[28]

The Extent of Concentration in U.S. Industry.   To show the general extent of concentration, it can be helpful to use the standard four-firm ratios. Caution is needed: the average of the **unadjusted** official four-digit industry ratios strongly understates the true degree of concentration. Once the ratios are corrected, the weighted-average degree of true concentration in U.S. markets has probably been between 50 and 60 percent, rather than the 40 percent that has been indicated by the raw census ratios.

Trends of Concentration.   Since the ratios are defective, only rough estimates are possible. From 1947 to 1967, there was a significant rise in average (unadjusted) concentration from 34 to 40 percent. Much of this rise was in consumer-goods markets, where television advertising probably had an increasing effect favoring larger firms.

After 1967, the official ratios showed little change, but these ratios do not include imports. Since imports have risen significantly in scores of industries, the true degree of concentration has probably decreased, possibly back to the patterns of the 1940s.[29]

Entry Barriers.   As noted earlier, barriers may arise from more than twenty sources (presented in chapter 9). Estimating their individual heights and their combined size is extremely difficult. One must evaluate each source for each industry. Then one must combine them, using some sort of weighting, even though research has not developed any weighting method at all.[30]

Bain and Mann attempted to derive measures for about forty industries in the 1950s.[31] Many industries have changed since then, and earlier editions of this book attempted to revise and extend their findings using a variety of sources and exercising rough judgments. But no estimates are offered in this edition, as barriers are such a confused topic, lacking an objective basis for estimation.

One retreats to intuition: certain utilities (electricity, telephones, most dominant-firm markets like computer software and newspapers) probably have high barriers. Entry into the railroad industry is virtually closed by difficulties in gathering rights of way and building roadbeds; likely retaliation by existing railroads would add to the barriers. Most retail and other services probably have low barriers because small size is the rule and little capital is needed to get started. Some minerals are tightly controlled, and some are not. Many professional services have sizable barriers of credentials and access to crucial facilities (e.g., hospitals, for doctors).

4.   OTHER MAIN QUESTIONS

Rates of Entry.   Most competitive markets have a good deal of entry and exit going on, but most of it is by small firms. Most of these little entrants have minor impacts and short lives.[32] So illusions of rapid entry often exist even when nothing significant is happening. In highly concentrated markets, fringe entry and exit may also occur, but major entry (taking, say a 5-percent or larger market share) is rare. Any such substantial entry is, moreover, usually slow. For example, the entry by Japanese automobiles into the U.S. market began with mere footholds in the 1960s, and it grew gradually by only a point or two a year until 1979–80.

Redefining Markets? Allowing for imports in U.S. markets tends to reduce U.S. concentration, as was noted earlier (unless an importer is among the four largest sellers). But as imports take an ever-larger share of a U.S. market, we eventually need to redefine the market on a regional or world basis.

A few markets are genuinely global, but the hard choices are in the middle range. For example, as imports approach 25 percent of new car sales in the United States, are we really looking at a worldwide market, or at least one that includes all Japanese producers? The answer is seldom obvious; there is no simple threshold value for switching from a U.S. market with imports to a global market.

Imports may have impacts that go beyond their bare market shares. Foreign sellers commonly have different attitudes and objectives from domestic ones. Outsiders do not usually cooperate as readily as home firms do; indeed, they often break local price-fixing rings. Neither can they be as easily punished or disciplined to force compliance with collusion. Therefore foreign sellers often enforce competition more strongly than their mere market shares would indicate.

QUESTIONS FOR REVIEW

1. Show how the Schumpeterian competitive process is the exact opposite, point by point, of the neoclassical perfectly competitive situation. Can both be valid?

2. Explain why higher concentration tends to encourage collusion in tight oligopoly.

3. Explain why a four-firm concentration ratio of 23 percent for newspapers seriously understates true market concentration. How about sheet metal work (6 percent) and radios (77 percent)?

4. Choose three industries and try to estimate the height of their entry barriers. What types of data would you try to use?

5. Japanese and other foreign cars now hold an important share of sales in the U.S. Should we (1) merely include them in calculating U.S. market shares in the U.S. automobile market, or (2) redefine the market as one worldwide market, including all cars made in the world? What threshold conditions (import shares, transport costs, similarities of products, etc.) justify switching to the larger market in this and other cases?

6. Try appraising these industries as dominant firm, tight oligopoly, or loose oligopoly: beer, baseball, automobiles, fast-food restaurants, banking in your town, television broadcasting, newspapers, movie theaters in your area, and long-distance telephone service.

7. Do high market shares usually decline rapidly or slowly? What conditions may speed that decline?

ENDNOTES

[1] The auto market would not include other machines for travel such as bicycles, roller skates, semi-trailer trucks, and airplanes, even though they all can be used to get from one place to another. Even though they all provide transportation, consumers simply don't regard them as substitutable for each other.

[2] Moving closer, what about bread sold in Chicago and Des Moines? No. Chicago and Milwaukee? Maybe in some degree, because bread can be shipped (at some cost) between those cities. Chicago and its suburb Glencoe? Probably; the distance is only a few miles.

[3] After 1995 Jerry Hausman and others developed the use of scanner data from checkout lines, such as in supermarkets and drugstores. In theory, they could apply abundant data about prices and quantities to measure demand elasticities. That would bypass efforts to define markets using cross-elasticities. The demand elasticities could, theoretically, reflect (inversely) the degree of market power (recall the Lerner index).

But problems of designing the research and interpreting its results have limited its value. The method has not produced large gains as its authors hoped. See Jerry Hausman, Gregory Leonard, and J. Douglas Zona, "Competitive Analysis with Differentiated [sic] Products," *Annales d'Economie et de Statistique* 34 (1994): pp. 159–78. *Annales* is not a mainstream journal.

[4] Yet the converse is not necessarily true. Two goods' prices may move in parallel if one good is an important input to the other but not substitutable for it. For example, the prices of raw copper and copper wire move very closely together because copper is the main input for making copper wire. But they are in a vertical relationship (input and product) rather than being substitutable.

[5] After two later revisions, the latest version is *Horizontal Merger Guidelines* of the Antitrust Division and Federal Trade Commission, Washington, DC: 1992, reprinted in *Trade Regulation Reporter* (CCH): Para. 13,104. The Guidelines have weaknesses. For a thorough critique, see George B. Shepherd, Helen S. Shepherd, and William G. Shepherd, "Sharper Focus: Market Shares in the Merger Guidelines," *Antitrust Bulletin* 45(4) (Winter 2000): pp. 835–85. See also Robert D. Willig, "Merger Analysis, Industrial Organization Theory and Merger Guidelines," Special Issue, *Brookings Economic Papers* (1991): pp. 281–312, with comments by F. M. Scherer and Steven C. Salop.

[6] In some rather odd jargon, one examines a SSNIP (a "small but significant nontransitory increase in price"). So this is the "SSNIP" method.

[7] That idea is central in the defense of the 1992 Guidelines by Janusz A. Ordover and Robert D. Willig, "Economics and the 1992 Merger Guidelines: A Brief Survey," *Review of Industrial Organization* 8 (April 1993): pp. 139–50.

[8] In odd cases, the share might better be based on other measures, such as assets, value added, or inventories of rental equipment. But sales revenue is almost always the preferred index, because it is based on the extent of sales won in the market by competitive efforts.

[9] Thus Procter & Gamble, with about 50 percent of the detergent market, has had much more market power than Lever Brothers with its 10 percent. And though Microsoft's 90-percent share of software is in the same market as its small rivals, Microsoft's market power is obviously far larger.

[10] Correlations between the HHI (see the next section) and profitability would also be inherently low.

[11] Economists can also consider the degree of change in market shares over time, reflecting competitive pressures; see John R. Baldwin and Paul K. Gorecki, "Concentration and Mobility Statistics in Canada's Manufacturing Sector," *Journal of Industrial Economics* 42 (March 1994): pp. 93–103.

[12] Albert O. Hirschman in 1945 and Orris Herfindahl in 1952 used an index similar to the HHI, so both names are attached to it.

[13] Also, the choice to square the market share, with an exponent of 2 rather than some other exponent such as 1.5, is strictly arbitrary.

[14] Others include replacing the term *excess profits* with the word *rent*, and *price discrimination* with *Ramsey prices*. These terms are discussed elsewhere in the book.

[15] Competitive balance—which is missing under dominance—has long been the focus of sports leagues. In 2002, for example, Major League Baseball avoided a strike by imposing a system that channels funds from rich teams to small-city poor teams.

[16] For example, when they were highly dominant, IBM and Xerox set higher price-cost ratios on the equipment that faced the weakest competition. Airlines since 1985 have fitted their fare

discounts thoroughly to differences in demand, especially between business travelers and others (see chapter 14).

[17] It was presented in his *Capitalism, Socialism and Democracy* (New York: Harper & Row, 1942). The presentation was actually rambling, diffuse and nontechnical, but the main ideas are reasonably clear.

[18] Until 1985, the main source of measures of the rate of erosion was Willim G. Shepherd, *The Treatment of Market Power* (New York: Columbia University Press, 1975), chapter 4. Paul Geroski's chapter "Do Dominant Firms Decline?" in Donald Hay and John Vickers, eds., *The Economics of Market Dominance* (Oxford: Basil Blackwell, 1987) presents and summarizes both recent and older research. See also George Pascoe and Leonard W. Weiss, "The Extent and Permanence of Market Dominance," Federal Trade Commission, Washington, DC, working paper, 1983; and R. Shaw and P. Simpson, "The Monopolies Commission and the Persistence of Monopoly," *Journal of Industrial Economics* 34 (1985): pp. 355–72.

[19] See Shepherd, *The Treatment of Market Power*, chapter 4. Conditions in these postwar Japanese industries were probably more turbulent than in either U.S. or U.K. industries (although the new import competition of the 1970s increased the turbulence of U.S. and U.K. industries).

[20] See Gerry Khermouch, "The Best Global Brands," *BusinessWeek* (August 5, 2002): pp. 92–99.

[21] See Joann Muller, "Autos: A New Industry," *BusinessWeek* (July 15, 2002): pp. 98–106.

[22] See Margaret C. Levenstein and Valerie Y. Suslow, "What Determines Cartel Success?" in Peter Grossman, ed., *How Cartels Endure and How They Fail: Studies of Industrial Collusion*, (Northhampton, MA: Elgar, 2002).

[23] This is similar to the product cycle, a basic concept in the analysis of business operations and strategy.

[24] See William G. Shepherd, *The Treatment of Market Power* (New York: Columbia University Press, 1975); and F. M. Scherer and David N. Ross, *Industrial Market Structure and Economic Performance*, 3rd ed. (Boston: Houghton Mifflin, 1991).

[25] Sources include the business press, especially the *Wall Street Journal*, which frequently reports evidence from private market research and other sources. Antitrust cases are often good sources of data. There are extensive private sets of market share measures, but they are not published or generally available, except at high fees.

[26] In this one area, the HHI excels over the four-firm ratio. Four 25-percent firms give an HHI of 2,500 (each market share squared is 625; together they equal 2,500). If there is a 97-percent firm and three 1-percent firms, their combined HHI is 9,412 (that is, 97 squared is 9,409, plus 3 ones). In this case, a 100-percent concentration ratio indeed masks sharply differing monopoly power.

[27] Here the two HHI values would be 900 and 3,252. Again, the contrast is sharp and the HHI is useful.

[28] This relationship has suggested to some researchers that a law of lognormal distribution and growth governs the formation of industry structure. If the growth of individual firms were randomly distributed by a lognormal distribution, then market shares would fit closely to a rule of two: that is, each firm would be twice the size of the next largest one. This law in fact does apply loosely, but there are many exceptions. Some dominant firms are four or five times larger than their nearest rival (a few examples are newspapers in most cities, Microsoft, IBM, Eastman Kodak, and Campbell Soup).

[29] On trends in the U.K., see A. Henley, "Industrial Deconcentration in U.K. Manufacturing Since 1980," *Manchester School of Economic and Social Studies* 62 (March 1994): pp. 40–59.

[30] It is important to avoid letting the amount of **actual entry** color one's appraisal of the height of the barriers; the two concepts are distinct, even though they may be related in actual industrial patterns.

[31] Joe S. Bain, *Barriers to New Competition* (Cambridge: Harvard University Press, 1956); and H. Michael Mann, "Seller Concentration, Barriers to Entry, and Rates of Return in Thirty Industries, 1950–1980," *Review of Economics and Statistics* 48 (August 1966): pp. 296–307.

[32] See Paul A. Geroski, *Market Dynamics and Entry* (Oxford: Basil Blackwell, 1991); and Timothy Dunne, Mark J. E. Roberts, and Larry Samuelson, "Patterns of Firm Entry and Exit in U.S. Manufacturing Industries," *Rand Journal of Economics* 19 (Winter 1988): pp. 495–515.

Part

3

Performance

Chapter

4

MARKET POWER'S EFFECTS ON PRICES, PROFITS, AND EFFICIENCY

Market power is evidently complex and intriguing, but does it really matter to the economy? If its harmful effects are actually weak, then market power could be merely a cardboard dragon, with only academic interest. Or perhaps instead, as free-market advocates say, its only effects may be good, not bad.

We'll review those effects in this chapter and the next. We start with the direct effects on prices and profits in section 1. Then in section 2 we examine the effects on efficiency. We consider the direction of causation—What really causes what?—that leading question that we posed in chapter 1. Other effects—on innovation, fairness, and other values—are held over to chapter 5.

I.   EFFECTS ON PRICES AND PROFITS

1.   SPECIFIC CASES SHOW IMPACTS ON PRICES

A monopoly's direct effect is to raise its prices above costs en route to its real goal of maximizing excess profits. That in turn translates into capital gains for shareholders. The impact on **price-cost ratios** and the impact on **profit rates** are both parts of the same basic monopoly impact.

Specific examples offer the most direct evidence, often showing deep impacts. But they might just be isolated freakish exceptions rather than the rule. To more accurately judge the full effect of monopoly, one also can turn to statistical cross-section studies, whose patterns are less dramatic but still clear.[1]

Cases.   Experts know that some firms with market power raise their prices to double, triple, or even much higher multiples of cost. Perhaps the all-time leading example is the OPEC oil cartel. Since the 1960s, the Organization of Petroleum Exporting Countries has set oil-production quotas for its members, which include many of the world's oil-exporting countries. In 1973–1974, OPEC dramatically raised the price of oil from about $3 per barrel to as much as $14; then in 1979 it pushed the price up further to over $30 per barrel.[2] This immense rise brought OPEC members over $100 billion each year in extra profits and caused severe economic instability in other countries.

In 1985 OPEC then cut the price deeply all the way down to the $13 to $18 range, reflecting a mix of Saudi Arabian strategic pricing and a decline in OPEC's control. As other suppliers (especially Russia) have emerged, OPEC has lost most of its power. Yet it still has punch; in 1999-2000 OPEC tightened its quotas, and world oil prices subsequently jumped from $16 to $24 per barrel and have since stabilized in the $30 range. Throughout, OPEC's impact and gains have been all the more striking because the organization has been a diverse and contentious cartel.

Small-scale examples also are instructive. In the 1960s, Miles Laboratories set the price for a medical kit at forty-three times cost. The kits, designed to prediagnose mental retardation in infants, were produced by Miles under an exclusive license. Miles's cost was about $6, but they set the price at $262 each.

The DeBeers diamond monopoly has controlled world diamond prices for over five decades.[3] Its Central Selling Organization can alter the price of diamonds across a wide range.

The leading airlines hold dominance in various hub cities. For example, Northwest controls over 80 percent of flights through both Detroit and Minneapolis, and USAir has a near-monopoly in Pittsburgh (see chapter 14 for details). Fares on these dominated routes average over 25 percent higher than others.

Eastman Kodak, with over 75 percent of film sales in the United States, was able to price "largely without regard to cost" (in one of its own officials' words) for over 90 years (see chapter 13). In Britain, Kodak, Ltd., held over 75 percent of the market for color film for several decades; it maintained prices at 35 to 55 percent above competitive levels.[4]

The drug industry offers many instances in which patented drugs, protected against effective competition, are produced at costs of 10 cents or less per pill but are priced at high multiples of the cost.

Archer-Daniels Midland officials participated with Hoffmann-LaRoche and Bayer AG officials in price fixing of lysine, a food additive for hogs, a $500 million industry. In the early 1990s, the price was apparently raised from 60 cents to over $1 a pound.[5]

Local hospitals joined in 1995 with doctors in Danbury, Connecticut, and St. Joseph, Missouri, in price-fixing schemes that kept out lower-cost managed-care companies.[6] Fees were raised substantially.

The price of cellophane was raised substantially by Du Pont during the many years it held a virtual monopoly on this product in the United States.[7] Collusion in a series of tight oligopolies in American electrical equipment markets probably maintained prices 20 percent above their long-run competitive levels during the 1950s. When fixed brokerage fees were made competitive on the New York Stock Exchange in May 1975, prices dropped by 43 to 64 percent.

Examples like these can be multiplied many times over, in many countries, sectors, and specific markets.[8]

Price Discrimination.   Monopoly power also enlarges price discrimination, which sets a structure of different price-cost ratios depending on customers' differences in demand elasticities (chapter 10 gives details).[9] Such demand-based "charging what the traffic will bear" can generate surprisingly large volumes of profits, raising the whole company's profit rate.

2.   CROSS-SECTION STUDIES CONFIRM BROADER PATTERNS

Logically, the task is simple: to test whether monopoly structure causes changes in either prices or profits. Prices or profits are the **dependent** variable (the effect), while structural conditions are the **independent** variables (the possible causes).

One assembles data on an array of markets or firms, including facts on all conditions that might strongly affect prices or profits. Then one runs statistical regressions to estimate the coefficients between structure and prices or profits.

Scores of such cross-section studies have been published during the last five decades. They have divided into two main approaches: (1) **industry-based** studies of price-cost margins and (2) **company-based** studies of rates of profit on investment.

Price-Cost Margins.   Serious research began with Joe S. Bain.[10] From 1951 until 1968, research focused on **industrywide** analysis of **price-cost margins**, as explained by concentration ratios. The research effort then shifted more to **individual company** data, in an effort to explain the firms' profit rates with their market shares.

Generally the industrywide patterns turned out to be pretty weak. Price-cost ratios were only faintly related to concentration ratios, so that concentration seemed to raise prices only by about 10 percent at the most. Free-market writers could claim that concentration didn't matter much at all. But as chapter 3 noted, that weakness partly reflected poor data, which acted like static on a TV screen to make the patterns hard to discern. More recently, excellent studies in the airline, banking, and other industries have found stronger patterns.[11]

Company Profit Rates.   With more precision, research after 1968 focused more tightly on the market shares of individual companies. Much tighter relationships between profit rates and market shares were clearly shown.[12] The patterns also affirmed the business world's universal emphasis on market shares. Each 10-point increase in market share tended to yield a 2-point rise in profit rate; thus a 50 percent market share generally yielded a 10-point total rise in profit rate, above the competitive profit rate of about 10 percent.

After 1980 some researchers used q ratios in place of profit rates, and the same patterns emerged.[13] It emerged that profit rates are at least as useful as the complicated and imperfect q ratios.

3.   RISK DOES NOT EXPLAIN AWAY HIGHER PROFITS

Risk may also be involved. If investors are generally risk averse, then the equilibrium rate of return for risky firms and industries might be higher than for less risky cases. Differences in rates of return might just be "risk premiums" rather than monopoly gains. Drug companies, for example, say that their high profit rates aren't excessive but merely reflect their higher risk.

This theoretical possibility has been tested inconclusively in actual industries, because it is virtually impossible to measure risk. Risk is the danger of long-term financial loss, but actual measures of risk have relied instead on short-term fluctuations in firms' profits. Calculations of profit variance and the "beta coefficient" have been used as estimators of risk.[14]

Actually, risk's role is likely to relate **inversely** to market power, because a dominant firm usually will have less risk than its small rivals face. Therefore research is likely to show that dominant firms' high profits are not just risk premiums after all. On the contrary, allowing for risk is likely to accentuate the excess profits that high market shares yield.

Research does indeed show that pattern. In one study, a risk discount equal to the variance in yearly profit rates was subtracted from raw profit rates. That would reflect the lower true value of shakier profit rates. With this rough approximation, the resulting patterns in table 4.1 show that the relation between monopoly structure and profitability is even tighter.

Risk adjustment sharpens the measured effect of monopoly on profits. If long-term risk is ever reliably measured, that too would be expected to display the same basic patterns.

II.   EFFECTS ON EFFICIENCY

Because monopoly power appears to affect prices and profits, it may also shape real conditions. We turn first to efficiency, looking at X-efficiency and allocative efficiency. Then we review further evidence about the "efficient structure" hypothesis. In addition, natural resources need attention. The degree of competition may influence efficiency in the use of certain open-access natural resources.

1. X-Efficiency

Criteria.   Internal efficiency (X-efficiency) means keeping costs down to the minimum possible level. In a diagram of average and marginal costs, X-efficiency is reached by being *on* the average cost curve. Even a small rise above the curve can increase costs by 5 or 10 percent. Very large rises are not plausible, for the **stock market treadmill** and other pressures usually will not let them last (see chapter 8). Also, profit is a relatively small margin, often only a 10 or 15 percent sliver above cost. Squeezing down a 10 percent margin of X-inefficiency can often double the profit margin. Therefore the incentives against X-inefficiency are very strong. Against all these efficient pressures is human nature. Managers often have personal objectives that diverge from maximum company profit (see chapter 8). Excess profits enable these other objectives to come into play: growth and empire building, an easier life, the avoidance of risk, etc. Down the line, ordinary employees of a secure firm know that their company is lucrative and that there is a financial cushion. Keeping costs strictly at the minimum becomes difficult. Work effort also slips, since the pressure is lower. In short, costs rise above necessary levels.

Table 4.1   A Comparison of Risk-Adjusted Rates of Return

Industry	Market Share of the Leading Firm* (%)	Risk-Discounted Rate of Return, 1960–1969 (profit rate minus average yearly shift) (%)
Toiletries	45	25.0
Photographic	75	16.5
Drugs	(50)	17.1
Soft drinks	45	15.2
Office machinery	65	15.2
Automobiles	55	11.3
Tobacco	28	12.6
Electrical machinery	45	11.9
Soaps and detergents	45	12.1
Rubber	25	10.5
Petroleum	(25)	9.9
Glass	25	8.3
Steel	23	5.9
Meat packing	18	4.2

*Market shares are estimated. Parentheses indicate an approximate average value.

Source: Adapted from W. G. Shepherd, *The Treatment of Market Power* (New York: Columbia University Press, 1975), p. 112.

The topic can become quite complicated, because every inefficient action can be excused by some positive-sounding reason. But the simple lesson is that X-inefficiency can grow large and persistent.

Measurements.   Measuring X-inefficiency is still a primitive art.[15] There is no fully reliable method for measuring X-efficiency in firms.[16] For the time being, one needs to apply a reasonable judgment to the broad flow of commentary in the business press.[17] Though not scientific, published opinions do provide a fairly reliable guide to the general scope of X-inefficiency.

Two lessons emerge. First, X-inefficiency is a common problem that often raises costs by more than 10 percent above their efficient levels.[18] Second, X-inefficiency is closely related to market power. Monopolies, dominant firms, and tight oligopolists are likely to develop marked X-inefficiency. Some avoid it, but many do not. Most firms under strong competitive pressure do not display slack.

Examples.   Before we turn to specific cases, one period strongly shows large X-inefficiency in the past: the severe downsizing of many U.S. firms during the 1980s. The cuts commonly reduced company costs by 15 percent, or even by 25 percent or more. These cuts are a rough indicator that X-inefficiency was large.

Turning now to examples, they illustrate patterns and show you the kind of opinions that often dominate the business press. In this small sample, there is no intention to single out specific firms for criticism. In fact, X-inefficiency is usually publicized only after a firm has turned the corner under new managers.[19]

Recent instances include International Harvester in the decades before 1970: "We were large, lethargic, lacking in new ideas, and inbred."[20] Hershey Foods was said in 1975 to have a "structural disease" of complacency.[21] Du Pont "became stuck in an old mold, with too much reliance on historical ways" in the years before 1973.[22] Kennecott Copper was for many years a secure "sleeping giant content to liquidate itself through generous contributions to its shareholders as long as its mines held out."[23]

IBM in the 1980s offered spectacular X-inefficiency. After dominating computers for three decades, IBM had become "a giant, calcified institution" with "bad habits and inefficient processes that had taken root over seven decades." "[The] colossus has one of the world's most luxuriantly thick bureaucracies" with "layer upon layer upon layer."[24] After the company nearly failed in 1993 under $8 billion in losses, Louis Gerstner was brought in to save it, and he did. But he brought IBM's "suffocating" and "hermetically sealed" corporate culture back to life.[25]

General Motors, Ford, and Chrysler came under severe new competitive pressure from Japanese imports during 1979–1981. Spurred by that threat, they managed to reduce their costs by no less than 20 to 30 percent, suggesting that their X-inefficiency had been that high. By 1992 GM was cutting even more deeply amid a recognition that it had become thoroughly inefficient. Its mediocrity and financial losses caused major reductions in its stock price.[26]

When AT&T consented (under antitrust pressure; see chapters 13 and 16) to be divided in 1984, it kept its manufacturing operations, thinking that they offered high growth and profits. Its old Western Electric equipment company was combined into an information systems subsidiary. But half of the former Western Electric capacity and employment were soon closed down under the pressure of direct competition in the marketplace after a century of sheltered monopoly.[27] AT&T itself now extols the change, and during both 1995–1996 and 2001–2002 it repeated the process, dividing itself into three or more units (see chapter 13 for more).

In 1987, Boeing (the dominant aircraft maker: see chapter 14) embarked on an arduous reorganization after recognizing that its costs were unnecessarily high. It aimed to cut its employee costs by 25 percent.[28] In fact, Boeing remained deeply plagued by inefficiency even after 2000; it still uses several incompatible computer systems, and its production methods are suffused with waste.[29]

X-inefficiency also arises outside conventional manufacturing industries. Stockbrokers were less efficient under the fee-setting cartel before 1975. Rate cutting by the Russian shipping fleet during 1974–1976 exposed excess costs in many private ocean shippers. Regulated utilities have long been recognized as tending toward X-inefficiency. Weapons production in the United States has often been notoriously X-inefficient because of lax Defense Department purchasing.

The U.S. health-care industry has contained large degrees of inefficiency in a patchwork of markets. Resource use has varied by more than double in different sections of the country, involving all aspects of medical treatment.[30]

The list can easily be lengthened by searching further in the business press. The opinions are often debatable, but they usually express what is widely known in the trade. Firms will, of course, deny the appraisal at the time. Yet they often candidly acknowledge the situation later, after their management has changed.

A consensus view of average X-inefficiency would be roughly in the range of at least 10 percent of costs for firms with high monopoly power. The extra margin of cost scales down as competitive pressure increases. This tendency would suggest about 5 percent of extra costs for a typical tight oligopoly.

2. ALLOCATIVE EFFICIENCY

The loss of allocative efficiency caused by market power is the welfare triangle noted in chapter 2. Some economists regard it as *the* main burden of monopoly. Actual misallocation has of course been kept low by many past decades of antitrust actions. If antitrust were removed, the misallocation would probably grow far larger.

To measure misallocation, one needs to know the elasticity of demand, the increase in price caused by market power, and the slope of the average cost curve for each firm exerting market power in each market. The loss from this triangle would (by simple plane geometry) be 1/2 times the rise in price, times the change in quantity. If demand elasticity equals 1, prices are raised by 20 percent, and average costs are constant, then the triangle would represent about 2 percent of total revenue.

In actual markets with substantial market power, the average increase in price is often above 10 percent. Scale economies are probably not a strong factor in most markets, as will be noted in chapter 7. Elasticities of demand will differ sharply across industries, of course. The convention has been to assume that, on average, demand is approximately unit elastic.[31]

On this basis, the estimated misallocation effect would be slightly under 1 percent of GNP. This is a lower bound on the true value, because:

1. Some market power is not known.

2. The data tend to underestimate its effect.

3. The price effect of market power probably exceeds the assumed value.

Moreover, a low estimated misallocation may merely show the benefits of past antitrust actions in enforcing competition, rather than the misallocation that would occur if there were no antitrust.

Some earlier studies reached varying estimates of misallocation.[32] Harberger in 1954 used averages of profits from 1920 to 1929 in eighty industry groups. The misallocation burden came out at about 0.2 percent of GNP. Yet this figure is widely regarded as too low.[33]

Cowling and Mueller have given a contrasting estimate based on a different approach.[34] They treat monopoly profit itself as a social cost, and they focus on the before-tax levels of profit. To it they add advertising, on the suggestion (by Harberger and others) that advertising is a social cost. The initial level of monopoly profit is therefore as follows:

Monopoly profit = recorded profit (above the cost of capital) + advertising − taxes

The costs spent by the firm in monopolizing activities may absorb some of the monopoly profit, and in that sense, the estimate of actual social loss may be too low.

Cowling and Mueller offer a variety of estimates of the loss, based on varying assumptions, using more complete, refined data than Harberger employed. Their estimates, ranging roughly from 4 to 13 percent of corporate output, can be considered the upper bound of possible levels. The true value probably lies between their estimates and Harberger's, probably between 1 and 2 percent of national income.

Like X-inefficiency, the misallocation burden may have decreased in recent decades as competition has risen.[35] The consensus is that it probably has been about 1 to 2 percent of GNP, but that it may be closer to 1 percent now.

One policy lesson is clear. If antitrust has indeed kept this burden low, then antitrust should presumably be kept strict.

3.   THE FREE-MARKET "EFFICIENT-STRUCTURE" HYPOTHESIS

Recall the free-market claim that causation is reversed, running from performance to structure. The main evidence offered as proof was given by Harold Demsetz in 1973.[36] The data, shown in table 4.2, were slender; Demsetz included just 99 three-digit industries. The small firms are separated from the larger ones. Size is a crude basis for separation; it would be better to use relative size, to show the largest four, the next four, and the rest. Some small industries have no big firms, while some big industries have no small firms.[37]

Also, Demsetz's use of raw concentration ratios injects error, because those ratios are often based on poor market definitions.[38] For all these reasons, results were likely to be unclear.

A mild pattern did emerge. Larger firms seem to make higher rates of return than others. That might reflect greater efficiency, and Demsetz claimed that it did. But instead, it could simply reflect the greater market power held by firms with higher market shares.

Therefore, the results do nothing to separate market-power effects from efficiency effects. Demsetz asserted instead that the higher large-firm profits reflect economies of scale or superior performance by those firms. Despite its weaknesses and mixed results, this study has been the main "proof" that dominance reflects only superior efficiency. Only if all imperfections were absent, in every market, might that assertion be permissible.

Table 4.2   Concentration and Profit Rates, 1963

Number of Industries	Four-Firm Concentration Ratio (%)	Rate of Return on Assets (firms with assets over $50 million) (%)
3	60+	21.6
11	50–60	12.2
21	40–50	9.4
24	30–40	11.7
22	20–30	10.6
18	10–20	8.0

Source: Evidence in Harold Demsetz, "Industry Structure, Market Rivalry, and Public Policy," *Journal of Law and Economics* 16 (1973).

There has been no further persuasive evidence for that claim.[39] In 1977, Sam Peltzman attempted a statistical test relating growth to cost differences. He tried to correlate changes in concentration with differences in price-cost patterns, saying that it was an indirect indicator of efficiency. But the data and coefficients were extremely weak (he used uncorrected census ratios, for example), and a critique by Scherer in 1980 showed that the results indicate little about efficiency.[40]

Claims About Correlations.   Free-market advocates have also simply claimed that the correlations between market shares and profit rates show only superior performance, not market power.[41] Yet that is mere speculation. Even if the correlations were entirely caused by superiority, there would have to be sustained superiority by **all** firms with high market shares to fit the claim. And that kind of universal sustained superiority is simply not true.

Cases.   This can be seen from actual cases, such as Microsoft, IBM, Boeing, and Eastman Kodak. As chapters 7, 13, and 14 will note, economies of scale do not explain their market positions. Those firms have held large amounts of excess market share. Moreover, these markets are known to have significant imperfections, and the companies have had periods of substantial inefficiency.

Microsoft gained its powerful near-monopoly over operating software around 1980 by cleverly getting IBM's approval for DOS as the standard IBM system. Its Windows software has some excellent features, but was widely regarded as ramshackle and unreliable until about 2001. Microsoft kept and extended its monopoly by tenacious and dubious stratagems, leading to the antitrust case in the late 1990s that convicted it for anticompetitive actions (see chapter 13). Microsoft does not fit the free-market hypothesis.

IBM has dominated the mainframe computer market for some thirty-five years. It gained dominance partly because of special advantages; it already held 90 percent of the tabulating machine market and a powerful sales force that visited most large businesses.[42] Its innovation fell behind its rivals in the early 1960s, and it retained its dominance only by a series of actions widely regarded as anticompetitive.[43] It retained dominance in the 1980s long after it developed severe internal inefficiency.

Boeing Aircraft became the dominant aircraft firm after World War II (see chapter 14). Its dominance has risen from good airplane designs and also by complex behind-the-scenes maneuvering to capture sales. But its internal efficiency is known to be low, and occasionally even chaotic. That helped to cause slippage, allowing Airbus to rise to near-equality. Therefore Boeing departs from the free-market hypothesis.

Eastman Kodak has held over 75 percent of the U.S. amateur film market for about 90 years.[44] It retained that share partly through its strong position in related markets for cameras and for film processing. The company's innovativeness has been regarded at times as mixed and mediocre, especially in the 1970s (see also chapter 13). It has been struggling recently to shift to the digital photography era.

Altogether these cases conflict with the efficient-structure hypothesis rather than confirm it.

Variance Analysis.   A research approach in the 1980s used variance analysis to estimate the relative importance of industry-specific and market-share effects on profitability.[45] It did show that market-share effects are significant. But the method is indirect, applying a simple model to estimate conditions that vary within industries in complex ways.

The results are doubtful: that industry-specific conditions explain most of the variation among firms' profits. Instead, profitability is known to vary directly with market shares in a wide range of typical industries. These strong **intraindustry** patterns coexist with some **interindustry** variations in profits, reflecting differing industry characteristics.

Indeed, past research and common observation suggest that intraindustry variation is at least as strong as interindustry differences. Schmalensee's and Wernerfelt-Montgomery's results are therefore dubious, and it is likely that their method masks the complexity of the patterns. Moreover, Ioannis Kessides found three sources of error when rechecking Schmalensee's data and calculations.[46] In the upshot, Kessides finds ". . . that market share is both statistically significant and quantitatively important."

Altogether, the indications of market power's effects continue to be widespread and strong.

4. FUNCTIONLESS ADVERTISING[47]

Advertising comes in two main types: informative and persuasive. **Informative advertising** expands buyers' knowledge so that they can apply their preferences more effectively when making choices that will maximize their welfare. By improving choices, informative advertising adds to welfare.

Persuasive advertising instead attempts to change consumers' preferences. Because it interferes with the exercise of innate preferences, it alters choices away from the efficient lines that "consumer sovereignty" would yield. Thus persuasive, image-instilling advertising is largely a form of economic waste. That applies to both the bulk of television advertising and much magazine advertising, at the least.

Standoff Advertising. A subcategory of advertising is standoff advertising among oligopolists. It occurs when each firm would be willing to forego the expenditure but all are afraid to stop for fear of losing ground to the others. Much oligopoly advertising may be of this sort, with no net gain. Indeed, advertisers often say that there is little evidence that any kind of advertising strongly affects consumer spending.

No precise measures of the functionless types of advertising have been made, but there is an approximate consensus that it includes perhaps half of all advertising. If that is true, then at least $70 billion annually may represent economic loss.

5. CONSERVATION OF NATURAL RESOURCES

Competition has some unusual effects on natural resources. It can handle some resources with great efficiency but destroy others. That depends on special features, which we consider first.

Natural resources range across two basic spectrums:

1. **Renewable to Fixed.** Fish, forests, water, and other resources will renew themselves if not cropped too heavily. Ores, oil, and coal are gone forever once they are taken out. Many resources are intermediate

on this spectrum. Topsoil and wilderness, for example, are often renewable, but only at great cost.

2. **Mobile or Immobile.** Some resources are fixed in place; they can be precisely owned and controlled. Others—such as fish, whales, and oil—can move, so they are open for capture.

For all resources, the efficient rate of use will maximize their total value over the whole span of time.[48] Decisions about resources rest on speculations about their future values. Thus petroleum can be used at present prices or held in the ground for use at future prices. The choice often is to convert the resource into some other form (such as turning iron ore into steel and thence into a machine) that will give further value in production.[49]

Private Choices.   Private market choices may reach the optimum with no special guidance. Owners of resources wish to maximize their assets' value. If markets are reasonably perfect, then private choices will bring resource use into line with social criteria. The key variables—interest rates, predictions, and relative prices—will emerge in markets and guide decisions by the resources' owners and users. Present and expected future scarcities will be reflected and balanced in the market result.

Competitive processes may yield conservation, but only if markets are reasonably perfect. If the owners are monopolists, they will restrict present usage somewhat by setting prices at higher monopoly levels. Yet the owners still wish to maximize the long-run value of their resources, and thus their restrictive effect may distort their choices only slightly.[50]

Mobility and Open Access.   Mobile resources and certain others will not be optimized by competition. Each firm will have an interest in maximizing its own take. The whole outcome can be to deplete the resource entirely, at far above the optimal rate. Whales, oil, fresh water in the western U.S.—these are famous, urgent examples, among many.

Early oil drilling in the United States gave many owners joint access to unusually large pools. Each owner then tried to take oil as fast as possible. Certain international fishing resources have been "ravaged by decades of overfishing," reduced to one-tenth or less of their sustainable levels.[51] Unifying (that is, monopolizing) is necessary to avoid overfishing. The optimal rates of harvest for whales, anchovies, tuna, various white fish, and many other major fish categories are already well known, but open access distorts the incentives.

Scenic and wilderness areas also involve the open-access problem. Here the resource is fixed rather than mobile. If it is open to more than one user, its use will reduce its natural character and value. Conversion to a single-owner park status (usually under public ownership) has been the usual answer, from the Great Wall and Machu Picchu to Yosemite, Yellowstone, and the Grand Canyon.

The correct general solution is to unify or actually to monopolize ownership of the resource. Then the optimum rate of use can be carefully applied, using the minimum amount of inputs to harvest the resource at the best rate.

QUESTIONS FOR REVIEW

1. Draw a demand curve and cost curves diagram to illustrate a firm raising its price 20 percent above the competitive level. Then draw and explain

another diagram with curves to illustrate a drug company that set a price that is five times higher than the constant marginal cost of $1.

2. Explain why industry-based statistical studies relating concentration and price-cost margins tend to yield much lower correlations than do firm-based statistical studies relating market shares and profit rates.

3. A close correlation of market shares with profit rates may reflect market power, efficiencies, or some of both. Use examples to illustrate the range of these factors. Do you have a general view about the market-power and efficiencies interpretations?

4. Do General Motors' and IBM's dominance and deterioration before 1992 and recovery since then fit the free-market view that dominance lasts only if the firm is superior? Explain.

5. Discuss (a) two actual instances where X-inefficiency has arisen in firms with market power and (b) two instances where new competitive pressure has squeezed X-inefficiency down.

ENDNOTES

[1] One major set of studies provides statistical case studies of a number of industries: Leonard W. Weiss, ed., *Concentration and Price* (Cambridge: MIT Press, 1989).

[2] Among the outpouring of writings about OPEC, see James M. Griffin and David J. Teece, *OPEC Behavior and World Oil Prices* (London: Allen & Unwin, 1982); John M. Blair, *The Price of Oil* (New York: Pantheon Books, 1976); Steven A. Schneider, *The Oil Price Revolution* (Baltimore: Johns Hopkins Press, 1983); and Paul W. MacAvoy, *Crude Oil Prices* (Cambridge: Ballinger Press, 1982).

[3] See Debra L. Spar, *The Cooperative Edge: The Internal Politics of International Cartels* (Ithaca: Cornell University Press, 1994); David Koskoff, *The Diamond World* (New York: Harper & Row, 1981); and Godehard Lenzen, *The History of Diamond Production and the Diamond Trade* (London: Barrie and Jenkins, 1981).

[4] U.K. Monopolies Commission, *Color Film* (House of Commons, No. 1, London: Her Majesty's Stationery Office, April 21, 1966).

[5] See the authoritative coverage in John M. Connor, *Global Price Fixing: Our Customers Are the Enemy* (Dordrecht, the Netherlands: Kluwer Academic Publishers, 2001).

[6] Thomas J. Lueck, "Illegal Price-Fixing Charged in Danbury Hospital Suit," *New York Times* (September 14, 1995): p. B6.

[7] See George W. Stocking and Willard F. Mueller, "The Cellophane Case and the New Competition," *American Economic Review* 45 (March 1955): pp. 29–63.

[8] A curious related development is for firms to hide their identity by changing their names. Standard Oil of New Jersey became Exxon; hundreds of banks, health-care firms, baby Bells, electric utilities, and others joined the craze. This confronts the student with serious difficulties in understanding what companies really do.

[9] Prominent examples include patented drugs, which are sold at sharply differing prices to different groups. Another example is airline fares; the same plane may contain customers getting equal service (including scheduling convenience) but paying prices varying by multiples of three or four.

[10] Joe S. Bain, "Relation of Profit Rate to Industry Concentration, American Manufacturing, 1936–1940," *Quarterly Journal of Economics* 65 (August 1951): pp. 277–98.

[11] See especially Leonard W. Weiss, ed., *Concentration and Price*; Stephen A. Rhoades, "Market Share as a Source of Market Power: Implications and Some Evidence," *Journal of Economics and Business* 37 (1985): pp. 343–63; Ralph Bradburd, T. Pugel, and K. Pugh, "Internal Rent Capture and the Profit-Concentration Relation," *Review of Economics and Statistics* 73 (August 1991): pp.

432–40; Timothy F. Bresnahan and P. C. Reiss, "Entry and Competition in Concentrated Markets," *Journal of Political Economy* 99 (October 1991): pp. 977–1009; and for import effects, M. M. Katics and B. C. Petersen, "The Effect of Rising Import Competition on Market Power: A Panel Data Study of U.S. Manufacturing," *Journal of Industrial Economics* 42 (September 1994): pp. 277–86.

[12] William G. Shepherd, "The Elements of Market Structure," *Review of Economics and Statistics* 54 (February 1972): pp. 25–37; Richard Schmalensee, "Do Markets Differ Much?" *American Economic Review* 75 (June 1985): pp. 341–51; E. W. Eckard, "A Note on the Profit-Concentration Relation," *Applied Economics* 27 (February 1995): pp. 219–23.

[13] A q ratio is a firm's market value divided by its asset, or replacement, value. If stock market activity reflects rational, accurate evaluations, then q will be superior to mere backward-looking profit rates. But the q ratios are not easy to derive from company data. Also, they inevitably incorporate some of the same errors that infect accounting profit rates. See Michael Smirlock, Thomas Gilligan, and William Marshall, "Tobin's q and the Structure-Performance Relationship," *American Economic Review* 74 (December 1984): pp. 1051–60, and the sources cited there. For a critique of q ratios and their use, see W. G. Shepherd, "Tobin's q and the Structure-Performance Relationship: Comment," *American Economic Review* 76 (December 1986): pp. 1205–10.

[14] Variance is a weak measure because it is superficial and possibly biased. Thus, everyone may already allow for the yearly jumpiness in profits, and so no real risk is involved. Also, variation may be *upward*, which means desirable high profits and lower risk.
The beta coefficient is the ratio of the firm's own stock-price fluctuations to the entire *stock market's* fluctuations. It suggests whether this firm's stock has been more volatile than the whole market, on average. But that too is strictly short term, and it is backward looking. The right measure would look ahead, considering the risk that the firm now faces.

[15] More directly, studies of performance are frequently done by professional business consulting firms, and these management audits are occasionally published. Their value lies in their directness and professional quality. Yet they are fallible, and often they have been commissioned for purposes other than a broad-scale appraisal. So one should consider their lessons cautiously.

[16] But see Richard E. Caves and David R. Barton, *Technical Efficiency in U.S. Manufacturing Industries* (Cambridge: MIT Press, 1990).

[17] Good sources include the *Wall Street Journal* and general-purpose business magazines that report on company affairs and current opinions, including *BusinessWeek, Forbes,* and *Fortune*. Investment analysis' opinions are circulated in brokerage house newsletters and the financial press.

[18] Scherer and Ross, *Industrial Market Structure and Economic Performance*, chapter 18, 3rd ed. (Boston: Houghton Mifflin, 1991).

[19] The cautious observer may therefore discount the new-CEO claims about previous mismanagement as possibly being self-serving.

[20] The quotation is from the executive vice-president of the company. See "New Spur for a Sluggish Giant," *BusinessWeek* (March 17, 1975): pp. 50–54.

[21] "Melting Profits," *Forbes* (November 1, 1975): p. 40.

[22] According to its chairman, Irvin S. Shapiro, quoted in "Pattern Breaker," *Forbes* (July 1, 1975): pp. 24–25.

[23] *BusinessWeek* (December 7, 1968): pp. 104–108.

[24] *Wall Street Journal* (November 11, 1988).

[25] His withering account of IBM is in Louis V. Gerstner, Jr., *Who Says Elephants Can't Dance? Inside IBM's Historic Turnaround* (New York: HarperBusiness, 2002).

[26] See William G. Shepherd, "Antitrust Repelled, Inefficiency Endured: Lessons of IBM and General Motors for Future Antitrust Policies," *Antitrust Bulletin* 39 (Spring 1994): pp. 203–234.

[27] "AT&T Chairman Sees More Cost Trims but No Further Job Cuts or Restructuring," *Wall Street Journal* (November 1985): p. 4; and "Why AT&T Isn't Clicking," *BusinessWeek* (May 19, 1986): pp. 88–95.

[28] *Wall Street Journal* (September 7, 1987): p. 1.

[29] See Jerry Useem, "Boeing vs. Boeing," *Fortune* (October 2, 2000): pp. 148–60; and Stanley Holmes and Mike France, "Boeing's Secret," *BusinessWeek* (May 20, 2002): pp. 110–20.

[30] Ron Winslow, "Study Finds a Crazy Quilt of Health Care," *Wall Street Journal* (January 30, 1996): p. 135; the report in the Dartmouth Atlas of Health Care is comprehensive and detailed.

[31] Actually, elasticity would have to be greater than one, for marginal revenue must be positive and equal to marginal cost. The unit elastic assumption is only a rough approximation.

[32] See Arnold Harberger, "Monopoly and Resource Allocation," *American Economic Review* 44 (May 1954): pp. 77–87; George J. Stigler, "The Statistics of Monopoly and Merger," *Journal of Political Economy* 64 (1956): pp. 33–40. Also Scherer and Ross, *Industrial Market Structure and Economic Performance*; and William G. Shepherd, *Market Power and Economic Welfare* (New York: Random House, 1970).

[33] Harberger's large industry groups masked the range of profits among the true markets. Also, he ignored X-inefficiency. Furthermore, he dealt only with deviations from the average profit rate, assuming that low and high rates would move toward the average. The correct method is to assume that all profits are moved down toward the minimum competitive level.

[34] Keith Cowling and Dennis C. Mueller, "The Social Costs of Monopoly Power," *Economic Journal* 88 (August 1978): pp. 727–48.

[35] For one study of this topic, see T. H. Oum and Y. Zhang, "Competition and Allocative Efficiency: The Case of the U.S. Telephone Industry," *Review of Economics and Statistics* 77 (February 1995): pp. 82–96.

[36] Harold Demsetz, "Industry Structure, Market Rivalry, and Public Policy," *Journal of Law and Economics* 16 (April 1973): pp. 1–9; for criticism, see F. M. Scherer and David Ross, *Industrial Market Structure and Economic Performance*, 3rd ed. (Boston: Houghton Mifflin, 1991), chapter 11.

[37] Or the small firms are in different submarkets from the big ones, because three-digit industries are far broader than real markets.

[38] Any research that finds only three industries with concentration over 60 percent is not very reliable or inclusive.

[39] See Scherer and Ross, *Industrial Market Structure and Economic Performance*; Stephen Martin, *Industrial Economics: Economic Analysis and Public Policy* (New York: Macmillan, 1994), chaper 7; and Dennis C. Mueller, ed., *The Dynamics of Company Profits: An International Comparison* (New York: Cambridge University Press, 1990).

[40] See Sam Peltzman, "The Gains and Losses from Industrial Concentration," *Journal of Law and Economics* 20 (October 1977): pp. 229–63; and F. M. Scherer, *Industrial Market Structure and Economic Performance*, 2nd ed. (Boston: Houghton Mifflin, 1980), pp. 288–92. See also John S. Heywood, "Market Share and Efficiency: A Reprise," *Economics Letters* 24 (1987): pp. 171–75, for further confirmation that the relationship between market share and profit rate reflects market power.

[41] Perhaps the most ambitious empirical claims in this direction have been by Michael Smirlock et al., "Tobin's q and the Structure-Performance Relationship," *American Economic Review* 74 (December 1984): pp. 1051–60.

[42] See Shepherd, "Antitrust Repelled," 1994.

[43] These include anticompetitive price discrimination, the use of money-losing "fighting ships" to drive out specific competitors, and unduly early announcements of new models in order to deter sales of superior computers by Control Data Corporation; see chapter 13; Gerald W. Brock, *The U.S. Computer Industry* (Cambridge: Ballinger, 1975); and Richard T. DeLamarter, *Big Blue* (New York: Dodd, Mead, 1986).

[44] Don E. Waldman, *Antitrust Action and Market Structure* (Lexington, MA: Lexington Books, 1978), chapter 7; James W. Brock, "Structural Monopoly, Technological Performance, and Predatory Innovation: Relevant Standards under Section 2 of the Sherman Act," *American Business Law Journal* 21 (1983): pp. 291–306; and Gerald W. Brock, "Persistent Monopoly and the Charade of Antitrust: The Durability of Kodak's Market Power," *University of Toledo Law Review* 14 (Spring 1983): pp. 653–83.

[45] Richard Schmalensee, "Do Markets Differ Much?" *American Economic Review* 75 (June 1985): pp. 341–51; and Birger Wernerfelt and Cynthia A. Montgomery, "Tobin's *q* and the Importance of Focus in Firm Performance," *American Economic Review* 78 (March 1988): pp. 246–50. For an effective critique of the Schmalensee paper, see Ioannis N. Kessides, "Do Firms Differ Much? Some Additional Evidence," *American Economic Review* (1990).

[46] First, a very few observations (55 of the total 1775) had extreme values, strongly affecting the computed patterns. If they are deleted, the expected firm-based effects do become quite strong after all. Second, Schmalensee's results were distorted by heteroscedasticity (differences in the degree of variation, across the size ranges of firms and industries). When that is corrected, the firm-based effects again are strong. Third, Schmalensee's model constrained the market-share effect to be identical among industries, whereas in fact it undoubtedly varies in some degree. Kessides concludes that the model is "misspecified." When that misspecification of the model is corrected, market-share effects emerge from the data.

[47] Chapter 12 discusses advertising more thoroughly.

[48] See the excellent summary in Gardner M. Brown, "Renewable Natural Resource Management and Use Without Markets," *Journal of Economic Literature* 338 (December 2000): pp. 875–914. Also Thomas H. Tietenberg, *Environmental and Natural Resource Economics* (New York: HarperCollins, 1996); and Anthony C. Fisher, *Resource and Environmental Economics* (Cambridge: Cambridge University Press, 1981).

[49] The optimum rate of use for each resource depends on (1) the costs of using it, (2) current prices compared with predicted prices, (3) interest rates, and (4) ethical weights used in comparing our use with our posterity's use. The predictions will also cover future technology, for new methods can make a resource more valuable or, conversely, obsolete. The whole choice is complex and difficult, for it rests on many factors, some of which are obscure.

[50] Tietenberg, *Environmental and Natural Resource Economics*, especially chapter 12.

[51] See, for example, Susan Diesenhouse, "In New England, Battle Plans for Survival at Sea," *New York Times* (Sunday, April 24, 1994): p. F7; and Robert Langreth, "Commercial Fish Stocks Could Rebound with Oversight of Industry, Study Says," *Wall Street Journal* (August 25, 1995): p. B3.

Chapter

5

Innovation, Fairness, and Other Values

Now we come to some rather more dramatic effects of monopoly and competition. **Innovation** is dynamic and often spectacular; monopoly's retarding of it is deadening. The **unfairness** caused by facing a monopoly angers many people much more than losing a few percentage points of inefficiency. And when you have no **freedom of choice**, as in facing just one cable TV company, the Yellow Pages, or the local newspaper, it can be very disturbing.

These broader harms often are hard to measure, but they may be much more important than any effects on static inefficiency, especially the retarding of innovation. First, section 1 presents innovation; we note eight features of innovation and review theories about competition's stimulating role. Section 2 sums up the empirical research on innovation and examines the role of the patent system.

Section 3 assesses monopoly's impacts on fairness, section 4 considers competition itself as a value, and section 5 reviews some even broader effects.

I. INNOVATION

Innovation probably far outranks static efficiency in economic importance.[1] Even just a few years of fast innovation can quickly exceed the results from fine-tuning current efficiency. Innovation is after all dynamic rather than static, creative rather than repetitive.

The basic issue is whether competition or monopoly is more favorable to technological progress.[2] The mainstream hypothesis favors competition, but there are exceptions, as well as an opposing free-market view. And Schumpeter urged that the pursuit of market dominance creates progress, as noted in chapter 3.

1.   CONCEPTS AND RELATIONSHIPS

The nature of technological progress is clarified by eight basic sets of concepts.

1. Invention, Innovation, and Imitation.   There are three phases in bringing out new products and processes.

First, invention creates the new idea. The act is intellectual: seeing a new image, a new connection between old conditions, or a new area for action. It can range from basic scientific concepts to strictly practical ideas (such as a new notch in a gear). Much productive invention is accomplished by single thinkers and tinkerers, not just big research teams.

Second, innovation applies the idea in production and practical use. The innovator establishes production facilities and brings the new product or process to the market. This often displaces previous products or processes. It often takes big volumes of money capital, plus large-scale masses of people, to innovate well.

Imitation then follows, as the innovation is copied by others.

This triple-I sequence is easy to remember; often the term **innovation** is used broadly to refer to all three stages. Each stage requires different skills and resources, and the incentives are distinct for each. Invention is usually a lonely activity requiring intensive mental exploration.

Innovation, by contrast, is a business act. Financing, creation of real production, and taking risks may be difficult. Such entrepreneurship goes beyond the management of old processes. By contrast, the imitator copies, often only after the innovation has become safe and routine.

2. Process and Product Innovations.   Changes may be divided into two categories. **Process innovations** simply alter the way given products are made; examples include a new way to use a drill press, lay out a factory floor, or using the Internet instead of other methods. **Product innovations** create a new good for sale without any change in process; examples include the Palm Pilot or a new car model.

The two kinds of change are distinct in concept, though they often mix in actual cases. Each kind of change can occur in varying degrees, ranging from trivial variations to whole new approaches.

3. Autonomous and Induced Changes.   This contrast is very important. **Autonomous inventions** arise naturally from the ongoing flow of new knowledge and technology. Discoveries in areas 1 and 2 often make inevitable an advance in areas 3 and 4, which in turn causes progress in areas 5 and 6.[3] Autonomous inventions also come from the sheer curiosity of creative geniuses, who invent even if there is no chance to get wealthy from it.

By contrast, **induced inventions** are stimulated strictly by the hope of making money. Without that spur, they would come more slowly or not at all. Much commercial R & D activity fits this type. Teams of scientists in drug-company laboratories, for example, working under carefully budgeted plans, seek inventions that will pay: without the payoff, there is no inventive effort.

Many inventions mingle both features, of course. The advance of knowledge makes them inevitable, but money may make them happen a little sooner. Very broadly, process inventions tend to be autonomous, while product inventions are more likely to be induced.

The distinction is crucial in appraising social policies toward technical change. **A patent system, for example, has no social value whatsoever if inventions are autonomous** (see section 2). Even if instead some inventions are induced, one needs to ask what share of all inventions these comprise, whether they are important or trivial inventions, and how much they are accelerated by money rewards.

4. *Normative Issues.* The distinction between positive and normative conditions is particularly important in evaluating technological change. **Positive** issues relate to facts; they define and measure the various parts of the process.

Normative lessons are the ultimate purpose of the subject: to judge how good changes have been compared with what might reasonably have been expected. For example, the vast improvements in computers after 1955 might be credited to IBM, the leading firm. But much of that was autonomous, and industry experts often say that IBM slowed down progress, rather than speeding it up. Another example: Microsoft's Windows has been widely criticized as ramshackle and mediocre, subject to crashing. Microsoft instead insists that it has been marvelous. But the normative evaluation is definitely a two-sided debate.

One compares the **net gain** in total productivity with its cost. The cost is the R & D effort, in money, talent, and tangible resources. It often involves a degree of uncertainty, of gambling that a project will pay off. Also, the efforts may not neatly be assigned to one innovation or another. Only the net gain helps one say whether innovation has been close to optimal lines. There may be too little innovation or too much (using too many resources) in any given industry.

5. *Technological Opportunity.* This important concept is crucial for all normative evaluations. Industries differ in their opportunities for progress. Some are bursting with new possibilities, such as the Internet during the 1990s. In others, technology is pretty much fixed. Since the 1980s, information technology has been crammed with high technological opportunity. In contrast, concrete, brick-making, papermaking, and cloth-weaving have had little chance for progress. When you compare actual trends with the degree of opportunity, faster changes often seem actually to have been normal or even slow. Without such a comparison, one simply cannot make intelligent normative appraisals.

Estimating opportunity is a sophisticated task, inherently unsure. Large-seeming opportunities often turn out to be barren (nuclear power is a good example). The leading firms in an industry will commonly rate opportunity lower (and will claim credit for higher net gains) than will outside observers.

6. *The Replacement Effect.* While innovation creates the new, fundamentally, **it also destroys existing values**. A firm may have a fine product now, but its newer and better product may eliminate all of the old product's value. For example, the onset of optical fiber for transmitting telephone messages destroyed most of the value of older copper telephone wires. The Internet has destroyed vast amounts of value of older information technology. Audiotape cassettes eclipsed vinyl records, compact disks have partly eclipsed audio tapes, and those disks themselves have recently been under threat.

This **replacement effect** is crucially important. In response, firms with large market positions often innovate slowly and cautiously so as not to harm their own existing asset values too sharply. Of course they wish their own innovations to replace *other* firms' products; firm A doesn't mind eliminating the values of firms B through Z. Indeed, that is often precisely the way to succeed and to raise one's market share.

7. Economies and Diseconomies of Scale. Technical progress may be affected by economies (and diseconomies) of scale of innovation. There may be a distinct optimal scale for a firm in inventing or innovating. That scale may require a large market share, or perhaps, instead, a small scale.

Consider **inventing** first. Much of it is lonely thinking by independent thinkers, working on their own or in small laboratories, although some inventions require teams of researchers and large-scale resources. Conditions will differ from industry to industry. Also, inventions can arise outside an industry and then be sold to the firms for production. In that case, any economies of scale are not relevant to industry structure.

Innovating uses different skills and resources. It often requires new investments and large engineering changes. The incentives involve (1) net gains after allowing for the replacement effect, (2) the chances for sharply increasing the firm's market share, and (3) the internal economies involved in the process of change itself.

These conditions will vary from case to case and even among differing innovations within a given industry. For example, small firms may be adequate for handling minor innovations, but other innovations may be so large that only a large firm can mass the needed funds, equipment, talent, and sustained effort. Also, the risk may be so high that only secure dominant firms can take the chance. Major new aircraft types are one possible instance where managers of Boeing or Airbus may feel they have to bet the company on a new model. Others sometimes include large computers, new automobile models, and complex communications equipment. These conditions are often noted by free-market writers as reasons for dominant firms.

Yet be cautious. Among the examples just given, the best large computers have been designed and built by small firms (Control Data, Cray Research, Apple, and others). Small automobile firms (the early Honda and Chrysler) have been at least as creative as giant General Motors, and often much more so. Large innovations can often be divided into parts that small firms can handle, either in parallel or in sequence. Competitive capital markets generate ample funds for all productive innovations, regardless of size.

Moreover, innovation usually occurs more rapidly when several firms race to invent or innovate first. The resulting gain in competitive speed may offset any loss of economies of scale in innovation.

8. Appropriability and Free Riders. The awkward term **appropriability** refers to the ability of a firm to capture (or appropriate) enough gains from its new ideas and products to make it worthwhile. New inventions and innovations may be copied so quickly that the inventor or innovator cannot garner enough rewards to justify the cost of creating them. Incentives to invent or innovate may then become too low, and progress may dry up.

Gains may instead be reaped by "free riders" who merely copy the original creations.[4] The free-rider problem has therefore been posed as a threat to innovation, with the blame laid squarely on competition. Innovators need a period of monopoly, it is claimed, so they can reap enough gains to justify their costs before free riders can capture the rest.

This free-rider problem could in theory discourage innovation. But its net effect is a matter of degree.[5] Free riding does not retard autonomous innovations. It only threatens induced innovations. The degree of any disincentive is always open to doubt. Free riding may only be a scattered, minor phenomenon. And the innovator might reap a large gain even if free riding is extensive.[6] Indeed, the monopoly rewards for creating a patented innovation can be much larger than they need to be. Competitive rates of return, skimpy though they are, may be quite enough to induce efficient rates of innovations.[7]

2. Optimal Technological Change

Optimum Choices at the Margin. Like most activities, innovation incurs costs, and it should be pursued only up to the level where its marginal benefits equal its marginal costs. Each rational firm reaches this result as it manages its R & D and innovation activities.

The typical firm has an array of possible projects. The payoffs for each project are expressed in rates of return. Cost is the cost of the funds required to buy the R & D resources. The optimal level of R & D activity is where the marginal capital costs and returns on R & D spending are just equal. All projects up to that level should be undertaken; they add net profits. Beyond that level, all projects subtract from profits.

It is assumed that the R & D resources are being employed with utmost X-efficiency: no bureaucracy, waste, or loss of effectiveness occurs. That strict assumption may often be violated in practice.

R & D is a costly input; **it is not, of course, to be maximized.** Instead, its level is to be optimized in this direction, by this firm, in order to yield the efficient amount of progress. R & D cost is to be **minimized** for any given level of yield. Students often mistakenly suppose that R & D is inherently a good thing, which ought to be maximized. High levels of R & D spending do *not* prove that a firm is a good innovator.

Monopoly's Effects. The basic question is as follows: Which generates more progress for given R & D resources, competition or monopoly? The answer has generally been competition, because it gives higher rewards and it forces firms to innovate. There are two possible exceptions. Monopoly may promote innovation if (1) there are large economies of scale in R & D, or (2) the free-rider problem discourages induced innovation.

Competition versus Monopoly: Comparing Net Profits. Competition tends to result in a maximum rate of progress by offering higher rewards to invention and innovation. The **replacement effect** of innovations operates on all firms, possibly destroying the value of their existing products and facilities.

But the monopolist feels this damage most completely: innovation will destroy some or all of the value of its existing technology. Because the firm holds all of its market, it has no room to add market share. **The replacement effect falls on its own products.** Therefore the **monopolist** will usually bring in new processes and products slowly, more slowly than the socially optimal rate.

For the **competitive firm**, in contrast, the possible gains from innovation are one-sided and may be very large. It takes market share away from others, not just from itself. Under competition, firms tend to innovate at maximum speed so as to capture maximum profit before their competitors move in.

Dominant Firms: The "Time-Cost Trade-off" and a "Fast-second Strategy."
Since innovations involve both time and cost, a time-cost analysis can compare the choices of dominant firms with those of their lesser rivals. Figure 5.1 presents the comparison, distilled from a complex discussion by Scherer.[8]

There is assumed to be a basic time-cost trade-off curve for a given innovation in a given industry. Suppose, for example, the innovation is a radically new type of television. It can be undertaken quickly by a vastly expensive crash program of R & D, or it can be done slowly, letting the technology ripen gradually and only spending modest amounts of R & D resources.

It also can be done at any speed in between, along a smooth curve as shown in Figure 5.1. The slower, cheaper pace is cheaper partly because it permits **autonomous** innovations to occur in related fields, so that this innovation becomes easier as time passes. The time-cost trade-off curve will vary for each specific innovation, but its general shape is likely to be as shown in figure 5.1.

Now consider two alternative innovators, a dominant firm and a competitor with a small share. The dominant firm can expect to gain most of the benefits of the innovation over a long future period. This is shown by a total revenue curve labeled *A*, indicating the revenues that this firm can obtain from this innovation. The curve is set high to reflect the large size of revenues. Also, its slope is nearly horizontal, because the dominant firm has little fear that large rivals will pursue the innovation and capture its future revenues. The dominant firm can undertake the innovation slowly and still reap most of the revenues.

Not so for the small competitor. It can expect to reap smaller benefits simply because it starts out as a much smaller firm. And it also must fear that other small firms will innovate first or imitate quickly to capture revenues. Therefore this small firm's revenue curve (labeled *B*) is lower and much more steeply sloped. It is barely above the time-cost trade-off curve for a short interval.[9]

Each firm will maximize its profits where marginal cost and revenue values are equal. That occurs where the slopes of the time-cost and revenue curves are equal. At those points the vertical distance between the curves (the net profits) are maximized. For the dominant firm, this is time (TM), which is shown as fifteen years. For the small firm, the time is much shorter, at five years. The small firm's cost is also greater, at $50 million, which is double the $25 million spent by the dominant firm.

Yet the dominant firm is able to reap a larger revenue of $100 million, because it has a high degree of market control. The small firm charges its customers $60 million, making only a $10 million profit. The dominant firm's net profit is much larger, at $85 million.

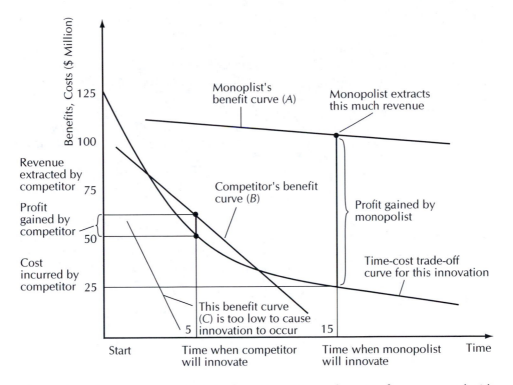

Figure 5.1   Time, costs, and benefits for an innovator: a dominant firm compared with little companies.

By the narrow criterion of the amount of resources used to accomplish the innovation, monopoly is less costly. **But the innovation occurs much more slowly, and consumers are made to pay much more in order to obtain it ($110 million rather than $60 million).** By a consumer-surplus criterion, the small, quick innovator is definitely superior. If this is a sharply better product, then the monopoly-imposed extra delay of ten years, plus the extra consumer payment of $50 million, is a decidedly inferior result.

The revenue curves have been drawn to illustrate the most likely general conditions. In actual cases, they might differ in location, slope, and shape. Yet the dominant firm would usually have a higher, flatter curve than any small rivals, and that gives the slowness and high price.[10]

The concepts illustrated in figure 5.1 suggest a general lesson, which is borne out repeatedly in actual markets. **Innovations tend to be led by the smaller firms in a market.** The dominant firm commonly **invents actively**, discovering ideas that may eventually prove useful. But it usually chooses to **delay the innovation phase**, letting smaller firms take the risk of trying out the new ideas. When one seems successful, the dominant firm will then move quickly to imitate, trying to catch up to and supplant the small innovator. This is sometimes called the fast-second strategy.

Examples of it abound. Digital watches and personal computers were rejected by dominant firms when first developed. Small or new firms innovated them instead. Eastman Kodak neglected or opposed many of the major innovations in its markets, including the 35mm camera, compact cameras, cartridge-loading films, and amateur flash devices.[11] IBM (then the tabulating-equipment monopoly) rejected an offer of plain-paper copying technology in 1946, and it started out slowly in computers from 1945 to 1953. Also, it completely missed the prospects for the personal computer around 1980.

Gillette in the 1950s decided against offering a stainless steel razor blade until a small outsider firm, Wilkinson Sword, came out with one. Then Gillette rushed out its own blade. The pre-1984 Bell Telephone System was notorious for doing lots of inventing but then holding back on applying the ideas.

This pattern is not universal; there are a number of exceptional cases. Also, unusually large innovations might require large firms with large market shares to provide large-scale financing.

But generally, effective competition speeds up innovations and charges consumers less for them. Monopolists tend instead to retard innovations and to charge more for them. That is also what Schumpeter claimed. Dominant firms become stagnant, so they are displaced when a new firm creates some major new innovations and pushes out the slothful old firm. The dominant firm tries to block innovation. The new entrant makes it happen.

The same lesson applies to new entry.[12] In duopoly theory, the entrant assumes the same role as an existing rival in applying pressure for innovation. In long-run analyses, the same effect emerges. The fear of an innovating entrant stimulates monopolists to innovate more rapidly.

II. EMPIRICAL ANALYSIS OF R & D AND INNOVATION

First, some facts to set the issues in perspective. Technical progress has generated about a 2 percent yearly rise in total output compared with total inputs during the last century. This is not a high rate, even though it does accumulate over many decades into a substantial gain. Certain surface indicators, such as media claims and business commentary, may suggest that change is rapid, even radical. Yet many of these product changes are matters of style rather than content.

Change varies sharply among industries. Some are virtually static, while others change processes or products rapidly. Examples of such waves of innovation are steel in 1860 to 1880, electricity in 1880 to 1910, pharmaceuticals in 1940 to 1960, electronics since 1960, and information technology since 1990 or so. The pulse often coincides with the early growth stage of the industry, when new opportunities are large and untapped.

1. PATTERNS OF R & D

Total U.S. R & D spending has been over $200 billion per year in recent years, nearly 3 percent of gross domestic product. In all manufacturing industries, total R & D funds are just over 4.0 percent of sales. Although government pays most of the R & D bills in certain aerospace industries, most other industries generate their own funds.

Note the problems in assessing R & D's effects. It is an **input** for innovation, **not the output**. High R & D spending may reflect inefficiency or waste in innovation rather than high gains. Also, R & D is itself a slippery category. Some firms put only strictly scientific expenses in it; others include maintenance and repair costs as well.[13]

The key question for our purposes is as follows: Does monopoly improve the amounts and yield of innovative activity or does it restrict and distort it, as theory generally suggests? There are several main ways to analyze evidence on the question: case studies, small samples, and large-scale cross-section analyses of data. One can study R & D patterns (the input), patents (an inventive output), or major innovations (another output). These and other methods have been tried since the 1950s, and the literature offers fairly consistent findings.

2. SOURCES OF INVENTION

Do inventions come mainly from small operators or from large-scale industrial laboratories? Jewkes, Sawers, and Stillerman evaluated the sources of some seventy major inventions from the 1880–1965 period.[14] The inventions were carefully chosen to include the most important ones (some were actually clusters of related inventions). Each invention was researched thoroughly to discern whether its source was an individual, a small firm, or a large company.

Thirty-three of the seventy came from individuals, whereas only twenty-four came from industrial research laboratories, either large or small. Table 5.1 includes a selection of the two groups. Among those accomplished by individuals are air conditioning, catalytic cracking of petroleum, the electron microscope, the jet engine, radio, and xerography—all substantial inventions.

When the authors assessed whether the proportions have changed in recent decades, they found they had not. There was no general basis for believing that important inventions come mainly from large-scale laboratories.

Table 5.1   Selected Major Inventions 1880–1965 by Source

By Individuals	By Industrial Firms
Air conditioning	Acrylic fibers
Automatic transmissions	Cellophane tape
Catalytic cracking of petroleum	Continuous hot-strip rolling
Cyclotron	Fluorescent lighting
Electron microscope	Neoprene
Helicopter	Polyethylene
Jet engine	Silicones
Kodachrome	Synthetic detergents
Penicillin	Television
Instant photography	Transistor
Power steering	
Radio	
Synthetic light polarizer	
Xerography	

Source: Drawn from John Jewkes, R. Sawers, and R. Stillerman, *The Sources of Invention,* rev. ed. (New York: St. Martin's Press, 1968), pp. 71–90.

Of the twenty-five main innovations put forth by the Du Pont Company in the United States between 1920 and 1950, only eleven were initially discovered by Du Pont itself. The rest came from outside inventors.

These and other studies converge on a common pattern that is suggested by theory. Inventions are predominantly still accomplished by individuals, usually working **outside** of large corporate research establishments in their own facilities or at academic or nonprofit units. Some innovations may require larger resources, but most innovations can be accomplished by small or medium-size firms. Only an occasional, very large innovation seems to require a big company.

Statistical Analysis of R & D and Patents.   **R & D intensity** may be positively related to concentration. If this hypothesis is true, it could suggest that concentration fosters innovative effort, or that innovative effort causes concentration. It might be that oligopoly firms in concentrated industries tend to use excess R & D resources through inefficiency or duplication of effort.

When R & D data became available in the 1960s, several tests of the hypothesis that R & D is positively related to concentration were done.[15] Yet all of them had a basic flaw. R & D is an input. High levels of it can indicate energetic progress, or instead excess amounts of R & D effort or a waste of R & D resources. So even a tight correlation between R & D and concentration would give no normative lesson or distinguish cause from effect.

In fact, the tests mainly suggest a slight negative correlation: R & D intensity declines as concentration increases above about 60 percent. But the concentration data are faulty, and the correlations are faint. The pattern gives no economic lesson.

Patents might serve as a rough measure of inventive output. One could test whether they are related to company size or concentration. This might suggest how monopoly affects inventive activity.

Unfortunately, patents are a notoriously weak measure. Most of the 120,000+ patents issued each year have little practical value and are not used. Many others are of moderate value. Only a few are important with high yields. Some have negative social value; they are used as blocking patents to stop innovation, or they are developed simply to keep competition out.

Various weighting schemes for patents have been discussed, but none works very well. The research so far has simply counted all patents, assigning each equal value. Most recently a weighting scheme has been developed that weights each patent by the frequency of its being cited in subsequent patent descriptions. This gives more importance to patents that are related to later inventions. Key and important inventions may accurately be indicated by this method. But it is time-biased; it is sensitive to time elapsed, so that it works best for older patents that have existed for many years rather than for new patents.

Note, too, that patents are only one way to protect new ideas. The other is secrecy. Many—perhaps most—ideas are used secretly rather than revealed in a patent. Patent data miss this process entirely.

There have been some studies comparing company size and patents, along with other factors. Scherer has suggested that, among large firms, patenting activity increases up to moderately large size, and then tails off among the very largest firms.[16] Other researchers have suggested the same for concentration; patenting activity increases as concentration rises toward 40 percent, and then tapers off at higher concentration.

Sources of Innovations.   One can evaluate the main innovations in a series of major industries and then judge which firms did them. This approach corresponds to the research on the sources of invention discussed in the preceding section. Mansfield et al. studied the steel, automobile, petroleum, drug, and other industries.[17] They drew on expert appraisals of the main innovations in recent decades in each industry. The innovations were assigned to the firms that did them, and then the patterns were analyzed statistically.

Most of the patterns show that small-share firms lead and dominant firms follow. The research indicates that innovative activity is greatest in firms with roughly 5- to 20-percent market shares. Below that, firms may be too small to fund significant innovations; above 20 percent, they tend increasingly to wait to innovate until forced by other firms.

The Role of Patents.   A patent traditionally gives its owner exclusive control for seventeen years over producing and marketing an invention.[18] It might not provide a true economic monopoly in a relevant market, because the invention competes closely with other products or production methods. Yet the essence of a patent is (1) to confer a degree of market power upon the owner and (2) to permit an unrestricted capture of excess profits from the patented idea.[19] In practice, as noted earlier, many patents are impractical, valueless, and unused. Many others are valuable but have effective lives of only three to seven years before competitors displace them by inventing around them or developing superior ideas. Fewer patents have full seventeen-year lives and generate large profits. Still others provide a basis for capturing even longer lasting degrees of monopoly than the seventeen-year term.

The patent system stirs hot debate because it creates definite monopoly positions in return for uncertain gains from stimulating invention and innovation. It has also become a focus for a new industrial-organization theory, duopoly modeling, in which alternative settings are posited in order to define the profit inducements for invention and innovation.[20] In these models, it is assumed that inventions and innovations are strictly **induced** and extremely sensitive to prospective profits; a higher profit reward always yields more inventive or innovative activity. This view ignores **autonomous** inventions.

That assumption fits the logic of patents, which dangle the bait of a lucrative monopoly. The resulting profit rewards range from zero (with a loss of the invention's original cost) to very high sums, occasionally hundreds of times larger than the efficient reward.

Yet the logic may be flawed. Many patented inventions are autonomous, so that inducements and patent monopoly are irrelevant. Even where inventions are induced, the gains are only matters of degree, which may be small (perhaps just weeks or months).[21]

For example, xerography is often cited as a case of major innovation induced by profit hopes (indeed, in the 1960s, there was a spectacular rise in Xerox Company stock prices). Yet xerography was bound to be created sometime in the 1960s by the maturing of technology, perhaps only a few years later than it did emerge. Therefore the high gains to the stockholders of the innovating company may have far exceeded the social gains from having xerography available a few months or years earlier.

An important contrasting case is the silicon chip, which was invented almost simultaneously by two people in 1959. Neither of them obtained fame or a large fortune from this vastly important invention. Yet the chip was invented, as it was bound to be soon, by other inventors if not by these two. In short, skepticism is in order about claims for the supposed need to reward innovation lavishly.

In any event, the patent system is based on a basic economic error: the belief that invention needs to be stimulated by **indefinite** rewards rather than by finite, **efficient** rewards. As noted earlier, competitive profit rates (as adjusted for risk and other factors) are the correct inducement level. Supracompetitive profits tend to induce lesser amounts of innovation because the creative activity is voluntary rather than compelled by strict competition.

III. FAIRNESS

We turn now to broader values, which may be less precisely definable and measurable than efficiency and technological change. They can be analyzed, how-ever, and in the ultimate reckoning they may be the most important effects of market power.[21]

1. SHIFTS IN WEALTH

Market power shifts wealth from the many customers to the few monopo-lists (recall chapter 2). That makes wealth more unequal, as the colossal wealth of William Gates nicely illustrates; his $50+ billion has come largely from his finan-cially hard-pressed fellow citizens.

Wealth effects reflect (1) the degree of monopoly held by a firm and (2) the size of the firm. Past wealth effects are the sum of many thousands of market positions, ranging from petty local monopolies and oligopolies up to full-blown nationwide monopolies. Other forces also have shaped wealth, of course, such as genius and effort, luck, personal investment yields, inheritance, and taxation.

The research problem is complicated. Ideally, one could calculate the size and degree of each position of market power since 1890 (e.g., Standard Oil, IBM, newspapers, Xerox, Microsoft), then allow for their relative innovation and effi-ciency to arrive ultimately at the net effect of market power on wealth in each case. These effects could be summed up and compared with the total rise in industrial wealth in order to evaluate the extent of the monopolies' impact.

Two methods have been used in actual research. One models the process, reaching estimates from various assumptions about the key conditions. The other simply sifts the mass of evidence about actual market power and family wealth. Although the two approaches differ sharply, their findings are in accord.

A Model. Comanor and Smiley's pathbreaking study posited that the wealth effect reflected several conditions since 1890.[22] First was the degree and duration of market power; this condition generated the estimated flow of monop-oly profits. Next was the rate of return on wealth. The third condition was the dis-persal of family holdings: current spending as a share of the wealth and other forces dissipating wealth (taxes, bequests, etc.). Comanor and Smiley tried reasonable upper- and lower-bound assumptions about these factors in order to derive the range of plausible estimates. The wealth effect would be smaller if (1) monopoly were slight, (2) the return on assets were small (so they would not build up rapidly), and (3) the rate of dissipation of fortunes were high.

The estimates bracketed the most likely values. For example, suppose that monopoly profits were 3 percent of GNP and monopolies lasted forty years. Then calculations show that 13 percent of the 41 percent of wealth held by the top three wealth classes would have come from monopoly gains. On these and other plausible assumptions, about one-fourth to one-half of the highest family wealth in the 1960s traced back to monopoly.

Other Evidence.   There is much other evidence to sift through. One category is the known instances of dominant firms, especially from 1870 to 1910.[23] Many are still well known. The Rockefeller family drew billions from Standard Oil (along with the Morrows, Pratts, and other inside members); Du Pont wealth came from gunpowder and chemicals; American Tobacco created the Duke family fortune; the Mellons mined the Alcoa aluminum monopoly; Vanderbilts, Harrimans, Morgans, and others grew rich from dominant positions in railroads and other sectors; Armours and Swifts dominated Chicago society with wealth from meatpacking. Nearly every sizable city has had one or more families that created a large newspaper fortune, from Scripps, Hearst, and Pulitzer to Cowles (Minnesota and Iowa) and Chandler (Los Angeles).

These are just the upper tip. Fortunes of the second rank arose from hundreds of market positions in steel, newspapers, cameras and film, aluminum, soap, razor blades, and scores of other markets, and of course banking. In fact, nearly every dominant firm in finance, utilities, insurance, and retailing has bred at least one family fortune. In the third rank, thousands of smaller local wealthy families drew their fortunes from a local bank, hotel, department store, newspaper, lumberyard, or the like.

The correlation of family wealth with market power is not tight, for wealth arises from other sources such as luck, effort, and innovation. In Britain and Australia, also, the role of monopoly seems to have been significant but to have created only a minority of total wealth.[24]

But monopoly power has been an important source, not a marginal one. And often the monopoly wealth is enlarged for the family's children, grandchildren, and later generations via favored portfolio investment and real estate.

2. INCOME

Wealth generates income, so the wealth effect is paralleled by a redistribution of income toward the owners of new monopolies. The extent of this shift depends on the wealth effect itself, as discussed previously.

More visible is the effect on wages, salaries, and bonuses paid to employees. One possibility is that firms with market power pay more to their workers. The extra payment can be in the form of rates of pay, various perks, or easier work for given pay. These can all be forms of X-inefficiency (recall chapter 4). Evidence regarding this possibility is mixed. Many dominant firms do provide better pay, benefits, and security and do permit a certain degree of slack in their employees.

This pattern, often described as paternalism, often is designed to forestall the formation of unions among workers. Yet paternalistic pay and benefits may not exceed what union activity would provide.

Some research has been done on the interactions among concentration, union power, and wage rates, but here, too, the results have been inconclusive.[25] Even if the overall effect were strong, income would not be disequalized by very much. It would only alter the benefits between those employees (from top to bottom) who work for monopolists and those who do not.

The other possibility is that pay differentials are sharpened *within* firms holding market power. In particular, the managers' share may be increased, perhaps sharply. In the U.S., top managers do obtain much higher pay relative to workers than in other countries. That became an acute issue in the 1990s, and it is widely thought that many top officials wield monopoly control over their boards.

3. OPPORTUNITY

Opportunity has long been an attractive measure of fairness. In theory, even if wealth and income are unfairly distributed now among the assets of older people, the opportunities for future gains by young people can and should be fair. Then current inequities seem more benign, because they would eventually be replaced by fair conditions.

Opportunity does appear to be an unequivocal standard—more equality of opportunity is always better than less. Still, there are the following technical problems with the criterion:

1. Opportunity is intangible and virtually impossible to measure.
2. Not all people have equivalent endowments and abilities to strive. Instead, talents differ, so that some children have sharply greater opportunities than others.
3. Many, perhaps most, people are not temperamentally suited to unremitting competition.
4. The criterion assumes that the rewards to differing talents are equivalent. In fact, some human talents draw great prizes (ruthlessness, shrewdness, willingness to take risks), while others usually make one unfit for commercial success (kindliness, artistic ability, generosity toward others).

Monopoly power usually reduces opportunity and makes it less equal. In extreme cases, it shrinks the number of firms to just one. In all cases, it reduces the variety and responsiveness of firms, both as sellers to consumers and as employers choosing among diverse talents. Finally, it may increase discrimination by race, sex, and ethnic origin.[26]

Opportunity may be relatively equal in the United States compared to many other countries. This openness reflects many factors: the lack of hereditary aristocracy, ethical traditions, the sheer size and regional variety of the country, and its financial markets. Therefore market power has not shut off opportunity. Business opportunities (to set up a firm or to rise within existing firms) are relatively open.

Yet market power does reduce opportunity in many ways. Family connections and wealth from older and existing monopolies give many young people a head start in business and finance. Undoubtedly, family status strongly affects one's chances for success.[27]

Job discrimination is of particular interest. It is the use of race, sex, or other merit-irrelevant features in hiring, promotion, or pay levels. Major biases have existed against women, blacks, and various other ethnic and age groups. Market power may intensify discrimination or instead possibly alleviate it. The key is **white-collar** jobs; being more desirable they represent higher levels of opportunity and directly reflect a company's hiring policies.

Under effective competition, firms can not indulge any irrelevant prejudices, because doing so would incur extra costs and possibly even endanger the firm's existence. Indeed, if a disfavored group received low wages because of discrimination, competitive firms would hire *more* people in that group.

Under market power the outcome is not determinate. Since profit maximizing is partially voluntary, managers may place importance in other areas. If white male managers share common prejudices (e.g., against women and blacks), then market power would facilitate discrimination; managers could substitute in favor of other white males, even at some sacrifice in profits. Some managers, of course, may prefer instead to emphasize neutrality or even implement affirmative action.

Statistical tests might discover which pattern is more common. One study has compared industry concentration with the percentage of blacks in upper-level jobs.[28] Figure 5.2 shows one of the comparisons. While the data have certain weaknesses,[29] the patterns for 1966 consistently suggest that open hiring of blacks occurred mainly in competitive industries.

Another study examined the hiring of women and blacks in 300 large firms and banks in 1966 and 1970.[30] The patterns were complex, but the main conditions emerged clearly. Large firms as a group had virtually no women or blacks in upper-level jobs. Certain "women's" industries (such as cosmetics) were exceptions. At the other extreme were the insurance, banking, and computer industries, where small armies of women clerks and programmers were supervised by small groups of white male executives. Certain other heavy industries (metals, engineering) were almost totally white and male in upper white-collar jobs.

The typical large firm had virtually no women or blacks in upper-level jobs in 1970. Market power intensified this effect slightly, but size was the main factor. Growth and other conditions that might change the patterns played only a small role. These patterns have softened, but they continue, as confirmed by widespread commentary in the press.[31]

IV. COMPETITION ITSELF: BENEFITS AND COSTS

Competition is not just a neutral means to other ends. It provides value in itself, even beyond the effort, efficiency, innovation, and fairness that it promotes.

1. BENEFITS

Competition provides the following two deep values:

1. a valid process for developing and expressing personal excellence

2. protection against monopoly control and exploitation

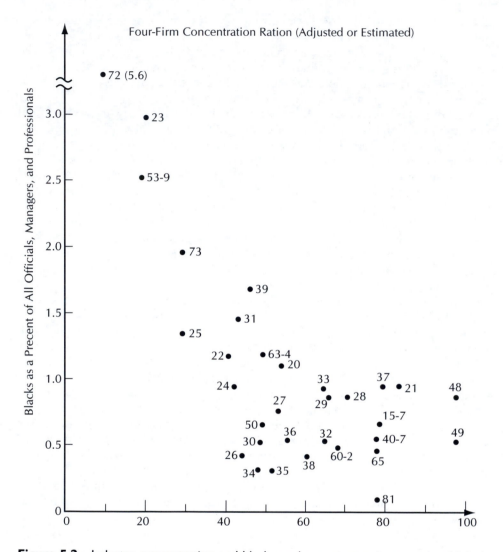

Figure 5.2   Industry concentration and black employment rates in upper-level jobs in 1966.

Note: The number by each observation is the Census Standard Industrial Classification code number for the industry group.
Source: W. G. Shepherd, "Market Power and Racial Discrimination in White-Collar Employment," *Antitrust Bulletin* 14 (Spring 1969): p. 156.

Competition is a fundamental social process that expresses (and shapes) basic attitudes. It fosters beliefs in diversity, tolerance, and individual initiative, all of which are blocked by monopoly. Competition promotes independence, self-reliance, and greater mobility among social classes.

When competition is the organizing principle of an economy, it becomes a basis for an open, flexible society in which merit and personal values take primacy over control from the top. It also permits political democracy to flourish, because power and information are dispersed rather than concentrated. The ancient contrast between Athens and Sparta is a striking example: Athens—open, spontaneous, experimental; Sparta—closed, regimented, autocratic.

The contrast can also be seen by imagining an economy composed solely of one colossal conglomerate firm that possesses a monopoly in every market. Suppose that this diversified firm generates good performance in all specific dimensions, including efficiency, innovation, and distribution.[32] It would still be defective, because it would be rigid and closed, excluding the crucial process that allows variety and a sharing of power among the populace.

Even if such centralized power is exercised benevolently, it diminishes individual values. Competition is the classic individualistic process, reflecting classical liberal (or libertarian) values. Yet, paradoxically, its value is denied most firmly by many free-market advocates, who profess to favor classical liberalism.[33] They argue that as long as **the results** of competition are obtained (especially static efficiency), it does not matter to a society whether competition or monopoly **actually exists**.

In their thinking, **competition** has lost its meaning.[34] If monopoly provides the *benefits* of competition, they say, then monopoly really *is* competition—or at least the equivalent of competition.[35] This view rejects the core belief of the original Chicago-school leaders. It also ignores both common sense and careful technical analysis.

2.   COMPETITION'S LIMITS AND HARMS

Competition does have certain drawbacks, especially at the level of relentless personal competition **among individuals**. The following limits and harms can be important.

Shallow and Myopic?   Competition sometimes becomes a series of small, intensive, and short-sighted episodes in which each player aims for specific goals. The pressure for immediate victory and survival can preclude longer-run objectives and larger possibilities. People become stressed, narrow, and limited. Firms adopt a myopic perspective and become tyrannized by short-term financial pressures.

Anticreative?   The harsh forces of competition can choke creativity and imagination as players are forced to struggle merely to survive. Millions of small-business owners face such relentless pressures every day. Tight competition can set narrow zones for action in the short run, such as cutting costs and responding to immediate conditions. The larger and richer results that creativity makes possible may become an unaffordable luxury.

Divisive?   Competition often has an either-or outcome; one competitor triumphs, the other is defeated. Therefore competition often requires a strict exclusion of competitors' interests from each player's considerations. One wins by defeating others, eliminating them whenever possible. Any consideration of the interests of one's competitors reduces one's own chances of success; a boxer wins by knocking out his opponent, not by assisting him. In setting **people** against one another, competition can be harmful. Yet company-level competition is different; in setting **firms** against one another, the positive effects probably far outweigh the negative.

Exhausting?   Because it requires maximum effort and exclusive attention, competition tends to exhaust the players. Since further effort can always enhance one's chances of winning, the demands are ultimately unlimited. Small-business managers know this endless pressure only too well. Sports competition is different: each game is followed by a period for recovery, and there is rest between seasons. But market competition permits no such letup. Unrestrained **personal** competition therefore produces maximum stress. As with divisiveness, though, competition among enterprises does not involve this problem.

Destructive Sequences?   Sometimes the results of competition are socially harmful rather than beneficial. Examples include arms races, the destruction of open-access natural resources, and the selling of harmful products. With competition driving the destructive process, no one player has responsibility for the outcome. Excess is harder to contain when individual responsibility is absent.

Winner-Take-All Results?   Competition may give extremely skewed prizes, with a few winners hugely enriched while others are pauperized. Sports offer varying examples. Superstars amass incredible wealth from playing games for a few years. Michael Jordan and a few top boxers are examples. In contrast, some golf tourneys scale prizes generously among players. Economic competition can be equally fair or cruel.

A Cause of Insecurity?   Competition leaves participants at risk of severe penalties for failure. Little companies may fail. Workers may lose their jobs with no notice.

Cruel and Harmful to Social Interests?   Competition grinds out production at low prices, possibly also at low wages. It may make no provision for social cohesion, mutual interests, and other elements of a good society.

All these costs can be genuinely harmful in **personal competition**. In **competition among firms**, however, the costs do not generally fall directly on people.[36] Myopia, anticreativity, and destructive sequences *can* be harmful in industrial competition, but these costs are usually outweighed by the important benefits of competition.[37] Therefore **maximal competition should prevail among enterprises in all markets**, so as to generate high levels of corporate performance.

V. OTHER VALUES

1. FREEDOM OF CHOICE

Freedom of choice is an important social value. Its simple meaning in markets is clear: freedom to buy what one wants at reasonable prices, to change jobs, to set up a business, and so forth.

Market power reduces freedom of choice, often starkly. A monopoly blocks the choices of consumers, of workers, of suppliers, and of people aspiring to compete. Competition usually maximizes freedom of choice, even though there may be the special problems we have just noted.[38]

2. SOCIAL EFFECTS

A healthy political process is a major benefit of industrial competition, as already noted. Corrupting effects may occur in Washington, DC, or down to the smallest local levels. Large firms often exercise economic power to extract special concessions from local officials by playing localities against one another. Powerful firms are commonly able to wield great power at the state and national levels, and large multinational firms have done so on an international level in dealing with entire small nations.

Political competition is the essence of a democratic process, which is highly vulnerable to economic monopoly. Political competition for votes is an entire parallel system that interacts with economic competition in the market system.

The problem can run deeper; concentrated economic power can corrupt, distort, and destroy political democracy, replacing it with power blocs, syndicalism, and autocratic regimes. That probably occurred in Germany and Japan before World War II.[39] The Philippines under Ferdinand Marcos from the 1970s; Haiti under the Duvaliers from the 1950s to 1970s; Indonesia under Suharto from 1999 to 2000—these and others have been corrupt systems in which political monopoly created economic monopolies and mercilessly exploited the people. Other such banana republics and one-party tyrannies are still common around the world even now.[40] They always seek to fuse political monopoly with economic monopolies and exploitation.

Some degree of this political impact already exists in certain states and in the United States as a whole, where big business often calls the shots and squeezes favors from local government.[41] Big-business political action committees exert strong influences over some elected officials at all levels. Henry Simons' dark fears that monopoly will destroy democracy may not yet be fully realized, but some such effects do continue.

Economic security means primarily an avoidance of abrupt job losses. Layoffs have always had major impacts on people's lives, and during 1985-91 they were especially deep and widespread in the United States. Tight oligopoly generally increases the severity of recessions, especially in heavy industries, though the degree of extra instability is a matter of debate. Market power generally has given managers more discretion in cutting the ranks of employees.

Cultural diversity involves a broader set of issues. Competition can promote and reward diversity, for free-market activity is often especially responsive to the full range of human interests and talents. Competitors seek out market niches and special interests to serve.[42]

Market power, on the other hand, is mostly negative in several ways. Monopolies and tight oligopolies commonly narrow the range of products and services. They reduce the scope for varieties of styles and interests.[43] They also tend to reduce the civic roles and contributions of company branches in their local areas; that has become a major feature of nationally based firms. In addition, severe downsizing cuts have affected almost every U.S. community since 1985.

QUESTIONS FOR REVIEW

1. "Patent systems can be worthwhile if induced innovations are important and if the rewards from patents speed them up." Explain why this statement is true.

2. Explain why under normal conditions of time-cost trade-offs and benefit curves, a dominant firm will usually lean toward imitating rather than innovating.

3. Discuss three industries with high degrees of technological opportunity and three industries with very low technological opportunity. What evidence helps you to make these judgments?

4. Explain the replacement effect, which may cause monopoly firms to innovate less rapidly.

5. Discuss three leading families whose wealth arose at least partly from monopoly. Is their wealth still important?

6. Discuss the values that are provided by competition itself.

ENDNOTES

[1] See John Sutton, *Technology and Market Structure* (Cambridge: MIT Press, 1998), for recent analysis of technology's role. Back in 1957, Robert Solow noted that technological progress caused about 90 percent of economic growth from 1870 to 1950; see his "Technical Change and the Aggregate Production Function," *Review of Economics and Statistics* 39 (1957): pp. 312–20. A few recent examples include the Internet, a colossal innovation in communications. Continuous innovations have raised the capacities of optical fibers by factors of thousands.

[2] The literature on this subject is large, as F. M. Scherer and David Ross note in their *Industrial Market Structure and Economic Performance*, 3rd ed. (Boston: Houghton Mifflin, 1991), chapter 17; see also Edwin Mansfield, et al., *Research and Innovation in the Modern Corporation* (New York: Norton, 1971); John Jewkes, R. Sawers, and R. Stillerman, *The Sources of Invention*, rev. ed. (New York: St. Martin's Press, 1968); and Morton I. Kamien and Nancy L. Schwartz, "Market Structure and Innovation: A Survey," *Journal of Economic Literature* 13 (March 1975): pp. 1–38.

[3] The automobile, for example, became thoroughly inevitable after oil was discovered, motors became small and precise, and rubber for inflatable tires was developed. Hand calculators and digital watches were a natural outcome of new semiconductor technology in the 1970s. Once the computer chip was invented by 1960, the vast progress in computers and electronics just followed naturally.

[4] The problem has long been recognized; see Scherer and Ross, *Industrial Market Structure*; Fred S. McChesney, and William F. Shughart, eds., *The Causes and Consequences of Antitrust* (Chicago: University of Chicago Press, 1995); A. Michael Spence, "Cost Reduction, Competition, and Industry Performance," *Econometrica* 52 (January 1984): pp. 101–22; and Jean Tirole, *The Theory of Industrial Organization*, 2nd ed. (Cambridge: MIT Press, 1993), chapter 10.

[5] See E. W. Eckard, Jr., "An Empirical Test of the Free Rider and Market Power Hypothesis: A Comment," *Review of Economics and Statistics* 76 (August 1994): pp. 586–89, and sources cited there.

[6] See for example Richard M. Brunell, "Appropriability in Antitrust: How Much is Enough?" *Antitrust Law Journal* 69(1) (2001).

[7] See William G. Shepherd, "Efficient Profits vs. Unlimited Capture, as a Reward for Superior Performance: Analysis and Cases," *Antitrust Bulletin* 34 (Spring 1989): pp. 121–52.

[8] The analysis is adapted from F. M. Scherer, "Research and Development Resource Allocation Under Rivalry," *Quarterly Journal of Economics* 81 (August 1967): pp. 359–94; see also Scherer and Ross, *Industrial Market Structure and Economic Performance*, chapter 15.

[9] An even smaller firm might have curve *C*, which is entirely below the time-cost curve. That firm cannot profitably make this innovation. Only if it can imitate at a much lower level of cost might it eventually adopt the innovation.

[10] A possible variation is that the competitive firm might have a lower time-cost curve because it is more efficient at R & D. If that is true, it would enhance the superiority of the competitive situation compared to dominance.

[11] See the critical evaluation in James W. Brock's "Structural Monopoly, Technological Performance, and Predatory Innovation: Relevant Standards Under Section 2 of the Sherman Act," *American Business Law Journal* 58 (1983): pp. 291–306.

[12] See Tirole, *The Theory of Industrial Organization*, chapter 10; and Kamien and Schwartz, "Market Structure and Innovations."

[13] One old adage about R & D concerns efforts to fix a machine. "If the machine works, put the cost in Maintenance. If it doesn't work, put the cost in R & D."

[14] Jewkes, Sawers, and Stillerman, *Sources of Invention*.

[15] See Scherer and Ross, *Industrial Market Structure and Economic Performance*.

[16] Scherer and Ross, *Industrial Market Structure and Economic Performance*, chapter 17.

[17] The resulting rewards are often high; the dominance of the Bell Telephone System, Xerox Corporation, the Aluminum Company of America, and many drug firms (among other prominent examples) was built upon key patents. See Scherer and Ross, *Industrial Market Structure and Economic Performance*.

[18] See also William D. Nordhaus, *Invention Growth and Welfare* (Cambridge: MIT Press, 1969); and Mansfield, *Industrial Research and Technological Innovation*.

[19] See Tirole, *The Theory of Industrial Organization*, chapter 10; and Kamien and Schwartz, *Market Structure and Innovation*. For a review of "memoryless" patent races, see Jennifer Reinganum, "Practical Implications of Game Theoretic Models of R & D," *American Economic Review* 74 (May 1984): pp. 61–6; and G. Grossman and C. Shapiro, "Dynamic R & D Competition," *Economic Journal* 97 (1987): pp. 372–87.

[20] For other criticisms of the patent system, see Scherer and Ross, *Industrial Market Structure and Economic Performance*, chapter 16, and the sources noted there.

[21] The original Chicago-school leader on these issues, Henry C. Simons, was particularly eloquent about the value of the competitive system as a means of controlling power and promoting effective democracy; see Simons, *Economic Policy for a Free Society* (Chicago: University of Chicago Press, 1948).

[22] William S. Comanor and Robert H. Smiley, "Monopoly and the Distribution of Wealth," *Quarterly Journal of Economics* 89 (May 1975): pp. 177–94.

[23] See John Moody, *The Truth about the Trusts* (Chicago: Moody Publishing, 1904); and the many sources given in the polemical survey by Ferdinand Lundberg, *The Rich and the Super-Rich* (New York: Lyle Stuart, 1968). Recent surveys are in *Forbes* magazine's annual "The Forbes 400," a survey of the richest Americans.

[24] See John J. Siegfried and A. Roberts, "How Did the Wealthiest Britons Get So Rich?" *Review of Industrial Organization* 6 (1991): pp. 19–32; and John J. Siegfried, Rudolph C. Blitz, and David K. Round, "The Limited Role of Market Power in Generating Great Fortunes in Great Britain, the United States, and Australia," *Journal of Industrial Economics* 43 (September 1995): pp. 277–86.

[25] See Ralph Bradburd, T. Pugel, and K. Pugh, "Internal Rent Capture and the Profit-Concentration Relation," *Review of Economics and Statistics* 73 (August 1991): pp. 432–40, and sources cited there; also Leonard W. Weiss, "Concentration and Labor Earnings," *American Economic Review* 56 (March 1966): pp. 96–117; and J. A. Dalton and E. J. Ford Jr., "Concentration and Labor Earnings in Manufacturing and Utilities," *Industrial and Labor Relations Review* (October 1977): pp. 45–60.

[26] The counterpossibility is that large dominant firms may be neutral arenas in which qualified people have equal opportunities to rise. Yet that is doubtful: it is size rather than market power that would provide the neutrality.

[27] John A. Brittain, *The Inheritance of Economic Status* (Washington, DC: Brookings Institution, 1977) is one of many studies that show the role of family advantages. At least half of the wealthiest Americans (as listed in the "Forbes 400," etc.) began with family fortunes and other advantages.

[28] William G. Shepherd, "Market Power and Racial Discrimination in White-Collar Employment," *Antitrust Bulletin* 14 (Spring 1969): pp. 141–61. See also William S. Comanor, "Racial Discrimination in American Industry," *Economica* 40 (November 1973): pp. 363–78.

[29] Concentration is not precisely measured, nor does it fully represent market power (recall chapter 3). The officials, managers, and professionals categories are not homogeneous. They range from presidents down to executive trainees and assistant plant managers.

[30] William G. Shepherd and Sharon G. Levin, "Managerial Discrimination in Large Firms," *Review of Economics and Statistics* 55 (November 1973): pp. 412–22. See also William A. Luksetich, "Market Power and Sex Discrimination in White-Collar Employment," *Review of Social Economy* (October 1979): pp. 21–24; and William R. Johnson, "Racial Wage Discrimination and Industrial Structure," *Bell Journal of Economics* 10 (Spring 1978): pp. 70–81.

[31] Only one-third of the largest 500 U.S. corporations in 1995 had two or more women on their boards; only 21 out of the 500 had three women. Boards typically have over fifteen members in total, so females are a mere sprinkling. See Joann S. Lublin, "Survey Finds More Fortune 500 Firms Have at Least Two Female Directors," *Wall Street Journal* (September 28, 1995): p. B16.

[32] Various new-Chicago writers would in theory accept this megamonopoly even if it delivered only static efficiency.

[33] See Robert H. Bork, *The Antitrust Paradox* (New York: Basic Books, 1978); the same effect emerges from the contestability-school approach (recall chapter 1).

[34] Recall the fascinating review of the new-Chicago lexicon of competition, as contrasted with the mainstream usage of terms, by Eleanor M. Fox and Lawrence A. Sullivan, as cited in chapter 1.

[35] A similar lesson is drawn by contestability-school writers, including Baumol and Willig; recall chapter 1.

[36] The distinction is not absolute, of course. Firms are composed of people, and therefore extreme competitive pressures among firms can have some personal impacts. This is especially true of small businesses, which are often little more than extensions of a single owner or a few people. But the distinction is quite important for larger firms, which pose the main problems of market power.

[37] An exception may occur when a lucrative dominant firm is benevolent to its locale. A rise of competition may squeeze out these benefits, leaving the citizens deprived. An example is Eastman Kodak in Rochester, New York, which as "Uncle Kodak" provided a large variety of civic benefits. Under new global competitive pressures in the 1990s, it scaled back its contributions sharply; see Milt Freudenheim, "A Doting Uncle Cuts Back and a City Feels the Pain," *New York Times* (October 8, 1995): sec. 3, p. 1. Of course many lucrative firms have made little social contribution at all (see chapter 8), and some become excessively paternalistic in their company towns.

[38] Religious competition offers particular benefits. Many countries have had a single official religion (e.g., Catholic, Lutheran, Muslim, etc.), or a choice between just two, and these organizations often control parts of the educational process. The basic U.S. policy of open entry and no direct support for specific religions is about as pro-competitive as possible. The result may ultimately be even more important for the country than the industrial benefits of antitrust policy.

[39] The German and Japanese dictatorships had a complicated and shifting relationship to business power groups during the 1930s and World War II. Yet observers agree that economic concentration facilitated the autocratic regimes and their military ventures. The relationship was symbiotic. See T. A. Bisson, *Zaibatsu Dissolution in Japan* (Berkeley: University of California Press, 1954); Johannes Hirschmeier and Tsunehiko Yui, *The Development of Japanese Business* (London: Allen & Unwin, 1981); Takatoshi Ito, *The Japanese Economy* (Cambridge: MIT Press, 1992); and H. Mayajima, "The Transformation of Zaibatsu to Postwar Corporate Groups: From Hierarchically Integrated Groups to Horizontally Integrated Groups," *Journal of Japanese International Economics* 8 (September 1994): pp. 293–328.

[40] Mafia control in Sicily spread to corrupt Italian politics and society after the 1950s; Alexander Stille, *Excellent Cadavers: The Mafia and the Death of the First Italian Republic* (New York: Pantheon Books, 1996).

[41] For example, the spread of casino gambling in the United States has created local impacts of monopoly-related money; see Kevin Sack, "Gaming Lobby Gives Lavishly to Politicians," *New York Times* (December 1995): p. 1.

[42] In some situations, relentless competition can instead shrink and deaden a culture, squeezing out human elements and enshrining the cruelty of Gradgrinds and the shallowness of Babbitts. The participants may be forced to be selfish, insecure, and anonymous. Universal competition can produce a cultural wasteland. So competition's cultural impacts may be mixed.

[43] One related instance is the 1995 purchase by William Gates (of Microsoft) of the Behman Archive, the premier visual archive source with 16 million images. It shows how a dominant-firm billionaire can use wealth from one dominant position to extend control over a culture's central icons. The issues are significant, even if Gates does not apply monopoly pricing to his cultural treasures. See Steve Lohr, "Huge Photo Archive Bought by Software Billionaire Gates," *New York Times* (October 1995): pp. 1, D5.

Part

4

Determinants of Market Structure

6

CAPITAL MARKETS, MERGERS, AND OTHER INFLUENCES ON STRUCTURE

Many forces shape market structures. Economies of scale are the traditional focus of attention; dominant firms usually claim them to justify themselves (the next chapter considers them in detail).

But first, this chapter clears the way by considering other possible influences on market structure. Section 1 covers critical financial markets. High levels of competition in financial markets promote competitive structure in all other markets. Conversely, market power in finance can encourage monopoly in the rest of the economy.

Section 2 discusses mergers, which can—and often do—raise market shares sharply. Especially during merger booms, such as in the 1890s, 1920s, 1960s, 1980s, and 1990s, mergers can sharply reshape some markets.

Section 3 considers other possible forces: life cycles of products and firms, rapid growth, random processes, and public policies.

I.   CAPITAL MARKETS

Finance is the controlling sector of the modern economy. It contains two main parts:

1. *commercial banking, which deals in credit* (that is, loans and bonds); and

2. *investment banking in securities markets, which deals in equity* (that is, stock ownership and corporate control).

These suppliers of capital supervise and influence firms in all other markets. Their dealings range from close one-on-one exchanges by banks and their main clients, all the way over to the anonymous masses of market transactions by millions of investors.

The critical concept here is **perfect capital markets**. This section explains that concept before discussing banking and securities markets.

1.   THE ROLES OF CAPITAL MARKETS

Capital is the controlling input of capitalism. Each firm's access to funds is critical to its survival as well as to its ability to compete effectively. Capital markets allocate funds among firms. Their decisions involve amounts and costs of funds and the rates of return on them, usually in light of risk. In allocating funds, financial markets shape the degree of competition throughout the rest of the economy.

Perfect Capital Markets.   Competitive capital markets are necessary for effective competition in the economy. Indeed, perfectly competitive capital markets are essential to the free-market efficient-structure hypothesis.

A perfectly functioning capital market would overcome all market imperfections by providing complete funds to every efficient firm. All projects whose prospective returns exceed the cost of capital would be funded.[1] All firms (big and small, dominant or tiny competitors) would have equal access to funds strictly on the basis of their efficiency. A long-established monopolist would have no better access to outside funding than any potential competitor, for the perfect capital market would supply them impartially, in line with their objective efficiency. If capital markets are perfect, or nearly so, the invisible hand theoretically guarantees an efficient outcome.

This process would reduce market power to the bare minimum dictated by technology. Any pecuniary gains or other yields of market power would attract new competition, supplied amply with funds. Any monopoly profit not arising from technical economies of scale, superior quality of management and innovation, or artificial devices for monopoly (patents, franchises) would be eliminated. Conversely, imperfect capital markets are likely to induce imperfections and monopoly power in other markets.

Are real capital markets close to perfect or marked instead by market power? The short answer is that there are obviously some imperfections. But how large are they? A full answer requires us to review several concepts, some history, and some data.

Types of Capital Markets.   All financial enterprises, commercial and investment, share the same basic function. They judge the financial prospects of firms under varying degrees of uncertainty and risk, and they allocate funds among firms in return for stocks or interest-bearing securities. Though centered in Wall Street, these financial operators are spread throughout the United States, operating everywhere by means of instant telecommunications. They contain some of the sharpest, most energetic minds in the economy, playing for the highest stakes.

These financial units play three main kinds of roles: (1) credit, that is, the supplying of funds; (2) counsel in the form of advice, connections, and support; and (3) control by enforcing efficient decisions. Consider these three functions in turn.

Credit: The Supply of Capital. Capital markets channel savings into investment by firms. The flow of funds is very large, and nearly all firms draw significantly on outside capital of various kinds, especially loans from banks and new issues of bonds and stocks. Firms also have internal funds available: profits plus depreciation from the firm's cash flow, which can be used for investment (or for dividends). Supplying capital funds is probably not the major role of capital markets for the larger mass of established firms. However, that role can be crucial for young, smaller, fast-growing firms, which need outside capital.

Counsel: Advice, Connections, and Support. Each firm exists in a set of banking and other relationships that connect it with its main advisers and sponsors.[2] This continuity and support provide a degree of direct supervision over company choices, and they help to determine the firm's future opportunities.

Control: Enforcing Efficiency. Capital markets enforce efficiency in two ways. First, the stock market continually evaluates each firm's prospects and performance. Second, a company can be taken over if its behavior is especially inferior.

2. Capital Markets as Taskmaster: The Control System and Enforcer of Efficiency.

Capital markets function as an enormously powerful and comprehensive taskmaster. The all-important result is that **capital-market supervision tends to enforce efficiency throughout the economy**. This is perhaps the most important role of financial markets, as the central control system of capitalism.

Evaluating firms is a continual process. Millions of investors judge companies and compare them with other firms as they make innumerable investment choices, minute by minute, every day. Stock markets are the main focus for this evaluation, as investors buy and sell stocks. But bond markets and rating services also respond to company prospects.

Despite their serious imperfections, stock markets do conduct a widespread, rapid, and continuing process of evaluation. Since the evaluations reflect choices by all investors among the whole array of firms, they are comparative, realistic, and comprehensive. The entire evaluation process is wide, including the infinitude of small trading deals as well as dramatic takeover attempts.

A firm's stock price reflects its investors' best evaluations of the firm's true earning power. The process is prospective: it looks ahead, discounting each firm's future prospects into the current market value of its stock. Finally, it is comprehensive, reaching into every corporation to render continuing judgments about the quality of current and expected performance.

The evaluation process puts firms' managers on a treadmill, under continuing pressure to perform as well as investors expect. Any serious managerial letup should, in theory, lead to a relative fall in the firm's stock price. That angers investors because it reduces their assets. And angry investors can mobilize to remove managers from their jobs.

Ultimately, a lagging firm may face a takeover—the public seizure of one firm by another (we discuss it later in the book). The threat of takeover often scares even the most inept or unruly managers into efficient behavior. If that is not enough, the buyer may succeed in gaining control and make the improvements directly. Therefore takeovers can be the capital markets' visible hammer in enforcing control and efficiency—though in practice they often fumble the opportunity.

3.   BANKING RELATIONSHIPS: THE REPLICATION HYPOTHESIS.

The ties between banks and their prime clients are important. Banks prefer secure, lucrative clients to risky, low-profit ones, so their relationships with the former involve a degree of mutual reliance. In seeking low-risk clients, banks inevitably offer favorable terms to the more attractive.

Their link gives advantages for both the bank and the firm. The firm gets funds in larger amounts and at lower interest costs. It also gets valuable advice and information from the bank, plus a degree of potential support against future stresses. On its end, the bank reduces the costs of getting information and making decisions, which would be substantial with new, unfamiliar customers. It also gains continuity and security for its own operations.

The situation is circular: more funds at lower interest rates improve the security, profitability, and prospects of the client firms. Banking factors can therefore both create and reinforce the disparities in market position and profitability.

Banking monopolies therefore tend to maintain market power in other markets and to deter lesser firms and entrants. More precisely, banking structure tends to replicate itself throughout other markets. To analyze industry in isolation from finance is to ignore this basic determinant.

The Supply of Capital.   Evidently U.S. banking markets diverge from the model of perfect capital markets, but in the larger cities are not highly monopolistic. Yet much local and regional banking still occurs under conditions of tight oligopoly.

How might this affect the supply of capital? Mainly by providing more funds at lower interest rates to firms with the best banking relationships. Studies of actual interest rates show that rates are inversely related to the size of the borrower; bigger firms get cheaper loans.[3] This may be due in part to the lower risks and transaction costs of loans to large firms. Yet again there is circularity, because the secure, favorable banking relationship itself lowers risks and transaction costs.

4. INTERNATIONAL COMPARISONS

Banking structure is tighter in other industrial economies. In Britain, France, Germany, Switzerland, Japan, Italy, Sweden, and other countries, there are fewer dominant banks, which thus have higher shares. There are usually only three or four truly national banks in each country. Structure has been relatively stable for several decades, with little turnover or decline in concentration. Entry of new banks is generally limited, but behavior is less aggressively competitive than in the United States. The move toward greater European integration has increased competition. Though most leading French and Italian banks are state-owned, this appears to make little difference in cooperative behavior.

II. MERGERS

In the market for corporate control, whole companies are routinely bought and sold. The main result is mergers, which combine two or more firms into one. The firms may differ in size, with one absorbing the other. The merger may occur amicably or under hostility (as most takeovers do). The merger may affect competition. "De-mergers" also occur, spinning off parts of companies or splitting up whole companies.

Mergers and spinoffs occur by the many thousands each year, but they are only a small fraction of the endless wheeling and dealing in the market for corporate assets. Perhaps ten mergers or spinoffs are considered and started for every one that is actually accomplished.

Mergers may cause two main economic harms: market power and inefficiency. Mergers have often been blamed for raising concentration. They certainly did so in the first great merger wave of 1897 to 1901, and they may have added to concentration during the later merger waves of the 1920s and 1960s. They did so again during the immense 1980s merger wave and the current even-larger wave. Mergers also may cause inefficiency, sometimes even leading firms into bankruptcy.[4] We consider both possible effects in what follows.

Mergers are of three main kinds: horizontal, vertical, and conglomerate, as illustrated in figure 6.1. Each poses distinctive issues; each may provide greater efficiency and/or reduce competition. We focus on horizontal mergers here because they reduce competition directly.

Besides pure mergers between two free-standing firms, there is also much divestiture (selling off) of branches by firms. This is a way to dispose of a weak

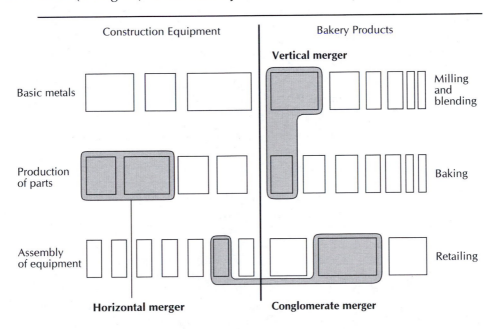

Figure 6.1   The three main types of mergers.

operation, prune back the firm, or simply adopt a different company strategy. Such divestiture is part of the normal functioning of capital markets. Indeed, about half of all asset exchanges from 1970 to 1985 and during the 1990s wave of mergers have actually been divestitures. They reflected a disposal of thousands of dubious acquisitions made during the conglomerate wave of the 1960s and the takeover wave of the 1980s.

Do mergers usually achieve scale economies, or perhaps so-called "synergies" among diverse operations? Or instead, do they mainly create higher market shares—or simply larger, sluggish bureaucratic companies—or worse, clashes and confusion? In covering these issues, we first consider the motives for mergers and then their actual patterns. Takeovers are discussed next, followed by the failing-firm problem. Finally, we look at the effects of mergers.

1. MOTIVES FOR MERGERS

The main underlying motive for mergers is, of course, to gain profits.[5] Firm A believes it can gain more from buying Firm B than the price it will have to pay to get Firm B. Mergers may also serve other managerial objectives. The three main profit-increasing reasons for mergers are market power, technical economies, and pecuniary economies. A merger may have one or all of these effects—or none.

Straight Market Power and Profits. If a merged firm has more market power, it can achieve higher profitability. Horizontal mergers invariably raise market power; by definition they eliminate side-by-side competition between the two firms. The effect may be small or large, depending mainly on the two firms' market shares.

Vertical mergers tie together firms located along the chain of production. Commonly they have little or no effect in raising market power (see chapter 12). A "conglomerate," diversified merger is a more subtle matter. It combines two unrelated activities, such as bulldozers and books, or rugs and steel. It may somehow enlarge the scope of the new combined firm's strategies beyond what the two firms could do before merging. It might also create synergies. Pure conglomerate mergers do not change the structure of either market directly, so usually there is no increase in market power.

Technical Economies. Several kinds of technical economies may be achieved by merger. One is **economies of scale**, which horizontal mergers may provide if the merging firms were both below the minimum efficient scale.

A second is **vertical economies**, gained by joining firms at two levels of production. A classic instance is the merging of iron and steel operations so that pig iron and steel ingots can be sent on to the next processing level directly without losing heat.

Third, **economies of diversification** may arise from conglomerate mergers. The whole firm may be stabilized by combining diverse activities, rather than having "all its eggs in one basket." The activities' fluctuations will tend to even each other out, making total operations less risky. Also, financial guidance and flows may be more efficient in diversified firms. In addition, so-called "synergies" may occur from interactions among different technologies and managers within a conglomerate. But synergies rarely occur; "reverse synergies" are more common, resulting from clashes and chaos.[6]

The net real gains from merger are the only relevant basis for judging the efficiency contribution of mergers. A merger is just one among three main ways to achieve technical economies. The firms could instead choose internal growth or long-term contracts. Compared to them, in fact, the net technical gain from merger is often small, zero, or even negative.

A firm that chooses internal growth invests its funds to create new capacity rather than buying an existing company. Managers prefer mergers because they are quicker than setting up a new unit, and horizontal mergers reduce competition. Yet almost any true technical economy available through merger can also be achieved by internal growth (that is, enlarging the firm's existing capacity or setting up a new firm).

Long-term contracts among firms are another way to achieve technical economies. Vertical economies, in particular, can often be realized by twenty-year or thirty-year supply contracts, which provide for complete security and precision of supplies. In comparison, the net gains from merger may be small or nil.

Pecuniary Economies. Pecuniary economies provide monetary benefits without improving the use of real resources. Mergers yield several main kinds. First, the merged firm may be able to enforce lower prices for the inputs it buys. Second, tax laws and accounting rules may raise the profitability of mergers. Third, the merger may provide promotional advantages.[7] If marketing power (via advertising, sales networks, and other promotional devices) is transferable, then pecuniary gains result.

2.   Actual Merger Patterns and Waves

Though mergers have occurred ever since business activity began, we will focus on those of the last century. There have been five main waves, the last of which continues at this writing.

Many large railroad and industrial firms were formed by mergers between 1850 and 1890. Indeed, the early stock markets from 1870 to 1900 often were dominated by spectacular struggles, alliances, and mergers among the robber barons of railroads, steel, shipping, oil, meat, and other companies.

The First Wave. The first mass of large modern corporations emerged from the huge trust movement that peaked in 1897–1901 (see figure 6.2). This wave of horizontal mergers, which sometimes united scores of competitors at one stroke, formed near-monopolies in a variety of industries both large and small. In 1904, John Moody counted over 300 such dominant firms.[8] Large aggregate concentration in the economy emerged, along with high market shares in many individual industries.

Some of this activity reflected the claim that modern industry required the stability provided by dominant firms. Instead, though, many mergers were instigated by promoters merely for the purpose of creating high fees and paper gains from watered stock. The merger fever was cooled in 1901 by Theodore Roosevelt's antitrust actions and by a slump in the stock market.

Many of the new monopolies faded quickly because of internal dissension, inefficiency, or entry by new firms.[9] Others (such as American Tobacco and General Electric) retained dominance for decades or were reduced by antitrust

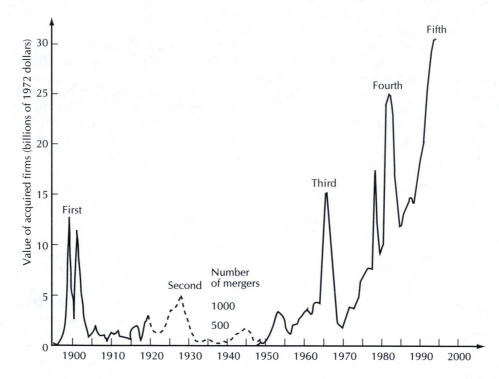

Figure 6.2 Constant-dollar volume of manufacturing and mineral firm acquisitions, 1895-1985.

Note: Data on the value of manufacturing and mineral company acquisitions are not available for the years 1921-1947. The broken line reflects the number of acquisitions in those years. Source: Ravenscraft and Scherer, *Mergers, Sell-offs, and Economic Efficiency* (Washington, DC: The Brookings Institution, 1987): p. 21; and current business press.

actions. Parallel merger waves in Canada, Britain, and elsewhere also created many lasting dominant firms. Yet because collusion was legal in those countries, there was less incentive for firms to merge, so the U.S. wave was more expansive than the others.

Since then, there have been four merger waves in the United States—the 1920s, 1960s, 1980s, and 1990s. Merger activity usually rises in a bull market and drops in a bear market.

The Second Wave. The 1920s wave included a large volume of utility mergers that set up pyramid forms of control. At the top were holding companies, which held multi-utility groups, which in turn controlled many actual electric companies. These pyramids were shaky, and that made the 1920s boom especially unstable.

The Third Wave. Another long rise in mergers reached a peak in the "go-go" boom of 1964 to 1969. About four-fifths of the mergers in this period were classified as conglomerate by the FTC, and many 1980s and 1990s mergers were conglomerate.

The Fourth Wave. Relaxed Reagan antitrust policies in the 1980s unleashed another merger boom. Many were horizontal mergers, some of which reduced competition markedly.[10]

The Fifth (and Biggest) Wave. The 1990s brought an even larger merger boom, shown in figure 6.2. It included all types of mergers, especially major horizontal mergers in banking, drugs, health care, and telecommunications. As much as half of the 1980s and 1990s mergers were in recently deregulated industries.[11] Many of the facts and issues eerily repeated the first merger wave of the 1890s. Scores of major mergers created dominant positions, or raised them further. A mild example was the AT&T-Comcast merger of 2002, creating the largest firm in cable and broadband services. The merged firm probably held over half of that market.

The meltdown in dot com companies and in telecommunications after 1999 brought this boom to a halt.[12] In addition, the biggest merger—that of AOL and Time Warner in 2001—became a spectacular failure.[13]

In most other countries, the public's distrust of horizontal and vertical mergers has been minor. In fact, governments frequently promote horizontal mergers with the rhetoric of strengthening firms against foreign competitors. Accordingly, horizontal mergers are often a large share of mergers abroad.

The volume of mergers abroad has been large, parallel to the U.S. waves in the 1960s and 1980s. From 1956 to 1972, one-fourth of the growth of large British firms was by merger,[14] and French and Japanese patterns were similar. The 1980s and 1990s brought merger booms to Britain similar to the U.S. booms.

3.   TAKEOVERS

Two types of mergers and issues require special analysis: takeovers and mergers that fail.

In a takeover, one firm seizes another against its managers' will. The acquiring firm makes a sudden tender offer to buy the target firm's stock at a price well above the going stock market price. If 51 percent of shares are offered, the target firm is taken over.

Takeovers often occur when a firm is thought to be managing its assets so poorly that its stock price is low and a new owner could achieve better returns and raise the stock price. The extent of takeovers is often not clear, for there are all degrees of surprise, stress, and force. Many mergers are partly takeovers. Others that seem amicable are actually takeovers; the target firm has caved in before the takeover was made public. A spectacular fight by the target managers may merely be a strategy to force the acquirer to raise its bid price.

Takeovers theoretically lead to higher efficiency, but the actual results since 1965 have often been poor, sometimes even chaotic. The earlier free-market confidence in takeover benefits was belied by takeovers in the 1960s, 1980s, and 1990s; many of them were dismal failures.

4.   FAILED MERGERS AND SPINOFFS

There is a rich research literature on the harms and failures of many mergers.[15] The business press, too, often reports mercilessly on the many mergers that fail. Often these mergers were poorly planned, were undertaken merely for egoistic empire-building motives, were based on false hopes of synergies, or involved conflicting corporate styles.

Table 6.1   The Role of Imports, Antitrust, and Deregulation in Increasing Competition, 1958–1980

Industry (category)	Industry's National Income, 1978 ($ million)[a]	Industry (category)	Industry's National Income, 1978 ($ million)[a]
1. Antitrust		**2. Increasing Imports**	
Meatpacking	$2,469	Steel and products (A)	$16,269
Baked goods	3,310	Automobiles	15,844
Drugs	4,735	Aircraft	6,823
Aluminum and products	3,754	Tires and tubes	3,534
Metal cans	2,521	Shipbuilding	3,287
Shoe machinery	50	Television tubes	3,156
Heavy electrical equipment	6,422	Artificial fibers	2,246
Telephone equipment (D)	3,416	Television sets	2,090
Cable TV equipment	(120)	Cameras	(1,000)
Photographic equipment and supplies	4,905	Copiers (A)	(3,900)
		Vacuum cleaners	361
Telephone service long distance (D)	17,843	Motorcycles	284
		Sewing machines	181
Radio and television broadcasting	4,741	Total	$58,975
Banking (D)	24,649	**3. Deregulation**	
Security, commodity brokers (D)	5,428	Telephone equipment (A)	3,416
		Railroad transportation (A)	14,217
Real estate agents	13,677	Trucking	25,917
Photofinishing labs	1,435	Air transportation (A)	12,054
Automotive rentals	2,807	Telephone service long distance (A)	17,843
Motion pictures and theaters	3,347		
		Banking	24,649
Commercial sports	1,426	Security, commodity brokers (A)	5,428
Legal services	16,232		
Total	$123,287	Total	$103,524

[a]Figures in parentheses are estimates

Note: (A) means antitrust was also important; (D) means deregulation was also important

Sources: Adapted from William G. Shepherd, "Causes of Increased Competition in the U.S. Economy, 1939–1980." *Review of Economics and Statistics* 64 (November 1982): 613–26, Table 3.

Split-ups and spinoffs are a natural process for curing merger failures and for overcoming excess diversification. A "whirlwind breaking up companies" spread in the 1990s, as the emptiness of many synergy claims became evident.[16] It led many huge firms to divide themselves up voluntarily. A partial listing begins with AT&T (revenues $75 billion) in 1995 and again in 2002, ITT ($24 billion), Tenneco ($13 billion), Melville ($11 billion), Dun & Bradstreet ($5 billion), and Dial ($4 billion).[17] Other firms divested large chunks of their operations; examples include General Motors, Sears Roebuck, Viacom, Union Pacific, 3M, Ralston-Purina, Hilton Hotels, and Matsushita.

5. THE EFFECTS OF MERGERS

Ravenscraft and Scherer assessed merger activity from 1950 to 1977.[18] They found that "operating efficiency fell on average following merger."[19] Indeed, even purely financial returns to the merging companies were not good; ". . . the average acquisition, if not downright unprofitable, was not highly profitable."

Moreover, the supposed disciplining effect on management does not show through clearly. Most acquired firms were already well managed, not in need of improvement. The ballyhooed synergies typically did not develop, and improved funding from the internal capital market within conglomerate firms did not occur.

They find, in fact, that most of the popular justifications for mergers did not operate strongly during the 1950–1977 period. Many mergers seemed to reflect empire-building urges rather than clear efficiencies. The 1980s and 1990s mergers also involved more extensive conglomerate activity, with equally mixed results followed by a large volume of corrective divestiture activity.

The 1990s wave included many mergers doomed to fail. A study in 2002 showed unsparingly that many of the biggest mergers had yielded only trouble and reduced value to the acquiring firm.[20]

6. IMPACTS ON RIVALS

Free-market writers developed a new claim in the 1970s: any complaint by a rival about a merger merely proves that this rival is inefficient. Therefore, the claim goes, any added pressure on the rival is automatically a good thing, because the pressure forces the rival to perform better.[21] The complaint, by a catch-22 illogic, is said to prove the virtue of the merger and the falsity of the complaint. This view was popular among Reagan antitrust officials, who refused to heed rivals' complaints about mergers that sharply increased market shares and market power.

But that claim depends entirely on an extreme free-market assumption—the lack of imperfections. With imperfections, a merger can have anticompetitive impacts, and the rival's complaint may be valid and important.[22] A dominance-raising merger can enlarge the scope for strategic price discrimination and other anticompetitive actions.

III. OTHER DETERMINANTS OF STRUCTURE

1. LIFE CYCLES

In the most general life cycle, markets begin with one or a few firms, but their market power declines because others enter as the industry grows. No comprehensive or sophisticated study of this has yet been done, but many markets have some sort of life cycle.[23] Cases vary in original degree of monopoly and rate of decline in concentration. Also, odd departures can occur under a public policy that increases or reduces monopoly, or a large merger that interrupts the decline in concentration. The life cycle is more a tendency than a law or a rule.

First-Mover Situations. During the early development of a market, one firm often forges ahead, becoming the first mover that develops the product, stimulates demand, and achieves dominance.[24] Such first movers often exploit their advantages and retain their dominance for a long time.

2.   NETWORK INDUSTRIES AND ECONOMIES OF SCOPE

Certain industries contain networks that serve a variety of customer locations and groups; examples are railroads, airlines, electricity, telephone systems, and local water supply.[25] The technology of such networks often imposes a natural monopoly. The network involves so-called economies of scope, in which each supplier tries to attract all customers to its network, so as to achieve a high intensity of demand. That makes competition unstable or even impossible.

A humble example is garbage removal. Each hauler sends trucks on routes along city streets to pick up the garbage. It naturally wants to get all the customers that its trucks go past, because the marginal cost of stopping for each customer is very low. The haulers use intense tactics (especially price discrimination) to win customers so that their routes are filled out.

Telephone systems are similar. Each system wants to have all customers, to enhance the use of its system and to let everybody call everybody else. Likewise with airlines; they can add flights to marginal destinations at little cost from their existing routes.

Economies of scope arose as a popular topic in the 1980s, and they can be significant. But their practical importance needs careful evaluation. In some industries scope economies may actually be small, but the system uses them as an excuse for taking anticompetitive actions. That has probably occurred in garbage removal, trucking, and telecommunications.

Before 1980, networks and scope economies were thought to preclude competition, as in local electricity and telephone service. It is now recognized that open access can make competition entirely viable even in single-network situations.

For example, local customers may all be connected physically to the wires of the local telephone or electricity system. But the customers can be allowed to choose freely among alternative suppliers if the local network is required to function as a highway, letting competitors serve customers through its network. That is precisely the basis for possible future competition in those two industries. The full outcome is still to be seen.

3.   PUBLIC POLICIES

Several kinds of public policies probably influence market structure in predictable directions. Whether these policies are imposed on industries or are instead controlled by firms in the industries themselves is often an open question. Frequently both directions of control are mixed together. The following policy influences appear to exist in some degree.[26]

Antitrust policies have three main parts (see chapter 15). They are against (1) established high concentration, (2) mergers that may create new market power, and (3) collusion among firms to control the market.

In practice, the *balance* of strictness among these three directions of policy affects market structure. Thus U.S. antitrust policy since 1899 has been more stringent against collusion among firms. That may have induced many firms to merge, creating more market concentration. In a similar example, British rules against collusion tightened sharply after 1955. This probably induced a wave of mergers, which raised the degree of concentration in British industry. These broad effects have arisen in a wide range of industrial structures. U.S. antitrust actions have also made direct trustbusting changes in quite a few specific industries (see chapter 16).[27]

Direct controls on structure are also fixed by policy for some industries (see chapter 17). In utilities sectors, one firm has traditionally been given an exclusive franchise in each area, as in electricity and local telephone service. Entry into many other industries has been limited. Such controls range from airtight monopoly franchises to general licensing standards. They are found in a variety of national, state, and local markets.

Patents grant exclusive rights over inventions for seventeen years in the United States and certain other countries (recall chapter 5). By conferring monopoly, they can shape a market from its birth. They can also be amassed and used in various legal strategies as a way of gaining and retaining market control. Among the industries strongly influenced by patents have been telephone service, pharmaceuticals, copying equipment, electrical equipment, glass, and photographic supplies. Patents may therefore have significantly increased monopoly in the U.S. economy.

Evidently there are many determinants of market structure besides economies of scale. They might well account for much or all of the variation in actual structure. One would need to filter out these other determinants in order to define and estimate the true role of scale economies.

QUESTIONS FOR REVIEW

1. Explain how the stock market is like a taskmaster, tending to put managers on a treadmill.

2. Explain the replication hypothesis, that banking structure tends to replicate itself in other markets.

3. Why might mergers occur, other than for technical economies?

4. Summarize a recent takeover. Was the target company inefficient? Was the purchase price low or high? Did the target company damage itself in its efforts to resist?

5. How can many of the 1960s, 1980s, and 1990s mergers have been unwise, if capital markets operate efficiently?

ENDNOTES

[1] There is no comprehensive discussion of perfect capital markets. But see Frank H. Knight, *Risk, Uncertainty and Profit* (New York: Harper & Row, 1921); and George J. Stigler, *The Organization of Industry* (Homewood, IL: Irwin, 1968), chapter 10.

[2] These include the firm's accountants, investment banker, underwriter, outside legal counsel, and advertising agency as well as its banker.

[3] See, among others, Donald P. Jacobs, *Business Loan Costs and Bank Market Structure* (New York: National Bureau of Economic Research, 1971).

[4] See, for example, "The Case Against Mergers," *BusinessWeek* (October 30, 1995): pp. 122–30.

[5] See David J. Ravenscraft and F. M. Scherer, *Mergers, Sell-offs, and Economic Efficiency* (Washington, DC: Brookings Institution, 1987).

[6] The term "synergies" has no economic basis; usually it is just a glib claim trying to justify a dubious merger. For one case where "synergies" were a harmful illusion, see John Motavalli, *Bamboozled at the Revolution: How Big Media Lost Billions in the Battle for the Internet* (New York: Viking Press, 2002), reviewed by Tom Lowry, "The Sinkhole of Synergy," *BusinessWeek* (August 26, 2002): p. 22.

[7] For example, Procter & Gamble bought the Clorox company in the 1950s, but was forced to divest itself of this company in 1968. The FTC decided, and the Supreme Court affirmed, that

P&G's advertising power would strongly assist Clorox, which had over 50 percent of the bleach market, to hold or increase its market power. The merger would probably have reduced competition without providing technical benefits.

[8] Among the newly merged firms were International Harvester, American Sugar Company, General Electric Company, American Can Company, and U.S. Steel Corporation. John Moody's survey is required reading for students of the subject; see his *Truth about the Trusts* (Chicago: Moody Publishing, 1904); see also Anthony P. O'Brien, "Factory Size, Economies of Scale, and the Great Merger Wave of 1898–1902," *Journal of Economic History* 48 (1988). For an affirmation that this merger wave shaped the structure of U.S. industry, see Naomi Lamoreaux, *The Great Merger Movement in American Business, 1895–1904* (New York: Cambridge University Press, 1985).

[9] For a lively textbook case, see Alfred S. Eichner, *The Emergence of Oligopoly: Sugar Refining as a Case Study* (New York: Columbia University Press, 1971); see also William Z. Ripley, ed., *Trusts, Pools and Corporations*, rev. ed. (Boston: Ginn, 1916); and Lamoreaux, *The Great Merger Movement*.

[10] See Walter Adams and James W. Brock, *Dangerous Pursuits* (New York: Pantheon Books, 1991) and sources cited there. For a defense of mergers' efficiency during the 1980s and 1990s, see Gregor Andrade, Mark Mitchell, and Erik Stafford, "New Evidence and Perspectives on Mergers," *Journal of Economic Literature* 15(2) (Spring 2001): pp. 103–20.

[11] Even labor unions joined the wave with a blockbuster merger; see "Unions of Auto Workers, Steelworkers and Machinists Agree to Merge by 2001," *Wall Street Journal* (July 27, 1995): p. A3.

[12] See Robert Frank, "Where Have the Masters of the Big Merger Gone?" *Wall Street Journal* (June 25, 2002): pp. C1 and C3; and Robert Frank and Robin Sidel, "Firms That Lived by the Deal In '90s Now Sink by the Dozens," *Wall Street Journal* (June 6, 2002): pp. A1 and A8.

[13] See Matthew Rose, Julia Angwin, and Martin Peers, "Failed Effort to Coordinate Ads Signals Deeper Woes at AOL," *Wall Street Journal* (July 18, 2002): pp. A1 and A6; Bruce Orwall and Martin Peers, "The Message of Media Mergers: So Far, They Haven't Been Hits," *Wall Street Journal* (May 10, 2002): pp. A1 and A5; and Motavelli, *Bamboozled at the Revolution*.

[14] S. Aaronovitch and Malcolm C. Sawyer, "Mergers, Growth and Concentration," *Oxford Economic Papers* 27 (March 1975): pp. 136–55.

[15] See various chapters of Harry First, Eleanor M. Fox, and Robert Pitofsky, eds., *Revitalizing Antitrust in Its Second Century*, (New York: Quorum, 1991).

[16] "The Whirlwind Breaking Up Companies," *BusinessWeek* (August 14, 1995): p. 44; Laura Landro, "Giants Talk Synergy but Few Make It Work," *Wall Street Journal* (September 1995): pp. B1, B10; Jim Carlton, "Reverse Synergy," *Wall Street Journal* (September 15, 1995): p. R10.

[17] Joanna S. Lublin, "Spinoffs May Establish New Companies, but They Often Spell the End of Jobs," *Wall Street Journal* (November 21, 1995): pp. B1, B8.

[18] Ravenscraft and Scherer, *Mergers, Sell-offs, and Economic Efficiency*. Another extensive study is Dennis C. Mueller, *The Determinants and Effects of Mergers* (Cambridge: Oelgeschlager, Gunn & Hain, 1980).

[19] Ravenscraft and Scherer, *Mergers, Sell-offs, and Economic Efficiency*, pp. 195–204.

[20] See the extensive coverage in David Henry, "Mergers: Why Most Big Deals *Don't* Pay Off," *BusinessWeek* (October 14, 2002): pp. 60–70.

[21] Robert H. Bork, *The Antitrust Paradox* (New York: Basic Books, 1978); and Fred S. McChesney and William F. Shughart, *The Causes and Consequences of Antitrust* (Chicago: University of Chicago Press, 1995).

[22] See also the discussion by Kenneth D. Boyer, "Mergers That Harm Competition," *Review of Industrial Organization* 7 (April 1992): pp. 191–202.

[23] For one view, see B. Jovanovic and G. M. MacDonald, "The Life Cycle of a Competitive Industry," *Journal of Political Economy* 102 (April 1994): pp. 322–47.

[24] See the survey by William T. Robinson, Gurumurthy Kalyanaram, and Glen L. Urban, "First-Mover Advantages from Pioneering New Markets: A Survey of Empirical Evidence," *Review*

of Industrial Organization 9 (February 1994): pp. 1–24; and Comments by F. M. Scherer and David F. Lean in *Review of Industrial Organization* 9 (April 1994): pp. 173–80.

[25] Harry M. Trebing, "The Networks as Infrastructures-The Re-establishment of Market Power," *Journal of Economic Issues* 28 (June 1994): pp. 379–89; and M. L. Katz, "Systems Competition and Network Effects," *Journal of Economic Perspectives* 8 (Spring 1994): pp. 93–115.

[26] For an inclusive survey and analysis of such policies, see William G. Shepherd, *Public Policies Toward Business*, 8th ed. (Homewood, IL: Irwin, 1990); see also chapters 15–17 in this book.

[27] The industries include petroleum, tobacco products, gunpowder, broadcasting, aluminum, tin cans, shoe machinery, and the entire telecommunications sector in 1984. There have been indirect effects in other markets. For evaluations, see Simon Whitney, *Antitrust Policies*, 2 vols. (New York: Twentieth Century Fund, 1958); and William G. Shepherd, *The Treatment of Market Power*, (New York: Columbia University Press, 1975): pp. 304–20.

Chapter

ECONOMIES AND
DISECONOMIES OF SCALE

Economies of scale are always a hot issue. Is bigger usually better in most markets? Or is small usually beautiful? Waves of contrary claims have swept over the field since the 1890s, and ideas continue to fight it out more than a century later.[1]

Careful research has generally favored smallness in most markets, but advocates for big business have presented their claims, especially in the 1890s, the 1920s, the 1950s, and since 1970. Their primary model is the "efficient-structure hypothesis," that is, that the current structure in each market is said to be—invariably—the best structure.

If economies of scale really are that large, then an "antitrust dilemma" may exist. In order to achieve effective competition with at least five comparable rivals, those five firms might be too small to be efficient.

But if technology favors small sizes in most industries (say, 5 percent or 10 percent market shares), then competition could be fully effective *and* fully efficient. The antitrust "dilemma" would be imaginary or false, and actual high-concentration markets might have large amounts of excess market share.

In judging this, only **technical cost conditions** are relevant; **pecuniary elements** should be filtered out. And only **net economies** compared to the possible gains from using other methods (long-term contracts, etc.), are to be considered. The three main conditions to be measured are **minimum efficient scale** (MES), **cost gradient**, and possible **diseconomies of scale**.

What does research show? To briefly sum up this chapter, **most markets are naturally competitive, with considerable room for competition**. Market shares exceed the minimum efficient scale in many important U.S. markets. Accordingly, **many markets have substantial excess market share**.

Section 1 opens by explaining the basic trends in technology since the Civil War: a trend toward giantism until the 1930s and then a reversal toward small size. Sections 2 to 4 present the concepts of scale economies at the plant level and companywide level. Then sections 5 and 6 review the methods and results of past research into the economies of scale.

I.   HISTORICAL SHIFTS IN TECHNOLOGY TRENDS

The Industrial Revolution began in Britain in the 1770s, powered by the early steam engine. U.S. industrial development boomed after 1850, changing a small-scale, rural-oriented society into an industrial, urban economy. But in the twentieth century, heavy industries yielded after the 1930s to the rise of services and electronics industries, which soon became the majority activity of the modern economy.

Several forces have shaped technology during these major periods—primarily power, materials, transportation, and electronics. From 1850 to the 1930s, changes mainly favored large size for factories and for whole companies. They provided technical economies of scale both at the plant level and in multiplant operations. Then this tide waned and reversed, as several powerful forces converged favoring small-scale technology.

Power for Production.   The powering of factories has undergone vast changes, from human and animal muscles on down to modern high-tech uses of electricity and electronics. After 1770, the steam engine largely replaced ancient sources of power, such as human beings, draft animals, and falling water. Steam was much more powerful, enabling machines to be larger and operate faster than before, by orders of magnitude. Steam power also favored bigger factories, where many machines were powered by belts or gears attached to just one or a few large steam engines. These "dark satanic mills" typified industrial progress for over a century.

After 1880, electricity provided an increasing force toward small-scale operations. Electric motors of many sizes became available, delivering power more flexibly. Electrically powered machines were more adaptable and, in many operations, much smaller and more precise than those powered by steam. Smaller factories became more feasible in a wider variety of locations. As electronics spread after 1950, further miniaturization of production has occurred.

Materials.   The Industrial Revolution brought about an iron age—or rather, a metals age. Metals such as iron, steel, copper, and aluminum were highly exact, homogeneous substances with uniform properties. New metal alloys provided a further range of strength and other properties. Unlike leather and wood, metals lent themselves to standardization and mass production. Chemicals, oil, and other minerals also fitted this trend. Changes in materials favored large-scale, uniform processes in place of earlier small-scale crafts and workshops.

Since about 1920, one counterforce against bigness has been the increasing complexity of industrial products and services. Advanced electronics and aircraft, for example, cannot be churned out as simply as tons of steel or bricks. Services, especially, tend to require a small scale. Even in older, simpler industries, the limits of scale have often been fully reached or even overshot.[2] In oil, chemicals, metals, meatpacking, machine tools, and other industries—even the generation of electricity itself—the trend toward larger plants has faded or reversed, in part because the materials for production are far more refined. Also, such newer industries as electronics involve extremely refined materials and precision methods, often best achieved at a small scale.

Transportation.   The two great steam-powered transport modes—railroads and steamships—also fostered increases in industrial scale in the 1800s. Rail lines linked large cities and resource deposits (coal, ores). Along these routes, factories tended to be few, large, and centrally located. Shipping was done in large batches, or even by the trainful, which again favored large-scale factories.

The truck reversed this trend after 1920. Trucks are more flexible for loading, smaller in scale, and able to rove almost everywhere. The rise in truck transportation reopened whole sets of industries and geographic areas to small-scale production. Further, much truck traffic involves composite loads, with many small individual shipments, which extends efficiency to very small sizes. The spread of the interstate highway network after 1950 greatly deepened this effect, and since trucking deregulation in 1980, millions of trucks have roamed everywhere delivering almost anything.

The automobile furthered the trend by enabling workers to reach a wide range of work places, both large and small. Before, workers had to cluster in dense areas in large cities, where the big labor pools favored large-scale factories.

Communications and Computers.   Advances in communications also shaped technology and optimum size. The telephone made possible the close and extremely refined coordination of distant activities. This favored smaller plants and also large, multiplant firms.

The onset of computers after 1950 made managerial controls far more extensive and precise. Computer systems also replaced whole armies of service workers (such as telephone operators and filing clerks). In the 1950s, giant computers seemed likely to favor giantism in business. But since the 1960s, miniaturization has made increasingly powerful computer functions available to small firms, plants, and individual machines (in process controls).

The net effect of the computer now fully supports very small-scale plants and firms. And the Internet and its features have since 1990 made small firms even more efficient.[3]

Worker Skills.   The great waves of immigration during 1880–1920 provided masses of modestly educated, non-English-speaking workers, who could be organized for mass physical work. They could be regimented in simple tasks and in massive operations. The top-down forms of authoritarian management prevalent at the time favored large plants and firms.

Now most workers are much better educated, more self-reliant, and less tolerant of large-scale autocratic controls. This intelligent sharing of responsibility has raised productivity relatively in smaller, more worker-sensitive firms.

After 1980, the economy was swept by conflicting managerial doctrines. The business press widely praised smallness for its liberating, creative forces. A wide array of business interests, reporters, and commentators directed withering criticism at many large mergers. They stressed the virtues of small-scale nimble and flexible firms. Meanwhile, a number of giant firms encountered spectacular troubles during 1980–1993, including IBM and General Motors.[4] Previously they had been celebrated as models of superior giant-firm efficiency.

Merger promoters have continued to praise giantism and the supposed synergies from combining polyglot activities. Reagan antitrust officials openly favored big business under new-Chicago doctrines.

The need for skepticism and caution continues amid self-serving and overheated claims.[5] One begins by learning the concepts carefully, in order to weigh the evidence wisely.

II. BASIC CONCEPTS

Basic scale-economic theory is simple and traditional. The average cost curve declines over some range of output until the lowest-cost point is reached.[6] That **minimum efficient scale** may be at a low or high output level, as illustrated in figure 7.1 by curves 1 and 2. The **cost gradient** (that is, the downslope of the cost curve) may also vary between steep (curve 1) and shallow (curve 2). Firms are not usually at an output level below MES, because that would raise their costs and squeeze their profits.

Economies can arise at the **plant** level in the operation of factories and shops, or at the **multiplant** (or companywide) level, in the coordination of many plants and in other activities undertaken by the whole firm. Above the MES size, there may be diseconomies of scale that cause average cost to slope up. Or instead, average cost may be flat for an interval above MES or even possibly at all sizes above MES. The gradient of any diseconomies can be shallow or steep. Figure 7.1 also illustrates these possibilities.

The main contrasts are drawn in figure 7.2, where total market demand is shown by curve 1. Curve A has steep cost gradients and a distinct low-cost size at q_A. That is the **optimal scale** for the firm. At production much above or below q_A, average cost is much higher, so the firm is confined to that (approximate) size. Curve B has the same MES at q_A, but its cost gradient is lower and its average cost is constant at higher outputs. There is no single level of best size. Firms as small as q_A can compete evenly with any and all larger firms up to size q_D.

Both A and B give plenty of room for competition. Well over five comparable firms can coexist, each at least as big as the minimum efficient scale.

Curve C has an optimal scale at q_C, which is a substantial share of the market. Since the cost gradients are rather shallow, the cost penalties from being above or below q_C are not heavy. Finally, curve D has scale economies throughout the size range, up to a size large enough to meet all market demand. Since the cost gradient is steep, any firm below the monopoly share q_D suffers a large cost penalty.

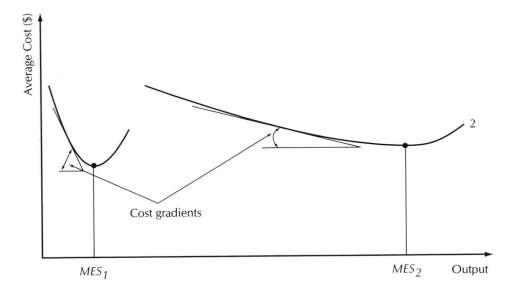

Figure 7.1   Two contrasting overage cost curves.

1. NATURAL COMPETITION AND NATURAL MONOPOLY

Curve *A* embodies **natural competition**. All firms must have small market shares, and therefore competition will occur naturally and be intensive. Curve *C* is **natural oligopoly**. Four firms will tend to evolve, each with 25 percent of the market. Curve *D* is **natural monopoly**. The first firm to expand can cut its price below any smaller firm's costs and therefore eliminate it. Only one firm will survive. Monopoly is unavoidable and also desirable for its cost efficiency.

In Curve *B*, the most efficient size is indeterminate because any size between q_A and q_D is equally efficient. There is room for effective competition, but costs do not determine market structure. The actual structure depends on the interplay between competitive pressures and the gains from monopolizing the market. A full monopoly could occur, or instead a dominant firm or tight oligopoly. Or market shares could all be driven down to q_A, giving low concentration and effective competition.

For curve *B*, any size above q_B involves **excess market share**: the amount of market share that is above MES. Larger size does not provide lower costs, and it usually leads to those harmful costs of monopoly power (X-inefficiency, allocative inefficiency, retarded innovation, unfair distribution, etc.) that are familiar to you.

Excess market share is an important problem. It usually inflicts social costs without providing any cost savings to the firm and the economy. To measure its extent, we turn to the concepts of scale economies and then to the evidence.

2. TECHNICAL VERSUS PECUNIARY GAINS

Before analyzing technical economies of scale, we must distinguish carefully between them and pecuniary gains to scale.

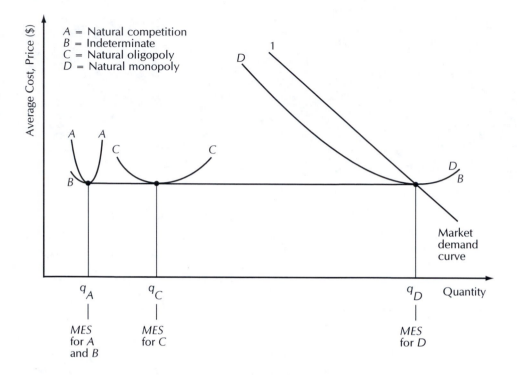

Figure 7.2   Four alternative versions of the average cost curve.

Technical economies of scale are those arising from the actual physical organization of production activities. They reduce the ratio of inputs to outputs, thereby achieving a genuine increase in economic efficiency and a reduction of costs. These are true social gains, whether they are captured by the firm as profit or passed on to customers by means of lower prices.

Pecuniary gains are merely a matter of money, not of real efficiency. They occur mainly from lower input prices paid by the firm. The firm's accounting costs are reduced, but not from any change in the real methods of production.

Two points about pecuniary gains need mention. First, the lower prices might reflect technical economies **realized by the supplier** (for example, when General Motors buys large volumes of tires). If the large firm's orders for inputs are fewer and larger, then the unit costs of producing and handling these larger batches may be lower.

Second, the supply of capital may involve subtle mixtures of pecuniary and technical gains. Firms often obtain funds at lower costs (in interest rates or dividend payout ratios) because they are genuinely superior: their risks are lower, justifying lower interest rates.

3. Costs Are Often Unclear Rather Than Precise Lines

Although economists draw bright-line cost curves in concept, they often have great difficulty measuring them in fact. Measured cost curves are often blurred, or moderately wide bands, rather than lines. The exact sizes of MES and gradients are often fuzzy and unsure.

III. PLANT-LEVEL ECONOMIES AND DISECONOMIES

Finally we have arrived at the core of the topic. We start at the level of the individual plant. What factors may cause the average cost curve of the plant to decline and then, perhaps, turn up?

Points of Definition.   Consider what a **plant** is. It is a physical facility at a single location. There is usually a building sitting on some land, with machines or other equipment inside. There are transport facilities for bringing in inputs and sending out outputs. These conditions are common to a wide variety of plants. Despite their differences, a steel mill, a warehouse, a theater, a barber shop, and a university campus are all plants.

Finally, we are concerned here with **long-run cost curves**. They reflect the choices available when all inputs can be varied. Short-run curves, by contrast, are much more steeply U-shaped; once a plant is built for a given optimal level, short-run departures from that level are difficult.

1. THE THREE MAIN SOURCES OF ECONOMIES OF SCALE

Specialization.   Specialization has long been known as a basic cause of scale economies, and Adam Smith set it at center stage in 1776 in his *Wealth of Nations*.[7] As a plant hires more workers, each can be put to more specialized tasks. They hone their narrow skills, getting more-than-proportionally faster as a team; ten specialized workers may do a hundred times as much output as one jack-of-all-trades worker.

Specialization lets workers learn to do their specific tasks much more rapidly and precisely. It also avoids the loss of time and effort from having to shift workers among tasks. **Specializing may make jobs more complex (like brain surgery) or, instead, extremely narrow and simple (like turning the same bolt all day long).**

Machines can also be made more specialized and thereby more efficient. Specialized machines are often complex, expensive, and capable of long production runs. With long runs, the fixed costs of the machine are spread out thinly per unit of output.

Physical Laws.   Physical laws often favor larger size. Geometrical relationships of volumes to surfaces are one type of law. For example, as a pipe's size increases, its flow capacity rises more than proportionally to its circumference. Hence long-distance pipelines for gas or oil use just one big pipe rather than a bundle of little pipes. Certain forces of pressure operate most efficiently at large scale. For example, a 20-ton stamping machine can outdo 500 workers pounding with hand-held hammers. High-temperature processes often work more efficiently at large scale. For example, from 1920 to 1970, ever-larger electric generators were built, using higher heat and pressure.

Management.   Management efficiencies are often realized at larger plant sizes. An excellent manager often is capable of supervising hundreds of workers, especially where the technology involves routine tasks. This ability is reinforced by modern methods of processing information, such as computers and telephone. Management gains can often reduce costs over a significant size range.

2. SOURCES OF DISECONOMIES

Paradoxically, the very same three sources of economies can become causes of diseconomies of scale for plants if they are pushed too far. If **specialization** becomes excessive, it may foster workers' alienation, careless work, and frequent breakdowns. The levels of workers' efforts may also be reduced, as bored workers gravitate toward the minimum levels of required effort. Dull jobs in many large factories have bred so much alienation among workers that efficiency and quality have declined.

Also, **physical laws** usually turn against one eventually. For example, too-large pipes will burst, and super-critical temperatures can become unstable and dangerous. As size increases, it usually encounters unfavorable physical laws of some sort, even if some other relationships are still favorable.

Management is the third cause of diseconomies. It often has the effect of a fixed factor, causing average cost to rise as plant size grows. A plant usually does best when there is one manager on the spot, able to catch problems and resolve them decisively. Increasing size dilutes this ability, causing other inputs to display diminishing marginal productivity. This is evident, for example, in many restaurants and family farms, where close control by a manager-on-the-spot seems essential. It also operates generally, in virtually any plant.

Bureaucracy is a related problem. As size increases, managers must delegate tasks. Committees, staffs, and layers of middle managers arise. Information is passed on, but it is subject to distortion in the process. In short, there is no complete substitute for firsthand contact.

3. EXTERNAL MULTIPLANT COSTS AND LEARNING CURVES

Now we step outside the conditions internal to the plant, which govern the average cost curve. Two other concepts are important but quite separate from these technical economies and diseconomies. One concept is the external costs of transport. The other is the learning curve. They do not affect the shape of the plant's production cost curve.

External But Intrafirm Costs, Particularly Transport Costs.   For some goods, transport costs are important, along with production costs. Usually these are heavy, bulky products whose ratio of value to weight is low. Good examples are bricks, ready-mix concrete, and milk, but there are many other middle-range cases.

When markets are focused in a small area, transport costs do not matter much. But when the market for a good is spread out geographically, transport costs can influence the total cost curve of the plant.[8] As the quantity of production rises, more distant customers must be sought over geometrically widening areas; the average costs to move the product to these distant customers are a rising proportion of total costs. This relationship reflects plane geometry: as a circle's radius increases, its area increases more than proportionally.

Figure 7.3 illustrates this effect. When high transport costs are added to the production costs set by internal factors, the average total cost curve has a smaller optimal size (at Q_2) and a steeper upslope toward the right. Analogous conditions hold for the transport costs of inputs.

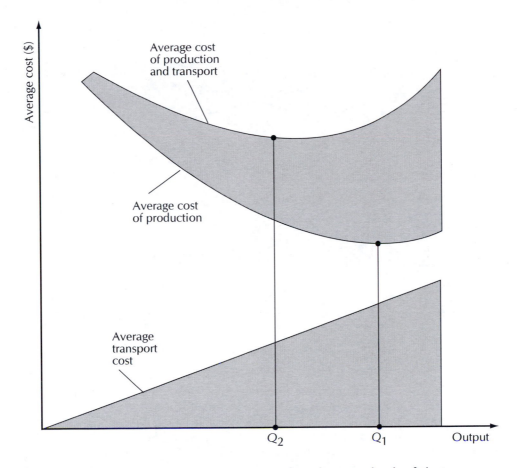

Figure 7.3 Rising overage transport cost can reduce the optimal scale of plants.

The Learning Curve. So far we have presented static analysis, showing the cost levels for a variety of alternative possible output levels in a given period. Time-related conditions also can be important, especially as embodied in the learning curve.[9]

When a new product or process is started, a learning process begins. The first units usually involve a degree of trial and error as new methods are established and people are trained. Initial costs per unit are therefore high. As production accumulates, people become quicker and smoother at their tasks. Machines are debugged and adjustments are made toward the best possible system of production.

The result is a learning curve, showing a decline in the current average cost of production as **total production** mounts. The phenomenon is an obvious one and has been known for many centuries, but it was first observed and formulated as an economic concept in the mass production of aircraft during World War II. More recently, economists have stressed that the first mover (the first firm to gain substantial size and experience with a product) will have an advantage over late-

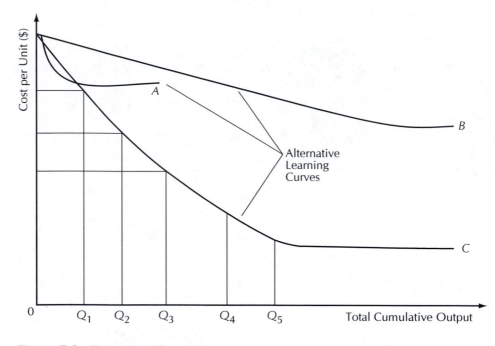

Figure 7.4   Illustration of learning curves.

comers. The late-comers can chase the first mover down the learning curve, as it were, but they may never catch up.

The outcome will depend on the slope of the learning curve for each specific case. Three forms are illustrated in figure 7.4. Notice that the horizontal axis is the total cumulative amount of production from the first unit on, not the level of production to be chosen during one period. A learning curve may have a short, steep slope (curve *A*); a long, shallow slope (*B*); a long, steep slope (*C*); or still other forms. Curve *C* will give the first mover a large advantage over other firms compared to curve *A*.

IV. MULTIPLANT ECONOMIES AND DISECONOMIES

In the simplest multiplant case, a firm could add one plant after another as it grows. This would yield a virtually flat firm-level average cost curve to the right of the MES level of the plant. Figure 7.5 illustrates this situation.

If there are economies of scale in the firm-level activities, the successive plants could be added at decreasing average costs. Instead, there may be diseconomies at all levels. Perhaps most commonly, a range of declining cost may be followed by an MES for the firm and then a range in which diseconomies prevail.

Technical Conditions.   The shape of the multiplant cost curve depends on how various companywide activities change with larger size. Extending the

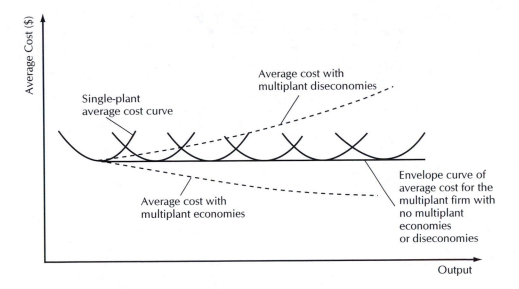

Figure 7.5 Constant costs for the multiplant firm that grows just by adding plants, showing economies and diseconomies.

firm's scope reduces duplication, but it also causes bureaucracy. For each activity, how do these balance out?

These activities divide into several main types. The most basic category is **management**. Generally, thorough management control requires a hierarchy of officials and reporting activities. Paradoxically, this tends to frustrate its own purpose by diluting information and authority and often sowing confusion. The same problem arises for plants. Such bureaucracy can be mitigated by technical improvements: instant computerized reporting, profit centers, and so on. Yet bureaucracy will always add layers of administrative costs to production costs, so the firm must somehow save enough on other activities to offset these extra costs.

V. METHODS OF RESEARCH

To study economies of scale, one must measure the average cost curve for plants and firms in each market. One would then know the MES, the cost gradient, and the upslope (if any) at higher output levels above MES. **All pecuniary elements would, of course, be filtered out,** because we are seeking to measure only the **technical** economies of scale. That would provide a normative basis for evaluating actual scales of plants in the market, comparing what is with what ought to be.

Yet it is very difficult to factor out pecuniary elements. Several methods for measuring cost curves have been developed since the 1930s. All leave some degree of pecuniary elements in, though one technique, engineering estimates, seems to be somewhat better than the others.

One strictly unsuitable method is to compare the profitability of different-sized units.[10] Because this method leaves in all pecuniary economies, the comparisons have no normative value. Profitability data have their uses, but they cannot help in evaluating efficiency.

We now turn to the research studies and their results. Your main task is to learn the methods and their weaknesses so that you can make your own judgment about actual trends and specific cases. The estimates themselves, which are rather few and doubtful, are mainly a vehicle for mastering the concepts.

The first efforts, starting in the 1930s, used average cost data for cross-section and time-series analysis. Studies of this sort continued through the 1950s. Joe S. Bain introduced the use of what he called **engineering estimates** in 1956, followed up by Pratten's and Scherer's results in the 1970s and later.[11] The **survivor technique** was advanced by George J. Stigler in 1958, and it has seen several uses.[12] Some analysts have also used **existing size distributions** to make a rough approximation of efficient size. Research continues on specific industries as well as on broad patterns.

None of the methods gives clear answers, especially for firmwide conditions. Roughly speaking, engineering estimates are regarded as the best all-around method. Survivor tests give some useful hints about plant-based economies. Existing size distributions are used mainly for crude data to be included in large regression equations. Average-cost data have generally been abandoned, being scarce and unreliable.

Each method has serious limitations, and all are expensive and arduous. The wise researcher tries to use at least two of them in any project as a supplement and cross-check to each other.

VI. EMPIRICAL FINDINGS

1. ENGINEERING ESTIMATES

Advantages. In this approach, one assembles expert opinions about the shape and position of the cost curves, both for plant and for multiplant activities. The experts are engineers and managers in the firms themselves, people who work directly with these issues as they design new plants and operate whole companies. One conducts personal interviews with, and sends questionnaires to, as many well-placed officials as possible. One also searches the specialist trade journals and any other informed sources to double-check the opinions.[13]

With these various judgments in hand, one estimates the cost curves for the best-current-practice capacity. The method's strength is that it draws on evidence from professionals who are solving problems on a daily basis, under the pressure of the profit motive. Also, it uses several sources, which can be checked against each other to reach the most reasonable estimate.

Problems. The method is arduous, requiring scores of interviews and much other effort for a study dealing with more than a few industries. To cover a really broad range of industries (say 80 or 100) would take more expert economists than are now available.

Another weakness is that the experts' opinions are in fact just opinions. Each is likely to believe that their own plants and firms are about the right size.

Finally, the method works *least* well when there is only one or a few major firms in the industry, because in that case independent judgments are very difficult to obtain. Yet those are the very industries (near monopolies and tight oligopolies) where good estimates are most acutely needed to guide antitrust policy.

Results. Bain's pioneering study covered twenty industries as of about 1950. His interviews were heavily supplemented by other less direct sources, such as trade journals. The results are rather rough and approximate. In most of the industries, optimal plant size was a small percentage of total industry size, cost gradients were small, and multiplant economies were said to be slight. Actual concentration in most of the industries contained a lot of excess market share.

In 1975, Scherer and several colleagues provided new estimates of plant scale economies in twelve industries, both in the United States and in five other countries (Canada, Germany, France, Sweden, and Britain).[14]

The researchers tried to separate the internal production costs of the plant from such external factors as transport costs (recall section 2). They also compared MES with regional markets where those were more relevant than national markets (as in cement and beer). Finally, they tried a number of statistical regressions to test the sources and effects of scale economies. Later, similar studies were done by C. F. Pratten and Leonard W. Weiss.[15]

Their main results, summarized in table 7.1, are estimates rather than precise cost curves. The broad lessons are similar to Bain's. **Excess market shares are extensive, and the cost gradients are usually small. Multiplant economies were generally slight or absent** (see columns 2 and 3 in table 7.2). Only advertising appeared to be a significant source of multiplant economies in beer, cigarettes, and refrigerators.

In other smaller countries, scale economies appear to make a degree of concentration more necessary. In roughly half the industries covered, the existing concentration abroad, regional or national, did not exceed the estimated MES for the firm.

Though engineering estimates are important, they have covered only a limited share of the important industries, and their results are debatable. For leading dominant-firm industries such as computers and newspapers, no engineering estimates are available for conditions since 1950 at either the plant or the firm level. The estimates of plant economies are reasonably strong; estimates of multiplant economies are rather weaker and scarcer. Since 1970, the MES levels for both plants and enterprises have probably declined further, as electronic technology and communications have increasingly favored smaller scale operations.

2. Survivor Tests

The survivor technique, current since 1958, relies on actual trends in plant sizes rather than on opinions.[16] The idea is simple: if plants in a size range X are surviving or increasing their share, then they must be efficient in all essential activities. The researcher ignores actual costs, expert opinions, and other direct measures of efficiency. Instead one compares the size distribution of plants over a series of years, identifying those size groups that survive.

One can evaluate just one industry in depth over many decades, or one can compare a few years' shifts in sizes (say from 1978 to 1986) for many industries.

Table 7.1 Measures of Scale Economies, 1967

	MES as Percent 0f 1967 U. S. Demand	Gradient: Precent by Which Cost Rises At 1/3 of MES
Scherer's Estimates		
Leather shoes	0.2	1.5
Cotton and synthetic broadwoven fabrics	0.2	7.6
Paints	1.4	4.4
Antifriction bearings	1.4	8.0
Glass bottles	1.5	11.0
Portland cement	1.7	26.0
Automobile batteries	1.9	4.6
Petroleum refining	1.9	4.8
Beer brewing	3.4	5.0
Cigarettes	6.6	2.2
Refrigerators	14.1	6.5
Pratten's and Weiss's Estimates		**At 1/2 of MES**
Machine tools	0.3	5.0
Bread baking	0.3	7.5
Iron foundries	0.3	10.0
Bricks	0.3	25.0
Flour mills	0.7	3.0
Tufted rugs	0.7	10.0
Bicycles	2.1	n.a.
Soybean mills	2.4	2.0
Detergents	2.4	2.5
Sulfuric acid	3.7	1.0
Passenger auto tires	3.8	5.0
Liner board	4.4	8.0
Printing paper	4.4	9.0
Synthetic rubber	4.7	15.0
Transformers	4.9	8.0
Nylon, acrylic, and polyester fibers	6.0	7–11
Commercial aircraft	10.0	20.0
Automobiles	11.0	6.0
Cellulosic synthetic fibers	11.1	5.0
Computers	15.0	8.0
Electric motors	15.0	15.0
Turbogenerators	23.0	n.a.
Diesel engines	21–30	4–28

n.a. = Not available

Source: F. M. Scherer, *Industrial Market Structure and Economic Performance* (Chicago: Rand McNally, 1980): pp. 96–7; see also Leonard W. Weiss, "Optimal Plant Size and the Extent of Suboptimal Capacity," in *Essays on Industrial Organization in Honor of Joe S. Bain,* Robert T. Masson and P. D. Qualls, eds., (Cambridge, MA: Ballinger, 1978): pp. 128–31; and C. F. Pratten, *Economies of Scale in Manufacturing Industry* (Cambridge: Cambridge University Press, 1971).

Using data readily available in census reports, one can seemingly make estimates of the optimal size range for hundreds of four-digit industries. The technique appears to be both fast and objective.

Table 7.2   Multiplant Scale Economies in U.S. Markets, 1967–1970

	Multiplant Cost Gradient	MES as Percent Of U.S. Market, 1967	U.S. Big-Three Firms, 1970	
			Average Market Share (percent)	Average Excess Market Share (percent)
Fabric weaving	Slight	1	10	9
Shoes	Slight	1	6	5
Paints	Slight	1.4	9	7.6
Cement	Slight	2	7	5
Automobile batteries	Slight	2	18	16
Steel	Very Slight	3	14	11
Petroleum refining	Slight	4–6	8	3
Glass bottles	Slight to Moderate	4–6	22	17
Bearings	Slight to Moderate	4–7	14	8
Cigarettes	Slight to Moderate	6–12	23	14
Beer	Moderate	10–14	13	1
Refrigerators	Moderate	14–20	21	4

Source: Adapted from F. M. Scherer, *Industrial Market Structure and Economic Performance* (Chicago: Rand McNally, 1980): pp. 188–89.

But there are tight limits to its usefulness. The method is worthless for evaluating firm-level economies, because it automatically includes pecuniary economies. Even some plant estimates may be tainted by pecuniary conditions. This problem is most acute in precisely those problem industries (those with few firms holding high market shares) for which good normative measures are most urgently needed. Moreover, the technique does not clarify the shape of the cost curve either outside or inside the estimated range of optimal scale.

There are also sharp practical problems. The Census Bureau bases its plant data on the number of workers in each plant, not on output. If innovation is labor saving, then all plants may appear to be shrinking faster than their true output levels are. Also, actual survivor tests have been unable to discern coherent shift patterns in most industries. Instead, most shifts appear to be erratic and meaningless.[17]

Accordingly, only a handful of survivor results from numerous past studies can be regarded as reliable. They fit the findings from the engineering estimates quite well; MES appears to be less than 2 percent of the industry's total size in most cases.

Existing Size Distributions.   The present sizes of plants give a possible hint of what the optimal size is. At the extreme, if *all* plants are size *y*, that is likely to be the optimal size. If no plants are size *z*, that is almost certainly not the optimal size. Thus a careful researcher begins by at least inspecting the actual size distribution of plants for any strong patterns.

3.   An Antitrust Dilemma?

Altogether, economies of scale appear to be limited, so that market shares above 20 percent will usually embody a substantial degree of excess market share.

That is true of nearly all dominant firms in nationwide industrial markets in the United States in recent decades (recall chapter 3): General Motors, IBM, Eastman Kodak, Campbell Soup, Xerox, and Gillette are leading examples.[18]

A 10-percent market share is quite consistent with effective competition. Consequently **there has been virtually no important antitrust trade-off,** which might theoretically require a hard choice between competition and economies of scale. The new-Chicago attack on antitrust policies has evidently come partly from ideological leanings rather than from a sound scientific basis.

QUESTIONS FOR REVIEW

1. Explain how physical laws may favor larger size but then be harmful at still larger sizes.

2. Explain how high transport costs usually make the MES of plants larger than it would be from internal factors alone.

3. Explain the larger trends that have favored small-scale operations since the 1930s.

4. Explain why engineering estimates are the best all-around method, to be supplemented from other sources.

5. Explain the difference between technical and pecuniary economies of scale.

6. Show and discuss what is meant by *room for competition* and *excess market share*. Try to indicate what those values might be for several real markets.

ENDNOTES

[1]Among the important treatments are Charles J. Bullock, "Trust Literature: A Survey and Criticism," *Quarterly Journal of Economics* 15 (February 1900–01): pp. 167–217; John M. Clark, *Studies in the Theory of Overhead Costs* (New York: Macmillan, 1922); W. Arthur Lewis, *Overhead Costs* (London: Allen & Unwin, 1948); Joe S. Bain, *Barriers to New Competition* (Cambridge: Harvard University Press, 1956); and F. M. Scherer, Alan Beckenstein, Erich Kaufer, and R. Dennis Murphy, *The Economics of Multiplant Operation: An International Comparisons Study* (Cambridge: Harvard University Press, 1975).

[2]Thus Ford's giant pre-1920 automobile plant at River Rouge near Detroit was far oversized as soon as it was built. The scale of most automobile plants today is but a small fraction of that one.

[3] A further layer to the Internet's role is the "declustering" effect. The Internet allows colleagues in many firms to locate almost anywhere. That further dissolves the supposed advantages of large plants and firms. See Joel Kotkin, *The New Geography: How the Digital Revolution is Reshaping the American Landscape* (New York: Random House, 2001).

[4]See also Walter Adams and James W. Brock, *The Bigness Complex* (New York: Pantheon Books, 1985); and Adams and Brock, *Dangerous Pursuits* (New York: Pantheon Books, 1991).

[5]See also T. A. Abbott and S. H. Andrews, "The Structure of U.S. Manufacturing: A Technological Perspective," *Journal of Social and Economic Measurement* 19 (1993): pp. 241–79.

[6]See especially Scherer et al. *Economics of Multiplant Operation*. Scale economies differ from possible economies of scope in network industries (recall chapter 6); see Borje Johansson, Charlie Karlsson, and Lars Westin, eds., *Patterns of Network Economy* (New York: Springer, 1994) for a wide survey; and F. M. Scherer and David Ross, *Industrial Market Structure and Economic Performance*, 3rd ed. (Boston: Houghton Mifflin, 1991), chapter 10.

[7] Adam Smith, *The Wealth of Nations* (New York: Random House, Modern Library ed., 1937), book 1, chapters 1–3. Smith used a pin factory as his illustration, but the process can be seen in virtually every modern factory or shop. For example, a restaurant with a cook and waiter instead of two cook-waiters involves specialization; a factory with 20,000 workers will have specialization among assemblers, supervisors, secretaries, janitors, drivers, and scores of other jobs.

[8] See Scherer et al., *Economics of Multiplant Operation*, chapter 2, for analysis of the transport factor.

[9] See the sources in Scherer and Ross, *Industrial Market Structure and Economic Performance*, pp. 98–99; William J. Fellner, "Specific Interpretations of Learning by Doing," *Journal of Economic Theory* 1 (August 1969): pp. 119–40; and L. E. Yelle, "The Learning Curve: Historical Review and Comprehensive Survey," *Decision Sciences* 10 (1979): pp. 302–28.

[10] This method was popular from the 1890s through the 1930s. Among a number of studies, no clear pattern emerged; high profitability was registered variously by firms with low and high market shares. Such inconclusive results were, in any case, irrelevant to the normative issue.

[11] Bain, *Barriers to New Competition*; Scherer et al., *Economics of Multiplant Operation*; Cliff F. Pratten, *Economies of Scale in Manufacturing Industry* (Cambridge: Cambridge University Press, 1971); and Pratten, *The Competitiveness of Small Firms* (New York: Cambridge University Press, 1991).

[12] Stigler, "The Economies of Scale," *Journal of Law and Economics* 1 (October 1958): pp. 54–71, extols the method. Limits are noted in William G. Shepherd, "What Does the Survivor Technique Show about Economies of Scale?" *Southern Economic Journal* 36 (July 1967): pp. 113–22; and Joe S. Bain, "Survival-Ability as a Test of Efficiency," *American Economic Review* 59 (May 1969): pp. 99–104.

[13] Within this approach, there are differing methods. Some researchers use interviews mainly, some use questionnaires, others prefer elaborate analysis of the factors affecting optimal scale, and still others rely heavily on searches of the journals that engineers and other experts read. All four tactics have value, and the best studies use all to some degree.

[14] Through interviews with 125 companies, plus journal reading, they estimated MES and cost-gradient conditions as of the late 1960s. Since there were seventy-two industry-country cases, they averaged less than two actual interviews per each. Still, their project was a major effort. It also explored some features of multiplant conditions.

[15] Weiss relied on interviews or questionnaires covering from three to fourteen sources per industry. See Leonard W. Weiss, "Optimal Plant Size and the Extent of Suboptimal Capacity," in Robert T. Masson and P. David Qualls, eds., *Essays on Industrial Organization in Honor of Joe S. Bain* (Cambridge: Ballinger, 1976), chapter 7.

[16] It was actually pioneered by Thorp and Crowder in the 1930s, well before Stigler proposed it in 1958. See Willard F. Thorp and Walter F. Crowder, *The Structure of Industry*, Monograph 27, Temporary National Economic Committee (Washington, DC: U.S. Government Printing Office, 1941), part 1, chapter 2, pp. 19–57.

[17] To take one example, a research study on 1947–1958 patterns began with 140 important industries. Yet there were reasonably clear "efficient-size" ranges for only ten of those 140 cases. And several of these estimates conflicted with estimates by Weiss and Bain. See Shepherd, "What Does the Survivor Technique Show?"

[18] See also William G. Shepherd, "Monopoly Profits and Economies of Scale," in John Craven, ed., *Industrial Organization, Antitrust and Public Policy* (Boston: Kluwer Nijhof, 1982).

Part

5

Behavior and Related Topics

Chapter

8

THE FIRM: CONCEPTS AND CONDITIONS

Few human inventions have had the vitality and variety of the enterprise. It is the building block of the economy's production. Its officials' decisions drive the competitive process or, in varying degrees, create and maintain monopoly.

This chapter could easily have been placed earlier in the book to clarify these basic conditions at the outset. However, **industrial organization studies firms' behavior in their market settings.** The inner workings of the enterprise are mostly a different topic.

The firm is analyzed here mainly to ensure that conditions of motives, profit risk, and corporate organization—**as they affect competitive and monopoly conditions**—are adequately covered. Therefore this is something of a survey chapter, focusing on organization in section 1, motivations in section 2, and real-world patterns in section 3.

I. CONCEPTS OF THE FIRM[1]

The essence of the enterprise is clear and simple: it is any unit where people produce a good or service. The enterprise may consist of one local plant (a factory, an office, or even a restaurant) or of many hundreds of such plants. The corner drugstore is an enterprise, and so are Microsoft, the Chicago White Sox, the hospital where you were born, and your own college.

Each firm has its own independent life, form, and powers of decision.[2] It is also embedded in a system of market processes, supply and customer relationships, and financial supervision. We start by considering purely internal conditions.

Each firm extends its boundaries to include activities that it can do more efficiently by **internal** controls than by **external** market transactions. If internal controls were always superior, each firm would try to expand to replace all market activities.

In theory, the contrast is extreme; internally, control is complete, whereas externally, market choices are free and fluid. In practice, however, there are shadings. Internal control ranges between being quite tight (in small unified firms) and being very tenuous (in many large diversified holding companies). External transactions range widely too, from brief and simple anonymous exchanges over to complicated and tight long-term commitments.

1. Choices and Forms

Choices.   The private firm's main purpose is to create profit.[3] It does this by feeding inputs into a production process and then selling the outputs, as shown in figure 8.1. If its sales revenues exceed what the firm pays for inputs, there is profit. Profit is a key measure of success. Profit is a vector of the firm's two main activities: (1) **producing outputs from inputs and then selling them,** and (2) **owning and managing the assets of the firm.**

These two activities are controlled mainly by the firm's top managers. They decide policy, and they not only order lower-level employees to carry out their decisions but also supervise the employees' work. If the firm is a corporation, its board of directors is legally responsible for its activities. The board may have a broad influence, but top managers usually dominate.

Production is a **flow concept,** a process through time. Its outcome is summarized in the firm's yearly income statement of revenues, costs, and profits. There are many inputs at certain prices and outputs at certain prices. The income statement embodies the following basic equation for profit (or net income):

$$\text{Profit} = \text{total revenue} - \text{total cost}$$

The firm's actual costs and revenues represent single points on its cost and demand curves. Good management minimizes the actual costs for a given level (or perhaps bundle of levels) of outputs.

Ownership is a **stock concept** involving control of a firm at each point. Financial values appear in a firm's balance sheet of assets and liabilities. The firm's capital assets embody its tangible production core: physical capital (land, buildings, equipment), inventories, and working capital. The firm also exists in the human capital of its workers and in the ongoing organization of the whole business. **Capital is the tangible form in which the firm's private owners bear risk and draw profit.** Profits are earned for the owners, as shown in the **income statement**, and are transferred to the **balance sheet**.

The owners are the stockholders; the board of directors is supposed to supervise the firm solely in their interests. The pivotal identifying fact of private corporate ownership is the **issuance of voting stock to private holders.** Shareholders want rising profits. The actual and/or expected future rises of profits usually lead investors to bid up the price of the company stock, providing **capital gains** to the shareholders.

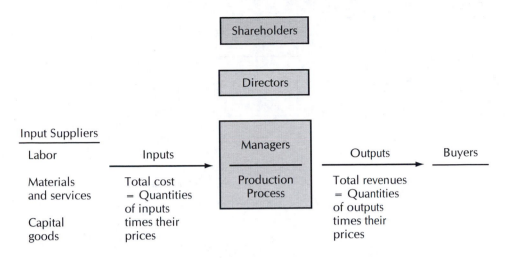

Figure 8.1   The basic economic elements of an enterprise.

Profitability is the percentage rate of return on the owners' capital, as follows:

$$\text{Rate of return} \ = \ \frac{\text{profit}}{\text{equity capital}}$$

For any given level of capital, stockholders want the rate of return to be maximized. In the long run, the level and pattern of investment are to be optimized, which will maximize the present value of the firm. **This present value in turn is, ideally, reflected at every moment by the stock market's evaluation of the firm and its prospects.** The company's total market value at each time simply equals the current share price times the number of shares outstanding. Therefore profits and the stock price are the two main success indicators of the corporate firm (more details are given later).

The firm is a complex and changing set of activities going on within a corporate shell, which itself can be changed by the company's officials. Managers evolve certain forms, techniques, and rules for their firm from among many possibilities. Profit maximizing is the animating and guiding force, but day-to-day judgments and actions by managers are often debatable.

Indeed, there is always room for choice and debate about all aspects of every firm. Efficient, lively firms do in fact have a continuing process of internal debate and change. The formal, legal conditions of the firm (e.g., owners' rights or organization charts and responsibilities) may appear fixed and rigid from the outside, but they only express human efforts and experiments, which are changeable.

What happens within the standard business setting is richly human. The marvel of the modern corporation is that it channels the unruly variety of human behavior along relatively consistent and productive lines, which we study here. Those lines evolve, and the degree of efficiency is always an open issue.

Forms.   Figure 8.2 depicts typical corporate structure. The basic functions in all firms are similar, but in larger firms, they are more specialized and complex.

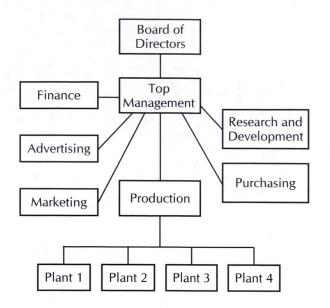

Figure 8.2   A functional structure.

A basic dilemma arises: **Specializing** permits a gain in the efficiency of doing a specific task, but it requires a **separation of activities** among people. That separation makes it more difficult for upper managers to coordinate production and to obtain accurate information about what is happening. The separation also diffuses responsibility. In short, high specialization breeds bureaucracy.

In a one-manager firm, all activities are done by one person—amateurish perhaps, but certainly coordinated! Any sizable firm has to divide its activities among tens, hundreds, or thousands of employees. There are two basic ways to delegate authority over these activities: along **functional** lines or along **divisional** lines. Figure 8.2 shows a functional division. Each subunit is specialized to its task and is the only part of the firm that does it. A three-branch divisional form is depicted in figure 8.3. Each division (really a separate firm under the holding company) combines many functions and operates in parallel with the others.

2.   Success Indicators: Profits and Stock Prices

1.   *Profitability* is the main index of a private firm's economic performance. The company may boast about its socially attractive activities, such as the number of jobs it creates, the high-quality outputs it produces, its exports, its innovations, and so on. But these are all secondary to the firm's main goal: to earn a large and increasing flow of profits for its investors.

Profitability is a matter of degree, not of absolute amounts. The simple total of dollar profits is not enough to show how profitable a firm is. **Profit as a percentage of capital or rate of return on equity is the correct measure of profitability,** for that shows how well the firm is managing its owners' capital.

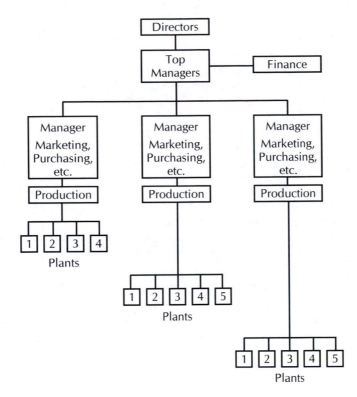

Figure 8.3 A three-branch decentralized divisional firm.

The simple formula for profitability is as follows:

$$\text{Rate of return} = \frac{\text{net income after taxes}}{\text{capital}}$$

$$= \frac{\text{total revenue} - \text{total cost and taxes}}{\text{invested capital}}$$

For example, a large firm might have the following figures for a year:

$$\text{Rate of return} = \frac{\$433 \text{ million}}{\$1,302 \text{ million}} = 33.3 \text{ percent}$$

This is a remarkably high rate of return, but it only covers one year. To judge the firm's profitability carefully, you must consider the average profit over some three to five years to even out any odd yearly fluctuations.

Profits must average higher than the cost of capital 8 to 10 percent for interest and the average rate of return in competitive markets. The nightmare is to run losses.

2.   *Stock prices* are the other main success indicator for the private firm. Each share of stock offers its owners a chance to gain future dividends and **capital gains** (that is, a rise in the price of the share itself). Firms' managers want to satisfy investor-owners by making the company prosper so that dividends will grow and/or the stock price will rise and provide capital gains. The share's price depends on demand and supply in the stock market. Both supply and demand, in turn, depend on what most investors think of the company's profit performance, both now and expected in the future.

Since most large-scale investors are pretty well-informed, they act quickly (recall chapter 6). Therefore stock prices usually move swiftly and sensitively. Accordingly, the market value of a stock largely depends both on the firm's future prospects and on its current performance in maximizing profits.

Current stock prices are a comprehensive, sensitive index of investors' judgments about each firm's whole performance, both present and expected. For managers and owners, this is *the* index of company performance. It is a powerful lever—or treadmill—forcing managers to perform well.

3.   Corruption and False Information

This discussion assumes honest accounting and full information as the bedrock of well-managed firms and informed stock-market decisions. Such integrity has been common, under enforcement by the Securities and Exchange Commission. But the stock-market bubble of the 1990s bred sharp deviations by some leading companies. Enron became the most notorious example.[4] Managers devised ways to abuse their companies, workers, and investors while fabricating huge capital gains for themselves.

This distorted the usual structure of incentives, in which managers' interests were aligned with their companies' profits. The distortions required dishonest accounting, and a reassertion of accounting standards after 2001 probably cured much of the problem. But the problems, and possible abuses, are endemic.

4.   Other Types of Firms

Much of this chapter's content applies not only to private profit-making firms but also to public, nonprofit, and cooperative firms.[5] All firms need to make efficient choices about inputs, outputs, and investments. But for these other types of firms, profit is not the single overriding motive. They usually have social goals as well. Some of these firms seek to supply goods to needy people at low prices. Others provide important services that no private firm could supply at a profit. Still others furnish utility services (such as city water and basic postal service) for which private operators, having a monopoly position, might charge too high a price.

Taken together, these non-private firms are a diverse and important group of enterprises, covering nearly one-fourth of all U.S. economic activity. Economists have studied them very little, however. The four main types follow.

Public enterprises are found in all sizes at the national, state, and local levels. They provide schools and universities, libraries, parks, electricity, ports, courts, health care, cemeteries, and much else.[6]

Not-for-profit enterprises also include a great variety of firms owned by charitable groups that often have some special social purpose. Examples are many charitable hospitals, private schools and private colleges (Harvard, Yale, Earlham, Wabash, Pomona, and hundreds of others), the Red Cross system, city orchestras and cultural centers, and thousands of day-care centers. Many of these units sell their services, but most also rely heavily on contributions. Some struggle, always short of funds; others enjoy ample financing and rapid growth.

Cooperatives are enterprises owned by their customers or suppliers.[7] Millions of farmers sell their crops, livestock, and milk through farm cooperatives, and they buy much of their supplies from them too.[8] Electric-utility cooperatives have been important since the 1930s.[9] In the retail sector, cooperative stores are common near or on many campuses (the Yale Co-op, the Harvard Co-op, etc.). In all cases, cooperative enterprises try to cover their costs with sales revenue, and they channel their profits back to their owners (customers or suppliers).

Worker-owned firms in the U.S. include United Airlines and the Avis car rental firm, as well as scores of lesser ones. They were the prevalent form in Yugoslavia before 1990 (and the transition to standard forms is gradual). The Mondragon enterprises in Spain are another example, and there are others in various countries.

II. MOTIVATION

1. OWNERSHIP AND CONTROL

Most literature focuses on standard **owner-manager** topics: Who owns and controls the firm? What are their motives?[10] **Entrepreneurship** may also be important—inspiration, complex creative actions, and larger-than-life sagas, as celebrated by Schumpeter.[11] Because that is a relatively unsystematic topic, more difficult to dissect and test, this section deals with traditional topics.

In the millions of small businesses, ownership and control are combined in one person who makes decisions and also benefits from whatever financial success the firm achieves. **As size increases, ownership tends to become divorced from control.** Stocks are bought and sold among many investors, while managers become a more specialized group who draw salaries and may own little of their company's stock.

This divorce of ownership from control evolved after 1890 as large corporations grew and stockholding became diffused. In a landmark book published in 1932, Berle and Means argued that this divorce—a "managerial revolution"—had changed the nature of large corporations.[12] Managers were now free from tight control and able to run their firms pretty much as they wished. Since 1932 the trend has continued, so that in many of the largest 1,000 corporations there is no major controlling block of shares.

Boards of directors still supervise the executives and have to approve all major decisions, but the board and the executives are often largely independent of stockholder control and can select their own members and set their own guidelines. Indeed, as the scandals of 2000–2002 made clear, top executives have dominated many boards of directors, holding key positions, selecting other members, and controlling discussions. Single owners or large financial institutions (banks, insurance firms) may hold 2, 5, or even 10 percent of the stock in some of these companies, but control is still firmly in the hands of managers.

Such firms may still perform virtually all their activities and make decisions just as if control and ownership were unified. Indeed, a number of studies have shown that the divorce is not as great or as influential on behavior as has been claimed.[13]

Moreover, managerial control need not be harmful. It may encourage continuity and professionalism by replacing the old-style industrial buccaneer with the skilled modern manager. Actions may be more predictable and objective, rather than reflecting the whims of a single owner. However, managers may focus less on maximizing profits for the owners and more on growth and managerial perquisites for themselves.

2. Managers' Goals

Managers are not automatons who make mechanical decisions that maximize profits. Their own personal motivations may influence corporate outcomes, and so these motives need to be examined.

Most managers are rewarded for good performance by extra pay, bonuses, and promotions.[14] Their performance is rated by various criteria, such as personal efficiency, growth, or profits of their unit or specific actions. At lower levels, there are fairly objective tests and comparisons for finding out who is doing well. The criteria are usually designed to fit the policy goals laid down by the top managers.

At higher management levels the criteria for performance are less precise, and personal differences in style and judgment come to the fore. Upper managers settle complex issues of judgment that are unique, nonrepeatable, and uncertain. Moreover, the upper manager's pay is a complex matter of bargaining and personal assertion that is not neatly tied to actual contribution. In the 1990s, that arrangement became an acute issue as many top managers essentially gave themselves yearly pay of over $10 million.

Agency Theory.   The practical difficulties of judging top management's performance have given rise in recent years to theories about the principal-agent problem.[15] The basis of agency theory is the fact, known since Berle and Means's 1932 book, that managers, though acting as agents for the stockholders (the principals, or owners of the firm), may have motives that diverge from those of the principals they are supposed to serve. The theory notes that these divergences can be examined under various assumed conditions.

Agency theory assumes that managers vary in their effort levels, and that valid judgments on their performance depend on having access to information about the firm's performance possibilities. In plain English, managers may try to hide the firm's real opportunities so they can ease up in their work. Some of the analysis also uses insurance and risk concepts, in which owners seek to attain maximum profits subject to various constraints about the risk of capital losses.

Much of the theory has focused on ways to design management pay so as to align managers' interests with those of the owners. The results have been predictable: pay and bonuses should be tied to profits and/or capital gains through

Table 8.1   Directions for Managers' Motivations

Direction of Preferences	Comments
Profit	This is traditionally the primary criterion.
Time preference	This may vary sharply but still be consistent with long-run profit maximizing.
Risk	Is risk aversion "normal"? Managers differ in attitudes toward risk.
Expense preferences	These are a form of nonpecuniary rewards—"the good life." They may also include simple sloth and slack, or "the quiet life."
Sales maximizing	Or growth maximizing. Sales may just be a rule of thumb for seeking maximum long-run profits.
Social values	These may tip occasional close decisions. "Goodwill" from social actions may increase profits, too.

profit-sharing or stock option schemes. Those two devices are in fact widely used, and they help keep most managers close to the profit-maximizing goal.

Directions of Managers' Motivations. Still, managers' styles and motives may explain some of the striking differences in performance among real firms. Table 8.1 notes some main points from the growing research on the topic.

Managers' time preferences will set companies' long-run profit strategies. Replacing a farsighted president with one with a more short-term focus can shift the strategy sharply.

Risk is that part of future uncertainty that is relatively systematic and predictable, but which is still dangerous because it can bring financial ruin. Managers often have strong preferences concerning risk; most are risk averse, but some actually prefer risk.[16]

Expenses may be preferred by managers, rather than squeezed to the minimum. Any company has many directions in which a slight increase in inputs can be used to add to the managers' sense of status and affluence. The results can be opulent, especially in things seen and used by top managers. Or they may be subtle and easy to justify as higher quality, as good for the company's image, as necessary to attract good managers, and so forth. X-inefficiency and slack are concepts that include this effect. In extreme cases, the added expenses can soak up much of the available profits.

Sales maximizing may also occur. Managers may choose to enlarge their sales as a criterion of success, because large and growing sales enhance their own sense of importance, and/or greater sales may tend to result indirectly in maximum long-run profits. Research on this idea has been inconclusive.

Social contributions often are implicit in a company's actions. Every important decision has impacts on jobs, sales, and prices, which help some and hurt others outside the firm. Managers might temper their private profit-maximizing decisions with these social concerns.

Normally, profits are reduced when such social aims alter managers' choices. One instance is keeping an unprofitable plant going—or locating a new plant in a distressed region—in order to provide jobs. Others are voluntary avoidance of pollution, buying American, helping in urban redevelopment, and contributing to education, churches, and other worthy groups.

Yet the corporate system leans strongly against social motives. The stock market treadmill effect tends to squeeze them out. Managers are rarely trained or encouraged to perform with social awareness on the job, though social actions may be approved as a spare-time hobby. Therefore any seeming corporate philanthropy is usually intended to create goodwill as part of a larger strategy for long-run profit maximizing.

3. PROFITS AND RISK

The return to capital contains several distinct economic elements: (1) **the pure interest rate on invested capital,** which would be earned if investment had no risk; (2) a **risk premium,** which is an additional return required to reward investors for risky investment; and (3) any remainder, which is **economic profit** (or excess profit; excess above the cost of capital to the firm).

When funds are invested, the owner bears some risk about the outcome. Since risk is normally viewed as unpleasant, investors must be rewarded with extra returns. A risk-return relationship is, accordingly, a basic feature of investment decisions. To analyze it, we must first define risk (recall the discussion of risk in chapter 4).

Risk means a degree of hazard. For the firm, the hazard is financial. Bankruptcy and insolvency are the extreme cases, but there are lesser degrees of distress. If the bad result can be defined, then risk is the probability of its occurring. Thus risk has two components: severity and probability.

Risk actually takes two forms: long-term and short-term.

Long-term risk is the danger of a basic change that may damage or kill the firm. Examples are electronic calculators that wiped out the slide rule, the CD and audio tapes that terminated the old vinyl record, or optical fiber that rendered most copper telephone wires obsolete. Risk exists when these deadly changes are not foreseen.

Short-term risk is the rapid fluctuations of profits as time passes. In some firms, this jumpiness in profits is sharp, and that seems to make the firm risky. This concept can be useful in guiding portfolio choices made by investors, and it also clarifies some choices made by managers.

Long-term risk is usually much more important: the basic position of the firm will be shaken or eliminated by big changes in technology, taste, or competitive conditions. Defining risk is controversial. Yet even if measurement is difficult, one can still analyze risk-return choices in theory.

The Risk-Return Relationship. As chapter 4 noted, risk is unpleasant, and people will usually accept it only if they expect compensating rewards. The result is the concept of a risk-return relationship: Investments with higher risks usually tend to offer higher average returns.

III. REAL FIRMS

Turning now to real enterprises in real markets, we discuss mainly private corporations, for they handle most of the market activity in Western economies.

1. CORPORATIONS

Private corporations conduct over three-fourths of U.S. economic activity, dominating manufacturing and utilities. In farming, retailing, and services, other business types (partnerships, small proprietorships, cooperatives, nonprofits, public firms, etc.) also are common. The shares have been steady for several decades.

Almost all really large enterprises are corporations, for several familiar reasons. Shareholders' liability is limited to the value of their investment. Large volumes of capital can be raised more easily. And the corporation need not be reorganized when mere mortals pass on. Therefore most goods are actually produced in corporations, though consumers may do most of their personal dealings with noncorporate retailing firms.

In the size distribution of all U.S. corporations, the relatively few largest ones do *not* dominate. Firms below $1 billion in assets do some 60 percent of sales by all corporations. The patterns are not much different in Britain, France, and other Western countries. We may visualize several kinds of corporations, ranging from small to medium, large, and very large. Small and medium corporations often are managed by the main owner and relatives. Company structure is simple and the product line is usually narrow.

As size increases, these patterns grow complex. Managers are often largely free of tight shareholder control, and they often dominate the board of directors. That can invite abuses, and it led at the turn of the millennium to abuses, fraud, and scandals.

2. TRENDS AND SHARES AMONG CORPORATIONS

Large private corporations are important. But what is their scope? What causes their position to change? What kind of ties exist between them? And how do U.S. corporations compare to foreign ones in these respects?

The Largest Firms. The few really giant industrial corporations are a special group, not an archetype for other enterprises. Several of the very largest (including General Motors and IBM) have had dismal inefficiency and poor innovation after 1970 thanks to their market dominance and sheer size. Not-so-large firms do not generally share these problems. In short, giantism in the megacorp is a specialized situation; it is subject to X-inefficiency and poor innovation rather than being a fine cutting edge of best practices.

Causes of Change. Large firms may display two kinds of change: (1) trends in their aggregate share in the economy and (2) changes in their individual rankings. Both changes arise from the same four main causes:

1. *Industry Growth Rates and Price Trends Differ.* In recent decades, such industries as electronics, communications, copiers, and computers have enjoyed rapid growth, pulling up firms in these industries. By contrast,

slow growth in steel, meatpacking, copper, and other industries has exerted a downward pull on their firms.

2. ***Mergers Have Caused Big Shifts In Company Rankings,*** particularly after 1980. But mergers have not strongly affected aggregate concentration. From 1909 to 1947, mergers' role was modest, and from 1947 to 1980, mergers equaled only about 15 percent of all the asset growth of the 200 largest firms. Even the 1980s and 1990s merger booms have probably affected the totals only slightly.

3. ***Government Agencies Are Decisive For Some Industries.*** The Pentagon and the Department of Energy have paid for a large share of all industrial R & D, and in some industries they pay for nearly all of it (recall chapter 5). They are also large buyers of the outputs from certain industries. The effects on growth and size are often mixed, but they can be strong, as in the aircraft and communications industries.

4. ***The Relative Efficiency of Large Firms May Be Decisive.*** When large corporations' share rose from 1947 to 1965, it was said to reflect their superior efficiency. Yet the real cause could have been pecuniary economies. At any rate, the steadiness of total shares after 1965 suggests a general absence of superior efficiency.

Comparisons with Other Countries. There are contrasting possibilities. Foreign firms may reflect a smaller-scale technology, and therefore be smaller and less dominant in their own economies. Or, since foreign economies are smaller than the United States, the shares of large firms in them may be larger.

The data are inconclusive on this issue. In fact, there are only a few sets of data, and these deal only with the manufacturing sectors. The clearest basis for comparison is with Britain. Aggregate British concentration matched that of the United States from 1910 to 1955. Between then and the 1970s, British concentration rose sharply, to one-third higher than the U.S. level. Meanwhile, West German concentration rose to about the U.S. level in the 1970s. Japanese aggregate concentration has long been higher than in the United States, and now is probably about the same as in Britain.[17] On this and other evidence, American concentration emerges as probably comparable to foreign levels.

Informal connections among companies may also affect the true degree of economic power. Ties between firms and bankers—and within family groupings—are more extensive in many other countries than they are in the United States. Japan, Germany, and Sweden have especially extensive networks of this sort.

In Japan, the extraordinary **zaibatsu** combines extended by 1940 to all sectors of the economy (as chapter 5 noted). The largest seven combines held one-fourth of all Japanese assets.[18] Facing one another in hundreds of markets, they often adopted diplomatic coexistence instead of competition. The three largest combines (Mitsui, Mitsubishi, and Sumitomo) were partly dissolved between 1946 and 1948 under MacArthur, but by 1960 they were largely reassembled. Though looser than before, these combines still provide a degree of unity and control.

German banks hold large blocks of company shares, acting as centers of support and control. In Sweden, there are also important family groupings. No thorough measures of such connections have been made, so we do not know their precise extent and strength. Yet these factors might well make effective aggregate concentration higher abroad than in the United States.

Questions for Review

1. "Corporations exist to produce; profits are a byproduct." Or: "Corporations exist to make profits; production is a byproduct." Discuss these views.

2. "The key identifying fact of private ownership is the issuance of voting stock to private holders." Explain this statement.

3. Explain how, even if a firm's profit volume is large, its managers may genuinely believe that they have little room for discretion.

4. What determines the boundary between the firm and the market process?

5. What criteria determine if a 10-, 15-, 25-, or 45-percent rate of return on capital is good?

6. Explain how managers as agents may deviate from the interests of stock-owners as principals. Are the deviations very large, in your judgment?

Endnotes

[1] Among the rich variety of writings on the nature of the firm, see Sharon Oster, *Modern Competitive Analysis* (New York: Oxford University Press, 1999); Alfred D. Chandler, Jr., Peter Hagstrom, and Orjan Solvell, eds., *The Dynamic Firm: The Role of Technology, Strategy, Organization and Regions* (New York: Oxford University Press, 1998); Ronald H. Coase, "The Nature of the Firm," *Economica* 4 (November 1937): pp. 386–405; Kenneth J. Arrow, *The Limits of Organization* (New York: Norton, 1974); and Alfred D. Chandler, Jr., *The Visible Hand: The Managerial Revolution in American Business* (Cambridge: Belknap Press, 1977).

[2] On the larger style and responsiveness of firms, see two excellent conceptual studies by Michael E. Porter, *Competitive Advantage: Creating and Sustaining Superior Performance* (New York: Free Press, 1985); and *Competitive Strategy: Techniques for Analyzing Industries and Competitors* (New York: Free Press, 1980).

[3] Other types—public firms, nonprofit enterprises, cooperatives, etc.—are discussed below in subsection 3.2. Many of their features, such as accounting, structure, and technology, are identical with those of private firms.

[4] See for example Loren Fox, *Enron: The Rise and Fall* (New York: John Wiley & Sons, 2002); Robert Bryce, *Pipe Dreams: Greed, Ego and the Death of Enron* (New York: Public Affairs Press, 2002); and Brian Cruver, *Anatomy of Greed: Unshredded Truth From an Enron Insider* (New York: Caroll & Graf, 2002).

[5] Charles T. Clotfelter, ed., *Who Benefits from the Nonprofit Sector?* (Chicago: University of Chicago Press, 1992); Avner Ben-Ner and Benedetto Gui, eds., *The Nonprofit Sector in the Mixed Economy* (Ann Arbor: University of Michigan Press, 1993).

[6] The nature of public enterprises has been clarified by the wave of "privatizing" since 1980 that converted many of them to private enterprises. Chapter 17 discusses this transition. Among the large literature, see Bill Bradshaw and Helen Lawton Smith, eds., *Privatization and Deregulation of Transport* (London: St. Martin's Press, 2000); David M. Newbery, *Privatization, Restructuring and Regulation of Network Utilities* (Cambridge: MIT Press, 1999). See William L. Megginson and Jeffrey M. Netter, "From State to Market: A Survey of Empirical Studies on Privatization," *Journal of Economic Literature* 39 (June 2001): pp. 321–389, for a extensive review of the subject; also Elliott D. Sclar, *You Don't Always Get What You Pay For: The Economics of Privatization* (Ithaca, NY: Cornell University Press, 2000), for a strong critique of privatization's flaws; and Mitsuhiro Kagami and Masatsugu, eds., *Privatization, Deregulation and Economic Efficiency: A Comparative Analysis of Asia, Europe and the Americas* (Northampton, MA: Elgar, 2000).

[7]See Jeff Bailey, "Co-ops Gains as Firms Seek Competitive Power," *Wall Street Journal* (October 15, 2002): p. B5; and Richard J. Sexton and Julie Iskow, "What Do We Know About the Economic Efficiency of Cooperatives: An Evaluative Survey," *Journal of Agricultural Cooperation* 8 (1993): pp. 15–27.

[8]Richard T. Rogers and Lisa M. Petraglia, "Agricultural Cooperatives and Market Performance in Food Manufacturing," *Journal of Agricultural Cooperation* 10 (1995): pp. 1–12.

[9]Mitchel Benson, "As Woes Mount for Utilities, Cities Try to Take Charge," *Wall Street Journal* (November 4, 2002): pp. A1, A8; and *Electric Cooperatives: On the Threshold of a New Era* (Public Utilities Reports, Congers, NY: 1996); see also various issues of *Public Utilities Fortnightly.*

[10]For example, H. Mehran, "Executive Compensation Structure, Ownership, and Firm Performance," *Journal of Financial Economics* 38 (June 1995): pp. 163–84.

[11]See Bruce A. Kirchhoff, *Entrepreneurship and Dynamic Capitalism* (Westport, CT: Praeger, 1994); R. T. Hamilton and D. A. Harper, "The Entrepreneur in Theory and Practice," *Journal of Economic Studies* 21 (1994): pp. 3–18; E. J. O'Boyle, "On the Person and the Work of the Entrepreneur," *Review of Social Economy* 52 (Winter 1994): pp. 315–37; and for more advanced analysis, William J. Baumol, *Entrepreneurship, Management, and the Structure of Payoffs* (Cambridge: MIT Press, 1993).

[12]A. A. Berle and Gardiner C. Means, *The Modern Corporation and Private Property* (New York: Macmillan, 1932); rev. ed., Harcourt, Brace & World, 1968.

[13]See F. M. Scherer and David Ross, *Industrial Market Structure and Economic Performance* (Boston: Houghton Mifflin, 1991), chapter 2, and sources there; Philip H. Burch, Jr., *The Managerial Revolution Reassessed* (Lexington, MA: Heath, 1972); and William A. McEachem, *Managerial Control and Performance* (Lexington, MA: Heath, 1975).

[14]R. L. Lippert and W. T. Moore, "Compensation Contracts of Chief Executive Officers: Determinants of Pay-Performance Sensitivity," *Journal of Financial Research* 17 (Fall 1994): pp. 321–32; M. J. Conyon and D. Leech, "Top Pay, Company Performance and Corporate Governance," *Oxford Bulletin of Economic Statistics* 56 (August 1994): pp. 229–47.

[15]J. E. Garen, "Executive Compensation and Principle-Agent Theory," *Journal of Political Economy* 102 (December 1994): pp. 1175–99; an early principle-agent discussion is Harvey J. Leibenstein, *Beyond Economic Man* (Cambridge: Harvard University Press, 1976); see also Jean Tirole, *The Theory of Industrial Organization* (Cambridge: MIT Press, 1988), pp. 51–55.

[16]For example, see J. Zwiebel, "Corporate Conservatism and Relative Compensation," *Journal of Political Economy* 103 (February 1995): pp. 1–25.

[17]See Takatoshi Ito, *The Japanese Economy* (Cambridge: MIT Press, 1992); H. Mayajima, "The Transformation of Zaibatsu to Postwar Corporate Groups—From Hierarchically Integrated Groups to Horizontally Integrated Groups," *Journal of Japanese International Economies* 8 (September 1994): pp. 293–328; and Richard E. Caves and Masu Uekusa, *Industrial Organization in Japan* (Washington, DC: Brookings Institution, 1977).

[18]See T. A. Bisson, *Zaibatsu Dissolution in Japan* (Berkeley: University of California Press, 1954); Johannes Hirschmeier and Tsunehiko Yui, *The Development of Japanese Business* (London: Allen & Unwin, 1981); and Kozo Yamamura, *Economic Policy in Postwar Japan: Growth versus Economic Democracy* (Berkeley: University of California Press, 1967).

Chapter

9

MONOPOLY,
DOMINANCE, AND ENTRY

Dominant firms are the foremost real situations of large monopoly power. They include famous firms, such as the notorious Standard Oil combine during 1870–1920 and General Motors and IBM from the 1930s to the 1980s. Current leaders are Microsoft, the Baby Bells in local telephone markets, Anheuser-Busch in beer, Eastman Kodak, your local newspaper—all those listed in table 3.4 and many others too.

They may capture their dominance by implementing anti-competitive actions, by their superior efficiency, or by still other methods. Often they rise by having better products or some special advantage, and then they hang on tenaciously.

In this chapter, we present the main ways in which **market dominance** starts and evolves.[1] First we review the main cases and trends of dominance, including how fast it fades away (chapter 13 will present case studies of actual dominant firms). Section 2 then explores how dominance starts, and section 3 considers some theories about how dominance evolves.

Section 4 then turns to a tangential topic: **potential competition and entry barriers**. Such entry conditions might set limits on how much power the dominant firm really has. Section 5 discusses dominant firms' reactions to those barriers. Although the topic of entry is often linked to oligopoly, it is clearer when instead it is related to dominant firms. Section 6 concludes with the extreme case of "ultrafree" entry (or "contestability").

I. LEADING CASES AND TRENDS OF DOMINANCE

1. LEADING CASES

In the United States, many leading dominant firms were created a century ago, back in the first great merger wave of 1897–1901. To see how widespread and brazen those changes were, see John Moody's fascinating survey of 1904.[2] He describes approvingly the several hundred dominant firms that were rapidly assembled by mergers across the whole range of U.S. industries.[3] Their later evolution was presented in 1965 by A. D. H. Kaplan.[4]

Many of these dominant firms faded quickly, but some (including General Electric, DuPont, and the Aluminum Company of America) are still prominent.

Table 3.4 presented some leading dominant firms of today, and tables 3.6 and 3.7 showed many of the biggest ones from 1910 down to the 1970s. Those lists are not complete, because the data on dominance are not fully available. Also, the hundreds of newspapers that dominate their city-area markets are too numerous to include individually. And hundreds of other dominant market positions are hidden within large diversified enterprises, which do not report them separately.[5]

2. TRENDS

The long trend of dominance in the economy has probably gone downward, as chapter 3 noted. In particular, single-firm dominance in industrial markets seems to have faded, especially since the rise of imports in the 1970s. Some utilities have evolved back toward naturally competitive technology, and many of those were deregulated after 1975. Yet deregulation has often led to dominance, and new dominant near-monopolies like Microsoft continue to emerge. Moreover, weak U.S. merger policies since 1980 have permitted hundreds of mergers that actually increased market dominance. Striking examples include banking, health care, drugs, telecommunications, electricity, accounting, and the information technology sector.

3. HOW FAST DOES DOMINANCE FADE?

The rate of erosion has been slow, as chapter 3 noted. Before 1970, high market shares receded at an average rate of only about half a percentage point per year, if the decline was not hastened by antitrust. Standard Oil, American Tobacco, Corn Products Co., and DuPont did decline substantially, but not from natural causes; they lost antitrust cases and were required to divest some of their capacity. The other firms listed in tables 3.6 and 3.7 generally declined slowly, or not at all, during the years up to 1970.

Since then, declines in U.S. dominant firms' market shares have been mixed or unclear, and some shares keep rising. Microsoft, for example, is extending its dominance into many new adjacent markets. Dominant firms do not, as a rule, decline very much.

II. SOURCES AND SUSTAINING FACTORS OF MONOPOLY AND DOMINANCE

How do firms achieve dominance, and what makes dominance persist? Free-market advocates credit it all to the firms' large-scale economies and superior innovations. Any other dominance, they say, comes from abuses of government power. But instead, dominance often has come from mergers, luck, anticompetitive actions, and maneuvers to exploit market imperfections. You must judge each situation skeptically for yourself.

Chapters 6 and 7 broadly reviewed the determinants of structure in all market types. Here we focus on specific determinants as they relate to dominance.

1. TECHNICAL SCALE ECONOMIES

Technical scale economies have mostly shrunk since the 1930s, under the long-run trends that chapter 7 explained. These economies are now large only in a few exceptional cases.

Natural Monopoly. During 1900–1960, technical economies of scale seemed to create natural monopolies in utility sectors, such as electric power, telephone service, Western railroads, and postal service.[6] But since then natural monopoly has been a shrinking phenomenon, which now occurs mainly within city areas in urban systems of supply. The local distribution of water, electricity, natural gas, cable TV, bus and subway service, and ambulance service may be remainders from the earlier numerous natural monopolies.

Dominance. The same is true of other sectors; technical economies of scale have usually been minor for dominant firms, as tables 7.1 and 7.2 suggested. Instead, dominant firms usually have excess market share, and there would be much room for more competition.

2. SUPERIOR PERFORMANCE

Little research has been done on this favorite free-market claim. Instead, there are prominent cases where *inferior* firms held on to their dominance for a long period: Chapter 4 noted IBM (1960s–1993), General Motors (1950s–1990s), and Microsoft (1980s–1990s) as just a few conspicuous instances. Market imperfections, sharpened by firms' adroit use of excess profits, has allowed dominance to continue long after inferiority has set in.

3. PURE LUCK AND FIRST-MOVER ADVANTAGES

By luck or skill, one firm often will move ahead of others to dominate a new market, as we saw in chapter 6. That drove the 1990s dot com bubble; each new market had hordes of start-up firms desperately scrambling to become the dominant firm. Once the leader got ahead of the pack, it could cash in its advantages to maintain its lead over equally capable rivals. Virtually all lasting dominant firms had some such advantages from being a "first mover," often by sheer luck.

4. MERGERS

Though mergers were a notable cause of dominance during the first great wave of 1897–1901, they had by 1950 receded to minor importance. Large horizontal mergers were effectively prevented after 1920 in many leading industries, though explicit merger constraints were not applied until the 1950s. The 1960s merger boom also involved few major horizontal mergers.

But the 1980s and 1990s merger booms brought back the dominance-creating merger. The wild merger wave during 1991–2000 especially brought an instant growth of dominant positions in airlines, newspapers, banking, health care, telecommunications, weapons, and scores more industries. Weak antitrust restraints continued even in 2002, when, for example, the AT&T-Comcast merger was permitted to combine the 1st- and 3rd- ranking firms.

5. TACTICS AND STRATEGIES

Dominant firms use a variety of devices to maintain or enhance their position. Strategic price discrimination has been very important for such leading cases as the old Standard Oil, United Shoe Machinery, IBM, Xerox, airlines, AT&T, and Microsoft. When timed well and carried far enough, price discrimination can become anti-competitive. These two types of price actions are covered in chapter 10.

III. MODELS OF DOMINANT FIRMS

Each dominant firm faces continuing choices about whether to increase, hold, or yield its market share. It weighs the benefits and costs of each alternative, perhaps adopting a long-run profit-maximizing strategy. Of course, external events also affect these choices, as when a small rival or new entrant suddenly challenges the dominant firm with a major new product.

This section describes some of the major models applied to these strategies.

1. THE DECLINING DOMINANT FIRM

Worcester noted in 1957 that dominant firms often decline, and he offered an analysis to explain why this may be so.[7] He posited the existence of fringe firms, each being tiny and all of them collectively adding up to a minor share of the market. But in his theory, dominant firms were entirely passive to the fringe firms. The dominant firm indeed declined, because it was (by assumption) helpless to stop the process.

This model was flawed because it assumed the result in advance. The fringe firms were assumed to have lower costs, so they would easily eat away the dominant firm's position. But the model had a fatal defect: it was unreal. Important real conditions like imperfections, fierce resistance by dominant firms, and price discrimination were all assumed away. Any of those three could permit the dominant firm to defeat or eliminate the fringe firms, even if the fringe had lower costs.

Dominant firms do not hold up a single-price umbrella while letting small firms steal their market position, as Worcester assumed. Instead, they sharpshoot their prices precisely, so as to meet and punish the fringe competitors in their market niches. They retain high prices elsewhere, so as to fund the sharpshooting and create other imperfections.

Real imperfections, retaliation, and price discrimination therefore nullify both the assumed decline and the rosy efficient-structure lesson. A realistic model will in fact include all of those three conditions, because they are usually important when there is dominance.

Yet Worcester's declining-dominance idea was widely accepted: "if dominant firms do not decline, it must be because they are equal or superior to fringe firms in efficiency." Instead, the model has no proof, and its assumptions were biased.

2. MODELING OPTIMAL CHOICES OVER TIME

In this more sophisticated analysis, dominant firms design their market-share strategy within a setting of constraints created by small rivals and/or new entrants. The pioneering work in this area was done by Darius Gaskins, but there have been some modifications.[8]

The dominant firm's choices are simplified to the following form:

$$\frac{dX}{dt} = k[P(t) - P_O]$$

where d is the incremental difference in, X is output, k is a constant, t is time, P is price, and P_O is the fringe firms' price. The ratio on the left-hand side of the equation is the rate at which the fringe firms will expand their total output in each time period (it is also the rate at which the dominant firm's output will contract). $P(t)$ is the dominant firm's single price at time t, while P_O is the level of cost (and, equally, price) of the fringe firms.

If the dominant firm sets its price $P(t)$ above the fringe firms' price P_O, then the fringe firms will take away market share from the dominant firm. The bigger the price gap, the faster the shift of market share. The k coefficient governs the general rate at which a given price difference causes a shift of market share.

This process involves dynamic shifts of market shares, which continue over time. But the model can only be as reliable as the information about k and the degree to which it fits actual market conditions.

Unfortunately, this model contains the same biases as Worcester's analysis. It ignores imperfections, retaliation, and price discrimination. It assumes that the dominant firm declines if the fringe firms have a cost (and price) advantage. Conversely, if the dominant firm persists, then it is assumed to be equal or superior in efficiency rather than exploiting imperfections.

In short, models of this sort assume that there are no interactions or price discrimination. Therefore they assume away much of the heart of the problem: the complex impacts which actual dominant firms impose on their small competitors.

The third approach has involved new entry by potential competitors from outside the market. It has inspired many papers, and so it is given a whole section, which follows.

IV. CONCEPTS OF ENTRY AND LIMIT PRICING

Now we turn to the topic of potential entry and barriers against new competition. They are said by their enthusiasts to be important, perhaps the dominant feature of markets. Viewed purely as a theory, entry can indeed be interesting. But as a guide to real markets, the "potential competition" topic has limited relevance and practical use. It's simply peripheral to the issues of real competition **inside** the market.

The main idea behind potential-competition theory is simple, as chapter 2 noted.[9] Dominant firms may spur new entry if they raise their prices high enough. So their choices will determine how "high" the barrier against potential competition may be. The barrier height can range from zero ("free entry") to very high ("blocked entry"). The incumbent firm's price can be raised up to a particular height (the limit price) without stimulating new entry; above that limit price, entry will occur. In the extreme case of free entry, there is no significant barrier at all. The threat of quick, powerful entry scares the dominant firm from raising prices at all. Free entry could nullify market power.

As we noted in chapter 2, this theory is controversial because it diverts attention away from markets' internal conditions out to its periphery. Also the theory has technical problems, as we will shortly explain. Yet entry became a popular topic after Bain stressed it in 1956. First we will consider the validity of this approach, and then we will review some of its results.

The topic of entry barriers has frequently been treated as an oligopoly subject, on the idea that several leading firms adopt a common strategy toward possible entrants. That idea fit the interest of Bain, who reintroduced barriers in 1956 as a factor likely to raise the market power of oligopolists.[10] But the theory's main relevance is probably for the single dominant firm. Therefore barriers are introduced in this chapter.

1. THE NATURE OF ENTRY

The concepts of entry and barriers have the surface intuitive appeal of a simple, clear metaphor: barriers are like sturdy dikes, holding back the sea of competition. However, the technical character of entry and barriers are actually quite complicated.[11]

The Extent of Entry. Entry is the addition of one or more new sellers to a market. It creates new capacity, adding to the market's whole capacity. Entry is therefore partly defined by the extent of the new firms' sales. Yet there is more to the topic. Other firms may **exit** from a market at the same time that new firms are entering it. Therefore only **net entry**—the entrants' combined new market share **after** subtracting the combined market share of any firms that exited during the period—is relevant.

Yet entry and exit among fringe firms are largely irrelevant to the position of the dominant firm. What matters is the bite that the new entrants take out of the dominant firm's market share. Accordingly, entry is correctly defined not in terms of the new entrants' own market shares, but rather **in terms of how much market share the dominant firm loses.**

The nature of the entrants is also significant. If twenty tiny fringe firms with 1-percent market share each are replaced by one entrant with a hefty 20-percent share, the competitive situation is likely to change, and vice versa.

Speed of Entry.   Entry may occur at any speed, from instantly to a glacial pace. Rapid entry has a greater impact, so an analysis ought to include speed of entry in estimating entry's effects.

Unfortunately, economists have not solved these complex issues or devised accurate measures of entry. There have been numerous studies of entry.[12] Yet entry remains a complicated and largely intuitive topic, whose technical conditions have not been resolved. Note that small-scale entry blends in with the host of small moves made by those fringe firms already inside the market. Potential competition can therefore be hard to separate from actual competition by small rivals. In fact, entry is just one element among all the conditions that dominant firms routinely deal with. And as we note below, neither the degree of entry nor the "height" of barriers has ever been measured reliably.

2.   BARRIERS AGAINST ENTRY

Barriers are the conditions—of all kinds—that make entry difficult. Bain emphasized just four main sources of barriers, which influence their height. Four decades of further analysis have added many other sources, all of them plausible and possibly important.[13] The list now numbers at least twenty-two, as presented in table 9.1.

The Sources of Barriers.   The sources come in two main categories: exogenous and endogenous. Exogenous sources are embedded in the underlying conditions of the market: technology, nature of the products, need for large-scale capital, and vertical integration, for example. Bain's pioneering discussion in 1956 stressed these familiar basic factors. Because they exist outside the leading firms' control, they are fundamental causes that cannot be altered.

Endogenous conditions and strategic actions are much more complicated, subtle, and sophisticated. They are within the dominant firm's own discretion; they are done strictly voluntarily. The firm can create barriers simply by choosing to take (or perhaps just threatening to take) actions against an entrant. These endogenous barriers are intangible and impossible to measure. They merely express the (unpredictable) willingness and ingenuity of the firm in taking actions against its little rivals and newcomers.

At a deeper level of meaning, such voluntary barriers merely reflect the degree of imperfections inherent to the market, which the dominant firm can exploit against existing rivals as well as against any possible entrants. Caves and Porter's concept of mobility barriers recognizes this point.[14] If those imperfections are large, then entry barriers will be high.

Ultimately, such barriers and imperfections simply blur together to entrench the dominant firm. With these cautions in mind, we can review the main sources of barriers in table 9.1.[15] First are thirteen exogenous sources.

1. ***Capital Requirements.*** The most general cost advantage is cheaper and more ample capital, which the established firm may get because of its greater size and security. This barrier inhibits entry into large, capital-intensive industries where minimum efficient scale is large (examples are oil refining and automobiles).

2. ***Scale Economies.*** These may force an entrant to come in, if at all, at a large market share. This will increase total industry capacity and the vol-

Table 9.1   Common Causes of Entry Barriers

I.   Exogenous Causes: *External Sources of Barriers*

1. ***Capital Requirements:*** related to the MES of plants and firms, capital intensity, and capital market imperfections.
2. ***Economies of Scale:*** both technical and pecuniary; require large-scale entry, with greater costs, risks, and intensity of retaliation.
3. ***Absolute Cost Advantages:*** many possible causes, including lower wage rates and lower-cost technology.
4. ***Product Differentiation:*** may be extensive.
5. ***Sunk Costs:*** any cost incurred by an entrant that cannot be recovered upon exit.
6. ***Research and Development Intensity:*** requires entrants to spend heavily on new technology and products.
7. ***Equipment is Highly Durable and Highly Specialized ("Asset Specificity"):*** makes entrants install costly, highly specialized equipment; entrants suffer large losses if the entry fails.
8. ***Vertical Integration:*** may require an entrant to enter at two or more stages of production; raises costs and risks.
9. ***Diversification by Incumbents:*** may make it possible to move resources around to defeat entrants.
10. ***Switching Costs:*** complex systems may entail costs of commitment and training, which impede customers from switching to other systems.
11. ***Special Risks and Uncertainties of Entry:*** entrants' higher risks may raise their costs of capital.
12. ***Gaps and Asymmetries of Information:*** incumbents' superior information helps them bar entrants and may raise entrants' cost of capital.
13. ***Formal, Official Barriers Set by Government Agencies or Industrywide Groups:*** examples are utility franchises and foreign-trade duties and barriers.

II.   Endogenous Causes: *Voluntary and Strategic Sources of Barriers*

1. ***Preemptive and Retaliatory Actions by Incumbents:*** include selective price discounts targeted to deter or punish entry.
2. ***Excess Capacity:*** lets incumbents retaliate sharply and threaten retaliation credibly.
3. ***Selling Expenses, Including Advertising:*** increase the degree of product differentiation and make entry harder.
4. ***Segmenting of the Market:*** segregates customer groups by their demand elasticities, and makes broad entry into the whole market more difficult.
5. ***Patents:*** may provide exclusive control over critical or lower-cost technology and products.
6. ***Exclusive Controls over Other Strategic Resources:*** examples include the best ores, the best locations, and various unique talents of people.
7. ***Raising Rivals' Costs:*** require new entrants to incur extra costs.
8. ***Packing the Product Space:*** may occur in industries with high product differentiation, like cereals.
9. ***Secrecy about Crucial Competitive Conditions:*** specific actions may create secrecy about key conditions.

Sources: These categories are extracted from the larger literature, as discussed in the text.

ume of supply, and therefore the market price is likely to fall, which alone reduces the gain to the entrant. In addition, established firms are likely to threaten retaliation against such a large entrant in order to prevent its entry. If the economies of scale are large, the established firms are likely to have large market shares and be able to inflict sharp penalties on the newcomer (chapter 7).

3. *Absolute Cost Advantages.* These advantages can arise from differential wage rates, superior talent, random luck, and historical accidents. Other cost advantages come from patented processes, special access to raw materials, and favorable locations.

4. *Product Differentiation.* This barrier arises from advertising, marketing strategies, and other conditions (see chapter 12). Some advertising is persuasive, aiming to create preferences for brand names. Once such preferences are formed, the established firm has an advantage over newcomers, so potential entrants may decide not to try to establish their brands. Moreover, an established firm may be able to meet an entrant with selective advertising campaigns that neutralize the newcomer. The newcomer must then advertise so heavily that its costs (including selling costs) are raised well above the established firm's costs. Advertising is only one of several selling expenses; the same reasoning holds for all (chapter 12).

5. *Sunk Costs.* Certain costs may be unavoidable for firms to be in the market, and they may be impossible to recover if the firm leaves. Such sunk costs may be investments in physical capital, advertising to create brand images, spending to create a marketing network, or others.[16]

6. *Research and Development Intensity.* Large R & D spending may be necessary in order to get started in a market (examples are advanced electronics, automobiles, and complex chemicals). Moreover, the expenditures may need to be long-term in order to build up sufficient R & D capacity (chapter 5).

7. *Asset Specificity.* The various assets used by a firm will usually have some degree of specificity for this purpose. They may not be adaptable to other uses, and therefore they cannot be sold and converted. That imposes high risks and costs, and failed entry results in large losses.

8. *Vertical Integration.* If it is efficient for firms in the industry to be vertically integrated, then an entrant must enter on two or more levels in order to match the existing firms' costs. That requires assembling more capital, R & D and staff talent, and that larger commitment raises the degree of risk in case of failure (chapter 12).

9. *Diversification by Incumbents.* Diversified firms may be able to deploy their massed resources at any one branch where needed to prevent entry. These resources may include funds, marketing staff advertising resources, and R & D capacities (chapter 12).

10. *Switching Costs.* Purchasers of complex equipment often must invest in specific training and associated equipment, which can be used only

with that complex equipment. The buyer becomes locked in to the equipment. Switching to different systems becomes costly, and so prospective entrants have to spend heavily to help their new customers switch from their old equipment.

11. *Special Risks and Uncertainties.* New entrants commonly face higher risks than incumbents, because they have less reliable knowledge about the market's conditions. That can raise their costs of raising capital.

12. *Less Information.* Entrants inherently have less information than incumbents. Acquiring information can be costly. Entrants therefore are riskier, and that will raise their cost of capital.

13. *Formal, Official Barriers by Governments or Industry Groups.* Many industries are protected by government limits, requirements, and other restraints, or by preconditions and rules set by industrywide groups. A dominant firm will shape such industrywide rules to its advantage so as to make entry difficult.

Next come the nine endogenous sources of barriers, which incumbents can influence or wholly control.[17]

1. *Retaliation and Preemptive Actions.* This category embraces a large category of strategic devices, all of which can be applied (or merely threatened) in varying degrees of severity. Prices are only one weapon; others include advertising, targeted innovations of various kinds, and counteractions in related markets.

2. *Excess Capacity.* By creating and carrying excess capacity, a dominant firm warns other firms that it can block entry easily by expanding its output quickly. This method has been used in prominent cases.

3. *Advertising and Other Selling Expenses.* Selling expenses can accentuate the effects of brand loyalties beyond what is intrinsic to the market (exogenous source 4). Firms commonly exercise total discretion over their advertising and marketing activities, fitting them to general or specific competitive needs (see chapter 12).

4. *Creation or Accentuation of Market Segmentation.* The leading firm may segregate customers by their demand and other attributes, so as to treat them differently in pricing and other ways. By deepening the boundaries within the market, it makes across-the-board entry more difficult.

5. *Patents.* These are specific voluntary devices that firms seek in order to gain exclusive control over inventions. Strategic patenting (in place of secrecy or other tactics) is important in many industries, such as the drug industry, to prevent or control new competition.

6. *Controls over Strategic Resources.* Many critical resources can be controlled, either through strategic acquisitions or in other ways. By getting control of the best ores, the best locations, or the best managers or inventors, incumbents may be able to deter new competition.

7. *Raising Rivals' or Entrants' Costs.* The incumbent may have a variety of ways to impose extra costs on rivals or entrants (see chapter 10).

8. ***Packing the Product Space.*** In some industries, the product space can be "packed" by a proliferation of branded items, so that new firms have no niches in which to gain a foothold. Although this tactic may seem to enhance consumer choice, it also blocks entry (see chapter 14).

9. ***Secrecy.*** Often knowledge about crucial market conditions and opportunities is decisive for entrants. A dominant firm often controls the knowledge and may be able to alter conditions so that existing knowledge is made obsolete.

Each of these sources includes a variety of specific forms. They operate in many dimensions, such as dollar volumes, types of talent, degrees of product variety, and amounts of excess capacity.

3. PROBLEMS PLAGUING THE EFFORTS TO MEASURE BARRIERS

If barriers exist and are important, then scholars should be able to measure and verify them. Also, if policies are to deal with barriers in a useful way, then it is necessary to assess their size and the ways to decrease them.

Measuring the Individual Elements. But more than forty years after Bain's initial work, barriers remain poorly specified and poorly estimated. Nor can entry or barriers be measured reliably at all. There is no agreement about the methods for measuring either the endogenous nor the exogenous elements.

Merging the Measures into Overall Estimates of Barrier Size. Even if some of the elements could be measured well, combining those measures into a total estimate of the barriers' "height" is even more difficult and unscientific. Should the elements be added to each other, or is each independently sufficient to create a high barrier? Do two medium-strong elements create a high barrier equivalent to one very-strong element? Should the elements be multiplied by one another in some fashion because they are strongly reinforcing?

There are few systematic studies of actual barriers, but even they do not begin to solve the measurement problems.[18] The occasional barriers research still relies on rough categories, such as "high, medium, or low," and it relies merely on educated guesses.

Internal and External Conditions Are Correlated with Each Other. High barriers mainly can occur with a dominant firm. Research on actual cases has been unable to tell whether the causation runs from market shares to barriers, vice versa, or a mixture.

Potential Entrants Can't Really Be Identified. It is important to know the pool of potential entrants, because they set the competitive force exerted by potential entry. If there are few candidates in the wings, then entry may exert little pressure even if barriers are low.

Yet scarcely any research has been done on identifying potential entrants. Most analyses simply assume that potential entrants are abundant and strong. But in many cases, that is not true.

In short, entry and barriers are interesting to some theorists, but so far they have little practical use. They are complicated matters, which are closely linked to the structure inside the market. Because they are mentioned in debates on competition, we need to note the ideas.[19]

V. FIRMS' CHOICES IN LIGHT OF POTENTIAL ENTRY

For theory's sake, assume that entry and barriers *can* somehow be defined and measured. Under those assumptions, we can specify in theory the conditions and choices that entry may involve for dominant firms.

The entry barrier gives the established firm a chance to raise price above its long-run average cost without attracting new competition from outside. (Of course, the existing rivals may react, but they're ignored in this theory.) The height of the barrier is shown by the gap between the average cost and the "entry-inducing price." Figure 9.1 illustrates the theory. For simplicity, average costs are assumed to be constant. When price is set above the entry-inducing price level, new competition takes away some of the firm's customers.

Therefore the demand curve has a kink at the limit price. The kink will be sharp if entry is quick and big as soon as price rises even a shade above the limit price. In this extreme case, the possible entry (an external condition) will dominate the market power (an internal condition of the market).

We will now summarize the way Joe Bain discussed three separate forms of barriers: product differentiation, scale economies, and an absolute cost advantage.

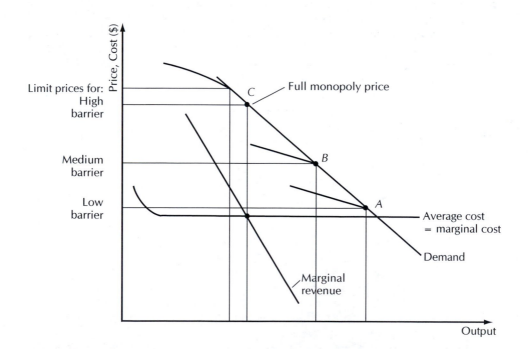

Figure 9.1   General patterns of barriers and the effects of entry.

Product Differentiation.   If products differ (because of advertising or other selling activities), then their prices can vary. Existing firms can raise price some distance above cost before drawing in new firms (as chapter 12 considers).

Scale Economies.   If minimum efficient scale is large, the new entrant may have to be so big that the older firms are bound to retaliate. Also, a large entrant adds to the industry's total capacity, shifting the supply curve down, which also lowers price. The effect is shown by line *R* in figure 9.2; its height is the change in price that each level of entry will cause. Add this to the average cost curve itself to get curve *E*. *E* is not an average cost curve, but only the curve of the lowest possible price that will just permit entry at any given scale.

Any price below the minimum point on curve *E* will deter entry. Older firms are able to price in range *B* without drawing entrants into the market. *B* therefore represents the height of the barrier caused by economies of scale.

Cost Differences.   Finally, the absolute cost barrier, depicted in figure 9.3, is any cost advantage that the established firm has, such as better ores or cheaper capital. These advantages are likely to be sharper at greater sizes. The entrants' and existing firms' cost curves will look like those in figure 9.3. The interval marked C shows the height of this category of barrier.

These three conditions may combine in quite complex ways. They may reinforce or be neutral toward each other. High economies of scale and product differentiation may make for very high barriers or even blockaded entry. There is no method yet to disentangle these factors. The analysis only permits one to speak broadly of the height of the barrier, whatever its parts and sources may be.

A low barrier plus powerful threats of potential entry could force the dominant firm to keep price down close to average cost. That is shown by point A in

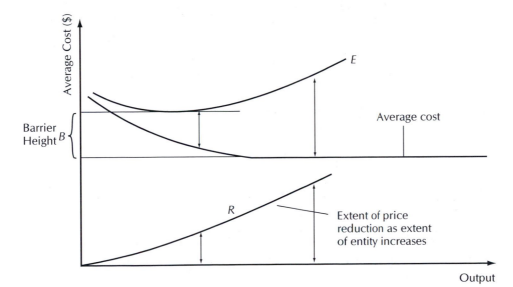

Figure 9.2   Economies of scale as a barrier to entry.

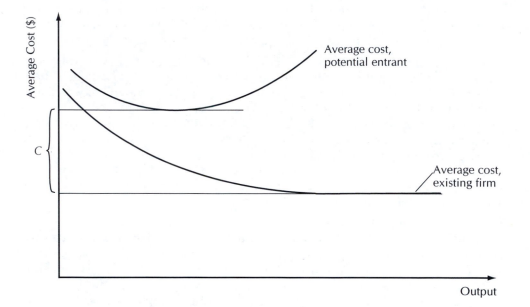

Figure 9.3   An absolute cost advantage as a barrier to entry.

figure 9.1, just above the competitive level. At the other extreme, a high barrier can permit full monopoly pricing by the firm, as at point C in figure 9.1. The firm adopts the price strategy that fits its preferences. A price just at the entry-limiting level will often be chosen, but sometimes a firm will prefer to take higher profits now and yield up its market share over time.

The choice will depend on several conditions, such as the sharpness of the kink at the entry-limiting price, the shape of the cost curve, and the dominant firm's particular expectations about other firms' plans and expectations. Also, a higher time discount rate will incline the firm to take profits immediately.

The Theory In Perspective.   To ignore potential competition entirely would be too narrow. It plays some role—perhaps in some cases, a major role. As we have seen, however, **actual competition** is usually the decisive factor. Three specific points help to put the role of barriers in perspective.

Several Firms.   A single dominant firm with a pricing strategy toward entry is easy to imagine. The idea of several firms practicing a unified limit-pricing policy is less plausible. Such oligopolists naturally face possible competition among themselves as well as from lesser firms in the market. They *may* focus on potential competition from outside, but this approach would require them to decide that competition among themselves is of little or no importance. An oligopolists' joint limit-pricing strategy is therefore implausible. The whole issue depends also on the degree of concentration, since a tight oligopoly can be more cohesive than a loose oligopoly.

Rate of Entry.   Entry may range from as slow as molasses to as quick as lightning. The faster the rate of entry, the flatter the firm's demand curve above the entry-limiting price. The slower the rate of entry, the less the entry barriers will matter in any event. The role of barriers therefore depends not only on their height but also on the vigor, resources, and responsiveness of potential entrants.[20]

The size and profitability of the potential entrants probably affect how much of a threat they are. Also, some potential entrants are in closely adjacent or similar industries, and such technological nearness may make them more likely to move in forcefully.[21] Moreover, one can see how many potential entrants there are. A large group can exert more discipline than just one or two.

The height of barriers and the rate of entry are two separate concepts; you must learn to keep them clear and distinct. The degree of constraint that potential competition may exert depends on both.

A Curve Instead of a Kink?   The theoretical kink in the demand curve at the limit price is far too simple for most situations. A smooth bend in the demand curve is more sensible, since entry would probably happen by degrees rather than on an either/or basis. Figure 9.4 illustrates such a continuous relationship between price and entry.

Remember, entry is often a matter of uncertainty. As price rises, the probability of entry normally will rise. But all the various real conditions may not work out. Conversely, entry may occur even at lower prices. Strategy toward entry often involves risk and gambling on the odds, as is illustrated in figure 9.4 by the scatter of possible outcomes around the demand curve.

These two features—a continuous entry-price relationship and the element of probability—make entry more plausible. They also blur and fade its role. Entry now tends to shade in with other competitive actions. Indeed, entry is best seen as a modifier of the central conditions in the market.[22]

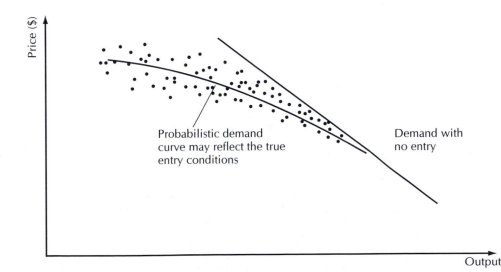

Figure 9.4   Potential entry may operate by degrees and with uncertainty.

VI. THE SPECIAL CASE OF ULTRAFREE ENTRY (CONTESTABILITY)

In 1982 Baumol, Panzar, and Willig claimed to offer an important new theory, focusing on an extreme case which they called "contestability." They suggested that perfectly free, absolute, reversible entry is the best basis for defining efficient allocation. It was, they said, "a new theory of industrial organization" that "will transform the field and render it far more applicable to the real world" and be "extraordinarily helpful in the design of public policy."

Since "contestability," they said, took the place of competition itself, it sought to displace the heart of the field of industrial organization. It naturally met sharp criticism.[23] They continue to promote the idea actively, but its defects remain.[24]

The theory rests on three assumptions:

1. *Entry Is Free and Without Limit.* The entrant can immediately duplicate and entirely replace any existing firm, even a complete monopolist. With no costs or significant lags in entry, the entrant can match all dimensions of size, technology, costs, product array, brand loyalties, and other advantages of all existing firms.

2. *Entry Is Absolute.* The entrant can establish itself immediately, before an existing firm makes any price response. If the entrant obtains any advantage, even a tiny price difference, it will displace the existing firm, with no interaction or sequence of moves. This result occurs even if a pure monopolist faces elimination.

3. *Entry Is Perfectly Reversible.* Exit is perfectly free, at no sacrifice of any cost. Sunk cost is zero.

These conditions are pure, and the deductive results hold only when they hold. For such markets they coined the term *contestable*, but the phrase *ultrafree entry* is more precise. Its pure, abstract conditions appear to nullify even a total monopoly, **scaring it into setting prices at competitive levels.** Like Bain's simple free-entry case, ultrafree entry places a sharp kink or truncation in the demand curve; now the kink is down exactly at the competitive price. If the incumbent raises price even by just a penny, it will be instantly and totally ousted by a newcomer.

Yet the model's assumptions are contradictory. If entry is sufficiently trivial, it may indeed avoid a response. But ultrafree entry also assumes total entry. The two assumptions are in direct contradiction of each other. If entry is trivial, it has no force. If it is total (or even merely significant), then the no-response assumption is not tenable: the incumbent firm will take all possible efforts to prevent the entry.

Moreover, the theory is naive and static, with only one price. It ignores possible strategic price discrimination by the incumbent, which could decisively defeat entry while permitting excess profits.[25] Also, sunk costs are usually difficult to measure.[26]

Baumol and Willig have tried to apply the theory to large-scale cases involving airlines, long-distance telephone service, and railroads. However, none of these markets permits ultrafree entry (see chapters 13 and 14). In fact, the theory applies to no known actual market. Nor is the theory robust: if actual conditions depart even slightly from any of the assumptions, then the theory's lessons are false.

It is easy to dismiss ultrafree entry (or contestability) because its key elements contradict reality. If the extreme assumptions don't hold precisely, then fear of entry will not nullify a monopoly; the theory is not robust. As before, an actual competitor is usually more important than a potential entrant. Potential competition is still merely secondary, blending in with other conditions.

As often happens, a bright idea has been exaggerated and oversold by its enthusiastic authors. The ensuing debate trims the concept and claims down to their proper niche, taking their place among all the other ideas. In this instance, contestability offers insights, but it does not affect the central role of market structure.

QUESTIONS FOR REVIEW

1. Discuss two cases of dominance in which superior performance may have been the main cause, contrasting them with two cases where it was not.

2. Are dominant firms likely to adopt a passive stance toward smaller rivals? Explain the resulting decline of dominance when the firm is passive.

3. Bain suggested that entry barriers intensify the effects of oligopoly market power, but now entry is often said to weaken or eliminate market power. Does your judgment lean one way or the other?

4. How is entry to be defined: in terms of numbers of firms, entrants' market shares, net entry, declines in the incumbent firms' market shares, the speed of entry, or other elements?

5. Contrast the exogenous and endogenous sources of entry barriers, with examples. Which are usually more important?

6. How can the endogenous sources of barriers be measured? If they could be measured, how could they be combined into a single measure of barrier height?

7. Choose two industries and estimate the height of entry barriers into them. Explain your estimates.

8. Show with diagrams how scale economies and product differentiation give rise to specific heights of entry barriers. Contrast cases of low and high barriers.

ENDNOTES

[1] See particularly David I. Rosenbaum, ed., *Market Dominance: How Firms Gain, Hold or Lose It and the Impact on Economic Performance* (Westport, CT: Greenwood, Praeger, 1998), for a review of the many dimensions of the problem.

[2] John Moody, *The Truth About the Trusts* (Chicago: Moody Publishing, 1904).

[3] There also was an outpouring of research highly critical of the trusts. Some of it was noted in chapter 1. The leaders were Richard T. Ely, *Monopolies and Trusts* (New York: Macmillan, 1900); Charles J. Bullock, "Trust Literature: A Survey and Criticism," *Quarterly Journal of Economics* 15 (February 1900–01): pp. 167–217; and William Z. Ripley, ed., *Trusts, Pools and Corporations* (Boston: Ginn, 1916).

[4] See A. D. H. Kaplan, *Big Enterprise in a Competitive System* (Washington, DC: Brookings Institution, 1965).

[5] For example, such diversified companies as Procter & Gamble, General Foods, and General Mills have had a number of products that dominate specific markets, but they do not publish details on these lines.

[6] See Alfred E. Kahn, *The Economics of Regulation*, 2 vols. (New York: Wiley, 1971); Richard Schmalensee, *The Control of Natural Monopolies* (Lexington, MA: D.C. Heath, 1979); and William G. Shepherd, *Public Policies Toward Business*, 8th ed. (Homewood, IL: Irwin, 1990).

[7] Dean A. Worcester, "Why 'Dominant' Firms Decline," *Journal of Political Economy* 65 (August 1957): pp. 338–47. See also the survey in F. M. Scherer and David Ross, *Industrial Market Structure and Economic Performance*, 3rd ed. (Boston: Houghton Mifflin, 1991).

[8] Darius W. Gaskins, Jr., "Dynamic Limit Pricing: Optimal Pricing Under Threat of Entry," *Journal of Economic Theory* 3 (September 1971): pp. 306–22. Gaskins' analysis includes existing smaller firms as well as new entrants. More recent analysis is discussed in Scherer and Ross, *Industrial Market Structure and Economic Performance*; and Jean Tirole, *The Theory of Industrial Organization*, 2nd ed. (Cambridge, MA: MIT Press, 1993).

[9] See especially Joe S. Bain, *Barriers to New Competition* (Cambridge: Harvard University Press, 1956); and Scherer and Ross, *Industrial Market Structure and Economic Performance*, chapter 10.

[10] See also Stephen Martin, "Oligopoly Limit Pricing: Strategic Substitutes, Strategic Complements," *International Journal of Industrial Organization* 13 (1995): pp. 41–65.

[11] Paul A. Geroski and J. Schwalbach, eds., *Entry and Market Contestability: An International Comparison* (Oxford: Basil Blackwell, 1991). For a review of the growing evidence about entry, exit, and turnover, see Richard E. Caves, "Industrial Organization and New Findings on the Turnover and Mobility of Firms," *Journal of Economic Literature* 36 (December 1998): pp. 1947–1982.

[12] John J. Siegfried and Laurie Beth Evans, "Empirical Studies of Entry and Exit: A Survey of the Evidence," *Review of Industrial Organization* 9 (April 1994): pp. 121–55.

[13] See also Paul Geroski, Richard J. Gilbert, and Alexis Jacquemin, *Barriers to Entry and Strategic Competition* (New York: Harwood Academic, 1990); Richard Schmalensee, "Ease of Entry: Has the Concept Been Applied Too Readily?" chapter in Harry First, Eleanor M. Fox, and Robert Pitofsky, *Revitalizing Antitrust in Its Second Century* (New York: Quorum, 1991), pp. 338–48; and D. S. Bunch and Robert Smiley, "Who Deters Entry? Evidence on the Use of Strategic Entry Deterrence," *Economic Statistics* 74 (August 1992): pp. 509–21.

[14] Richard E. Caves and Michael E. Porter, "From Entry Barriers to Mobility Barriers," *Quarterly Journal of Economics* 91 (May 1977): pp. 241–61.

[15] Their main authors and researchers have been discussed at various places in this book; see also Scherer and Ross, *Industrial Market Structure and Economic Performance*, chapter 10.

[16] William J. Baumol, John Panzar, and Robert D. Willig, *Contestable Markets and the Theory of Industry Structure* (San Diego: Harcourt Brace Jovanovich, 1982).

[17] See also chapter 10's discussion of price discrimination.

[18] Two important studies are Joe S. Bain, *Barriers to New Competition*; and H. Michael Mann, "Seller Concentration, Barriers to Entry, and Rates of Return in 30 Industries, 1950–1960," *Review of Economics and Statistics* 48 (August 1966): pp. 296–307.

[19] Both Bain and Mann tried to include several elements to make approximate judgments about barrier heights, but their data were often roughly estimated and they provided no general, objective formula or technique for combining the data on individual barrier elements. To recognize this roughness is not to criticize it; the estimates were probably about as good as could be made then, now, or in the future.

[20] For example, see Ronald W. Cotterill and Lawrence E. Haller, "Barrier and Queue Effects: A Study of Leading U.S. Supermarket Chain Entry Patterns," *Journal of Industrial Economics* 40 (December 1992): pp. 427–40.

[21] Most entry is done by adjacent firms, who simply add to their existing product lines; see Michael Gort, *Diversification and Integration in American Industry* (Princeton, NJ: Princeton University Press, 1962); and Charles H. Berry, *Corporate Growth and Diversification* (Princeton, NJ: Princeton University Press, 1975).

[22] As a final example, entry by foreign firms often has an uncertain effect; see Robert M. Fein-

berg and Joseph Shaanan, "The Relative Price Discipline of Domestic Versus Foreign Entry," *Review of Industrial Organization* 9 (April 1994): pp. 211–220.

[23] This section draws on William G. Shepherd, "'Contestability' versus Competition," *American Economic Review* 74 (September 1984): pp. 572–87. The main sources on contestability are William J. Baumol, "Contestable Markets: An Uprising in the Theory of Industry Structure," *American Economic Review* 72 (March 1982): pp. 1–15; and Baumol et al., *Contestable Markets*. For further praise of the idea, see William J. Baumol and Robert D. Willig, "Contestability: Developments Since the Book," *Oxford Economic Papers* (November 1986), Special Supplement. Marius Schwartz, "The Nature of Contestability Theory," *ibid.*, shows that contestability is not a robust concept.

[24] A recent version is William J. Baumol and J. Gregory Sidak, *Toward Competition in Local Telephony* (Cambridge: MIT Press, 1994); a critique is in William G. Shepherd, "Contestability vs. Competition—Once More," *Land Economics* 71 (August 1995): pp. 299–309.

[25] John S. Heywood and Debashis Pal, "Contestability and Two-Part Pricing," *Review of Industrial Organization* 8 (October 1993): pp. 551–66.

[26] See, for example, Timothy F. Bresnahan and P. C. Reiss, "Measuring the Importance of Sunk Costs," *Annals of Economic Statistics* 34 (April-June 1994): pp. 181–217.

Chapter

10

PRICE DISCRIMINATION AND PREDATORY ACTIONS

What do the following have in common? *Newsweek* costs 45 cents per copy by student subscription, 69 cents by regular subscription, but $3.88 at the newsstand. You pay $8.75 for a movie ticket to see *Frankenstein: Love and Kisses*, but the child sitting next to you pays only $5.75. On a flight from Chicago to New Orleans, your round-trip discount ticket cost $229; the businesswoman sitting next to you paid the full coach fare of $960, while a passenger across the aisle paid only $115.

These multiple prices all probably involve **price discrimination,** but not just because the prices differ: If the ratios of price to cost are *different* among buyers, *then* it is price discrimination. For example, if every movie customer costs the theater $3.00, then your price/cost ratio is 2 to l, whereas the child's ratio is only 1 to 1. That difference in the ratios is price discrimination, and in this instance it is quite sharp.

Discrimination occurs because firms can make more money by charging isolated customers (or groups of customers) "what the traffic will bear." Differences in demand elasticities rather than (or in addition to) cost then determine prices, with inelastic-demand customers getting charged the most. In contrast, efficient prices fall in line with cost, as you have seen throughout this book. Every firm tries to set its prices selectively, extending discounts in line with demand conditions. But its ability to discriminate is limited by market conditions.

The 1990s brought far more multiple pricing and discrimination to the U.S. economy than in the past in almost every market. Price discrimination has also become much more important as a dynamic strategic weapon to use against smaller competitors.

This chapter trains you to identify price discrimination. That judgment is often more complicated than you think. For example, a "cheap-ticket" $75 standby airline passenger may actually be discriminated *against*, as you will shortly see. You will learn to judge when discrimination is **pro-competitive** or **anti-competitive**.

This chapter summarizes the main concepts and real-world versions of price discrimination. Section 1 gives the basic theory. Section 2 shows the effects of discrimination on competition, monopoly, and efficiency. Extreme discrimination may become predatory, as section 3 discusses. Section 4 reviews a variety of real cases.

I. THE NATURE OF PRICE DISCRIMINATION[1]

1. PRECONDITIONS FOR DISCRIMINATION

Price discrimination can occur when the following three conditions hold:

1. *Demand Elasticities Differ Sharply* among groups of buyers.
2. *The Seller Can Identify and Separate Buyers* on the basis of these differing elasticities.
3. *The Seller Can Prevent Low-Price Buyers From Reselling* the good to high-price buyers.

The seller then divides the buyers into two or more groups and charges higher prices to the buyers with less elastic demand. Remember that inelastic demand means stronger **preferences** for the good (perhaps from urgency) and/or high **purchasing power** (that is, affluence). Those who are willing to pay more **are made to pay more**. Other buyers with more elastic demand—those who have good substitutes or are too poor—are charged less.

The classic instance has been the old-time town doctor who treated everybody from the bottom to the top of the local social ladder—and knew their income and wealth. For the same appendectomy, the doctor might ask the banker to pay $2,500 but the poor widow only $50, or perhaps provide it for free. Nineteenth-century railroads also were masters at charging what the traffic would bear, for example, 10 cents per ton-mile out on the plains and 2 cents per ton-mile alongside rivers with competing roads and barge lines.

Perhaps the most familiar instance today is half-price movie, bus, train, and airplane tickets for children. The costs of supply are much the same for both children and adults, yet adults pay a much higher ratio of price to cost. Other examples are automobile models and airline fares on all routes (we discuss these toward the end of this chapter).

When discrimination occurs, elasticity of demand—*not* cost—governs the prices. A price discriminator follows the basic profit-maximizing rule: set price and output at the level where marginal revenue equals marginal cost. A single-price firm simply considers the demand and marginal-revenue schedules for all its sales. A price discriminator sets a price for **each group of customers** on the basis of the demand and marginal revenue for that particular group.

The seller must keep the low-price buyers from reselling the product to the high-price buyers. Otherwise the low-price buyers simply buy more and then resell it to the high-price buyers. That pulls the high price down toward the low price.

Note that uniform prices can actually be discriminatory if costs differ. For example, a stamp costs 37 cents for a first-class letter sent anywhere in the United States, either a mile across town or 3,000 miles from Maine to California. Because that uniform price ignores the greater costs to more remote locations, it is discriminatory. It is not necessarily bad; indeed it is quite good, because it unifies the country.

One always judges possible discrimination by comparing **price-cost ratios,** not just prices. Cost differences can justify price differences.

2. ANALYSIS OF PRICE DISCRIMINATION

Identical Costs, Differing Prices.   Consider the simple case where prices differ but costs are uniform, illustrated in figure 10.1. Marginal cost is the flat line *MC*, which is assumed for simplicity to be constant and identical for the two customer groups; in other words, the product being sold is precisely uniform in its costs. Group A has relatively inelastic demand, while group B's demand is more highly elastic. Each demand curve has a corresponding marginal-revenue curve, marked *A* and *B*.

The firm maximizes its total profit by setting output to each group at the level where marginal revenue equals marginal cost. The resulting two prices are sharply different. Group-A buyers pay $100, whereas group-B buyers pay only $20 for the same good. Inelastic demand leads to a higher price-cost ratio.

In condensed form,

$$\frac{\text{price A}}{\text{marginal cost A}} > \frac{\text{price B}}{\text{marginal cost B}}$$

This automatically deviates from the marginal conditions of efficient allocation. Even if the equality of price and marginal cost does not hold closely in the rest of the economy, at least *one* of the two price-cost ratios must be out of line, and here the deviation is sharp.

Or let figure 10.1 illustrate the pricing of a lifesaving drug, say for heart attacks. The same drug is sold to two groups: (1) to local druggists for resale to patients with doctors' prescriptions and (2) to large hospitals for dispensing to patients. The druggists' customers have **inelastic demand**, because they merely buy what their doctor tells them to. In contrast, the hospitals have **elastic demand**. They are big buyers, bargaining shrewdly and playing the drug companies against one another to get a low price.

Thus the identical drug, costing perhaps $3 per dozen pills to make, might sell for $15 per dozen to retail druggists and $5 per dozen to hospitals. (In practice, the ratios of price to cost may differ more or less sharply.)

Prices Differing Less than Costs.   Now consider a more complicated case, as illustrated in figure 10.2. Costs differ sharply. Suppose that marginal cost *C* is for regular provision of airline passenger service on a reserved, guaranteed-seat basis. Marginal cost *D* is for standby service, for people (students, backpackers) who are willing to take a chance that there will be an empty seat.

Marginal cost for *C* is high at $75, because it involves the provision of guaranteed service on a plane, even if the demand for that plane on that day is low. The cost includes all of the expenditures for capital, maintenance, staffing, and

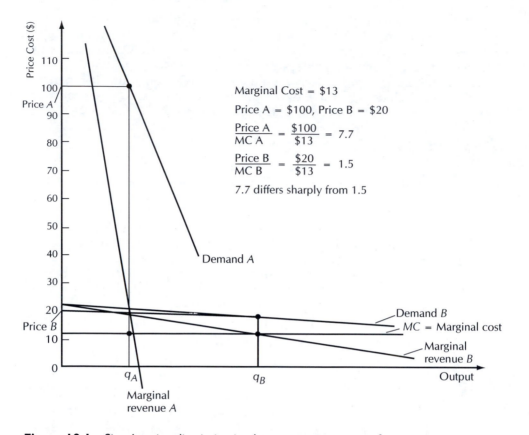

Marginal Cost = $13

Price A = $100, Price B = $20

$$\frac{\text{Price A}}{\text{MC A}} = \frac{\$100}{\$13} = 7.7$$

$$\frac{\text{Price B}}{\text{MC B}} = \frac{\$20}{\$13} = 1.5$$

7.7 differs sharply from 1.5

Figure 10.1 Simple price discrimination between two groups of customers.

fuel that are required to provide this guaranteed-seat airline service. Marginal cost for *D* is lower, at $10, because the airline incurs little extra cost from letting someone walk on and take a seat that would otherwise have been empty. The marginal cost involves hardly more than the extra fuel to carry one more body.

As always, the airline seeks to maximize its profits from each of the two groups by setting output for each group where marginal revenue equals marginal cost. That approach results in a fare of $100 for regular passengers and $50 for standby passengers, as shown in figure 10.2. A regular passenger might be irritated to see a standby rider pay only half fare, but in fact **this instance of discrimination runs the other way.** It is the standby passengers in group D who are discriminated **against**, because the ratio of price to cost for that group is higher than group C's ratio. The price-cost ratios are exactly 4 to 3 for group C and 5 to 1 for group D.

If the airline instead chose a single fare for both groups in figure 10.2, that, too, would be discrimination. Price P_E is such a single discriminatory price. The price-cost ratios would be about 1.1 for the buyers in group C and 5.0 for those in group D. P_E is an irrational choice for the airline, for it does not maximize the firm's profits. This airline would *always* try to discriminate in order to maximize its profits.

Table 10.1 presents standard conditions that can make elasticities sharply different. The differences may be stable and predictable or instead rapidly shift-

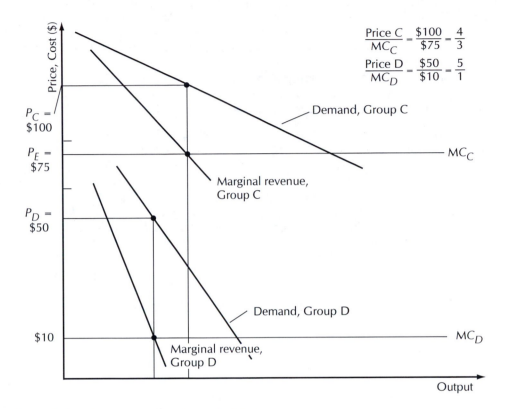

$$\frac{\text{Price C}}{MC_C} = \frac{\$100}{\$75} = \frac{4}{3}$$

$$\frac{\text{Price D}}{MC_D} = \frac{\$50}{\$10} = \frac{5}{1}$$

Figure 10.2   Price discrimination with differing costs.

ing. (Examples: stable variations are found in electricity demand by time of day, day of the week, and seasons. Fashion clothing and toys often have less stable, but still sharp, variations in elasticity.)

3. TYPES OF PRICE DISCRIMINATION

Discrimination is not limited to the simple case of a single product sold to two groups of buyers. The number of products and of buyer groups both range up to high levels. What matters is that firms may sell related products at differing price-cost ratios.

Buyer groups can be ever more finely divided until at the extreme the seller reaches perfect discrimination among every unit sold to every one of its customers. The prices then fit the market demand curve itself, so that all consumer surplus is taken by the seller.

In his classic analysis of price discrimination, A. C. Pigou called this **first-degree** price discrimination. Examples of it are the old-time small-town doctor (noted earlier) who neatly set each bill for each item in line with each patient's ability to pay. Also a rug merchant may haggle the maximum price from each rug sold, one by one; the same approach holds for many automobile dealers and piano stores.

Second-degree discrimination is simply a cruder version, in which the seller can only array prices by descending price groups. **Third-degree** discrimination involves functional groupings of customers (such as residential versus industrial customers, or separate geographical areas). Figure 10.1 gave a simple two-group third-degree case.

In short, price discrimination varies from simple groupings to comprehensive, highly refined systems. There is also variation in who makes it happen; the seller may impose it, the buyers may force it or the seller, or mixtures of both may occur.

Static or Dynamic?   Discrimination can be a rigid, comprehensive system or an ongoing process of changes and dynamic responses.

This variety of conditions has given rise to a number of common names for price discrimination, including price discounting, demand-based pricing, selective pricing, value-of-service pricing, loss leaders, pinpoint pricing, price sharpshooting, cherry-picking, and of course charging what the traffic will bear. The ordinary retail sale often involves a degree of price discrimination. All these phrases usually refer to the same basic fact: a variation among the price-cost ratios for a seller's identical or related goods.

II. PRICE DISCRIMINATION'S EFFECTS

Each firm that sets prices selectively has two main aims:

1. *Static Maximizing of Profits.* The price structure is set to yield the maximum total profit from the whole set of varying buyers. From the firm's whole market position, the multiple pricing extracts the biggest total profit.

Table 10.1   Conditions Influencing Demand Elasticities

1. *Customer conditions*	a. Preferences. b. Income and wealth. c. Knowledge.
2. *Technical limits*	a. Physical connections and apparatus usually make demand less elastic. b. Ability to shop around.
3. *Competition*	a. Extent of competition. Intense competition causes the firm's demand curve to be highly elastic for that specific product; lack of competition will permit demand to be inelastic. b. Threat of entry.
4. *Vertical conditions*	a. Monopsony power causes demand to be more elastic. b. Ability to self-supply lets buyers have more choice, so demand is more elastic.

2. ***Dynamic Strategic Impacts.*** Discrimination can also be a key weapon to raise or defend the firm's market position against competitors. The dominant firm implements a complicated process of quick pricing actions as conditions change among all of the various buyer groups.

You already know the static maximizing choices. Now we focus on the dynamic process, using discrimination as a complex weapon to increase market share and/or entry barriers.

1. THE DYNAMIC COMPETITIVE WEAPON

Each firm (large or small) tries to take customers from its competitors. Selective, discriminatory pricing is a precise device to do that, much superior to broad price cuts. **Any price cut reduces revenue on preexisting sales, so it is painful to the firm. Selective price cuts (that is, discrimination) reduce that sacrifice.** They let the firm offer lower prices only to those buyers who require them.

Selective pricing can also be used to fight off (or scare off) a possible entrant. The firm keeps price cuts narrow so as to minimize its sacrifice of profits. As all these efforts proceed in the thick of complicated pricing battles, the firms limit one another's success. Ideally the whole process tears away at higher price-cost margins and forces all prices broadly down to cost. If so, then discrimination is a powerful enforcer of competition. But when that fails to happen, dominant firms with high market shares can milk higher profits by means of price discrimination and hit individual competitors with sharpshooting prices.

2. PROMOTING OR REDUCING COMPETITION

Price discrimination evidently can promote or reduce competition, depending on the situation. The two critical features are (1) the **market position of the firm doing the discriminating** and (2) **how systematic and complete the discrimination is**. The higher the firm's market share is, the more likely it is that its discrimination will reduce competition.

These two criteria are applied in figure 10.3. Price discrimination can occur in any combination of those conditions. The pricing is clearly pro-competitive in zone A: *sporadic* discrimination by firms with *small* market shares. In fact, many small-share firms—which hold no market power—rely heavily on selective price-discounting to compete. Such price cuts, often called *loss leaders*, are common in grocery, drug, and clothing stores. Several items are temporarily offered at special discounts to draw in customers. Once they're inside, the customers may buy other goods that have higher profit margins. Big newspaper ads for grocery and clothing sales often are full of such special discounts.

At the other extreme is the utility firm in zone B, holding a complete monopoly and selling across a spectrum of sharply differing buyers. Discrimination in zone B is *systematic* by a firm with a *high* market share. Such discrimination is deep, lucrative, and anticompetitive.[2] That danger is a main reason why utilities in electricity, gas, and telephones were regulated by public agencies, at least until recently (see chapter 17).

Discrimination can be the lifeblood of competition when it is sporadic and/or done by smaller firms, as in zone A. Indeed, if firms with small market shares try to keep some prices systematically higher than their costs, they will lose

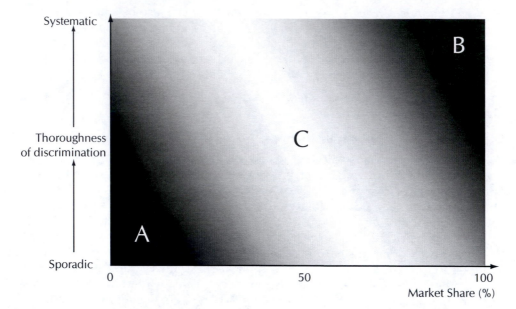

Figure 10.3 Price discrimination can be procompetitive or anticompetitive.

money and may go out of business. When price sharpshooting is done systemati-cally by dominant firms, as in zone B, it is usually anticompetitive.

Zone B discrimination can also forestall new competition. The dominant firm naturally meets competition where it arises; it sets low price-cost ratios where its rivals are strongest. The dominant firm can therefore hold comparably efficient competitors (or new entrants) to little or no profit in those parts of the market.

In contrast, **price discrimination in zone A (under effective competition) attacks the most lucrative markets, forces lower price-cost ratios, spreads to all submarkets, and drives prices down toward costs evenly throughout the whole market.** Systematic discrimination (which prevents that process) is a prime indi-cator of market power.

In the middle range (zone C), the effects are mixed. Here one must assess each case carefully, looking at the setting and the pricing actions.

Effects on Efficiency. Again, type-A (procompetitive) discrimination yields efficient allocation and X-efficiency. Type-B (anticompetitive) discrimination dis-torts allocation and causes other harms of monopoly.

There is one possible exception: the extreme case of **declining costs in an ultra-natural monopoly.** Suppose that scale economies are unusually extensive, so that the market demand curve cuts average cost at a lower output than mini-mum efficient scale (MES). In this odd case, the demand curve intersects marginal cost **below** average cost, as illustrated in figure 10.4. Then the standard static-effi-cient solution—setting price equal to marginal cost—would cause the firm to lose money. Profits are negative if the single price P_{mc} is set. A higher price (P_{ac}) could let the firm avoid financial losses and survive, but that would violate efficiency; P_{ac} is well above marginal cost, and Q_{ac} is well below Q_{mc}.

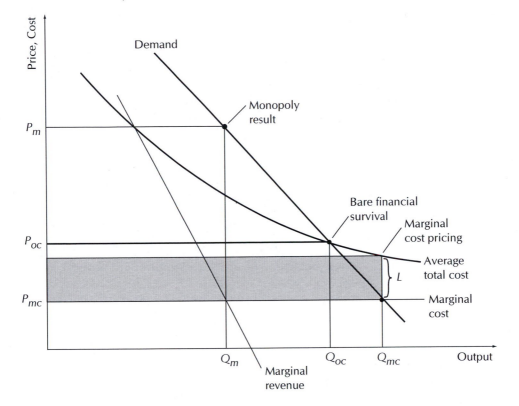

Figure 10.4 The declining-cost case.

This puzzle was lengthily debated by economists in the 1930s and 1940s. They eventually agreed that if different prices can be set for two or more groups (by an "inverse-elasticity rule"), then the firm can make a profit and the distortion will be kept as low as possible.[3] But if the monopolist were allowed a free hand in choosing those prices, it would gouge its customers and make excess profits. The hard task was to somehow constrain the firm to just competitive total profits.

Ramsey Prices. As we've seen, discrimination always involves setting price-cost ratios higher where demand is less elastic. In 1982, Baumol et al gave this familiar inverse-elasticity pattern of pricing a new label. They called it "Ramsey" pricing, after a little-known economist of the 1920s.[4] Ramsey prices, they said, are always efficient and must be accepted.

But their analysis had limits and gaps.[5] It lacked a reliable way to restrain the firm to reasonable profit levels company-wide. Therefore it gave monopolists a free hand to engage in anticompetitive price discrimination so as to gain excess profits. The method could not be applied in practice. And because it was strictly static, it ignored the key strategic impacts that discrimination can have toward reducing competition.

Primary-Line and Secondary-Line Effects. Discrimination can harm competition and efficiency on two different levels:

1. *First-Level Effects (among sellers).* First-level effects (often called primary-line effects) affect the competitive status of the discriminator and its own rivals.

2. *Second-Level Effects (among firms that buy this product).* Second-level effects (often called secondary-line effects) affect the competitive positions of buyers as they compete among each other. The differing prices of the good become differences in the firms' costs. If the good is an important input, then the price differences can harm the high-price buyers' ability to compete against the low-price buyers.

Video Renting.   Blockbuster, the dominant video rental chain, received steep discounts from movie makers in the 1990s. But the movie firms refused to give discounts to small local renters. Blockbuster could then set low rental prices, which drove out hundreds of small local renters throughout the United States. These second-level effects of discrimination by movie makers were severe, probably affecting the rental competition and prices that you pay in your locale.[6]

Book Retailing.   Large book publishers such as Random House, Puffin, and Houghton Mifflin have given large discounts to large book chains such as Barnes & Noble and Borders. That has let the large chains undersell small stores, often with fatal effects.[7]

Defending Discrimination.   Discriminators often point out that they are only cutting their prices where competition is sharp, which is a natural response. In fact, meeting competition in this way is legal under U.S. antitrust laws. But if prices are cut *below* the smaller rival's price, that can reduce competition by eliminating an efficient competitor. Therefore, dominant firms are supposed to keep their discrimination within limits.

3. PROBLEMS OF COST

Cost is the critical benchmark in judging if price discrimination is occurring. Marginal cost is the logically correct criterion, for it is the true measure of opportunity cost. Marginal costs are usually hard to measure, however, and average cost is often used instead. In long-run equilibrium, a competitive firm's marginal and average costs will be equal. Also, average cost is often much easier to measure than marginal cost. Therefore long-run average costs (or average variable costs, in the short run) are often used in evaluating whether discrimination has occurred.

Fluctuations.   As a firm's demand fluctuates, its level of marginal costs will change. This can occur regularly, as in peak and off-peak times for electric and telephone service. Fluctuations also occur over the business cycle.

Marginal costs are low in slack times and high during peaks. If prices shift in response to these changes, they may or may not involve discrimination. If capacity is idle, then a price cut down to the low-marginal-cost level might not be discriminatory (depending on what is done with other products and time periods). Yet if the price cut causes sales quantities to rise, then marginal cost may soon be back up above the price level.

Joint Costs.   Within a firm, many products share overhead or joint costs with other products.[8] For example, the costs of management, R & D and many other company-wide activities are often shared by a range of products. Often the same machine makes two or more products, and dividing the cost among them is difficult. Some processes yield byproducts (for example, petroleum refineries produce airplane and automobile fuel, kerosene, fuel oil, and tar products from one common process). Cost allocations among the products are necessary, but they are often arbitrary and debatable.

In short, marginal costs may be hard to measure in precisely those complex situations where price discrimination is likely to be sharp. You should grasp the concepts clearly, but expect trouble in applying them. Often one must use rough measures of average or variable costs as a first approximation for marginal costs.

4. TIE-INS

A tie-in requires you to buy good B, which you don't want, in order to get good A, which you do want. The tying product (good A) is often a patented product of some kind or a popular branded item. The tied item (B) is often a new product, an inferior one, or simply a complement. The firm holds more market power for good A than for good B. Tying B to A therefore transfers to B some of the selling power (or market control) of A. Even though this tactic causes less of A to be sold, it often permits the firm to raise its combined profits on the two goods.

Tying is an ancient custom, though a rather specialized one that crops up only in certain situations. Market processes usually undermine tie-ins, as new firms offer the tied goods separately. While it lasts, tying can extend market power from the tying product into the tied product and/or serve to extract more profit as a form of price discrimination. New-Chicago economists deny that market power can be levered in this way from product A to B, but there is agreement that discrimination can occur from tie-ins.

Market share is the decisive condition here, as in so many other issues. **Tying by dominant firms** (especially those with patents or some other special advantage in good A) **can reduce competition in good B's market.** Even if such leverage is not strong, the tie can raise entry barriers by forcing any new entrants to offer both products, not just one. Some benefits are possible, though less likely. The joint purchase might realize cost savings in ordering, shipping, or servicing. Also, tying makes it hard to identify the separate prices of the tied goods, so an oligopolist might use it as a device for quietly offering concealed price cuts.

III. "PREDATORY" ACTIONS, INCLUDING PRICING

Small firms often complain that they have been unfairly treated by larger competitors, who go too far by using "predatory" actions. The terms *predatory* and *predation* are merely lawyers' ominous terms for actions that reduce or eliminate competition. Economists have tried to give the phrase some economic meaning since 1972 in what has become a wordy, often-obscure, and inconclusive debate.[9] Though the term *predatory* itself is merely emotional with no economic content, the issue has been focused on selective actions (especially pricing) that do indeed go "too far." Such actions can hurt or promote competition, depending on the setting in which they occur. The lessons can be summed up as follows.

1. TESTING FOR ANTICOMPETITIVE ACTIONS[10]

1. Weapons.   Each firm can use many specific devices (or weapons) to compete. Price is one; its levels and structure can be changed. Changes in product quality and design are another type of action. The many other types of specific actions include advertising and other promotional programs. All of these can either be carried out concretely or merely threatened persuasively enough to affect rivals' choices.

2. Added Impacts.   Some of these competitive devices are selective; others are applied uniformly. Selective actions include price discounts to specific buyers or groups, product changes aimed at specific rivals, and promotional campaigns fitted precisely against one or several competitors in an area. Uniform actions include across-the-board price cuts and broad-scale advertising campaigns. Selectivity is a matter of degree; often there is no sharp break between selective and uniform actions. But selectivity is a condition that can be evaluated.

The economic task is to determine the conditions under which selective actions have anticompetitive effects. All selective actions can be procompetitive; only in certain settings do they reduce competition.

3. Universal Use.   All firms, all of the time, are ready to use any or all of these weapons (selective and uniform) in their efforts to defeat competitors and to gain market control. Competition itself comprises the totality of all such actions in the ongoing give and take of the struggle. When competition is effective, the competing firms have access to the same weapons, and their use of these devices gives healthy competition.

4. Going Too Far.   Some firms in some situations are able to harm competition by extending certain of their actions "too far," and they may do so systematically and successfully. Dominant firms with high market shares (in the range of 40 percent and above) dealing with much smaller competitors are usually in this category. Their resources are larger, and competitive parity is lacking.

5. One Step in a Strategy.   Such firms will indeed often choose to go too far, for two reasons. First, the firm may have a comprehensive strategy in which this first (money-losing) action is only **one step toward a larger total profit.** By sacrificing now to stop the newcomer, the monopolist may protect its larger monopoly and eventually gain larger profits. Many such strategies are routine in many markets: Loss leaders, deep discounts, two-for-one sales, etc., often involve small sacrifices now to make big gains later.

Second, the action may be intended as **a signal to other firms for the future.** By treating one competitor severely, a firm may scare others off from entering and also intimidate its small rivals into passive behavior. The sacrifice therefore has a multiple payoff.[11]

These two reasons refute the free-market claim that anticompetitive actions will not occur because profits recouped later cannot exceed the costs of the actions. In fact, the recoupment by the larger firm (in the related strategies or in other markets receiving its signals) can systematically exceed the actions' initial costs.

6. Not Self-Averting?   Actions that harm the competitive process are not self-averting. Dominant firms have inducements to intimidate or eliminate smaller competitors. They will presumably do so using the least costly method. That method involves selective actions with the least cost to the larger firm. Put in general terms, selective actions are the dominant firm's ideal device for adding market share profitably.

Selective actions are not equally available to smaller firms, because those firms face more complete, across-the-board competitive pressures than do dominant firms. Selective action is anticompetitive when it gives dominant firms a category of weapons that are unavailable to little rivals.

7. By a Dominant Firm. In short, selective actions are anticompetitive when they are taken by a firm whose market share is high *and* higher than the share of the target firm. The task is to design a policy fitted to those conditions. Only the specific category of **selective tactics by firms with high market shares** is anticompetitive. Restraining those actions will restore competitive parity.

2. Alternative Criteria

Three other much-discussed criteria are actually incomplete or nearly useless.

Price and Cost: Areeda and Turner. First is a method based on **prices and costs** only. Areeda and Turner argued in 1975 that actions might reduce competition only if the firm set price below cost (that is, incurred a definite financial loss). Once the rival was eliminated by the low price, the predator would recoup profits by later high prices. If no loss is suffered, they said, the action has not gone too far. This would be a special, extreme form of discrimination in which the price-cost ratio goes below 1.0.

This approach has been widely adopted because it seems objective and based on efficiency. One compares prices with true costs, which are supposed to be marginal costs. In the case of dominant-firm pricing, one usually takes its **long-run marginal costs** as the test, since the firm obviously expects to remain in the market in the long run. Pricing below the firm's own long-run marginal cost is presumed to be predatory, aimed at recouping long-run profits.

As noted already, marginal costs are hard to measure. One problem with this approach is that it is usually hard to measure costs reliably and to set the correct limits on prices in actual cases. The seeming objectivity of the price-cost tests is often illusory (as Areeda-Turner and many other writers admit).

Also, the test makes no sense when a **smaller firm** cuts its prices too low. That action cannot harm competition; instead, it can only promote competition by enhancing a small rival against a dominant firm. In short, the Areeda-Turner approach has some economic merit, but is incomplete because it omits the crucial competitive setting.

Anticompetitive Effects. Second, the **effects** of the larger firm's actions might be used as the test of anticompetitiveness. However, that approach will face impossible difficulties. As noted, all successful competitive actions by all firms will inherently harm their rivals' capital values. Any economist who tries to measure those effects and to separate excessive ones from the endless variety of impacts from fair competition and differences in the firms' efficiency will face a hopeless task. There would also be baffling questions about the severity of the effects. For example, if the smaller firm is crippled but not quite killed off, would the action be rated as not excessive?

One would need to estimate not only each action's effects as distinct from the effects of all other actions taking place, but also the relative efficiency and innovativeness of the two firms. Only then could one judge if the affected firm's difficulties were caused by the larger firm's tactics rather than by the smaller firm's own lesser competence. Any judgments would be hotly argued and inconclusive.

Intent to Harm Competition.   Third, policies might conceivably be based on judgments about the firm's **intent**.[12] But that approach is neither logical nor feasible. All firms naturally intend to defeat their rivals, and the actions they take to do so are usually part of healthy competition. Trying to determine when that intent goes too far is like trying to judge when an athlete is trying too hard.

What matters again, is the setting of the action and the weapons used by the rivals. If the setting and weapons are equivalent, then intent is irrelevant. If the setting and weapons are in imbalance, intent also is irrelevant. In any event, intent is usually a complex mixture of attitudes that are virtually impossible to discover and to measure against an objective scale.

3. The Basic Criterion

The basic economic criterion is therefore simple and based on type-B (anticompetitive) actions in figure 10.3. The policy would prevent **systematic selective actions** by firms whose **market shares are sharply larger than their rivals'**. There is no need for price-cost tests, measures of effects or intent, or evaluations of relative efficiency. Though there are some complexities, they usually will be smaller than those of the other tests.

If the attacking firm is smaller or only a little larger than the other, then its actions are part of fair competition. However, if its market share is, say, 30 points higher than the other firm's, then important selective actions can clearly be unfair.

Economists can therefore focus on anticompetitive actions in which a dominant firm takes selective actions. They may wish to add Areeda-Turner price-cost tests. If later prices were clearly high for recoupment, that could reinforce the type-B test. But by themselves, the three other tests are usually too narrow, too hard to apply, or not relevant.

4. Specific Instances and Rules

Creating the American Tobacco Monopoly.   Some early U.S. cases have been thoroughly mined for lessons. For example, John McGee argued that Standard Oil's actions were not predatory, but Scherer and others have noted strong contrary evidence.[13] Malcolm Burns studied the creation of the American Tobacco monopoly during 1890–1900.[14] He finds that the monopolizing actions had the predictable effect of driving down the value of the competitors' assets so that they could be acquired cheaply. This fits our general analysis, in which impacts show up in asset values, permitting monopolization and excess profits. At least one Bell Telephone company during 1894–1912 also adopted anticompetitive actions.[15]

Matsushita.   Leading Japanese electronics firms sold television sets in the United States at low prices from the 1950s to 1974. Motorola sued them for predatory pricing, alleging that they were driving Motorola out and would raise prices later to recoup. But the Supreme Court in 1986 exonerated the Japanese firms. Their opinion was largely theoretical, saying that predation was not a rational strategy because the Japanese could not gain a monopoly nor raise their prices to recoup.

The Court ignored that the Japanese had barriers against fair U.S. competition in Japan and that the Japanese had set prices below cost. The Court showed that it would usually reject predatory price complaints using facts or, if necessary, theory. After this decision, complaints about anticompetitive actions have mostly ceased.

A Stay-Low Pricing Rule.   Baumol has noted that a simple rule can frustrate attempts to price low with the intent of eliminating competitors.[16] If the price-cutter can be forced to keep the newly cut price down, then the payoff will be prevented. Knowing that this result will happen, firms will avoid such actions when they are anticompetitive.

The rule is simple and correct, but it faces practical problems. Also, it is valid only when the setting involves sharp market-share differences, as noted previously. Therefore, applying the rule requires careful study of the market setting.

Predatory Innovations.   Innovations also can have anticompetitive effects in certain situations. A leading case occurred in 1969 to 1971, when IBM redesigned certain computer components in ways that reduced the ability of rivals to make compatible equipment.[17] These small rivals were virtually eliminated from the market by this change and related actions. Their lawsuits against IBM alleged that the innovation was predatory. IBM was the dominant firm, with over 70 percent of the market. Although IBM won the cases (mainly on Areeda-Turner criteria, which were not wholly relevant), the possibility that product changes can harm competition is genuine and interesting.

Another such instance involved Berkey Photo's accusation that Eastman Kodak deliberately designed and introduced its new Instamatic Camera in ways that would remove Berkey as a competitor in film processing (see chapter 13).

Predation continues as a lively topic for modeling and empirical research and cases.[18]

IV. CASES OF PRICE DISCRIMINATION

Practical cases can convey the variety of price discrimination and illustrate how to evaluate it. But first, note that discrimination does not always clash with cost-based pricing. Supply to elastic-demand customers often happens to be at low cost, and therefore the demand-based and cost-based prices turn out to be roughly in line. The problem is to determine costs and then judge how far prices depart from them. Because costs are often hard to measure, one's judgment about discrimination must often be imprecise.

Airline Fares.   The airline industry consists of a mass of city-pair routes in the United States and abroad, served by a group of major and minor airlines (see chapter 14). Demand elasticities vary sharply among expense-account business customers, leisure travelers, and various others. Most business travelers and certain vacationers have low elasticity of demand, with last-minute urgent trips and expense accounts that cover the cost; some tourists have very high elasticity, as they plan long ahead and shop around for low fares.

Since the deregulation of airlines in 1978, price discrimination has become extremely widespread and thorough.[19] As computer reservations systems became more sophisticated, the airlines' ability to discriminate advanced, so that by 1985, the larger airlines were ready to make discounting more systematic. American Airlines led the way, hardening discounting in supersaver and other fare categories, each of which had firm limits on availability. Discounts were now available only if one stayed over Saturday night and bought the ticket in advance, and the degree of discounting tended to be uniform among the airlines. Tickets were usually not refundable, or were adjustable only at sizable cost.

By 1987, discrimination had become systematic rather than flexible, and it has remained in that general pattern. Large airlines employed hundreds of staff in yield management, whose job was to continually juggle the number of discount seats on each flight so as to extract the maximum revenue from passengers.

Hotel Prices.   Complex pricing also invaded the hotel industry in the 1990s. Discounts for large customers grew deeper and more common. Hotels developed "frequent-customer" discount programs. Even many individual customers have learned to ask routinely for discounts.

Automobiles.   Discrimination is universal in car prices. The sticker "price" is merely a suggestion; only naive buyers pay it. Smart buyers instead find the dealers' invoice price and then bargain up from that. The negotiated price depends on bargaining skill—as well as on the general scarcity and popularity of the car model.

Telephone Service.   Value-of-service pricing has permeated telephone pricing for many decades. Figure 10.5 illustrates one important discriminatory version. The familiar flat-rate monthly price for local service has made individual calls free, no matter how many are made, when they occur, or how long they last. One can make an hour-long local call during the business-hour peak period for no charge. Yet the real cost is normally high for such calls, since peak loads involve relatively high capacity costs. Figure 10.5 shows how strongly discriminatory the pricing might be: the peak-time cost level is over ten times as high as the off-peak cost level.

In contrast, long-distance telephone rates have fitted some of these cost differences. Busy-hour rates are naturally much higher than off-peak rates.

Some customers in large cities are now charged message rates, such as 10 cents per call above 70 calls per month, as is also shown in figure 10.5. The message rate also discriminates against off-peak callers. Only when calls are charged accurately by their duration and their time of occurrence can discrimination be eliminated.

Drugs. Drugs that are patented are typically produced by the patent-holding firm, plus one or two other licensed firms. The prices are set and adjusted so as to maximize profits during the patent's life. As we noted earlier, large, bulk-volume buyers are able to obtain low prices. In the 1950s to 1980s, the big buyers were the Veterans Administration and hospitals; since 1980, HMOs and mail-order retailers also have forced the drug companies to grant them lower prices.

The prices can differ by high multiples. The costs of packaging and distribution might account for some of the differences, but most of the price differences can be laid to discrimination. Patents protect most such discrimination by giving the holder virtually a free hand in exploiting the monopoly.

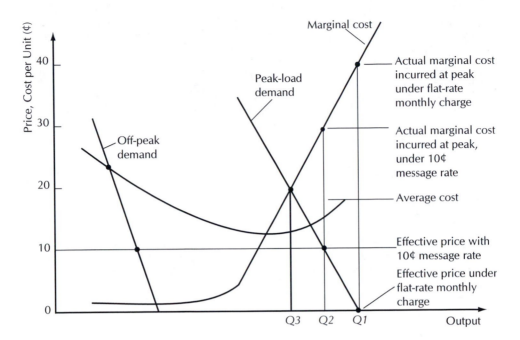

Figure 10.5   An illustration of local-service telephone pricing.

After 2000, sharp drug-price contrasts between the United States and Canada stirred intense efforts by U.S. consumers to acquire Canadian drugs, which average 67 percent below the U.S. prices. Table 10.2 illustrates some of the contrasts.

Standard Oil.   From 1870 to 1890, the Standard Oil Company's monopolizing of the new oil industry involved two main kinds of discrimination. One was selective price cutting in various regions, some of which may well have gone below costs. John S. McGee asserted in 1958 that the company's pricing was not anticompetitive, but others disagree (as noted earlier). Regardless, there was extensive, flexible discrimination, which aided in the absorption of competitors.

The second discrimination was done by railroads. Standard Oil pressured the railroads to provide it cheap freight rates for oil. Also, Standard made the railroads pay it a rebate for each barrel of competitors' oil that they carried! This was a main source of Standard Oil's monopoly, and it drew severe public criticism.

Magazines.   Magazine selling is packed with differential pricing. Each term, students are offered various special discount rates, and most magazines routinely offer a variety of discounts to new subscribers and various classes of renewal subscribers. Is this discrimination? Does it affect competition?

Consider two points. First, subscription prices usually differ sharply from newsstand prices, but so may costs. Subscription requires addressing and mailing costs; newsstand sales involve wholesale and retail markups. The publisher's net price per copy may be the same. Only a full cost comparison can tell.

Table 10.2. Samples of Price Discrimination in Drugs

Name	Price in U.S.	Price in Canada
Tamoxifen (breast cancer) 20 mg/90 pills	$287	$47
Prilosec 2 mg/100 capsules	$408	$175
Celebrex (arthritis) 100 mg/100 pills	$133	$68
Nexium 40 mg/84 capsules	$321	$144

Sources: Tara Parker-Pope, "The Ins and Outs of Getting Drugs (The Legal Kind) From Across the Border," *Wall Street Journal* (October 22, 2002): p. D1; and Sarah Lueck, "Upstart Texas Firm Makes Stir With Cheap Drugs From Canada," *Wall Street Journal* (October 21, 2002): pp. A1, A8.

Second, consider student discounts versus regular subscription rates. These usually *do* involve discrimination, because costs probably are about equal. The publishers' reasons for giving you special bargains are understandable. First, you are on a low budget, and you can easily borrow copies or use library copies; therefore your demand elasticity is relatively high. Also, they want you to become loyal readers, willing to pay the regular subscription rates for the rest of your life as your income rises.

Indeed, pricing involves a great variety of discounts, changing flexibly. Moreover, most magazines have modest or small market shares. Therefore discrimination is mostly type A, tending to promote competition.

Special Sales. Retailers often stage a sale to clear their inventory and/or to draw customers who might buy other items at regular prices. Clothing, groceries, furniture, automobiles—virtually every retail market—has a stream of such sales. Two kinds of discrimination might be present. One is between the sale items and others not on sale. The second is chronological, between the sale items before and during the sale. If the sale prices are cut 50, 60, or 70 percent below standard levels, the discrimination might even seem to go below cost.

Yet the actual discrimination may be much smaller, or not present at all. The key is the true level of cost. If the goods in stock are definitely surplus, the retailer will reappraise their true cost at a much lower level than if they were selling well and needed to be replaced. Indeed, if the goods are really a glut on the market, their marginal cost may be nearly or actually negative.[20] The ratio of the sale price to such costs may actually still be higher than the price-cost ratios of either the goods at a time before the sale or other regular goods.

All sellers face this recurrent problem of managing their inventories. As long as the discounts are sporadic rather than systematically planned, it is part of the competitive process. You can judge every local sale in your town from this perspective.

QUESTIONS FOR REVIEW

1. Suppose that demand elasticities vary sharply, but customers can resell the good freely among themselves. Can price discrimination occur? Discuss two real examples.

2. Explain how would you judge whether the following involve price discrimination: (a) Magazine subscriptions are half price for students. (b) First-class fares are twice as high as coach fares on the same plane. (c) Householders pay 7 cents per kilowatt-hour for electricity, whereas industrial firms pay 2 cents. (d) Some buyers get a PT Cruiser for $17,000, while others get it for $19,000.

3. Give three examples of procompetitive price discrimination. Then give and contrast three anticompetitive examples.

4. Does the phrase *predatory pricing* have any economic meaning? Explain that meaning.

5. Explain how Ramsey prices may maximize static consumer surplus for any set of demand elasticities. Now let competition increase for some goods and diminish for others; will the Ramsey prices now change? Will they be efficient?

6. Explain the strengths and limits of the stay-low price rule against predatory pricing.

ENDNOTES

[1] Basic references on the topic include A. C. Pigou, *The Economics of Welfare* (London: Macmillan, 1920); Joan Robinson, *The Economics of Imperfect Competition* (London: Macmillan, 1933); Fritz Machlup, *The Political Economy of Monopoly* (Baltimore: Johns Hopkins, 1952); and for public utility conditions, Alfred E. Kahn, *The Economics of Regulation*, 2 vols. (New York: Wiley, 1971; 1988 ed., MIT Press).

[2] The customer is often physically connected (by a wire or pipe, as in the cases of electricity, telephone service, and water), and reselling is impossible or illegal. Customers cover the whole array of types—households, businesses, and public agencies—so demands differ sharply. The utility service is a vital necessity for many, even most, customers (that is, demand is highly inelastic for many customers), so there is opportunity and incentive for steep overcharging.

[3] See Kahn, *The Economics of Regulation*, for thorough discussion. Discrimination may instead reduce static efficiency, under some conditions; see for example S. K. Layson, "Third-Degree Price Discrimination under Economies of Scale," *Southern Economic Journal* 61 (October 1994): pp. 323–27.

[4] William J. Baumol, John Panzar, and Robert D. Willig, *Contestable Markets and the Theory of Industry Structure* (San Diego: Harcourt Brace Jovanovich, 1982).

[5] See William G. Shepherd, "Ramsey Pricing: Its Uses and Limits," *Utilities Policy* 1 (October 1993): pp. 295–98; also Shepherd, "Competition and Sustainability," a chapter in Thomas G. Gies and Werner Sichel, eds., *Deregulation: Appraisal Before the Fact* (Ann Arbor: Bureau of Business Research, School of Business, University of Michigan, 1982); and also William G. Shepherd, "Contestability vs. Competition—Once More," *Land Economics* 71 (August 1995): pp. 299–309. For favorable discussion of Ramsey prices, see Jean Tirole, *The Theory of Industrial Organization*, 2nd ed. (Cambridge: MIT Press, 1993).

[6] The small renters sued Blockbuster and the movie makers, but were rebuffed in court.

[7] "Random House Sued by Booksellers Group," *New York Times* (January 6, 1996): p. C9. Other publishers agreed in 1995 to equalize their discounts to all booksellers. The book companies also subsidized advertising on books by the large chains only.

[8] Classic books on this crucial topic include J. M. Clark, *Studies in the Economics of Overhead Costs* (Chicago: University of Chicago Press, 1923); and W. Arthur Lewis, *Overhead Costs* (London: Allen & Unwin, 1948). The Baumol et al. analysis in *Contestable Markets* offers interesting insights on defining multiproduct costs and efficiency conditions.

[9] The main writings are Basil S. Yamey, "Predatory Price Cutting: Notes and Comments," *Journal of Law and Economics* 15 (April 1972): pp. 137–47; Philip Areeda and Donald F. Turner, *Antitrust Law*, 7 vols. (Boston: Little, Brown, 1978); and Frederic M. Scherer and David Ross, *Industrial Market Structure and Economic Performance*, 3rd ed. (Boston: Houghton Mifflin, 1991), chapter 13. See also M. R. Burns, "Predatory Pricing and the Acquisition Cost of Competitors," *Journal of Political Economy* 94 (1986): pp. 266–96; D. Fudenberg and Jean Tirole, "A 'Signal-Jamming' Theory of Predation," *Rand Journal of Economics* 17 (1986): 366–76; Janusz A. Ordover and Garth Saloner, "Predation, Monopolization, and Antitrust," in Richard Schmalensee and Robert D. Willig, eds., *Handbook of Industrial Organization* (New York: North-Holland, 1989).

[10] This section draws on William G. Shepherd, "Assessing `Predatory' Actions by Market Shares and Selectivity," *Antitrust Bulletin* 31 (Spring 1986): pp. 1–28.

[11] For example, suppose it cost the early Standard Oil $1 million to cut its price in one region to drive out its small rival, and it could only make $900,000 in profits there later by raising its price. If ten other rivals in other regions were frightened by this display of ferocity, Standard Oil might be able to buy them all out at lower prices, saving it many millions.

[12] See the discussion in William S. Comanor and H. E. Frech III, "Predatory Pricing and the Meaning of Intent," *Antitrust Bulletin* 38 (Summer 1993): pp. 293–308.

[13] John S. McGee, "Predatory Pricing: The Standard Oil Case," *Journal of Law and Economics* 1 (October 1958): pp. 137–69; also Ronald H. Koller II, "The Myth of Predatory Pricing," *Antitrust Law and Economics Review* 4 (Summer 1971): pp. 105–23. See also Scherer and Ross, *Industrial Market Structure and Economic Performance*, pp. 468–79, and sources cited there.

[14] Malcolm R. Burns, "Outside Intervention in Monopolistic Price Warfare: The Case of the 'Plug War' and the Union Tobacco Company," *Business History Review* 56 (Spring 1982): pp. 33–53; and Burns, "Predatory Pricing and the Acquisition Cost of Competitors," *Journal of Political Economy* 94 (April 1986): pp. 266–96.

[15] David F. Weiman and R. C. Levin, "Preying for Monopoly? The Case of Southern Bell Telephone Company, 1894–1912," *Journal of Political Economy* 102 (February 1994): pp. 103–26.

[16] William J. Baumol, "Quasi-Permanence of Price Reductions: A Policy for Prevention of Predatory Pricing," *Yale Law Journal* 89 (November 1979): pp. 1–26.

[17] *California Computer Products, Inc., et al. v. International Business Machines Corp.*, 613 F. 2d 727 (9th Cit. 1979). See Richard T. DeLamarter, *Big Blue* (New York: Dodd, Mead, 1986).

[18] Still another instance is Y. J. Yung, J. H. Kagel, and D. Levin, "On the Existence of Predatory Pricing: An Experimental Study of Reputation and Entry Deterrence in the Chain-Store Game," *Rand Journal of Economics* 25 (Spring 1994): pp. 72–93.

[19] See especially Steven A. Morrison and Clifford Winston, *The Evolution of the Airline Industry* (Washington, DC: Brookings Institution, 1993), and sources there; also chapter 14 in this book; and Severin Borenstein and Nancy L. Rose, "Competition and Price Dispersion in the U.S. Airline Industry," *Journal of Political Economy* 102 (August 1994): pp. 653–83.

[20] That is, a warehouse full of unwanted goods is a burden, which one might pay to have hauled away.

Chapter

11

Tight Oligopoly: Theories and Real-world Patterns

Tight oligopoly falls just below dominance on the scale from monopoly to effective competition. Tight oligopoly has been a favorite topic of theorists since it emerged in the 1930s. Yet economists still find it baffling.

When a market contains only a few main rivals, their behavior and the results are always difficult to predict. The rivals are **interdependent**, with a wide and shifting variety of possible strategies. The action gets complicated; imagine a chess game among three players who are simultaneously playing in a three-dimensional space rather than a flat chessboard, are thinking at least five moves ahead, and are constantly forming or breaking coalitions, both with each other and against each other.

Or, to change the metaphor, every oligopolist is like a general waging war on the battlefields of commerce, trying to outwit, bluff, and bludgeon its rivals. Yet, since oligopoly also always rewards cooperation, the generals are constantly tempted to form alliances with their "enemies." The warfare then may give way—possibly just for a little while, or instead perhaps for decades—to collusion among some or all of the combatants.

Collude or Fight? The leading policy question is whether tight oligopolists tend to **collude to fix prices,** to **fight each other,** or to oscillate between those extremes. Free-market theorists say that price-fixing always fails, but we note that there are strong exceptions. Tight oligopoly may indeed create collusion that often comes close to full monopoly.

Game Theory.   Some economists have hoped to capture oligopoly's variety in a single comprehensive theory or, at most, in several theories. That theorizing has waxed and waned since 1930 in several waves of oligopoly theorizing, focusing increasingly on game theory. The first wave began as far back as 1838 with Augustin Cournot. Game theory and strategic analysis boomed during 1944–1960, and they revived during 1975 to the late 1980s.[1]

All these models have always ignored direct collusion in favor of indirect non-collusive behavior. That is a steep bias and limitation. The strengths and uses of the models remain limited, as we will see, and game theory has faded since its peak in the 1980s.

A Shrinking Problem?   The extent of actual tight oligopolies in the U.S. economy has dropped sharply in recent decades, from about 35 percent to about 18 percent, as we saw in chapters 1 and 3. Oligopoly variations may ultimately be merely a minor matter; after all (as figure 2.12 illustrated), oligopoly simply gives a range of variation around the basic patterns caused by market shares.

Predicting oligopoly is much like predicting the weather. Rough averages and ranges can be guessed at, but reliable and precise answers simply can not be obtained. Yet theorizing continues, and this chapter conveys several simple models. Sections 2–5 focus on analysis when direct cooperation is ruled out by assumption. Section 6 reviews conditions favoring or discouraging collusion, and sections 7–8 review some conditions in real oligopoly markets.

I.   CONFLICTING INCENTIVES: COOPERATION VERSUS CHEATING

The basic question regarding cooperation is simple: Can it stick? If it succeeds, the group of colluders raises prices and gains excess profits. But paradoxically, the stronger its success in raising prices, the larger the rewards are to each member for cheating. And that cheating eventually destroys the collusion. However, the cartel tries to detect and punish defectors, and that may sustain the collusion.

Some free-market theorists say that cheating quickly defeats every price-fixing ring. At the other extreme, some experts say that cartels can enforce tight, long-lasting collusion. In fact, success will vary with the conditions.[2]

Incentives to Cheat.   It is easy to show the incentives to cheat. Figure 11.1 illustrates a typical firm (panel A) within a whole market (panel B). Under competition, price is P_1 and total market output is Q_1 (in panel B). Our typical firm's profit-maximizing output is at A in panel A.

Price fixing raises the price to P_2, which requires cutting total output to Q_2. Everyone must sell less, and this firm is assigned to cut back to output B. If all the firms follow orders, then the collusion works and each makes profits as shown by the shaded rectangle E.

Once price is fixed higher, however, the firm's maximum profit point is instead at X, where its marginal cost equals the fixed price (which therefore is its

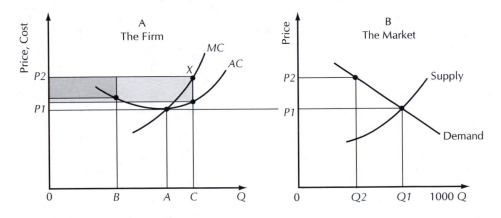

Figure 11.1   The incentive to cheat on collusive price-fixing.

marginal revenue). If it decides to cheat and sell an amount C, its profits are E *plus* the crosshatched area. Even if it doesn't go as far as point X, it gains from every extra unit it sells.

II. BASIC THEORIES OF INTERDEPENDENCE

Oligopoly involves **interdependence** among several firms (actually from two firms up to as many as eight).[3] Members of the group can either coordinate or compete.

Oligopoly therefore also involves **indeterminacy**, because it provides a wide range of possible outcomes.[4] Outcomes vary because there are infinite varieties of both oligopoly structures, which differ in concentration, inequality among leaders, and other elements; and attitudes and motives among the rival firms.

The shining hope of theorists has been to find **determinate solutions** to the slippery, smoke-and-mirrors indeterminacy of the oligopoly problem. Augustin Cournot pioneered these studies, writing lucidly about **quantity-setting duopolists** as early as 1838. His analysis went unread by economists until discovered in the 1880s by J. Bertrand, a Frenchman, who suggested in a brief paper that each duopolist might take action by **setting its price** rather than its output.[5]

The subject then lay largely neglected again until 1932, when Edwin Chamberlin placed it at the center of the newly discovered oligopoly problem. Next John von Neumann and Oskar Morgenstern offered their formidable *Theory of Games and Economic Behavior* in 1944. A boom in research and debates then followed, but by 1960 it was realized that oligopoly theory was of little use in explaining or predicting real market behavior, such as in the automobile or steel industry.[6]

In 1959 Kaysen and Turner studied extensively the tight-oligopoly riddle in theory and fact, with suggestions for strong U.S. antitrust policies toward it. But oligopoly remained stubbornly unsolved, except in abstract specialized blackboard games. By 1970, oligopoly was a passé topic, while tight oligopoly was also fading from actual markets.

But then, surprisingly, oligopoly modeling revived after 1975 for more than a decade. It suited the rising tide of mathematical analysis by young theorists as a vehicle for talent. It then settled down as a business strategy topic, primarily relevant to business-school courses. Nevertheless, game theory has provided the tools to define the strategic environment in which firms operate. In the process of formulating the game theoretical model, the theorist benefits from considering variables he may not otherwise consider and scrutinizing the applicability of the model to the real world.

However, game theory has not yielded a single model to explain oligopoly behavior. In fact, industrial-organization game theory is comprised of as many models as there are industries. Each model is used to describe behavior in different industries, and several models are required to describe different behaviors within each industry. Given any behavior observed in the marketplace, there is likely to be at least one model that explains it. By explaining everything, does game theory actually explain nothing?

Additionally, the results of game theoretical models often depend delicately on the precise form of the model. Different assumptions, variables, or constraints often produce very different results within the same model. The diverse outcomes obtained simply by altering one variable or assumption do little to build confidence in the validity of the models.

Moreover, the results of oligopoly models merely confirm intuitively obvious points. For example, basic Cournot analysis indicates that (under certain assumptions) an increase in the number of equal rivals will move the outcome closer toward the competitive level of prices. That is of course obvious from intuition, wider experience, or simpler theory, but the pure theory satisfies the urge of theorists to prove something, even if only in an abstract model.

III. GAME THEORY: MODELS OF NONCOLLUSIVE DUOPOLY

If the setting is narrowed down to two rivals, it is possible to reach determinate results under certain assumptions about costs, demands, and the rivals' decision rules. There are some markets with just two main players: athletic shoes (Nike and Reebok), some airline markets, aircraft (Boeing and Airbus), some railroad markets, some telecommunications markets (AT&T against Baby Bells), garbage haulage, locomotives (General Motors and General Electric), some ambulance markets, disposable diapers (Kimberly-Clark and Procter & Gamble), and certain toys (Mattel and Hasbro).

In trying to clarify such real markets, game-theory models have **three severe weaknesses**:

1. They are short-run.

2. They assume that each firm is myopic, incapable of learning and adjusting when its assumptions are falsified in practice.

3. They assume that firms never think about any directly collusive actions.

Games analysis, for all its limits, can illustrate how firms arrange joint-maximizing outcomes if they cannot collude directly or even semidirectly.[7]

1. Using Payoff Matrixes to Illustrate Duopoly Choices

Some main insights about joint maximizing, interdependence, and stability can be illustrated by simple game situations, such as those that we have concocted for the payoff matrix in figure 11.2. The matrix is strictly artificial, and it is also imaginary, with no pretense of fitting any real market. In fact, nobody has yet been able to fit matrix values to a real market with any success.

In figure 11.2's typical games matrix, there are two firms or players.[8] Their prices can differ briefly, we assume, but they will have to be equal in any equilibrium.

Interpreting a Matrix. Prices range along the two price axes, from low prices (top left) to high (bottom right). Suppose that the two firms are Nike and

Prices that Nike can choose ($)

Prices that Reebok can choose ($)

Reebok \ Nike	10	20	30	40	50	60	70	80	90	100
10	−300 / −300	−200 / 0	−10 / 2	−20 / 4	−30 / 7	−42 / 11	−55 / 16	−70 / 22	−90 / 30	−120 / 38
20	0 / −200	−5 / −5	−1 / 6	−5 / 9	−11 / 15	−18 / 20	−26 / 25	−50 / 31	−65 / 38	−80 / 46
30	2 / −10	6 / −1	10 / 10	8 / 25	6 / 29	0 / 33	−10 / 37	−23 / 41	−37 / 45	−50 / 55
40	4 / −20	9 / −5	25 / 8	22 / 22	20 / 38	17 / 42	10 / 46	4 / 50	−5 / 55	−15 / 70
50	7 / −30	15 / −11	29 / 6	38 / 20	33 / 33	31 / 55	28 / 60	24 / 65	19 / 70	15 / 80
60	11 / −42	20 / −18	35 / 0	42 / 17	55 / 31	48 / 48	75 / 70	31 / 75	28 / 80	25 / 90
70	16 / −55	25 / −26	37 / −10	46 / 10	60 / 28	70 / 35	75 / 61	55 / 80	48 / 90	38 / 100
80	22 / −70	31 / −50	41 / −23	50 / 4	65 / 24	75 / 31	80 / 55	75 / 75	62 / 97	40 / 105
90	30 / −90	38 / −65	45 / −37	55 / −5	70 / 19	80 / 28	90 / 48	97 / 62	88 / 88	78 / 93
100	38 / −120	46 / −80	55 / −50	70 / −15	80 / 15	90 / 25	100 / 38	105 / 40	93 / 78	77 / 77

Figure 11.2 An illustrative payoff matrix for duopolists Nike and Reebok.

Reebok, which are actually the current leaders in the athletic-shoe market. The resulting payoff matrix has one cell for each pair of prices for the two firms. Thus, with Nike shoes at $80 and Reebok shoes at $60, the numbers are 75/31 in the corresponding cell. The numbers mean that Nike gets $31 million in profits, while Reebok gets $75 million. That comparison is plausible; the lower-price firm gets higher profits.

The numbers in figure 11.2 are merely illustrative, but they do fit common sense. Together the two firms can raise their combined payoff by raising their prices simultaneously, but this is true only up to a point.

Now let's examine the basic nature of this matrix. It is a **variable-sum, symmetrical matrix**, as shown by the following properties. First, as with any matrix, it can best be interpreted by focusing on **the diagonal going from low to high price values;** in figure 11.2, that is from the upper left to the lower right corner. Along the diagonal, market equilibrium is possible, because the two firms' prices are equal.

The matrix is not **zero-sum**, because the total amounts of the two firms' profits do vary throughout it. You can verify this by comparing cells around the matrix. The matrix is **symmetrical**, as you can test by comparing corresponding cells on its opposite sides.

Solutions. Now look along the diagonal to identify the two interesting solutions: (1) **the joint-maximizing price** and (2) **the competitive-equilibrium outcome.** They are the two shaded cells.

First, the joint maximum. If both Nike and Reebok set a price of $90 per pair, then each makes $88 million and the jointly maximized profit is $176 million. No other cell gives a combined total profit that large (the next largest is $171 million, when prices of $90 and $100 are simultaneously chosen: 78/93 or 93/78).

This joint-maximum result is an equilibrium at the full monopoly price, but, unfortunately for the firms and fortunately for consumers, it is an **unstable equilibrium**. Nike and Reebok must arrange it by direct cooperation, and it must be enforced by trust and/or penalties. It would not emerge by independent voluntary choices. You can verify that by starting at any low price on the diagonal. If either firm raises its price, it makes less profits while its rival makes more. So neither firm would raise prices first.

The joint-maximum result at $90 illustrates the general truth that two duopolists (or, more generally, all oligopolists) may luckily attain a monopoly. But the monopoly outcome may not last, however. As section 1 noted, each firm can instead gain higher profits for itself by cutting price a little, as long as the other firm does not also cut its price.

In the matrix, each firm makes $97 million if it cuts its own price from $90 to $80 while the other stays at $90. In the matrix, Nike is shown as the price cutter, getting the circled $97 million profit by cutting its price to $80. Reebok must now reconsider its choices; while Nike is at $80, Reebok can raise its profit from $62 million to $80 million by cutting price to $70, as shown by the arrow. Once Reebok cuts its price to $70, Nike must reconsider and respond; by cutting to $60, it can raise its profit: from $55 million to $70 million.

This price war continues, ratcheting down to the competitive equilibrium price of $30 per pair. There the two rivals will stay, because neither can gain by raising its price while the other does not. This resting point represents a famous concept in game theory: a **Nash equilibrium**. In a Nash equilibrium, no individual player can improve by changing his behavior as long as the other players do not change theirs either.

The matrix illustrates that noncollusive actions can yield competitive results, whereas a higher equilibrium price might come about only by direct collusion. And the collusive price will be subject to instability from cheating.

The degree of instability cannot be told from the matrix alone. It is a complicated matter, depending on the duration of short-run profits and the severity of retaliation by the rival. Finally, bear in mind that the instability is strictly made up; other payoff values could easily be written in that would stabilize it. (Indeed, it is a good review exercise to make up your own matrices with contrasting outcomes.)

Note that the players could adopt a larger strategy against price cutting. Each could threaten to cut price immediately to the $30 competitive level as an instant punishment for any price cutting at all. This approach could eliminate any prospect of gains from price cutting, thereby making the joint-maximum equilibrium more stable.[9]

Games analysis also has been applied in some experiments in which students or other volunteers play games by preset rules.[10] These tests have borne out the same lessons. The student oligopolists try to collude, often with remarkable success, but often the games quickly degenerate into price wars, at least for a while. Your own experience in a four-person Monopoly game might confirm the variety of outcomes and shifts as the players repeatedly form alliances and change them.

2. COURNOT AND BERTRAND MODELS

Strategic thinking obviously can be valuable in many situations.[11] Often it is merely a business choice, however, not a full normative basis for setting public policies.

The two contrasting approaches most commonly used are **Cournot models**, in which each firm sets only its **quantity**; and **Bertrand models**, in which price is the only decision variable. In each case, we begin with just two firms of equal size and industrial conditions. Average costs are constant, and therefore equal to marginal cost. Consequently, each firm has no specific capacity; it can produce just one unit or all of the industry's output at the same cost per unit.

Cournot Output-Setting Models.   Cournot analysis is similar to the passive dominant-firm analysis in chapter 9. We begin with the market demand curve and horizontal cost curves, as shown in figure 11.3. Each firm is assumed to maximize its profit by accepting the other firm's existing output level and then choosing its own best output level.

Suppose that firm 2 has chosen output level Q_2, as shown. Firm 1 then has a residual demand curve, which is to the left of the market demand curve by the amount Q_2. Firm 1's demand curve also defines a marginal revenue curve, as shown in figure 11.3. In this case, firm 1's maximum profit point, where its marginal revenue is equal to its marginal cost, is at output Q_1.

The same exercise can be done for every other level of output that firm 2 may choose. As Q_2 rises, firm 1's demand curve is shifted farther left, and its chosen Q_1 value is lower. At one extreme, firm 2 may choose to supply all the market

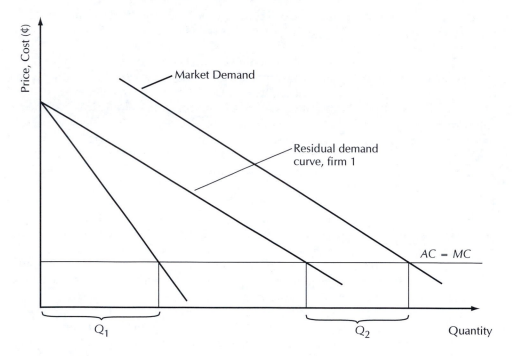

Figure 11.3   Marker demand and firm 1's residual demand curve.

output, as shown in figure 11.4. Firm 1 is then left with a residual demand curve so far left that it supplies nothing. At the other extreme, firm 2 may choose to supply zero. Firm 1 then has the whole market demand to itself, and it will set output at Q_1, as shown in figure 11.5.

Generally, firm 2 must set its output at the competitive level—where price equals marginal cost—in order to drive its rival from the market (as in figure 11.4). If firm 2 chooses instead to withdraw from the market (as in figure 11.5), then firm 1 can set the monopoly output with the monopoly price.

The result is a **reaction curve** for firm 1, which relates the output it chooses to firm 2's prior output level. This curve is shown in figure 11.6, with the extreme cases as we just derived them. When firm 2's output is at the maximum level (consistent with a price that covers costs), then firm 1 produces zero, as shown by point 1. That is the competitive level for the market. When firm 2 produces zero, then firm 2 is able to set the monopoly level of output (at point 2). It is just half of the competitive level, because average costs are constant.

Between these two extreme cases, we can interpolate intermediate points. For a straight-line demand curve, they lie along the straight-line reaction curve shown in figure 11.6.

Because the situation is assumed to be symmetrical to both firms, firm 2 will have a reaction curve that is the mirror image of firm 1's reaction curve. It is derived by the same steps we went through for firm 1. Both reaction curves are shown in figure 11.7. Each has a competitive and monopoly extreme, but in reversed locations.

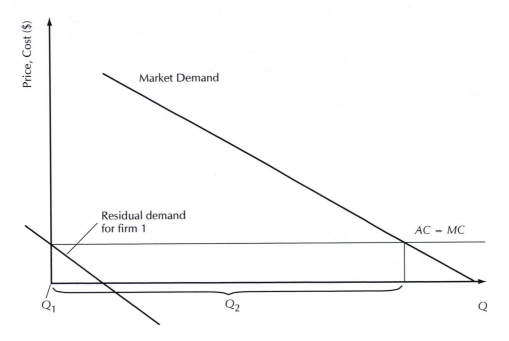

Figure 11.4 Firm 2 supplies all output.

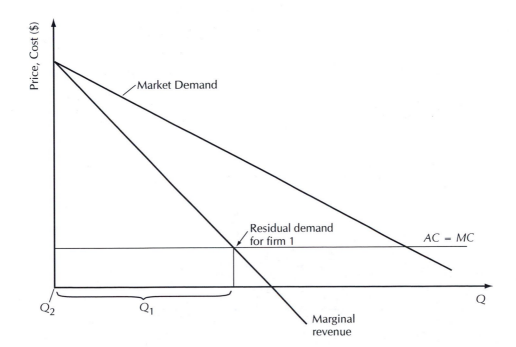

Figure 11.5 Firm 2 supplies zero output.

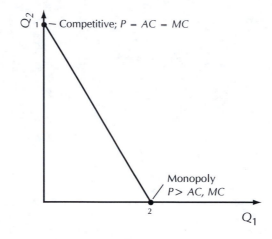

Figure 11.6 Firm 1's reaction curve.

These two curves define the possible outcomes. At all points except where they cross, they involve a conflict between what the two firms expect of each other. That conflict can be seen by considering a sequence of moves, as illustrated in figure 11.8. For example, suppose that firm 1 produces zero because firm 2 has been producing the competitive market output at point 1. Now that firm 1 is producing zero, firm 2 will react by cutting its output in half, to the monopoly level Q_m. Firm 1 now reacts in turn by moving to point 3 on its reaction curve, firm 2 reacts by moving to point 4, and the process converges on the point common to both curves. That is the point of Cournot equilibrium, with the two rivals dividing the market equally. Because each firm sells the level expected by the other, no change occurs in this stable equilibrium.

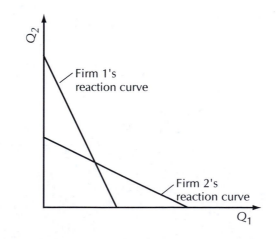

Figure 11.7 The two firms' reaction curves.

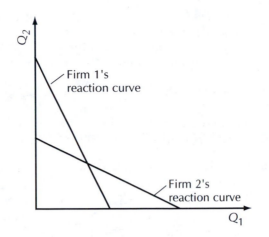

Figure 11.8   Convergence on the equilibrium point.

We can also find the Cournot equilibrium using equations of the market demand and firm marginal cost curves. Suppose the market demand curve is given by:

$$Q = 110 - P$$

Each firm has a marginal cost curve given by:

$$MC_1 = MC_2 = 10$$

Because firm 1 accepts firm 2's existing output level, the demand curve facing firm 1 is:

$$Q_1 = (110 - P) - Q_2$$

For a linear demand curve, the accompanying marginal revenue curve is twice as steep as the demand curve. Therefore, firm 1's marginal revenue curve is:

$$MR_1 = 110 - Q_2 - 2Q_1$$

Setting $MR_1 = MC_1$ yields the profit-maximizing output for firm 1:

$$Q_1 = 100 - Q_2 / 2$$

This is the equation for the reaction curve because firm 1's profit-maximizing output choice depends on firm 2's choice of output. The symmetrical reaction curve for firm 2 is:

$$Q_2 = 100 - Q_1 / 2$$

The output decisions of firm 1 and firm 2 are consistent only at the point where each firm is producing what the other firm expects. This occurs at the intersection of the reaction curves:

$$Q_1 = Q_2 = 33.33$$

The result is in the middle of the range between pure monopoly and pure competition. The pure-monopoly output Q_m could be sold by one firm or the other, or divided between the two along the dashed line between Q_m1 and Q_m2, as shown in figure 11.9. To move onto that line, the two firms would have to coordinate their actions carefully and deliberately. Conversely, the pure-competitive output could be provided by any combination lying along the dashed line between Q_c1 and Q_c2.

Compared to these extremes, the combined equilibrium output (Q_1 plus Q_2) is below the competitive level toward the pure-monopoly level. Indeed, it is closer to monopoly than competition; in this case, Cournot behavior tends to give a degree of monopoly pricing, albeit monopoly pricing reached by strictly independent choices.

This result fits intuition, of course. We expect high concentration to yield a degree of monopoly behavior, even if not by direct collusion. But the assumptions underlying the model are certainly exotic. Firms are always independent but passive, never challenging each other. Neither do they cooperate with each other. This passivity is the underlying assumption that makes it possible to derive a result that includes a degree of monopoly effect.

More oddly, these firms are strictly myopic, never looking beyond each period, even though any normal firm in a situation of rivalry would quickly learn to anticipate future adjustments. That is, after all, the essence of the interdependency.

Thus the sequence shown in figure 11.8 involves dimwitted behavior in which the same error is repeated over and over again. For that matter, the whole approach assumes the two firms are operated by dimwits, because they obviously could quickly coordinate to reach full monopoly results.

Also, the meaning of identical size is peculiar when, by assumption, costs are constant. When that is true, any firm can freely produce any amount of output at the same cost. Accordingly, the firm has no well-defined capacity or size. These firms are really not producers so much as wholesalers who can acquire any amount of output to sell at the going cost level. Such firms have little to do with real enterprises producing with specific capacity and costs in real markets.

Still, the model gives an interesting insight—a degree of monopoly can occur even without no direct collusion. Some theorists take comfort that sensi-

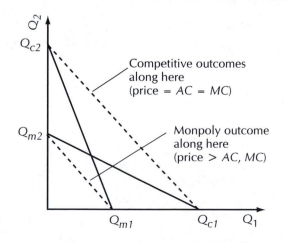

Figure 11.9 Contrasting competitive and monopoly outcomes.

ble conclusions can be derived rigorously, even if in a surreal model. Moreover, one can add more firms to the situation. If all are assumed to be of equal size, then each firm is passive toward a larger total output set by all its rivals. Under these conditions, each firm sets a smaller quantity for itself, but the summed total of all firms' output is larger than when there were only two firms. As the number of (equal-size) firms rises, the equilibrium more closely approaches the competitive output.

The analysis can also cover two **unequal-size** firms, but only by a further restrictive method, that is, by assuming different cost levels for the two firms. Returning to figure 11.3, suppose that firm 1 is able to adopt a superior method of production, which reduces its costs to cost B, well below the original level at cost A. This change is shown in figure 11.10, where firm 2 remains stuck with the old, higher-cost method, cost A.

Firm 2's reaction curve will remain unchanged, but firm 1's will not. For any output level chosen by firm 2, firm 1 will now choose a higher output level for itself: Q_{1B} rather than Q_{1A} in figure 11.10. Therefore firm 1's reaction curve will shift to the right by these amounts, using the same approach as before.

As shown in figure 11.11, the equilibrium now will have firm 1 producing more than before while firm 2 produces less. Firm 1's cost advantage has led it to take a larger market share while firm 2 accepts a smaller share. Whether price is proportionally closer to monopoly levels than before is not determined.

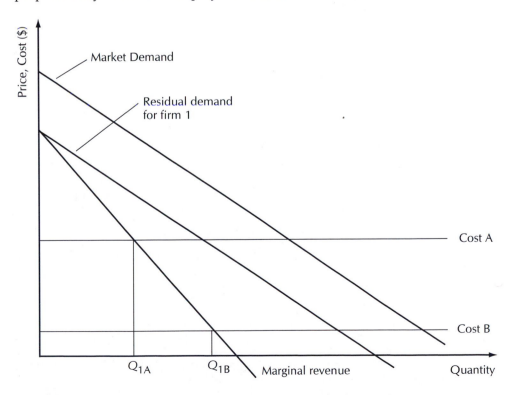

Figure 11.10   Firm 1's lower cost (at Cost D) leads it to set a higher output.

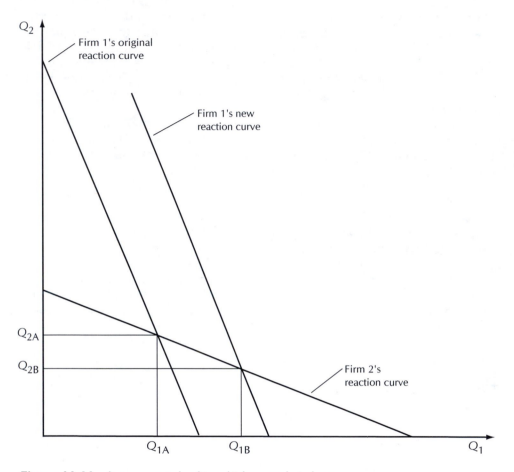

Figure 11.11   Lower costs lead to a higher market share.

In analytical terms, the cost drop has given firm 1 a higher degree of market power. Recall that the Lerner index of monopoly is (P - marginal cost) / price.

It can be shown that

$$P - MC \,/\, P = \text{market share} \,/\, \text{demand elasticity} = MS \,/\, E_D$$

for each firm. A lower cost gives a higher Lerner index, which is expressed by the role of market share in the right-hand side of the equation. This can be extended to the whole market, using an industrywide average of firms' marginal cost (MC_{AV}) and the HHI. It can be shown that

$$\text{price} - MC_{AV} \,/\, \text{price} = \text{HHI} \,/\, E_D$$

for the market. Such results make the HHI more attractive to theorists as the measure of concentration, because the results seem to show rigorously that the HHI is valid and can be directly linked to other market conditions.

Yet these insights should be interpreted cautiously. The market power is derived solely from cost superiority; therefore the analysis is narrowly limited to market power that stems solely from lower costs. It excludes the many other possible sources of market power. Indeed, this analysis instills the bias that monopoly power really does arise only from cost superiority. That is only true in the ideal new-Chicago school of thought.

Moreover, to achieve large market-share differences, there must be impossibly large differences in costs. A degree of market dominance involving market shares of 60 percent for one firm and 10 percent for four others would require that the lesser firms' costs be six times as high as the dominant firm's. Such extreme differences are quite implausible, except when the dominant firm excludes rivals from technology by monopolistic means (e.g., patents). In that case, dominance would then not arise strictly from market forces and superior efficiency. Rather, cost superiority would reflect imperfections and monopoly controls.

Once again, you need to cautiously evaluate the insight provided by the analysis. Cournot models assume narrow and dimwitted decisions in a strange setting of cost and demand. Even at its best, the analysis merely confirms a few obvious points more easily arrived at through intuition and experience.

Bertrand Price-Setting Duopolists.   Assume that the duopolists continue to be myopic and dimwitted, but that they now set prices rather than outputs. This model may be somewhat more realistic, because it involves the possibility of differences between the two firms' products. However, it also assumes that the two firms accept each other's price as a given when setting their own price, never learning to anticipate or to design strategies. As before, this artifice is adopted because it yields definite answers, even though it makes little sense.

Price-setting duopolists require a somewhat different technique of analysis, but it will also lead to reaction curves for the two duopolists. We begin by assuming that the two firms' outputs are differentiated and there is some brand loyalty, so that a price difference will lead some buyers to shift to the cheaper seller. The two sellers are assumed to maximize their profits by choosing their best price while expecting that the other firm's price will stay where it is.

How differentiated the two products are is the key condition governing each firm's residual demand curve. If they are highly differentiated (e.g., two goods with strong brand loyalties), then each firm's demand will be relatively close to the market demand curve. At the other extreme, similar products will have much higher elasticities of demand, because buyers will shift drastically even if only small price differences occur.

Firm 1 will have a different residual demand curve for every given price already chosen by firm 2. Figure 11.12 illustrates two such curves, one if firm 2's price is high (panel A), and another if firm 2's price is low (panel B). Firm 1's profit-maximizing choices then follow routinely, as shown by the MC = MR points in each diagram, at Q_A and Q_B. Generally, a higher price by firm 2 elicits from firm 1 a price that adjusts in that direction, and vice versa when firm 2's price is low. Intuitively, if firm 2 prices monopolistically, firm 1 will have more scope to do so also, but a low firm-2 price will put pressure on firm 1 not to raise its price very far out of line.

If the demand curves are straight lines, and *if* they shift strictly in parallel (rather than rotating or twisting in some other way), then firm 1's reaction curve can be derived in terms of the two firms' **prices**, as shown in figure 11.13. The

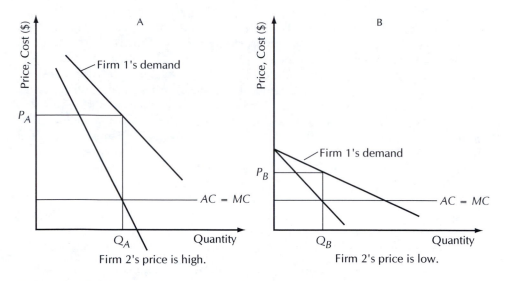

Figure 11.12   Bertrand duopoly: Firm 2's price affects firm 1's demand.

same is done to derive firm 2's reaction curve, which is a mirror image of firm 1's curve. Figure 11.13 shows three sets of reaction curves for rising degrees of differentiation between the two products. The curves in panel A illustrate slight differentiation. **Both are upsloping, because the two prices tend to move together, not in reverse to each other, as in the Cournot output-setting model.**

As the degree of differentiation between the products increases (panel B), firm 2's curve rises and becomes flatter, while firm 1's curve moves to the right and becomes steeper (they are still mirror images of each other). The extreme case of complete differentiation is shown in panel C. Of course, in that case, the two goods are not really in the same market because (by assumption) they are not mutually substitutable. To that extent, what we really have here is a pair of monopolists, not duopolists competing in the same market.

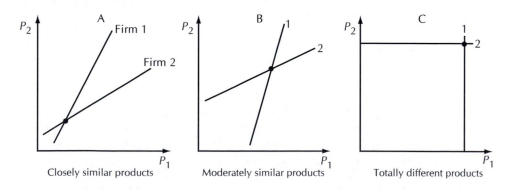

Figure 11.13   Bertrand analysis: Reaction curves depend on the degree of difference between the firms' goods.

In any event, the crossing point of the two reaction curves defines the equilibrium result for each case. When the products are closely similar (that is, more directly competitive), the outcome is near the competitive price level. At the other extreme, total differentiation permits each firm to price as if it were a pure monopolist, which indeed it is. In the middle range, greater degrees of differentiation will move the result closer to monopoly pricing levels.

This Bertrand price-setting analysis provides a nice contrast to the Cournot model. Product differentiation is now included, at least as a matter of degree, and the logic differs in certain respects. The reaction curves take contrasting, positive slopes, and the outcome depends on product differentiation rather than on the numbers of (equal-size) firms.

But the intellectual limits of this model are narrow. The two firms' myopia is complete. The assumption of product differentiation violates the requirement that products in the same market are close substitutes. In the end, both analyses merely illustrate what is known from intuition and mainstream experience: namely, that fewness, cost advantages, and product differentiation tend to breed monopoly behavior. Even so, some interesting practical evidence about game-situation behavior has been developed, in real cases and in experimental situations.[12]

IV. TACIT COLLUSION AND PRICE LEADERSHIP

Where price fixing is illegal (as in the United States), tacit collusion may evolve in tight oligopolies. Though rarely as forceful as direct price agreements, it can be significant.

Tacit Collusion.   Tacit (or implicit) collusion requires that the oligopolists build up a degree of shared knowledge and trust. The coordination is often precarious, for the firms cannot legally apply explicit controls and penalties. Yet such controls and penalties must be present, if only in the shadowy form of shared expectations about what will happen to price cutters. The main penalty is some form of retaliation to match or undercut the price cutter. It must be applied often enough to be believed and feared.

Such price wars are costly to the enforcers. In each industry, the length to which the punishment will occur reflects a balance between the gains from collusion, the individual rewards to price cutters, and the profits lost by enforcing penalties on price cutters.

Among industry conditions, **concentration** favors tacit collusion. So do **homogeneity** of products, **stable industry conditions**, and long **familiarity** among the firms. Shifts in cost and demand require frequent adjustments in the fragile coordination.

Price Leadership.   Price leadership is one form that tacit collusion may take. The phrase is merely a loose intuitive one. It refers to the process by which one firm leads a price increase with other firms following. Each follower gains individually by *not* following. Why, then, would the leader boldly raise price, unless it were reasonably confident that the rest would follow? This implies tacit collusion.

Especially during 1890 to 1940, many concentrated industries did seem to display collusive price leadership. Prices would remain stable for a period, then one firm would raise price sharply. The others would quickly match the rise, often in exact detail. The new price would hold for a long period until the next round, which was often led by the same firm. The meatpacking industry from 1890 to 1920 and the cigarette and steel industries during the 1930s showed such patterns strikingly. Early analysts of oligopoly in the 1930s took it for granted that such price leadership was tacit collusion at work. Later, in the 1950s, steel and autos also followed this pattern. Again, collusion seemed to be at work.

We can also model collusive price leadership using a market demand equation and the firms' marginal cost equations. The model assumes that the price leader sets a market price that is followed by all the other firms, the other firms choose what quantity to supply based on the market price, and the price leader supplies the remainder of the market demand at this price.

Suppose that a market has a price leader and 1000 other identical, price-taking firms. The total demand in the market is given by:

$$Q_D = 50{,}000 - 1{,}000P$$

The price leader has a marginal cost curve given by:

$$MC_L = 10$$

The price-taking firms in the market have identical marginal cost curves given by:

$$MC_{PT} = q + 5$$

The price-taking firms set $MC = P$ or $q + 5 = P$. Because there are 1000 identical firms, the supply curve of the price taking firms is:

$$Q_{S,PT} = 1000P - 5000$$

The price leader supplies the remainder of the market demand that is not supplied by the price-taking firms. Therefore, the demand for the price leader is the market demand minus the quantity supplied by the price-taking firms:

$$Q_{D,L} = 55{,}000 - 2{,}000P$$

From this demand curve, we can derive the marginal revenue curve for the price leader:

$$MR_L = -Q_L/1{,}000 + 27.5$$

The price leader chooses the market price where his profits are maximized at $MC_L = MR_L$:

$$10 = -Q_L/1{,}000 + 27.5$$
$$Q_L = 17{,}500$$
$$P = \$18.75$$

Each price-taking firm then supplies the quantity where $MC_{PT} = P$ or 13.75 units. The total supplied in market is the sum of the price leader's supply and the price takers' supply: 31,250.

Yet the process may instead be barometric price leadership. The firms themselves routinely claim at the time that the price rises are required in order to cover rising costs, investment requirements, and so forth. They may be right. If so, the process itself matters little.

Price leadership is an imprecise phrase, and the collusive and barometric types are not clearly distinct. Actual cases are likely to mix some attributes of both.

V. CONDITIONS FAVORING OR DISCOURAGING COLLUSION

Costs. When oligopolists' costs differ, agreement on prices becomes more difficult. The cost differences can arise from many causes. The firms may differ in their locations, in their access to cheap inputs, or in their quality of management. They may have built plants of differing sizes at differing times.

Demand. When demand curves differ, preferred prices will usually differ, even if costs are identical. When both costs and demand vary, the chance that firms will prefer the same price is remote. Oligopoly pricing therefore tends to be unstable, and agreement is difficult except in odd cases.

Shifting demand over the business cycle is an important special case. As demand falls during a recession, price warfare often breaks out among oligopolists. Why don't they instead maintain prices, or perhaps reduce them gradually? The main reason is cost differences. Some firms are capital-intensive with low marginal costs. Other firms have less machinery, relying more on labor, which gives them a higher marginal cost at below-capacity levels of output. Those with lower marginal costs will wish to cut prices more deeply.

Therefore, oligopoly pricing is likely to be especially fluid during recessions, as differences in costs come into play. Conversely, any stable and uniform pricing by oligopolists during recessions is likely to reflect direct collusion.

Nonprice Competition. This aspect can be a substitute for price competition. In many markets, the leaders indulge in a variety of nonprice interactions (in product design, advertising, and so on) while carefully avoiding price warfare. Competition is thus channeled in safer directions. The room for this secondary competition varies among industries. Some industries are rich in nonprice dimensions, or at least the nonprice features can be cultivated. Others are bare of the nonprice frills; simple, homogeneous products are the obvious instance.

Information. Information can make cooperation easier. **When sellers are better informed than buyers,** they can detect price cutting more quickly and penalize it more fully. This puts a chill on price cutting and shifts the range of likely prices upward. If information is tilted the other way, **then buyers can induce more price cutting,** since detection and retaliation by sellers will be slower.

The tilt toward buyers is likely to occur in markets for simple and uniform products, for which buyers can easily comparison shop. By contrast, more complex products for which special-order contracts are the rule give sellers the advantage on key information. Colluding sellers will set up systems to force quick disclosure among themselves (but *not* to buyers) of the prices being set in the market.

VI. COLLUSION IN REAL MARKETS

How do these concepts play out in real markets? There are three main questions: Does price-fixing last? How extensive are the cooperative efforts? What specific forms do they take? The first two questions can be answered briefly and broadly. The third involves details that occupy the rest of this chapter.

Collusion Often Is Extensive, and It Can Last For Long Periods. Cooperation in price-setting *is* extensive. Most forms of price fixing are illegal in mainstream U.S. industries under antitrust laws (see chapter 15), and yet collusion does occur in many cases. As one experienced executive put it in 1975, "The overwhelming majority of businessmen discuss pricing with their competitors." Said another, "Price-fixing has always been done in this business, and there's no real way of ever being able to stop it—not through Congress, not the Justice Department. It may slow down for a few years. But it will always be there." And still another: "It's just the way you do business. There's an unwritten law that you don't compete. It's been that way for 50 years."[13]

These tendencies may have yielded to new pressures, including tougher antitrust penalties after 1976 and stronger import competition in many markets. That is not reliably known, however. And recent research shows a wide range of price fixing and formal cartels in U.S. and European markets that have lasted for many years even when they are illegal.

Table 11.1 indicates some patterns of industrial price fixing in U.S. markets.[14] Hay and Kelley found that formal (and illegal) price fixing is frequent even in very tight oligopolies in which tacit collusion might be expected instead.

In some other countries, where such cooperation has been legal, the degree of control and detail has been much greater than in the United States. From 1930 to 1956, some 2,500 schemes for price fixing and market sharing emerged in British industries.[15] Numbers were comparable for other Western European countries.[16]

VII. TYPES OF COLLUSION

The main categories of collusion (from the strongest to weakest) are: cartels, controls on entry and market areas, price-fixing agreements, and tacit collusion. There is space here only to describe and then illustrate each type with examples.

1. CARTELS

Cartels have come in many varieties. The standard cartel had written rules and penalties that the parties agreed to, plus a staffed organization to see that the rules were followed. Almost every conceivable device has been tried at some time and place. Some cartels have been arranged and enforced by the state itself; others have been supported by the courts.

Table 11.1 Selected Price-Fixing Conspiracies in U.S. Industries, 1961–1970

Market	Geographical Scope	Four-Firm Concentration in the Market (%)	Number of Conspirators (and their share of sales) (%)	Number of Firms in the Market
Wrought steel wheels	National	85	5 (100)	5
Bedsprings	National	<61	10	20
Metal library shelving	National	60	7 (78)	9
Self-locking nuts	National	97	4 (97)	6
Refuse collection	Local	–	86	102
Women's swimsuits	National	<69	9	–
Steel products (wholesale)	Regional	66	5 (72)	–
Gasoline	Regional	>49	12	–
Milk	Local	>90	11 (>80)	13
Concrete pipe	Regional	100	4 (100)	4
Drill jig bushings	National	56	9 (82)	13
Linen supplies	Local	49	31 (90)	–
Plumbing fixtures	National	76	7 (98)	15
Class rings	Regional	<100	3 (90)	5
Tickets	Regional	<78	9 (<91)	10
Baked goods (wholesale)	Regional	46	7	8
Athletic equipment	Local	>90	6 (100)	6
Dairy products	Regional	>95	3 (95)	13
Vending machines	Local	93	6 (100)	6
Ready-mix concrete	Local	86	9 (100)	9
Carbon steel sheets	National	59	10	–
Liquid asphalt	Regional	56	20 (95)	–

The omitted figures are not available.

Source: Adapted from George A. Hay and Daniel Kelley, "An Empirical Survey of Price Fixing Conspiracies," *Journal of Law and Economics* 17 (April 1974). Adapted from the appendix table.

In Europe and most global markets since 1960, cartels have been removed or forced into weaker forms, but they often persist more informally. Among less complete cartels, the marketing cartel (called a syndicate in Germany) has been a common type. It handles all its members' sales and manages their revenues, controlling every aspect but profit pooling and investment.[17]

2. CONTROLS

Specialized controls may be firm but are incomplete. The most common type in the United States is control on entry. Definite standards are set, which all sellers in the market must meet. These controls can be applied by the sellers on their own or by a public regulatory agency.

Among many examples, one has been commercial banking. Entry was restricted after 1935 by chartering; new entrants have had to prove that more banking services were needed. Over twenty states have prohibited branching by a bank into more than one physical location. Despite loosening since 1970, some controls on bank entry are still significant.

Various professions—medicine, law, and accounting, for example—have major restrictions on who can enter. Others (beauticians, barbers, and morticians, for example) are controlled by state licensing laws. The restrictions often underpin effective price fixing by the professionals' associations.

3. AGREEMENTS

Next is the large realm of price-fixing agreements, ranging all the way from tight pacts to loose, wishful efforts. They are a frequent occurrence, even where illegal. Table 11.1 suggests their variety. Price is the key element controlled. Price agreements may be reinforced by market divisions and other controls. Among many hundreds of instances, the following are classics.

Electrical Equipment.   In 1960, an extensive price-fixing ring among U.S. producers of heavy electrical equipment was discovered and penalized.[18] In many submarkets, elaborate control mechanisms had evolved as a way of life over at least several decades. The methods of fixing prices were designed to preserve market shares, usually with the sellers rotating by phases of the moon and other devices. At the industry's trade association meetings there were private gatherings upstairs to keep the price arrangements going.

Despite frequent acrimony and occasional breakdowns, the schemes variously raised prices by 10 to 30 percent over long periods of time. Their eventual exposure in 1960 was a spectacular event. After 1960, some cooperation continued in the form of tacit collusion (discussed later).

Cast-Iron Pipe.   The six leading producers divided the market into several regions and established a price-fixing committee. They controlled two-thirds of sales outside the eastern seaboard. Prices were raised, and an auction pool was run to settle who would be the lowest bidder at public lettings. The conspiracy ran for many years until the mid-1890s, when it was the target of the first landmark antitrust opinion, which in 1899 declared price fixing to be flatly illegal.[19]

Collusion by Elite Colleges: The Overlap.[20]   After 1954, the leading Ivy League colleges began conspiring to set the scholarships that they would offer new students who had applied to several of them. Their admissions officers met during March to decide together exactly what dollar offer was suitable for each student, based on need. Then the colleges all offered each student exactly that agreed amount, with no chance to adjust it.

This collusion, called the overlap, may have had a laudable purpose at first—to hold the line against students bargaining for higher scholarships, so that the funds could be spread as widely as possible to needy students. But as time passed the overlap became instead a run-of-the-mill cartel, simply holding down prices paid to students. It prevented free choice by students seeking to get tuition discounts from the leading colleges. It also hurt the lesser colleges, who could have made high scholarship bids to attract top-quality students away from Harvard, Yale, etc. And it encouraged inefficiency in the colleges.

Eventually, in the 1990s the scheme was finally sued for violating antitrust law, and the collusion stopped in 1994. Pricing became more flexible, as top students were able to bargain for better offers. Yet there was no evidence that the funds for needy students were reduced.

4. TACIT COLLUSION[21]

The only way tight oligopolists in the United States can adopt common prices legally is to do so tacitly. They can give indirect signals, such as a series of public statements about the need to raise prices, which then develop a consensus for an actual rise. The firms may simply learn to coexist and adopt price leadership.

Cigarettes.   In a classic instance, the three main cigarette sellers kept virtually identical prices from 1923 to 1941 and stuck to a tight pattern of price leadership. Prices held steady for long periods—despite large shifts in costs—and then changed suddenly, usually within a day's time. The firms earned an 18 percent return on investment. After 1946, the industry became somewhat less concentrated and pricing became less rigid.

Turbine Generators.   After the 1960 convictions of electrical-equipment firms for price fixing, competition prevailed in the industry for three years. Then in May 1963, General Electric announced a new system of pricing, with four parts. (1) GE greatly simplified the formulas for setting prices, and it published its method in detail. (2) GE added a simple multiplier (.76, to be precise) for converting book prices to actual bids. (3) GE promised to put a price protection clause into all sales contracts, whereby if GE lowered price for any customer, it was bound to extend the discount (retroactively) to all sales made during the preceding six months. This sharp self-penalty assured Westinghouse that GE would not give selective discounts. (4) All orders and price offers were to be published so Westinghouse would not fear secret price cuts.[22]

This ingenious plan surrendered all the secret methods and strategies of price competition that make oligopoly competition work for a system of open coordination.[23] Westinghouse quickly copied GE's plan, even down to the precise numbers in it. Each firm now could coordinate confidently with the other. From 1964 on, the firms used the same multiplier applied to identical book price levels. There was no price cutting, no flexibility.

The parallel pricing was therefore reinforced by an awareness that price cutting would not occur, and that if it did, it would be easily detectable. Eventually the firms gave up the system in 1976, after one large buyer sued (American Electric Power, in 1971) and the Antitrust Division threatened to sue.

5.   OTHER DEVICES: TRADE ASSOCIATIONS AND
JOINT VENTURES TRADE ASSOCIATIONS

Trade associations and related technical cooperative activities also promote cooperation in many cases, but they are too diverse to permit simple judgments. Trade associations are numerous; virtually every industry has at least one. There are about 2,000 national associations, 3,000 state and regional ones, and 8,000 local ones. Some seventy of these associations have full-time staffs of over 400. Many of them have extensive operations that are bound to increase cooperation.

Trade associations are focused in certain industries, particularly lumber products, electrical equipment, textiles, aerospace industries, and alcoholic beverages. The largest are in utilities, various branches of transport, and, above all, the many lines of insurance. Most local trades (such as laundries, real estate, and construction) have frequent meetings and other mutual customs. Generally, trade associations are minimal in very tight oligopolies and merely nominal in very loose oligopolies and atomistic markets. Some of the tightest have been in professional associations of lawyers, doctors, and the like.

Trade associations have frequently increased cooperation among sellers. At their regular meetings, members have sometimes gone upstairs to fix prices (as in the electrical-equipment conspiracies). The associations' programs can affect the amount of information disseminated among sellers as a basis for limiting price cutting.

Some procompetitive effects can occur. The associations' information reporting can help buyers, though it is usually tipped in favor of sellers. Some associations are among lesser firms, aiming to strengthen them against dominant firms. Others try to exert countervailing power on behalf of their many small members (for example, the purchasing associations of small grocers).

6. JOINT VENTURES

Many **joint ventures** have been created by competing firms, usually for some laudable purpose, such as to perform research or operate mines. They have been extensive in many industries, especially steel, copper, oil, computers, and chemicals. They have spread rapidly in the 1990s; the Antitrust Division received only twenty-one petitions for clearance of joint ventures in fiscal 1986, but the number quadrupled to 89 in 1995.[24]

The usual claim is that the resources of two firms (or more in some cases) are needed to support the activity. This claim may be true in some situations, so that net increases in production or innovation do result, yet it is perfectly clear that joint ventures can coalesce interests and inhibit competition.

The desired effect would be a balance between these two directions. Most joint ventures are rather small units held by large firms, which suggests that the concentration effect is relatively strong compared to the possible increase in production and innovation.

Oil.   In the U.S. oil industry, over sixty joint-venture pipelines for oil and oil products have knit together all large oil firms shipping to virtually all significant markets. The lines are built to fit their owners' locations and needs. Also, the partners have to coordinate their flows in each pipeline. This approach ensures that the firms cannot take sharp competitive moves against one another and that outsiders cannot use the pipelines to enter the market.

GM-Toyota.[25]   In 1982, a major joint venture was announced by General Motors and Toyota Motors of Japan involving a West Coast plant that Toyota would operate to produce cars to be sold by General Motors. This was a quasi-merger of the leading U.S. producer with its leading foreign competitor. The tie reduced competition between these major competitors and increased their joint influence over the market. Ford and Chrysler both challenged the venture, but it was approved (after intense debate) by the Reagan Federal Trade Commission.

Its net technical benefits turned out to be minimal, giving little technical gain to GM. Therefore the anticompetitive effect was not offset by efficiencies. Even in the worldwide automobile industry, the two partners still held nearly 50 percent of it. By 1990, GM had declined sharply, reflecting the failure of this joint venture to add to efficiency.

QUESTIONS FOR REVIEW

1. Why don't oligopolists always engage in complete joint maximizing of profits?

2. Suppose a market faces a market demand given by $Q_D = 6,000 - 200P$. The price leader in the market has constant marginal costs of $MC_L = 15$, and the 100 identical, price-taking firms have marginal costs given by: $MC_{PT} = q + 5$. Compute the market price, quantity supplied by the price leader, and total quantity supplied in the market.

3. Make the positive case for Cournot analysis as a valuable way of clarifying market outcomes.

4. Explain why higher concentration provides more information to enforce collusion.

5. Prepare your own payoff matrix for a non-zero sum duopoly with (a) a stable joint maximum, and then (b) an unstable joint maximum. For (b), show step by step how the outcome degenerates to a competitive outcome. Does your matrix fit an actual industry?

6. What items of behavior does a complete cartel need to control? Is that identical to a monopoly?

7. A group of bidders for highway paving contracts never submits identical bids. Yet somehow they spread the work evenly among all of them in a regular rotation. Explain how bid-rigging might proceed.

8. Suppose that in the 1960s, General Electric had sold $100 million of generators every month. It considers cutting price by $20 million. Show and explain how much its six-month price protection policy would cost it for such a price cut. Explain how that might discourage price cutting.

9. When General Motors and Toyota set up a joint venture to make cars in California, what anticompetitive effects might that have had?

ENDNOTES

[1] Useful summaries of pure oligopoly theory can be found in Stephen Martin, *Industrial Economics*, 2nd ed. (New York: Macmillan, 1994). See Jean Tirole, *The Theory of Industrial Organization*, 2nd ed. (Cambridge: MIT Press, 1993); and Richard Schmalensee and Robert D. Willig, *Handbook of Industrial Organization*, 2 vols. (Amsterdam: North Holland, 1989), for high-tech versions.

[2] For example, R. Cyert, P. Kumar, and J. Williams, "Impact of Organizational Structure on Oligopolistic Pricing," *Journal of Economic Behavior and Organization* 26 (January 1995): pp. 1–15.

[3] That is for roughly equal-sized firms. Above ten firms, the firms progressively lose their sensitivity to individual rivals.

[4] Important earlier sources on oligopoly behavior include: Edward H. Chamberlin, *The Theory of Monopolistic Competition*, 6th ed. (Cambridge: Harvard University Press, 1962); John von

Neumann and Oskar Morgenstern, *Theory of Games and Economic Behavior* (Princeton, NJ: Princeton University Press, 1944); William J. Fellner, *Competition Among the Few* (New York: Knopf, 1949); Joe S. Bain, *Barriers to New Competition* (Cambridge: Harvard University Press, 1956); A. D. H. Kaplan, Joel B. Dirlam, and Robert F. Lanzillotti, *Pricing in Big Business* (Washington, DC: Brookings Institution, 1958); Carl Kaysen and Donald F. Turner, Jr., *Antitrust Policy* (Cambridge: Harvard University Press, 1959); and Schmalensee and Willig, *Handbook of Industrial Organization.*

[5] See Augustin Cournot, *Researches into the Mathematical Principles of the Theory of Wealth* (Homewood, IL: Irwin, 1963); and J. Bertrand, review of Cournot's book in the *Journal des Savants* (September 1883): pp. 499–508.

[6] See Martin Shubik, *Strategy and Market Structure* (New York: Wiley, 1959).

[7] Still another recent application has been in FCC auctions of airwave frequencies in 1995 and 1996. Both the FCC and the participants used gaming concepts in preparing the rules and actual bids.

[8] To model three rivals would require a three-dimensional cube; that would be highly confusing and not much more instructive.

[9] See Tirole, *The Theory of Industrial Organization*, chapters 6 and 9, and the sources noted there; and Donald Hay and John Vickers, eds., *The Economics of Market Dominance* (Oxford: Basil Blackwell, 1987), chapter 1.

[10] See James W. Friedman, *Oligopoly and the Theory of Games* (Amsterdam: North-Holland, 1977).

[11] See for example Avinash K. Dixit and Barry J. Nalebuff, *Thinking Strategically: The Competitive Edge in Business, Politics and Everyday Life* (New York: Norton, 1991); a very practical summary is in F. William Barnett, "Making Game Theory Work in Practice," *Wall Street Journal* (February 11, 1995): p. A14. On a more complex technical level, see Jorgen W. Weibull, *Evolutionary Game Theory* (Cambridge: MIT Press, 1995).

[12] A good sample would include D. D. Davis and C. A. Holt, "Market Power and Mergers in Laboratory Markets with Posted Prices," *Rand Journal of Economics* 25 (Autumn 1994): pp. 467–87; T. N. Cason, "The Impact of Information Sharing Opportunities on Market Outcomes: An Experimental Study," *Southern Economic Journal* 61 (July 1994): pp. 18–39; J. A. Brander and Z. Zhang, "Dynamic Oligopoly Behaviour in the Airline Industry," *International Journal of Industrial Organization* 11 (September 1993): pp. 407–35; S. Domberger and D. G. Fiebig, "The Distribution of Price Changes in Oligopoly," *Journal of Industrial Economics* 41 (September 1993): pp. 295–313; J. Cave and Steven W. Salant, "Cartel Quotas under Majority Rule," *American Economic Review* 85 (March 1995): pp. 82–102; and G. Ellison, "Theories of Cartel Stability and the Joint Executive Committee," *Rand Journal of Economics* 25 (Spring 1994): pp. 37–57.

[13] These quotations are among many in this vein from an excellent survey article, "Price-fixing: Crackdown Under Way," *BusinessWeek* (June 2, 1975): pp. 42–48. One could find comparable articles in almost any current year. See also Simon N. Whitney, *Antitrust Policies* (New York: Twentieth Century Fund, 1958), 2 vols., for extensive accounts of activities in twenty major industries in the years before 1958.

[14] See the excellent study by George A. Hay and Daniel Kelley, "An Empirical Survey of Price Fixing Conspiracies," *Journal of Law and Economics* 17 (April 1974): pp. 13–38.

[15] Most were abandoned by 1962, under the Restrictive Trade Practices Act of 1956. See R. B. Stevens and B. Yamey, *The Restrictive Practices Court* (London: Weidenfeld and Nicolson, 1965); and annual *Reports* of Registrar of Restrictive Practices (London: Her Majesty's Stationery Office).

[16] See Corwin D. Edwards, *Cartelization in Western Europe* (Washington, DC: Department of State, 1964); and John P. Miller, ed., *Competition, Cartels and Their Regulation* (Amsterdam: North Holland, 1962), especially chapters 4 and 5. The European cartel craze arose in the 1930s under the stress of economic stagnation. The corresponding U.S. version of cartels—the National Recovery Administration (the NRA)—lasted only a few years in the 1930s.

[17] One prominent international cartel, the Organization of Petroleum Exporting Countries (OPEC), achieved startling success in the 1970s (recall chapter 4). See John M. Blair, *The Control of Oil* (New York: Pantheon Books, Random House, 1976). For comparison, see also A. N. Madhavan, Robert T. Masson, and W. H. Lesser, "Cooperation for Monopolization? An Empirical Analysis of Cartelization," *Review of Economics and Statistics* 76 (February 1994): pp. 161–75.

[18] See Richard A. Smith, *Corporations in Crisis* (Garden City, NY: Doubleday, 1962), chapters 5 and 6; and Ralph G. M. Sultan, *Pricing in the Electrical Oligopoly*, 2 vols. (Boston: Harvard Business School Division of Research, 1974). This case provoked some 1,900 damage suits by utility firms that had bought electrical equipment. There were conspiracies in nine related markets, covering billions of dollars in sales over many years.

[19] The case was *Addyston Pipe and Steel Co. v. United States* 175 U.S. 211 (1899). Old as it is, the conspiracy was preceded by many hundreds of others in other industries in many earlier decades.

[20] See Donald R. Carlson and George B. Shepherd, "Cartel on Campus: The Economics and Law of Academic Institutions' Financial Aid Price-Fixing," *Oregon Law Review* 71 (Fall 1992): pp. 563–629; and George B. Shepherd, "Overlap and Antitrust: Fixing Prices in a Smoke-Filled Classroom," *Antitrust Bulletin* 40 (Winter 1995): pp. 859–84.

[21] Recall that other terms for the same behavior are shared monopoly, conscious parallelism, price signaling, indirect collusion, administered prices, and, in the United Kingdom, parallel pricing.

[22] As the Antitrust Division memorandum in support of the consent decree in 1976 pointed out, customers were even permitted to audit GE's and Westinghouse's own sales books in order to ensure that no secret price cutting was occurring. The memorandum is in *U.S. v. General Electric Co. and Westinghouse Electric Corp.*, U.S. Dist. Ct., Eastern Dist. of Penna., Civil No. 28228.

[23] To understand this plan, imagine that GE and Westinghouse have both sold fifteen turbines in six months for $20 million each, but GE wishes to get a major new contract for five turbines by bidding only $18 million each. The retroactive price cut (to $18 million each on the fifteen earlier turbines) would cost it $30 million, besides the $10 million on the five new turbines. That extra $30 million penalty will discourage GE from making the price cut. Moreover, since Westinghouse would know exactly what GE would do, the chances for avoiding competition would be high.

[24] Neal Templin, "Strange Bedfellows: More and More Firms Enter Joint Ventures with Big Competitors," *Wall Street Journal* (November 1, 1995): pp. 1, A8.

[25] See the thorough coverage by John E. Kwoka, Jr., "International Joint Venture: General Motors and Toyota (1983)," a chapter in John E. Kwoka, Jr. and Lawrence J. White, eds., *The Antitrust Revolution: The Role of Economics*, 2nd ed. (New York: HarperCollins, 1994), and the sources cited there.

Chapter

12

Vertical Conditions, Size and Diversification, and Advertising

Vertical and conglomerate issues have always been secondary to the main horizontal conditions inside markets. These secondary conditions can sometimes be important, and they pose interesting questions. But they are tricky to measure and to evaluate. We give them brief coverage here.

First, **vertical patterns** include monopsony (or countervailing power), vertical integration, vertical mergers, and vertical restrictions on markets (including resale price maintenance). Sections 1–3 discuss them.

Large size and diversification are noted in sections 4 and 5. **Advertising** is covered in section 6; does it affect competition in those consumer-goods industries where it is prominent?

I. MONOPSONY AND BILATERAL MONOPOLY[1]

Pure monopsony consists of one **buyer** for an entire market, exerting power backwards against the sellers. We usually assume the opposite condition: there are many buyers, and none holds any monopsony power. Most analysts ignore monopsony, assuming that it is rare; yet many degrees of monopsony are possible.

1. PRICING WITHIN A RANGE

Buyer concentration is probably much lower than seller concentration, on the whole.[2] Few important monopsony shares over 40 percent are known (apart from some small local instances).

Theory suggests that monopsony can promote an efficient outcome if certain conditions are favorable.[3] Consider the bilateral monopoly illustrated in figure 12.1. Firm A sells its product to firm B, which simply resells it to final consumers. Demand B is the final demand curve faced by firm B. It has a marginal revenue curve MR_B, but that curve is also the effective demand curve (demand A) for firm A's output. It has a corresponding marginal revenue curve MR_A. To simplify the analysis, firm A's cost of supply is assumed to be constant, so that average and marginal cost are identical at that constant level.

The monopsonist firm B prefers to buy from firm A at the competitive price P_C. It can then resell the output at the higher (monopoly) price P_M, but this action clashes with firm A's choice. Firm A wants to collect the price P_M in selling to firm B so its profits will be maximized. If firm A prevails, it gains the excess profits shown by area I. If firm B wins (and buys at price P_C rather than P_M), its excess profits are areas I and II.

The price paid to firm A by firm B is not determinate; firm A prefers price P_M, while the monopsonist firm B prefers to pay as little as possible, at price P_C. The matter is strictly a private struggle between them. The final price and output levels are given; the firms simply fight over the spoils.

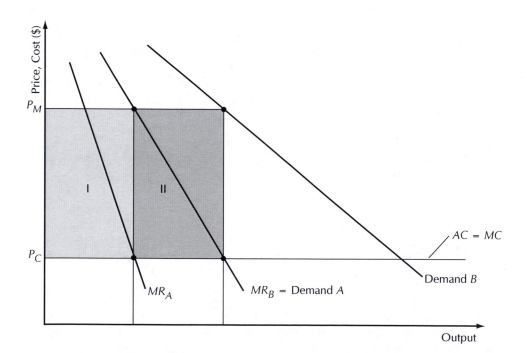

Figure 12.1 Bilateral monopoly.

If monopsonist firm B faces effective competition in selling its outputs, then that may lead firm B to exert pressure back on firm A so as to neutralize firm A's monopoly power. Suppose that firm B's competitors can sell at price P_C (drawing their supplies from other sources). Then firms A and B must meet price P_C if they are to survive. So firm B's status as a seller can be crucial. Though it may seem improbable that a **monopsonist** would turn around and sell its outputs under **competitive** conditions, a little thought should satisfy you that it is quite possible. Wal-Mart and Kmart could be good examples. It is from the final level that pressure may be exerted backward to hold the bilateral monopoly to competitive results.

2. COUNTERVAILING POWER

Note that monopsony is an attractive position to hold. Locate a monopolist, interpose yourself as a monopsonist retailer, and then you can skim off some or all of the monopolist's profit for yourself. J. K. Galbraith urged in 1952 that this would indeed happen to most oligopolies: "As a common rule, we can rely on countervailing power to appear as a curb on economic power."[4] The result could be ideal; oligopolies would achieve economies of scale and the rivalry would stir innovation, but their market power would be neutralized. Strong retailers were among the countervailers that Galbraith envisioned.

Later debate has shrunk the likely scope of such spontaneous countervailing power. Some dominant firms have been able to prevent monopsony power by elaborate sales networks (drugs, copiers, and IBM in computers during the 1950s–1970s), well-controlled dealer systems (automobiles), and other marketing policies (Microsoft). Some other monopolies (such as most utilities, physically connected to the customer) have technology that automatically excludes new monopsonists from arising.[5]

Yet the process of countervailing power is often at work. Where technical conditions permit, it can be important, as confirmed by the buying power and low prices of Wal-Mart and other discount chains.[6] Monopsony plus competitive retailing can be efficient.

II. VERTICAL INTEGRATION

Whether integration can affect monopoly power is a hotly disputed issue. New-Chicago economists argue that integration cannot transfer (or lever) monopoly power from one level to another, nor create more market power than exists from horizontal conditions. The opposite view is that when integration displaces open transactions it often forecloses the market and excludes rivals.

To assess integration, we first define and measure it and note the reasons why firms adopt it. Then we consider its likely effects and the antitrust policies that have been applied to vertical mergers.

1. DEFINING AND MEASURING INTEGRATION[7]

Definition. The production of any good usually involves a series of stages in which raw materials are extracted, processed into intermediate goods, assembled, finished, and eventually distributed as final products. For example, steel goes through many stages, whereas bread is often both baked and sold by the same retail unit.

Vertical integration joins two or more of these successive stages. In practice, virtually all firms combine some successive operations, but they also buy inputs from other firms, and their own outputs are sold to others for further processing or distribution. Both upstream (backward) integration and downstream (forward) integration are common.

Between nonintegrated firms, goods pass from one stage to the next by arm's-length market transactions at going market prices. In contrast, integrated firms transfer the goods by internal shifts, valuing them at internal transfer prices.[8] Those prices need not equal current market prices; they can be arbitrarily set according to the firm's internal motives and systems.

There are many reasons to integrate, as we will shortly see, but many firms remain independent. A market may contain firms with widely differing degrees of vertical integration. The determinants of the scope of vertical integration are a complex matter, and there is often much blurring.

Measurement. Though the meaning of vertical integration seems intuitively simple, it is surprisingly hard to measure. One method is to count stages of production, but defining stages is often a matter of judgment and debate. Instead, one can take the ratio of a firm's value added to its final sales revenue as an index of its degree of integration.[9] However, the ratio of value added to sales tends to be smaller for industries farther along in the chain of production. Therefore comparisons of industries using this simple ratio may be biased.[10]

2. REASONS FOR VERTICAL INTEGRATION

The main reasons why firms adopt vertical integration are to achieve efficiencies and to take advantage of monopoly-related conditions.

Efficiencies. These divide further into two main types: technical conditions and savings on transactions costs.

Technical savings are **physical**. Heat and transport resources can be saved by, for instance, smelting iron in blast furnaces adjacent to steel mills. Pig iron can be fed in immediately rather than having to be shipped over distances and reheated. Other metals may also be combined more efficiently.

Other savings come from better **organization**. Operations at the two (or more) stages may be coordinated more smoothly. Scheduling can be directly planned among all operations without risk of default or external failures.

Williamson has stressed the value of reducing transactions costs. By owning and directly controlling their own operations, integrated firms can avoid the costs of searching for the best and cheapest suppliers, negotiating the complex terms of contracts, monitoring the flows and qualities of inputs, and enforcing contractual provisions on less-than-reliable suppliers. Williamson cites several basic conditions that favor integration, including what he labels "bounded rationality" and "opportunism."[11]

Monopoly-related Incentives to Integrate. Over six specific types of monopoly-related incentives have been identified. They either raise the firm's ability to charge monopoly prices or they strengthen its ability to avoid paying monopoly prices for its inputs.

Barriers are often the most important competition-reducing effect. If integrated firms control most or all of a market's supply, then independent and new firms may find it necessary to do the same. Otherwise they fear that they will be unable to obtain sufficiently secure and reasonably priced supplies. Such integration may impose increased costs, which raise barriers. The integrated firm may accentuate the effect by taking strategic actions that raise their rivals' costs.[12]

Free-market theorists have for over forty years emphatically denied any monopoly effects with a flat counterhypothesis: **that integration does not raise monopoly power at all, ever.**[13] This hypothesis assumes a frictionless, well-functioning market system; integration would then be undertaken only when it gives technical economies. Integration never serves as a lever to extend monopoly power from one level to another. Monopoly might exist at one or more levels and have its usual effects, but that horizontal condition is the only proper focus for concern. Vertical conditions are irrelevant.

Markets usually do not have pure conditions, as we have seen in earlier chapters.[14] Substantial market shares and significant imperfections increase the likelihood of some monopoly-raising effects. The real question is, at what market share are the effects likely to become important: 10 percent, 25 percent, 40 percent, etc.?

The answer depends on concepts and facts that came up in earlier chapters: the degree of competition in capital markets, the role of entry barriers, and the extent of uncertainty and market imperfections generally. It would depend also on a thorough analysis of actual behavior in industries with vertical integration. No such full study has yet been done.[15]

3. VERTICAL MERGERS

Mergers for integration have posed the relevant issues with special clarity. Antitrust decisions have stopped some vertical mergers and shed some light on their role.

For decades, the U.S. Supreme Court said that vertical mergers excluded competition and may raise monopoly, barring them even when they involved as little as 5 percent of market sales. Later, rules eased, and by the 1970s the limits were at about 10 to 20 percent.[16] After 1980, Reagan officials applied free-market doctrine and withdrew all resistance to vertical mergers (see chapter 16). The avoidance of vertical cases continues.

III. VERTICAL MARKET POWER AND RESTRICTIONS

Powerful firms may be able to exert power forward to downstream markets. One form of this is imposing vertical restrictions on later markets.

1. VERTICAL MARKET POWER

Firms often try to extend control to the next level. One noted example is Alcoa, which tried to extend its near-monopoly position in aluminum to improve its position in aluminum products. Two other recent instances are toys and aftermarkets.

Toys. The two leading toy companies are Mattel and Hasbro, each with an array of favorite toys (Barbie, GI Joe, Monopoly, etc.). In 1995–1996 Mattel attempted to merge with Hasbro, but Hasbro successfully resisted. It was widely believed that the merged Mat-Bro firm would have been able to exert control over distribution, even over such powerful chains as Toys 'R Us.[17]

Aftermarkets. Companies that buy complex equipment (such as computers, control systems, or machinery) usually invest heavily in knowledge, layout, and other features in order to knit the equipment into their operations. That commitment locks in the user because of high switching costs. The high switching costs give the equipment producer a chance to charge high price-cost margins on aftermarket services such as repairs and parts.

This process applies market power from one level to the next, and it became an active antitrust issue in the 1990s.[18] Other firms tried to enter the aftermarkets, but the equipment producers resisted fiercely (see chapter 16).

2. VERTICAL RESTRICTIONS

Vertical restrictions became hotly disputed in the 1970s, as free-market economists sought to prove that vertical restraints are usually beneficial rather than anticompetitive. The discussions included mainly territorial restrictions and resale price maintenance.

Just as with vertical integration, vertical restraints may create market power and/or promote efficiency.

1. **Creating Market Power.** Restraints eliminate competition, often by direct price fixing enforced by specific contracts.

2. **Promoting Efficiency.** Restrictions may reduce transactions costs and/ or support high-quality dealer networks. Supply contracts might involve high costs in locating good dealers and making sure that they promote the product. Restraints permit organizing and enforcing dealer networks to reduce such costs.

There are actually two dealer-quality reasons as follows:

a. *Building up a small firm.* The supplier may be trying to develop a new market position. To attract retailers, it may reward them with protected market areas and extra profits. If this strategy succeeds in helping the supplier build up its market share and challenge existing market leaders, then restrictions will promote competition at both levels, though only during the buildup phase.

b. *Supporting quality service against free riders.* The supplier may seek to have its products carried by high-quality dealers (as in bookstores, automobiles, cameras and supplies, and stereo equipment). Quality involves extra advice and service for customers, stocking more models and parts, and reliability in backing the products. These extra-quality services are costly, and it may not be possible to price them out separately so as to charge customers for them.

Smart customers learn to rely on good dealers for some of the extra services (e.g., advice), but then they go across the street to buy the actual products (cameras, stereos, books, etc.) from cut-price discounters. Eventually this free riding drives the good dealers out of the market, leaving only discounters and other lower-quality dealers. The product's reputation and sales will suffer.

This free-rider case for vertical restraints is a familiar free-market idea.[19] In this view, the restrictions don't create market power; they merely respond to the free-rider problem so as to promote better service. Therefore the restraints are beneficial.

Free-market writers also generally argue that free-market choices develop specific pricing of all valuable items, in all markets. Such an unbundling occurs routinely for many products in the form of specific warranties and service contracts. Also, many dealers do manage to confine their extra services to their own customers. Furthermore, many customers remain loyal to good dealers over the course of many purchases and repurchases. Finally, suppliers often can pay directly to subsidize the extra services if they believe them necessary.

A lack of unbundling can only reflect market imperfections, which also could underlie market power. Restricting competition to make good dealers more profitable is only one way to support high-quality service, and its monopoly costs may be high. As yet, there's little reliable research showing big free-rider problems in any market. Therefore the free-rider case for vertical restraints in real markets is not very persuasive.

Territorial Restrictions. Manufacturers often confine their dealers to specific areas. For example, the Coca-Cola and Pepsi-Cola companies have long set exact local areas in which each of their bottlers is permitted to deliver. Any delivery outside the area (that is, any competition with another outside bottler) can trigger a removal of the franchise. With such territorial restrictions, the producer reaches forward to prevent competition among its sellers at the retail level. That clearly reduces competition within the brand.

The **local distributors** usually prefer to be given large, **exclusive** franchise areas. In fact, they press the national suppliers to grant such franchises. Yet the distributors also have conflicting incentives: If they could invade their neighbors' areas, they could raise profits, but counterinvasions by those neighbors would hurt profits.

The **national supplier** (e.g., the Coca-Cola company) normally wants a maximum of competition downstream at the wholesale and retail levels, because that expands the level of output that it can sell at its profit-maximizing price. Franchise restrictions reduce competition, the levels of output, and the supplier's profits. The restraints seem to hurt their interest. In fact, producers often are forced by dealers to accept them.

The FTC investigated Coca-Cola and Pepsi-Cola's restraints in the 1970s. Their market shares have ranged between 25 and 45 percent, high enough that the restriction on **intrabrand competition** (i.e., among Coca-Cola bottlers) would substantially reduce competition in the market as a whole. In 1978, the FTC adopted that reasoning in holding the territorial restrictions illegal under antitrust laws. The companies immediately obtained an antitrust exemption from Congress, so the restrictions are still in full force.

Leading beer companies place similar restrictions on their wholesalers in many states, as noted in chapter 14. They too may reduce competition.

Resale Price Maintenance. Resale price maintenance, or RPM (often called by the euphemism "fair trade"), happens **when the original manufacturer sets retail prices**. Many familiar items have been fair-traded, including books, cameras, clothes, appliances, and toiletries. In fact, manufacturers print suggested prices on the labels, or circulate them privately to retailers, for just about every kind of consumer product.

Often the suggested prices have no force; automobile sticker prices, for example, are just a starting point for you to negotiate a lower "real" price. Yet fair-trade laws were in force in many states from 1937 to 1976, prohibiting retailers from selling below the RPM price. Thus price fixing was backed up by the power of the courts.[20]

RPM is basically an agreement among retailers, enforced by the producer, not to compete on price. Although manufacturers select the actual price, they often do not really want RPM to be strong.

However, RPM might have three benefits for them. One is possibly a building of a new dealer network. A second is a need to support high-quality dealers (as just explained for territorial restrictions). The third reason is to support a high-quality brand image. Manufacturers often seek to prevent the discounting and rack-jobbing of their branded products, which undermines the quality of those products by equating them with leftovers.

RPM has frequently maintained prices 20 percent or more above competitive levels, and its excesses actually held up price umbrellas, which encouraged the spread of discount chains during the 1960s. It is still at the center of ongoing guerilla warfare in thousands of retail markets. Though fair-trade laws were formally repealed in 1976, the practice of suggesting prices is still widespread.

Free-market writers mounted a campaign in the 1970s and 1980s to justify and rescue RPM, and Reagan officials sought to use the Spray-Rite case in 1983 to make the case for RPM.[21] However, most economists believe the strict policy line against vertical price fixing is still correct. The effort to rehabilitate RPM has receded as extreme free-market thinking has faded.

IV. THE EFFECTS OF BIGNESS

Now we turn to conditions that have repeatedly stirred popular anxiety: giant corporations and conglomerates. Both are peripheral to the problem of real monopoly within markets, but they may have larger society-wide impacts. Free-market analysts say that these two conditions have nothing to do with market power. In each case, we must first define the condition—not a simple task—and then consider its benefits and costs.

Absolute size (or size per se) is distinct from **relative size** (the firm's share within the market). Size means bulk or sheer mass, and economic mass may give a degree of economic power and influence economic results. There are several indexes of size. Sales revenue, capital, employment, value added, and profits have been used.[22] Which index to use depends partly on context. If the firm's financial power is in question, for example, then the size of its capital or profits could be decisive, rather than the number of jobs or volume of sales.

In practice, sales and assets are the most commonly used measures of size. For many purposes, either measure is good enough, and of course the two measures are closely related for the normal run of firms. Yet they can diverge; a firm may have giant-sized assets but small ranks of employees (oil firms and banks lean that way), or high sales and low assets (as most retailers).

What effects might size have? Several possible effects have been advanced during the century.

Market Power.   Ever since the United States' first monopoly crisis in 1885–1920, bigness has been said to provide market power. A counterargument after 1945 urged that size per se is entirely irrelevant to market power.[23] This in turn was countered by Bain's stress on entry barriers.[24] A "capital barrier against new competition" can be caused by sheer size if a new entrant must assemble large-scale financing. Therefore a big firm gains some market power from its size per se.

This fits common sense: General Motors has more power than an otherwise identical but tiny firm producing toy cars. The effect of size may be small, especially if barriers are only a minor element of structure. The issue is open.

X-Efficiency and Economies of Scale.   Size *has* made it harder to avoid internal inefficiency. In small firms, the manager sees everything and can directly enforce efficient operations. Large enterprises always involve a degree of bureaucracy with several layers of management. Although valid information is crucial for managers, the bureaucratic process instead often sends up false information and unreliable proposals. Size breeds mistakes, and it weakens controls on costs. It also tends to weaken employees' identification with their firms and therefore undermines their effort levels and efficiency.

Political Power.   Large size also can yield political power, for two main reasons. First, large firms hold large-scale financial resources, which can be quickly mobilized and deployed for lobbying. Second, their large employment rolls give them some influence over voting patterns. Trade associations among smaller firms (such as druggists or grocers) can also sometimes assemble sizable funds and voting influence. But their actions are more fragmented and cumbersome than the direct actions of large firm.

V.   DIVERSIFICATION

Most firms produce a variety of products. Britain's East India Company from 1700 to 1850 was a very early vastly diverse enterprise, and by 1900 various diversified firms spread into many sectors and regions of the United States. By 1950 many diversified firms had long been well established, from Procter & Gamble and RCA to General Electric and General Foods. The spectacular merger waves of the 1960s, 1980s, and 1990s greatly increased the extent of conglomerates, epitomized by AOL-Time Warner in 2001, which by 2002 was notoriously unwieldy.

Most diversification is not pure; typically the firm creeps into adjacent markets rather than leaping randomly into new sectors.[25]

Since diversification is neither horizontal nor vertical, some observers, especially free-market advocates, deny that it ever reduces competition and instead often improves performance. A contrary view is that diversification can increase market power while impairing efficiency.[26] The literature has tended toward polemics, and the business press itself veers between favoring diversification and denouncing it. In the 1990s, for example, massive conglomerate mergers occurred at the same time as major voluntary break-ups of AT&T and other firms.

1. Possible Benefits

There are several possible benefits (or so-called "synergies") from diversification, as well as several possible social costs. Consider first the benefits and then the costs. For each benefit, only the **net benefits** compared to other methods are relevant.

Transfer of Technology. The firm may extend its proven technology into new markets.

Allocating Capital. The managers of a diversified firm allocate capital among its branches. This control over investment policy is often the main power and role of top-level managers. By knowing its branches well, top management may allocate capital better than the market process.

Pooling Risk. If the branches' risks are randomly distributed or follow offsetting cycles, then their combined risks are lower. Hence the diversified firm tends to have stable total profits. The gains are limited; above five branches, the riskpooling gain is usually slight.

2. Possible Harms to Competition

Cross-Subsidizing. Cross-subsidizing permits using profits from branch A (or the rest of the firm) to support deep, unfair price cuts by branch B.

The competitive effect of such support depends mainly on market position. If branch B is dominant, the support will tend to entrench it further. But if branch B has a small market share, the support will increase the competition it is able to apply to the other, more dominant firms.[27] Yet if the diversified firm is dominant in most markets, its pooled resources are likely to strengthen the dominance.[28] In contrast, a firm holding small-share branches is likely to promote competition rather than reduce it.

Mergers Reducing Potential Competition. Potential competition may be important for some markets, as earlier chapters noted. If a potential entrant merges with a firm already inside the market, the ranks of actual plus potential competitors are reduced by one. That decreases the total degree of competitive constraint, even if only slightly.

There are two special reservations:

1. Potential entrants are hard to identify.

2. The acquired firm's position in its market can make it either anti- or procompetitive. If a dominant firm is acquired, its new parent's resources may help entrench it further, but if a minor firm is taken over, its parent's

support will build it up and raise competition. Conglomerate mergers that give such toeholds in the market can improve competition.

Spheres of Influence. Now step back and consider the big picture rather than market-by-market effects. Imagine an extreme situation with five big diversified firms extending into all major sectors. They coexist in parallel, touching one another within hundreds of markets.

This will lead them to think in terms of spheres of interest, where diplomatic behavior replaces competition. Each firm would weigh the actions in one market in light of the possible retaliations by the other firms in that market *and* in other markets. Generally, coexistence and mutual restraint would replace robust competition.[29]

Local Effects. Finally, although the impacts of absentee ownership upon localities are less technically proven, they may ultimately be important. One impact occurs through plant closures decided by distant officials who are unaware of, or insensitive to, local strengths. Conglomerate mergers frequently have that effect. Often these decisions ignore the true values offered by the work force and the locale.

The other category of impacts is more subtle. Local firms are normally knit into their communities, with the companies' officials contributing and participating in local affairs, such as fund drives, schools, and city government.[30] When taken over by large firms, companies typically stop their local involvement. Indeed, there is often a shift toward pressuring the city for tax reductions and other favors.

VI. PRODUCT DIFFERENTIATION, ESPECIALLY ADVERTISING

Advertising is always a provocative topic, and from 1965 to 1975 it was both criticized for stifling competition and praised for promoting competition.[31] The debate continues, though less urgently.

Competition is most rigorous when products are identical: buyers can compare goods precisely and switch freely among them. When goods are differentiated, competition is often less effective. Comparisons are harder to make, and buyers may become loyal to specific brands of goods. Advertising seeks precisely to create that loyalty—to tie people to their favorite brands, reducing competition.

Only a relatively few consumer-goods industries have intensive advertising, so the problem is a focused one.[32] We consider the anti- and pro-competitive effects in turn.

1. SELLING EXPENSES

There are many ways to promote sales. **Advertising** is the most visible device, and it often is important. **Sales forces** are another major technique. A third form is the use of **promotional discounts, samples, and special pricing.** Such methods do not alter the product. They try instead to change demand conditions. These methods are substitutable to varying degrees. Many firms use all three all of the time. Here advertising will be the main focus, but the analysis applies to the other forms of selling expenses as well.

Effects of Advertising.   All selling expenses operate on a simple concept: They add to costs in order to add to demand.[33] They serve as an alternative to price cutting as a competitive tactic. They are "softer" and safer than price cutting. Since selling activities usually run into diminishing returns for any given product, they are not likely to cause as much mutual harm among rivals as price cutting would.

One simple view is that if consumers are willing to pay for advertising (in the price of the good), they must want it. This assumes that consumer preferences after being shaped by sales effort are more valid than the preferences that existed before the sales effort was applied. That could be, but its premise—that prior preferences are necessarily inferior—is stronger than most analysts are willing to accept.

Note also that the customer cannot buy the good without paying (implicitly) for the advertising. That is, advertising is tied to the good. If customers cannot buy just the good, then little can be said about the value of advertising to them.

Defining Advertising Intensity.   The advertising/sales ratio is commonly used to indicate advertising intensity. This is generally a good index, but it can be deceptive.[34] One alternative index is expenditure per customer or per capita of the population. Another is the number of messages received by buyers, but these too have problems of measurement and interpretation. The advertising/sales ratio is likely to continue to be the workhorse index of advertising intensity.

Market Setting.   In **pure competition**, selling expenses are irrelevant. Price is simply given by the market, and the firm's selling effort cannot alter the flat demand curve. In **pure monopoly,** selling expenses may play a limited role. True, they can be used to reduce demand elasticity to raise the amount of profit taken in. Advertising may also sharpen market segments and increase the scope for price discrimination; yet, on the whole, a monopolist need not make much selling effort. Some regard this as one benefit of monopoly: It avoids excess selling expenditures.

Standoff Advertising.   It is in the intermediate range—especially with dominant firms and oligopoly—that selling expenses flourish. They are valuable to the sellers as a safer method of competition than price cutting. Demand can be altered, and a firm can hope to raise its market share and profits sharply by many kinds of promotional blitzes. Defensive advertising often becomes routine for oligopolists. Even if they plan no aggressive promotional campaigns, they find it wise to nourish their customers' brand loyalties against the possibility that other firms might attack them.

Since all oligopolists in a market will share these incentives, the result is widely believed to be standoff advertising, in which oligopolists engage in very little price competition but are responsible for a large flow of parallel advertising. The advertising largely cancels itself out among the firms. Each is willing to stop advertising, but is too afraid to do so because the others might not. In the end, all are engaging in partly functionless expenditures.[35]

Informative and Persuasive Advertising.   This brings us to the basic point that some selling effort is **informative**, whereas some is **persuasive**. The information part is socially beneficial. It genuinely adds to consumers' knowledge of what is available; it improves competition and consumer choice. An example is classified advertisements in newspapers.

Persuasive advertising, by contrast, merely tries to change consumer preferences or to divert attention from facts to images. It occurs most obviously in image advertising. It either impairs consumer choice or is irrelevant to it. If it helps a new competitor enter the market, it might have social value.

Since their values and impacts are different, the distinction between information and persuasion is important. Many sales efforts mix the two, however, so it is hard to factor out the components in practice. (Even a classified ad often contains a sales pitch, for example.)

2. ADVERTISING'S EFFECTS ON COMPETITION

How Advertising Raises Barriers to Entry.   Advertising makes it more expensive to enter a market. To enter a market of advertised goods, a new firm must spend a lot just to get started.

Three cases suggest the anticompetitive effect. **The cigarette industry** has led the way in intensive advertising for over fifty years. The several major sellers are locked in classic conditions of standoff advertising, most of it of a persuasive kind. That may be costly, but it discourages entrants. Few firms have, in fact, entered this market since 1920, other than the generic brands since the mid-1990s.

In **the bleach market,** Clorox has been dominant for decades, with a market share above 50 percent. The company uses intensive advertising to build strong brand loyalties, even though bleaches are chemically uniform. Despite the attracting power of Clorox's high profit rates, new firms have found it difficult to enter the market in the face of Clorox's advertising power. Clorox's main rival, Purex (with about a 15 percent market share), also has been limited by advertising. In one episode, Purex attempted to raise its share by regional sales promotion, whereupon Clorox mounted its own promotional blitzes in the same regions, blocking Purex and deterring it from further efforts.

The cereals industry presents a more subtle version of sales effort on two levels. First, the three major cereals firms (Kellogg, General Mills, and General Foods) advertise heavily, raising the familiar barrier to new entrants. Entry has in fact been minor in the last four decades. Second, they have joined in a practice of packing the product space. As explained in detail in chapter 14, advertising has helped to bar new competition by supporting a proliferation of brands. The result has been high profit rates for the Big Three.

The Big Three reject this view, stressing they offer a diversity of choices to consumers. The packing was merely a full response to consumer preference, they say.

Advertising May Be Procompetitive or Neutral.   There are two main reasons why advertising may *not* increase market power. First, advertising can be a powerful device by which new or small firms succeed. This obvious point could hold even when the barriers effect exists. Business history offers many examples. Conceivably they could more than offset the barriers effect. A full appraisal would require a census of all such cases, and that has not remotely been done.

Second, advertising may just be a process of investing in customer loyalty. That investment is costly, and it needs to be refreshed. High profits may just be a stream of normal returns to advertising investments. Weiss noted that the investment feature accounts for little, if any, of the profits arising from advertising.[36]

In short, the research consensus so far is that advertising does tend to raise market power and monopoly profits, especially persuasive advertising of experience goods. And persuasive advertising is a large share of the total.

Advertising's effect in raising entry barriers does not seem to be overwhelming. Also, the effect clusters in relatively few consumer-goods markets rather than spreading across the whole economy. Selling expenses are a rather specialized problem, and their effects are often mixed.

QUESTIONS FOR REVIEW

1. Which conditions of bilateral monopoly yield competitive prices?

2. Show that vertical integration does not affect competition in perfectly functioning markets. Then discuss three conditions under which vertical integration does reduce competition.

3. You have been asked to judge whether a merger will foreclose potential competition. What data would you try to use, both about the firms and about the market?

4. What is the best measure of absolute size? Explain your answer.

5. Explain the free-rider justification for RPM. Which industry conditions favor it? Discuss three actual industries for which it may be valid and important.

6. Explain why market shares are important in judging the interbrand and intrabrand effects of vertical attempts at control.

7. Explain why tight oligopoly is likely to develop heavy selling expenses.

8. Make the case that all advertising is valuable and procompetitive.

ENDNOTES

[1] Leading sources include Frederick R. Warren-Boulton, *Vertical Control of Markets: Business and Labor Practices* (Cambridge: Ballinger, 1978); Roger D. Blair and Jeffrey L. Harrison, *Monopsony: Antitrust Law and Economics* (Princeton, NJ: Princeton University Press, 1993); "Special Issue on Vertical Relationships," *Journal of Industrial Economics* 39 (September 1991): pp. 445–620.

[2] There are no reliable data. No data corresponding to the census concentration ratios for sellers are prepared. Also, informal information about prominent cases is much less extensive than it is for dominant-firm sellers (recall chapter 9).

[3] Early discussions in the literature include A. L. Bowley, "Bilateral Monopoly," *Economic Journal* 38 (December 1928): pp. 651–59; and James W. McKie, *Tin Cans and Tin Plate* (Cambridge: Harvard University Press, 1959).

[4] John Kenneth Galbraith, *American Capitalism: The Theory of Countervailing Power* (Boston: Houghton Mifflin, 1952).

[5] There, new competition arises by letting customers get supply from outside over the utility's system; see chapter 13.

[6] An example is private-label brands. Many food items (such as soup, coffee, and flour mixes) are sold by dominant firms under their own brand names at premium prices. At the same

time, these firms often supply exactly the same products but with the chain grocers' own brand labels pasted on, at much lower prices. The producer competes (under vertical pressure) with itself, in part. Yet the pressure doesn't work in a lot of markets; retailers have failed in this effort with most cereals, soda pop, beer, and razors, among many others.

[7] Among the leading treatments of this topic, see Morris A. Adelman's chapter on integration in George J. Stigler, ed., *Business Concentration and Price Policy* (Princeton, NJ: Princeton University Press, 1955); Michael Gort, *Integration and Diversification in American Industry* (Princeton, NJ: Princeton University Press, 1962); Frederick R. Warren-Boulton, *Vertical Control of Markets*.

[8] Integration can be a matter of degrees and shadings rather than strict yes-no conditions. The market transactions can be tight long-term contracts that provide nearly as much control as does direct ownership. The controls actually applied under integration can be highly delegated with little actual exertion of authority.

[9] An integrated producer adds value by processing at many stages, so its ratio would be high. A retailer, by contrast, adds little value, so its ratio would be low. Yet this method also has its faults. Some one-stage industries have high value added (that is, the processing is extensive, though simple); bricks are an example.

[10] Another method using input-output data is suggested by S. W. Davies and C. Moms, "A New Index of Vertical Integration: Some Estimates for UK Manufacturing," *International Journal of Industrial Organization* 13 (1995): 151–77.

[11] Oliver E. Williamson, *Markets and Hierarchies*, (Glencoe: Free Press, 1985). Jargon sometimes obscures real meanings. *Bounded rationality* means the limits on knowing what is happening in markets. Humans cannot process and interpret unlimited details about market conditions while at the same time seeking to make rational profit-maximizing decisions. Integration offers a way to reduce that burden. *Opportunism* means the wayward tendencies of suppliers to mislead, cheat, and generally underperform. An integrated firm minimizes these hazards by owning and directly controlling its own suppliers.

[12] See Steven C. Salop and David Scheffman, "Raising Rivals' Costs," *American Economic Review* 73 (May 1983): pp. 263–71.

[13] Original statements of the hypothesis are by Morris A. Adelman, in "Integration and Antitrust Policy," *Harvard Law Review* 63 (November 1949): pp. 27–77; and Joseph J. Spengler, "Vertical Integration and Antitrust Policy," *Journal of Political Economy* 58 (August 1950): pp. 347–52. Robert H. Bork restated the ideas in full free-market form in "Vertical Integration and the Sherman Act: The Legal History of an Economic Misconception," *University of Chicago Law Review* 22 (Autumn 1954): pp. 157–201. Richard A. Posner, *Antitrust Policy* (Chicago: University of Chicago Press, 1976) offers a more balanced discussion.

[14] In addition, Arrow notes that vertical integration to reduce uncertainty of supply may commonly eliminate competition, even if no other vertical economies exist. See Kenneth J. Arrow, "Vertical Integration and Communication," *Bell Journal of Economics* 6 (Spring 1975): pp. 173–83.

[15] An example of empirical study is S. Suominen, "Effects of Vertical Integration on Price and Volume," *Empirica* 16 (1992): pp. 203–19.

[16] See Philip Areeda and Donald F. Turner, *Antitrust Policies*, 7 vols. (Boston: Little, Brown, 1978); Blair and Harrison, *Monopsony*; and Warren-Boulton, *Vertical Control of Markets*.

[17] Joseph Pereira, "Toy Retailers Fear Playing with 'Mat-Bro'," *Wall Street Journal* (January 26, 1996): pp. B1, B5.

[18] For example, see Wendy Bonds, "Jury Says Kodak Monopolized Service Market," *Wall Street Journal* (September 19, 1995): p. A4.

[19] The original statement is in Lester Telser, "Why Should Manufacturers Want Fair Trade?" *Journal of Law and Economics* 3 (October 1960): pp. 86–105. For more complex assessments, see Frederick R. Warren-Boulton, "Resale Price Maintenance Reexamined: *Monsanto v. Spray-Rite*, (1984)," a chapter in John E. Kwoka and Lawrence J. White, eds., *The Antitrust Revolution*, 2nd ed. (New York: HarperCollins, 1994); William S. Comanor, "Vertical Price Fixing and Market Restrictions in the New Antitrust Policy," *Harvard Law Review* 98 (March 1985): pp. 983–1102; and F. M. Scherer, "The Economics of Vertical Restraints," *Antitrust Law Journal* 52 (September 1983): pp. 687–718.

[20] Some RPM laws extended enforcement to retailers that had not signed as participants in fair-trade schemes. The price fixing therefore reached out to include all retailers, not just those actively joining in the scheme.

[21] The case was *Monsanto Co. v. Spray-Rite Service Corp.*, 104 S.Ct. 1464 (1984). See Kwoka's coverage in Kwoka and White, *The Antitrust Revolution*.

[22] Measures have been judged and used by many writers, including A. D. H. Kaplan, *Big Enterprise in a Competitive System*, rev. ed. (Washington, DC: Brookings Institution, 1965); and John M. Blair, *Economic Concentration* (New York: Harcourt Brace Jovanovich, 1972). For an early pioneering discussion, see A. A. Berle and Gardiner Means, *The Modern Corporation and Private Property* (New York: Macmillan, 1932).

[23] See Morris A. Adelman, "The Measurement of Industrial Concentration," *Review of Economics and Statistics* 33 (November 1951): pp. 269–96; and the debate stirred by Adelman's article in that *Review* May 1952.

[24] Joe S. Bain, *Barriers to New Competition* (Cambridge: Harvard University Press, 1956).

[25] See John T. Scott, *Purposive Diversification and Economic Performance* (New York: Cambridge University Press, 1993); early studies include Michael Gort, *Integration and Diversification in American Industry* (Princeton, NJ: Princeton University Press, 1964); and Charles H. Berry, *Corporate Growth and Diversification* (Princeton, NJ: Princeton University Press, 1975).

[26] The business press frequently stresses the harms of conglomerate mergers. Among academic research showing that diversification often reduces company profitability, see L. H. P. Lang and R. M. Stulz, "Tobin's *q*, Corporate Diversification, and Firm Performance," *Journal of Political Economy* 102 (December 1994): pp. 1248–80.

[27] For example, in the 1970s and early 1980s, Phillip Morris injected funds for major advertising blitzes by its Seven-Up subsidiary. That was procompetitive on balance, because it raised competition with the larger Coca-Cola and PepsiCo firms.

[28] ITT became a prime instance of a conglomerate holding a string of firms with leading positions in their markets; see James S. Campbell and William G. Shepherd, "Leading-Firm Conglomerate Mergers," *Antitrust Bulletin* 13 (Winter 1968): pp. 1361–82. Of course, many older firms also hold a series of leading positions: General Motors, DuPont, General Electric, and Procter & Gamble are examples.

[29] O. R. Phillips and C. F. Mason, "Mutual Forbearance in Experimental Conglomerate Markets," *Rand Journal of Economics* 23 (Autumn 1992): pp. 395–414; A. van Witteloostuijn and M. van Wegberg, "Multimarket Competition: Theory and Evidence," *Journal of Economic Behavior and Organization* 18 (July 1992): pp. 273–82.

[30] A good example has been the Eastman Kodak Company's various contributions to the city of Rochester, New York, where its headquarters and extensive production facilities are. Scores of other cases are well known.

[31] Important early sources include Joe S. Bain, *Barriers to New Competition* (Cambridge: Harvard University Press, 1956), chap. 4 and app. D; William S. Comanor and Thomas A. Wilson, *Advertising and Market Power* (Cambridge: Harvard University Press, 1975); and Julian L. Simon, *Issues in the Economics of Advertising* (Champaign: University of Illinois Press, 1970). An excellent survey of all arguments is provided in William S. Comanor and Thomas A. Wilson, "The Effect of Advertising on Competition: A Survey," *Journal of Economic Literature* 17 (June 1979): pp. 453–76. See also Richard E. Caves and Peter J. Williamson, "What Is Product Differentiation, Really?" *Journal of Industrial Economics* 34 (December 1985): pp. 113–32; and Scherer and Ross, *Industrial Market Structure*, pp. 436–38.

[32] An important study focusing on advertising also looks at a relatively few advertising-intensive industries—John Sutton, *Sunk Costs and Market Structure: Price Competition, Advertising, and the Evolution of Concentration* (Cambridge: MIT Press, 1991).

[33] See John Beath and Yannis Katsoulacos, *The Economic Theory of Product Differentiation* (New York: Cambridge University Press, 1991).

[34] For example, the U.S. automobile industry is very large and it advertises heavily. Its frequency of messages per potential customer is high because of its large absolute spending on

advertising (over $2 billion per year). Yet the total sales revenue of the industry is so very high that the advertising/sales ratio is actually rather low; it is around 1 percent, compared with over 10 percent for cereals, beer, and other advertising-intensive industries.

[35] See Comanor and Wilson, *Advertising and Market Power*. For further analysis of excess advertising, see Avinash Dixit and Victor D. Norman, "Advertising and Welfare," *Bell Journal of Economics* 9 (Spring 1978): pp. 1–17.

[36] Leonard W. Weiss, "Advertising, Profits and Corporate Taxes," *Review of Economics and Statistics* 51 (November 1969): pp. 421–30; see also Harry Block, "Advertising and Profitability: A Reappraisal," *Journal of Political Economy* 82 (March/April 1974): pp. 267–86.

Part

6

Industry Case Studies

Chapter

13

CASE STUDIES OF DOMINANT FIRMS:
MICROSOFT, NEWSPAPERS, BABY BELLS, COMPUTERS, BEER, ELECTRICITY, AND OTHERS

Dominant firms provide lively, contentious, and complicated topics of study. Only when you consider dominance in a "case study" do the meaning and effects of market power stand out in clear focus. We now consider a series of famous dominant firms, followed by a few of the best-known tight oligopolies in chapter 14.

Each situation presents standard patterns, along with some special conditions of its own. Several are in transition, and their dominance may fade away. In all cases, the dominant firms have used dramatic tactics to obtain, defend, and increase their dominance.

The major cases include the following (selected from table 3.4):

1. Microsoft in operating software and other digital markets

2. Newspapers in hundreds of towns and cities

3. Baby Bells in local telecommunications-service markets

4. IBM in mainframe computers

5. Anheuser-Busch in beer

6. Electricity.

Also, we give two briefer capsule cases: Ticketmaster (the dominant distributor of tickets for events), and Yellow Pages (the dominant classified directory in hundreds of cities and areas).

Read on to hone your skills. Is each case of dominance solid and able to exploit imperfections, perhaps lasting at least another several decades? Or instead is it fragile and fleeting, perhaps being ousted quickly by "creative destruction" in a free-market or Schumpeterian competitive process?

I. MICROSOFT

Microsoft's dominance was established in 1980, when it obtained control over programming IBM's personal computers.[1] Microsoft has since extended and deepened its monopoly, and it continues to extend into a number of adjacent markets.[2] It is deeply involved in severe competitive strategies and in a long series of mergers with firms in adjacent and emerging markets.

1. THE MARKET

There is wide agreement that Microsoft's relevant market is operating software—the crucial software that operates personal computers and many other digital activities. Growth since the market's origins in 1980 has been explosive. Microsoft's DOS system became the basis for virtually all PC's in the 1980s, except for Apple's Macintosh computers. Its dominance continues.

2. STRUCTURE

Among the vast array of software, operating systems are critical. When IBM was still dominant, it accepted the DOS system provided by the new Microsoft company and ceded control over it. Microsoft soon enlarged its initial position with Windows, edging out Apple, Lotus, and other creative forces.

By 1992, Microsoft had emerged as the dominant software company, with about 90 percent of the market. It largely controls the evolution of new technology, partly by aggressive actions it has taken to subdue rivals. Its strong position and prospects have raised its market value even above IBM's—and indeed above nearly all other corporations in the world.

3. DETERMINANTS

There may seem to be some "natural-monopoly" basis for Microsoft's dominance, since computers need to be reasonably compatible—particularly so since the rise of the Internet. That is a basic feature of "network" industries that link customers (as in telephones, electricity, and railroads). Users want a single standard.

But the network basis is separable from the process of innovating new methods, and also from the control of common technology. Microsoft captured the near-exclusive position of the industry standard. It has worked to retain its dominance and control over innovation. But much of its near-monopoly is not dictated by technology. Since the mid-1990s, alternative systems to Windows—especially the independent and free Linux system—have attracted away some of Microsoft's customers. Therefore, whatever natural-monopoly conditions may have existed at the start have largely faded away.

4. BEHAVIOR

Microsoft has tested—and sometimes exceeded—the limits of what dominant firms are permitted to do to their small rivals. Microsoft thoroughly copied IBM's early basic strategies to deter competition. Like IBM in the 1960s, Microsoft controlled new technology so as to make competition difficult. It also used strategic price discrimination to compete especially hard in specific parts of the market. It also extended its monopoly into related markets by bundling different services. Finally, Microsoft used giveaways (including Internet Explorer, and the "free" inclusion of on-line service in its Windows 95 programs) to extend its control.[3]

Microsoft's pricing of Windows was aggressive, extracting the value from its dominant position. In 2002, Microsoft grew even more aggressive; it increased Windows' price sharply to $500 and set a new policy that prevents buyers from using the Windows program on more than one computer. Microsoft sets tight controls on users to enforce its restrictions.

5. PERFORMANCE

Microsoft is widely regarded as a lucky opportunist, thanks to IBM's carelessness in giving Microsoft a dominant role. Such innovations as the Windows 95, 98, and later programs have been moderate improvements, not breakthroughs. Until 2002, Windows had generally been regarded as a ramshackle and unreliable program, prone to crashing. Other firms are regarded as being better innovators, as with Linux.

Microsoft provided relatively poor quality of support services to customers needing help.[4] The aggressiveness of its leader, William Gates, may have overcome some of the usual retarding effects of dominance, or it may have merely exploited imperfections to offset declining innovative ability.

Meanwhile, Microsoft's rise and monopoly profits created colossal wealth for the relatively few members of the founding group, such as Gates and Paul Allen.[5] That wealth in turn spread into other crucial sectors, just as the early Rockefeller and DuPont fortunes were used to gain control of other dominant firms such as General Motors.[6]

6. IN SUMMARY

Microsoft has copied many of IBM's strategies. It too gained dominance partly by luck, and it used a variety of tactics to deter competitors.

Because of this dominance and its history, antitrust actions against Microsoft have been inevitable and important. But they have had virtually no significant effects, as chapter 16 summarizes.[7]

II. NEWSPAPERS IN LOCAL MARKETS

If you read an off-campus newspaper, it is probably dominant in its market (that is, in your city's area). The U.S. newspaper industry is a vast honeycomb of specific local and regional markets, and dominance is nearly everywhere. It is found from the *Boston Globe, Washington Post,* and *Philadelphia Inquirer* in the east to Phoenix's *Arizona Republican* and the *Los Angeles Times* in the west; from the sober, news-heavy *New York Times* and the daily business encyclopedia *Wall Street Journal* down to many hundreds of small-town papers.[8]

The march toward newspaper monopoly raises problems not only of economic monopoly but also of media control.[9] Some cities contain cross-media monopolies controlling both newspapers and television stations. In addition, large newspaper chains such as Capital Cities and Gannnett own scores of local newspaper monopolies. These chains' controls may reduce the freedom of the press and diversity of views. Because local monopolies and chain ownership are growing, the problem is increasing.

This industry's most interesting questions focus on market definition, economies of scale, and the meaning of good performance.

1. The Markets

Newspaper markets are mainly local for two reasons: their readerships are interested in local issues, and advertising usually is focused locally.

Products and Areas. Economists have regarded newspapers as the relevant product and localities as the correct area. The papers compete directly and usually are closely substitutable within their city areas.

The market might instead really be a **local advertising market, including all local media** such as television, radio, coupon flyers and other promotional activities, along with newspapers. If so, then newspapers would compete with the other media for advertising dollars.

The expert answer has usually denied this view. Newspapers offer distinctive services (news, opinions, columns, comics, sports, etc.), are sold through different channels, and are used differently. The local all-media market may be relevant to some narrow issues, but those are generally separate from the broad question of newspaper market power.

Quality. Newspapers range from the highbrow news encyclopedia of the *New York Times* to the tabloid press like the *New York Post* and *Boston Herald*—and for that matter, the *National Enquirer* (the highest circulation paper of all in the United States!). Do readers substitute freely among them in response to price? Rarely, because contrasting newspapers provide distinct services; therefore the serious newspaper market is distinct from the tabloid paper market. The same applies to most suburban newspapers and weekly advertising papers. Their coverage and readerships are largely distinct from regular city newspapers.

Morning and Evening Editions. Many cities used to have separate morning and evening papers, which were quite distinct. Many readers would buy both papers as complements. That difference has faded recently, because television now provides the evening news for most people. Most papers are now issued in the morning, often with similar evening editions. Even where there are two papers, they are often partially merged under a joint operating agreement.

National Newspapers. Among prominent papers of true national scope are the *Wall Street Journal* and the *National Enquirer*, among others. Each works in a product niche, sometimes as the dominant paper. They usually function as complements to local papers rather than as substitutes.

2. STRUCTURE

Dominance is pervasive, and it is reinforced by chain ownership.[10] Among the 100 largest cities, most have one dominant paper and some have two. In twenty of these largest cities, the two newspapers have actually been partially merged; they have one owner and one printing system, but maintain two separate editorial staffs. Therefore single-firm dominance has become common, with just a few duopolies also still in being. There is also a fringe of suburban papers and weekly advertisers, but they are not very important in most cities.

There are a few significant exceptions to the march of dominance. Little Rock, Arkansas, long had two comparable, vigorously competing newspapers, as do some other cities. The case for natural dominance in the technology of newspaper markets is not yet established.

The trend toward dominance has been especially strong since about 1960. In the 1950s, many cities had at least three papers. Mergers have been widespread, however, often as papers faced (or claimed to face) financial failure.

Barriers to entry into newspaper production are extremely high. There may be exceptions for small market niches such as suburban papers or advertising-based weeklies, but even these are largely filled and blocked by existing papers.

3. DETERMINANTS

The news function of the newspaper appears to involve relatively small economies of scale. Many cities would probably support four or five newspapers if only news reporting and features were needed. That is partly because wire services and other sources are so ample and accessible.

Scale economies (and pressure toward monopoly) instead appear to come mainly from production and distribution activities, advertising, and gains from forming newspaper chains. It is generally cheaper to have just one large printing press, and delivery trucks and personnel also involve economies of scale. The cost gradients on these may not be steep, so that the cost penalties of having several newspapers per city might be rather small. The main direct determinant of newspaper-market structure has simply been mergers, which have eliminated competition in scores of cities.[11]

Advertising is commonly cited as the main cause of newspaper monopoly. Advertisers are said to apply pressure for one newspaper to emerge as victor, because some advertisers inherently prefer to have one main vehicle. The claim is debatable. Smaller-circulation papers can offer lower rates to attract advertisers. If newspapers can survive handily in cities of 100,000 population and less, there seems no strong reason why they cannot do so in larger cities just as well.

Chains achieve some technical economies of scale in coordination and providing services, but the pecuniary gains are perhaps larger. Chains can offer irresistible bids to independent papers to sell out.[12] Chains can make entry impossible, thereby raising market power and permitting higher advertising rates.[13]

4. BEHAVIOR

Collusion has not been a main pattern. Instead, unilateral efforts to defeat rival papers have been common. A full range of pricing, advertising, and other strategies has been typical.[14]

One anticompetitive tactic has tended to prevent new entrants from competing fully. The leading paper makes exclusive deals with national syndicators that bar smaller rivals from access to such popular syndicated services as the best news-wire services, comic strips, columnists (including Dear Abby, etc.), crosswords, and the like. In Chicago, those exclusive deals have impeded the ability of suburban newspapers to expand toward competition on a citywide basis.[15]

5. PERFORMANCE

Newspapers have commonly raised their advertising rates and copy prices substantially upon attaining dominance (or after making quasi-mergers).[16] Their profit rates also rise substantially. Many leading newspapers have been among the most secure and profitable enterprises in the economy.

No systematic information is available about actual X-efficiency, rates of innovation, or quality of news coverage. There has been a narrowing of news and editorial coverage as the number of alternative papers has dwindled to one or two in each city. Chain ownership has brought standardization and central editorial control.

6. IN SUMMARY

Dominance in local newspaper markets has become greater than in any other important unregulated industry in the entire U.S. economy. Some newspapers have near-complete monopolies, while few city markets have more than two significant competitors.

Although some economies of scale exist, they are probably generally moderate. The dynamics of advertising and of artificial exclusions from the best syndicated features may be stronger causes.

The effects of dominance on prices and profits have usually been substantial. The effects on larger social dimensions, particularly on the quality of news coverage, may eventually prove more harmful.

III. LOCAL TELEPHONE-SERVICE MARKETS (THE BABY BELLS)

Since the 1950s, the telecommunications sector has changed with rapid shocks, and it still has an aura of rapid change. Yet these markets—mainly local and long-distance telephone and transmission services, cable TV and broadcasting, and equipment—are familiar, as close as your own telephone and TV set. AT&T's dominance of the telephone system began in the 1880s, and its monopoly behavior was virtually a caricature of the pure monopolist.[17]

The Bell system's eventual breakup in 1984 (see chapter 16) is perhaps the greatest single antitrust event in U.S. industrial history, but AT&T and the Baby Bells continued to dominate their markets. The 1990s brought large changes, including the 1996 Telecommunications Act, which aimed to unleash competition among all of the sector's parts. Also, the industry has been devastated by shocks of deceptive accounting and severe impacts of change. Yet the industry offers striking examples of the Baby Bells as dominant firms that repel new efforts to encourage competition.[18] AT&T's dominance of long distance has finally been eroded, but the Baby Bells continue to hold tight dominance.

1. THE MARKETS

Although there is a reasonably well-coordinated system of communications throughout the United States, there is a patchwork of hundreds of genuine local-service markets. **Product dimensions** of the market include personal and large-scale telephone and data transmission services; cable TV transmission; Internet-type computer access information services; and related services such as broadcasting and local alarm services. Its **geographic dimensions** include local and intercity markets, with the necessity for long-distance providers to have access to local systems (either telephone or cable TV). But wireless service cuts across both market dimensions. Wireless is, in fact, the main competitive threat to the local-service near-monopolies.

Although these myriad markets were largely kept separate until the 1990s, the 1996 law tried to fuse them by allowing free entry among them all. The hope—now admitted to be unsuccessful—was to promote full competition in all of them.

2. STRUCTURE

Before 1984, AT&T dominated the sector as the Bell system. It provided nearly all long-distance service and about 80 percent of local service, but each locality had pure-monopoly conditions. Television broadcasting had its three networks and unaffiliated stations and, after 1970, local cable-TV systems (which increasingly merged after 1980 into chains).

Long Distance.   During 1970–1984, the FCC fostered competition in long distance under pressure from the pioneering MCI company.[19] But as late as 1984, MCI and Sprint still held only about 15 percent of all traffic. By 1989, AT&T's share receded to about 60 percent, but then it stabilized until 1995 both in the national market and among cities within states. Meanwhile MCI managed to raise its share toward 25 percent and Sprint toward 10 percent. The meltdown of the telecommunications sector after 2000, including WorldCom's scandals and bankruptcy in 2002, has brought still more competition to long-distance markets.

Local Exchanges.   In local city markets, the Baby Bells, GTE, and other established systems retained virtually complete monopoly into the 2000s, despite FCC policies trying to encourage entry by TelePort, MSF, and others. Free-entry policies had minor results. By 2002, the Baby Bells were still overwhelmingly dominant. They were developing wireless systems as well and, in some cases, put them in separate units.

3. DETERMINANTS

For a century, from the 1880s to the 1980s, AT&T claimed overwhelming economies both of scale and of vertical integration. That, AT&T said, made its unified control of the entire telephone sector necessary.

By the 1970s, however, technology had evolved markedly. Long-distance capacity went from copper-wire systems to satellites and microwave towers, and then to optical fibers. Local systems changed from crude electromechanical switching devices to advanced computers, and parallel cellular and other systems began spreading. User equipment advanced to complex electronics for handling message content, as the telephone handset began to overlap with computers. Vast data volumes could be compressed into optical fibers.

Technology no longer favored monopoly at any point; rather, it offered ways to prevent monopoly in virtually all parts, if the rules were opened up, as the 1996 Telecommunications Act tried to do. The existing dominant firms might be able to entrench themselves and extend their control, however, if the rules were unbalanced or too lenient. For local markets, the Baby Bells have kept control. The main challenge is from cell phones, which have spread rapidly since 1995.

4. BEHAVIOR

Before 1984, the Bell system's behavior fit its monopoly position closely. It extracted a maximum of revenue from telephone service, using thorough price discrimination. It also controlled the adjacent equipment markets by prohibiting its customers from owning their own telephone equipment; instead AT&T rented the equipment at high fees. That permitted AT&T to extract high profits from its vertically integrated and unregulated equipment-producing monopoly, named Western Electric; the local Bells had to buy all their equipment from Western.

The Bell system extended its monopoly into other adjacent markets as well, such as alarm-monitoring systems.[20] It reaped extremely high profits on long-distance service, using them to set local service fees relatively low so as to maximize its political standing. It tried to monopolize alarm services, recycling, and other related markets.

Cable-TV systems, on their part, extracted monopoly profits so openly that Congress twice required the FCC to regulate them, in the 1970s and 1990s. Regulation was generally weak, however, especially after many systems formed large chains. Cable systems have been free of regulation since the mid-1990s.

5. PERFORMANCE

The unified Bell System delivered good performance in many dimensions, particularly reliability and clarity of transmission, but it was a sheltered, sleepy, and X-inefficient monopoly. As a result, AT&T later suffered huge internal strains while converting itself into an efficient enterprise from 1985 to 1990. It actually repeated the break-up twice, recognizing that its own monopoly slowed innovation.

The old Bell Laboratories made important scientific discoveries and inventions, but AT&T fitted monopoly behavior by delaying innovation. AT&T was slow to introduce dial switching, to develop variety in handsets and company-premises equipment, to adopt electronics, to introduce computerized switching, and to adopt microwave transmission in the 1940s and optical fibers in the 1970s.

In 1984, the Bell breakup stirred some popular resistance to "dismantling the world's best telephone system," as some claimed. But the separation did not in fact reduce service quality, and it vastly enlarged innovative activities in all parts of the sector. For nearly two decades, Americans have routinely had choices and quality far greater than would have evolved.

Long-distance prices declined as competition spread until 1992; then as the dominance/oligopoly settled further, prices began rising.[21] Baby Bells have tried urgently to enter long-distance markets, but by 2002 they received permission to enter only a small minority of them. Meanwhile, long-distance firms have had little success in entering local markets.

6. IN SUMMARY

The old Bell system behaved and performed just as the economics of monopoly predicted. The new competition after 1984 gave the predictably large beneficial results. But dominance remained overwhelming in local markets, as the Baby Bells have repelled most efforts to enter. Their mergers have strengthened their dominance.

IV. MAINFRAME COMPUTERS (IBM)

As the near-monopoly supplier of tabulating equipment from the 1930s to the 1950s, IBM easily captured dominance of the computing industry after 1950.[22] It mined its dominance for high profits and extraordinary capital gains for its stockholders. But soon, even in the 1960s, IBM was struggling to keep up with its competitors' innovations. Also Big Blue, as it was known, grew increasingly bureaucratic, and by the 1980s IBM was displaying classic dominant-firm ossification and blunders.[23]

IBM was from 1950 to 1990 one of the most powerful, profitable, and controversial companies in American industrial history. It has regained its health and power since then as the dominant large-computer firm. A major antitrust case during 1969–1982 brought many of its inner conditions out into full view, and so the brief summary here has more than the usual array of facts to rely on.[24]

1. THE MARKET

From the 1950s to about 1980, the mainframe computer was the correct basis for defining the computer market. This market subdivided in the 1980s as minicomputers and personal computers increasingly grew at the expense of mainframes. They are complementary for many uses. On the whole, it is still meaningful to treat mainframes as a market that is largely separate from the market for personal computers.

2. STRUCTURE

Computer Hardware.   IBM's market share in mainframes has been generally in the 60- to 70-percent range since the 1950s, and it remained high even as PCs grew rapidly after the early 1980s.[25] Other mainframe producers have had market shares below 10 percent from the 1960s on, and so IBM's dominance has been extreme.

In PCs, IBM was able to gain only a minor role at first, though its ThinkPad series gained a solid niche in the 1990s. Meanwhile Apple Computer initially took leadership in personal computers with a 25-percent share. It then yielded to several vigorous competitors, and the PC market became a relatively loose oligopoly.[26]

3. DETERMINANTS

Sales forces were the original source of IBM's dominance. It was able to move from its dominance of tabulating equipment into dominating computers in the 1950s because the same powerful IBM sales force simply added the new equipment to its product array. That sales force remained important until the 1980s, when distribution unraveled into a variety of marketing channels.

The second influence is production economies of scale, in supplying individual computer models and whole families of systems, but these never explained IBM's dominance. There was great creativity among small firms in this industry. IBM recognized this explicitly in 1980 by devolving some of its development work in order to avoid bureaucracy.

The production economies are limited, as reflected in the farming out of much production to small firms in Asia. The best recent estimates are that MES is well below 20 percent of the market in all branches of the computer industry, from mainframes down to personal computers.

Therefore, IBM has probably had a large degree of excess market share for decades. That is attested by the continuing ability of very small rivals to compete.

4. BEHAVIOR

Two patterns of IBM behavior stand out.[27] One is the raising of prices to yield high rates of return. Until 1986, IBM steadily earned profit rates above 18 percent on invested capital; from 1977 to 1985, the rate of return was between 21 and 26 percent. For two decades, IBM stabilized its profitability by using pricing strategies that tilted customers toward leasing machines rather than buying them. The flow of lease revenues from IBM's large fleet of equipment provided its main profits, and the policy encouraged customers to stick with IBM. It also forced competitors to match the strategy, and so they had to build up large inventories of equipment for leasing. That imposed extra costs of entry and made it more costly for small rivals to start up and to gain market share. IBM eventually shifted toward a higher ratio of sales to leases, after which its profit rose strongly until 1986.

IBM also adopted extensive price discrimination among its products.[28] Among computer models, IBM set prices to attain different profit rates, reflecting differing degrees of demand elasticity. The 360 family of computers in the 1960s is a good example.[29] For smaller models, for which buyers are less expert and more likely to pay more to get the IBM name, IBM set prices about 40 percent above costs. On larger models, for which buyers are sharper and rivals had better machines than IBM, prices were set just barely above or even below costs. When IBM desperately fought back against two specific types of superior machines from 1967 to 1970, they lost money heavily on the so-called fighting ships.

Further, IBM set much higher price-cost ratios on its peripheral equipment (where competition was expected to be weak) than on the core units of its computers. Moreover, IBM has always offered different special deals to individual customers (such as free programming and other assistance) in order to win specific contracts. Finally, IBM has virtually given away computers to many universities and colleges in order to instill students with a lifetime loyalty to their products.

5. PERFORMANCE

IBM earned a high 28% on equity every year during the 1960s, reflecting its dominance. But its profits plummeted after 1985 to an $8 billion loss in 1992. IBM had a mixed record of efficiency and innovation. In the 1980s, it was falling behind just as its claims for superiority were strongest. It tried in 1987 to 1989 to reverse decades of bureaucracy by cutting its work force and facilities deeply and eliminating entire layers of management.

IBM generally did poorly as an innovator. It was a follower, not a leader, in the 1960s. After the 1970s IBM was unable to keep up in several kinds of computers, including personal computers (competing against Compaq and Apple). For another example, "IBM's workstation, the three-year-old RT-PC, has been a highly visible failure. . ." And IBM's diversification into telephone equipment (by buying Rolm Corp.) also "failed."[30] Despite IBM's many successes, its general record of innovation declined as its dominance grew.

By 1991–1992, IBM was virtually a failing company, and a wholesale shake-out of managers led to the arrival of Louis Gerstner. He installed standard forms of efficiency and coordination, although he too had failures and questionable actions.[31] IBM's dominance was reasserted, and it now seems unshakeable.

6. IN SUMMARY

IBM has been a complex enterprise with an ambiguous economic history. Its dominance is in a major section of the entire computer industry. Though IBM displayed severe X-inefficiency and slow innovation at times during the 1960s to the mid-1990s, it was able to maintain high growth and profitability for over thirty years. And its dominance was reasserted after 1993.

V. BEER (ANHEUSER-BUSCH)

Anheuser-Busch rose to dominance of U.S. beer markets from the 1970s to the 1990s. Beer is an ancient traditional product, widely used since at least the earliest ancient Egyptian kingdoms. Though producers try to instill strong brand loyalties, most beers cannot be distinguished reliably in a blind taste test, and every brewer can duplicate any other brewer's flavor.

Brewing was an extensive local-regional industry, with hundreds of companies, before the Prohibition era of 1918 to 1933. Since 1933, industry ranks have thinned to a few major national brewers plus a fringe of regional and local ones. Despite the emergence of chic microbreweries in many locales over the last decade, the market is dominated by the heavily advertised national brands such as Budweiser and Miller. Have the mergers reduced competition? Is competition effective in national and/or regional markets?

Also, the leading brewers enforce exclusive distribution territories in many states, just as Coca-Cola and Pepsi-Cola do in the soft-drinks industry. Is that practice anticompetitive?

1. THE MARKET

The product is largely standardized: a pale gold fermented drink, sold mainly in small bottles or cans as well as in kegs. Ales, lagers, and beers are largely substitutable to many buyers, although the darker, strong-tasting versions may be a (much smaller) separate market. Possibly higher-priced brands and imported beers are distinct from the mass brands, but the physical differences are generally minor and there is extensive substitution among them.[33]

Geography poses harder questions. Are beer markets local, regional, or national in scope? Transport factors suggest regional markets; shipping costs are important relative to total costs, and actual shipping is mostly within 300 miles. Yet since the major standard brands are produced in multiple plants across the country, interactions among the main corporate producers are often national in scope.

An equivocal answer seems unavoidable. Some competitive conditions occur within regional markets or when a national brewer adopts strategies against one or several strictly regional sellers. The main market is a national one, however, in the struggle for sales among Anheuser-Busch, Miller, Coors, and Stroh.

Distribution.   A second market level is in the retail distribution of beer. Trucks deliver to retail outlets such as package and grocery stores. These delivery-market areas range between roughly the largest urban areas and middle-size states. Deliveries can range as far as 150 miles or so, though ordinarily they are within 50-mile areas that trucks can easily reach in a day's run.

2.   STRUCTURE

Earlier local markets were tight oligopolies among local leaders, but they have been replaced by a set of leading national companies led by Anheuser-Busch and joined by Miller and Coors. In 1955 four-firm concentration was 22 percent; it rose strongly and steadily to 90 percent in the 1990s. This rise was led by Anheuser-Busch, which rose from about 20 percent in 1970 to at least 50 percent in the 1990s.[34] Advertising has been a major force for Anheuser-Busch, but it grew mainly internally. Its main rivals are Miller with 20 percent and Coors with 11 percent.[35]

Entry barriers are high, raised mainly by advertising. Newcomers can find local market niches, but they are crowded and under pressure from the national companies. To go national, a small firm must mount a major advertising campaign against the retaliation of the leading firms. Like the cereal market, the beer market illustrates the power of advertising as an entry barrier (recall chapter 12). Although a heroically large market blitz may establish a new product, the barrier effects are always present.

3.   DETERMINANTS

Scale economies in brewing are not small, with MES probably at about 1 to 1.5 million barrels per year.[36] That is some 5 percent of national output, and it is large compared to the size of many local-regional markets. Advertising is the other main factor; it may provide pecuniary economies up to 20 percent of the national market. Mergers were especially important from the 1950s to the 1970s (though not to Anheuser-Busch), stirring hot debate whether they reflected monopolizing or efficiency. In fact, many of them mainly reflected advertising's effects, and therefore they may have been inevitable.

At the distribution level, the technology is simple and leaves large scope for competition. There can be many overlapping delivery firms in any area, and these can freely move into adjoining areas by adjusting their central shipping points.

4. BEHAVIOR

The firms have followed tight-oligopoly and dominant-firm behavior in avoiding direct price competition. There is some price discounting by all firms, but price stability is the general pattern. Advertising, devising new brands, and special promotions are softer methods that skirt the mutual dangers of price wars.[37]

As for unilateral anticompetitive actions, a much-discussed example occurred in the 1950s. Anheuser-Busch was charged in the 1950s with price discrimination in the Missouri area market, which allowed it to increase its market share there from 17 to 39 percent.[38] Anheuser-Busch has continued to take selective pricing actions, even though it is the dominant firm. Price discrimination may not be critical to its continued leadership, but it helps.

At the distribution level, the leading brewers have set rigid territorial limits on their distributors in many states. Any sales to adjoining areas are forbidden, on threat of terminating the franchise. This blocks intrabrand competition. This type of action is neutral or even procompetitive when market shares are small, but when undertaken by Anheuser-Busch, it prevents a large amount of intrabrand competition.[39] The FTC held Coca-Cola's and Pepsi-Cola's similar systems to be illegal in 1970 (as noted in chapter 12), but those firms obtained a special exemption from Congress. During the Reagan administration and since then, antitrust officials have shown no concern about vertical restrictions in beer.

5. PERFORMANCE

Prices have probably been held significantly above competitive levels. Anheuser-Busch's profits have been high, averaging over 18 percent returns on equity capital since 1970.

Beer advertising is virtually all of the image-forming, persuasive type, so it is largely an economic waste (recall chapter 12). Most of it is also mutually canceling among the oligopolists. The resources involve over $1 billion per year.

Innovation has been slow. Aluminum cans were developed from the outside by the container industry. Lower-calorie beers caught on in the 1980s. Little other innovation has appeared for forty years, except for new brands. That may seem natural for a product that originated thousands of years ago, and technological opportunity in this industry is probably limited. Even so, the rate of innovation has been slow.

In distribution, the limits on intrabrand competition have probably raised prices significantly. That conclusion is disputed by industry sources, who say that free competition would eliminate smaller dealers, permitting the few survivors to raise prices further. Though doubtful, this outcome might apply for some areas.

6. IN SUMMARY

The beer industry is not simple. It now has dominance by Anheuser-Busch and regional markets that co-exist with a national-brand market. Heavy advertising has shaped its structure toward higher concentration, and it provides Anheuser-Busch with a way of minimizing direct price competition. It also accounts for the main monopoly loss in the industry. Tight territorial restrictions on beer distribution in many states also probably cause significant monopoly effects.

More effective competition might not increase innovation by very much in this ancient industry. Nor is it clear how advertising could be reduced. Technology, however, would permit lower concentration, more efficiency, and faster innovation.

VI. ELECTRICITY

The electricity industry began in the 1990s an historic shift from natural-monopoly regulated "utilities" toward what eventually might become competitive markets. Most electric companies still hold monopoly or dominant positions in some of their markets. The main question was: will competition become effective or be trapped in dominance?

When Thomas Edison invented the light bulb in 1879, he created the basis for widespread use and commercial supply. By 1900 the industry had developed its main features: local privately-owned monopolies supplying businesses and residences. Transmission widened as the industry grew, so power was sent over increasing distances. Regulation of these utility firms began in Wisconsin in 1907, and by the 1930s most states had regulatory commissions; federal regulation also was in formation.

The local-monopoly basis continued, but regulation was generally light. Costs tended to decline over time, as the technology explored the economies of ever-larger scale in generation and transmission. After 1960 nuclear power became a major innovation, but it turned sour after 1978 as risks, costs, and the problems of winding down generating plants became excessive.

In the 1980s, competition developed in regional markets for short-run surplus power.[40] But many white-elephant nuclear plants still posed huge costs for many utility firms, and many old monopoly patterns continued in the 1990s as regulation receded. Deregulation seemed to advance in many states, but the prospects for effective competition were dim.

Then in 2000–2001, California erupted in a spectacular crisis. Electricity prices multiplied by 10 times over, with frequent blackouts. A major cause was that marketers like Enron had manipulated prices severely by cheating and fraud, as well as cooking their accounts. The scandals and fiascoes traumatized deregulation over much of the country, although some states continued cautiously ahead.[41] The industry's future form was placed in doubt.

1. THE MARKETS

The industry is complicated, with **three stages of production** and a nationwide patchwork of regional and local geographic markets.[42] For over a century, all three stages have been vertically integrated into the local monopoly utility. But each stage is different, both in economic and physical forms. They have diverged increasingly since 1960.

Each stage's markets are now recognized to be distinct from the others.

Generation. The first stage is generation, which creates electricity by using steam heat to spin generators. "Conventional" generation uses coal-fired boilers, but oil, gas, water power, wind power, and nuclear fuel can also be used (solar cells are a final alternative).

Markets for generation services involve the wholesale supply of bulk power. But power comes in several kinds. The basic one is long-term **firm power**. This power is guaranteed to be available if it is needed. That is essential for the buyer, which cannot tolerate any chance that its distribution system will go dark. This long-term power is often contracted for 20 or more years. **Non-firm power** comes in various gradations, in which the buyer agrees that the power may not be available under specified conditions. Such power is, of course, cheaper than fully firm power. Finally **spot power** is the moment-to-moment supply of surplus electricity, involved in short-term transactions among many systems in a region.

Generators commonly engage in all three types of markets, and so do buyers as they seek to minimize the costs of the electricity they buy.

Geographic markets for these forms of generated power are regional, often reaching well over 500 miles. Thus power is sold and exchanged over the western U.S., from Washington to Arizona. Power from eastern Canada is sold as far away as Virginia and Ohio.

Transmission. Transmission is like electricity highways; it moves high-voltage electricity from the generating sites over large wires to the areas where it will be used. Its markets are less complex than generating markets, because the services are fewer and simpler.

Product markets are for transmission services. Geographic markets are generally regional.

Local distribution. Local distribution uses sets of wires throughout towns and cities to bring electricity to all the individual local customers.

The product markets reflect the great variety of customers, from the biggest industrial factories down to small residential buyers. Their demand conditions are extremely varied, from elastic to highly inelastic. The main market divisions are three: large-industrial power at high voltages, commercial buyers, and residential customers.

The geographic markets have always been simply the local distribution areas. But currently these markets are being fundamentally altered by a change in regulatory rules. The eventual purpose is to create competition by letting final customers buy their power from anywhere rather than being locked in to a local supplier. This change is just beginning, so the borders of these markets are not well defined.

2. STRUCTURE

For about a century, the electricity industry was a set of complete, government-franchised monopolies.

Generating-services markets. But markets for generating services began to emerge and widen in the 1960s, and by the 1990s the spot-power markets had become effectively competitive. Firm-power markets are not yet effectively competitive, because they remain mostly in dominant-firm or tight oligopoly patterns, often with effective agreements not to compete.

Entry into the firm-power markets is difficult. To supply genuinely firm power, a generating firm must have a complete system of assured capacity. That can be extremely expensive for a new entrant to create. In addition, the supplier must have a complete set of long-term contracts for the power so as to avoid risks that the power cannot be sold.

Therefore, many firm-power markets are still highly monopolistic, with dominance and difficult entry. In contrast, short-term spot-power markets are generally highly flexible, fast-adjusting, and competitive. But competition in those markets does not make the firm-power markets any less monopolistic.

Transmission-services markets. These are usually region-wide, though some smaller pockets exist.

Local distribution. As of 1995, these markets are still monopolies, but competition may become important in coming years. State commissions in California, Massachusetts, Wisconsin, and New York, among others, are moving their companies toward open purchases by electric customers. Federal regulators also are developing policies to promote open competition at the local level.

Entry is a key condition. It is now difficult, and its evolution will depend on the policy rules that are adopted by regulators.

Mergers. In anticipation of competition, a wave of electric-utility mergers began in the mid-1990s, reaching flood proportions. They tended to reverse the shift to competition by combining firms which would be competitors. But the stock-market collapse and the scandals after 1999 brought this merger mania to a halt.

3. Determinants[43]

Economies of integration. Since the industry's early days, there have been economies from the coordinated planning of all three stages, giving a reason for tight vertical integration. But these benefits have increasingly been offset by the costs of monopoly. Also, it has been increasingly possible to coordinate by competitive markets rather than internal controls. That has made vertical integration less acceptable, and so new policies are moving away from it.

Economies of scale. Until the 1960s, the economies of scale in generation seemed to grow endlessly, and ever-bigger plants were built. In transmission, too, size and voltages rose ever higher, seeming to maintain natural-monopoly conditions. Transmission areas grew larger and larger.

But since the 1960s, the natural-monopoly basis has faded at both these stages. New generating equipment is generally smaller, thanks to new technology. And transmission lines often offer complex patterns for selling power across large areas; although large size still gives lower costs, the markets themselves are so much larger that there is little natural monopoly.

At the local distribution level, there is of course no real basis for duplicate physical systems. But regulators could dilute the local distributor's control by requiring free access at fair prices, enabling customers to look outside for suppliers.

In short, the determinants are primarily rules, not basic economic conditions. These markets could be effectively competitive, **if** the correct rules were set and enforced.

4. Behavior

The utilities naturally resisted new competition, both by regulatory hearings and lobbying and by trying to bar new competition. They refused to wheel power from others, and when required to wheel, they tried to set prices for wheeling which effectively exclude the power. When new U.S. policies after 1978 promoted the entry of alternative power sources (so-called co-generators), many utility firms resisted sharply.

Yet as competition became more vigorous, many utilities shifted their policies to take advantage of it. In the 1990s, some made sweetheart deals with major customers—under regulatory approval—to lock them in and head off the oncoming competition.[44] This involved dynamic price discrimination, perhaps precluding effective competition in the future. Regulation's ability to promote competition is incomplete.[45]

5. Performance

Until the 1960s, regulated electric utilities were widely thought to be subject to significant X-inefficiency. In 1963, new economic theories of regulation raised the further possibility that the regulated utilities would waste capital by investing too much. There were also doubts that electric firms were innovative; they seemed to do little but tend their assets and build a new plant and transmission line every so often. It was a placid, rather stodgy industry.

But later research has not confirmed that these tendencies have caused any major excess costs.[46] The worst performance was in buying scores of nuclear plants, many of which imposed large "stranded costs."

After 1968, the industry faced severe new pressures, including tight environmental limits on pollution and on locations for new facilities, a meteoric rise in fuel prices after the 1973 oil embargo, and the costly collapse of nuclear power programs.[47] Firms adjusted somewhat, though many still clung to monopoly rather than shifting to creative, competitive behavior.

6. In Summary

This industry contains dominance in important markets, and even "competitive" markets in the west were manipulated during 2000-01 by fraudulent marketers. Most utility firms have tried to maintain their dominance while engaging in standard forms of price discrimination.

Deregulation has been checkered. Some firms adjusted toward flexible, competitive behavior, but others pursued mergers or fraud. How far the mergers will restore market controls is still unsure. But antitrust will need to take special steps to keep reducing market dominance and to reduce entry barriers.

VII. CAPSULE STUDIES

1. Ticketmaster[48]

The Market and Structure.   Ticketmaster is the exclusive ticketing agent for nearly 70 percent of entertainment and sports events in halls and arenas around the United States. Regionally, its share is lowest in the Sun-belt and border states. Its share is over 70 percent in California, 89 percent in Michigan, 95 percent in

Florida, and 73 percent in New York. Its small rivals include such minor factors as Dillard's in Phoenix and Protix in Madison, Wisconsin. The events range from operatic stars and professional sports to Disney's World on Ice, the Holocaust Memorial Museum in Washington, DC, and nearly all rock music concerts.

Founded in 1982 and led aggressively by Frederic Rosen, Ticketmaster soon overcame Ticketron, the previously dominant ticketing firm. Ticketron was inefficient, and Ticketmaster was able to nail down long-term exclusive deals with halls and arenas from the start. By 1991 Ticketron was failing, and Ticketmaster was able to buy it out.

Behavior.   Exclusive deals continue to be Ticketmaster's key method, tying up sites of all kinds, driving whatever bargain is necessary in order to secure the contract. That amounts to extensive and systematic discriminatory pricing. Ticketmaster is widely accused of anticompetitive practices. Now that it is dominant, Ticketmaster's price discrimination patterns are in fact inevitably anticompetitive, because they quell competition from its smaller rivals.

Profitability.   Ticketmaster says that its service fees average only 14 percent of the ticket price, but its charges probably are close to 30 percent. This far exceeds the charges of its small rivals. Profits therefore amply fit the dominant-firm situation.

In 1993, the new wealth created by Microsoft took over Ticketmaster. Paul G. Allen, the billionaire co-founder of Microsoft, bought Ticketmaster in 1993. Ticketmaster still relies on 1970s computer technology, but the Microsoft connection may bring improvements. That is likely to maintain or increase Ticketmaster's dominance.

2.   YELLOW PAGES

Yellow Pages are universally familiar as the comprehensive, classified reference directory to local businesses. Everyone uses the local Yellow Pages to locate sellers after they've decided what they want. Larger businesses typically have a boxed advertisement with details.

Markets.   The market for Yellow Pages is distinct and confined closely to these directory services. It might be thought instead that Yellow Pages are just a small item within the larger general market for local advertising. That is not correct; general advertising seeks to make people want to buy the advertiser's services.

Yellow Pages are used instead *after* the decision to buy has been made; now you need to find a renovator, car dealer, or plumber. The Yellow Pages are almost universally relied upon, and they are used repeatedly and thoroughly, rather than just tossed aside as most advertising is. Yellow Pages are widely trusted, partly because the compilers apply standards of accuracy, checking on claims and details. Finally, Yellow Pages advertisements do not give prices; that also contrasts with most advertising, which often treats prices as the main feature.

Structure.   Yellow Pages directories usually are local monopolies, with no serious competitor; they hold above 90 percent in virtually all towns and cities. These near-monopolies are further reinforced by being linked directly with the "official" telephone company.

In a few areas, some new directories have emerged in recent years, but most are inferior and weak. Even the R. R. Donnelly company, which prints many of the Yellow Pages volumes around the United States, was repelled in a major effort to enter markets in Virginia. If such an experienced and well-situated entrant fails, it is not surprising that others do worse or do not try. Entry barriers are high.

Profitability. The Yellow Pages virtual monopolies have been extremely profitable. Revenues are probably a high multiple of costs, and the rates of profit on investment may be close to 100 percent in many cases. Local telephone companies cling tightly to their Yellow Pages monopolies because the profits are high and beyond the regulators' restraints.[49]

QUESTIONS FOR REVIEW

1. Is Microsoft's near-monopoly tightening and spreading or instead fragile and vulnerable?

2. How might effective competition against the Baby Bells develop?

3. In defining "newspaper" markets, are they really local "multimedia" markets? Discuss the conditions in at least one city you know about.

4. What possible ways can you suggest for promoting competition in newspaper markets?

5. Will open access for local customers really lead to effective competition in electricity markets?

ENDNOTES

[1] See Daniel Ichbiah and Susan Knepper, *The Making of Microsoft* (Rocklin, CA: Prima, 1991).

[2] For coverage of Microsoft's role in the United States, see Stan J. Liebowitz and Stephen E. Margolis, *Winners, Losers and Microsoft: Competition and Antitrust in High Technology* (Oakland, CA: Independent Institute, 1999). They focus on Microsoft's competitive actions, and they argue that the firm has inferior products but "locks them in" to defeat superior competitors. On global conditions, see David C. Mowery, *The International Computer Software Industry: A Comparative Study of Industry Evolution and Structure* (New York: Oxford University Press, 1996).

[3] For an argument that Microsoft's power may lead to a much wider monopoly, see James Gleick, "Making Microsoft Safe for Capitalism," *New York Times Magazine* (November 5, 1995): pp. 50–64.

[4] See Don Clark, "Microsoft Beefs Up Customer Services," *Wall Street Journal* (May 4, 1995): p. B7. Service is "woefully inadequate" compared to competitors; computer managers in 1994 rated it as 1 on a scale where 5 is best. Microsoft in 1995 had 600 staff members to assist customers, while Oracle Corp. had more than 4,000.

[5] Gates in 2002 held over $50 billion in assets from his Microsoft gains. Other Microsoft founders also hold fortunes numbering in the many billions.

[6] For example, in 1995 Gates bought the Bettman Archive, the dominant collection of photographic and related images in the world. This allows him to set lucrative prices for access to these central social and cultural images. Allen bought control of Ticketmaster, the near-monopoly ticket-vending company.

[7] On the futility of the case that ended in 2002, see the major story by Steve Lohr, "For Microsoft, Ruling Will Sting But Not Really Hurt," *New York Times* (November 2, 2002): pp. B1, B4–B5; and John Markoff, "Rivals Are Resigned to Life With a Dominant Microsoft," *New York Times* (November 3, 2002): p. 15.

[8] See Robert G. Picard et al., eds., *Press Concentration and Monopoly: New Perspectives on Newspaper Ownership and Operation* (Norwood, NJ: Ablex, 1988); and Kenneth C. Baseman, "Partial Consolidation: The Detroit Newspaper Joint Operating Agreement (1988)," a chapter in John E. Kwoka, Jr. and Lawrence J. White, eds., *The Antitrust Revolution* (New York: HarperCollins, 1994), and sources listed there.

[9] See Ben H. Bagdikian, *The Media Monopoly,* 2nd ed. (Boston: Beacon Press, 1987), and sources there.

[10] Extensive data on local newspaper circulation are in the basic journalism source, "The Working Press of the Nation," *Newspaper Directory,* issued periodically.

[11] Among monopoly-creating mergers in 1995, the *Baltimore Sun Times* bought and closed the *Evening Sun,* and the *Houston Chronicle* bought and closed the *Post.* See William Glaberson, "Times Mirror Will Close the Baltimore Evening Sun," *New York Times* (May 26, 1995): p. D4.

[12] Susannah Patton, "Family Newspapers Struggle to Hang On," *Wall Street Journal* (February 27, 1995): p. A7A.

[13] Among industry leaders is the Gannett chain with ninety-three dailies, ten TV stations and eleven radio stations; see Patrick M. Reilly, "Keeping Low-Tech Profile, Gannett Co. Puts Its Faith in the Newspaper Business," *Wall Street Journal* (October 3, 1995): p. B1.

[14] An unusual form of collusion between two newspapers may also have occurred in some cases. If both newspapers can seem to be losing money and facing closure, then pressure can be put on government officials to approve a merger or quasi-merger. The "failing firm" would seemingly cease to be a rival anyway. This apparently happened in Detroit in the 1980s, as the *News* and *Free Press* engaged in a circulation battle that predictably put them in current losses. Their demands for a quasi-merger to rescue them from this self-inflicted difficulty were finally granted in 1988.

[15] The author studied this issue as an adviser to the *Chicago Daily Herald,* a suburban daily that sought after 1985 to compete citywide against the *Chicago Tribune* and the *Chicago Sun-Times.* Among other effects, the exclusions covered nearly all of the twenty-five best comic strips, as well as leading opinion columns, Dear Abby and other advice columns, and the *New York Times* and *Los Angeles Times* news services.

[16] James N. Dertouzos and William B. Trautman, "Economic Effects of Media Concentration: Estimates from a Model of the Newspaper Firm," *Journal of Industrial Economics* 39 (September 1990): pp. 1–14.

[17] For detailed facts on the industry and the effects of the breakup, see Robert W. Crandall, *After the Breakup: U.S. Telecommunications in a More Competitive Era* (Washington, DC: Brookings Institution, 1991). See also Bridger M. Mitchell and Ingo Vogelsang, *Telecommunications Pricing: Theory and Practice* (New York: Cambridge University Press, 1991); and Gerald W. Brock, *Telecommunications Policy for the Information Age* (Cambridge: Harvard University Press, 1994).

[18] For global comparisons with countries trying all manners of policies, see Bjorn Wellenius and Peter A. Stem, eds., *Implementing Reforms in the Telecommunications Sector: Lessons from Experience* (Washington, DC: World Bank, 1994), with forty papers on all regions and topics.

[19] For MCI's fascinating history, see Philip L. Cantelon, *The History of MCI 1968–88, The Early Years* (Dallas: Heritage Press, 1993).

[20] Crandall, *After the Breakup*; and see Erwin Blackstone, A. J. Buck, and S. Hakim, "An Analysis of Telephone Company Entry into Unregulated Markets: The Electronic Security Case," *Antitrust Bulletin* 39 (Fall 1994): pp. 727–52.

[21] The soft-competition tendencies were increased by the formation of joint ventures and alliances by all three companies with various systems abroad. The quasi-mergers developed rapidly after 1994 as major reform gained momentum.

[22] See Gerald Brock, *The U.S. Computer Industry* (Cambridge, MA: Ballinger Publishers, 1975); and Brock, "The Computer Industry," a chapter in Walter Adams, ed., *The Structure of American Industry,* 8th ed. (New York: Macmillan, 1990); Neil B. Niman and Manley R. Irwin, "Computers," a chapter in Walter Adams, *The Structure of American Industry,* 9th ed. (New York: Macmillan, 1995); Richard Thomas DeLamarter, *Big Blue: IBM's Use and Abuse*

of Power (New York: Dodd, Mead, 1986), which gives thorough coverage to IBM's pricing and product strategies; and William G. Shepherd, *Market Power and Economic Welfare* (New York: Random House, 1970), chapter 15.

[23] See Paul Carroll, *Big Blues—The Unmaking of IBM* (Chicago: Crown, 1993); and Charles H. Ferguson and Charles R. Moms, *Computer Wars* (New York: Random House, 1993).

[24] The case was *U.S. v. International Business Machines Corp.*, 69 CIV 200, So. Dist. of N.Y. It was filed in 1969, tried in court from 1975 to 1982, and dropped by the government's antitrust division in 1982. For statements of IBM's views by economists hired to defend it in this and other antitrust cases, see Franklin M. Fisher et al., *Folded, Spindled and Mutilated: Economic Analysis and U.S. v. IBM* (Cambridge: MIT Press, 1983); and Fisher et al., *IBM and the U.S. Data Processing Industry: An Economic History* (New York: Praeger, 1983).

[25] Ironically, when the major U.S. antitrust lawsuit against IBM's dominance was dropped in 1982, it was widely expected that the restructured AT&T would become a powerhouse in computers. Thus IBM would come under severe attack by AT&T, bringing effective competition to the market. In fact, AT&T proved incapable of mounting a powerful computer operation, and by the 1990s it was a marginal, unprofitable factor. In 1995 AT&T announced plans to split itself in three partly in order to shed its computer-industry failures.

[26] By 1995, the PC market shares were Packard Bell, 13 percent; Compaq, 11 percent; Apple, 10 percent; IBM, 9 percent; and Gateway 2000, 5 percent—see the *Wall Street Journal* (May 1, 1995): p. B4. These market shares had not changed much by 2003.

[27] See Shepherd, *Market Power and Economic Welfare*; and DeLamarter, *Big Blue*; for an opposite view, see Fisher et al., *Folded, Spindled and Mutilated*.

[28] See Shepherd, *Market Power and Economic Welfare*; and DeLamarter, *Big Blue*.

[29] See Shepherd, *Market Power and Economic Welfare*. As DeLamarter shows (*Big Blue*, chapter 6), IBM also set highly discriminatory prices among the components of each system.

[30] *BusinessWeek* (May 29, 1989): p. 77.

[31] He failed at consumer markets and home PCs, and the expensive takeover of Lotus had little result. Gerstner also extracted immense payments from IBM as incentives and bonuses.

[32] To start on this industry, see Kenneth G. Elzinga, "Beer," a chapter in Walter Adams, eds., *The Structure of American Industry*, 9th ed. (New York: Macmillan, 1995), and the sources there. Also John Sutton, *Sunk Costs and Market Structure: Price Competition, Advertising, and the Evolution of Concentration* (Cambridge, MA: MIT Press, 1991), especially pp. 285–303 and 515–32; Douglas F. Greer, "Beer: Causes of Structural Change," a chapter in Larry L. Deutsch, *Industry Studies* (Englewood Cliffs, NJ: Prentice Hall, 1994); W. John Jordan and Bruce L. Jaffee, "The use of Exclusive Territories in the Distribution of Beer," *Antitrust Bulletin* (Spring 1987): pp. 137–64; Victor J. Tremblay and Carol Horton Tremblay, "The Determinants of Horizontal Acquisitions: Evidence from the U.S. Brewing Industry," *Journal of Industrial Economics* (September 1988): pp. 21–45; Tim R. Sass and David S. Saurman, "Mandated Exclusive Territories and Economic Efficiency: An Empirical Analysis of the Malt Beverage Industry," *Journal of Law and Economics* (April 1993); and Richard Gibson, "Anheuser-Busch Makes Price Moves in Bid to Boost Sales of Flagship Brand," *Wall Street Journal* (February 28, 1994).

[33] In blind taste tests, most people cannot distinguish among most of the popular and high-priced brands.

[34] Though Anheuser-Busch's share of beer volume is 49 percent, its share of revenue and profits is much higher. See Nina Stechler Hayes, "Brewer SABMiller's Profit Rises, Boosted by Entry Into U.S. Market," *Wall Street Journal* (November 22, 2002): p. B4. See also Christopher Lawton, "Anheuser-Busch Rolls Out the Price Jump," *Wall Street Journal* (October 23, 2002): p. B4.

[35] Richard A. Melcher, "Is It Finally Miller Time?" *BusinessWeek* (February 12, 1996): p. 37.

[36] See F. M. Scherer et al., *The Economics of Multi-plant Operations* (Cambridge: Harvard University Press, 1975); E. Elyasiani and S. Mehdian, "Measuring Technical and Scale Inefficiencies in the Beer Industry: Nonparametric and Parametric Evidence," *Quarterly Review of Economics and Finance* 33 (Winter 1993): pp. 383–408; and the sources noted in Elzinga, "The Beer Industry."

[37] See, for example, W. P. Culbertson and D. Bradford, "The Price of Beer: Some Evidence from Interstate Comparison," *International Journal of Industrial Organization* 9 (1991): pp. 275–89.

[38] Details are in *Federal Trade Commission v. Anheuser-Busch*, 363 U.S. 536, an antitrust case that dealt with the episode.

[39] For further detail, see W. John Jordan and Bruce L. Jaffe, "The Use of Exclusive Territories in the Distribution of Beer: Theoretical and Empirical Observations," *Antitrust Bulletin* 32 (Spring 1987): pp. 137–64.

[40] Good sources on the industry's shape and prospects are Paul Joskow and Richard Schmalensee, *Markets for Power* (Cambridge: MIT Press, 1985); Mark W. Frankena and Bruce M. Owen, *Electric Utility Mergers* (Westport, CT: Praeger, 1994); and Carl Pechman, *Regulating Power: The Economics of Electricity in the Information Age* (Boston: Kluwer, 1993.)

[41] For example, most electric companies renamed themselves during the 1990s, replacing factual names like "Edison" and "Power & Light" with empty words ending in "-ergy," etc. For example, "Commonwealth Edison Co., Chicago, looked at a lot of 'ergies,'" an official says, "but settled on something else nonsensical: Unicom Corp." Illinois utilities became "Ameren" and "Illinova." See Jeff Bailey, "Electric Utilities," *Wall Street Journal* (November 16, 1995): p. 1. This mimics the earlier trends of banks, oil companies, Baby Bells, health-care firms, and others in seeking anonymity through meaningless names (recall chapter 4). In the later scandals after 1999, the jazzier names were correlated with the more severe troubles, with Enron leading the way.

[42] D. Gegax and K. Nowotny, "Competition and Electric Utility Industry: An Evaluation," *Yale Journal on Regulation* 10 (Winter 1993): pp. 63–87.

[43] See Herbert G. Thompson et al., *Economies of Scale and Vertical Integration in the Investor-Owned Electric Utility Industry* (Columbus, OH: National Regulatory Research Institute, 1996); and David L. Kaserman and John W. Mayo, "The Measurement of Vertical Economies and the Efficient Structure of the Electric Utility Industry," *Journal of Industrial Economics* 39 (October 1991): pp. 483–502.

[44] See for example J. A. Herriges et al., "The Response of Industrial Customers to Electric Rates Based Upon Dynamic Marginal Costs," *Review of Economics and Statistics* 75 (August 1993): pp. 446–54.

[45] For example, see Benjamin A. Holden, "California's Struggle Shows How Hard It Is To Deregulate Utilities," *Wall Street Journal* (November 28, 1995): pp. 1, A11.

[46] For an assessment, see William G. Shepherd, *Regulation and Efficiency: A Reappraisal of Research and Policies* (Columbus, OH: National Regulatory Research Institute, Ohio State University, 1992).

[47] Rodney Stevenson, "Social Goals and Partial Deregulation of the Electric Utility Industry," *Journal of Economic Issues* 28 (June 1994): pp. 403–13.

[48] See Anthony Ramirez, "Ticketmaster's Mr. Tough Guy," *New York Times* (November 6, 1994): bus. sec. pp. 1, 6; and Ralph Blumenthal, "Oddities Continue in Pearl Jam's Feud with Ticketmaster," *New York Times* (August 23, 1995): pp. B1, B2.

[49] In 2002, the Qwest company (owner of US West, the northwest US Baby Bell) sold its Yellow Pages rights for $7 billion, reflecting its high profitability.

Chapter

14

CASE STUDIES OF TIGHT OLIGOPOLIES:
PASSENGER AIRCRAFT, AIRLINES, SPORTS, READY-TO-EAT CEREALS, AND TRASH REMOVAL

Tight oligopoly is important in the U.S. economy, but less so than it was before 1970. It is still only modestly clarified by economic theory, despite endless efforts using game theory.

Some tight-oligopoly markets are interesting, instructive, and very familiar. Think, for example, of Boeing and Airbus in jet aircraft; the leading airlines themselves; leading sports (baseball, football, basketball, and hockey); and Kellogg's and others in ready-to-eat cereals. Even the humble local garbage truck is part of a gritty tight oligopoly, with Waste Management and Browning-Ferris as the duopolists in nearly every U.S. city. These five cases suggest the rich variety of situations and outcomes.

I. PASSENGER AIRCRAFT (BOEING AND AIRBUS)

The Boeing Aircraft Company was the dominant U.S. aircraft producer during most of the period after World War II. From numerous competitors in 1945, the industry narrowed down to just three main rivals by 1967 (Boeing,

McDonnell-Douglas, and Lockheed). By the 1970s, Boeing stood alone among U.S. firms, with McDonnell-Douglas a distant second. Then European governments jointly created the Airbus Industrie consortium, and it became a substantial competitor in the 1980s. By 2002 Airbus had pulled nearly even with Boeing, resulting in a duopoly.

Boeing's biggest rise came with the jet age, beginning in 1959. Its planes were generally superior, and Boeing was also aided by military resources and technology developed under favorable contracts for the Pentagon.

1. THE MARKET

The market includes full-size civilian passenger aircraft for use by airlines. This is distinct from military aircraft, small aircraft (20 seats or less), helicopters, and other such equipment. Since 1959 the main aircraft in this market have been jets, but turboprops are also a significant section of the market.

Since 1985 three distinct markets have been emerging: jumbo jets, above 300 seats; midsize jets; and commuter aircraft, below 100 seats and often with prop-jet power. In recent decades, Boeing has held an actual monopoly at the top level, with its 747 model. Airbus is about to leap-frog that size with a giant "jumbo jet" for 600-plus passengers. Both rivals are also in the middle range, while other firms (such as Canadair and Fokker) compete in the smaller-plane short-hop market.

Geographically, the market expanded by 1975 to a worldwide basis, as all airlines became largely free to buy from any producer. Although aircraft are the tangible product, sales often also involve vastly complex financing and parts-supply deals, negotiated between the airlines and the producers but often with intimate involvement by the governments on both sides.[1]

2. STRUCTURE

Boeing's market share was in the range of 50 to 65 percent in the 1960s and 1970s, even as the market grew rapidly. Other firms faded, though Airbus Industrie was formed. By 1980, Boeing's share of current sales revenue was nearly 80 percent. In 1994, Boeing had 57 percent of commercial transport jets revenue, Airbus had 28 percent, and McDonnell-Douglas 10 percent. Boeing's 747 model has virtually monopolized jumbo jets since 1969, with total production now at over 1,100. In 1996, the U.S. government allowed Boeing to take over McDonnell-Douglas, raising its market share to 70 percent. But Airbus pulled nearly even with Boeing in 2002.

Entry barriers appear to be extremely high. Reputation is important, including a full backup of personnel, technical capacity, and finances for fixing any problems that arise. The capital requirements for entry are very high because of scale economies, industry size, and R & D needs. Connections with governments are important for three reasons. First, U.S. military contracts have provided important technology, profits, and product spinoffs for Boeing. Second, U.S. officials' support behind the scenes can help sway plane purchases abroad. And third, foreign governments are also often involved in purchase decisions by foreign airlines, because there are large financial and job impacts, plus military aspects.

When Airbus entered, it initially required large financial resources and governmental support for decades. No further entry appears possible under any realistic circumstances.

3. DETERMINANTS

Scale economies are important, though the MES level for firms is probably not more than 20 percent of the market, with room for perhaps five comparable competitors.

Many airlines prefer to standardize and unify their fleets so as to reduce the costs of servicing and repairs. Still another determinant is reputation. Airlines lean toward larger, established suppliers, which can assure them of future continuity and aircraft safety.

Risk comes from new technology, as well as from difficulties in predicting demand many years ahead. Economic recessions, oil price shocks, and other random factors may also continue to make aircraft purchasing unstable. Such risks favor the dominant firm.

4. BEHAVIOR

Boeing's actions have been largely unilateral in its continual battle to obtain plane sales. Most of the action occurs out of public view, and there have been few charges of unfair tactics directed specifically at Boeing. In turn, Boeing alleges unfair governmental backing and favoritism for Airbus. Collusion seems to be absent.

5. PERFORMANCE

Boeing has set highly profitable prices on its 747 aircraft, with their virtual monopoly. On the current price above $150 million per plane, about $30 million per plane is operating profit.

But Boeing is not efficient. Year after year, Boeing is scaldingly criticized in the business press for being highly X-inefficient and slow in innovation.[2] A thorough review in 1995 noted "gross inefficiencies and astronomical defect rates in its manufacturing," and a "sprawling bureaucracy" with a production process that is "out of control" because it has "800 different computer systems" and involves "manually—*manually!*—tracking which parts go into which plane." Altogether, the X-inefficiency was probably at least 10 percent of costs, and possibly over 15 percent.[3] By comparison, Airbus has been aggressively innovative as the hard-pressed entrant, and it apparently has kept costs and prices low.

In innovation, Airbus has led Boeing. It has adopted electronic controls and other advanced technology, and some of its aircraft design features are superior. That superiority has recently lifted Airbus to parity with Boeing.

6. IN SUMMARY

Boeing has followed the dominant-firm theory. It rose in part from its own innovations and fortunate governmental help, and it was dominant for decades. Then it encountered X-inefficiency, slowed innovation, and effective new competition from Airbus. New pressures may finally force Boeing to improve its efficiency and innovation.

II. AIRLINES[4]

Airlines were a spectacular leading policy case in the 1980s, after deregulation in 1978 led to a dramatic rise of competition. But the industry reverted during 1984–1988 to a patchwork of dominance and competition, leaving the industry mixed and controversial. Some observers see strong competition, efficiency, and innovation, whereas others see much market power and anticompetitive pricing.[5]

Especially among those who fly, airline deregulation is still an endlessly debated topic. There is strong competition on some routes but high degrees of monopoly on others. The hub-and-spoke system allows one or two airlines to dominate many large-city airports, from Dallas, Newark, Denver, and Philadelphia to the airports at Washington, DC. Price discrimination is probably anticompetitive on many routes and areas.

1. BRIEF HISTORY

A brief historical survey may help. Through the 1920s and most of the 1930s, air travel grew from a small business run by a group of hedgehopping daredevils into a new industry dominated by about six trunk airlines.

By 1938, the biggest airlines were seeking friendly regulation as a way to minimize competition. They got it in the form of the Civil Aeronautics Board. From 1938 until 1975, the CAB froze the industry's structure, permitting virtually no entry or shifting among routes. Structure was tight; 90 percent of city-pair routes, with 59 percent of all passenger miles, were genuine monopolies. The airlines behaved like a market-rigging cartel, agreeing on fares among themselves and then obtaining CAB approval and enforcement. This practice prevented effective competition.

The airlines did compete indirectly on amenities (such as fancier decor and tastier meals) and by scheduling more frequent flights, even though planes flew half empty on average. Salary levels for workers also were generous. CAB regulation therefore tended to raise costs, possibly by 30 to 50 percent above efficient levels.

Economists documented these costs, and by 1975 a political momentum had developed to remove regulation. It was an early step in the larger deregulation movement, to be discussed in chapter 17.

Airline deregulation in 1978 led to chaotic, effective competition, with some fifty new airlines taking off. Hub-and-spoke patterns developed, with each airline routing most of its traffic through one, two, or several airports. Fare discounts spread to most tickets by 1983. The gains included higher productivity, lower fares, and greater diversity, along with some "union bashing" that allowed the airlines to cut work forces and rates of pay.

From 1984 to 1986, the industry reverted partway to monopolistic patterns. The leading airlines set rigid rules for most fare discounts (all requiring Saturday stayovers, advance reservations, nonrefundable tickets, etc.), and they initiated large mergers that increased their dominance over hub airports. National concentration rose.

Traffic varies from huge volumes in the largest cities down to mere trickles in the many smaller cities. The map is dominated by the hub-and-spoke pattern; most flights go to a hub city, and most long flights are broken in the middle by a transfer at a hub.[6]

These parts combine in a vast set of operations. Several thousand flights take place in the United States each day, for a total of over 400 million passenger trips a year.

It has been estimated that deregulation has reduced fares sharply below their likely levels under regulation: Morrison and Winston rated the savings at $6 billion to $12 billion a year. By 1986, however, there were strong complaints that deregulation had been subverted by mergers and pricing.

After 1990.   Another phase began, as competition revived on many routes. Southwest Airlines extended its cut-price coverage in the country, and other low-price airlines entered, including ValuJet in the east. The industry was in transition, possibly to more intensive competition.

After 2001.   The terrorist attacks of September 11, 2001, plunged the industry into reduced demand and extreme, congestion-creating procedures to screen every passenger. Public loans have kept America West flying, and possibly others. The stresses have predictably stirred plans for mergers to "consolidate" and "streamline," but they have not been permitted. Yet quasi-mergers have occurred: an "alliance" to coordinate United Airlines and US Airways was approved in 2002, and another between Delta, Northwest, and Continental is pending. These alliances would substantially reduce competition.

2. DEFINING THE MARKETS

Product features are relatively simple in the airline sector, whereas geographic features are complex and debatable.

Product Substitutability.   Airline travel is highly distinct from alternative forms of travel. Bus, train, or automobile travel may be marginally substitutable for plane trips below about 150 miles, but above that distance they are entirely distinct. In general, there is no close (or even remote) substitute for air travel.

Geographic Substitutability.   This is quite complicated. The whole area of the United States is clearly not one big market, because each traveler's needs are extremely precise between city destinations. Some observers go to the other extreme, saying that *each* city-pair route is an entirely separate market. Since there are hundreds of cities, that would mean that there are thousands of individual-route markets within the whole U.S. airline industry. But that goes too far, because some city-pair routes overlap others quite closely.

City pairs are often only parts of larger regional or multicity area travel markets. There is no simple pattern to this. Many of the spokes on the airline hubs are true individual markets.

One can also think of major hub airports as being local markets of their own, because they influence access along their spoke routes into and out of the hub airport. Those hub markets too are not simple or rigid, because some of the spoke routes are paralleled by the spoke routes of other hubs.

To economic experts, the industry is a great patchwork of markets. Many city pairs are pretty clear markets and many hub cities can be regarded as meaningful markets or as cores of regional air-travel markets. Each case needs to be inspected on its merits.

3. STRUCTURES AND DEGREES OF COMPETITION

Shares of Traffic. In this complex industry, the degrees of competition vary sharply. Some markets are dominated by one airline, particularly the fortress hubs at many major airports, as table 14.1 indicates.[7] Trunk routes tend to have low concentration, especially if parallel routings are considered. Lesser routes often show high dominance, and some spoke routes are virtual monopolies.[8] In addition, eastern shuttles (Boston-New York-Washington) have been sheltered duopolies.[9]

Moreover, the leading airlines are well aware that they are spread across a complex sector where fare cutting that breaks out in one part often catches fire and hurts them all. High national concentration has increased the incentives to avoid price cutting.

Conditions of Entry. Entry into the entire market by new airlines is not easy, although several newcomers such as ValuJet in the east and Reno in the west have come in since 1985.[10] Entry into individual routes also can be difficult, because existing suppliers often punish entrants with deep price cuts on their routes.[11] In addition, American and United Airlines originally owned the leading computer reservations systems, which in the 1980s helped them steer travel agents and passengers their way.[12]

Since 1995, Southwest Airlines has led a rise by low-frills airlines that has eroded the high-cost leaders' positions. Often these low-cost airlines can only enter nearby airports, rather than the main hubs. But they have put increasing pressure on the leaders with their much higher costs.

Taken together, the industry's concentration, hubbing, entry barriers, and reservations systems have reduced competition significantly. There is tight oligopoly in most of the industry, with high dominance in many individual markets and fortress hubs, but they are mingled with strong competition on some routes.

4. DETERMINANTS

Before 1978, it was assumed that open competition would be unstable and destructive, because the large airlines would be able to exploit economies of scale to drive out others.

Table 14.1 Shares of Passengers in Selected U.S. Markets, 1994 Data

City	USAir	American	United
Baltimore	46.6%	11.2%	6.8%
Charlotte, N.C.	84.5	1.2	0.8
Chicago	1.8	34.2	47.5
Los Angeles	6.1	11.2	24.0
New York (La Guardia)	24.0	17.4	7.8
Philadelphia	56.2	10.2	7.2
Pittsburgh	81.9	1.9	1.4
San Francisco	6.1	6.5	56.5
Washington, DC (National)	24.9	13.0	7.5

Source: U.S. Department of Transportation

Economies of Scale. By 1970, however, research had showed that economies of scale in the industry were pretty much exhausted at a relatively small scale. There was no technological advantage to large size. Indeed, the emergence of many smaller regional commuter airlines after 1977 and cut-price airlines after 1990 have affirmed the absence of large scale economies. The industry was and is naturally competitive.

Economies of Scope. There are significant economies of scope, or network effects. Once an airline has established a hub with a number of routes extending out, it can often add new routes at relatively low cost. Dominated fortress hubs became a prominent feature.

Mergers and Affiliations. Mergers have strongly shaped industry structure since 1980. First, the large carriers either bought or subordinated most of the smaller airlines. Then during 1985–1988 they merged together extensively. Some of these mergers created management problems rather than efficiency.

Cost Differences. The older major airlines have high average costs, as indicated in table 14.2. The newer no-frills airlines (Southwest, ValuJet) have much lower costs, which have driven their rise and spread.

5. Behavior

The industry contains a wide range of behavior, from periodic fare wars to collusion to local-monopoly tactics. Airlines often tend to match each other's prices quickly, keep them for significant intervals, and then change them quickly together. That reduces uncertainty and avoids deep fare-cutting.

After 1984, the leading airlines adopted the same structure of fare discounts, with similar restrictions about advance payments, Saturday-night stayovers, and nonrefundability. That rigidity softened moderately after 2000, as Internet buying spread.

Price Discrimination under Yield Management. Fare discounts became, at least among leisure customers, common. Airline pricing contains much price discrimination, in which seats are sold at varying ratios of prices to costs. Every large airline has hundreds of pricing staff working on yield manage-

Table 14.2   Airline Costs, 1995

Airline	Costs per Mile (cents)	Labor as % of Expenses
American	10.7	34.7
Continental	9.8	22.6
Delta	10.7	32.7
Northwest	10.8	31.8
Southwest	5.6	32.7
TWA	—	30.6
United	10.6	31.3
USAir	11.3	37.2
ValuJet	6.2	—

Source: U.S. Department of Transportation, 1995

ment. They maximize the revenue from each flight by repeatedly adjusting the number of seats offered on discount.[13] This approaches the extreme result of perfect price discrimination.

The structure of discounts segments the market, rather than giving free play for flexible price cutting. The whole pricing pattern has anticompetitive effects, for reasons explained in chapter 10. Within the leading airlines' pricing structure, the system milks customers for maximum revenue, and it makes entry difficult.[14] Under some conditions, the behavior roughly approximates that of a single monopolist.

Predatory Actions. In addition, there have been anticompetitive pricing actions directed against specific airlines. From 1980 to 1985, large airlines eliminated some small rivals from the market by setting extremely low prices on key routes.[15]

6. PERFORMANCE

Airlines markets, behavior, and performance have been studied with extraordinary thoroughness. The patterns fit the concepts of industrial organization with high fidelity.[16]

The effective competition of 1978 to 1985 brought significant gains. Airline load factors went up, from 56 percent in 1977 to 62 percent in the mid-1980s and 66 percent in the mid-1990s. Ticket prices rose less rapidly, saving passengers perhaps $6 billion to $12 billion annually.[17] The volume of air travel rose far more rapidly, since more people could now afford to fly.

Service quality declined because of crowding, more waiting during earlier check-ins and midtrip plane changes, risks of missing connections, and baggage problems. Flying became more like downscale bus travel. To some extent, cost savings occurred mainly from cutting employees' pay rates. That was a transfer of money, not a reduction in true costs.

The 2001 attacks severely degraded service quality, by forcing massive inconveniences and instability on passengers. Whether these policies can be scaled back to the level of true risks is unclear.

Deregulation brought more rapid innovations in service quality, hub-and-spoke formats, and varieties of aircraft. Since 1990, the new competitive airlines have revived innovation in fares and service.

7. IN SUMMARY

The behavior and performance of the airline industry have reflected its changing structure, just as basic theory would predict. The 1990s revival of competition has restored some of the price cutting and innovation that had abated from 1984 to 1990.

III. SPORTS

The United States can safely be said to be happily sports crazy. For many Americans, sports are the economy's most important sector of all; they play, watch, debate, gamble, and generally dote on sports. Sports are diverse, from hang gliding to golf, yachting to bowling, polo to rooster fighting, and chess to tractor pulls.

Sports are also big business.[18] The main economic elements include the costs of putting on games, ticket sales, advertising, and broadcasting of games, as well as support services such as arenas. There are also large ancillary activities, such as gambling, insignia clothing and other loyalty items that are sold to fans, and the whole sports-reporting culture bred by newspapers, sports magazines, and broadcasters.

This section follows the literature in focusing on the big four professional sports: baseball, football, basketball, and hockey.[19] Though they are the backbone of commercial sports, these four sports' total yearly ticket sales (over $100 million in recent years) are actually *lower* than those for horse racing and dog racing. A hidden economic role of the four sports is gambling; total annual betting on these four league sports was estimated at over $50 billion in the 1980s.

The four sports are all formed into **leagues,** which are run as private cartels. They organize their sports under common rules, which are elaborately designed to make competition balanced and exciting rather than one-sided blowouts.[20] Each cartel also takes complex actions to exclude new competition (that is, rival leagues).

The leagues have high degrees of market power. Do they abuse it? The main issues are player drafts, rights, and salaries; the large flows of television funds; and the controls over moves of teams from one city to another. The team owners have a stranglehold on the nation's principal sports. Are these monopolies benevolently and efficiently managed, giving excitement to the populace at minimal cost? Or are they classical monopolies: narrow, restrictive, inefficient, exploitative, and slow to innovate?

1. THE MARKETS

The basic product is the **game.** It has three elements: a display of talent, an entertainment, and a drama whose outcome is in doubt. The game is part of an ongoing yearly season, which climaxes in a championship playoff.

The basic producer is the **team,** although the **league** is ultimately the true decision group. Teams are partly independent firms making their own decisions and partly mere units (like plants) of the league enterprise. In any event, the league can be considered a natural monopoly within its sport's market.

Defining the markets for these sports is a complex task. Each professional sport can be considered a distinct market, because each is separately organized, involves contrasting types of games, operates in its (partly) separate season, and is generally regarded as distinct. Moreover, the leagues carefully minimize their overlaps with college and other sports.[21]

Their seasons do overlap during parts of the year, however, so that interested TV viewers can substitute among them if they wish. Moreover, as advertisers (e.g., beer and car companies) deploy their advertising among them, sports may compete for broadcasting revenues. Indeed, as visual entertainment, sports may be just part of the whole amusement market.

At the narrowest extreme, each city with a team can be considered a market, because that is the zone of the local team's loyal customers for tickets; yet that definition is probably too narrow. At the other extreme, "all professional sports" is generally agreed to be too broad a market definition. All in all, "each professional sport" is the most meaningful market definition, generally agreed in the literature.

2.   STRUCTURE

Each league holds a monopoly of its sport, operating as a tight cartel. There is potential competition from lower leagues in the sport (e.g., minor leagues in baseball and hockey), but these are kept subordinate and minor. Indeed, major-league baseball teams usually own the minor-league teams, averting potential competition.

The leagues have high barriers against entry by any new teams or leagues.[22] The sports arenas in major cities are owned or exclusively contracted for by the teams. If new teams did emerge outside the established leagues, the latter would exclude or boycott them and probably threaten to leave any city that permitted such a new team to start.

Some of the league monopolies face some countervailing power. Players are organized in unions, and stars are able to bargain for maximum pay for themselves. The resulting battles (with holdouts, disputes, and even player strikes as in baseball during 1994–1995) often create more drama than some of the games on the field. The leagues also face strong broadcasting groups (networks and cable sports systems) in hard bargaining over TV payments and exclusive rights.

In addition, the owners deal with their host cities over stadium provisions and costs and other forms of support. The teams usually whipsaw the cities with threats to move away. Because so many cities are kept starved for teams, the threat to leave can be extremely effective. Generally speaking, the vertical pressures are only modest.

3.   DETERMINANTS

The market structure is partly shaped by inherent forces, especially the owners' high incentives to monopolize each sport. They control the players' entry to the sport as well as their moves among teams. Such control helps the leagues to keep players' salaries down, which they did quite successfully before the 1970s. When there are two leagues, the players' bargaining position is far stronger, as during the two-league NFL-AFL situation in 1960–1967 and the NFL–USFL episode in the early and mid-1980s. Those are now neatly locked up, however.

Thus the monopoly structure is largely an artifact. There could well be two or more leagues in each sport, as indeed there are in Europe, where soccer and basketball players move freely among soccer and basketball teams in Britain, France, Italy, Germany, Spain, and so on.

There could also be several tiers of leagues, from the top leagues on down to minor ones, so that teams could rise to higher leagues as their quality improves. That is the case in British soccer's relegation system (more about it later). A mix of private and city-owned teams is also possible, as in Europe. In sum, the current patterns do *not* reflect true economic determinants or efficient requirements.

These self-imposed rules are claimed to be necessary in order to maintain competitive parity among the teams. The top draft choices of players go to the previous season's lowest-ranking teams. Some leagues set limits on the teams' salary budgets. Television revenues and home-game ticket revenues are (usually) divided in ways that tend to equalize team quality. By renewing parity, the leagues attempt to ensure that games are suspenseful.

Major league baseball added a set of leveling devices in 2002 as part of a compromise to avoid a players' strike. The New York Yankees, in particular, are taxed to reduce their large payroll and to spread resources among poorer teams in smaller cities.

Yet altogether, the various leagues' rules suppress competition more than parity requires. Professional sports' structures are motivated by profit-maximizing under monopoly rather than by underlying economic conditions, which would permit far more competition and increased efficiency.

4. Behavior

Behavior mainly concerns the endless efforts to create parity and competitive balance among teams. The main controls are on **players' choices in joining and changing teams** and on **the division of revenues between the host team and the visitors.**[23] There is great variety among the leagues, with changes over time as well. The main trend has tended toward greater freedom to choose for players, but within controls that are still quite tight.

The teams' owners obtain new players by a yearly **draft,** in which the choices are in reverse order of the teams' success the previous season.[24] This gives a tendency toward competitive balance within the league. It also clashes with each owner's urge to amass the most talent and with players' freedom of choice in selecting employers, a fundamental right in a nonslave society. This conscription reduces the players' ability to obtain a salary and signing bonus in line with true economic value, and so this unified management behavior strongly affects the pay levels of new players.

Players are further required to stay for a period with the teams that conscripted them, again abridging freedom of choice. Under pressure, the various leagues have reluctantly adopted various schemes for players to seek free-agent status. This permits the better players to seek salaries up to their true commercial value.

Owners can gain by conspiring to avoid a full bidding process for free agents, as they did in baseball during the 1985–1986 and 1986–1987 seasons. Mutual restraint is still in the owners' collective interest, and some degree of it may be endemic.

Generally, basketball has had the least degree of market control by the owners, whereas football and baseball (which has had an explicit exemption from most antitrust enforcement since 1922) have had the most. Each situation is subject to change, under almost daily changing pressures and new legal challenges.[25]

As for the actual parity within leagues, there is usually much imbalance. In baseball, for example, the Yankees' 2003 payroll was $150 million, with the others ranging down to the Devil Rays at $20 million.

5. Performance

Teams' financial success is influenced by several standard factors, especially their win-loss record, their signing of stars, and the population and income level of the cities they play in. Star athletes often raise team revenues (attendance times ticket price) by $5 million or more per year. Therefore stars seek to capture their commercial value when they bargain for high salaries. Presumably, the owners do not pay them more than that value.

Winning records also can be crucial. Teams that had been playing to near-empty stadiums suddenly find the seats crowded when they become playoff contenders. Levels of population and income have the expected effects. Teams in New York and Los Angeles are often the most profitable, simply because their pools of potential customers are so large. Television revenue reflects the winning and star effects, because national viewers want to watch winning teams and the most famous players, and advertisers respond to these mass viewership patterns.

Are teams highly profitable? Team accounts are mostly kept secret and, in any event, usually reflect arcane accounting manipulations to minimize profits and taxes. Teams in such large cities as New York and Los Angeles are usually highly profitable, and most other teams probably do turn solid profits. The multiplication of franchise values in all leagues is perhaps the clearest evidence of monopoly pricing and profits. Vertical power has also been exerted, as teams brazenly manipulate cities into bearing large costs of new stadiums.

Pricing behavior in sports fits many monopoly predictions. Many football stadiums are small with relatively few games (16 regular-season football games compared to 82 basketball and 162 baseball games). The football team owners use this advantage to set high prices and tight conditions for season tickets.

The pricing of players also fits monopoly predictions. In sports with looser controls on players (especially basketball), salaries have risen much faster than in the more tightly controlled sports (especially football). Bilateral monopoly therefore has differing effects, depending on the owners' relative power.

Of course, the competitive equilibrium salaries of each sport may differ according to skills, talent pools, length of career, injury risks, and other nonmonopoly factors.[26] The sharp relative rise in basketball salaries when controls eased in the 1970s shows how important vertical power is. Indeed, the salary rise in all four sports reflects the rise in players' bargaining power compared to the owners'.

It is impossible to judge X-inefficiency scientifically, but most experts regard the quality of team and league management as low. As for innovation, the leagues have made continuing adjustments in rules and format to sustain spectator interest. They are helped by the extensive sector of sports journalism, whose thousands of writers, filling thousands of daily sports pages, stimulate and sustain the fans' interest even in the minutiae of each sport.

The one major failure of supply and innovation is seen in the relative fewness of teams. Over thirty-five cities with populations above 500,000 lack any significant team in baseball, football, *and* basketball. Only fifteen cities have teams in all three of those sports. The lack of a baseball team in Washington, DC, and a football team in Los Angeles are striking examples, among many, of restricted supply.

The leagues restrict supply not only by limiting the numbers of their own teams and controlling their locations, but also by blocking the creation of other leagues and teams. The reservoir of sports demand in nearly all cities below 1.5 million in population is probably very large, and it will continue to be unmet as long as the current leagues maintain their exclusive control.

A Superior Alternative System. An effective solution is readily available, but it would loosen the entrenched monopoly controls. Its model is the British soccer relegation system based on four league levels, arranged in tiers. Any town or group can form a team in the low-level county leagues, build it up gradually, and seek to boost it to the higher leagues. Each year the two top teams in each league rise to the next league up, while the two lowest teams are relegated to the next league below.

Small-town teams can and do rise to the very top league by skill and resources. Many of these top-quality teams are from towns much smaller than American cities that have no team whatsoever in the four top professional sports. The biggest city teams sink down to lower leagues when they perform poorly; incompetently run U.S. teams are instead guaranteed perpetual big-league status. Moreover, suspense is intense throughout the season in all levels of the British system, as losing teams fight desperately to avoid relegation. By contrast, losing teams in U.S. leagues play out the end—or even the majority—of their seasons in dull, meaningless games.

The relegation system generates a maximum of spectator interest, because even losing teams involve drama all season long. If the system were adopted in the United States, sports would be open, fluid, and far more responsive to both demand and supply than the current tight, limited monopolies. The approach would provide hundreds of cities with a chance to form strong teams that aspire to the top leagues. Seasons could be exciting throughout for nearly all teams.

Instead, the major-league teams have subordinated the lower leagues, especially by limiting their access to television coverage as well as to larger cities.[27] Cities' and fans' freedom of choice is limited to a relatively few teams playing— once one team pulls far ahead—in partly meaningless seasons.

6. IN SUMMARY

These markets are controlled by tight, profit-maximizing cartels that have many features of monopoly firms. The results appear to fit predictions from the theories of collusion, exclusion, and unequal bilateral monopoly. Though each league maintains its balance and continuity fairly well, a larger perspective suggests that performance falls far short of the results that an open, flexible, genuinely competitive structure would give.

IV. BREAKFAST CEREALS[28]

Behind the crowded cereals shelves, crammed with their 50-plus brands of cereals, stand just three main companies. They form one of the longest-established and most lucrative tight oligopolies.

It started a century ago with Shredded Wheat and Grape-Nuts, which are still staple cereals. In the 1890s, led by the health eccentric George Kellogg, crisp cereals first challenged the old tradition of hot porridge. By 1905 corn flakes, puffed wheat, and puffed rice had also been brought to market, and the industry has grown steadily ever since. Basic change comes slowly; four of the five main production methods (extrusion was introduced in 1941, with Cheerios) have existed for at least eighty-five years.

In the 1950s, sugared cereals were marketed in a variety of forms, reinforced by increasingly intensive advertising to children. The addition of small candy bits and fruits, plus further advertising intensity, followed in the 1960s. The rise of "natural" cereals in the mid-1970s was succeeded in the 1980s by a variety of brands claiming to be more healthful (with bran, for example).

Altogether, the industry's basic products and technology have been stable since 1910. The ranks of competitors changed during the early days, but they, too, have changed little since the 1930s. Kellogg took the lead in the 1930s and has kept it. Its two main rivals, General Mills and General Foods, have joined Kellogg in forming a tight, stable, and highly profitable oligopoly.

This industry's special features are intensive advertising (mainly directed at children), brand proliferation, small-scale economies, and sustained high profit rates. In an experimental antitrust case that ran a rocky course from 1972 to 1981, the Federal Trade Commission sought to test whether the oligopoly was really a shared monopoly whose tacit collusion approximated the essential outcomes of monopoly. The case was eventually dropped under political pressure, and cereal prices have risen strongly since then.

1. THE MARKET

There is wide agreement that dry ready-to-eat breakfast cereals sold in the United States is the correct market definition. Hot cooked cereals are quite distinct, and so are Pop-Tarts, diet bars (with or without chocolate coverings), and, of course, toast, ham and eggs, and pancakes. Though there is much product variety, the best-selling products have changed little since 1950, or even since 1910.

2. STRUCTURE

The early firms in the market included Quaker Oats, Post (later part of General Foods), and Kellogg; they were later joined by General Mills (which bought the maker of Wheaties in 1928). Each specialized in its original product and then added other forms of cereals. During the 1950s to 1980s, Kellogg maintained about a 45-percent share, with General Mills at approximately 20 percent and General Foods at about 15 percent. But after about 1990 Kellogg slipped steadily, sinking to a market share of about 30 percent, while General Mills moved up toward 30 percent.[29] Ralston Purina (Chex) and Quaker Oats are significant but small factors.

Three-firm concentration is in the 80- to 90-percent range, where it has remained for many decades. Entry barriers are generally regarded as high, thanks mainly to brand names and intensive advertising. Any significant entrant (or attempt by smaller sellers to increase market share) faces sharp retaliation in the forms of advertising and selective price cuts. Moreover, the incumbents have filled virtually all of the product space (discussed in the following sections).

3. DETERMINANTS

Economies of scale in production are known to be limited, with MES reached at about a mere 5-percent market share.[30] That scale provides for several production and packaging lines for sufficient flexibility. Because MES is small, Kellogg and the other leading producers have extensive excess market share.

Advertising also affects the existing tight-oligopoly structure. It is intensive, often over 15 percent of total revenues. It has probably hardened the tight-oligopoly structure since 1950 by favoring existing firms with large market shares (recall the logic given in chapter 12).

Structure also has been shaped by distribution, interacting with scarce grocery shelf space. The major sellers maintain extensive delivery systems, which give them direct influence over the use of shelf space in grocery stores. Shelf space acts as a bottleneck in reaching final customers, because new access to it is effectively restricted by the leading cereals firms. Many supermarkets now charge "slotting fees" for shelf space, with the most desirable shelf space costing the most. The major cereals sellers, with their large quantities of available cash, are able to outbid small sellers for the most desirable space. The only way that a small or new producer can gain access to the desirable shelf space is to outbid the major sellers or buy the property rights from a major seller that already owns the slot.

The difficulty of small cereals sellers in getting into supermarket shelf space can be contrasted sharply with the snacks industry (potato chips, etc.). Convenience stores carry a much wider selection of snacks made by small, unknown producers, because they do not charge the slotting fees of supermarkets. Thus, small and new snacks sellers are much more easily able to reach the customers of convenience stores.

4. Behavior

The main behavior has been a packing of the product space with proliferating brands; it appears to have been implicitly collusive. The extent of brand proliferation has indeed been great; in 1973, the six leading producers had a total of eighty brands, and many brands have been added since then.

They fill the product space, leaving only tiny niches to new entrants. Because newcomers and small rivals are forced to incur extra advertising costs in order to enter with new brands or raise market share, it follows that competition from either can be averted by packing the product space in advance.

The existing firms portray their actions as being innovative and responsive to consumer demand. To an extent, that is true. Nonetheless, the effect of brand proliferation in excluding competition is powerful, and it is fully known among the main cereals companies.

5. Performance

The three firms' profitability has been high and sustained, with rates of return on investment averaging about 20 percent since the 1940s.[31] When the FTC's shared-monopoly case against the three oligopolists was ended in 1981, retail prices of cereals quickly rose by approximately 20 percent. They have continued rising faster than any index of costs or general prices.

There has been no general lapse of X-efficiency, although General Foods' "acknowledged inefficiencies" were large and sustained in the 1960s.[32] The advertising of cereals absorbs from 10 to 15 percent of sales and is almost exclusively of the persuasive type. If that spending is regarded as a welfare loss, then this oligopoly causes a waste of many hundreds of millions of dollars per year.

Innovation has consisted mainly of creating new combinations of grains and sugars in differing shapes, with brand names and images. This innovation is partly a response to changing consumer demand, as when bran and whole-grain cereals were added to take advantage of the health and fitness boom that began in the 1970s. Much demand is induced by advertising aimed at children, and much brand innovation has simply packed the product space.

The nutritional value of cereals came under attack in 1970.[33] Critics noted that the products had little food content, while the heavy use of sugar damaged children's teeth. Though nutritional brands were added in the 1980s, the companies still rely heavily on sugared cereals eaten by children.

6. IN SUMMARY

Although the shared-monopoly antitrust action was withdrawn, the big three cereal makers continue to exemplify tight oligopoly, with strong differentiation and an ability to influence buyers by advertising. On balance, misallocation and waste of advertising resources have probably been substantial.

V. TRASH REMOVAL

Few industries are homelier than garbage disposal. In earlier times, most trash was simply thrown out onto the streets; now things are tidier. Modern packaging, rushed lifestyles, and current technology mean that homes and businesses now generate large volumes of solid wastes, which have to go somewhere. They are now picked up by trucks running regular routes, and then the trash is usually left at nearby dumps or, less frequently, incinerated.[34]

Haulage and dumps used to be a government activity in most towns and cities, as a local public monopoly, but since the 1960s there has been widespread privatizing. Seizing this opportunity after 1960, two private firms have moved aggressively, making hundreds of mergers (and creating some new capacity) in cities and towns nearly everywhere in the United States. They are **WMX**, formerly Waste Management Inc., and **BFI**, formerly Browning-Ferris Industries. They now dominate nearly every locale in the United States, turning the industry into a vast linked patchwork of duopolies.[35] Look for WMX's and BFI's trucks working the streets.

This downscale industry has seen much seamy activity and guerilla warfare. In some cities (including New York), there has been municipal corruption over awarding and defending garbage-hauling franchises.[36] Hundreds of small rivals are regularly negotiating to be bought out and/or suing the two leaders for alleged anticompetitive tactics.

Do these nationwide chains really provide effective competition in some, most, or all towns? Is duopoly natural and inevitable because of economies of scale and scope? Have WMX and BFI chronically taken unfair actions?

1. THE MARKETS

The markets' scope is usually reasonably clear. The product types include two distinct groups:

1. **Residential Haulage.**   Residences are dispersed, and few have large volumes. Serving them requires more driving and labor activity.

2. **Commercial and Industrial Haulage.**   Businesses differ by being fewer and typically having larger volumes of trash. Business service therefore focuses on large customers, uses different technology (larger dumpsters, etc.), and has less driving and labor effort.

The geographic markets are usually set by the driving distances for pickup and dumping. Trucks rarely travel more than fifteen miles from their town or city in order to reach a dump, so most markets are virtually congruent with city areas.

Very large cities may contain two or more geographic markets; middle-sized cities are usually clear markets; and some small towns are parts of larger, multi-town markets.

2. Structure

WMX and BFI emerged in the 1960s, and by the 1970s they dominated most cities. Usually there is also a fringe of several small rivals, often with only one or two trucks. Typically the two leaders each have about 40 percent. Their shares have generally continued to rise as they have continued to buy out small rivals. More such mergers are likely under current antitrust standards.

Entry barriers are hotly debated. The leaders assert that entry is easy—just rent a truck. Entry barriers may be high, however. To survive after entry, a newcomer must win enough customers away from the leaders to sustain regular truck routes in much or all of the citywide market. Also, the leaders have incentives to offer deep selective discounts in order to prevent losses of the best customers; the next subsection explains those incentives.

Therefore, newcomers often face severe problems in gaining enough customers to survive; the barriers caused by the leaders' pricing responses can be high. That is attested by the rarity with which any firms have substantially entered any significant markets since 1980.

3. Determinants

Pickup routes are the central technology of the industry. The ideal is to have short, dense routes including every house in every block. Then the drivers can pick up large volumes quickly, minimizing their time and effort. At the extreme, there may be natural monopoly, but the economies may be only moderate (with a mild cost gradient), so that competition may be viable.

The situation does offer economies of scope, because these are networks in which one more customer can be handled very cheaply. Accordingly, the marginal cost for each customer is low; the passing truck merely takes a minute or less to serve each customer. This gives each rival a powerful incentive to offer deep discounts, if necessary, to get or hold a customer. The best customers are, of course, the largest-volume customers.

A second determinant is the dump. The trash must go somewhere, typically a landfill where trucks simply leave the waste. Some cities have their own public dumps that are priced fairly to all users (that is, the competing haulers). In many cities, WMX and/or BFI own their own dumps, and that can provide a distinct competitive advantage. The dump may reduce the owner's total cost. It may also be priced so that little rivals have to pay more, thereby raising entry barriers and giving the duopolist higher profits to support more strategies.

A third determinant is the gains from operating nationwide, with units in many hundreds of cities. That gives added support and protection to each local unit. It also means that WMX and BFI face each other in stable, entrenched duopolies nearly everywhere in the United States.

4. BEHAVIOR

Behavior has been a mix of rough sharpshooting tactics and mutual forbearance between WMX and BFI. They have imposed restrictive contracts in most cities, which limit customers and raise entry barriers. The contracts last for three years with automatic renewal and penalties for dropping service. That has effectively "locked out smaller trash haulers."[37]

Pricing is the main strategic weapon, by means of selective price discounts. Although most companies have standard price lists for service, they usually depart freely from them by offering sharp discounts wherever they wish.

Each city is therefore the scene of deep dynamic price discrimination. Each firm tries to hold most customers to high prices but also cuts its prices sharply for specific customers where it seems necessary. For example, the discounts may dip to 50- or 60-percent below the standard price for the most attractive customers.

The resulting pricing warfare is often brutal, and it has forced many small haulers to sell out cheaply or quit. Discounts have probably frequently dropped below specific costs. To the duopolist, there may be a large net gain from cutting below cost if the impact helps eliminate the competitor entirely.

Some discounting is inevitable, caused by underlying economies of scope. That poses the question of whether the industry is often really a natural monopoly, where effective competition simply can't be sustained.

The question is reinforced by the tendency of the two leaders to avoid price warfare against each other. In each city, there are powerful incentives to stabilize market positions and engage in a joint maximizing of profits. That is accentuated by the nationwide situation, with the same duopolists facing each other in hundreds of cities. If WMX takes severe actions in one city, then BFI has many opportunities to fight back with severe actions in other cities. That provides strong added incentives for both firms to avoid mutual price cutting in every city.

Actual behavior has fitted these conditions. WMX and BFI have routinely adopted deep selective price discounting against their small rivals, and this added pressure has led hundreds of them to sell out at reduced asset values. WMX and BFI have generally avoided sharp price discounting against each other.

5. PERFORMANCE

Price and cost levels are difficult to evaluate with common standards of efficiency, because most cities have only the WMX and BFI duopoly. There are strong indications from scattered evidence that small rivals have often had significantly lower costs and prices. It is doubtful that WMX and BFI derive significant true economies either from their ownership of dumps or from their nationwide chain basis.

Innovation has not been clearly aided or retarded by the multiple-city duopoly conditions. Fairness has been reduced, by reducing or eliminating the asset values of many smaller rivals. Higher haulage prices have also probably occurred, with transfer effects away from customers to the duopoly. Competition and freedom of choice also have probably been reduced.

6. IN SUMMARY

This industry is controversial, and effective competition in it may simply not be viable. Tighter limits on mergers and on selective price discounting might strongly increase the degree of competition by letting small and new haulers compete more effectively. Currently, the two leaders appear to be deeply entrenched, perhaps so much so that effective competition will not recover. Here as elsewhere, the emergence of market power may be irreversible.

QUESTIONS FOR REVIEW

1. Why has Airbus been able to approach equality with Boeing in recent years?

2. Explain the definition of air-travel markets. Is there one national oligopoly, a series of large-city dominant firms, or some mix? If a mix, what is it, mostly?

3. Explain how scarce gates and slots affect the degree of contestability of many airline markets. Explain how airline mergers and the channeling of fare discounting into standard patterns have reduced competition.

4. Define the markets inhabited by the four main professional sports. Do they overlap with each other? With collegiate and high-school sports? Or divided among local monopolies, by teams?

5. Evaluate how strong the countervailing forces are for (a) players, (b) cities, and (c) television networks. Do they differ markedly among the sports?

6. Are these sports really natural monopolies, which must have league monopolies? Discuss the effects of organizing new leagues to vie with existing ones.

7. Discuss one of the main professional sports. Has it been X-efficient and innovative, in your judgment?

8. Explain how economies of scope (or of density) occur in trash-removal markets.

9. If you held dominance in a city trash-removal market, wouldn't you use special discounts to prevent a new competitor from growing?

ENDNOTES

[1] Many foreign airlines are owned by their governments, in contrast to the United States where all airlines serving civilians are privately owned. Even private foreign airlines often are closely affected by their governments when working out deals to purchase aircraft.

[2] For example, see Alex Taylor, "Boeing: Sleepy in Seattle," *Fortune* (August 7, 1995): pp. 92–8; and Jerry Useem, "Boeing vs. Boeing," *Fortune* (October 2, 2000): pp. 148–60. Both stories detail Boeing's inefficiencies and blames them on the complacency that came with dominance of the market.

[3] From 1993 to 1995, for example, Boeing cut nearly 15 percent of its employees.

[4] A thorough review is in Steven A. Morrison and Clifford Winston, *The Evolution of the Airline Industry* (Washington, DC: Brookings institution, 1993). See also James W. Brock and William

G. Shepherd, "The Airline Industry," a chapter in Walter Adams, ed., *The Structure of American Industry*, 9th ed. (New York: Macmillan, 1995); and Richard H. K. Vietor, "Contrived Competition, Airline Regulation and Deregulation, 1925–1988," *Business History Review* (Spring 1990): pp. 61–108.

[5] Among the optimists, see especially Alfred E. Kahn, "Surprises of Airline Deregulation," *American Economic Review* 78 (May 1988): pp. 316–22; and Elizabeth E. Bailey, David R. Graham, and Daniel P. Kaplan, *Deregulating the Airlines* (Cambridge: MIT Press, 1985); also Steven A. Morrison, "Airline Services: The Evolution of Competition Since Deregulation," a chapter in Larry L. Deutsch, *Industry Studies*.

[6] On hub-and-spoke patterns, see Lisa Saunders and William G. Shepherd, "Airlines: Setting Constraints on Hub Dominance," *Logistics and Transportation Review* 29 (September 1993): pp. 201–20.

[7] See Alfred E. Kahn, "The Competitive Consequences of Hub Dominance: A Case Study," *Review of Industrial Organization* 8 (August 1993): pp. 381–406; William N. Evans and Ioannis Kessides, "Localized Market Power in the U.S. Airline Industry," *Economic Statistics* 75 (February 1993): pp. 66–75; and Saunders and Shepherd, "Hub Dominance."

[8] Morrison and Winston, *The Evolution of the Airline Industry*; and A. S. Leahy, "Concentration in the U.S. Airline Industry," *International Journal of Transportation Economics* 21 (June 1994): pp. 209–15.

[9] Edwin McDowell, "Shuttles in Northeast Thrive and Keep Fares Up," *New York Times* (May 8, 1995): p. D3.

[10] Bridget O'Brian and Rick Brooks, "No-Frills Approach Propels ValuJet to Quick Success," *Wall Street Journal* (May 4, 1995): p. B4; and Bryan Gruley and Scott McCartney, "Flock of New Low-Fare Carriers Means Savings for Consumers, U.S. Study Says," *Wall Street Journal* (November 2, 1995): p. A4.

[11] See A. S. Joskow, Gregory J. Werden, and R. L. Johnson, "Entry, Exit, and Performance in Airline Markets," *International Journal of Industrial Organization* 12 (December 1994): pp. 457–71; also J. M. Joesch and C. D. Zick, "Evidence of Changing Contestability in Commercial Airline Markets During the 1980s," *Journal of Consumer Affairs* 28 (Summer 1994): pp. 1–24.

[12] The computer listings can easily be set to favor one airline over another; see Morrison and Winston, *Evolution of the Airline Industry*, and sources noted there. The bias is powerful; because marginal costs per passenger are low, the shifted revenues are virtually all net profit.

[13] For example, American's yield managers "monitor and adjust the fare mixes on 1,600 daily flights as well as 538,000 future flights involving nearly 50 million passengers," in "The Art of Devising Air Fares," *New York Times* (March 4, 1987): p. DI.

[14] In one part, the northeast shuttles, duopoly pricing by Delta and USAir fits classic lines, with high prices (far above corresponding west-coast shuttle fares) that yield sustained high profits.

[15] For example, in June 1984 People Express entered the Newark-Minneapolis route at fares of $99 on weekdays and $79 on evenings and weekends. Previously, the lowest fare had been $149, and the standard coach fare was $263. Northwest, the dominant firm, promptly cut its fares to $95 and $75, for service that was much better (in seating, meals, baggage handling, etc.). Therefore Northwest undercut People's fare. Desperately, People cut its fares further, to $79 and $59; Northwest also matched those cuts. Unable to survive such deep cuts, People Express eventually was bought by Texas Air. After merging with Republic, Northwest had over 80 percent of the traffic into Minneapolis. It then increased its fares sharply.

[16] See generally Morrison and Winston, *The Evolution of the Airline Industry*; and Evans and Kessides, "Structure, Conduct, and Performance." The impact of hub dominance, for example, is now well known; see also M. Dresner and R. Windle, "Airport Dominance and Yields in the U.S. Airline Industry," *Logistics and Transportation Review* 28 (December 1992): pp. 319–39; and Margaret A. Peteraf and R. Reed, "Pricing and Performance in Monopoly Airline Markets," *Journal of Law and Economics* 37 (April 1994): pp. 193–213.

[17] The figure is controversial because it compares actual prices with those that might have occurred under certain assumed conditions. See Morrison and Winston, *The Evolution of the Airline Industry*.

[18] Good sources include William S. Kern, ed., *The Economics of Sports* (Kalamazoo, MI: W. E. Upjohn Institute for Employment Research, 2000); James Quirk and Rodney Fort, *Hard Ball: The Abuse of Power in Pro Team Sports* (Princeton: Princeton University Press, 1999); Stefan Kesenne and Claude Jeanrenaud, eds., *Competition Policy in Professional Sports: Europe After the Bosman Case* (Antwerp: Standard, 1999); and Roger C. Noll and Andrew Zimbalist, *Sports, Jobs and Taxes: The Economic Impact of Sports Teams and Stadiums* (Washington, DC: Brookings Institution Press, 1997). Also Gerald W. Scully, *The Market Structure of Sports* (Chicago: University of Chicago Press, 1995); Scully, *The Business of Major League Baseball* (Chicago: University of Chicago Press, 1989); Scully, *Advances in the Economics of Sports* (Greenwich, CT: JAI Press, 1992); James Quirk and Rodney D. Fort, *Pay Dirt: The Business of Professional Sports Teams* (Princeton, NJ: Princeton University Press, 1992); and Andrew Zimbalist, *Baseball and Billions* (New York: Basic Books, 1992).

[19] Of course, these pro sports are paralleled by the major intercollegiate sports, which pose most of the same issues, in lesser forms. Collegiate sports are analyzed thoroughly in Francis X. Dealy, *Win at Any Cost* (New York: Carol Publishing Group, 1990). The NCAA's rules enable universities to exploit the better college athletes for high money yields, while paying the players much less than their economic value. The amateur rules therefore involve hypocrisy and are of course difficult to enforce. The NCAA's role as a cartel is shown in Arthur A. Fleischer, Brian L. Goff, and Robert D. Tollison, *The National Collegiate Athletic Association: A Study in Cartel Behavior* (Chicago: University of Chicago Press, 1992); see also John J. Siegfried, "The National Collegiate Athletic Association: A Study in Cartel Behavior; Review Article," *Antitrust Bulletin* 39 (Summer 1994): pp. 599–609.

[20] The critical condition of competitive balance is analyzed thoroughly in Rodney Fort and James Quirk, "Cross-Subsidization, Incentives, and Outcomes in Professional Team Sports Leagues," *Journal of Economic Literature* 33 (September 1995): pp. 1265–99.

[21] Thus football game times are neatly segregated: high school on Friday nights, college on Saturdays and Thursday evenings, and professional mainly on Sundays and Monday evenings.

[22] That is illustrated by the sad fate of the would-be-entrant World Football League in the early 1970s and the United States Football League during 1983–1986. The established leagues have also been helped by their ability to sign exclusive contracts with the major television networks.

[23] Good sources include Ira Horowitz, "The Reasonableness of Horizontal Restraints: (NCAA) (1984)," a chapter in Kwoka and White, eds., *The Antitrust Revolution* (New York: HarperCollins, 1994); and, for a wide coverage of legal issues and cases related to sports, Paul C. Weiler and Gary R. Roberts, *Sports and the Law: Cases, Materials and Problems* (St. Paul: West Publishing, 1993).

[24] K. B. Grier and R. D. Tollison, "The Rookie Draft and Competitive Balance: The Case of Professional Football," *Journal of Economic Behavior and Organization* 25 (October 1994): pp. 293–98.

[25] For example, in 1995–1996 the owner of the Dallas Cowboys (Jerry Jones) took disruptive actions to end the system of revenue sharing among teams: "Dollars and Dallas: For Cowboys, a League of Their Own?" *New York Times* (September 24, 1994): pp. 1, 13, sports section.

[26] Thus players' high salaries are usually earned only for a few years and are highly taxed. The players constantly risk injuries that can terminate their careers. After retirement, their remaining years are usually spent at relatively modest-paying activities. In addition, multiyear contracts usually have present discounted values well below their nominal dollar values. Thus a star may have a $40 million ten-year contract at $4 million per year. Discounted at 10 percent and taxed at 33 percent, that stream of earnings has a much smaller present capitalized value after taxes, even ignoring the added dilution caused by future price inflation.

[27] For example, see Stefan Fatsis, "Major Leagues Keep Minors at a Distance," *Wall Street Journal* (November 8, 1995): pp. B1, B9.

[28] Leading analyses of this industry are F. M. Scherer, "The Breakfast Cereal Industry," a chapter in Walter Adams, ed., *The Structure of American Industry,* 6th ed. (New York: Macmillan, 1982), pp. 191–217; and Richard Schmalensee, "Entry Deterrence in the Ready-to-Eat Cereal Industry," *Bell Journal of Economics* 9 (Autumn 1978): pp. 305–27. They grew out of a complex Federal Trade Commission case involving the leading cereal makers from 1972 to 1981; *FTC: In re Kellogg Company et al.,* Docket No. 8883, filed 1972, decision January 1982. John Sutton also

covers cereals thoroughly in his *Sunk Costs and Market Structure* (Cambridge: MIT Press, 1991), especially at pp. 229–47 and 455–60.

[29] Greg Burns, "Has General Mills Had Its Wheaties?" *BusinessWeek* (May 8, 1995): pp. 68–69.

[30] See Scherer, "The Breakfast Cereal Industry"; Louis W. Stern, Technical Study Number 6, *Studies of Organization and Competition in Grocery Manufacturing* (Washington, DC: National Commission on Food Marketing, 1966); also the testimony of Michael Glassman in the FTC cereals case: transcript at pp. 26319–72.

[31] From 1958 to 1970, the average returns on cereal division assets were as follows: Kellogg, 18.9 percent; General Mills, 29.5 percent; and General Foods (Post), 15.1 percent, for a combined weighted average of 19.8 percent. See *In re Kellogg et al.*, CX-701A.

[32] The quote is from Scherer, "The Breakfast Cereal Industry," p. 211.

[33] A detailed analysis of sixty cereals' content was given in U.S. Senate, Committee on Commerce, Subcommittee for Consumers, Hearings, *Dry Cereals* (Washington, DC: U.S. Government Printing Office, 1970), pp. 2–43.

[34] A good basic source on this industry is Edward J. Savas, *The Solid Waste Removal Industry* (New York: Columbia University Press, 1972).

[35] Christopher Williams, "Solid-Waste Concerns Are Expected to Post Strong Earnings for 3rd Period," *Wall Street Journal* (October 9, 1995): p. B3B, provides a broad survey of economic results.

[36] For the unattractive realities, see Richard Behar, "Talk About Tough Competition," *Fortune* (January 15, 1995): pp. 90–100; Selwyn Raab, "Texas Company Seeks to Acquire Garbage Business Linked to Mafia," *New York Times* (January 23, 1996): pp. BI, B3.

[37] See James P. Miller, "WMX Unit, Browning-Ferris Settle U.S. Charges of Unfair Competition," *Wall Street Journal* (February 16, 1996): p. B2. In addition, there was a "... 'right to compete' clause in contracts, which required customers to tell Waste Management of a competing offer for dumpster service, and to let the company make a counter-offer."

Part

7

Public Policies toward Monopoly

Chapter

15

ANTITRUST POLICIES:
STANDARDS AND METHODS

A **policy** seeks to change business structure or behavior. Ideally, it applies consistent criteria, rules, and enforcement to the wide variety of market situations. A policy may correct deep problems, giving high **benefits.** Every policy also involves **costs,** which offset some or even all of the benefits. Any significant policy usually stirs active debates. Some (its beneficiaries) often say the policy is too timid, whereas others (its targets) may denounce it as harsh and destructive.

From the 1890s to the 1980s, the United States used two distinct policies to deal with the problem of monopoly: **antitrust** for ordinary markets, and **regulation** for natural-monopoly utility markets (recall figure 1.3). They have been unique American experiments with important effects.

Policies have also been hotly debated, topic by topic and case by case, often leading to sharp changes as the decades pass. Frequently they are banner headlines in the daily news (e.g., the Microsoft case and electricity deregulation in California during 2000–2001). Often policy decisions have been manipulated by the target companies themselves.

After 1970 both antitrust and regulation were cut back, first moderately and then severely after 1980, when free-market ideologues captured Washington. The 1990s brought a slight revival in antitrust but further cutting of regulation. By 2002, both policies were in unusual turmoil.

Nonetheless, **antitrust—weak or strong—remains the basic industrial policy of the United States**, driven deep into the bedrock of the American economy.[1]

It reaches into most sectors, seeking to make competition so effective that other more intrusive types of controls on monopoly will not be needed. It is antitrust's task to stop price fixing, reduce dominance, and prevent competition-reducing mergers. Regulation's task is to set limits on utility firms' prices in order to obtain the natural-monopoly efficiencies while preventing monopoly impacts. Deregulation has tried to shift regulated industries back under antitrust supervision.

These policies attract intense debate because the issues are complex, the facts are unsure, and hundreds of billions of dollars are at stake. For example, the Reagan administration's dropping of merger restraints in the 1980s—and equally permissive Clinton policies in the 1990s—unleashed massive merger booms, with major effects (recall chapter 6). Antitrust and regulatory decisions can cause billions in capital gains or losses to the shareholders of the firms.

Free-market advocates and big-business groups claim that most markets are already fully competitive, and so most antitrust policies are unnecessary and harmful.[2] In contrast, mainstream economists often urge stronger antitrust actions, partly to deal with deregulated industries that are not yet fully competitive (recall telecommunications and electricity from chapter 13).

We first present the mainstream antitrust policies that have evolved since the Sherman Act became law in 1890, and then note the severe 1980s cutbacks and timid revival after 1988. Section 1 summarizes how antitrust and regulation have evolved since the 1890s. It also explains the economic guidelines for efficient policy choices. Section 2 presents the settled main lines of actual pre-1980 antitrust policies, and it notes the extent of the Reagan-era reductions.

Section 3 briefly describes antitrust policies in other countries. After these general features, chapter 16 will present details of the three specific parts of antitrust: toward dominant firms, toward mergers, and toward conduct.

I.   ORIGINS AND STANDARDS OF U.S. ANTITRUST AND REGULATION POLICIES

Since 1890, U.S. antitrust and regulatory policies have been hammered out amid turbulent political action, and so the policies are naturally imperfect rather than ideal. The task is to discover the economic content of these policies, what they are really doing to the economy, and which parts may need changing.[3]

1.   THREE WAVES

There have been three major waves of antitrust policies.[4] Recall table 1.3, which shows some of the main antitrust and regulatory events. Figure 15.1 suggests the spectacular waves of mergers and of antitrust actions. Action causes responses; each new wave of mergers stirred anxiety in the populace that corporate power was being enlarged and abused. Politicians responded by enlarging antitrust resources, and antitrust officials then renewed and increased their efforts.

The first wave came in 1885–1920, when antitrust policies and regulatory agencies began. Then from 1933 to 1950 a second wave occurred; antitrust cases attacked several dominant firms, and airlines, telephones, and electricity came under regulation. Finally, between 1965 and 1975 a modest set of antitrust cases were tried, and Congress created a variety of social regulations. Doubts grew, however, and the 1980s brought a political reaction, with deep cutbacks in both antitrust and regulation.

Each wave reflected the public's discontent with recent business events and its belief that government action was needed. Many of the actions were inadequate, went too far, or applied incorrect incentives.

Early Conditions and Policies.   The crucial formative period for policies was 1890 to 1910. Before 1890, there had been a scattering of common-law rules and customs dealing with early forms of business, mostly at the local and state level. In cities, gas and water utilities were controlled in various ways, often under city ownership. The charges for using turnpikes and canals presented problems of monopoly pricing, met in diverse ways by the various states.

The U.S. industrial revolution burst with great force upon this localized scene from 1865 to 1900. Railroads spread across the country, forming monopolies in some regions and charging discriminatory prices. Stirred by the Civil War and the railroad boom, heavy industries expanded rapidly. Gold rushes, land rushes, the invention of electric light systems and telephones, the dramatic growth of the oil industry from 1870 to 1890—these and other new developments transformed the economy toward large-scale manufacturing industries. Price rigging became common in many industries. Moreover, after 1890 the great financiers like J. P. Morgan were busy forming trusts in many industries by merging scores of little firms into big ones. Workers, farmers, consumers, and small businessmen were harmed in all regions of the country.

Regulation.   The 1880s saw rising public agitation against these changes. Farmers organized to fight price gouging by the railroad monopolies. They and other citizens increasingly denounced the new industrial trusts. Amid sharp

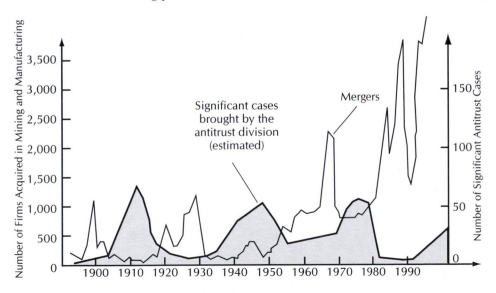

Figure 15.1   The pulses of merger and antitrust activity.

political debates, two kinds of policy action were initiated. First, regulation was established, starting with the Interstate Commerce Commission in 1888 to regulate railroads.

Then state regulatory commissions were created from 1907 on to regulate the new electricity and telephone systems, as well as railroad traffic within the states. These steps accepted **private ownership** of the basic utility operations, in contrast to **public ownership** of the railroads and utilities that was common in other countries.

These small state regulatory commissions were supposed to control private utilities strictly, permitting only fair rates of return and just and reasonable prices (without too much price discrimination). By the 1930s, most states had their own regulatory commissions, and new federal commissions had been created to cover interstate operations in the main utility sectors.

Antitrust.   Second, antitrust policy was created in 1890 to reduce and constrain monopoly in the rest of the economy. It was called *antitrust* because it was aimed against the creation of industrial trusts (which were combinations of independent firms). The Sherman Act of 1890 outlawed both monopolizing by one firm and collusion among competitors. After some delay, the law was applied firmly to price fixing in 1899 and to some dominant firms in 1911. As further enlarged in 1914 and 1950, the U.S. antitrust laws became a uniquely thorough method for curing industrial monopoly and price fixing.

Antitrust and regulation have had checkered careers since 1920, reflecting larger economic trends and political swings. Antitrust has veered between waves of action (1904–1920, 1938–1952, and 1968–1980) and relatively inactive periods (the 1920s, 1952–1968, and particularly during the Reagan-Bush years of 1981–1990). Since 1990, antitrust has been weak by historical standards, and European antitrust is recognized as stronger.

The regulation of natural-monopoly "utilities" began in 1888, but it took a long time to get established. Its full coverage and moderate powers were reached only in the 1950s. At most times, both antitrust and regulation have been sharply criticized, by business for being too harsh and "anti-business," and by others for being too permissive.

Selections of people to run the agencies are often political choices made under political pressure; that often results in mediocre appointments. The agencies' budgets also are limited by the political budgetary process. Frequently, the target companies engage deeply in lobbying and public advertising, swaying voters and public opinion against the policies. In these and other ways, the companies may control policies, rather than being controlled by them.

Public enterprise also continues as a strong policy element. It includes many hundreds of city and regional electricity systems (the Tennessee Valley Authority, the New York State Power Authority, the State of Nebraska, etc.), bus and subway systems in cities great and small, many city water-works systems, major ports, national parks, health-care and social-insurance systems (Medicare), and many other cases to be noted in chapter 17. It has scarcely been attempted in U.S. manufacturing and finance. This contrasts with many other countries. Since 1980, a privatization movement has shifted many enterprises to private hands, and free-market efforts continue to close government agencies and shift jobs to private firms.

2. STANDARDS OF EFFICIENT POLICIES: MARGINAL COSTS AND BENEFITS

Economists commonly judge policies by some version of cost-benefit analysis, using the familiar comparisons of costs and benefits at the margin.

The Efficient Cost-Benefit Margin.   When public-policy choices are efficient, each action is set at the level where its marginal benefits just equal its costs. The public **benefits** when monopoly's effects are reduced or prevented. The result: greater efficiency, lower prices, more rapid innovation, and other goals.

There are also policy **costs**, both direct and indirect. Ideally, the official weighs all the benefits and costs, at least approximately, in such marginal cases and decides to pursue those with the larger yield. Figure 15.2 illustrates the ideal choice. At point A, the marginal benefits of added degrees of competition will just equal their costs. Any level below A is too little; at A_1, for example, the marginal benefits of more policy action are well above the marginal cost. Therefore, doing more is just "worth it" at the margin. That holds for successive levels up to A. Beyond A, further action is not worth it. At A_2, for instance, the marginal cost of greater competition is well above the marginal benefits.

Design and Amount.   Policy choices have two main elements: design and amount. Each policy should be well designed, yielding the maximum benefits for a given amount of cost. It will apply the correct set of incentives to the firm to induce its behavior to fit optimal lines. For example, an antitrust treatment of a monopolist might deftly negotiate compliance at little cost, rather than launch a vast, costly court battle that may eventually achieve little.

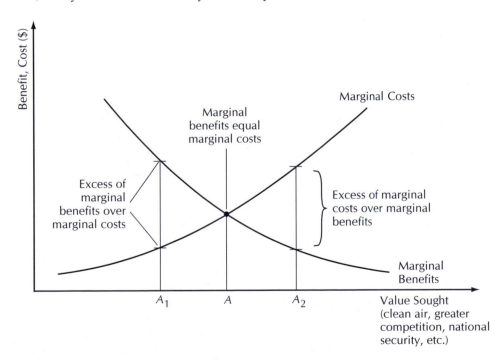

Figure 15.2   Simple cost-benefit analysis.

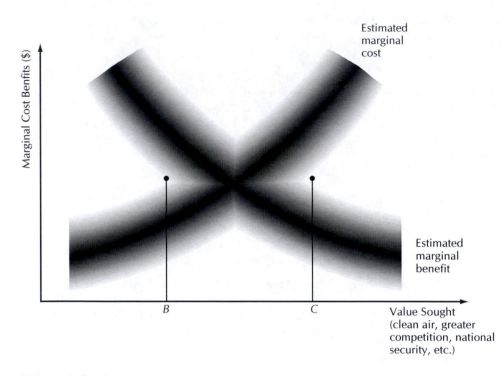

Figure 15.3 Cost-benefit choices can be uncertain when the amounts are uncertain.

The best-designed policy is then to be carried out to the efficient amount, just up to the efficient margin. Accordingly it will be just extensive or strict enough. These concepts are rarely applied precisely in practice, because there are several types of important problems:

1. The facts are often unsure, so that the benefits and costs can't be measured accurately.

2. Officials' judgments may be biased.

3. The groups who have to bear the costs are often not the same as those who reap the benefits. That may create major problems of unfairness.[5]

When the facts about costs and benefits are vague, the situation looks like figure 15.3; instead of bright-line curves for benefits and costs, there are fuzzy broad bands of estimated possible values. That leads to sharp contrasts in efficient choices, even by people using the same logic. Conservative, pro-big-business analysts usually estimate **benefits to be low and costs to be high.** That will lead them to choose point *B*, a minimal policy effort.

In contrast, a liberal, pro-small-business analyst will do the opposite, rating **benefits as high and costs as low.** That will lead to level *C*, which is far more strict. In general, new-Chicago analysts lean toward point *B* results, with minimum action, while most others would go higher. There may be intense debate between the two viewpoints, even though they both use the same logic. The conflict arises because they make contrasting judgments about the facts.

Costs of Policies. Now consider the costs of policies in more detail. Broadly speaking, there are two types: direct and indirect.

Direct costs are the dollar budgets spent for public agencies. These can be substantial, but some agencies have tiny budgets compared to the interests they supervise. For example, the two U.S. antitrust agencies spend only about $100 million yearly in dealing with markets totaling some $6 trillion of gross national product.

Indirect costs are of several kinds. One is conflict-resolution costs, such as for operating the courts where antitrust cases are tried. Another is **private-firm response costs.** These are spent by defendant firms in resisting and/or influencing the public actions. For example, a firm may spend $10 million defending against an antitrust case while the FTC only spends $1 million on it. Or a utility may spend $2 million on a rate hearing that costs the regulatory commission $300,000 to hold.

Another indirect cost is **public supervision**: the scarce ability of the political process to evaluate and exert control in the public interest. Information is costly, and the ability of citizens to acquire, weigh, and act upon it has high opportunity costs.

Costs of interference are the third type of indirect cost. Policies set limits, preventing some private firms from taking actions they would prefer. Firms may also lose efficiency when their profits are restrained. The result can be a loss of productivity. Of course, a well-designed policy can also increase the efficiency of firms.

These effects vary from case to case. Often, too, they are hard to measure and predict, which is why they are highly debatable.

Benefits of Policies. Policy benefits also require careful weighing. They include the full range of benefits that competition provides, from technical efficiency and innovation to broad values of fairness, freedom, and others noted throughout this book.

3. BIAS IN POLICIES

In the ideal public agency, officials would seek and apply optimal policies, but real agencies often depart from the ideal. Several theories have been offered to explain the defects of real regulation.

Compromise. Agencies' policies are usually just compromises among the interests involved in each market: companies, consumers, workers, suppliers, and the like. These groups could thrash the matter out in Congress or in the courts by a pluralistic bargaining process. An agency often is more efficient, however, in weighing complex evidence and reaching a balanced outcome.

Generally, officials give other reasons for their choices, claiming that they have been determined by clear logical criteria. But economists looking for the real effects beneath surface words often find a practical attempt to split the difference or to minimize political trouble.

Compromise need not be wrong, either as an approach or as a result. However, compromise is a different conceptual basis from the ideal of efficient control applied by public authorities.

Capture. Agencies often come effectively under the control of the firms they supposedly control. The degree of capture can vary, but some observers believe that it is usually nearly complete. A captured agency acts like a tool of the firms. It is one-sided, rather independent, and guided by social goals.

The capture concept is consistent with both right-wing and left-wing views—that is, with free-market opinions and with Marxian theories that the state is merely the arm of capitalist interests. A capture theory also is consistent with a third, more cynical, view: that many officials are simply corrupted by the firms. Actually, corruption is not necessary for capture; the officials in charge of captured agencies often have high personal standards of integrity.

Inefficiency and Lags.   Another theory is that agencies develop as much bureaucratic fat and slowness as is permitted. Officials seek to build empires, to minimize their own risks, and to prolong their careers. Accordingly agencies may make mistakes and operate poorly because of sheer ineptitude and bureaucracy.

Spending What Is at Stake.   A firm being treated by a policy will consider how much money it should spend to resist (that is, to bend the policy to its own interests). As a general rule, **the rational firm will ultimately be willing to spend as much as the profits at stake in order to protect those profits.** The resulting spending may be quite large. For example, a firm making $20 million a year in monopoly profits would, as a sound, routine business decision, be willing to spend up to that amount in legal and other costs to try to block antitrust policies that would remove the monopoly power.

Taxes.   Accentuating this effect are taxes. The firm's resistance costs are usually tax-deductible business expenses, so the firm's opportunity cost of spending on resistance is less than the accounting expense. For example, a firm that has $20 million per year in after-tax monopoly profits at stake will have an incentive to spend much more than that to protect those profits from policy actions. The tax rate makes resistance dollars seem cheaper to the firm, so it is willing to spend them more freely.

The resulting spending can dissipate in advance the very benefits that the policy is intended to gain for consumers and the public. Moreover, the firm can merely threaten to overspend on resistance, which could eliminate all of the public benefits. If that threat scares off the agency from acting, then it frustrates the policy action in advance, at no cost at all.

Time Bias.   Often one side (the agency or the firm) can impose delays on the proceedings and gain benefits from doing so. Stalling thus distorts the outcome.

The time bias is strengthened by the brevity of most policymakers' tenure. New policies often require at least three years to prepare and ten years for benefits to be fully harvested. Most top antitrust and regulatory decision makers are in office less than four years. Inexperience often neutralizes them for the first year or two, and after that they are eager to show results. Therefore they tend to take quick, visible, and shallow actions rather than thoughtful, effective ones. They may abandon actions that will last beyond their own tenure.

Probability Bias.   An uneven burden of proof can bias an outcome sharply. Thus the laws and traditions of private-property rights normally set the burden of proof against changes in the status quo. An even burden of proof presumes, of course, that there is equal access to critical data. Without such equality of access, the actual burden of proof may be tilted. In fact, the burden of proof is decisive in a wide range of cases, and it often prevents correct actions.

Information Bias. Public agencies need complete and timely information on all sensitive variables (market shares, prices, costs, innovation choices, competitive tactics, and alternative treatments), both past and future. But they often have only scanty information. Most of that information is known directly and intimately by firms, and when it endangers their profits, it will naturally be secreted. Because firms also try to influence public fact-gathering policies, the data released in the public realm often are skimpy. This imbalance between company knowledge and agency ignorance can cause steep biases in specific policy choices, as well as in the general evaluation of policy needs and urgency.

Taken together, these biases have three effects. First, industrial policies are less complete than they would otherwise be because the problems and potential yields are underestimated. Second, whole problems, areas, and cases are probably slighted because of ignorance. Third, a large share of agency resources must be spent on mere fact-gathering; investigating and assessing facts is actually what takes most antitrust and regulatory resources. These biases may cumulate to cause large distortions in the resulting policies.

Some observers, therefore, regard many policy actions as harmful on balance, because they are imperfectly informed. That fits the standard free-market view. But the opposite view may be more correct more often. If biases all tend to hold policies below their efficient levels, then the right cure is to enlarge policy efforts so as to offset them.

4. ANTITRUST: BENEFITS AND COSTS OF ACTIONS

Each antitrust case aims to restore full competitive results more quickly than natural market forces would, or antitrust tries to prevent a drop in competition by merger or price fixing. If antitrust can do that, then there is more competition, with its many benefits. In figure 15.4, the economic gain is the shaded area, where competition is greater than it otherwise would be.

How Fast Does Dominance Decline? If the natural decline of monopoly power would be slow, then a fast-acting antitrust case may create large net gains. If monopoly's natural decline would be fast, then antitrust may not speed it up at all, so that antitrust's benefits would be small or zero. This issue ties directly to figure 2.13, which shows contrasting views about the speed of monopoly's decline.

Also, there is a sequence of costs and benefits that needs to be considered when setting policies. Figure 15.5 illustrates the benefits and costs of an antitrust action. The costs of litigation and transition occur first, and then the benefits begin to flow. The resulting flow of benefits, it is hoped, will be large enough to justify the costs. Discounting the values for time usually shrinks the benefit-cost ratio, because the benefits come later, often after many years.

The benefit-cost results of these cases are usually debatable. Free-market advocates theorize that monopoly power declines rapidly and cases are so slow that antitrust action brings little net gain in competition. Moreover, because they regard monopoly as weak, they regard the flow of benefits in figure 15.5 as small. Therefore they favor few or no Section 2 cases or merger restraints.

Other experts theorize that natural declines of market power are usually so slow that antitrust cases can bring about large net gains in competition. Since they also think that benefit flows will be large, they favor extensive Section 2 actions.

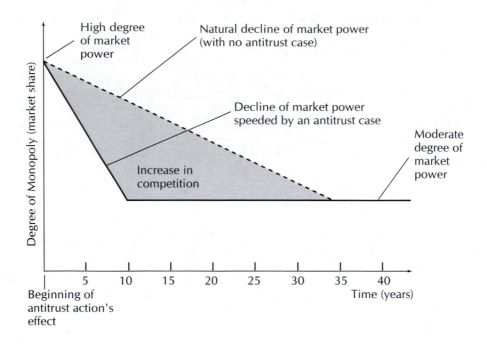

Figure 15.4   The net effect of an antitrust case in raising competition.

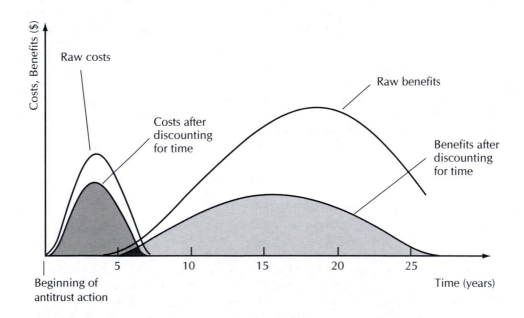

Figure 15.5   The sequence of costs and benefits from an antitrust action (with discounting for time).

Merger Analysis.   A narrower analysis has been applied to mergers.[6] If a merger raises market power, the effect may be to raise price, as illustrated by a rise from A to B in figure 15.6. The efficiency loss is the welfare triangle, as chapter 2 noted. The merger might also reduce costs, such as shown by the shaded rectangle in figure 15.6. If the efficiency gains exceed the welfare loss, then it might be efficient to let the merger occur, even if it reduces competition.

This simple conclusion needs numerous adjustments:

1. The cost gains may just be unfounded claims, not real results.

2. Higher monopoly may cause harm throughout the rest of the market, even though any efficiency gains will be achieved only in this firm.

3. The firm may keep the gains as excess profits, so that consumers get no benefit.

4. Higher monopoly may foster X-inefficiency, retard innovation, cause unfairness, and impose all the other costs of monopoly (recall chapters 1 and 2). These losses may far exceed the narrow efficiency gains in figure 15.6.

5. The merger may set legal precedents for many others. The gains here may be offset a hundredfold by losses in future mergers.

Thus the simple comparison is just a first step, which may be grossly biased in favor of allowing mergers that are actually harmful.

5.   REGULATION: BENEFITS AND COSTS OF ACTIONS

Regulation tries to hold down the prices of natural monopolies so as to prevent excess profits while gaining the benefits of economies of scale. In theory the

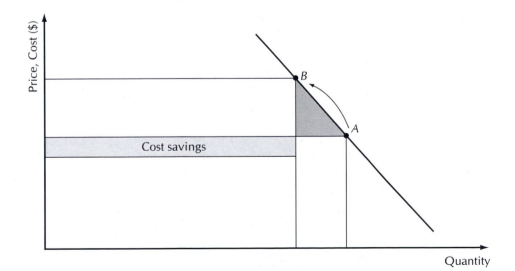

Figure 15.6   Mergers: comparing welfare loss with cost gain.

constraints are applied with minimal administrative costs. The utility complies and is fully efficient, while the economies are passed on to consumers in low prices.

Direct Costs. In practice, regulation has often had substantial direct costs of hearings and administration. The firms have often spent significant amounts on legal and expert-testimony costs, and utility managers have focused much of their efforts on influencing the regulatory outcome.

Indirect Costs. Economists have identified two indirect costs. One is **cost inflation**, under the incentives of cost-plus regulation, which lets utilities pass cost increases on to consumers in higher prices. A second is an induced **rise in investment** under the incentives of rate-base regulation. Both effects are explained in chapter 17. Their logic is clear, but their actual size is hotly debated.

II. U.S. ANTITRUST POLICIES: FORMS AND COVERAGE

Now we turn to antitrust policies, especially in the United States. There is no single best set of laws, agencies, or procedures to bring about optimal patterns of competition. There are many possible tools, which can be combined in various ways and degrees of strictness. American antitrust is one specific set of techniques, which has developed since 1890. It has gone through big changes, with waves of action and many shifts in techniques.

1. LAWS AND AGENCIES

Laws. The Sherman Act of 1890 is the basic antitrust law, prohibiting both unilateral monopoly and collusion among firms in broad terms. In 1914, the Clayton Act made certain specific actions and mergers illegal. It was amended in 1936 to limit certain kinds of price cutting, in 1937 to permit fair trade (the Miller-Tydings Act), and in 1950 to tighten up on mergers (the Celler-Kefauver Act). Table 15.1 codifies the main laws.

The Sherman Act has two main sections: 1 and 2 in table 15.1. The standard section 1 target is price fixing. Section 2 makes market dominance illegal: Every monopolization or attempt is a misdemeanor.

The Clayton Act of 1914 outlawed four specific practices (discrimination in prices, exclusive and tying contracts, intercorporate stockholdings, and interlocking directorates), and added a general rule against unfair methods of competition. None of these prohibitions was absolute; the three practices were forbidden only where their effect, in the words of the law, "may be to substantially lessen competition or tend to create a monopoly. . . ."

To sum up, the Sherman Act is the basic law, whereas the Clayton Act (as further amended) has refined it. Many states have some form of antitrust law (often called "baby Sherman Acts"), but in most states these laws are weak or dormant, with only one or several staff members to apply them.

Scope. Despite their broad language, these laws have a limited reach. Many sectors are exempt by law or by custom, as table 15.2 shows.

Table 15.1   The Basic U.S. Antitrust Laws

1. **Restraint of Trade** (Sherman Act, Section 1)
   Collusive actions, such as price-fixing, market rigging, and sales-allocating schemes and other restrictive actions, are all forbidden.
2. **Monopolizing** (Sherman Act, Section 2)
   Both monopolizing and attempting to monopolize a market are illegal.
3. **Mergers** (Clayton Act, Section 7, amended in 1950)
   Any merger that may substantially reduce competition in any market is illegal.
4. **Other Actions That Are Prohibited:**
   a. Interlocking directorates (one person serving on the boards of two competing companies).
   b. Price discrimination that harms competition (Robinson-Patman Act of 1936).
   c. Exclusive and tying contracts (Clayton, Section 3). (If good A can be bought only by also buying good B, the two goods are tied.)
   d. Unfair methods of competition (FTC Act, Section 5). These are unspecified in the law, but would include abusive or extreme actions.

The "rule of reason" is another tight limit on antitrust. The formal laws are flat and complete; they proscribe **every** monopoly or attempt to monopolize and **every** conspiracy to restrain trade. In 1911, the Supreme Court injected a rule of reason into Section 2 in the Standard Oil case. Reasonable (i.e., non-abusive) monopolies were exempted. This limit has become precedent for nearly all cases. In fact, a degree of "reasonableness" pervades antitrust in its use of resources and decisions about actions.

Table 15.2   Departures from Antitrust: Exemptions and Policies That Reduce Competition

1. **Exemptions**
   Much local and statewide activity: construction, shops, repairs, services.
   Labor unions at all levels.
   Local utilities and urban services: electricity, gas, telephone.
   Social services and health services: schools, hospitals.
   Public enterprises: many electric, transit, and water systems at the local and regional levels.
   Farm and fishery cooperatives: dairy cooperatives.
   Many military suppliers: aircraft, missile systems, tanks, ships, ammunition.
   Baseball and, to a lesser degree, other professional sports.
   Newspapers' joint publishing arrangements in many cities.

2. **Policies That Reduce Competition**
   Tariffs and other barriers to international trade, such as quotas and agreements to limit imports.
   Patents: They provide a monopoly for seventeen years.
   Banking regulation that prevents new entry in many banking markets.
   Price raising for certain farm products (milk, tobacco) is enforced by the U.S. Department of Agriculture.
   Shipbuilding and shipping: Price fixing is permitted by the Federal Maritime Commission.

Agencies. The laws are merely formal words; they need to be enforced by tangible actions of well-staffed and sophisticated agencies. There are two federal enforcement agencies: the Antitrust Division within the Department of Justice and the Federal Trade Commission, an independent agency created in 1914.

The Division is a standard law-enforcement unit, pursuing lawsuits to try firms for illegal actions.[7] The FTC as an "independent agency" is supposed to bring full technical resources to bear in a specialized, expert court, so that the FTC itself decides on violations and penalties.[8] In practice, the two procedures are not so distinct. The Division actually negotiates extensively and tries to get compliance informally as well as through lawsuits. The FTC's rulings are often appealed to the federal courts in important cases; therefore the FTC does not always have the final say.

Both units were small until the late 1930s—a mere "corporal's guard," in one view.[9] They grew to about 300 lawyers each by 1950, stabilized, and then expanded modestly again after 1970. Their budgets for antitrust enforcement were about $4 million each in 1950, and were still below $12 million in 1970. In 1980, the budgets were less than $40 million each, still tiny compared to an economy of $4.8 trillion and a federal budget of over $600 billion. Since 1976, fees charged for merger applications have given the Division larger budgets during merger booms (even though little action was taken toward mergers). But both agencies have had modest actual resources and staffing.

The resources have always been thinly spread, even when they are more adequate.[10] Major industries may be monitored by only four or five equivalent full-time lawyers and economists. Many other sectors, especially new industries, are given only passing attention or are neglected. A single big case can absorb a sizable share of the whole agency's resources. At the top, the agencies are run by political appointees, who are usually in office for only three years or less. Because many significant actions take between five and fifteen years to run their course, the top officials often can have little effect, and they focus on cases with quick payoffs.

The agencies are run by lawyers, applying "the law." Economists are brought in on many cases, but only to give some economic advice. As recent appointees, many of the staff economists hold free-market views. Therefore they usually urge minimal actions and avoidance of some entire antitrust areas, such as vertical problems and "predatory" prices.

The Antitrust Division can take firms to court, seeking to try, convict, and change them. It also does much bargaining behind the scenes, and it settles many cases with consent decrees before a final judgment is reached. The FTC staff takes firms before the commission itself for rulings (often with a first-round decision by an FTC administrative-law judge, which the commission then affirms, overrules, or modifies).

The two agencies usually operate in harmony. They overlap in authority, and often one agency takes up a matter that the other has declined.[11] The Division focuses generally on heavy industries; the FTC specializes in lighter, consumer-oriented industries. Both roam over the whole spectrum of markets.

Because they are so small, the two antitrust agencies mainly try to develop a series of relatively few precedent-setting cases, rather than to pursue and catch every firm that might be breaking antitrust laws. We will present some of those landmark cases in the next chapter.

Setting.   The setting for the agencies includes the rest of the government and private antitrust resources. Though they are nominally free from outside interference, in actuality the agencies are subjected to various outside pressures. Their budgets are set by the executive branch and Congress. Firms constantly try to use officials (in the White House, Defense Department, and elsewhere) and congressional members to influence the agencies. Court decisions can be appealed to the appellate courts and the Supreme Court, either to reverse decisions or merely to delay the process.

On the private side, the large defendant firms often have large resources to resist or manipulate policy efforts. The private antitrust bar employs about 10,000 lawyers. Large firms often apply five, ten, or even twenty times as many lawyers and experts to a case as the agencies do. This fits their large stakes in the outcomes, often running into hundreds of millions of dollars. Their interests will induce them to spend up to the total amount of profit at stake in order to win, as noted earlier. For small firms, the situation may be reversed; they have small resources, so the agencies often have the upper hand against them.

Private antitrust suits—by one firm against another—often trigger or supplement actions by the public agencies. These suits were few before 1960, but they rose to about 1,200 new cases per year in the 1970s. Reagan policies in the 1980s deliberately sought to stop them, and they fell to only about 400 to 500 new cases per year in the 1990s. These cases arise in a great variety of markets.[12] In theory, they provide spontaneous private enforcement of competition, and they could neatly fill any gaps when the Division or FTC are lax. But in practice, private cases are often lacking precisely where they are most needed.

Private cases are induced partly by treble damages, as was written into the Sherman Act in order to give it teeth. After winning a case, the plaintiff tries to prove the extent of financial harm it has suffered from the anticompetitive actions. It is then entitled to triple (or treble) the amount of the damages. Defendants' advocates say that trebling is harmful from overstimulating private lawsuits. If trebling were eliminated, they say, private suits would correctly pursue only the genuine, full amount of the real harms.[13]

Private cases face strong disadvantages. They often are high-risk gambles, where the defendant usually has far greater resources and skills at stalling. Defendants often play rough, countersuing and inflicting costly legal actions on the plaintiff. Plaintiffs often are unable to stand these pressures, even with the prospect of triple damages. Therefore it is possible that private cases are understimulated by treble damages, not overstimulated. Despite aggressive arguments against trebling, research has given no reliable basis to alter this long-standing policy.

Courts.   The lines and precedents of enforcement are ultimately set by the federal courts. Both agencies have to win their cases by persuading judges, and both can be reversed. Historically, judges have often been inexpert on the fine points of antitrust, but they have been broadly unbiased.

In the 1980s Reagan officials sought to change that, by appointing large numbers of free-market judges. Appointees by Reagan and both Bushes are a large majority of all sitting federal judges at all levels. Most met strict tests of conservative doctrine, including antitrust. Many are still young, and most have gone through a free-market-tilted schooling program on "correct" economics.[14] Therefore the courts now present a significant deterrent to strong antitrust. They will apply free-market doctrines to reduce its impacts, even if the agencies' officials try to become more strict.

Sanctions.   The agencies' powers boil down to several kinds of economic penalties that they can inflict, as follows:

1. **Investigation.**   The study process can be large, long, and costly to the firm, by choice either of the agencies or of the firms themselves (if the firms choose to mount a win-at-any-cost defense).

2. **Suit.**   A case inflicts the direct costs of litigation. These can run up to $10 million and more, even in medium-size cases. It also results in diversion of executive attention. Chief officers often spend a large share of their time on major cases. And the bad publicity can affect a company's image and goodwill.

3. **Stoppage of Company Actions.**   The contested action is often stopped as soon as it is challenged, though it may be eventually exonerated.

4. **Guilty Decision.**   This is only a decision on the legal outcome. It leads to fines, constraints on behavior (injunctive relief), and/or changes in company structure (perhaps by divestiture). The plaintiffs in private damage suits often claim damages of over $100 million but settle for $5 million or less.

The right levels of fines, penalties, and other sanctions have at least two dimensions: (1) the size of fines, other money penalties (including damages), and jail sentences, and (2) the probability of getting caught and penalized. Much of this chapter and the next are about probabilities, which vary among the types of violations and among industries and companies.

As for fines, they have been so minor for most large defendants that experts have long recommended raising their ceilings.[15] The $5,000 limit set in the Sherman Act was finally raised to $50,000 in 1955, and raised again in 1974 to $500,000 for individuals and $1 million for firms. Most actual fines levied by judges are far below those limits and are negligible expenses for large firms.[16]

Jail.   Since 1976, officials have applied criminal penalties more severely, with jail sentences in some price-fixing cases. Over twenty officials are typically sentenced to some prison time each year. But they are usually small-time violators, often with poor legal advice and caught in rough-and-tumble business situations.[17]

Damages, Especially Private Treble Damages.   Violators can also be made to pay compensation for the economic damage they have caused. Antitrust agencies can try to prove the dollar amount of the harm done so as to collect those dollars for the public treasury.

Private plaintiffs are (as noted already) entitled to triple the amount of the dollar damages they can prove. Most private suits are motivated by these yields. The typical trial of a private case has a liability phase, to judge if the defendant is guilty of an antitrust violation. If it is found guilty, then the damage phase allows the plaintiff to try to prove the amount of true damages.

The design and calculation of damages is an interesting practical use of economics. The violation may have been an excessive monopoly price charged to the plaintiff that inflated its cost; some anticompetitive action that put the plaintiff out of business; or a wide variety of other impacts that raise costs, cut revenues, or both. The plaintiff must show that it suffered lost profits for some definite period. The basic format is shown in figure 15.7; the lost profits are a series over some past period (and possibly on into the future). The defendant tries the opposite; to show that the yearly loss was small or even nil, and that the correct time period of the losses is much shorter.

The basic idea is simple, and a straightforward estimate based on reasonable strength and length of impact is often successful. Defendants' witnesses often prepare elaborate models and calculations to prove small damages, but they are often disregarded.

Taken altogether, antitrust is applied by small, hard-pressed agencies, operating in a large and complicated domain, with huge responsibilities but only modest resources. They are under many pressures and limits, but they can also apply some serious penalties. The outcomes may or may not fit the ideal balance between competitive benefits and possible true economies of scale. Both the general force of antitrust and the inner balance among its various parts are open to question. Experienced observers expect only that antitrust approximates the main lines of correct policies at least for some periods of time. Some scholars regard antitrust as radically mistaken, and almost none believe that it is regularly close to ideal.

The Economic Meaning of High Winning Percentages. Agencies seek to win their cases, and so a high batting average in cases that reach the Supreme Court is often taken as a sign that policies are successful and very strict. "They win all their cases, so the Court must be on their side and extremely stringent."

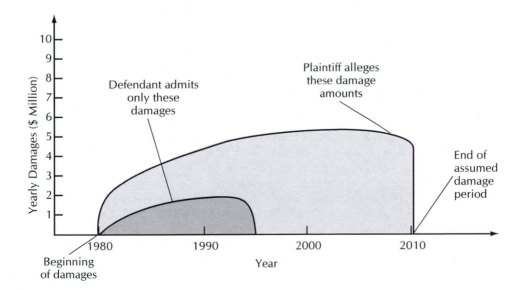

Figure 15.7 Antitrust damages.

But the opposite lesson is probably true. High win rates may show weak policies, because the agencies select from a wide variety of possible cases when choosing their actions. Normally, they try a range of possible cases, so that the Supreme Court can select among them in setting the lines of precedent.

Agencies may instead pull back and play it safe, pursuing only the most obviously winnable cases and avoiding cases with more even chances of winning or losing. Then the Supreme Court will indeed decide these too-few cases for the agencies, and business interests will claim that policies and courts are far too strict. The truth will be the opposite; winning all of the cases will display a weak policy.

Critical Attacks on Antitrust.   Free-market advocates and the "entry" group have blamed antitrust scathingly for being "excessive" and "anti-efficient." Those attacks led to the 1980s Reagan-era cutbacks, but the attacks continue, seeking to let all dominance, mergers, and conduct except blatant price fixing go untouched. Your view on that will reflect your assessment of monopoly conditions as well as policy actions that have been taken.

2. THE DEVELOPMENT OF ANTITRUST

The Sherman Act was actually first applied in the 1890s to attack labor-union strikes. After that shaky start it was applied firmly against price fixing in 1899 in the Addyston Pipe case (this case and others are summarized in the next chapter). That strict prohibition of price fixing is still enforced. No longer able to collude with one another after the district court's decision in 1897, many of these pipe firms simply merged, as did far more firms in scores of other industries.

The First Wave.   Recall that figure 15.1 showed waves of antitrust. First came Theodore Roosevelt's trustbusting campaign starting in 1904, which was mainly carried through later during William H. Taft's presidency in 1909 to 1913. The Standard Oil Company untied its separate statewide monopoly units, the American Tobacco Company divested some assets, Du Pont was forced to divest some gunpowder capacity, and AT&T agreed to avoid monopolizing the telephone sector (which it then proceeded to do anyway).

Because the Sherman Act is so brief and broad, business interests soon demanded more details about exactly which actions were illegal. Under Woodrow Wilson's "progressive" approach, the Clayton Act in 1914 was written to try to cover those details, though only a few specific offenses were spelled out. The Federal Trade Commission was created at that time to enforce the new law. In 1920, US Steel barely escaped a Section 2 conviction in the Supreme Court. That decision unfortunately prevented an efficient reshaping of that firm, and so it staggered on with poor performance for many decades more.

Antitrust was then cut back deeply during the Roaring Twenties, even as the second great merger boom mounted to its peak in 1929. The balance of antitrust actions then actually swung in favor of mergers and cooperation among firms. But then the crash of 1929 and the Great Depression of the 1930s renewed pressure to act against what was seen as rising corporate power.

The Second Wave.   The second antitrust wave, from 1938 to 1952, touched many dominant firms. The aluminum monopoly (Alcoa: the Aluminum Company of America) was challenged in 1937, and two new competitors were finally added in 1950. The duopoly in metal cans (American Can Company and National Can Company) was subjected to restraints by a court decree in 1950. The dominant National Broadcasting Company (NBC) was required to sell one of its two radio networks in 1943, thereby creating the American Broadcasting Company (ABC). Movie companies were forced by the Paramount Pictures decision in 1948 to sell their theater chains. There were also major cases against some tight oligopolies, including the leading cigarette companies.

The pace of antitrust slowed again from 1953 to 1968. The only exception was the application in 1962 (the Brown Shoe case) of strict new limits against mergers among competitors. On other antitrust fronts, little was done to reduce market power or to discourage conglomerate mergers during the "go-go" merger boom of the 1960s.

The Third Wave.   During 1968–1974, the antitrust pulse quickened moderately, especially with several large cases alleging that IBM, Xerox, AT&T, and the big cereal companies had monopolized their markets. Only the AT&T case resulted in significant changes, although those gains were spectacular.

Antitrust Virtually Stops in the 1980s.   From 1981 to 1988 the Reagan administration brought antitrust nearly to a halt.[18] Actions against market dominance were stopped; while the AT&T divestiture was carried out, the IBM case was dropped. Horizontal merger rules were relaxed from about 7 plus 7 percent, to well over 20 plus 20 percent. At times in the 1980s, virtually all horizontal mergers seemed to be permitted or even welcomed.

Price-fixing cases diminished mainly to those with petty offenders caught arranging identical bids for public projects like roads and buildings. Cases against vertical mergers and restraints, strategic actions, predatory prices, and conglomerate mergers were almost entirely stopped. Moreover, Reagan officials opposed all private cases and actually intervened to stop some of those.

Bush officials after 1988 restored some moderate antitrust activities; Clinton officials after 1992 went only a little further, and they retreated on mergers. Since 2000, Bush officials have pulled back, more in line with the free-market theories of the Reagan administration.[19] In 2001 the Microsoft settlement was seen as a virtual sell-out, and the criticism was even sharper in 2002 when the settlement was confirmed by the judge. Mergers between major competitors, and code-sharing arrangements among Northwest, Delta, and Continental airlines were not challenged.

3.   ANTITRUST CRITERIA

Economists try to see through the legal details of antitrust, in order to discern its true economic criteria and real economic effects. The main antitrust criteria have evolved in the courts since 1890 in hundreds of precedent-setting cases and decisions.

The wording of the statutes sounds broad and conclusive, but the laws have come to be applied only within reasonable limits in line with a rule of reason. In practice, "reasonable" means what the agencies can feasibly try for and what the courts will accept. The limits of enforcement often shift markedly as the courts and the country's political complexion change. For example, the Supreme Court under Earl Warren in the 1960s tightened criteria against mergers and dominant firms, even though the agencies did not pursue cases strongly. In contrast, the Burger Court of the 1970s and 1980s pulled back the margin of antitrust enforcement toward lenient treatment of mergers and the pricing tactics used by dominant firms.

Currently the courts are quite conservative, while the political climate is more liberal. The Bush agencies might consider strictness toward dominance or mergers, but they know that it would be rejected by the Reagan-Bush selected higher courts. Although free-market viewpoints have mostly been discredited among economists, their backwash in the courts continues to set close limits on policies.

Defining the Market.   Defining the market is, of course, a pivotal issue, as it also is in research. The plaintiff (an agency or a private company claiming to be a victim of monopoly) urges a narrow definition, which gives the defendant firm a high market share. The defendant claims instead that the market is much larger so that its share of that market is small.

The Court's decision on this point often governs the outcome of the case, for if it accepts a large market, then harmful market power could not exist. Generally the Warren court defined markets narrowly from 1960 to 1970, whereas the later Burger court accepted broad market definitions. The Rehnquist court is even more favorable to big-business interests.

4. PRECEDENTS

Policy is applied by individual cases, which agency lawyers develop, bring to trial, and try to win. Some cases become huge, involving scores of lawyers, years of preparation, and millions of documents, as we will soon show. Many others are compact and clear, taking only a year or two from the violation to the final decision. The courts' decisions in these cases set precedents, which then govern most or all later cases. The precedents all reduce to fairly simple patterns.

Toward Existing Structure.   After the Alcoa decision in 1945, the threshold criteria for prosecuting dominance was a 60-percent market share, plus some evidence that the firm had taken some unfair or abusive action to gain its dominance. Since any firm with a market share under 60 percent would almost certainly be acquitted, no cases were brought against firms below that threshold. Since 1980, the threshold value seems to have risen to about 80 percent. Virtually every dominant firm is now immune from antitrust action. Microsoft, with its 90-percent market share and series of hardball actions, compelled a challenge.

Even if its market share is above the threshold value, a firm can escape by arguing that its position arose only from Asuperior skill, foresight, and industry" (that is the usual legal phrase), so that it deserves every bit of its dominance. Judges often are persuaded by that argument. IBM had particular success with it in winning a series of cases after 1968, and Microsoft also asserts that claim.

Mergers.   From 1966 to 1980, horizontal mergers were usually stopped if the resulting firm would control more than 15 percent of the market. Accordingly, very few mergers with a combined market share above 15 percent were even attempted.

Then Reagan officials announced more lenient limits, plus a willingness to permit high-share mergers if they would lead to improved efficiency. The merger limits fluctuated in the 25- to 45-percent range, often without any visible basis. After 1992, Clinton officials were also mainly permissive. They stopped a few mergers, but they permitted many other mergers that created market shares well over 50 percent. Current Bush officials have loosened merger constraints even further.

Price Fixing.   Price fixing has usually been treated strictly. The courts will not permit a defense based on the claim that it was reasonable. The agency merely needs to show at trial that price fixing occurred, even without proof that its effects were strong. The courts will then usually convict *per se* (that is, guilty "in itself"). Since 1980, cases have been fewer and smaller, often clustering in petty violators. Reagan antitrust officials actively tried to legalize vertical price fixing in the form of resale price maintenance.

5.   ECONOMIC EFFECTS OF ANTITRUST

Antitrust actions have reduced the size of a number of important dominant positions, mainly through actions taken before 1950. The AT&T divestiture in 1984 was the biggest Section 2 result of all time, which even AT&T later fully agreed was appropriate and brilliantly successful.

Price fixing has been sharply reduced, although some has simply been driven underground. Secret collusion continues in many industries and in a variety of tight oligopolies. Tight-oligopoly indirect collusion has scarcely been touched.

A large range of horizontal and vertical mergers—and even some conglomerate mergers—were forestalled during 1958–1980. Since 1980, constraints on horizontal mergers have been loose and uncertain, while constraints on vertical and conglomerate mergers have ended.

Altogether, antitrust policies have probably kept U.S. industrial concentration and the extent of price fixing much lower than they would have been otherwise. It is inconceivable that antitrust would be abolished, because its basic forms are central to American capitalism.

If antitrust *were* somehow removed, monopoly would rise markedly. An immense merger boom would immediately roar ahead, raising concentration sharply in thousands of markets. Dominant firms would become common in markets of all sizes, able to take actions to quell their small rivals. Formal price-fixing cartels, with official staffs and binding contracts preventing price competition and allocating output and profits, would be created in thousands of markets just as they were in Europe during the 1930s to the 1960s.

In sum, antitrust has created large economic effects and benefits, which continue quietly because antitrust itself continues. Yet nearly all individual cases occur on the margins of policy. They are two-sided and often controversial. Some have been mistaken in some degree. Moreover, the economic effects of antitrust also display some awkward imbalances that favor powerful, established firms. Dominant firms are now largely free to set prices internally over their large shares of the market, even when their market shares are over 80 percent. But the smaller rivals of dominant firms can neither arrange to coordinate their price setting nor merge with each other.

In this way, antitrust does seem to coddle the already-powerful, while attacking small businesses that would copy their dominant competitors. Once a firm has gained dominance, it is largely immune from antitrust actions, free to do things internally that lesser firms cannot do. Ideally, antitrust would be equally strict toward dominant and smaller firms. But it isn't.

Antitrust's ultimate effects are debatable, then, perhaps promoting efficiency on the whole, but perhaps also lacking balance. The effects are also limited, for antitrust does not reach all of the economy. As table 15.2 shows, most local markets, newspapers, all labor unions, all patents, much weapons production, and most public enterprises are exempt from antitrust.

Meanwhile, various other policies directly reduce competition in many markets. They are summarized in part 2 of table 15.2. Not only is antitrust's reach incomplete; its resources are usually stretched thin.

Think of U.S. antitrust as **interacting with industry,** not standing above it and exercising lordly powers. Like any other policing agents, antitrust officials are influenced by industry, by Congress, by the executive branch, and by swings in popular attitudes. Policy choices are often political, mistaken, rash, or too cautious: in short, they are human, fallible, and changeable. Yet the basic economic effects against dominance, price fixing, and mergers have been important, and the struggles against price fixing remain relatively steady.

III. ANTITRUST IN OTHER COUNTRIES[20]

The 1930s brought a wave of cartels to Britain and western Europe in futile efforts to stabilize price, profits, and jobs against worldwide depressions. The price fixing continued into the 1950s, often with more than 2,000 cartels each in countries such as Britain and Sweden. Then the tide turned.

From 1956 to 1961, it put a stop to nearly all formal price fixing, and resale price maintenance was stopped in 1965. The U.K. Monopolies and Mergers Commission has deflected some mergers and required certain changes.[21] It has scarcely affected most dominant firms, though it has thoroughly studied many. British procedures for treating price fixing and market dominance are much more brisk than those in the United States, mainly because lawyers are not given a crucial role in the hearing process. After 1980, antitrust policies were eased under the conservative Thatcher government, in parallel with U.S. changes.[22]

Germany has applied mild limits against horizontal mergers, and since the 1960s it has also attacked industrial price fixing. Like other foreign countries, it has not moved against existing dominant firms. The European Union has moderately enforced several rules against dominance and price fixing.[23] French policies are dominated by a penchant for informal action between government and industries.[24]

For Europe, antitrust in the European Commission flowered in the 1990s, and it now exceeds the strength of U.S. antitrust. In many cases, European antitrust has taken stricter and more fact-based actions.[25] But by 2002, pressure from business interests and the Bush administration worked through European courts to cut back European antitrust.[26] Future directions are unsure.

Since 1950, Japan has had a Fair Trade Agency with formal powers to promote competition, but action has been largely negligible. Instead, the most important Japanese policy initiatives (much as in France) generally involve informal links between the government (especially MITI, the Ministry of International Trade and Industry) and industries, often encouraging mergers or temporary cartels.

Canada has agencies with formal powers to stop price fixing and anticompetitive mergers, but action has generally been minimal.[27] Canada's Competition Act of 1986 is the basis for current policy, with an emphasis on foreign trade in reducing domestic monopoly.[28] Merger policies have included the issuance of guidelines.[29] Actual constraints on mergers have been mild, with concern for important competition and possible merger efficiencies; mergers up to a combined 35-percent market share are generally permitted.[30]

Australia's modern antitrust policies began with the Trade Practices Act of 1974 and have developed with a wide consensus among experts and business interests.[31] The Trade Practices Commission has decided cases in the traditional areas, including dominance, mergers, and collusive behavior. As in other countries, Australia's procedures are more direct and effective than in the litigious United States. Maureen Brunt, a leader in the field and a member of the Commission, notes distinctive Australian treatments of market definition, market power, and efficiencies.[32] The policies rely on the 1980s doctrines of free entry and international competitive pressure.

Until the 1980s, the United States led the world in antitrust. Several others have now caught up, both in degrees of strictness and in the effectiveness of their procedures. For example, when post-apartheid South Africa considered major new antitrust moves in the 1990s, it borrowed procedures and criteria from a range of countries, not just from the United States. The same was true of former socialist countries in eastern Europe after 1989 as they privatized toward competitive markets. American consultants tended to inject the current fad for free entry as the cure-all, but these countries could draw on a variety of procedures.[33]

QUESTIONS FOR REVIEW

1. How have antitrust policies probably affected market structures in the United States?

2. Since U.S. antitrust has evolved and fluctuated over ten decades, and the country's needs and interests have also evolved, is it relevant to know exactly what Congress in 1889 intended antitrust to accomplish? Is static efficiency the only goal?

3. Does the capture theory of public agencies usually apply? Discuss an agency that seems to have been captured.

4. Explain three biases that may cause antitrust actions to be too strict or lenient.

5. Explain how the uncertainty over actual costs and benefits may lead new-Chicagoans to favor minimal antitrust while others, by the same logic, favor strict antitrust.

6. Explain how trebling of antitrust damages may (1) overstimulate private cases or (2) induce about the right amount.

ENDNOTES

[1] On antitrust, see F. M. Scherer and David Ross, *Industrial Market Structure and Economic Performance*, 3rd ed. (Boston: Houghton Mifflin, 1991); see also the excellent survey in Harry First, Eleanor M. Fox, and Robert Pitofsky, eds., *Revitalizing Antitrust in Its Second Century* (New York: Quorum Books, 1991); and Manfred Neumann, *Competition Policy: History, Theory and Practice* (Northampton, MA: Elgar, 2001). For legal details, see Eleanor M. Fox and Lawrence A. Sullivan, *Cases and Materials on Antitrust* (St. Paul: West Publishing, 1989). Global varieties of policy are shown in F. M. Scherer, ed., *Competition Policy: Domestic and International* (Northampton, MA: Elgar, 2000; in the U.S. by Brookfield, VT: Ashgate, 1993).

[2] For a full free-market statement, see Fred S. McChesney and William F. Shughart, eds., *The Causes and Consequences of Antitrust: The Public-Choice Perspective* (Chicago: University of Chicago Press, 1995). For a critique of free-market theory, see Rudolph J. R. Peritz, *Competition Policy in America*, rev. ed. (New York: Oxford University Press, 2001).

[3] Mainstream coverage of antitrust law, cases, and economics can be found in the *Antitrust Bulletin*, the *International Journal of Industrial Organization*, and the *Journal of Industrial Economics*. The *Journal of Law and Economics* provides a new-Chicago perspective. For thorough details on current cases and policy developments, use *Trade Regulation Reports* and *Antitrust and Trade Regulation Reporter*.

[4] See First, Fox, and Pitofsky, *Revitalizing Antitrust*; Scherer and Ross, *Industrial Market Structure*; also Tony Freyer, *Regulating Big Business: Antitrust in Great Britain and America* (New York: Cambridge University Press, 1992).

[5] An obvious example is when poor people are taxed to cover costs, while rich people get the benefits. This problem is widespread and acrimonious.

[6] It originated with Oliver E. Williamson, "Economies as an Antitrust Defense," *American Economic Review* 58 (June 1968). On the ensuing debate, see Scherer and Ross, *Industrial Market Structure*.

[7] See Suzanne Weaver, *Decision to Prosecute: Organization and Public Policy in the Antitrust Division* (Cambridge: MIT Press, 1977). See the Division's annual reports for details about size and ongoing activities. Past annual reports are assembled in the *Journal of Reprints in Antitrust*, 1995.

[8] See Robert A. Katzman, *Regulatory Bureaucracy: The Federal Trade Commission and Antitrust Policy* (Cambridge: MIT Press, 1980); also, see the FTC's annual reports, covering the latest activities in detail.

[9] Walton Hamilton and Irene Till, *Antitrust in Action*, vol. 26 of Temporary National Economic Committee, *Investigation of Economic Power* (Washington, DC: U.S. Government Printing Office, 1940).

[10] For example, the Antitrust Division in 1994 had 323 lawyers, which was one lawyer for every $21 billion of gross domestic product; Antitrust Division, *Annual Report for Fiscal Year 1994* (Washington, DC: U.S. Department of Justice, 1995). In addition, the FTC spends about half its resources on nonantitrust matters, such as consumer complaints, fur labeling, and fraud.

[11] For example, the FTC first investigated Microsoft's practices but backed off in 1992 from any action. The Division then took up the case and considered drastic cures, although in 1994 it negotiated only a modest settlement that left Microsoft's position virtually untouched. In 2002 there was an effort to "coordinate" by setting detailed areas for each agency. But it was recognized as an effort by the Bush administration to reduce control on the telecommunications sector, and was quickly abandoned.

[12] See Lawrence J. White, ed., *Private Antitrust Litigation: New Evidence, New Learning* (Cambridge: MIT Press, 1988), especially pp. 1–103.

[13] See White, *Private Antitrust Litigation*, which attempted to gather and present evidence in favor of removing the trebling feature. The evidence actually turned out to be ambivalent.

[14] The program, financed by an array of large corporations, has been operated for over two decades by Henry Marine, at Emory University and recently at George Mason University.

[15] On the general question of optimal fines, see the analysis in A. Mitchell Polinsky and Steven Shavell, "Enforcement Costs and the Optimal Magnitude and Probability of Fines," *Journal of Law and Economics* 35 (April 1992): pp. 133–48, plus the sources listed there.

[16] See also Edward A. Snyder, "The Effect of Higher Criminal Penalties on Antitrust Enforcement," *Journal of Law and Economics* 33 (October 1990): pp. 439–62.

[17] For example, in 1984–1985, some eighty-four people were convicted of criminal antitrust activities, and thirty-three were sent to jail; the longest sentence was fourteen months, the average was six weeks.

[18] For detailed explanations of this change, see the scholar's assessment by Philip Areeda and the insider's rationale by William Baxter (Reagan's first antitrust chief) in chapters of the massive review book by Martin Feldstein, ed., *American Economic Policy in the 1980s* (Chicago: University of Chicago Press, 1994).

[19] For a discussion of future antitrust choices in a post-Chicago-school environment, see Albert A. Fuer, "Small Business and Antitrust," *Small Business Economics* 16(1) (February 2001): pp. 3–20; and A. M. Colodner, "Antitrust, Innovation, Entrepreneurship and Small Business", in that same issue.

[20] Among recent reviews of European antitrust, see Michelle Cini and Lee McGowan, *Competition Policy in the European Union* (New York: St. Martin's Press, 1998); Roger Clark, Stephen Davies, and Nigel Driffield, *Monopoly Policy in the U.K.: Assessing the Evidence* (Northampton, MA: Elgar, 1998); and Stephen Martin, ed., *Competition Policies in Europe* (New York: Elsevier Science, 1998).

[21] See J. Denys Gribbin, "The Origins of Competition Policy," a chapter in Peter de Wolfe, ed., *Competition in Europe: Essays in Honour of Henk W. de Jong* (Dordrecht: Kluwer Academic Publishers, 1990).

[22] See George Symeonidis, *The Effects of Competition: Cartel Policy and the Evolution of Strategy and Structure in British Industry* (Cambridge, MA: MIT Press, 2002).

[23] See Williams S. Comanor, et al., *Competition Policy in Europe and North America: Economic Issues and Institutions* (New York: Harwood Academic, 1990); Alexis Jacquemin, "The International Dimension of European Competition Policy," *Journal of Common Market Studies* 31 (March 1993): pp. 91–101; and Donald Hay, ed., special issue on European and American Antitrust Policy, *Oxford Review of Economic Policy* 9 (Summer 1993): pp. 1–153.

[24] See William J. Adams and Christian Stoffaes, eds., *French Industrial Policy* (Washington, DC: Brookings Institution, 1986); and William J. Adams, *Restructuring the French Economy* (Washington, DC: Brookings Institution, 1989).

[25] See Simon J. Evenett, Alexander Lehman, and Benn Steil, eds., *Antitrust Goes Global: What Future for Transatlantic Cooperation* (Washington, DC: Brookings Institution, 2000), with chapters on merger policy, the Boeing-McDonnell-Douglas merger, and anticartel operations. Also Keith Cowling, ed., *Industrial Policy in Europe: Theoretical Perspectives and Practical Proposals* (New York: Routledge, 1999).

[26] Andy Reinhardt, "Trustbuster on Trial," *BusinessWeek* (November 11, 2002): pp. 52–53; and Paul Meller, "Court Deals New Setback to Europe's Antitrust Policy," *New York Times* (October 23, 2002): pp. W1, W7.

[27] See Christopher Green, *Canadian Industrial Organization and Policy*, 2nd ed. (Toronto: McGraw-Hill Ryerson, 1985); Bruce Dunlop, David McQueen, and Michael Trebilcock, *Canadian Competition Policy: A Legal and Economic Analysis* (Toronto: Canada Law Book, 1987); and Christopher Green, "Mergers in Canada and Canada's New Merger Law," *Antitrust Bulletin* 32 (Spring 1989): pp. 253–73.

[28] See Thomas W. Ross, ed., special issue on Canadian Competition Policies, *Review of Industrial Organization* (1997).

[29] Guidelines were actually issued on mergers (1991), predatory pricing (1992), and price discrimination (1992). See Robert D. Anderson and S. Dev Khosla, "Competition Policy as a Dimension of Economic Policy: A Comparative Perspective," Occasional Paper no. 7 (Ottawa: Bureau of Competition Policy, 1995).

[30] On the patterns of merger policies, see R. S. Khemani and D. M. Shapiro, "An Empirical Analysis of Canadian Merger Policy," *Journal of Industrial Economics* 41 (June 1993): pp. 161–77.

[31] David K. Round, ed., special issue on "The Australian Trade Practices Act 1974: Proscription and Prescription for a More Competitive Economy," *Review of Industrial Organization* 9 (October 1994): pp. 459–694.

[32] Brunt, "The Australian Antitrust Law after 20 Years—A Stocktake," in Round, ed., *The Australian Trade Practices Act 1974*, pp. 483–526.

[33] See R. M. Feinberg and Mike Meurs, "Privatization and Antitrust in Eastern Europe: The Importance of Entry," *Antitrust Bulletin* 39 (Fall 1994): pp. 797–811.

16

Antitrust Applied toward Dominance, Mergers, and Conduct

Antitrust's broad policy directions usually aren't simply announced. They have grown and fluctuated with a spectacular array of specific cases, which often have involved big human dramas.

The cases are selected by officials; studied by staff lawyers and economists; formalized as lawsuits, perhaps pursued and brought to trial (or perhaps not); decided; often appealed; and then (in a very few landmark cases) finally decided by the Supreme Court. These decisions then set precedents for policy.

Behind the dry legal terms and precedents are colorful events, often played out with many billions of dollars at stake. There have been scoundrels and statesmen of industry; some antitrust officials who were timid and others who were bold; and judges who were biased, foggy, or in some instances, positively superb.

Only by learning about the landmark cases can you understand the content and directions of antitrust—and also its limits and faults. We begin with market dominance, next turn to mergers, and then finish with collusion and other pricing behavior.[1]

I. TOWARD EXISTING DOMINANCE: SECTION 2 CASES

Standard Oil (1911) and AT&T (1984) stand out as the all-time leading Section 2 cases toward dominance. They decided large policy issues in the course of forcing large changes upon the leading monopolist of the era. Also important are two landmark cases which were "unsuccessful" and did *not* lead to needed changes: U.S. Steel (1920) and IBM (1982).

The first wave of Section 2 actions from 1902 to 1920 was extremely ambitious, and it did make changes in several prominent industries. The second wave from 1938 to 1953 had a smaller reach and less effect. The third wave during 1968 to 1982 touched a few conspicuous firms, but only one standout case (AT&T) had strong effects.

A case occurs only when there is a target: a dominant-firm position that needs curing even by the costly process of a Section 2 case. Agency officials must first study and decide whether two conditions prevail:

1. The dominant firm indeed has monopoly power and has violated the law.

2. A practical remedy can be applied

Then they must assemble the case, file it, press it through trial, and win a guilty verdict, then sustain that verdict against the firm's inevitable legal appeal, then get the court to apply an effective remedy, and finally monitor the remedy's effects.

1. ELEMENTS

First, consider what a Section 2 case involves. Typically the agency must present two parts: (1) proof that the firm holds monopoly power (especially in a high market share), and (2) some other evidence of abusive actions. From 1900 to 1980, the firm's market share had to be at least 60 percent (that is, a clear dominant-firm position) if the case was to be brought at all. Since 1980, the threshold value has been closer to 80 percent or higher.

Defining the Market. The case therefore must begin with a definition of the relevant market. The agency usually urges a narrow market, whereas the firm responds by claiming a very wide market. The two sides (through their experts) use the standard terms and methods (recall chapter 3) to assert what the **product** and **geographic** dimensions are, much as in the research literature. Reliable measures of the critical market-defining variables are rarely available, as chapter 3 noted. In the end, the court considers any SNIPP-approach evidence that either side may offer, but it usually makes a more direct reasonable judgment about the true market.

Dominant Market Share. The resulting market definition then determines the firm's market share, which is usually treated as the main indicator of its possible market power. Recently, claims about entry barriers have also become important. The agency will allege them to be high (reinforcing market power), whereas the firm will say that they are low or nil (so that potential competition eliminates any market power).

Abusive Conduct. If the court decides that the firm has a share well above 60 percent, it then considers possible abuse. The evidence may be a specific company memorandum, a course of action, or a pricing strategy. Systematic price discrimination often is used as proof that the firm deliberately set out to get and keep its dominance. Whatever it is, the additional information must show that the firm had a strong intent to achieve its dominance.

Superior Performance?   The firm commonly claims that its market position merely reflects its own superior performance (recall the free-market view that all dominance reflects superiority); the standard legal phrase is "superior skill, foresight, and industry." The firm usually claims also that it achieves economies of scale, and that any decision against it would "penalize success" and "sacrifice efficiency." The firm also stresses how innovative it has been, and it asserts that tampering with it would stop its progress and growth. Also, it points out, the chilling effect would occur in many other industries, as aspiring firms elsewhere observe that this firm is punished for its success.

A Long Process.   The process can be lengthy. Studying the market and preparing the suit can take several years. Then pretrial preparation can take two to four years more; the trial itself may last a year; and further appeals, remands, and decisions average about three to five years more. At that point, remedy may *begin*. From start to finish, it may take ten or more years to identify dominance, process the case, and start a cure. That gives the defendant a chance to assert that the industry has changed entirely, that the dominance and any abuses are long past, and that any remedy would not be appropriate.

Informal Criteria.   On top of these problems, a successful Section 2 case must also overcome several informal criteria. **Economies of scale** must be minimal rather than significant, so that the firm could be altered without losing efficiency. The firm must have been earning a lot of **excess, "monopoly" profits,** which make it look powerful and greedy. Its **technology** must be relatively simple, so that the courts are not overawed with its complexity nor afraid to consider changes in the firm.

Burden of Proof.   In short, the agency bears the burden of proof to show that a major shift toward competition is needed, is feasible, and will give large benefits. This burden of proof is heavy. At the least, large volumes of facts must be assembled and researched, which takes time and is usually resisted skillfully by the firm's lawyers.

Incentives to Stall.   The firm and its lawyers have extremely strong incentives to stall, exploiting legal procedures so as to delay the decision and any remedies. Stalling postpones the day when the dominance might be reduced; meanwhile the firm gets to make and keep monopoly profits. Moreover, stalling raises the chance that a sympathetic administration may later come into office and drop the case. For example, stalling tactics by IBM slowed its case, which began in 1969, until Reagan officials took office in 1981 and withdrew the case in 1982.

By the 1970s, Section 2 cases came to be seen as long, complex ordeals with uncertain outcomes. Since 1980, no new cases have been brought, and prospects for new ones are slight because of the generally hostile courts.[2] Yet the AT&T case shows that large complex changes can be achieved with remarkable speed and precision.

2.   WAVES AND CASES

The leading antitrust cases are grouped in table 16.1, reflecting the three waves.

Table 16.1   Major Section 2 Cases, 1905 to 1986

Cases	Time between Monopolization and Remedy	
	Years[b]	Interval (years)[b]
1904 to 1920		
American Tobacco	1890–1916	26
Standard Oil	1875–1918+	43+
Du Pont (gunpowder)	1902–1913	11
Corn Products	1897–1920	23
American Can	1901–	—
US Steel	1901–	—
AT&T	1881–	—
		—
Meatpackers (Armour, Swift, Wilson, Cudahy)	1885	
		—
American Sugar	1890–	—
United Show Machinery	1899–	—
International Harvester	1902	—
1938 to 1952		
Alcoa	1903–(1953)	(50)
National Broadcasting Company	1926–1943	17
Pullman	1899–1947	(65)
	1914–1948	34
Paramount Pictures		
American Can	1901–(1955)	(54)
Du Pont (GM holdings)	1918–1961	43
United Shoe Machinery	1899–1970	71
United Fruit	1899–1970	71
American Tobacco	(1920)–	—
Du Pont (cellophane)	1925–	—
Western Electric	1881–	—
IBM	(1925)–	—
Since 1968		
IBM (1969 case)	(1925)–	—
Cereals (1972 case)	(1950)–	—
Xerox (1973 case)	1961–1975	14
AT&T (1974 case)	1881–1984	103
Berkey v. Eastman Kodak[c]	1890s–	—
Aspen Skiing[c]	1978–1986	8

(continued)

Table 16.1   Major Section 2 Cases, 1905 to 1986 *(continued)*

Time between Beginning and End of Action[a]		Outcome
Years[b]	**Interval (years)[b]**	
1906–12	6	Divestiture of some assets.
1905–12	7	Dissolution into about a dozen regionally dominant firms.
1906–12	6	Mild dissolution; reversed quickly by effects of World War I.
(1910)–19	(9)	Slight changes from a consent decree
(1909)–20	(11)	No change.
(1907)–20	(13)	Acquittal, informal limits on further mergers.
(1909)–13	(4)	Compromise. AT&T retained its position; agreed to interconnect and avoid further mergers.
(1909)–20	(15)	Compromise. Packers agreed to stay out of adjacent markets and to cease coordination.
1908–14	6	No action. American Sugar's position had slipped already.
(1908)–18	10	USM leasing restrictions were modified.
1906–18	12	Compromise. Trivial divestiture.
1934–50	16	War plants sold to new entrants.
1938–43	5	Blue Network divested (became American Broadcasting Corp.)
(1937)–47	(10)	Divestiture of sleeping car operation. Manufacturing monopoly was not directly changed.
(1935)–48	(13)	Vertical integration removed.
(1945)–50	(5)	Compromise. Certain restrictive practices stopped to foster entry.
(1945)–61	(16)	Divestiture.
(1945)–69	(61)	Share reduced to 50 percent
1948–70	22	Moderate divestiture.
1938–46	8	Conviction but no significant remedy.
(1945)–56	(11)	Acquittal.
1946–56	10	Case effectively abandoned.
1947–56	9	Case effectively abandoned.
1965–82	17	Dropped.
1970–82	12	Acquittal.
1970–75	6	Compromise. Some opening of access to patents.
1965–84	19	Substantial divestiture.
1972–80	8	Kodak exonerated.
1979–86	7	Aspen Skiing held in violation, fined, and required to resume shared ticketing.

[a] Based on evidence of the start of official investigation and the end of official action.

[b] Parentheses indicate estimates.

[c] Private case.

Sources: S. N. Whitney, *Antitrust Policies* (New York: Twentieth Century Fund, 1958); and case records and decisions.

The First Wave, 1904–1920.   After a slow beginning during the 1890s, anti-trust burst upon the scene after 1903 in a wave of cases challenging many of the country's biggest companies. These cases tested the reach of the new law in reducing market dominance. The result was a compromise: Certain actual dominant firms were held in violation and forced to make moderate changes, but legal precedents were set that limited the law only to bad monopolies. Henceforth, the burden of proof favored dominant firms, and it still does.

In 1904, Theodore Roosevelt's first trustbusting case forced the dissolution of the Northern Securities trust, which merged two competing railroads in the Northwest. That opened the way—under Roosevelt and then Taft—to spectacular investigations, trials, and changes in a series of leading industrial firms. The oil, tobacco, sugar, telephone, steel, gunpowder, meatpacking, farm-machinery, shoe-machinery, and aluminum industries were among those affected, including no less than six of the ten largest industrial companies. The Bureau of Corporations was formed to do large studies of these industries, creating a large, detailed inventory of published evidence.

1911 was the landmark year: The Standard Oil Company and American Tobacco Company decisions were obtained expeditiously, and by 1913 remedies had been applied.[3] Each held about 90 percent of its market, had been ruthless, had not been innovative, and did not achieve economies of scale. Modest changes were achieved against Du Pont's gunpowder monopoly and AT&T's efforts to monopolize telephones, telegraphs, and related equipment. All of the remedies were actually moderate, not severe.

A series of other cases was stopped by the distractions of World War I and its conservative aftermath. In 1920, the Supreme Court buried the first Section 2 wave by acquitting the US Steel Corporation on a close 4 to 3 vote, saying that US Steel had been a "good trust."[4] In a final epilogue, in 1927, the Court acquitted the International Harvester Company on similar grounds.[5]

Standard Oil.   The Rockefeller oil monopoly, formed in the 1870s, had relied on ruthless anticompetitive actions, and it created immense fortunes for its founders. It had gained control of all of the important pipelines, mainly by exacting rebates from railroads on its own oil shipments as well as those of its rivals. Its selective local price cutting (that is, sharp and systematic price discrimination) had eliminated many rivals, in some cases by forcing them to sell out cheaply to Standard Oil. By 1910 Standard Oil's grasp was slipping, though it still held nearly 90 percent of the U.S. market.

Standard Oil's legal defense was inept, and there had been a wide groundswell of public dismay at its tactics. The company was still closely held rather than widely owned by the public. The product was simple, the offenses were shocking, and the Court found little difficulty ordering the trust dissolved.

The treatment was scarcely timely or severe. The monopoly had lasted nearly forty years. Though the trust was dissolved, the previous series of regional monopolies still existed, largely under shared ownership. During the year after dissolution, the shareholders actually reaped a 47 percent capital gain. It took some twenty years for competition to spread widely in the industry.[6]

This early peak of trustbusting immediately set tight future limits, clipping Section 2's wings. In a tortuously worded opinion, Chief Justice White inserted a rule of reason in Standard Oil as a precedent for future cases. Only "bad" trusts were said to violate the true meaning of Section 2. This rule of reason added the "plus" criterion to Section 2, and it placed the burden of proof on the Antitrust Division to prove the abuses.

US Steel.   The Court's failure in 1920 to treat US Steel was a clear economic error. Formed in 1901 by merging twelve steel firms (which had earlier combined 180 separate companies with over 300 plants), US Steel was notoriously inefficient from the outset, and it colluded indirectly with its competitors. Its market share had declined from 65 percent to about 50 percent in 1920. That, to the Court, was enough to indicate that it was a good (if inefficient) trust. A remedy in 1920 would have reintroduced competition to the ". . . sprawling, inert giant . . . ," avoiding the decades of deadening inefficiency and market control that US Steel (finally renamed USX) maintained into the 1970s.[7]

The Second Wave, 1938–1953.   Treatment ceased until 1938, when Alcoa was sued for the monopoly it had held since before 1900. Other cases followed under Thurman Arnold and on until 1952. The decisions on Alcoa in 1945 and United Shoe Machinery in 1953 partly revived Section 2. In doctrine, shares of 60 percent could be treated, though in practice large gaps remained. After 1952, treatment lapsed again.

Alcoa.[8]   Alcoa monopolized aluminum from its beginnings in the 1890s, first by controlling key patents and then by a series of astute actions to prevent new competition. The Antitrust Division sought to show that monopoly could be reduced by antitrust even if it had committed no single clearly abusive action. A prime charge was vertical price squeezes by Alcoa involving the price set for crude aluminum and the prices offered to customers for finished goods.

After a long process of preparation and trial, it was decided in 1945 with an opinion by Judge Learned Hand. Judge Hand rejected the rule of reason as the formal basis, saying that the Sherman Act forbade all monopolies, not just bad ones. Among several ways of defining the market, Judge Hand chose the use of new aluminum ingot as the relevant market, leaving Alcoa with a share of over 90 percent. He also noted incidentally that 60 percent might be a monopoly and that 30 percent surely was not. That remark became the rule of thumb for enforcement, ruling out cases below 60 percent.

Alcoa claimed that monopoly was "thrust upon it" by its excellence. Judge Hand said that Alcoa had not been "wholly inert," and that its whole course of action showed clear efforts to monopolize.

The decision was clear on doctrine, but the actual remedy for Alcoa's monopoly was moderate. Alcoa itself was not touched. New World War II aluminum plants had been built and run by Alcoa for the government, and Alcoa had expected to take them over. Instead they were sold off in 1950 to Kaiser and Reynolds, creating a tight oligopoly that has continued for five decades with little change.

NBC and Radio Broadcasting.   Radio broadcasting had been dominated by NBC, with only CBS as a substantial rival. NBC was forced to divest its Blue Network, which became the basis for ABC. That increased competition markedly, as the resulting three networks dominated television broadcasting into the 1990s.

1945 to 1952.   Then came a dramatic surge, with Section 2 actions toward AT&T, IBM, Du Pont, United Shoe Machinery, Eastman Kodak, American Can, and others. AT&T's vertical monopoly was attacked, presaging the successful divestiture in 1984. IBM's monopoly of tabulating equipment and cards was challenged, in a case that would have averted IBM's easy dominance of computers (discussed in a later subsection). Both cases were scuttled by Eisenhower administration officials.

United Shoe Machinery was held in violation in 1953, even though it now dominated only a small industry. Its market share was high and the plus included systematic price discrimination and a lack of superior efficiency. Yet the remedy was mild: It only limited certain exclusionary actions.

Eastman Kodak's control of film, processing, and cameras was challenged, but in 1954 the suit was settled informally. The company agreed to end its dominance of photofinishing and its tying of film sales and processing, but Kodak's dominance of film continued. By 1995, when the restraints were withdrawn, Kodak still dominated both film and processing.[9]

After 1952, Section 2 actions again languished. In the 1956 Du Pont cellophane decision, the Supreme Court by a 5-to-4 vote chose a broad market definition, embracing all packaging materials. Du Pont's share was held to be only 18 percent.[10] Though the Court soon shifted to drawing markets narrowly, the agencies virtually stopped bringing major Section 2 actions.[11]

The Third Wave, 1968–1982.   Five major cases were started in this period. IBM, AT&T, and Xerox were the three leading dominant firms in the U.S. The three cereals firms tested the tight-oligopoly tacit-collusion problem. The Du Pont titanium dioxide case challenged dominance as it was being created. Private cases against IBM and AT&T also proliferated, but the wave ebbed by 1982, with effects only on AT&T.

IBM.   IBM held substantial monopoly power and had taken aggressive actions toward its seven much-smaller rivals.[12] When the case was dropped in 1982, the range of permissible hard competition by all dominant firms was increased greatly.

After 1954 IBM held over 60 percent of the mainframe computer market, and it used bundling and deep price discounting to attack Control Data Corp. (a more efficient large-computer innovator) and to eliminate RCA (the innovator of computer time sharing) and Scientific Data Systems (a superior innovator in mid-level computers). Price discrimination was both **vertical** among machine types, with planned higher profit margins on the small computers where IBM had its greatest control, and **horizontal** among the various users of each computer model (as IBM sales reps promised free programming and other expensive help in order to capture desirable customers).[13]

After six years of IBM stalling and Antitrust Division difficulties, the trial began in 1975 and ran until 1982. IBM defended itself by (1) claiming a wide market, for all office equipment, (2) denying any predatory pricing, (3) claiming superior innovation and economies of scale, and (4) denying that its high accounting profits (18 percent on assets) reflected its true profitability.[14] Also, IBM's shares were widely held by small and large investors, an important interest group, which feared capital losses from any adverse ruling. IBM's relentless legal resistance was fortified by the prospect of large private damage claims if IBM were held guilty. Also, IBM gained from delay, probably by at least $1 million per day.[15]

Over twenty private suits also were filed by Control Data, Greyhound Corp., Western Union, Transamerica, and others making equipment designed to work with IBM computers. IBM generally lost the market-definition argument, but it successfully claimed that its actions were merely vigorous competition by an innovative leader, not anticompetitive actions by a laggard dominant firm. In fact, IBM by the 1970s had already developed the extensive bureaucratic inertia that was to cripple it in the 1980s, leading to its near-collapse in the early 1990s.

By 1982, the Reagan-appointed Division head, William Baxter, dropped the IBM case just weeks before the trial judge was expected to hold IBM guilty. IBM's delaying tactics had prevailed; it also won all the private cases.

But the cost to IBM was high. By pursuing a legal win obsessively, it averted the very conditions of effective competition that could have made it and the industry more efficient and innovative. "Unsuccessful" cases such as these illustrate the harm from *not* enforcing antitrust firmly enough.

Cereals. In 1972 the FTC charged Kellogg, General Mills, General Foods, and Quaker Oats with a "shared monopoly," seeking to test whether the law covered indirect collusion. The firms were accused of (1) packing the product space by proliferating brands, so as to deter new competition, and (2) jointly taking steps to avoid price competition and package premiums.[16] Lengthy preparations followed, along with intensive lobbying and political protests by the companies. The formal hearings ran from 1976 to 1979.

The case had a firm basis in economics and evidence—the firms were highly profitable, the products were simple, the innovations were not extensive, and there were no important economies of scale. Yet delay succeeded, and in the new conservative setting after 1980 the action was terminated.

Xerox. Xerox was the stock-market darling of the 1960s, propelled by its patent-based monopoly of plain-paper copiers. It developed extremely complex price discrimination (closely similar to IBM's methods) to exploit and protect its monopoly. The discrimination was based on number of runs, the numbers of copies per run, special large-user discounts, leasing machines rather than selling them, and related pricing patterns. Xerox also assembled a thicket of over 2,000 related patents.

Such actions succeeded in keeping Xerox's market share over 90 percent, even against entry by IBM and Kodak. Also, there were few scale economies, a lack of innovation after 1965, and monopoly profits averaging 27 percent on assets during the 1960s. Xerox countered that the true market was for all copying and reproducing, with Xerox holding less than 50 percent by 1973. Xerox also claimed that its scale economies and innovations were large and that its profitability was shrinking.

Unlike IBM, Xerox negotiated a quick settlement by 1975, which opened up some patents. Ironically, by 1976 Xerox was hit by powerful new Japanese competition (Canon and Ricoh) in small copiers. Xerox was quickly recognized to have grown sleepy and mistaken in its innovation and long-run plans—classic dominant-firm ailments. In the 1980s, Xerox settled into a defensive but ineffective mode. By 2000 Xerox's errors had sunk it to bare survival.

AT&T.   The epic exception to the Reagan-Bush freeze on Section 2 came to a climax during 1980 to 1984: the AT&T case. This brought the largest Section 2 divestiture of all time, and it showed that even the world's largest private enterprise—despite its great technological complexity, public esteem, widespread investor reliance, and political influence—could still be required by antitrust to make major structural changes.[17]

The case's after-effects continue to play out, as AT&T and the Baby Bells jockey over access to each other's markets. Moreover, AT&T itself has accepted the brilliance of the divestiture cure, and in 1995 it announced its own second, voluntary split-up. In 2001–02, AT&T again divided itself into parts, and it sold its broadband operation to Comcast.

The case proved that big cases can still succeed both procedurally and economically. Especially where a formerly regulated monopoly is applying vertical leverage to keep its monopoly, Section 2 can work well.

After the 1913 agreement and the 1949–1955 case, the issue of Western Electric was reopened in 1974 with a new suit by the Division. As a fifty-man FCC task-force report (of 1,500 pages) recommended, the division sought to separate Western Electric and possibly divide it into several competing firms within the whole market for telecommunications equipment. The new suit also contemplated separating out the long-lines department, some or all of the Bell operating companies, and Bell Laboratories. True natural monopoly could remain intact, but the Bell system would be prevented from using that advantage to capture other naturally competitive markets. Because the 1984 case succeeded in securing the most extensive (even astounding) divestiture ever attained, it requires a detailed discussion.[18]

It carried forward changes that had been developing for several decades—in new technology, in FCC actions, and in private antitrust suits. AT&T had frequently reached out to enter adjacent markets, ranging from telephone equipment, movies, and microwave transmission to copper scrap recycling. It had come under increasing pressure to let competition into its own domain, however, especially by FCC actions in 1968–1969 and 1977 and by the Supreme Court in 1979 in opening up long distance to competition. Technology now permitted competition in all but the local telephone calling market, where one set of wires and switches was still most efficient. The divestiture of 1984 simply forced AT&T into a new structure reflecting that reality.

Figure 16.1 shows the Bell System as challenged in 1974 to 1981. The case lay largely dormant for three years, but then a new judge (Harold H. Greene) sped it forward. He forced the two sides to agree on obvious points of fact, thereby identifying the main issues for trial. By preventing delay and excessive discovery procedures, Judge Greene forced the trial ahead briskly and brilliantly. After the Division's side was presented, he ruled tentatively that AT&T had probably committed violations. When AT&T's rebuttal case went poorly, AT&T realized that its back was to the wall. It decided that settlement was preferable to conviction (which would have triggered a flood of treble damage claims).[19]

AT&T was given the choice to keep either **all of its local operating companies** or **long-distance and Western Electric.** It chose the latter, thinking that they were more progressive and lucrative than the supposedly slow-growing, capital-intensive, and closely-regulated local firms. Though that choice was praised as

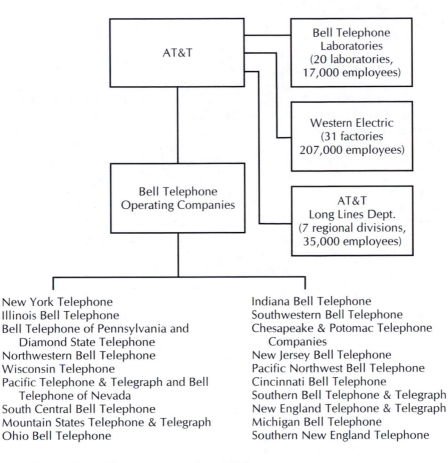

Figure 16.1 The AT&T structure before 1984.

brilliant at the time, it probably was the wrong choice. AT&T had great difficulty adapting to new competition, while the local firms (called Baby Bells) progressed rapidly and gave large capital gains to their shareholders.

The settlement was reached and announced (together with the IBM case withdrawal) in January 1982. After full hearings and some modifications by Judge Greene, the actual divestiture occurred on January 1, 1984.[20]

The main change was to detach the Bell operating companies (BOCs) from AT&T. The basic concept of the settlement identified two parts of the Bell system that needed to be separated: (1) **natural monopolies** (the local operations); and (2) the rest, which were regarded as **naturally competitive** or likely to become so. Dividing them would prevent the abuses of the past, in which the monopolies were used as a base for capturing and controlling other markets.

The twenty-one BOCs were grouped into seven regional firms (Nynex, US West, Bell South, Ameritech, Bell Atlantic, Pacific Telesis, and Southwestern Bell), as shown in figure 16.2. They operated in 164 LATAs ("local access and transport areas"), which covered all metropolitan areas. The regionals were also permitted to sell (but not produce) new equipment to customers, in competition with AT&T

and others, promoting competition in equipment sales. To avoid letting the regionals use their monopoly position to gain advantages in selling equipment, they had to sell through separate subsidiaries.

AT&T during 1984–1996 had two main parts: long-distance service (by AT&T Communications) and all others, including equipment production and marketing and foreign activities (by AT&T Technologies). The old Western Electric was dissolved and merged into four new units under AT&T Technologies. Long-distance service by AT&T covered all transmission among LATAs, so the coverage actually extended to a lot of intrastate calling. AT&T faced competition from MCI, Sprint, and others in long-distance service. It still held 60 percent of that market in 1995, but it has since dwindled below 50 percent.

Two main competitive issues came to a head in the mid-1990s. First, long-distance service seemed stuck with permanent dominance, as AT&T kept a 60-percent share after 1988, and price competition among AT&T, MCI, and Sprint faded. The only cure seemed to be letting the Baby Bells in, but that carried risks that they would use their gatekeeper controls over access to the local networks to sweep AT&T aside. Second, competition in local service might be possible if the Baby Bells' monopolies were opened up to all comers, including AT&T, cable-TV firms, and other cellular and related companies. The onset of new technology might make local service a free-for-all with effective competition, if no player had advantages.

In February 1996, a new Telecommunications Act permitted and promoted just such mutual invasions. But each side could invade the other only after strong competition was established in its own markets. Long distance was quickly approved to enter local markets. But the Baby Bells have fiercely repelled new

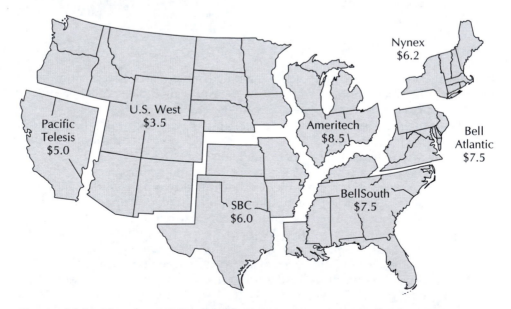

Figure 16.2 The seven Baby Bells (long distance revenues after subtracting local access fees). Source: Adopted from *Wall Street Journal* (February 5, 1996): p. B4.

entry into their local-service markets, and so the FCC and states have only allowed Baby Bells to enter relatively few long-distance markets.

But then telecommunications hit a "meltdown" by 2001. Too many companies had rushed to build optical fiber systems, and wireless phones suddenly boomed. That caused a glut of capacity, which bankrupted many of the new companies and squeezed demand for AT&T, MCI, and others.

The seven Baby Bells merged down to four. First, the FCC allowed Bell Atlantic to take over both Nynex and Continental (the old collection of small independents). When SBC then swallowed up Pacific Telesis and Ameritech, the FCC was caught with no basis for disapproving. The chances for new competition among the Baby Bells were thus sharply reduced. The industry was also swept by other mergers (see below).

In retrospect, the 1984 divestiture worked brilliantly, yielding the classical benefits of increased competition, especially innovation, and giving large gains to shareholders as well as consumers.[21] The old defenses of the Bell monopolies, such as the claims of large vertical economies and so-called "systemic integrity" were exposed as false. The gains from new innovation and higher X-efficiency swamped any possible static- efficiency losses. Natural monopoly had ceased, and the new competitive patterns fitted well the true emerging technology and scope for competition.

The case also disposed of claims that Section 2 actions have grown too large and complex to manage. Instead, a splendid judge proved that perhaps the most complicated sector of all could be assessed clearly at trial and reorganized efficiently by means of massive divestiture. Section 2 and the divestiture remedy were renewed as effective tools for the future.

Aspen Skiing. Against the official stoppage of Section 2 actions, the Supreme Court affirmed in a private case in 1985 that a dominant firm still must avoid deliberate actions to harm its smaller rivals. It dilutes somewhat the new-Chicago-UCLA line adopted by Reagan-Bush officials.

Aspen Skiing held over 80 percent of Aspen area skiing capacity, while Aspen Highlands had the rest. In the late 1970s, Aspen Skiing refused to continue a multi-area ticketing arrangement, thereby freezing its small rival out of most customers. Aspen Skiing offered no reason for the change, simply trying to increase its dominance and profits.

A jury, affirmed on appeal by the Supreme Court, held that Aspen's action violated Section 2. Aspen Skiing had abused its dominant position without offering any saving grace of efficiency or necessity for its action. Such a private case could yield only damages, not structural remedies. It contrasts with the carte blanche, hard competition view in IBM's case outcomes. Dominant firms do not, after all, have free rein to exploit all advantages over small rivals.

Eastman Kodak and Aftermarkets. In a lesser area, the Supreme Court's Eastman Kodak decision in 1992 resisted efforts by dominant firms to expand their power by capturing adjacent markets. Kodak had taken over the "aftermarkets" for the repair and parts for its main equipment. It claimed that free-market theory proved that it could not use "leverage" in capturing the aftermarkets. But the Court held that abusive leverage was a danger if there were market imperfections.[22]

Scores of other dominant firms had also tried to capture the aftermarkets for their products. This moderate decision slowed that process, but didn't stop it. It only gave competitors a chance to prove their case, which was still difficult to do.

Microsoft. Microsoft inevitably drew a major Section 2 case in the 1990s for possible monopolization.[23] As we saw in chapter 13, Microsoft was the country's leading entrenched industrial near-monopoly. Its market share had been over 85 percent for more than a decade, and it had inflicted a series of slashing actions that harmed competitors.

Though Microsoft's products were generally regarded as mediocre—as we've discussed earlier—it seemed to be extending its dominance into adjacent markets, especially some of the most interesting emerging new markets. Microsoft defended its actions as merely "tough but fair competition." The antitrust case tested whether instead Microsoft had abused its dominant position and suppressed competition.

After earlier tentative cases that amounted to little, the Division brought a major case in 1998.[24] Microsoft fought fiercely, through litigation, lobbying, and public relations. The case went to trial in the fall of 1999, under an independent-minded judge, Thomas Penfield Jackson. The main charge was that Microsoft had abused its dominance by taking predatory actions against Netscape and the Java language. Microsoft gave its web browser, Internet Explorer, away for free, virtually killing Netscape.[25]

When Microsoft's lawyers were outclassed at the trial and Judge Jackson held Microsoft in violation, it looked like Microsoft would follow Standard Oil. It had many of the marks of a Section 2 loser: poor lawyering; a groundswell of public resentment against a seemingly abusive monopoly; vast riches amassed by William Gates and his founding colleagues, who still closely controlled the company; a consensus on Wall Street that Microsoft might do better by being divided into parts; and an effective, fearless judge.

On appeal, Microsoft's violation was confirmed, but the Appeals Court rejected divestiture as a remedy.[26] Settlement discussions under the Bush administration led to a weak agreement. It provided only minor concessions by Microsoft. Eight of the nineteen states suing Microsoft tried for stricter limits, but a new judge affirmed the settlement.

Merely by delaying, Microsoft hardened its claim—which is always asserted by defendants—that the case had grown stale and irrelevant. Microsoft yielded nothing, and it won. It then seemed poised to spread its control into many adjacent markets.[27]

In perspective, this case seemed to be strangely ambitious for Division officials that were otherwise quite lax on mergers, predatory pricing, and other matters. The effort seemed merely symbolic, trying to look "tough" while never expecting any real result.

3. LESSONS OF SECTION 2 ACTIONS TOWARD DOMINANCE

Coverage. Section 2 cases have eventually covered many of the most prominent, acute instances of dominance. The suits, threats of suits, and settlements have abated many cases of dominance. Also, the rate of erosion of dominance has risen since 1960, making Section 2 less necessary for most situations.

Yields. The cases have yielded large benefits for their costs. One recent set of estimates places the benefit-cost ratio at 67 for the Standard Oil (1911) case, down to 5 for the United Shoe Machinery (1953) case.[28] The ratio for AT&T (1984) would also probably be very high, reversing the downward trend in yields. The highest yields have come with major structural changes.

Lags. Section 2 cases have generally lagged at least twenty years behind the monopolizing. No monopoly has been intercepted during its formation, and no case has recovered the monopoly gains from the offenders. In effect, there has been full amnesty for monopolizers.

Speed? As AT&T showed, well-managed Section 2 treatments can be reasonably swift. A firm facing a strong case may be induced to accept a fair settlement before the trial is completed (or even before it begins). Under good handling, the trial of the typical case might begin within three years of initiating; action and settlement might come soon after. Moreover, the firms' actions may be self-modified as soon as there is serious prospect of filing suit. A robust Section 2 policy could discourage the emergence of nonsuperior positions of dominance.

Strategic Pricing. A number of the cases have relied on strategic price discrimination as a sign of monopoly intent and abuse. The early IBM decision cited price discrimination in tabulating cards as a monopolizing action. The United Shoe Machinery decision treated the discrimination as a key anticompetitive process. The IBM case placed discrimination at center stage, and the FTC case against Xerox also cited it as important. Therefore the case decisions have accepted the central monopolizing role that strategic discrimination can play.

Defendants answer that they are merely meeting competition where it is strongest, and that is true. They inherently attune their pricing to varying pressures. As chapter 11 noted, however, that approach inherently suppresses competition, and the courts have recognized that effect. The 1975 Areeda-Turner argument set a narrower standard: that competition was harmed only if price went below cost. Earlier cases were broader.

4. POSSIBLE FUTURE CANDIDATES

Earlier chapters (3, 9, and 13) have noted the leading current dominant firms. They include some recent cases such as Microsoft and Ticketmaster; some formerly regulated monopolies such as airlines, local telephone service, and certain parts of electricity; and some old instances such as hundreds of local newspapers, and Anheuser-Busch in beer. Still others may come from new horizontal mergers, such as recently have been permitted in scores of industries including drugs, entertainment, health care, and banking.

For many of these situations, Section 2 has already been attempted (Kodak, telephone service) or is not easily adapted (newspapers, electricity). Other methods, including legislation (e.g., for telecommunications) may be needed, and a tightening of merger restraints could be important. Possibly, Section 2 has accomplished its main purposes by treating many past cases of dominance.

There are always new, emerging dominant situations, however, such as Microsoft, Intel, Ticketmaster, and parts of health care. Antitrust may have a crucial role to play by using the threat of Section 2 to prevent exclusions. Used astutely, Section 2 can still help to avert and ease the dominance problem.

II. TOWARD MERGERS

Mergers often have two negative effects, as chapter 6 showed: they may reduce competition, and they may cause turmoil and confusion rather than efficiencies and synergy. Antitrust policy should generally be strict on horizontal mergers, liberal toward vertical mergers, and largely inactive toward conglomerate mergers. Also, policy officials should be skeptical about companies' claims that mergers will yield efficiencies.

Merger policies developed slowly. After 1914, the Clayton Act's Section 7 forbade mergers that would reduce competition. But there was a large technical loophole permitting mergers, including many large horizontal mergers. Nevertheless, after 1920 many dominant firms prudently avoided big horizontal mergers. Finally, in 1950 the Celler-Kefauver Act plugged the loophole, and during 1958-1966 the Antitrust Division set a strict policy by several landmark cases.

In 1968 the Division issued Merger Guidelines, which codified the tight precedents that the Supreme Court just set. The Division, like the Supreme Court, regarded claims of merger efficiencies as unreliable. Instead, as in the 1950 law itself, the policy stopped mergers, which would "substantially reduce competition." Even when efficiencies might be considered, only the **net economies** were relevant (recall chapter 6).

After 1970, restraints were loosened moderately, and Reagan officials in 1982 issued new guidelines that abandoned most constraints and changed the methods. These guidelines actually set the new policies, rather than codifying the Supreme Court's precedents. Efficiency claims were now allowed. This radical shift opened the floodgates, and it encouraged the U.S. merger booms during the 1980s and 1990s.[29]

In 1992 the Division revised the Guidelines, but made them confusing and permissive.[30] Its "improved" use of "new-IO theory" had the effect of removing clear and important factors that could be measured. Instead, policy officials had to consider vague possibilities and unknowable "factors."

At least the policies can now be timely. Before 1976, the agencies had to scramble to discover and pursue mergers that might reduce competition. The 1976 Hart-Rodino Act required merging firms to prenotify the agencies, provide information as requested, and await approval. It also encouraged firms to discuss their mergers with the agencies in advance, seeking ways to adjust the companies so as to avoid legal challenges. The adjustments are often substantial.[31]

Also, certain technical improvements in defining markets and estimating market power are evolving, though they are still debatable.[32] In any event, the actual policies often proceed informally and privately, as well as by formal suits and trials.

1. HORIZONTAL MERGERS

From 1958 to 1966, the Warren Court tightened limits on horizontal mergers, eventually setting the restraints at 4 percent plus 4 percent in the Von's Grocery case. The tightness applied to markets where concentration was rising; claims of economies were not taken seriously, because internal growth could achieve them.

Bethlehem-Youngstown (1958). Bethlehem Steel Corporation, the second largest steel company, proposed in 1956 to merge with Youngstown Sheet & Tube Company, the sixth largest. Bethlehem was mainly an east coast firm, while Youngstown operated mainly in the midwest. Bethlehem portrayed the proposed merger as a geographic extension merger between two regionally separate firms that were not actual competitors. Bethlehem also denied that it was a potential competitor; it expressly said it would not enter the midwest market. Besides, it claimed, the merged firm would be better able to compete against the leading firm, US Steel.

The Antitrust Division proved that instead the two merger partners were already competing in many regional product markets. The merger was held to violate Clayton Section 7, and the decision was not appealed.[33] Two years later, Bethlehem *did* build a new plant near Chicago, reinforcing the wisdom of treating self-interested claims skeptically.

In its Brown Shoe (1962) and Philadelphia National Bank (1963) decisions, the Court developed tight limits. In 1966 the Von's Grocery decision tightened them to the current limit: to 4 percent plus 4 percent.[34] Von's involved the third and sixth largest grocery chains in Los Angeles, each of which held about 4 percent of the city's grocery trade. Though the decision was strict, it did not block any significant economies of scale nor cause economic harm. There has been no evidence that efficient mergers were stopped.

General Dynamics (1973). A merger among firms producing coal in and near Illinois raised the concentration of production in that region (in the top four firms from 43 to 63 percent during 1957–1967). The Supreme Court's decision in 1973 cleared the merger on two grounds.[35] First, the relevant market was held to be much broader than the Division alleged. This loosened the precedent that any significant market would demonstrate a violation. Second, the Court declared that other facts about the industry must also be considered in judging the competitive effect. Thus the simple clarity of the 1960s precedents was diluted, and the standard of proof for conviction was raised. The shift in policy was not sharp, since the changes were of degree rather than of kind: Roughly the four plus four percent rule went to seven plus seven percent.

The treatment of horizontal mergers was perforated by various exceptional cases.[36] Some failing-firm mergers were also permitted.

After 1980. Reagan officials soon issued complicated new merger guidelines, which changed policy rather than merely summarizing it. The SNIPP approach to market definition was announced, and HHI replaced concentration ratios (recall chapter 3). These were vague methods and empty indexes in place of clear standards. The allowance of efficiency claims also made evaluation more difficult.

Restraints on horizontal mergers soon virtually ended.[37] For example, General Motors and Toyota proposed a joint venture in 1983 to produce cars in California. The two firms could be regarded as the two largest competitors in the combined Japanese-American market or, for that matter, in a worldwide market. A significant reduction of direct competition was likely. Yet the FTC permitted the link on grounds that it would create added capacity and strengthen GM's ability to compete. In fact, the claims—and the FTC—were wrong: "The demonstrable benefits of the joint venture have been slight. . . ."[38]

In 1983–1984, two steel mergers stretched the limits still further. First, fourth-ranked Republic Steel proposed merging with third-ranked Jones & Laughlin (owned by LTV Corp.). Their combined share of total U.S. production would be as high as 50 percent in important specific steel markets, such as stainless steel and terne plate. Moreover, there were international restrictive agreements that impeded import competition into the U.S.

Nonetheless, the Republic-J&L merger was permitted. Almost immediately the rosy promises were belied, and the merged firm soon sank into bankruptcy. Reagan officials once again were gullible about self-interested claims of merger efficiencies.

From 1985 to 1988 several major airlines merged, increasing the dominance at many fortress hubs (recall chapter 14). The mergers were permitted by officials at the Department of Transportation, who had temporary responsibility for the industry and who believed the claims of contestability theory. Although the Antitrust Division opposed two of the mergers, they were allowed to occur.

A key policy element was the claim that any rival's objection to a merger should be ignored as the strictly self-interested pleadings of an inferior rival. Indeed, in catch-22 logic, the stronger the rival's complaint, the larger the merger's true efficiencies must be, proving that the rival was not only wrong but inferior. That of course reflected the rosy view that markets are perfect and that dominance reflects only superiority. That claim was baseless, however, if the market contained imperfections.[39]

The 1980s and 1990s merger booms created a number of high market shares, and no clear lines have been drawn. Therefore no useful landmark cases exist. Even under the mildly stricter Bush and Clinton policies, there appear to be no reliable, consistent constraints on mergers. Meanwhile, many mergers have probably reduced efficiency.

The 1992 Guidelines.[40] The 1982 guidelines had ignored the problem of market dominance, looking only at collusion. The 1992 guidelines addressed that problem, but it shifted policy toward a fixation on the peripheral features of potential entry and barriers. As we noted, it also blurred and confused the criteria for decisions. Market shares and concentration were essentially rejected as criteria. Though the HHI threshold of 2,000 was still to be considered, the Guidelines ignored that dominant market shares automatically violated the 2,000 level.

The Guidelines helped to reduce merger strictness even more, helping to fuel the explosive 1990s merger wave, with its many dominance-creating mergers (recall chapter 6). Some mergers were blocked. One between Staples and Office Max would have created high dominance in the chain-store office-supplies market. Another between MCI and Sprint would have created a 40% market share in long-distance telephone service and over 50% in Internet backbone services.[41] The Division also opposed a proposed merger of the two satellite companies, Echo-Star and DirecTV.[42] They would have held no less than 90 percent of satellite service, which was distinct from cable TV and other forms of connection. But the Division accepted a merger between the Carnival and Princess cruise companies in 2002. Carnival increased its first-ranked market share from 32 percent to 44 percent.[43]

Weak merger policies in the 1990s permitted scores of major mergers that created dominant market shares in a wide range of industries, from health care and drugs to banking, accounting, and cable TV.

Military Supplies Mergers. As U.S. weapons-procurement budgets receded after 1985, the shrinkage in the demand for weapons stirred a wave of horizontal mergers.[44] The rationale was that the room for competition had declined, making mergers inevitable. The logic was suitable for such large-economies-of-scale industries such as submarine building and aircraft. In many other markets the facts were debatable. But under Pentagon and political pressure, antitrust officials retreated in 1995, accepting many two-firm and one-firm outcomes. The re-expansion of military spending after 2001 encountered many firms with much more market power.

Health care firms also merged extensively after 1992, amid plans for health care reforms. Here too antitrust officials have been forced to set lenient policies for mergers among hospitals, HMOs, drug firms, and related units.

2. VERTICAL MERGERS

The current economic consensus is that vertical mergers reduce competition only when market shares are substantial (new-Chicago economists deny that *any* reduction will occur). Before 1970 some Warren-Court decisions reached down to small shares, but after 1980 Reagan officials stopped all vertical-merger cases.[45] No important vertical merger cases have been brought as of 2003.

Vertical merger policy has not had a steady evolution or rich set of precedents. Most cases present unique features, and claimed economies are often genuine. The Yellow Cab decision in 1947, Paramount in 1948, and A&P in 1949 established that vertical integration could not be used to foreclose competition at either level. Specific practices had been adduced in these cases; no general rule against vertical integration per se was applied. Subsequently, the Warren Court drew closer limits, saying that a large rise in vertical integration will per se foreclose competition and raise entry barriers. It is a fact that integrated firms usually avoid buying from independent suppliers.

Du Pont-General Motors (1957). The case was filed in 1949, alleging that Du Pont's holding of GM stock gave it preference in the market for automobile fabrics and finishes. GM's purchases comprised over half of the fabrics and finishes markets; Du Pont's sales to GM were about 30 percent of the market, a substantial share. The vertical tie had controlled GM's purchases, limiting Du Pont's competitors' ability to compete.[46] Vertical integration had only partially occurred, and the decision set a moderate limit on the market shares held by the firms.

Brown Shoe (1962). The Brown Shoe case had vertical aspects too. Brown made shoes and Kinney sold shoes. The Court looked less at the small market shares than at Brown's likely policy of requiring Kinney to carry Brown shoes, which would foreclose competition in a market that already had rising concentration. Before the merger, Kinney bought no shoes from Brown. Soon after, Brown had become Kinney's largest outside supplier, with 8 percent of Kinney's purchases. Despite the small shares, the merger was enjoined.

3. CONGLOMERATE MERGERS

Any policy toward conglomerate mergers must take place within a setting where many diversified firms have long existed in a wide array of markets (recall chapter 12). New conglomerates have often been corporate raiders (or trivial houses of cards). An efficient merger policy should reap the efficiency-inducing effects of conglomerate mergers while filtering out the possible reductions in competition.

Policy Criteria.   There were sharp turns in policy as the wave of mergers mounted in the 1960s. In 1969, the Antitrust Division made a broad-scale attack on mergers by new conglomerate firms, with LTV and ITT as main targets. This attack helped to stop the conglomerate-merger wave, but the attack was compromised before reaching the Supreme Court for a clear decision on its merits.

Because many of the 1960s mergers fell apart in the 1970s, the market-power effects of the mergers were shown to be probably weak or absent in most cases. Yet the agencies did explore various policy lines, including the danger of reciprocity, the reduction of potential entry, the unfair advantages that a giant firm's branch might acquire, and the toehold doctrine.

FTC v. Procter & Gamble (1967).   This controversial case offers striking details. When Procter & Gamble bought Clorox Chemical Company in 1958, P & G became the country's largest household-products firm. It did not sell bleach, but it had been planning to enter the bleach business. Some of its products were related to bleach, and P & G management had considered making a direct entry by building a new factory to produce bleach before deciding to enter the market by buying out the Clorox Company instead. Clorox itself was the dominant bleach firm, with a long-established share of 49 percent of the national market. Clorox's share in the Mid-Atlantic region was as high as 71 percent, compared to 15 percent for Purex, the next largest bleach producer.

The merger would clearly have subtracted a leading new potential entrant from the bleach market: P & G itself. That would have reduced competition and, by itself, should have been enough to lead the FTC to stop the merger. Yet the FTC (later affirmed by the Supreme Court) instead cited P & G's advertising advantages as the main grounds for preventing the merger.

The FTC and the Court stressed that P & G would be able to give Clorox overwhelming advantages in advertising and distributing its bleach. P & G was the nation's largest advertiser (spending over $175 million on advertising in 1967), and its discounts and market power were likely to entrench Clorox further as the dominant bleach firm.

If instead P & G had made a toehold acquisition of a small bleach company (say, Purex or smaller), that would probably have promoted competition, not threatened it. The loss of a potential competitor would have been more than offset by the increase in the small firm's ability to compete vigorously.

Since 1980, no cases against conglomerate mergers have been filed. One effect has been the flood of conglomerate mergers in the 1980s and 1990s, many causing inefficiencies and disorder.

III. TOWARD PRICE FIXING AND OTHER ACTIONS

1. PRICE FIXING

Price fixing is a per se violation: You did it, you're guilty. The agencies may catch only a small part of the price fixing that goes on in oligopoly markets. Even so, the range of cases and convictions is remarkably wide (recall chapter 11). In one six-month period, cases in the biweekly *Antitrust and Trade Regulation Report* (possibly in your college library) included the following: Korean wigs, ready-mix concrete, Hawaii package tours, paper labels, timber, Utah egg dealers, steel products, construction firms, bakeries in El Paso, liquid asphalt, plumbing supplies, and scores of others.

U.S. v. Addyston Pipe and Steel Company (1899).[47]   This landmark case dealt with a modest situation; six producers of cast-iron pipe in the region including Ohio and Pennsylvania had divided up their markets and operated a bidding ring. To prevent competition, they arranged to rotate the contracts among themselves, designating who would enter the lowest bid on each contract. Such a bidding ring ensures cooperation among sellers and gives buyers no real choice. Though the six firms held less than half of the markets, their price fixing was convicted as illegal per se by William H. Taft, then an Ohio judge and later a trust-busting president. Convicted, the firms soon merged and began to fix their prices internally and legally.

The flat prohibition of price fixing was followed for twenty years, with decisions against collusive bidding by purchasers of livestock, exclusion of competing railways from a terminal, the use of patent licenses to fix the prices of bathtubs, and the operation of a boycott by retail lumber dealers.

Other Landmark Cases.   In 1927 the Trenton Potteries decision reaffirmed the per se rule.[48] Firms producing 80 percent of vitreous enamel bathroom fixtures (bathtubs, sinks) had agreed to fix prices and to sell exclusively through jobbers. The Court refused to accept the defendant's claims that the prices fixed were reasonable.

The final landmark decision came in 1940 in the Socony-Vacuum case.[49] Major oil firms in ten Midwestern states arranged a scheme for avoiding periodic price cuts on excess oil. They did not control prices completely, and they urged in their defense that stabilizing prices was socially beneficial. Justice Douglas's opinion put the per se rule clearly and flatly:

> Any conspiracy which tampers with price structures is engaged in an unlawful activity. Even though the members of the price-fixing group were in no position to control the market, to the extent that they raised, lowered, or stabilized prices they would be directly interfering with the free play of market forces. The Act places all such schemes beyond the pale.

Even if agreements affected only a minor portion of the market, they were forbidden; any manipulation of prices, whatever its purpose, was against the law.

In 1960, sixty-one years after *Addyston* made price fixing flatly illegal, the electrical equipment conspiracy case showed that price fixing had been a way of life for decades in seven major markets for heavy electrical equipment (generators, transformers, switch gear); recall chapter 11.[50] There were fines and large damage suits by customers, and some officials served brief jail sentences.

A recent case illustrates the strictness. The five largest music labels and three national retailers reached settlement in the United States in 2002, in a case brought by 40 states alleging price fixing.[51]

These cases illustrate two features of policy toward price fixing. First, the agency simply had to show that price fixing occurred, not that its effects were bad. A normative evaluation would have required endless rummaging among debatable opinions. Second, the treble damage claims triggered by the cases provided the real economic punishment. This is still true for many cases.

The flat rule against price fixing and related devices is probably efficient. It avoids normative evaluations of each situation. Conceivably, this victimizes a few price-fixing schemes that do provide more social benefits than costs. Yet such good instances are probably rare. Moreover, many industries have managed to get themselves exempted from antitrust. Such exemptions may nicely take care of any "good" price-fixing cases.

For comparison, price-fixing may be more common in Europe, and it too draws big fines. The European Union fined seven Austrian banks $117 million in 2002 for violations that occurred from 1995 to 1998.[52] "The banks' chief executive officers met regularly at Vienna's Bristol hotel to exchange confidential information and coordinate rates and fees. The executives established a network of cartel committees that covered the whole of Austria." Nintendo paid $147 million in a price-fixing fine for colluding to set different prices in European countries.[53]

Tacit Collusion.   Policy is not so clear-cut toward other kinds of cooperative activities that are less explicit and tangible. Tacit collusion among tight oligopolists has proved especially hard to resolve. It could come under Section 1, as an indirect form of conspiracy, or under Section 2, as a shared monopoly. So long as it is strictly tacit, it is now virtually exempt from treatment.

From 1939 to 1946, the Court moved to define *conscious parallelism* as being equivalent to explicit collusion, where the effect was the same. The landmark case was American Tobacco (1946), in which the three leading cigarette firms were convicted under Section 1.[54] In delivered-pricing systems (1948)[55] and booking of movies (1950),[56] the Court drew the line against tacit collusion even more tightly. These convictions, however, were not followed by basic remedies. The structure and habits remained. After 1952, the Court and the FTC changed tack and rejected parallelism as a proof of conspiracy.

Despite calls for action, tacit collusion has been mostly ignored. Only extreme degrees of tacit collusion have stirred action; the General Electric-Westinghouse (1976) case was noted in chapter 11. In that case, there was no trial, conviction, penalty, or precedent. In the FTC's cereals case (discussed in chapter 14), the action failed.

2.   EXEMPTIONS

The trend has been to extend antitrust into formerly exempt sectors, such as regulated utilities, the professions, and sports (noted in chapter 13 and 14).[57] A leading sports case during 1981–1984 concerned collegiate football and television; it broke the NCAA's monopoly in 1984. Before then, the NCAA tightly controlled the broadcasting of games, and coverage was sparse. After the NCAA lost in 1984, coverage quickly became the now familiar virtual nonstop flood of games.

The NCAA had controlled all televising of games involving its 276 Division I colleges, as well as 574 others. Complex rules limited the volume of games broadcast (in good monopoly style), and they broadened coverage to include at least eighty-two member teams within each two-year period. Top teams wanted more exposure and revenues, so five major conferences banded together in the College Football Association (CFA) after some jockeying, and sued in 1981 to break the NCAA's monopoly.[58]

3. VERTICAL PRICE FIXING: RESALE PRICE MAINTENANCE

Resale price maintenance (RPM) was made unenforceable in 1975 after a short campaign that stirred virtually no resistance. Producers could print prices on their products as before, but now they could not legally force retailers to avoid discounting below those prices (nor could retailers band together to make the producer enforce the retail price fixing). In the 1980s, new-Chicago advocates and Reagan officials tried to make RPM enforceable after all, using the free-rider argument (recall chapter 11).

That effort failed in the 1983 Spray-Rite case, but it gained ground in the 1988 Sharp decision. Sharp Electronics had terminated a price-cutting dealer after the other dealer complained. Supreme Court Justice Scalia's majority opinion assumed that collusion is fragile. It applied a rule of reason; the plaintiff must show that RPM actually raised prices. The minority termed the action "a naked agreement to terminate a dealer because of price cutting," therefore a per se violation.[59]

Control of Aftermarkets for Service and Parts. In the 1990s a new topic arose, involving efforts by dominant firms to reach forward vertically to control the related markets for parts and repairs of their products. The Supreme Court saw some merit in a claim that Eastman Kodak tried to exclude other firms from servicing its equipment.[60] Those aftermarkets are lucrative, because Kodak (like many sellers of complex equipment) sets high discriminatory prices so as to harvest large profits from customers once they are locked in as committed users of the equipment. The customer's switching costs may be very high—retraining its staff, reorganizing its production, etc. Therefore it's too costly to react to Kodak's high service prices by switching to other equipment.

This is normal price discrimination, with the equipment-maker trying to use leverage from the equipment market to increase its position and profits in the service-and-parts markets.[61] Efforts of this sort are often routine and harmless, unless there is dominance in equipment along with high switching costs. The Kodak case stirred many other suits in similar situations, but the cases move slowly and the issues are unresolved so far. The cases seek to reinvigorate private-plaintiff actions against possible abuses by dominant firms.

Predatory Pricing. Recall from chapter 10 that anticompetitive predation involves diminished pricing now in expectation of recouping larger profits later. New-Chicagoans say that it is rarely a rational action, and so it rarely happens. Others note that a too-low price can have multiple impacts through signaling and that pinpoint discriminatory pricing can have sharp effects at minimal cost to the predator. More broadly, dominant-firm selective pricing is anticompetitive.

The Areeda-Turner price-not-below-marginal-cost test has been widely accepted in the courts since 1975. An even stricter line was set in 1986 in the Matsushita case.[62] As chapter 10 noted, the Court was willing to acquit Japanese firms of under pricing television sets in the United States by theory alone; predation was simply not likely to be rational. Related logic applied in the Brown & Williams case in 1993 involving generic cigarettes.[63] Though Brown & Williams had set prices below costs, the likelihood of successful recoupment was low because of the market's complex oligopoly conditions. Moreover, the impacts on the plaintiff had not been fatal. Therefore, the Court speculated, competition had not been harmed.

The precedent is virtually straight new-Chicago economics. Any victim of anticompetitive actions must meet strict burdens of proof in showing below-cost pricing *and* later recoupment *and* prove a large harmful impact on itself.

4. PRIVATE CASES

With treble-damages incentives, private plaintiffs pursue about 500 new cases per year, as noted in chapter 15. They often supplement public-agency cases.

A typical recent instance involved the Archer-Daniels-Midland (ADM) Company, which was widely reported in 1995 to have led a price-fixing ring in three markets totaling over $4.5 billion in sales: in fructose (a sweetener in soft drinks), lysine (a nutritional supplement for hogs and chickens), and citric acid (a flavoring agent). Even before its biggest customers (Coca-Cola and PepsiCo) filed claims, over seventy other companies had sued ADM by November 1995.[64]

Because the FBI apparently had detailed proof of the conspiracy from Mark E. Whitacre, an ADM official, the private plaintiffs expected to base their claims on strong evidence of ADM's guilt, as shown in the Antitrust Division's case. Against that, as is normal in such cases, ADM's counterstrategy was to close that path by denying everything, waging a relentless legal war, and trying to settle the case (on a nolo contendere basis, without admitting guilt), before it reached a decision. If ADM succeeded in that, then the private plaintiffs would face a much harder task: to mount their own cases, gather evidence, and prove ADM's actual guilt. Though such cases can have a big impact, most private cases are fragile and little more than minor nuisances.

IV. POLICY IMBALANCE?

Evidently antitrust policy is now rather strict toward price fixing, lenient toward horizontal mergers, and virtually nil toward existing concentration. Thus a firm with a 75-percent market share (e.g., Kodak, Campbell Soup, Ticketmaster, newspapers, Yellow Pages) is permitted to continue untouched, fixing prices pretty much as it pleases over its 75 percent of the market. Meanwhile other firms usually are not permitted to merge to acquire more than 40 percent of the market. Nor may they cooperate to fix prices in *any* part of the market.

This imbalance does not appear to fit research knowledge, as summarized in this volume. The imbalance tends to preserve the concentration; once it is formed, market power is largely safe from public action.

Questions For Review

1. Section 2 of the Sherman Act prohibits monopoly. Does this mean only pure monopoly? If not, how far down the scale of market share should Section 2 be applied: 70 percent, 55 percent, 40 percent?

2. The Reagan administration stopped bringing new Section 2 actions in the 1980s. Was this wise, in your view? If not, which cases are good candidates?

3. Describe the varying standards for bringing Section 2, Section 1, and horizontal-merger cases. Is there a gap among these standards that makes antitrust imbalanced?

4. If there is a gap, does it merely reflect the uncertainties in knowledge about market power's effects?

5. Assess the main benefits and costs of the AT&T divestiture case.

6. What are the correct limits on horizontal mergers, in light of international trade?

7. Should antitrust officials avoid all cases against vertical mergers?

8. Is a per se rule against price fixing a sound policy?

9. Discuss a real market where RPM might be justifiable, explaining the costs and benefits.

Endnotes

[1] Of course you can keep current with ongoing antitrust developments by using the *Antitrust and Trade Regulation Reporter* and *Trade Regulation Reports*. Also the *Antitrust Bulletin* covers changing ideas and cases.

[2] A rationale for stricter enforcement is offered in Walter Adams and James W. Brock, "Revitalizing a Structural Antitrust Policy," *Antitrust Bulletin* 39 (Spring 1994): pp. 2235–71; for a more minimalist view, see Oliver E. Williamson, "Delimiting Antitrust," a chapter in Harry First, Eleanor M. Fox, and Robert Pitofsky, eds., *Revitalizing Antitrust in Its Second Century* (New York: Quorum, 1991), pp. 210–45.

[3] *Standard Oil Co. of N.J. v., U.S.*, 221 U.S. 1; and *U.S. v. American Tobacco Co.*, 221 U.S. 106.

[4] *U.S. v. US Steel Corp.* 251, U.S. 417.

[5] *U.S. v. International Harvester Co.*, 274 U.S. 693, 708.

[6] See George W. Stocking, *The Oil Industry and the Competitive System* (Boston: Houghton Mifflin, 1925); and Simon Whitney, *Antitrust Policies*, 2 vols. (New York: Twentieth Century Fund, 1958).

[7] See Donald O. Parsons and Edward J. Ray, "The United States Steel Consolidation: The Creation of Market Control," *Journal of Law and Economics* 18 (April 1975): pp. 181–220; Whitney, *Antitrust Policies*; and Walter Adams and Joel B. Dirlam, "Steel Imports and Vertical Oligopoly Power," *American Economic Review* 54 (September 1964): pp. 626–55.

[8] *U.S. v. Aluminum Co. of America*, 148 F. 2d 416. See Merton J. Peck, *Competition in the Aluminum Industry* (Cambridge: Harvard University Press, 1961).

[9] See Wendy Bonds, "Kodak is Freed From Restraints on Marketing," *Wall Street Journal* (November 8, 1995): p. A4. "Kodak owns the nation's largest wholesale photofinisher—Qualex Inc.—which commands over 70% of the wholesale market and 30% of the entire photofinishing market. Wholesale photofinishers develop pictures for mass retailers such as K-Mart Corp. Kodak's ability now to include photofinishing costs in its film prices could boost its dominance in this market even more."

[10] *U.S. v. Du Pont*, 118 F. Supp. 41.

[11] In 1958 United Fruit Company agreed under pressure to end its old banana monopoly by creating from its assets a firm capable of handling 35 percent of the market by 1970. Thus encouraged, Castle & Cook and Del Monte entered the market strongly after 1964. By 1973, United Fruit (now United Brands) no longer led, and it had shifted mainly into other lines. In another modest case, Grinnell Corporation was convicted in 1966 for monopolizing the market in "accredited central station protective systems," but the market was small and the doctrine was not new.

[12] See Gerald Brock, *The U.S. Computer Industry* (Cambridge, MA: Ballinger Press, 1975); Richard T. DeLamarter, *Big Blue: IBM's Use and Abuse of Power* (New York: Dodd, Mead, 1986); and William G. Shepherd, *Market Power and Economic Welfare* (New York: Random House, 1970), chapter 15, for detailed accounts of IBM's strategic and related actions. For a defense of IBM, see Franklin M. Fisher, John J. McGowan, and Joen E. Greenwood, *Folded, Spindled and Mutilated: Economic Analysis and U.S. v. IBM* (Cambridge: MIT Press, 1983).

[13] The author was a principal originator of the economic heart of the case. See also William G. Shepherd, "Antitrust Repelled, Inefficiency Endured: Lessons of IBM and General Motors for Future Antitrust Policies," *Antitrust Bulletin* (Spring 1994): pp. 203–34. On the merits of the case, IBM's own chairman, Thomas J. Watson, Jr., admitted in his memoirs that IBM's innovations had lagged in the 1960s and IBM's actions had probably violated the law.

[14] Franklin Fisher was IBM's lead economic expert; the Fisher, McGowan, and Greenwood book, *Folded, Spindled and Mutilated*, sums up his antitrust defense.

[15] IBM's profits were about $1.7 billion yearly at the time. If only one-fourth were at stake under Section 2, then IBM's gain from delay was over $1 million per day.

[16] F. M. Scherer, "The Breakfast Cereal Industry," a chapter in Walter Adams, ed., *The Structure of American Industry*, 6th ed. (New York: Macmillan, 1982), pp. 191–217; and Richard Schmalensee, "Entry Deterrence in the Ready-to-Eat Cereal Industry," *Bell Journal of Economics* 9 (Autumn 1978): pp. 305–27.

[17] See the sources in chapter 13, and also Roger G. Noll and Bruce M. Owen, "The Anticompetitive Uses of Regulation: *United States v. AT&T*," a chapter in John E. Kwoka, Jr. and Lawrence J. White, eds., *The Antitrust Revolution*, 2nd ed. (New York: HarperCollins, 1994).

[18] Among many sources on the topic, see David S. Evans, ed., *Breaking up Bell: Essays on Industrial Organization and Regulation* (New York: North Holland, 1983), for lucid analysis supporting the Antitrust Division's case. On the other side, see William W. Sharkey, *The Theory of Natural Monopoly* (Cambridge: Cambridge University Press, 1982). On the aftermath, see Robert W. Crandall, *After the Breakup: U.S. Telecommunications in a More Competitive Era* (Washington, DC: Brookings Institution, 1991). On the rationale for the divestiture, see Timothy J. Brennan, "Why Regulated Firms Should Be Kept out of Regulated Markets: Understanding the Divestiture in *United States v. AT&T*," *Antitrust Bulletin* 32 (Fall 1987): pp. 741–91. Another excellent source is Peter Temin, *The Fall of the Bell System* (New York: Cambridge University Press, 1987).

[19] In a striking contrast with IBM's behavior, AT&T's Chairman Charles Brown took a far-sighted view, recognizing the possible benefits of competition. IBM officials instead were strictly combative. The subsequent gains for AT&T shareholders and large losses for IBM shareholders have confirmed the wisdom of Brown's stance.

[20] On the aftermath, see Crandall, *After the Breakup*; and Barry G. Cole, ed., *After the Breakup: Assessing the New Post-AT&T-Divestiture Era* (New York: Columbia University Press, 1991).

[21] Perhaps the ultimate praise came in the *Wall Street Journal* itself; see Bob Davis, "AT&T's Latest Moves Vindicate Trustbusters" (September 25, 1995): p. 1. "The AT&T case shows the value of old-fashioned trustbusting, where size is viewed with suspicion and market domination is the enemy. . . . The AT&T suit is now viewed as one of the government's smartest moves in industrial policy." See also R. Baker and B. Yandle, "Financial Markets and the AT&T Antitrust Settlement," *Eastern Economic Journal* 20 (Fall 1994): pp. 429–40; also the symposium, Paul W. MacAvoy, ed., "Telecommunications in Transition," in the *Yale Journal on Regulation* 11 (Winter 1994): pp. 115–240.

[22] The decision was *Eastman Kodak Co. v. Image Technical Services, Inc.*, 504 U.S. 451 (1992).

[23] For a full analysis, see Stan J. Liebowitz and Stephen E. Margolis, *Winners, Losers and Microsoft: Competition and Antitrust in High Technology* (Oakland, CA: Independent Institute,

1999). They refute Microsoft's defense, arguing that the firm has inferior products but locks them in against superior competitors.

[24] The decision is *United States v. Microsoft Corp.*, 253 F.3d 34 D.C. Cir. (2001). The FTC had investigated Microsoft in 1990, but the Commission deadlocked 2-2 on bringing a case. A contentious Division case followed, ending in mild restraints. Only in 1998 did the Division file a major case.

[25] On the economic merits, see Richard J. Gilbert and Michael L. Katz, "An Economist's Guide to *U.S. v. Microsoft*," *Journal of Economic Perspectives*, 15(2) (Spring 2001): pp 25–44.

[26] The appeals court seized on Judge Jackson's incautious comments to scold him for supposed bias, but the court flatly affirmed that Microsoft had violated Section 2.

[27] For example, Steve Lohr, "For Microsoft, Ruling Will Sting But Not Really Hurt," *New York Times* (November 2, 2002): pp. B1, B4, B5; and John Markoff, "Rivals Are Resigned to Life With a Dominant Microsoft," *New York Times* (November 3, 2002): p. 15. See also Steve Hannon, "What's a Rival To Do Now? Getting Out of Microsoft's Way Becomes a Key Survival Skill," *BusinessWeek* (November 18, 2002): pp. 44–46. "Already, Microsoft is attacking new worlds. Among them are 'smart' mobile phones for Web surfing and run-the-business applications for small and midsize companies. In each case, the company will leverage its monopoly products, Windows and Office, to get a leg up on the competition." AOL, Sun Microsystems, and Apple were noted to be vulnerable. Microsoft already held leading market shares of 93% in new PC operating systems, 49% in new server operating systems, 96% in browsers, and 24% in handheld operating systems.

[28] See William G. Shepherd, *The Treatment of Market Power* (New York: Columbia University Press, 1975).

[29] For example, from 1982 to 1987, some 3,000 mergers occurred each year, on average. Hundreds of these cases involved horizontal market shares above 30 percent, sometimes 40 or 50 percent, yet the two agencies filed no more than seven cases in total in any year.

[30] See George B. Shepherd, Helen S. Shepherd, and William G. Shepherd, "Sharper Focus: Market Shares in the Merger Guidelines," *Antitrust Bulletin* 45(4) (Winter 2000): pp. 835–85, for a detailed critique.

[31] In one recent example, Columbia/HCA Healthcare Corp. negotiated with the FTC to get approval for acquiring Healthtrust Inc., in the largest hospital merger to date. It agreed to divest seven hospitals, end a joint venture, and gain the FTC's advance approval for buying more hospitals in the six markets at issue; Bob Ortega, "Columbia/HCA, FTC Set Accord on Hospital Merger," *Wall Street Journal* (April 24, 1995): p. B4. In another example, Kimberly-Clark won approval of its acquisition of Scott Paper by agreeing to "divest itself of the Scotties facial-tissue business and baby-wipes businesses, which include Baby Fresh, Wash-a-Bye Baby, and Kid Fresh. . . ." and sell five mills. That avoided giving Kimberly-Clark a 60 percent position in facial tissue (it makes Kleenex) and 55 percent of baby wipes (it makes Huggies). See Matt Murray, "Scott's Purchase by Kimberly-Clark Clears Hurdles," *Wall Street Journal* (December 13, 1995): p. A4.

[32] See Daniel Hosken, Daniel O'Brien, David Scheffman, and Michael Vita, "Demand System Estimation and Its Application to Horizontal Merger Analysis," Working Paper No. 246, Bureau of Economics Federal Trade Commission, Washington, DC: April 2002.

[33] *U.S. v. Bethlehem Steel Corp.*, 168 F. Supp. 756.

[34] *Brown Shoe Co. v. U.S.*, 370 U.S. 294 (1962); *U.S. v. Von's Grocery Co.*, 384 U.S. 280 (1966).

[35] *U.S. v. General Dynamics Corp.*, 341 F. Supp. 534 (N.D. 111. 1972), affirmed 415 U.S. 486 (1973).

[36] These include the merger between the McDonnell and Douglas aircraft firms in 1967, the disastrous PennCentral merger in 1968, and the hasty merger of the two professional football leagues in 1967.

[37] See Walter Adams and James W. Brock, *Dangerous Pursuits* (New York: Pantheon Books, 1991).

[38] John E. Kwoka, "International Joint Venture: General Motors and Toyota (1983)," a chapter in Kwoka and White, *The Antitrust Revolution*, 2nd ed. (New York: HarperCollins, 1994), p. 73.

[39] See Kenneth D. Boyer, "Mergers That Harm Competitors," *Review of Industrial Organization* 7 (1992): pp. 191–202.

[40] See two major symposia about the new guidelines by experts on merger issues: David T. Scheffman, ed., "Symposium on New 1992 Merger Guidelines," *Antitrust Bulletin* 38 (Fall 1993): pp. 473–740; and "Special Issue: Merger Guidelines," *Review of Industrial Organization* 8 (April 1993): pp. 135–256 (including the text of the guidelines).

[41] European antitrust actually decided against the merger before American agencies did.

[42] See Andrew Ross Sorkin, "U.S. to Challenge Deal by EchoStar To Acquire DirecTV," *New York Times* (October 31, 2002): p. C19.

[43] See Evan Perez, "Carnival, Winning Princess Bid, Is Poised to Expand Dominance," *Wall Street Journal* (October 28, 2002): pp. A3, A14.

[44] See William E. Kovacic, "Merger Policy in a Declining Defense Industry," *Antitrust Bulletin* 36 (Fall 1991): pp. 543–92.

[45] For one response, see T. C. Willcox, "Behavioral Remedies in a Post-Chicago World: It's Time to Revise the Vertical Merger Guidelines," *Antitrust Bulletin* 40 (Spring 1995): pp. 227–56.

[46] *U.S. v. Du Pont*, 353 U.S. 586 (1957).

[47] *Addyston Pipe & Steel Co. v. U.S.*, 175 U.S. 211.

[48] *U.S. v. Trenton Potteries Co.*, 273 U.S. 392.

[49] *U.S. v. Socony-Vacuum Oil Co.*, 310 U.S. 150. ("Socony" was of course the old Standard Oil Company of New York, part of the old Standard Oil monopoly.)

[50] Producers of heavy electrical equipment had run secret bidding rings, using formulas based on phases of the moon to rotate orders among themselves. Some twenty-nine companies, including General Electric and Westinghouse, and scores of their officers were involved.

[51] The firms refunded $67 million to consumers who bought during 1995–2000 and gave $75 million in CDs to public entities. But no reduction in prices was expected. See Claudia H. Deutsch, "Suit Settled Over Pricing of Recordings at Big Chains," *New York Times* (October 1, 2002): pp. C1, C10.

[52] "The banks fixed fees on almost every service they offered, and fixed interest rates on nearly all their loans and saving accounts in the 1990s." See Pal Hofheinz, "Austrian Banks Are Fined by EU for Price Fixing," *Wall Street Journal* (June 12, 2002): page A14.

[53] Paul Meller, "Europe Fines Nintendo $147 Million for Price Fixing," *New York Times* (October 31, 2002): pp. W1, W7.

[54] *American Tobacco Co. v. U.S.*, 328 U.S. 781, 810.

[55] *FTC v. Cement Institute*, 333 U.S. 683.

[56] *Milgram v. Loew's, Inc.*, 94 F. Supp. 416.

[57] Leading cases opening up the professions to competition include *Goldfarb v. Virginia State Bar*, 421 U.S. 773 (1975) on lawyers and *FTC v. Indiana Federation of Dentists*, 476 U.S. 447 (1986). The FTC's program since the 1970s against restrictions by the professions has been aggressive.

[58] *National Collegiate Athletic Association v. University of Oklahoma*, 468 U.S. 85 (1984). See also John J. Siegfried, "The National Collegiate Athletic Association: A Study in Cartel Behavior," *Antitrust Bulletin* 39 (Summer 1994): pp. 599–609, and sources there.

[59] See Eleanor M. Fox and Lawrence A. Sullivan, *Cases and Materials on Antitrust* (St. Paul: West Publishing, 1989)

[60] See Carl Shapiro and David J. Teece, "Systems Competition and Aftermarkets: An Economic Analysis of Kodak," *Antitrust Bulletin* 39 (Spring 1994): pp. 135–62; also J. J. Voortman, "Curbing Aftermarket Monopolization," *Antitrust Bulletin* 38 (Summer 1993): pp. 221–91.

[61] Recall that new-Chicagoans deny that leverage can ever succeed. Others say that leverage can work strongly, if the markets have important imperfections.

[62] *Matsushita Electrical Industrial Co. v. Zenith Radio Corp.*, 475 U.S. 574 (1986). See Kenneth G. Elzinga, "Collusive Predation: *Matsushita v. Zenith*, (1986)," a chapter in John E. Kwoka, Jr. and

Lawrence J. White, eds., *The Antitrust Revolution* (New York: HarperCollins, 1994). On the other side, David Schwartzman, *The Japanese Television Cartel: A Study Based on* Matsushita v. Zenith (Ann Arbor: University of Michigan Press, 1993).

[63] *Brooke Group v. Brown & Williams*, 125 L.Ed. 2d 764 (1993).

[64] Scott Kilman, "Archer-Daniels Is Facing over 70 Lawsuits," *Wall Street Journal* (November 16, 1995): p. B 12.

Chapter

17

Regulation, Deregulation, Public Enterprise, and Privatization

Since about 1900, regulation has been the United States' unique method for dealing with "utility" industries like electricity and the telephone system. These were "natural-monopoly" markets; because their technology created large economies of scale, there was "room" for only one firm. To get the large size necessary for efficiency, the public would give a monopoly franchise to one company. Then it would try to keep that monopoly's prices down to competitive levels.

During the twentieth century, America's effort to regulate its natural-monopoly utilities—especially the telephone-service and electricity markets, and others such as railroads and airlines—used up a great deal of attention, emotion, and resources. In contrast, most other countries had put these industries under public ownership, usually as nationwide state monopolies.

After 1970 there was a great wave of "deregulation" in the United States, scrapping regulatory protections and relying instead on competition for good results. Deregulation has worked pretty well in some cases but quite badly in others. Prime examples were the electricity crisis in California in 2000–2001 and the telecommunications meltdown during 1999–2003. They showed how naive efforts at deregulation could lead to severe harms.

Meanwhile, since 1980 some other countries have been busily selling off many of their public-utility systems to private investors while removing constraints. Some privatizing has been successful, but others have given little gain, and still others have been huge failures.

These events range over a variety of sectors, situations, and details. The actions have filled the business press, as whole industries (such as airlines, cable TV, and electricity) have regularly been severely criticized. The economic issues involve several clear concepts of regulation, presented in this chapter. Competition is often portrayed as a magic wand to cure the inefficiencies of regulation. But in practice many kinds of troubles often erupt.

Section 1 considers how regulation has worked and what its real effects have been.[1] Sometimes new smaller-scale technology emerges and makes competition possible. If regulations are removed carefully and competition is promoted, enough competition may come in to be effective.

But instead deregulation may occur too fast or ineptly, as we discuss in section 2. That can let the old regulated monopoly stay on as a powerful dominant firm, but now free of control. Section 2 also reviews successful deregulation. Section 3 considers public enterprise, and section 4 covers the privatization of public firms.

I. REGULATION OF NATURAL MONOPOLY

In all economies, some markets have been natural monopolies, where the economies of scale leave room for only one firm. City water supply has always been such a utility: one set of pipes under the streets is much cheaper than two. Other early U.S. examples included the U.S. Post Office and town gasworks, often under public ownership. After 1840 railroads grew explosively in the United States as private ventures, and in the western prairie areas they often were monopolies. As electricity and telephones burst on the scene by 1880, they too became lucrative battlegrounds for private would-be monopolists.

Most other countries chose nationwide public enterprise as the way to organize their new railroads, electricity, and telephones. In the United States, these sectors were captured instead by buccaneering capitalists, often fighting each other. The owners then worked to have their firms declared to be natural monopolies and put under public regulatory commissions.[2] Especially at first, the regulation often was weak or simply a sham, with the utility firms themselves manipulating politicians to give the regulators only tiny budgets and weak powers. Even stronger regulation sometimes reduces efficiency, as we will note later.[3]

Regulation takes many alternative forms. The U.S. version has been an **independent regulatory commission.** It tries to limit the profit rates that the monopoly can earn by controlling its prices. This hybrid form spread between 1885 and 1930 with hopes of applying expert, nonpolitical control to the problems of natural monopoly.[4] But instead, it has often been weak, really being dictated by the "regulated" firm itself. The company often has had the upper hand over the commission, fending off controls and manipulating outcomes.

Table 17.1 lists some leading events and concepts as regulation has grown and receded in the United States.

Table 17.1   Leading Events in the History of U.S. Regulation

Years	Events
1888	Interstate Commerce Commission created to regulate railroads
1907–1930s	First Wisconsin, then other states set up regulatory commissions for utilities
1920, 1934	Federal Power Commission begins regulating electric power
1935	Federal Communications Commission created to regulate broadcasting and telephone service
1938	Civil Aeronautics Board created to regulate airlines
1944	Hope Natural Gas decision sets original cost as basis for rates, making effective regulation possible
1955, 1959, 1963	Adams-Gray, Meyer-Peck-Stenason-Zwick, and Averch-Johnson critiques of regulation
1965–1975	Rising calls for deregulation
1968, 1969	FCC issues Cartefone and MCI decisions opening up Bell systems to equipment and interconnection
1970s	Deregulation of banking begins
1975	Deregulation ends the New York Stock Exchange's fixing of brokerage fees
1978–1983	Deregulation of the airlines and abolition of the CAB
1980	Deregulation of railroads, trucking, buses, movers
1982–1984	Breakup of the Bell system
1985–1995	States increasingly withdraw regulation, even of local service monopolies
1992	Reregulation of cable TV
1994–1996	Electricity begins moving toward open-access competition, even for local distribution
1996	New telecommunications law seeks to open up competition in both long distance and local service, but it quickly faces blockage from Baby Bells.
1996-1999	California leads many states in deregulating electricity, but poor design and corrupt marketers cause huge price rises and chaos in 2000-2001. Deregulation is partly reversed or delayed in many states.
1997-2002	Major mergers: Baby Bells, electricity firms, AT&T-Comcast in cable TV. The FCC permits virtually all mergers.

The Interstate Commerce Commission (ICC) was the first federal commission. Though established in 1888, it was largely a mere shell until it gained real powers after 1910. Wisconsin Progressives started the first state-level commission in 1907, and other state commissions followed. By the 1930s, nearly all states had regulatory bodies of some sort. Other federal commissions date mainly from the 1930s.

Until 1944, most commissions were ineffective, stalled by debates over the value of company assets. The firms claimed that the **current** value of assets must be used in setting fair profits. That practice would have mired regulation in endless, obscure controversies over what the current values really were (since the regulators' actions themselves help to determine that value!). In 1944, a landmark Supreme Court decision made the original accounting cost of assets the standard basis for setting profits.[5] This immediately provided a relatively firm footing for commissions to set strict controls on profits, if they wish.

Only a few commissions have actually applied strict regulation, and only during some periods. Other commissions (including many state commissions) have been passive or strongly pro-company. Only in the 1960s did the FPC, FCC, and CAB begin to assert firm control over rate levels, rate structures, and the scope of monopoly.

At any rate, regulation was extensive from the 1930s until the 1980s, in contrast to the public ownership that was common abroad. The sun seemed to shine on regulation and its utility sectors (except railroads). Growth was achieving economies of scale, costs were steady or falling, and the problems to be solved were rather simple. Until 1968, regulation seemed to be reasonably well set and generally successful, especially in telephones and electricity.

But after 1968, severe new problems battered both the firms and their regulators: rapid inflation, ecological impacts on water and air, sharp increases in fuel prices, consumer activism, nuclear power fiascoes, and antitrust challenges. Regulation came under great stress, while deregulation grew more attractive as a way out.

In fact, utility sectors often tend to evolve toward natural competition. Once effective competition is fully established, regulation can then safely withdraw and leave the market to competitive forces supervised by antitrust. In the United States, some economists began pressing in the 1950s for the removal of much regulation, saying it was costly, passive, and distorting.[6]

Criticism spread, and finally after 1975 deregulation began in earnest.[7] By the 1980s, Congress removed most regulatory controls over transportation (airlines, air freight, railroads, trucking, and buses), telephones, cable television, banking, and natural gas.[8] This wave of deregulation was a watershed event as part of the general rise of competition.[9]

As deregulation began, new "incentive-oriented" partial regulation was often applied as a transitional method, and this helped to stimulate an outpouring of theoretical writings.[10] "Price caps" became a popular but debatable method after 1985.

Economists also began developing a mass of new static-efficiency analyses of conditions under regulation. Among many topics, they explored optimal incentive pricing under regulation, with varying conditions of information. The precision of the theory often reached far beyond any practical ability of rough, practical regulation.

Moving a monopoly market toward effective competition was much more difficult than just removing certain regulatory rules. Regulators typically came under immediate pressures to remove all regulation. They were always pushed toward **premature deregulation** of monopolies, long before effective competition was in place.

Even when regulators declared entry to be formally open, the old monopolist was still in place, ready to manipulate the regulators and quell any new rivals, but also to claim that actual or potential competition was severe. The dominant firm could use the standard monopoly devices to create and exploit imperfections, and the new entrants would often be few and fragile. The former monopolist actually preferred to accept a few small competitors so that it could now claim to be under strong competition. Dominance often continued to be stable and powerful, sometimes with 90% of the market and with only a few small rivals. Or sometimes, firms jumped in with new ways to corrupt and distort markets, as in the 2000–2001 electricity crisis in California and the western United States.

The process of deregulation continues to be intensely debated and full of surprises. In fact, few major full monopolists have been swiftly converted to fully effective competition—not the local Bell operating companies, nor cable-TV firms, nor electric distribution utilities.[11] Even so, deregulation and the advent of some competition can have strong effects.[12]

Meanwhile, public enterprise has been an important industrial-policy method. Where there is a distinctive public interest, public enterprise may serve it well, though it often becomes bureaucratic. After 1980, public enterprises in Britain and elsewhere became targets of a privatization crusade, selling off public firms to private investors. That crusade continues, though with modest impacts in the United States so far.

1.　CONCEPTS OF REGULATION

When regulation is set up, the economic question is whether the regulators have the resources, powers, willpower, and political support to apply constraints that are both tight and correct. The exclusive franchise is granted so as to achieve economies of scale; the monopolist is supposed to submit to effective control so as to keep prices down to its (minimized) costs. A minimum of public resources must create efficiency and a maximum of private enterprise.[13] But of course the firm is ensconced as the monopolist—lucrative, in control of key information, and determined to frustrate the regulatory process.

The first economic objective of regulation is **efficient prices**.[14] The situation is illustrated in figure 17.1 for electricity service in a normal situation. There are large economies of scale, with the average cost of electricity declining out to the output level Q_c. The demand curve for this whole market for electricity is shown intersecting the average cost curve at that same output level, if capacity has been well planned to coincide neatly with demand.[15]

Regulators now set the price of electricity at P_c. At that price, consumers want and receive the output level Q_c. In this ideal result, price just barely covers the firm's average cost so that the firm receives no excess profits. Capacity is fully used, economies of scale are achieved, and electricity is supplied at the lowest possible price and cost.

In some cases, economies of scale might be even bigger, as we saw in figure 10.4. The average cost curve then continues to decline beyond its intersection with the demand curve. The policy problem now grows more complex, posing a dilemma between average-cost pricing and marginal-cost pricing. The regulators will set price at P_{ac} to prevent excess profits, but marginal cost is still lower than

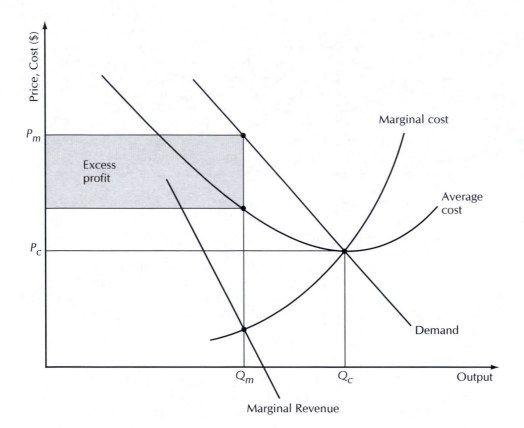

Figure 17.1   The basic economics of utility regulation.

that. If price were pushed down even lower to P_{mc}, so as to be equal to marginal cost, then the firm would suffer financial losses. This dilemma is an old, much-discussed puzzle.[16] But on the whole, the first case (shown in figure 17.1) is probably more common.

At its best, regulation applies its controls briskly and fairly. The economic task has two main parts:

1. to set price levels so that the firm does not earn excess profit and exploit its customers, and

2. to reduce price discrimination to a price structure that is just and reasonable.

The monopoly will try instead to discriminate sharply and systematically, along the lines discussed in chapter 10. Economic efficiency requires aligning prices with marginal costs instead, for maximum efficiency.

Ideally, the commission performs its two tasks with a minimum of cost and delay. If and when natural-monopoly conditions fade away, the regulation and the franchise are neatly and gradually withdrawn—no sooner, no later—so that competition can take over the job.

Regulation may, instead, go wrong. It may become a captive of the industry. It may be applied where natural-monopoly conditions do not exist. It may be slow, ineffective, and costly, and it can have inefficient side effects. It may last long after natural monopoly recedes.

In fact, deregulation has whittled regulation down so much that it now covers industries with small fractions of national income and total investment. Yet regulation raises important and complicated issues, as follows.

2. What Is To Be Regulated?

Ideally, regulation is applied to each **natural monopoly.** The firm's resulting monopoly power could be further enhanced if (1) the good is a **necessity,** with **highly inelastic demand** (such as electricity, water, and telephone service), and (2) users are **physically connected** to the supplier (as by wires or pipes). In those cases, consumers are especially vulnerable to exploitation and price discrimination.

These conditions are matters of degree, not yes-no issues. Economies of scale are often moderate rather than extreme, as we saw in chapters 7 and 9; industries do not divide neatly into natural-competition and natural-monopoly boxes. Moreover, technology may shift so that the economies of scale grow or recede. Or a new parallel industry may arise to inject competition, as with trucking invading railroads' markets, or cellular phones against wired telephones.

Unfortunately, these shifts are often unpredictable, unsure, and controversial. Also, the transition may take a long time. Therefore the proper scope of regulation is often uncertain and changing.

3. Commissions

There have been three main federal regulatory commissions:

1. the Interstate Commerce Commission (created 1888), over transportation[17]
2. the Federal Energy Regulatory Commission (1920, 1934), mainly over electricity[18]
3. the Federal Communications Commission (1935), over telecommunications[19]

There are nearly fifty state regulatory bodies covering intrastate issues. Most commissions have three to seven commissioners, who hear and decide issues brought before them by the regulated firms, customers, the commission staff, or other parties (usually called *intervenors*). Commission resources vary from scant to large. Housekeeping and peripheral tasks (such as safety at railroad crossings and the licensing of small operators) swallow up much of the resources of some commissions.

Commissioners are political appointees, generally either ambitious younger lawyers or operatives or older ones on their way out. Since more talented officials often rise to higher positions elsewhere, they are usually in regulatory office less than three years, with little time to develop or change basic policies. Staffs tend to be cautious administrators, carefully adjusting according to the conflicting interests of firms, customers, and other groups. The process is often run by lawyers, who use adversary procedures to turn out decisions meeting legal criteria. The formal legal powers of the commissions are usually large, but their duties and criteria are vague ("fair," "just and reasonable," the "public interest," and so on).

4. PROCESS

Commissions hold open hearings and render decisions. In the typical rate case, the firm announces a new, higher set of prices and asks the commission to approve them. Hearings are scheduled at which the company makes a detailed case for its request, using expert witnesses as well as company officials. The commission staff and/or public counsel then argue for a smaller increase, plus possibly a different structure of prices. Other intervenor parties may also join in, perhaps representing groups such as senior citizens, the poor, or large industrial users.

The hearings are often lengthy, and the ensuing decision may come many months after the original request. The commission usually grants a fraction of the request (half is the most common division) on the basis of its collective judgment.

The procedures provide extremely valuable due process, with an open forum for the views and evidence of all interested parties. Each group cites criteria and facts that favor it. The outcome is usually a compromise among the conflicting interests, stated in terms of some criterion or mix of criteria (fairness, efficiency, and so on).

5. DECISIONS ON PRICE LEVELS AND STRUCTURES

Commissions deal with three main kinds of economic issues: price level, price structure, and the scope of competition.

Price level is the usual topic, refined by decades of practice to a traditional litany of issues. The elements are summed up in the following equation, familiar to you as the basis of evaluating profitability:

$$\text{Rate of return} = \frac{\text{total revenue} - \text{total cost}}{\text{invested capital}}$$

The commission decides what the firm's rate base is (its amount of capital invested in the business). Next, it decides on a fair rate of return (usually in the range of 7 to 13 percent). Then the firm is allowed to set price levels that will generate enough sales revenue to provide the fair rate of profit on the rate base. Hence this approach is often called **rate-base regulation**.

If the commission permits higher output prices, that will raise total revenue, increase profits, and raise the rate of return. The company wants maximum profits, while the commission tries to hold profits (and prices) down to much lower levels.

As shown in figure 17.1's ideal case, setting price at marginal cost achieves economic efficiency. Marginal-cost pricing also avoids excess profits and achieves the lowest possible average cost.

The utility prefers a higher price, P_m, with large excess profits. But regulators try to set price at P_c, which gives the utility enough total revenue to cover its total costs. The utility is required to produce Q_c, the amount that people want to buy at the regulated price P_c.

6. ECONOMIC CRITERIA

Price Level. The commission sets some maximum permitted rate of return, but its level is controversial. The laws usually require a "fair rate of return," neither too high (unfair to customers) nor too low (unfair to the firm's shareholders). The profit rate should also be efficient, by several possible criteria:

1. It should equal the cost to the firm of its capital (the "cost-of-capital" criterion).

2. It should be high enough to attract just the optimal amount of new investment (the "capital-attraction" criterion).

3. It should be in line with risk-return conditions in other industries (the "comparable-returns" criterion).

These three criteria all relate to the same basic concept of efficient allocation of capital, but they are not precise guides to real conditions. Fair rates of return usually lie between 7 and 13 percent, but the correct level for each case can be debated endlessly without arriving at a definitive answer. The commission simply applies its judgment and picks a figure or range, such as 10.25 percent or 9.5 to 11.0 percent.

The value of the rate base is then fixed by the commission. The firm's invested capital includes both fixed capital, at various possible rates of depreciation; and other assets, including a range of short-term and liquid assets. Some or all of this capital value is allowed in the rate base, in what can be a complicated judgment by the commission.

Total costs are also usually reviewed to make sure that they are not inflated—in our terms, to assure that they are X-efficient. The specific price level then follows fairly directly, since it is the price change needed for the firm's profit rate to reach the maximum permitted rate.

These price decisions usually ignore two complications. First, demand may be elastic in some degree. Since price changes alter the amounts that people buy, the net revenue change may not be a simple matter at all. Second, future conditions may change, so that the new price schedule turns out to yield profits either above or below the permitted rate of return. Indeed, actual profit rates often do rise above the permitted ceilings.

Price Structure.   The structure of prices involves differences in the prices to various groups of customers. The structure is supposed to be "just and reasonable," as per the standard legal wording. Price discrimination by regulated firms is likely to be very sharp. These monopoly companies sell to a wide variety of customers (homes, shops, and factories of all kinds and sizes), often with radically different demand elasticities. Some degree of discrimination may be efficient, but that is a very complex issue, beyond the scope of this chapter.[20] Generally, optimal pricing contains much less price discrimination than the firm would prefer.

Instead, the proper criterion for prices is cost—specifically, marginal cost. When price equals marginal cost, the utility falls into line with efficient allocation in the rest of the economy (recall chapter 2).

The structure of utility costs is usually complicated. The regulatory commission must bring prices at least roughly into line with that cost structure. Overhead and joint costs (costs incurred supplying many or all customers) often make it unclear what the various marginal costs really are. Also, most utilities have sharp fluctuations in demand, as we note below. These fluctuations cause marginal costs to vary sharply between peak and off-peak times. Therefore the efficient price structure also needs to have marked differences—by seasons, by day, and by time of day—as we will analyze shortly.

What Should Be Regulated?   Natural monopolies often are not a distinct, neatly-defined group. Most regulated sectors (e.g., telephone services of all kinds) contain a variety of natural-monopoly and naturally-competitive parts, which often shift or evolve. Each firm naturally wishes to control the whole sector. Other firms often contest this, wishing to stay or expand in the market. The commission's task is to trim the franchise to the conditions, preventing any excess monopoly control.

The correct criteria include (1) natural monopoly, with its likelihood that (2) price discrimination will be severe among consumer groups with varying elasticities. Usually, also, a regulated sector has (3) fluctuating output, with costs and demand varying widely by time of use, and (4) physical connection to users, by wires, pipes, or other means, which make it difficult for customers to change suppliers or to resell the output. In practice, these matters of degree often defy clear answers, and the borders of regulation are strongly debated.

Fitting Prices to Marginal Costs.   Regulated firms usually have a variety of outputs, differing by physical features (size, weight, design) or by conditions of supply. Seemingly uniform products can vary sharply in costs. For example, the cost of a kilowatt-hour of electricity at midnight may be 2 cents, while it may be 20 cents at noon; off-peak production is usually much cheaper than peak-load output. That is illustrated by the typical daily load curve in panel I of figure 17.2.

Output peaks during the day, when factories and offices are busy, but then it falls to low levels during the off-peak nighttime hours. The best equipment is run continuously, giving low costs at off-peak times. That corresponds to low marginal cost in panel II. At peak times, the least efficient extra capacity must be started up and used for a little while, at high marginal costs. Therefore peak-load marginal costs are commonly a multiple of off-peak costs.

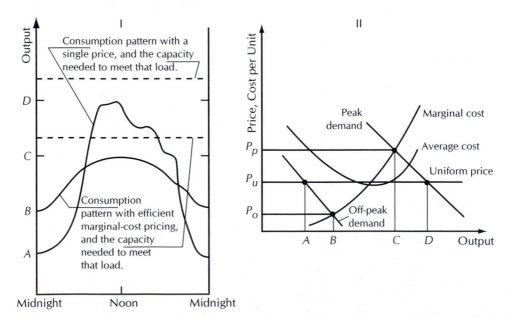

Figure 17.2   Load patterns, demand, and cost in utility pricing.

For efficiency, price should equal marginal cost. If price diverges sharply from marginal cost, then allocation is inefficient. Therefore utility regulators should strive for utility price structures in line with marginal costs. That calls for **peak-load pricing,** with prices set much higher at peak times than at off-peak times. In panel II of figure 17.2, the efficient prices are P_o and P_p, with outputs at B and C. A single price at P_u would instead lead to too much quantity at D, while cutting off-peak outputs to level A.

Such marginal-cost pricing is socially efficient, and often the regulated firm would gain greatly from adopting it. For example, setting prices too low for peak outputs encourages too much load at peak times and threatens the whole utility system with overload and collapse. Indeed, efficient marginal-cost pricing patterns often lie in the same direction as price discrimination, at least for parts of the utility's output.

Cost and demand conditions often diverge instead, so that regulators must force the firm to follow efficient, marginal-cost pricing rather than discrimination. Setting high prices at peak-load times is especially important, so as to avoid excess peak-load output. That is often hard to enforce, however, because it usually requires higher prices for the periods when the system seems to be most urgently needed. Also, rate-base regulation may encourage the regulated firm to add more capacity than is efficient (discussed later). Still, for the great mass of regulated outputs, marginal-cost pricing is both correct and feasible.

Nevertheless, before 1968 these lessons were largely ignored, for utilities were eager to grow by means of promotional pricing, which discriminates in favor of peak-load use. That gives sharp price-cut discounts even when costs are particularly high. Peak-load output was usually priced too low, both for electricity and telephone service. The new scarcities after 1967 suddenly made marginal-cost pricing seem wise, and there was some movement to adopt it.

Electricity prices used to ignore high peak-load costs almost entirely, and for some users they still do. That encourages overuse, and it requires companies to build too much capacity to meet those overstimulated peak-load levels. Local telephone pricing has been even worse. By charging a **zero** price for local calls, firms have encouraged an excessive level of use (as was shown in chapter 10).

Long-distance prices have always reflected marginal costs more closely. Therefore marginal-cost pricing has been routine in certain utility services, even though it was long avoided in others.

After 1970 there were new efforts toward marginal-cost pricing, especially in electricity. It is now often called "real-time pricing," designed to make customers realize the true cost of what they are buying. A typical price structure now defines peak times by business days, working hours, and seasonal peaks (either summer for air-conditioning load or winter for heating load). Off hours are generally nights and weekends.

A typical real-time pricing peak-load price might be 12.0 cents per kilowatt-hour, compared to 2.3 cents for off-peak power. That sharp difference fits figure 17.2, at least roughly. As long as customers know that peak power is markedly more expensive, a precise fine-tuning of the prices is not necessary.

Marginal-cost pricing is much more widely applied to large industrial users than ordinary small-use households. Despite moderate progress, much pricing of electricity, gas, and telephone service is still in the old uniform-price patterns.

Effects of Regulation on Costs.   After 1960, economists grew increasingly skeptical that the formalities of regulation actually had much effect. They also began saying that regulation actually had certain negative effects on efficiency.[21] Attention soon focused on two ways that regulation induces waste: **raising all costs** and **raising levels of investment.**

After much debate during the 1960s, some practical research emerged in the 1970s. Free-market economists urged that the wastes were so high that all regulation is destructive and should be scrapped. Reagan politicians agreed and pressed deregulation further.

But the research findings suggest only mild possible effects, and regulators quickly became much more careful in assessing utility costs and investment.[22] Though the CAB's regulation of the airline oligopoly probably raised costs before deregulation in 1978, there is no firm evidence of substantial wastes from other regulation. The following review of the issues is interesting, but the practical impacts are probably small.

Standard regulation lets the firm charge prices that will cover its costs plus a fair profit. This cost-plus approach may permit or even encourage X-inefficiency in the firm. With its monopoly position, the firm may be able to cover the higher costs.

This tendency is reinforced by firms' interest in providing high-quality, reliable service, which usually entails extra costs. Both the prices and quantities of the inputs may be raised. It is always tempting to set quality levels higher, and regulation's cost-plus-profit basis may lead utilities to adopt Cadillac-level quality too widely. There are strong limits on such cost-plus pressures:

1. **Regulatory Lag.** Regulation commonly lags behind the firm's cost changes. Therefore, the firm keeps substantial amounts of cost savings, giving strong incentives to keep costs down. In fact, regulatory lag usually injects such powerful incentives that it alone may prevent any inefficiency.

2. **Professional Standards.**   Managers and engineers generally apply good sense and technical criteria to what is needed in their system.

3. **Scrutiny By the Commissions.**   From the early days of regulation, officials and courts have recognized the need to guard against extravagant or unnecessary costs.

The rate-base method of regulation may induce the firm to increase the value of its rate base rather than minimize it.[23] Normally the permitted rate of return is set slightly above the cost of capital. The firm's shareholders, therefore, gain a little (or a lot of) profit from each extra bit of capital included in the rate base.[24] That may tilt the firm toward using too much capital.

The rise could come about in two ways:

1. Actual investment could be higher. When choosing new technology, the firm would lean toward more capital-intensive methods. Capacity to meet peak loads might also be higher because of the rate-base effect. This would give the firm (and the regulators) more protection against calamitous breakdowns at peak times.

2. Accounting choices would maximize the recorded value of assets. Depreciation methods would be adjusted toward writing down assets' value slowly. The firm might also permit overcharging in the prices of the equipment it buys.

The whole rate-base effect has never been accurately measured and, of course, firms have usually denied that it occurs at all. Though it could be significant, new awareness and safeguards against it probably keep it down to minor levels.

"Cream Skimming" and Competition.   All utility industries contain some markets that can be supplied competitively. The regulated firm, however, naturally wishes to encompass them in its exclusive franchise. Indeed, the rate-base effect encourages it; the firm wants to add the capital in the adjacent market to its rate base. Meanwhile, other firms want to get in to compete against the utility.

Newcomers naturally enter the most lucrative parts of the regulated firm's market, where the price-cost ratios are highest. This "cream skimming" (the British call it "picking the eyes out of the market") is regarded as an acute threat by the regulated firm.

The firm will claim that cream skimming strikes at the system integrity of the utility, for the creamy parts are necessary to support the skim parts. With the cream gone, either the whole system will go bankrupt, or at least prices for most consumers will have to rise. Such claims alarm customers in the skim markets, whose prices would rise.

The regulated firm therefore resists all competition. If competition is permitted, the original firm demands the right to meet the competition by selective price cutting. If that is permitted, the price cuts may be deep and systematic enough to keep out competition (recall chapter 10). The commission thus gets drawn into setting **floors** on specific prices as well as **ceilings** on the firm's whole price and profit levels. In doing this, regulators must rely on cost figures prepared by the regulated firm itself (which often seek to justify the prices by allocating costs to the high-price services used by captive customers).

Difficulties have been widespread in postal service, airlines, railroads, telephones, banking, electricity—anywhere that a commission has had to supervise a dominant firm facing differing degrees of competition. The specific cost and competitive conditions vary by gradations, rarely fitting into neat boxes.

II.   PARTIAL DEREGULATION AND PRICE CAPS

As deregulation spread in the 1980s, the British idea of price caps became popular.[25] Old regulation was said to be rigid, lumbering, and inefficient. Price caps avoid red tape by merely setting broad price constraints, leaving firms free to adjust their costs and prices efficiently.[26]

Many state commissions adopted this and other versions of partial regulation. The FCC applied price caps to AT&T's long-distance service in 1989, even though the actual enforcement was minimal. Price caps have virtues, including simplicity, but caps may fit poorly and they may permit anticompetitive actions by the dominant firm.

An ideal price cap would take the following form:

$$
\begin{array}{ccccc}
\text{Permitted} & & \text{rise in} & \text{savings from} & \\
\text{price} & = & \text{cost of} & - & \text{autonomous} & - \text{X (a squeeze factor)} \\
\text{rise} & & \text{inputs} & \text{progress} &
\end{array}
$$

It allows the firm to raise prices in line with rising costs, but it nudges and rewards the firm to take extra action to cut its costs by letting it keep the savings.

This general target needs to be supplemented by setting limits on how deeply the dominant firm can make selective price discounts to block its small rivals from the best customers (recall chapter 10). As dominance fades, limits can be relaxed; if dominance remains high, limits may need to be tight.

The three right-hand elements in the equation are actually controversial and may be set at incorrect levels.[27] If mistakes do happen, then the firm may soon be making profits that are far too high or too low. Also, the dominant firm may use price discounting to keep or increase its dominance, possibly even eliminating small rivals. In either event, regulators may then need to intervene after all, rather than let the price cap operate without supervision.

Price caps can be difficult and risky, especially because traditional regulation has not in fact been as harmful as is often claimed. Price caps work best when outputs are few, rivals are already near parity, reliable input cost indexes can easily be constructed, future technological trends are accurately known, and a correct squeeze factor can be applied.

III. FULL DEREGULATION

The full deregulation of a monopolist is a long, arduous, complicated, and hazardous task.[28] From 1975 to 1985, deregulation was started in a wide range of industries but concluded successfully only in a few. Deregulation made big changes in stockbrokers, most of the transport sector (airlines, railroads, trucking, and others), banks, broadcasting, telephones, and much of the electricity industry.[29] Some deregulation continues in the 2000s, but amid much wreckage and hot debate in the telecommunications and electricity sectors.[30]

Where the underlying technology was naturally competitive and competition was already strong, the act of opening up an officially protected oligopoly has easily led to fully effective competition. Examples are stockbrokerage, airlines, eastern railroads, banks, and trucking.

It has been far more difficult to shift the classic pure-monopoly utilities all the way over to effective competition.[31] In fact that has rarely succeeded, and it has often failed.[32]

1. CRITERIA FOR EFFECTIVE DEREGULATION

Market Share below 50 Percent. The dominant firm's market share must usually sink below 40 to 50 percent, and there must be at least four or five comparable competitors and easy entry, before competition can be effective.[33] A market share over 50 percent indicates the need to retain price constraints, both against excessive monopoly prices and against selective price cuts designed to eliminate smaller rivals.

Bottleneck Controls.   Competition is ineffective if there are bottleneck controls by which one or several firms exclude others or overcharge them for access to the market. Either such bottlenecks must be removed or placed in outside hands, or regulation must be retained to ensure that access is open and fairly priced.

Deregulation after Completion.   Premature deregulation is the cardinal error of deregulation policy.

Strict Antitrust.   After deregulation, the market usually becomes a tight oligopoly that can easily evolve back to dominance. Mergers must be carefully screened and selective pricing tactics must be monitored, so as to prevent a reversion to dominance. Entry barriers need to be kept low. These criteria fit the established, pre-1980 lines of U.S. antitrust policies.

2. RELYING ON ANTITRUST AGENCIES

Deregulators often have naive illusions about the effectiveness of antitrust. Merely remove regulations, the special interests claim, and antitrust will guarantee effective competition. The truth is much darker; deregulation often requires a complicated mingling of increasing antitrust controls and decreasing regulatory limits. Also, lax antitrust policies can quickly foster an outburst of mergers that restores monopoly power, as happened with airlines in 1985–1988 and in telecommunications and electricity in the 1990s.

Antitrust can be a weak reed to lean on for the following reasons (recall chapters 15 and 16):

1. The antitrust agencies are tiny units compared to their economy-wide responsibilities, with overstretched resources. Adding large, complex utility sectors to their burdens will almost guarantee weak treatments.

2. Their methods of enforcement are narrow. The agencies can only bring lawsuits to stop specific anticompetitive conditions or actions. They cannot exercise continuing formal or informal control over complex conditions, nor anticipate new trends. Strategic pricing and changing technology are particularly hard for antitrust to deal with.

3. The dominant-firm case is precisely the one that the antitrust agencies are least fit to handle. Effective deregulation requires sustained attention to move the monopolist down below 40 percent of the market, to prevent anticompetitive actions, and to enforce service responsibilities along the way. The agencies have often shown that they cannot persuade the courts to deal effectively with dominant-firm conditions, even in much simpler cases. In the 1980s, Reagan antitrust officials simply refused to bring Section 2 cases, and they chose a majority of federal judges who are known to be hostile to Section 2 actions. Since 1990 dominant-firm cases have been rare.

4. The agencies go through sharp changes in quality and political direction. Until 1980, these changes were usually only moderate, but the post-1980 reductions were severe. Antitrust is no longer reasonably reliable.

3. LESSONS OF DEREGULATION

Leading cases include airlines and telecommunications, which we already covered in chapters 13 and 14, and electricity.[34] The guidelines just discussed (market shares, selective pricing, and certain weaknesses of antitrust policies) should be considered in assessing those cases.

Major markets such as these (and railroads, also extensively deregulated) often contain sections that range from natural monopoly to competition. Any simple deregulatory treatment for the whole industry runs a risk of letting the old monopolist entrench and extend its control. The firm will use political muscle and rhetoric to demand complete deregulation, while preparing to deter entrants.

The process of deregulation requires regulators to rely increasingly on complex new antitrust skills; they do not just naively drop the old rules and retire. They must astutely adopt a realistic use of antitrust policies as they arrange for the dominant firm to recede below a 40-percent market share while at least four other substantial competitors grow.

The core task is to orchestrate and protect the influx of competitors as the controls on the dominant firm are gradually pulled back. Conflicting interests must be heard and allowed fair play in the marketplace. Further, the regulators often need to engage in complex legislative struggles that redesign the competitive setting.

A large example of that is the epic 1990s congressional struggle in reformulating rules for the telecommunications sector among AT&T, the local Bells, cable TV, cellular companies, computer-related firms of many kinds, major media firms, and still other large players. The 1996 Telecommunications Act was soon seen as a political deal that failed. Competition in long-distance markets continued to rise, but the Baby Bells have shut out nearly all competition in local-service markets.

In electricity, state-level deregulating has met some spectacular failures, especially in California. From May 2000 to June 2001, prices skyrocketed, both in California and in most of the western United States.[35] Both daily and futures prices rose to 10 or more times the normal price levels.

There were several main causes:

1. California's deregulation policies were badly designed, as the deregulation was hammered out in a political compromise in 1996.

2. Several accidental conditions of scarcity aggravated the shortages.

3. Corrupt actions to rig and distort the markets in many ways were made by Enron, El Paso, and other companies.

4. The Federal Energy Regulatory Commission (FERC) was under the control of the free-market ideologue Curtis Hebert, who simply refused to let FERC begin to take effective actions until April 2001. If FERC had taken curative actions earlier, the crisis would have quickly disappeared.

The crisis had large lingering effects, including scaring many states into reversing or delaying their own deregulation of electricity.[36] By 2002, the FERC had still not set policies on stable lines: "utility regulators in 15 states, primarily in the west and southeast, assailed FERC, asserting that deregulation is a catastrophic failure."[37]

Even airlines pose older issues, including large new proposed mergers (such as United Airlines and US Airways) that would raise monopoly power in major parts of the industry. The failure to remove frequent-flyer awards has let that dominance-favoring activity entrench itself further. It also links leading airlines with many other markets such as car rentals and hotels. Collusive pricing has posed difficulties. Deregulation has replaced old problems with new ones.

A Loss of Social Goals.   Regulated monopolies often serve important social goals, such as conservation of natural resources, service to poor citizens, and environmental protections. Deregulation poses a direct threat that competition will squeeze out these goals. That has particularly plagued efforts to promote competition in electricity, where there are fears that competition will lead firms to pollute, adopt resource-destroying technology, cut service to low-income families, etc.

IV. PUBLIC ENTERPRISE[38]

A public enterprise is owned by a government on behalf of its citizens. It can be identical to private firms in every respect, except that it does not have private stockholders. It uses inputs to produce outputs, and it keeps standard accounts of costs, revenues, and profits. Though it need not maximize its profits as a private firm does, it will often try to break even financially. It may pursue other goals, and so its economic performance may differ sharply from that of a private firm. Therein lies the fascination of public enterprise, for it offers a wide variety of possibilities and outcomes.

1. COVERAGE AND PURPOSES[39]

In many Western economies, public ownership typically has covered: most or all utility firms; one or several public banks; large social insurance programs; several major industries under partial public ownership; virtually all social services under public ownership; and in virtually no public enterprise in distribution.

Public enterprise also exists in many parts of the U.S. economy. There is a great variety of forms and behavior, ranging from conventional utility cases such as the Tennessee Valley Authority and the Port of New York Authority to industrial and service areas, certain subsidy programs, and important social enterprises such as public schools and universities, libraries, courts, and prisons. These public enterprises tend to be a phantom presence in the United States, not recognized for their real importance.

There are many reasons for creating public firms, but the most valid normative reason is that the enterprise can serve some social purpose that a private firm would ignore or eliminate.

Social and Political Preferences.   A society (city, state, or nation) may simply prefer public to private control, especially for certain leading sectors. For example, hundreds of U.S. cities (e.g., Los Angeles, Cleveland, Holyoke) have long had public electricity, whereas most others haven't. Nations too have differing traditions and views. Also the quality of civil service varies, and that can affect the performance of public firms (which in some societies may have corruption).

Inadequate Private Supply.   A new industry or project may seem too large and risky for private firms to invest in. They will demand government guarantees, grants, or other subsidies. It may seem wiser to put the unit under direct public ownership.

External Impacts.   Public firms may avoid various outside social harms or benefits, which private firms ignore. In the extreme, the service may be a pure public good calling for a full subsidy.

Sovereignty.   State ownership may be a way of avoiding ownership and control by foreign interests.

Some public firms are simply utilities providing infrastructure. Others have a special social element to serve, apart from the usual commercial goals (of producing services efficiently and selling them at prices that fit cost and demand conditions). For example, a local bus line is supposed to provide frequent, reliable service throughout the city more extensively than a strictly commercial bus line would provide. The nature and extent of the social element are usually debated intensely. What social element is provided by the Postal Service, for instance? Does it require daily deliveries, including Saturdays? Should junk mail be subsidized? If so, to what extent?

You may have noticed, for example, the hot debates over Amtrak's services and over costly city-financed sports stadiums that are used by private professional teams. Quieter debates continue endlessly about the financing of city services, public schools and state universities, airports, golf courses, state liquor stores in sixteen states, and all other public enterprises. In every case, the questions are: What is the valid social element? How much of it should the public pay for?

2. SUBSIDIES AND EFFICIENCY

The public pays for the social purpose by means of subsidies, which come from government tax revenues. The subsidy can be any amount, ranging from 100 percent to zero. Thus, public schools are subsidized totally from taxes, whereas local water supply is totally paid for by users. Most public universities are in between, supported partly by government subsidies and partly by students' tuition payments.

Each subsidy ought to be fitted precisely to the social element of the public firm. A small social effect calls for little or no subsidy, while a large social element might justify a total subsidy.

Size.   One danger is that a given subsidy will simply be too large, giving the users an undeserved free ride. Should library users, or bus riders, or students at public universities be subsidized heavily? Is there really a special social need? Are the users really needier than the cross-section of taxpayers?

Incentives.   A second danger is that subsidies will weaken the enterprise's incentives to cut costs. Whenever costs can be covered without effort, the firm may let them rise. Public firms as diverse as city transit, the Postal Service, and public schools are regularly accused of such wasteful subsidies.

These dangers are real, and they have no easy solution. But they are often exaggerated by free-market ideologues. Society must debate, trying to fit subsidies to their true social element and trying to avoid wasteful incentives. If the political process works well, it may supervise the firms and trim their subsidies to just the right patterns. Public enterprises can go beyond the narrow limits of profit in order to serve genuine public needs. But this capacity needs careful control to keep the firms from making wasteful mistakes.

3. ECONOMIC PERFORMANCE

Public enterprises come under the same general efficiency rules as private firms. They should minimize costs, and many do so with excellent efficiency.[40] Their prices should be aligned with their marginal costs (including social costs), just as for regulated privately owned utilities. Many public firms do, in fact, adopt efficient price structures. For example, British and French public firms were leaders in efficient utility pricing from the 1950s on.[41]

V. THE PRIVATIZATION OF PUBLIC FIRMS[42]

The "publicness" of firms depends on their ownership, the degree of outside subsidy and control, and the kind of policies the firm takes (e.g., strict profit maximizing or pursuing some public purposes). From 1950 to 1980, the degree of public enterprise in the United States and Western Europe was roughly stable.

Public enterprise has vigorous opponents, especially conservative politicians, free-market advocates, and private investor groups eager to take over assets at low prices and exploit their market positions. These groups have three main economic complaints about public firms:

1. **Public firms get public subsidies,** which are burdensome to taxpayers.

2. **Public firms' subsidies and other advantages enable them to set lower prices against private competitors.** Examples: tax-subsidized state universities have lower tuitions than private colleges, and public-power firms sell their power more cheaply than private electricity.

3. **Public firms may become bureaucratic and slow to innovate.** To serve competing private interests, or perhaps just to improve efficiency, a campaign to privatize public firms may arise, so as to "let market forces operate," "apply incentives for efficiency," and "get the government out of business."

Privatizing can take either or both of two directions: **ownership can be shifted to private hands and/or entry by new private rivals can be permitted.**[43] By itself, private ownership only shifts managements toward a narrower profit orientation.[44] Unless competition is effective, the privatized firm's actions can be doubly harmful; there will be monopoly pricing and retarded innovation, plus a withdrawal of the public firm's allowances for social impacts. A pure sell-off is therefore appropriate only when competition will be effective and the social elements are negligible.

The alternative method of privatizing is simply to open up entry in a way that maximizes competitive pressure as new private firms enter the market.[45] It will succeed only if entry is really free and the new competitors are forceful. Paradoxically, that very situation makes a sell-off unnecessary: the existing tight competition will force an efficient and innovative result even if the firm's ownership remains public. Free entry is therefore both necessary and sufficient for successful privatization, while a sell-off is neither. The British literature has noted the need for competition, but the British government's policies have not fully succeeded in creating it.

Actual Privatizing.   A privatization frenzy arose in Britain after 1979 and then spread to some other countries.[46] The United States has done only moderate privatizing at the national level, even under Reagan conservatives, but many state and local governments have privatized some operations (discussed later). A selection of leading results in various countries are noted in table 17.2; others could be added from countries ranging from the Philippines to Sweden.

British Privatizing.   Led by Margaret Thatcher's conservative government after 1979, privatizing was extended to the telephone system, gas supply, intercity buses, the British Airways airline, ports, airports, and British Steel; by the 1990s even the railroads and the electricity and water systems had been sold off.

Britain's experience suggests sobering, often calamitous lessons about the methods of privatizing public enterprises and the benefits realized from "getting the government out of the marketplace." The following brief summary only touches the main points of a large, growing literature.

British privatizing after 1979 drastically shrank the set of infrastructure firms taken over in the nationalizations of 1945 to 1950.[47] Privatizing could provide public benefits by reducing the costs of covering deficits incurred by poor private management. But the main change has been a selling off of ownership, inspired mainly by ideology and by pressures from investor groups seeking to acquire assets cheaply and make capital gains for themselves.[48]

Some privatized firms have indeed faced strong competition: British Rail Hotels and Jaguar (automobiles; now owned by Ford) are examples. The dominant firms have been much more numerous, however, and they have had it much easier. Though there are rosy predictions that new competitors will contain the monopolies, that has often failed to occur, leaving the private monopolies free to exploit the public.

In both telephone service and equipment supply, for example, British Telecom largely maintained its previous monopoly position into the 1990s.[49] British Gas has had similar experience. In inner-city bus travel, the virtual monopoly of the incumbent National Express was not sold off, but new entry was opened in 1980. Though many small chartered bus firms could enter in theory, actual entry has been slight. National Express has controlled access to terminals and has applied strategic pricing effectively to minimize the inroads of new bus rivals.

The sell-off of British Airways also failed to generate effective competition or new entry. The firm faces little competition on its domestic routes, and in 1987, it actually sought to buy out British Caledonian, its one rival. Its control of airport access in Britain as well as its use of strategic pricing has protected its virtual monopoly, with predictable results of high fares. British Airways has also continued its long-standing cooperation with its rivals in international routes so as to resist entry and maintain fare levels.

Electricity systems were privatized in 1990 as twelve regional electric companies. The companies immediately moved toward higher prices, and by 1995 were reaping very high rates of profit and large capital gains.[50] The profits made them takeover targets for many U.S. electric companies, and a wave of mergers ensued in 1995.[51] Privatization gave owners (including big American companies) large capital gains at their customers' expense. But the tide reversed; disasters under U.S. electricity deregulation led those American firms to sell off most of the same U.K. firms they had rushed to buy.

Table 17.2 Leading Examples of Privatizing since 1980

Enterprise	Activity	Year	Sale Price ($ billion)
United Kingdom			
British Telecom	Telephone system	1984	22.0
British electric companies	Electricity systems	1990	14.0
British Gas	Gas supply	1986	12.9
British Steel	Steelmaker	1988	4.2
France			
Elf-Aquitaine	Oil	1994	6.2
BNP	Banking	1993	4.9
Alacatel-Alsthom	Electrical engineering	1987	3.4
Italy			
INA	Insurance	1994	4.2
IMI	Banking	1994	2.3
Germany			
VEBA	Energy, telecommunications, chemicals	1984	1.7
Netherlands			
Koninklijke PTT	Telephone system	1994	3.8
Canada			
Petro-Canada	Oil and gas	1991	2.0
Japan			
NTT	Telephone system	1987	73.5
East Japan Railway	Railroad	1993	10.9
Japan Tobacco	Tobacco products, sales	1994	5.7
Japan Airlines	Airline	1987	4.7
Australia			
Comwealth Bank	Banking	1991	2.3
Qantas Airways	Airline	1992	1.5
New Zealand			
Telecom NZ	Telephone system	1990	2.5
Mexico			
Telmex	Telephone system	1990	7.0

Source: "The Big Deals," in special section "Sale of the Century," *Wall Street Journal* (October 2, 1995): pp. R12–R13.

Privatizing of water systems was "a disaster."[52] As one observer said, "Water privatization is a ripoff, a steal, a plunder, legalized mugging, piracy, licensed theft, a diabolical liberty, a huge scam, a cheat, a snatch, a grab, a swindle . . . a huge machine for taking money out of customers' pockets."[53]

The most spectacular failure was the railroads. The plan called for a firm to manage the rail system so that private railroad firms could run their trains over it. But rail safety and coordination instead descended into chaos, and there were a series of wrecks that outraged the country. The problems continued in 2002.[54]

Taken together, the British experiments demonstrate that privatization often causes severe abuses when private monopolies are created. As always, effective competition develops only slowly, if at all, in monopolized markets. The U.K. Monopolies and Mergers Commission had little effect, while efforts to constrain the monopolies were weak.

Moreover, the government often underpriced the stocks issued to the private buyers, giving away large windfall gains to large private investor groups at the expense of the public. The pressures to underprice the shares are strong, both from lobbying by private investors and from the government's anxiety to guarantee that all of the shares will be sold.

Privatization has worked best for firms with small social elements, which are already under competitive conditions. These cases have been the relatively minor ones in Britain, however, and the selling off of large monopoly utility firms has often hit consumers hard.

In Europe. On the continent, there has been less zeal to privatize, though some has occurred. Efforts to open up new competition have gone slower, with little more success than in British or U.S. markets. For example, in telecoms the old monopolies have yielded only slowly; their market shares in 2002 were still 80 percent or higher in Italy, Portugal, Spain, Germany, and France. "Telecom, gas and electricity in particular have proved devilishly difficult to liberalize. Former monopolies have enjoyed huge advantages over potential competitors because they already control networks, hold wide technological leads and have plenty of financial muscle to flex."[55]

In the United States. Some proposals for privatizing in the United States have been ill-conceived; examples include the FAA air traffic system, Social Security, the Tennessee Valley Authority, highways and bridges, and airports.[56] People have refused to trust private monopolies to serve public interests, and they have suspected that selling public assets will simply give large capital gains to private investors.

A quiet but striking conversion is taking place in many local water systems, with about 20 percent of drinking water and 2 percent of waste water now handled by private companies.[57] These utility operations run the risks of monopoly that have plagued Britain, requiring cautious but aggressive local regulation.

Still another kind of privatizing has made wide progress since 1980 at the state and local level: **replacing public services with contracting-out to private firms.** This displaces public workers rather than selling public assets. Table 17.3 suggests the broad shift; a familiar version on many college campuses is the conversion of dining halls to privately catered food courts.

These are significant but not radical changes. The broad shift in table 17.3 reflects mainly a widespread move against public-employee unions rather than a British-style campaign favoring capital gains for investors. Despite occasional fanatics' calls to sell off major public assets, the United States is likely to experiment with more moderate shifts in contracting, leasing, joint ventures, and other gradations.

Table 17.3   A Shift toward Privatizing Public Services

Service	Percent Contracted Out		
	1987	1990	1995
Janitorial services	52	62	70
Solid-waste collection	30	38	50
Building maintenance	32	37	42
Automobile towing	22	28	40
Security services	27	33	40
Street maintenance/repair	19	21	37
Parking garages	20	26	35
Park maintenance	18	25	32
Tree trimming	17	23	31
Data processing	16	21	31
Golf courses	16	18	24

Source: Adapted from *Wall Street Journal* (October 2, 1995): p. R8.

Failures in Japan?[58]   Japan has done four main privatizings: the telephone system (Nippon Telephone & Telegraph Corp., NTT) and Japan Airlines in 1987, East Japan Railway Co. in 1993, and Japan Tobacco in 1994. The government retains large holdings in NTT and Japan Tobacco.

In contrast to Britain's bonanzas for investors, Japan has set sale prices high, and that has left many investors with capital losses after privatizing. The efficiency effects have also been mixed, with government still keeping large holdings that affect the firms' decisions. Summarizing the record so far, the *Wall Street Journal* noted, "Even the most advanced countries can botch privatization. Just ask Japan."[59]

QUESTIONS FOR REVIEW

1. Explain why there are no simple criteria that clearly mark off sectors that should be regulated.

2. Why should prices for utility services usually be higher at peak than off-peak times? Show how this would apply to electricity pricing.

3. Explain how regulation may induce a waste of capital as well as X-inefficiency. Then explain how those effects may be minor.

4. Explain what price caps are and how they contrast with traditional rate-base regulation. Under what conditions will they work well (e.g., numbers and complexities of outputs, similarities of price trends in the economy, and knowledge about technological progress)? Or poorly?

5. For deregulation to be effective, what criteria must be met, especially regarding market shares? Do those standards square with the competitive conditions we have discussed throughout this book?

6. Discuss the two elements of successful privatization: private ownership and effective competition. Choose an actual public enterprise in the United States. Do you think it could be effectively privatized? Should that be tried?

ENDNOTES

[1]There is a large literature on the economics of regulation. Summaries include Richard Schmalensee, *The Control of Natural Monopolies* (Lexington, MA: Lexington Books, 1979); a clear statement of the economic issues is John Tschirhart, *The Regulation of Utilities: Pricing and Behavior* (New York: Cambridge University Press, 1991); for more extensive background, see Alfred E. Kahn, *The Economics of Regulation*, 2 vols. (New York: Wiley, 1971; reissued 1990 by MIT Press). On the ways that regulation is often distorted, see Bruce Owen and Ronald Braeutigam, *The Regulation Game: Strategic Use of the Administrative Process* (Cambridge, MA: Ballinger, 1978); and Roger Noll and Bruce Owen, *The Political Economy of Deregulation: Interest Groups in the Regulatory Process* (Washington, DC: American Enterprise Institute, 1983). On the history of regulation, see Marc Allen Eisner, *Regulatory Politics in Transition*, rev. ed. (Baltimore: Johns Hopkins University Press, 2000). Good sources of research findings and policy assessments also include the ongoing publications of the Institute of Public Utilities, Michigan State University; and the National Regulatory Research Institute, Ohio State University, especially its *Quarterly Bulletin*. *Public Utilities Fortnightly* gives detailed coverage of regulation and utility companies.

[2]For example, see Jeffrey E. Cohen, "The Telephone Problem and the Road to Telephone Regulation in the United States, 1876–1917," *Journal of Policy History* 3 (1991).

[3]Often, too, it was applied inappropriately to industries that were not natural monopolies. Examples include trucking, airlines, and natural gas production. American regulation was criticized very early. See Horace M. Gray, "The Passing of the Public Utility Concept," *Journal of Land and Public Utility Economics* 8 (February 1940): pp. 16–35; and Walter Adams and Horace Gray, *Monopoly in America* (New York: Macmillan, 1955).

[4]See Irston R. Barnes, *The Economics of Public Utility Regulation* (New York: F. S. Crofts, 1942); James C. Bonbright, *Principles of Public Utility Rates* (New York: Columbia University Press, 1961); and Kahn, *The Economics of Regulation* for thorough reviews of the history and concepts. Also R. L. Swartwout, "Current Utility Regulatory Practice from a Historical Perspective," *Natural Resources Journal* 32 (Spring 1992): pp. 289–343; and J. P. Tiemstra, "Theories of Regulation and the History of Consumerism," *International Journal of Social Economics* 19 (1992): pp. 3–27. On the analytical alternatives, see Richard Schmalensee, "Good Regulatory Regimes," *Rand Journal of Economics* 20(3) (1989): pp. 417–36; and M. Waterson, "A Comparative Analysis of Methods for Regulating Public Utilities," *Metroeconomica* 43 (February-June 1992): pp. 205–22.

[5]*Federal Power Commission v. Hope Natural Gas*, 320 U.S. 591 (1944).

[6]See especially Adams and Gray, *Monopoly in America*, 1955; followed by John R. Meyer, Merton J. Peck, John Stenason, and Charles Zwick, *The Economics of Competition in the Transportation Industries* (Cambridge: Harvard University Press, 1959).

[7]For an influential later set of discussions of the case for deregulation in many industries, see Almarin Phillips, ed., *Promoting Competition in Regulated Markets* (Washington, DC: Brookings Institution, 1975).

[8]Unfortunately, the botched deregulation of savings and loans—a grave failure of Reagan-era deregulation—led to huge losses and harm in the 1980s.

[9]For a perceptive appraisal of the first round of deregulation, see Leonard W. Weiss and Michael W. Klass, *Deregulation: What Really Happened* (Boston: Little, Brown, 1987).

[10]Some of the new theorizing was so abstract as to lack practical uses, but other parts were valuable; see for example David E. M. Sappington, "Designing Incentive Regulation," *Review of Industrial Organization* 9 (June 1994): pp. 245–72; and Schmalensee, "Good Regulatory Regimes." A good review of the new wave is J. J. Lafont, "The New Economics of Regulation Ten Years After," *Econometrica* 62 (May 1994): pp. 507–37. Among other analytical writings, see Daniel Spulber, *Regulation and Markets* (Cambridge: MIT Press, 1989); Glenn Blackmon, *Incentive Regulation and the Regulation of Incentives* (Boston: Kluwer, 1994); and Stephen J. Brown and Davis S. Sibley, *The Theory of Public Utility Pricing* (New York: Cambridge University Press, 1986).

[11]Airline competition became fully effective after deregulation during 1978–1984, but then monopoly elements were allowed to recur, as chapter 14 noted.

[12]See for example Richard H. K. Vietor, *Contrived Competition: Regulation and Deregulation in America* (Cambridge: Harvard University Press, 1994).

[13]See Paul L. Joskow, ed., *Economic Regulation* (Northampton, MA: Elgar, 2000), for a review with many perspectives; also Robert B. Ekelund, Jr., ed., *The Foundations of Regulatory Economics*, 3 vols. (Northampton, MA: Elgar, 1998), which provides 76 significant papers in regulation, covering its origins, modern approaches, and deregulation.

[14]See also Kenneth E. Train, *Optimal Regulation: The Economic Theory of Natural Monopoly* (Cambridge: MIT Press, 1991); advanced analysis is in Dieter Bos, *Pricing and Price Regulation: An Economic Theory for Public Enterprises and Public Utilities* (New York: Elsevier Science, 1994).

[15]Most utilities do in fact have a wide range of discretion in enlarging their systems as time passes, so that they keep capacity at least roughly in line with demand.

[16]See Kahn, *The Economics of Regulation*, Schmalensee, *The Control of Natural Monopolies*, and William J. Baumol, John Panzar, and Robert D. Willig, *Contestable Markets and the Theory of Industry Structure* (San Diego: Harcourt Brace Jovanovich, 1982).

[17]The ICC was formally abolished in January 1996, though some of its powers (and its commissioners) have been retained in the Department of Transportation. It has power to rule on railroad mergers, for example, with advice from the Antitrust Division.

[18]The awkward name replaced the clearer Federal Power Commission in 1978. The FERC also regulates gas pipelines, oil pipelines, and water power sites.

[19]There is also a U.S. Postal Rate Commission, covering postal rates, and a Maritime Commission, but they, and other units named commissions, do not have the standard regulatory tasks. Postal rates, for example, pose more specific, politically charged, and infrequent issues.

[20]The companies often advocate Ramsey prices (see chapter 10), but they have serious defects and are relevant only for special cases. See Baumol, Panzar, and Willig, *Contestable Markets*; and William G. Shepherd, "Ramsay Pricing: Its Uses and Limits," *Utilities Policy* 2 (October 1992): pp. 296–98.

[21]See Kahn, *The Economics of Regulation*; Schmalensee, *The Control of Natural Monopolies*; a retrospective survey of the benefits of deregulation by Clifford Winston, "Economic Deregulation: Days of Reckoning for Microeconomists," *Journal of Economic Literature* 31 (September 1993): pp. 1263–89; and Paul L. Joskow and Nancy L. Rose, "The Effects of Economic Regulation," a chapter in Richard Schmalensee and Robert D. Willig, eds., *Handbook of Industrial Organization* (Amsterdam: North-Holland, 1989).

[22]See William G. Shepherd, *Regulation and Efficiency: A Reappraisal of Research and Policies*, Occasional Paper 17 (Columbus, OH: National Regulatory Research Institute, 1992); and Robert W. Hahn and John A Hird, "The Costs and Benefits of Regulation: Review and Synthesis," *Yale Journal on Regulation* 8 (1990): pp. 233–78. Among specific estimates of regulation's efficiency effects, see Kenneth D. Boyer, "The Costs of Price Regulation: Lessons from Railroad Deregulation," *Rand Journal of Economics* 18 (1987): p. 408 ff; Ronald R. Braeutigam and Roger G. Noll, "The Regulation of Surface Freight Transportation: The Welfare Effects Revisited," *Review of Economics and Statistics* 66 (February 1984): pp. 80–87; Ann F. Friedlaender and Richard H. Spady, *Freight Transport Regulation: Equity, Efficiency, and Competition in the Rail and Trucking Industries* (Cambridge: MIT Press, 1981); Leon Courville, "Regulation and Efficiency in the Electric Utility Industry," *Bell Journal of Economics* 5 (Spring 1974): pp. 53–74.

[23]A classic discussion is in Harvey Averch and Leland L. Johnson, "Behavior of the Firm Under Regulatory Constraint," *American Economic Review* 53 (December 1963): pp. 1052–69.

[24]Suppose that the cost of capital is 9 percent and the permitted rate of return is 11 percent. Then every additional $100 million in the rate base will increase net profits by $2 million (that is, $11 million return minus $9 million cost of capital). Capitalized at a 10:1 ratio, that $2 million might equal $20 million in added stock value to the shareholders.

[25]See Mark Armstrong, Simon Cowan, and John Vickers, *Regulatory Reform: Economic Analysis and British Experience* (Cambridge: MIT Press, 1994); and Matthew Bishop, John Kay, and Colin P. Mayer, eds., *The Regulatory Challenge* (New York: Oxford University Press, 1995).

[26]For a comparison, see C. Liston, "Price-Cap versus Rate-of-Return Regulation," *Journal of Regulatory Economics* 5 (March 1993): pp. 25–48.

[27]The input-cost index may be difficult to devise. The savings from progress are hard to predict, and the squeeze factor may be too generous or tight.

[28]See Kahn, *The Economics of Regulation*, 1971; and Alfred E. Kahn, *Letting Go: Deregulating the Process of Deregulation* (East Lansing: Michigan State University, 1998). Another discussion is William G. Shepherd, "Entry as a Substitute for Regulation," *American Economic Review* 63 (May 1973): pp. 98–105. See also William B. Tye, *The Transition to Deregulation: Developing Economic Standards for Public Policies* (Westport, CT: Quorum Books, 1991).

[29]The CAB lasted from 1938 to 1978. After 108 years, the ICC finally went out of existence on January 1, 1996. The FCC and FERC continue.

[30]For an interpretation, see Alfred E. Kahn, "Deregulation: Looking Backward and Looking Forward," *Yale Journal on Regulation* 7 (1990).

[31]Winston, "Economic Deregulation," provides a good survey; see also R. D. Cudahy, "The Coming Demise of Deregulation," *Yale Journal on Regulation* 10 (Winter 1993): pp. 1–15.

[32]The failures have been especially in western electricity markets and in local telephone service (dominated by the Baby Bells). See William G. Shepherd, "Dim Prospects: Effective Competition in Telecommunications, Railroads and Electricity," *Antitrust Bulletin* 42(1) (Spring 1997): pp. 151–75. See also Edythe S. Miller and Warren J. Samuels, eds., *The Institutionalist Approach to Public Utilities Regulation* (East Lansing: Michigan State University Press, 2002); the chapters by John C. Spychalski (railroads), Kenneth D. Boyer (trucking), Eugene P. Coyle (electricity), Thomas C. Gorak, and William G. Shepherd give severe criticisms of deregulation in the United States.

[33]A contrary view is that in most cases the regulators merely need to declare that entry is open. The market becomes contestable, and the power of potential entry eliminates all possible market power; Baumol, Panzar, and Willig, *Contestable Markets*; also Baumol and Willig, "Contestability: Developments Since the Book," *Oxford Economic Papers*, special issue, (November 1986). Chapter 9 noted how extreme that view is for normal markets. In formerly regulated monopolies, the dominant firm has even more opportunities for deterring new competition.

[34]See Winston, "Economic Deregulation"; Wesley W. Wilson, "Market-Specific Effects of Rail Deregulation," *Journal of Industrial Economics* 42 (March 1994): pp. 1–22; R. A. Prager, "The Effects of Deregulating Cable Television: Evidence from the Financial Markets," *Journal of Regulatory Economics* 4 (December 1992): pp. 347–63; Mark W. Frankena and Bruce M. Owen, *Electric Utility Mergers* (Westport, CT: Praeger, 1994).

[35]See Richard F. Hirsh, *Power Loss: The Origins of Deregulation and Restructuring in the American Electric Utility System* (Cambridge: MIT Press, 1999); and Severin Borenstein, "The Trouble With Electricity Markets: Understanding California's Restructuring Disaster," *Journal of Economic Perspectives* 16(1) (Winter 2002): pp. 191–211. See also the major story by Scott Thurm, Robert Gavin, and Mitchel Benson, "As California Starved for Energy, U.S. Businesses Had a Feast," *Wall Street Journal* (September 16, 2002): pp. A1, A8.

[36]On the chaos, see David Armstrong and Andrew Caffrey, "Amid Collapsing Power Market, Energy Companies Are Reeling," *Wall Street Journal* (July 24, 2002): pp. A1 and A8.

[37]"The 600-page blueprint comes against the backdrop of an energy industry in convulsions with builders of power plants slashing construction budgets and power trading sharply curtailed." See Rebecca Smith, "FERC Unveils Plan to Reorganize Electric System," *Wall Street Journal* (August 1, 2002): pp. A2 and A4.

[38]R. Fare, S. Grosskopf, and J. Logan, "The Relative Performance of Private Mixed and State-Owned Enterprises," *Journal of Public Economics* 26 (1985): pp. 89–106, reviews strengths of public enterprise; for criticism, see A. E. Boardman and A. R. Vining, "Ownership and Performance in Competitive Environments: A Comparison of the Performance of Private, Mixed, and State-Owned Enterprises," *Journal of Law and Economics* 32 (April 1989): pp. 1–34. For a broad survey of economic issues relating to public enterprise, see W. G. Shepherd and associates, *Public Enterprise: Economic Analysis of Theory and Practice* (Lexington, MA: Heath, 1976).

[39]See Pier Angelo Toninelli, ed., *The Rise and Fall of State-Owned Enterprises in the Western World* (Cambridge: Cambridge University Press, 2000), for an extensive review of public enterprise's extent and history.

[40]See Fare, Grosskopf, and Logan, "The Relative Performance of Private Mixed and State-Owned Enterprises"; G. De Fraja, "Productive Efficiency in Public and Private Firms," *Journal of Public Economics* 50 (January 1993): pp. 15–30; and Henry Tulkens, "Economies and the Performance of the Public Sector," *Annals of Public and Cooperative Economy* 63 (September 1992): pp. 373–85.

[41]See for example Ralph Turvey, *Optimal Pricing and Investment in Electricity Supply* (London: Allen & Unwin, 1968); James R. Nelson, ed., *Marginal Cost Pricing in Practice* (Upper Saddle River, NJ: Prentice-Hall, 1964); and Robert L. Frost, *Alternating Currents: Nationalized Power in France, 1946–1970* (Ithaca: Cornell University Press, 1991).

[42]See also Matthew Bishop, John Kay, and Colin Mayer, eds., *Privatization and Economic Performance* (New York: Oxford University Press, 1994); William J. Baumol, "On the Perils of Privatization," *Eastern Economic Journal* 19 (Fall 1993): pp. 419–40.

[43]Actually there are other gradations and methods. For example, the public assets can be leased under a variety of alternative arrangements. In 1996, the New York Port Authority was considering such alternatives for the World Trade Center. See Caries Gasparino, "Port Authority Looks Into Sale of Trade Center," *Wall Street Journal* (February 23, 1996): p. A6A.

[44]Leroy P. Jones, Pankai Tandon, and Ingo Vogelsang, *Selling Public Enterprises: A Cost-Benefit Methodology* (Cambridge: MIT Press, 1990).

[45] The benefits of competition are analyzed in John C. Hilke, *Competition in Government-Financed Services* (Westport, CT: Quorum Books, 1992).

[46]See Bill Bradshaw and Helen Lawton Smith, eds., *Privatization and Deregulation of Transport* (London: St. Martin's Press, 2000); David M. Newbery, *Privatization, Restructuring and Regulation of Network Utilities* (Cambridge: MIT Press, 1999); and William L. Megginson and Jeffrey M. Netter, "From State to Market: A Survey of Empirical Studies on Privatization," *Journal of Economic Literature* 39 (June 2001): pp. 321–89. For a strong critique, see Elliott D. Sclar, *You Don't Always Get What You Pay For: The Economics of Privatization* (Ithaca, NY: Cornell University Press, 2000); and a world-wide review is in Mitsuhiro Kagami and Masatsugu, eds., *Privatization, Deregulation and Economic Efficiency: A Comparative Analysis of Asia, Europe and the Americas* (Northampton, MA: Elgar, 2000).

[47]On the earlier rise of British public ownership, see William G. Shepherd, *Economic Performance Under Public Enterprise* (New Haven: Yale University Press, 1965). On later experience and changes, see Christopher D. Foster, *Privatization, Public Ownership and Regulation of Natural Monopoly* (Oxford: Basil Blackwell, 1982).

[48]Dana Milbank, "Backlash," *Wall Street Journal* (October 2, 1995): pp. 17–18, notes how British privatization has enriched investors but done little for consumers.

[49]D. Parker, "A Decade of Privatization: The Effect of Ownership Change and Competition on British Telecom," *British Review of Economic Issues* 16 (October 1994): pp. 87–113.

[50]Suzanne Kapner, "British Reopening the Debate Over Privatization," *New York Times* (August 29, 2002): p. C4, presents new debates over electricity privatizing; and Kyle Pope, "Utility Privatizations Backfire in the U.K.," *Wall Street Journal* (March 30, 1995): p. A10.

[51]Tara Parker-Pope, "National Power Joins U.K. Utilities Fray as U.S. Firms, Others Search for Deals," *Wall Street Journal* (October 5, 1995): p. A17; and Agis Salpukas, "U.S. Utilities Buy in Britain to Learn Deregulation for Home Use," *New York Times* (December 1, 1995): p. D6.

[52]Barry Newman, "Taking a Bath," *Wall Street Journal* (October 2, 1995): p. R18, severely criticizes the water privatization.

[53]Joe Rogaly in the *Financial Times*; see Newman, "Taking a Bath."

[54]See Alan Cowell, "Britain Braces for Delays On Its Busiest Rail Line," *New York Times* (October 27, 2002): p. T3.

[55]See Keith Johnson, "Europe's Long, Long Last Mile," *Wall Street Journal* (November 13, 2002): pp. A20, A22, for detailed discussion.

[56]For example, Albert R. Karr, "Plan to Turn Over Air Traffic System to New Entity is Criticized in House," *Wall Street Journal* (February 15, 1995): p. A6.

[57]E. S. Browning, "French Companies Pour Into U.S. Waterworks Market," *Wall Street Journal* (February 25, 1994): p. B4. Even French water companies have been buying out some American cities' systems.

[58]See Robert Steiner, "Trepidation in Tokyo," *Wall Street Journal* (October 2, 1995): p. R20.

[59]Steiner, "Trepidation in Tokyo."

Chapter

18

FURTHER STUDY

The field you have surveyed is turbulent, important, and fascinating. Learning the current technical concepts and terms was just the first step. You also learned to see how they are evolving and how they apply to changing industrial conditions. This book has, we hope, helped you to understand complex economic problems and feel the exhilaration of dealing with colossal corporations and immense interests as routine, everyday matters.

By completing this course, you have extended your knowledge on several planes. You have learned the greater part of a new language, with technical terms and standards. The main lines of a large body of literature are now familiar to you. You are beginning to know how to test concepts and where to go for data on the subject. You have also acquired a certain amount of factual knowledge about U.S. and foreign conditions.

This has helped you achieve a more professional level of understanding. You should now be able to make sense of many journal articles and monographs by specialists, except perhaps for the most advanced. Better yet, you can apply a critical sense to these writings, judging for yourself how valid they are. You should be able to design ways to test concepts and industrial conditions, fitting the methods to the kinds of evidence available. And, of course, you are now keenly aware of how ignorant the experts are on many issues.

It is your level of skill that matters, not the specific views you now hold about competition and its effects. One's ratings of the quantitative "answers" must always be provisional rather than final. The evidence is usually weak, requiring a careful weighing of probabilities. Also, as new data emerge, old opinions must often be revised and sometimes discarded. One can only strive to use valid methods with a professional level of quality. You are now able to do that. Some of your research papers (or term papers) will be almost as good as some of those published in the journals.

Recognize this skill as a blessing, for it will enable you to handle the issues intelligently from now on. A few of you will go on to professional research careers in this field. Many of you will follow careers in law, business, accounting, or public agencies. They, too, will involve you deeply in the issues. The rest of you will encounter the problems described here month in and month out for at least forty years, as the issues develop and your own interests evolve. Understanding the nature of the competitive system—as it changes and you change—will be one of your continuing tasks. You can now approach it skillfully and skeptically.

Name Index

Aaronovitch, S., 148
Abbott, T. A., 166
Acs, Zoltan, 55
Adams, Henry Carter, 21, 29
Adams, Walter, 30, 52, 54, 57, 148, 166, 292, 293, 316, 369, 371
Adams, William J., 343
Adelman, Morris A., 29, 30, 267, 268
Allen, Paul G., 275, 290
Anderson, Robert D., 343
Andrade, Gregor, 148
Andrews, S. H., 166
Angwin, Julia, 148
Areeda, Philip, 29, 217, 218, 219, 224, 267, 343, 359
Armstrong, David, 400
Armstrong, Mark, 400
Arnold, Thurman, 351
Arrow, Kenneth J., 183, 267

Bagdikian, Ben H., 292
Bailey, Elizabeth E., 26, 314
Bailey, Jeff, 184, 294
Bain, Joe S., 22, 29, 52, 57, 74, 75, 87, 90, 95, 104, 162, 164, 166, 167, 190, 191, 196, 202, 250, 268

Baker, R., 370
Baldwin, John R., 89
Barnes, Irston R., 398
Barnett, F. William, 250
Barton, David R., 57, 105
Baseman, Kenneth C., 292
Baumol, William J., 26, 30, 53, 130, 184, 200, 202, 203, 219, 223, 224, 399, 400, 401
Baxter, William, 343, 353
Beath, John, 268
Beckenstein, Alan, 166
Behar, Richard, 316
Ben-Ner, Avner, 183
Benson, Mitchel, 184, 400
Berle, Adolph A., 29, 177, 178, 184, 268
Berry, Charles H., 202, 268
Bertrand, J., 227, 250
Bishop, Matthew, 400, 401
Bisson, T. A., 130, 184
Blackstone, Erwin, 292
Blair, John M., 57, 104, 251, 268
Blair, Roger D., 266
Blitz, Rudolph C., 129
Block, Harry, 269
Blumenthal, Ralph, 294
Boardman, A. E., 400

Bonbright, James C., 398
Bonds, Wendy, 267, 369
Borenstein, Severin, 224, 400
Bork, Robert H., 28, 30, 52, 130, 148, 267
Bos, Dieter, 399
Bowley, A. L., 266
Boyer, Kenneth D., 148, 372, 399, 400
Bradburd, Ralph, 104, 129
Bradford, D., 293
Bradshaw, Bill, 54, 183, 401
Braeutigam, Ronald R., 398, 399
Brander, A., 250
Brennan, Timothy J., 370
Bresnahan, Timothy F., 53, 105, 203
Brittain, John A., 129
Brock, Gerald W., 55, 106, 292, 370
Brock, James W., 52, 106, 129, 148, 166, 314,
    369, 371
Brooks, Rick, 314
Brown, Charles, 370
Brown, Gardner M., 107
Brown, Stephen J., 399
Browning, E. S., 402
Bryce, Robert, 183
Buck, A. J., 292
Bullock, Charles J., 21, 29, 166, 201
Bunch, D. S., 202
Burch, Philip H., 184
Burns, Greg, 316
Burns, Malcolm R., 218, 224

Cable, John, 30
Caffrey, Andrew, 400
Campbell, James S., 268
Cantelon, Philip L., 292
Carlson, Donald R., 251
Carlton, Jim, 148
Carroll, Paul, 293
Cason, T. N., 250
Cave, J., 250
Caves, Richard E., 57, 105, 184, 191, 202, 268
Chamberlin, Edward H., 22, 29, 227, 250
Chandler, Alfred D., 183
Cini, Michelle, 343
Clark, Don, 291
Clark, John Bates, 21, 29
Clark, John M., 21, 28, 29, 166, 224
Clark, Roger, 343
Clotfelter, Charles T., 183

Coase, Ronald H., 57, 183
Cohen, Jeffrey E., 398
Cole, Charles W., 29
Colodner, A. M., 343
Comanor, William S., 22, 120, 121, 129, 130,
    224, 267, 268, 269, 343
Connor, John M., 104
Conyon, M. J., 184
Cooper, Kerry, 55
Cotterill, Ronald W., 202
Cournot, Augustin, 23, 226, 227, 250
Courville, Leon, 399
Cowan, Simon, 400
Cowell, Alan, 401
Cowling, Keith, 99, 106, 343
Coyle, Eugene P., 400
Crandall, Robert W., 55, 292, 370
Craven, John, 167
Crowder, Walter F., 167
Cruver, Brian, 183
Cudahy, R. D., 400
Culbertson, W. P., 293
Cyert, Richard M., 30, 249

Dalton, J. A., 129
Daughety, Andrew F., 55
Davies, Stephen W., 267, 343
Davis, Bob, 370
Davis, D. D., 250
De Fraja, G, 401
de Wolfe, Peter, 343
Dealy, Francis X., 315
DeLamarter, Richard T., 55, 106, 224, 292,
    293, 370
Demsetz, Harold, 28, 100, 106
Dennis, Kenneth G., 29
Dertouzos, James N., 292
Deutsch, Claudia H., 372
Deutsch, Larry L., 293
Diesenhouse, Susan, 107
Director, Aaron, 28
Dirlam, Joel B., 250, 369
Dixit, Avinash K., 52, 250, 269
Domberger, S., 250
Dresner, M., 314
Driffield, Nigel, 343
Duetsch, Larry L., 54
Dunlop, Bruce, 343
Dunne, Timothy, 90

Eckard, E. W., 105, 128
Edwards, Corwin D., 250
Eichner, Alfred S., 148
Eisner, Marc Allen, 54, 398
Ekelund, Robert B., 55, 399
Ellison, G., 250
Ely, Richard T., 21, 29, 201
Elyasiani, E., 293
Elzinga, Kenneth G., 52, 293, 372
Epstein, Edward J., 55
Evans, David S., 55, 370
Evans, Laurie Beth, 202
Evans, William N., 314
Evenett, Simon J., 343

Fare, R., 400, 401
Fatsis, Stefan, 315
Feinberg, Robert M., 202, 344
Feldstein, Martin, 343
Feldstein, Paul J., 55
Fellner, William J., 29, 167, 250
Ferguson, Charles H., 293
Fiebig, D. G., 250
First, Harry, 202, 342, 369
Fisher, Anthony C., 107
Fisher, Franklin M., 30, 55, 293, 370
Fitch, Stephanie, 81
Fleischer, Arthur A., 315
Ford, E. J., 129
Fort, Rodney, 315
Foster, Christopher D., 401
Fox, Eleanor M., 130, 148, 202, 342, 369, 372
Fox, Loren, 183
France, Mike, 106
Frank, Robert, 148
Frankena, Mark W., 294, 400
Fraser, Donald, 55
Frech, H. E., 224
Freudenheim, Milt, 130
Frey, James, 55
Freyer, Tony, 342
Friedlaender, Ann F., 399
Frost, Robert L., 401
Fudenberg, D., 224
Fuer, Albert A., 343

Galbraith, John Kenneth, 255, 266
Garen, J. E., 184
Gaskins, Darius W., 202

Gasparino, Caries, 401
Gates, William, 120, 131, 275, 291
Gavin, Robert, 400
Gegax, D., 294
Geroski, Paul A., 78, 90, 202
Gerstner, Louis V., 98, 105, 293
Gibson, Richard, 293
Gies, Thomas G., 223
Gilbert, Richard J., 202, 371
Gilligan, Thomas, 105
Glaberson, William, 292
Glassman, Michael, 316
Gleick, James, 291
Goff, Brian L., 315
Gorak, Thomas C., 400
Gorecki, Paul K., 89
Gort, Michael, 202, 267, 268
Graham, David R., 55, 314
Gray, Horace M., 30, 398
Green, Christopher, 343
Green, Timothy, 55
Greene, Harold H., 354
Greenwood, Joen E., 30, 370
Greer, Douglas F., 293
Gribbin, J. Denys, 343
Grier, K. B., 315
Griffin, James M., 55, 104
Grosskopf, S., 400, 401
Grossman, G., 129
Grossman, Peter, 90
Gruley, Bryan, 314
Gui, Benedetto, 183

Hagstrom, Peter, 183
Hahn, Robert W., 399
Hakim, S., 292
Haller, Lawrence E., 202
Hamilton, R. T., 184
Hamilton, Walton, 29, 52, 342
Hand, Learned, 351
Hannon, Steve, 371
Harberger, Arnold, 99, 100, 106
Harper, D. A., 184
Harrison, Jeffrey L., 266
Hausman, Jerry, 89
Hay, Donald, 90, 244, 250, 343
Hay, George A., 250
Hayes, Nina Stechler, 293
Hebert, Curtis, 390

Henley, A., 90
Henry, David, 148
Herfindahl, Orris, 89
Herriges, J. A., 294
Heywood, John S., 106, 203
Hilke, John C., 401
Hird, John A., 399
Hirschman, Albert O., 89
Hirschmeier, Johannes, 130, 184
Hirsh, Richard F., 54, 400
Hofheinz, Pal, 372
Holmes, Stanley, 106
Holt, C. A., 250
Horowitz, Ira, 315
Hosken, Daniel, 371
Hunker, J. A., 55

Ichbiah, Daniel, 291
Irwin, Manley R., 292
Iskow, Julie, 184
Ito, Takatoshi, 130, 184

Jacobs, Donald P., 147
Jacquemin, Alexis, 202, 343
Jaffee, Bruce L., 293, 294
Jeanrenaud, Claude, 315
Jenks, Jeremiah, 29
Jewkes, John, 52, 117, 128, 129
Johansson, Borje, 166
Johnson, Arthur, 55
Johnson, Keith, 402
Johnson, Peter, 54
Johnson, R. L., 314
Johnson, William R., 130
Jones, Leroy P., 401
Jordan, W. John, 293, 294
Joskow, A. S., 314
Joskow, Paul L., 55, 294, 399
Jovanovic, B., 148

Kagami, Mitsuhiro, 54, 183, 401
Kagel, J. H., 224
Kahn, Alfred E., 22, 30, 54, 202, 223, 314,
    398, 399, 400
Kamien, Morton I., 128, 129
Kaplan, A. D. H., 186, 201, 250, 268
Kaplan, Daniel P., 55, 314
Kapner, Suzanne, 401
Karlsson, Charlie, 166

Karr, Albert R., 402
Kaserman, David L., 294
Katics, M. M., 105
Katsoulacos, Yannis, 268
Katz, Michael L., 149, 371
Katzman, Robert A., 342
Kaufer, Erich, 166
Kay, John, 400, 401
Kaysen, Carl, 22, 29, 227, 250
Kelley, Daniel, 244, 250
Kellogg, George, 307, 308
Kern, William S., 315
Kesenne, Stefan, 315
Kessides, Ioannis, 102, 107, 314
Khemani, R. S., 343
Khermouch, Gerry, 90
Khosla, S. Dev, 343
Kilman, Scott, 373
Kindem, Gorsham, 55
Kirchhoff, Bruce A., 184
Klass, Michael W., 53, 398
Knepper, Susan, 291
Knight, Frank H., 28, 29, 147
Koller, Ronald H., 224
Koskoff, David, 104
Kotkin, Joel, 166
Kovacic, William E., 372
Kwoka, John E., 54, 251, 267, 268, 292, 315,
    370, 371, 372

Lafont, J. J., 398
Lamoreaux, Naomi, 148
Landro, Laura, 148
Lang, L. H. P., 268
Langreth, Robert, 107
Lanzillotti, Robert F., 250
Layson, S. K., 223
Lean, David F., 149
Leech, D., 184
Lehman, Alexander, 343
Leibenstein, Harvey J., 22, 30, 57, 184
Lenzen, Godehard, 104
Leonard, Gregory, 89
Lerner, Abba P., 57
Lesser, W. H., 251
Letwin, William, 29
Levenstein, Margaret C., 90
Levin, D., 224
Levin, R. C., 224

Levin, Sharon G., 130
Lewis, W. Arthur, 166, 224
Liebowitz, Stan J., 291, 371
Lippert, R. L., 184
Liston, C., 400
Logan, J., 400, 401
Lohr, Steve, 131, 291, 371
Lowry, Tom, 147
Lublin, Joann S., 130, 148
Lueck, Sarah, 222
Lueck, Thomas J., 104
Luksetich, William A., 130
Lundberg, Ferdinand, 129

MacAvoy, Paul W., 55, 104, 370
MacDonald, G. M., 148
Machlup, Fritz, 22, 29, 223
Makowski, Louis, 57
Mann, H. Michael, 87, 90, 202
Mansfield, Edwin, 22, 30, 119, 128
March, James G., 30
Margolis, Stephen E., 291, 371
Marine, Henry, 342
Markoff, John, 291, 371
Marshall, Alfred, 29, 57
Marshall, William, 105
Martin, Stephen, 106, 202, 249, 343
Mason, C. F., 268
Mason, Edward S., 30
Masson, Robert T., 164, 167, 251
Mathewson, C. Frank, 53
Mayajima, H., 130, 184
Mayer, Colin P., 400, 401
Mayo, John W., 294
McCartney, Scott, 314
McChesney, Fred S., 30, 57, 128, 148, 342
McDowell, Edwin, 314
McEachem, William A., 184
McGee, John S., 28, 218, 221, 224
McGowan, John C., 30
McGowan, John J., 370
McGowan, Lee, 343
Means, Gardiner, 29, 177, 178, 184, 268
Megginson, William L., 54, 183, 401
Mehdian, S., 293
Mehran, H., 184
Melcher, Richard A., 293
Meller, Paul, 343, 372
Meurs, Mike, 344
Meyer, John R., 55, 398

Milbank, Dana, 401
Miller, Edythe S., 400
Miller, James P., 316
Miller, John P., 250
Mitchell, Bridger M., 292
Mitchell, Mark, 148
Moms, Charles R., 267, 293
Montgomery, Cynthia A., 102, 107
Moody, John, 29, 52, 129, 148, 186, 201
Moore, W. T., 184
Morgan, J. P., 21, 321
Morgenstern, Oskar, 227, 250
Morrison, Steven A., 224, 299, 314, 315
Motavalli, John, 147
Mowery, David C., 291
Mueller, Dennis C., 52, 99, 106, 148
Mueller, Willard F., 23, 104
Muller, Joann, 90
Murphy, R. Dennis, 166
Murray, Alan, 27
Murray, Matt, 371

Nalebuff, Barry J., 52, 250
Nelson, James R., 401
Netter, Jeffrey M., 54, 401
Neumann, John von, 227, 250
Neumann, Manfred, 342
Newbery, David M., 54, 183, 401
Newman, Barry, 401
Niman, Neil B., 292
Noll, Roger G., 55, 315, 370, 398, 399
Nordhaus, William D., 129
Norman, Victor D., 269
Nowotny, K., 294

O'Boyle, E. J., 184
O'Brien, Anthony P., 29, 148
O'Brien, Daniel, 371
Ordover, Janusz A., 89, 224
Ortega, Bob, 371
Orwall, Bruce, 148
Oster, Clinton V., 55
Oster, Sharon, 183
Ostroy, Joseph M., 57
Oum, T. H., 106
Owen, Bruce M., 294, 370, 398, 400

Pal, Debashis, 203
Panzar, John C., 30, 53, 200, 202, 223, 399, 400
Parker, D., 401

Parker-Pope, Tara, 222, 401
Parsons, Donald O., 369
Pascoe, George, 78, 90
Patton, Susannah, 292
Pechman, Carl, 294
Peck, Merton J., 369, 398
Peers, Martin, 148
Peltzman, Sam, 28, 101, 106
Pereira, Joseph, 267
Perez, Evan, 372
Peritz, Rudolph J. R., 342
Peteraf, Margaret A., 314
Petersen, B. C., 105
Petraglia, Lisa M., 184
Phillips, Almarin, 29, 398
Phillips, O. R., 268
Picard, Robert G., 292
Pigou, A. C., 209, 223
Pitofsky, Robert, 148, 202, 342, 369
Polinsky, A. Mitchell, 342
Pope, Kyle, 401
Porter, Michael E., 23, 52, 183, 191, 202
Posner, Richard A., 28, 30, 267
Prager, R. A., 400
Pratten, Cliff F., 162, 163, 167
Price, William H., 29
Pugel, T., 104, 129
Pugh, K., 104, 129

Qualls, P. David, 164, 167
Quirk, James, 315

Raab, Selwyn, 316
Ramirez, Anthony, 294
Ravenscraft, David J., 23, 53, 142, 145, 147,
    148
Ray, Edward J., 369
Reed, R., 314
Reilly, Patrick M., 292
Reinganum, Jennifer, 129
Reinhardt, Andy, 343
Reiss, P. C., 105, 203
Rhoades, Stephen A., 53, 104
Ripley, William Z., 29, 148, 201
Roberts, A., 129
Roberts, Gary R., 315
Roberts, Mark J. E., 90
Robinson, Joan, 29, 223
Robinson, William T., 22, 148

Rogaly, Joe, 401
Rogers, Richard T., 184
Rogowsky, Robert A., 52
Roosevelt, Theodore, 141, 336, 350
Rose, Matthew, 148
Rose, Nancy L., 224, 399
Rosenbaum, David I., 201
Ross, David N., 90, 106, 128, 129, 166, 167,
    184, 202, 224, 268, 342
Ross, Thomas W., 343
Round, David K., 129, 343, 344
Roussakis, Emmanuel N., 55

Sack, Kevin, 131
Salant, Steven W., 250
Saloner, Garth, 224
Salop, Steven C., 89, 267
Salpukas, Agis, 401
Samuels, Waren J., 400
Samuelson, Larry, 90
Sappington, David E. M., 398
Sass, Tim R., 293
Saunders, Anthony, 55
Saunders, Lisa, 314
Saurman, David S., 293
Savas, Edward J., 316
Sawers, R., 117, 128, 129
Sawyer, Malcolm C., 148
Scheffman, David T., 267, 371, 372
Scherer, Frederic M., 22, 23, 30, 53, 89, 90,
    101, 106, 114, 118, 128, 129, 142, 145,
    148, 162, 163, 164, 165, 166, 167, 184,
    202, 224, 245, 268, 293, 316, 342
Schmalensee, Richard, 30, 53, 55, 102, 105,
    107, 202, 224, 249, 250, 294, 316, 370,
    398, 399
Schneider, Steven A., 55, 104
Schumpeter, Joseph A., 28, 77, 78, 110, 116
Schwalbach, J., 202
Schwartz, Marius, 30, 203
Schwartz, Nancy L., 128, 129
Schwartzman, David, 373
Sclar, Elliott D., 54, 183, 401
Scott, John T., 268
Scully, Gerald W., 315
Sexton, Richard J., 184
Shaanan, Joseph, 203
Shapiro, Carl, 129, 372
Shapiro, D. M., 343

Shapiro, Irvin S., 105
Sharkey, William W., 370
Shavell, Steven, 342
Shaw, R., 78, 90
Shepherd, George B., 89, 251, 293, 371
Shepherd, Helen S., 89, 371
Shepherd, William G., 22, 23, 28, 30, 53, 89,
        90, 97, 105, 106, 124, 128, 130, 144, 149,
        167, 202, 203, 223, 224, 268, 293, 294,
        314, 370, 371, 399, 400, 401
Shooshan, Harry M., 55
Shubik, Martin, 30, 250
Shughart, William F., 30, 57, 128, 148, 342
Shy, Oz, 53
Sibley, Davis S., 399
Sichel, Werner, 223
Sidak, J. Gregory, 203
Sidel, Robin, 148
Siegfried, John J., 129, 202, 315, 372
Simon, Julian L., 268
Simons, Henry C., 28, 44, 57, 58, 127, 129
Simpson, P., 78, 90
Smiley, Robert H., 120, 121, 129, 202
Smirlock, Michael, 105, 106
Smith, Adam, 16, 20, 29, 38, 157, 167
Smith, Helen Lawton, 54, 183, 401
Smith, Rebecca, 400
Smith, Richard A., 251
Snyder, Edward A., 343
Solow, Robert, 128
Sorkin, Andrew Ross, 372
Spady, Richard H., 399
Spar, Debra L., 104
Spence, A. Michael, 128
Spengler, Joseph J., 267
Spulber, Daniel, 398
Spychalski, John C., 400
Stafford, Erik, 148
Steil, Benn, 343
Steiner, Robert, 402
Stem, Peter A., 292
Stenason, John, 398
Stern, Louis W., 316
Stevens, R. B., 250
Stevenson, Rodney E., 29, 294
Stigler, George J., 22, 28, 30, 57, 106, 162,
        167, 267
Stiglitz, Joseph E., 53
Stille, Alexander, 130

Stillerman, R., 117, 128, 129
Stocking, George W., 22, 29, 104, 369
Stoffaes, Christian, 343
Stulz, R. M., 268
Sullivan, Lawrence A., 130, 342, 372
Sultan, Ralph G. M., 251
Sumner, William Graham, 29
Suominen, S., 267
Suslow, Valerie Y., 90
Sutton, John, 30, 53, 128, 268, 293, 316
Swartwout, R. L., 398
Symeonidis, George, 54, 343

Taft, William H., 336
Tandon, Pankai, 401
Taylor, Alex, 313
Teece, David J., 55, 104, 372
Telser, Lester, 53, 267
Temin, Peter, 370
Templin, Neal, 251
Thompson, Herbert G., 294
Thorelli, Hans B., 29
Thorp, Willard F., 167
Thurm, Scott, 400
Tiemstra, J. P., 398
Tietenberg, Thomas H., 107
Till, Irene, 29, 52, 342
Tirole, Jean, 30, 53, 128, 129, 184, 224, 249,
        250
Tollison, Robert D., 315
Toninelli, Pier Angelo, 401
Train, Kenneth E., 399
Trautman, William B., 292
Trebilcock, Michael, 343
Trebing, Harry M., 149
Tremblay, Carol Horton, 293
Tremblay, Victor J., 293
Tschirhart, John, 398
Tsuji, Masatsugu, 54, 401
Tulkens, Henry, 401
Turner, Donald F., 22, 29, 217, 218, 219, 224,
        227, 250, 267, 359
Turvey, Ralph, 401
Tye, William B., 400

Uekusa, Masu, 184
Urban, Glen L., 148
Useem, Jerry, 81, 106
Utton, M. A., 53

Vickers, John, 28, 90, 250, 400
Vietor, Richard H. K., 314, 399
Viner, Jacob, 28
Vining, A. R., 400
Vita, Michael, 371
Vogelsang, Ingo, 292, 401
Voortman, J. J., 372

Waldman, Don E., 106
Warren, Earl, 337
Warren-Boulton, Frederick R., 266, 267
Waterson, Michael, 53, 398
Watkins, Myron W., 22, 29
Watson, Thomas J., 370
Weaver, Suzanne, 342
Wegberg, M. van, 268
Weibull, Jorgen W., 250
Weiler, Paul C., 315
Weiman, David F., 224
Weiss, Leonard W., 22, 53, 78, 90, 104, 129,
    163, 164, 167, 269, 398
Wellenius, Bjorn, 292
Werden, Gregory J., 314
Wernerfelt, Birger, 102, 107
Westin, Lars, 166
Weston, J. Fred, 28
Whitacre, Mark E., 368
White, Lawrence J., 54, 55, 251, 267, 268,
    292, 315, 342, 370, 372
Whitney, Simon N., 22, 29, 149, 250, 369

Wilcox, Clair, 29
Williams, Christopher, 316
Williams, J., 249
Williamson, Oliver E., 22, 30, 53, 256, 267,
    342, 369
Williamson, Peter J., 268
Willig, Robert D., 26, 30, 53, 89, 130, 200,
    202, 203, 223, 224, 249, 250, 399, 400
Wilson, Thomas A., 22, 268, 269
Wilson, Wesley W., 400
Windle, R., 314
Winslow, Ron, 106
Winston, Clifford, 224, 299, 314, 315, 399
Witteloostuijn, A. van, 268
Worcester, Dean A., 202

Yamamura, Kozo, 184
Yamey, Basil S., 224, 250
Yandle, B., 370
Yelle, L. E., 167
Yui, Tsunehiko, 130, 184
Yung, Y. J., 224

Zhang, Y., 106
Zhang, Z., 250
Zick, C. D., 314
Zimbalist, Andrew, 55, 315
Zona, J. Douglas, 89
Zwick, Charles, 398
Zwiebel, J., 184

Subject Index

Absolute cost advantages, 193, 198
Absolute size, and market power, 260
Advertising
    allocative efficiency and, 99
    as barrier to entry, 266, 284
    in cereal industry, 308–310
    changing demand through, 263
    defining intensity of, 264
    effects of, 264–265
    functionless, 102, 285
    informative and persuasive,
        264–265
    market setting and, 264
    in newspaper markets, 276–277
    research topics in, 56
Aftermarkets, 258, 357, 367
Agency theory, 178–179
Airbus Industrie, 112, 228, 296–297
Airline industry
    brief history of, 298–299
    cost differences in, 301
    defining markets of, 299
    economies of scale and scope in, 301
    market determinants of, 300
    mergers and affiliations in, 301

    structures and degrees of competition
        in, 300
Alcoa aluminum monopoly, 336, 338, 351
Allocative efficiency, 32–33, 99–100
American Broadcasting Company (ABC),
    337
American Can/National Can duopoly,
    337, 352
American Tobacco Company monopoly,
    21, 218, 350, 366
Anheuser-Busch, 283–285
Anticompetitive actions, testing for,
    216–219
Antitrust actions
    benefits and costs of, 327–328
    breakup of Bell System, 278, 354–357.
        See also AT&T
    compensatory damages, 334–335
    courts and, 333–334
    economic effects of, 339–340
    effect on competition, 144
    exemptions from, 331
    foreign, 340–341
    mergers and, 141–143
Antitrust actions. See also Antitrust policies

Antitrust agencies
    adoption of HHI, 72
    deregulation and, 389
    history and purpose of, 332
Antitrust Division, 26, 72, 248, 332, 351–
    352, 360–362, 364, 368
Antitrust policies
    advantages and disadvantages of, 325,
        329, 339–340
    benefits and costs of, 325, 329
    bias in, 325–327
    criteria for, 337–338
    development of, 336–337
    dominance and, 345–359
    economies of scale and, 165–166
    forms of, 330
    history of U.S., 321–322
    imbalance in, 368
    laws and agencies, 330–336
    effect on market structure, 146–147
    mergers and, 320, 360–364
    origins and history of, 320
    precedents for, 338–339
    price fixing and, 364–368
    purpose of, 319–320
    standards of efficient, 323–324
Antitrust policies. *See also* Antitrust actions
Appropriability and innovation, 112–113
Archer-Daniels-Midland case, 368
Areeda-Turner price-cost test, 217–219,
    359, 367
Aspen Skiing, Section 2 case of, 357
Asset specificity, 192–193
AT&T, 278–280, 337, 345, 352, 354–355–356.
        See also Baby Bells, creation of; Tele-
        communications industry
Authority, delegation of, 174
Autonomous innovation, 114
Autonomous invention, 110–111, 119

Baby Bells, creation of, 278–281, 354–357
Balance sheets, 172
Banking relationships in capital markets,
    138
Barriers to entry
    advertising as, 284
    cost differences, 197–198
    dominant firms as, 77
    endogenous sources of, 192, 194–195

    exogenous sources of, 191–194
    in aircraft industries, 296
    in trash removal industry, 311–312
    price increases by dominant firms, 196
    problems in measuring, 195–196
    product differentiation, 197
    scale economies, 197
    sources of, 191–194
Bertrand price-setting duopolists, 239–241
BFI (formerly Browning-Ferris Industries),
    310–312
Bilateral monopoly, 253–255
Boeing Aircraft, 98, 101, 112, 228
Brown & Williams, 368
Bureau of Corporations, antitrust research
    of, 21

Cable-TV systems, FCC regulation of, 280
Capital
    allocation, and diversification, 262
    economic elements of, 180
Capital gains, 93, 172, 176, 178, 320, 394,
    396
Capital markets
    banking relationships in, 138
    credit and, 137
    enforcing efficiency, 137–138
    perfect, 136
    types of, 136–137
Capture, 325–326
Cartels
    price fixing/collusion by, 82, 244–245
    research on, 22
Causation
    free-market advocacy and, 9
    structuralist premise of, 9
Celler-Kefauver Act, 360
Cereal industry, 307–310, 353
Chain ownership, 277
Cheating
    as common in oligopolies, 81
    cooperation vs., 226–227
Choice, freedom of, 35, 44, 109, 126, 305,
    307, 313
Clayton Act of 1914, 330–331, 336, 360
Collusion, 226–227
    conditions favoring or discouraging,
        243–244
    in cartels, 244–245

joint ventures and, 248–249
legislation regarding, 331
overlap (elite colleges), 246
price leadership and, 241–243
product space and, 309
in real markets, 244
tacit, 241–244, 247. *See also* Tacit collusion
in tight oligopolies, 79, 81–82, 225, 244, 246–247, 339, 366
types of, 244–249
Communications, technological trends in, 153. *See also* Telecommunications
Competition
actual vs. potential, 198
advertising's effect on, 265
antitrust policies' effect on, 328, 331
benefits of, 123–125
concept of, 5
core elements of effective, 5
core issues of, 6
cream skimming and, 387
cultural diversity and, 127
defined, 3
dominant firms' effect on, 77–79
effective, 3–6, 13, 17, 20. *See also* Effective competition
as test of excellence, 17
extent and trend of, 14–16
history of U.S., 19–23
Internet's effect on, 14–16
intrabrand, 259
job discrimination and, 123
limits and harms of, 125–126
limits on benefits of, 38–39
mergers' effect on, 262
modern debates and study on, 21
monopolistic vs. pure, 14
monopoly's effect on, 17
natural, 9, 47, 155, 355, 378
natural resources, effect on, 102–103
neoclassical equilibrium model of, 16
partial, degrees and concepts of, 75–83
perfect, 16, 36–38
performance and, 35–39
in political markets, 35
price discrimination and, 211–212
real market, degrees of, 83–88

realistic process of rivalry, 16
robust concept of, 16–17, 38
Schumpeter's process of, 16, 77–78
self-destructive nature of, 17
social effects of, 127
tight oligopolies and, 79–82
trends of, in U.S. economy, 15
unity among models of, 16–17
in Western society, 4
Computers, and technological trends, 153
Concentration
antitrust policies and, 339
gradations in, 72
market definition and, 85
market structure and, 10, 71–72
mergers and, 139
monopsony and, 254
profit rates and, 100
ratios, 56, 86–87
tacit collusion and, 241
tight oligopolies and, 81–82
trends of, 87
unadjusted industry ratios and, 87
Conglomerate mergers, 140, 142, 363–364
Conscious parallelism, 366
Consumer choice, 62, 85. *See also* Freedom of choice
Contestability theory, 9, 23, 26, 200–201
Cooperation
cheating vs., 226–227
trade associations and, 247–248
Cooperative enterprises, 177
Corporations
divorce of ownership from control in, 177
management of, 172–173
private, 181–183
trends and shares among, 181–183
See also Firms
Corruption/false information, 176
Cost curves, 36–37, 40–42, 45–48, 96, 99, 154–158, 160–163, 165
Cost gradient, 46–47, 151, 154, 161, 163–164, 277, 311
Cost-benefit analysis, 323–325
Costs
direct and indirect, 325, 330
effects of regulation on, 386
of interference, 325

marginal, 37–38, 40
of public policies, 325
of regulation, 329–330
sunk, 193
switching, 193–194
Cournot equilibrium, in game theory,
231–232, 234–239
Courts, as deterrent to antitrust, 333–334.
See also Supreme Court
Creative destruction, Schumpeter's process of, 16, 77–78
Creativity, effect of competition on, 125
Credit, and capital markets, 137
Cross-elasticity of demand, geographic
market areas and, 63–64
Cross-elasticity of supply, 68
Cross-media monopolies, 276
Cross-subsidizing, effect on competition,
262
Cultural diversity
as important value, 36
competition and, 127
effect of monopoly on, 44

Demand
cross-elasticity of, 63–64
elasticity of, 7, 33–34
inelastic, and monopoly power, 41
prices determined by elasticities in,
205–206
Democracy, 44, 124, 127
Deregulation, 23
of airline industry, 298
antitrust agencies and, 389
criteria for effective, 388–389
effect on competition, 144
full, 388–391
lessons of, 390–391
partial, and price caps, 387–388
premature, 378
purpose of, 320
of utilities industries, 286
Determinants of structure
of airline industry, 300–301
of Anheuser-Busch, 284
of Boeing Aircraft, 297
of cereal industry, 308–309
of electricity industry, 288
of mainframe computers, 282

of Microsoft, 274
of newspaper industry, 277
of sports industry, 304
of telecommunications industry,
279–280
of trash removal industry, 311
Direct costs, 325, 330
Diseconomies of scale, 46, 112, 151, 154
multiplant, 160–161
plant-level, 157–160
Diversification
as barrier to market entry, 193
definition/history of, 261
possible benefits of, 262
possible harms to competition,
262–263
spheres of influence and, 263
Diversity
competition and, 127
cultural, important value of, 36
monopoly's effect on, 44
performance value of, 36
Divestiture, in capital markets, 139–140
Dominance. *See* Market dominance
Dominant firms, 75–77
case studies of, 273–291
declining, 188–189
innovation and, 114–115
Internet's effect on, 15
market share and, 85–86
models of, 188–189
potential-competition theory and, 190
tactics and strategies of, 188
Dot com companies, 143
Du Pont
General Motors merger, 363
titanium dioxide case, 352
Duopoly
Bertrand price-setting model of,
239–241
in metal cans, 337
new IO theory on, 23
noncollusive, 228–241
quality-setting duopolists, 227
trash removal industry, 310
using payoff matrixes to illustrate
choices in, 229–231
Dynamic disequilibrium, 77
Dynamic innovation, 34

Eastman Kodak, 101, 352, 357
Econometric studies of profitability and
    structure, 23
Economic performance. *See* Performance
    values
Economic policies, time line of, 24–25
Economics
    contestability/free-entry, 9
    neoclassical, 20, 22, 78
Economies of scale
    in aircraft industry, 297
    in airline industry, 301
    as barrier to entry, 191, 197
    in brewing industry, 284
    debate over, 21
    effect on market structure, 9
    efficiency and, 261
    in electricity industry, 288
    management efficiency and, 157
    measures of, 164
    mergers and, 140
    misallocation and, 99
    monopoly power and, 46–47
    multiplant, 165
    natural monopolies and, 187
    in newspaper industry, 277
    pecuniary gains and, 155–156
    physical laws and, 157
    research methods on, 161–162
    in Section 2 cases, 347
    small vs. large, 151
    sources of diseconomies, 158
    specialization as cause of, 157
    technical, 156, 187
    technological progress and, 112
Economies of scope
    in airline industry, 301
    in network industries, 146
    market structure and, 146
    network industries and, 146
    in trash removal industry, 311
Economy
    of diversification, and conglomerate
        mergers, 140
    major sectors of, 11–12
    neoclassical vs. realist, 22
    pecuniary, 141
    plant and multiplant. *See* Multiplant
        economies; Plant-level economies

schematic outline of sectors in, 12
    technical vs. pecuniary, 21
    theories of, 9. *See also* Theories
    U.S. time line of, 24–25
Effective competition
    in airline industry, 302
    categories of, 82
    deregulation and, 298, 378–379, 389
    economies of scale and, 151
    IBM and, 353
    innovation and, 116
    job discrimination discouraged by, 123
    natural monopoly and, 155
    perfect capital markets and, 136
    three core elements of, 5
    in utilities industry, 378, 388
Efficiency
    allocative, 32–33, 99–100
    capital markets and, 137–138
    free-market "efficient-structure"
        hypothesis and, 100
    internal, 32
    mergers' effect on, 139, 145
    price discrimination's effect on, 212–213
    static, 32, 34
    vertical restrictions and, 258
    See also X-efficiency
Elasticities in demand
    conditions influencing, 210
    degree of monopoly and, 7, 41
    determining price by, 205
    misallocation and, 99
    price discrimination and, 206
    size of consumer surplus and, 33
Empirical studies, topics for research in,
    55–56
Endogenous conditions of entry, 74
Enron, 4, 176, 286, 390
Enterprise, 171, 173, 176, 322
Entrepreneurship, 177
Entry
    barriers against, 74–75, 77, 87, 190–195,
        187–198, 265–266, 284, 296, 311–312
    controlled/restricted, 245–246
    free, 26
    nature and extent of, 190
    net, 190
    rates of, 87
    speed of, 191

Equity, 34–35, 39
Excess market share, 47, 101, 151–152, 155, 163, 165, 187, 282, 308
Exit from market, 75, 87, 190, 200

Fairness
    opportunity and, 122–123
    shifts in wealth and, 120–121
    standards of, 34–35
Federal Energy Regulatory Commission (FERC), 381, 390
Federal enforcement agencies and regulatory commissions, 332–336, 381
Federal Trade Commission, 56, 248, 259, 285, 308, 332, 336
Firms
    capital assets of, 172
    corporate structure of, 173–174
    dominant. *See* Dominant firms
    external market choices of, 172
    foreign, 182
    internal control of, 172
    managers' goals in, 178–180
    motivation within, 177–178
    ownership and control of, 172, 177–178
    profitability of, 172–176, 180
    risk, long-term and short-term, in, 180
    types of, 176–177
First-mover advantage of dominance, 187
Flow concept, production as, 172
Free riders
    appropriability and, 112–113
    supporting quality service against, 258–259
    vertical restrictions and, 258–259
Freedom of choice, 109, 126, 305, 307, 313
Free-market "efficient-structure" hypothesis, 100–102, 136
Free-market theorists
    on antitrust, 320, 327, 338
    on benefits of monopoly, 9, 23
    on collusion, 81
    on competition, 4, 14, 125
    on deregulation, 319
    on diversification, 262
    on dominance, 187
    on integration and monopoly, 257
    on mergers, 145
    on unbundling, 259
    on vertical restraints, 258–259

FTC v. Procter & Gamble, 364
Functionless advertising, 102

Gains, technical vs. pecuniary, 155–156
Game theory, 9, 23
    Bertrand price-setting duopolist model, 239–241
    Cournot output-setting models, 231–239
    models of noncollusive duopoly, 228–241
    Nash equilibrium in, 231
    oligopoly and, 228
    payoff matrixes in, 229–231
    tight oligopolies and, 79, 226
    weaknesses of, 228
General Foods, 308
General Mills, 308
Generating-services markets
    in electricity industry, 287
Geographic market area, 62–66, 83–84, 284
Giantism, 154, 181, 260
Globalization, redefining markets by, 88
GM-Toyota joint venture, 248
Government agencies, effect on industry growth and size, 182
Gross national product (GNP), 12

Hart-Rodino Act, 360
Health-care industry, inefficiency in, 98
Hirschman-Herfindahl Index (HHI), 72–74, 86, 361
Horizontal mergers
    Bethlehem-Youngstown, 361
    Brown Shoe, 361
    effect on market power and profit, 140
    General Dynamics, 361
    military supplies mergers, 363
    public policies toward, 360–363
    Republic Steel/J&L, 362
    Von's Grocery, 360–361

IBM, 101, 281–282, 337, 346, 352–353
Imitation, 110
Imperfections, market, 9
Imports, effect on competition, 144
Income, 121–122
Income statements, 172
Independent regulatory commissions, 376
Indeterminacy, 81

Indirect costs, 325, 330
Induced inventions, 110
Industrial economics, further study in,
    403–404
Industrial organization theory
    contemporary, 26
    contestability theory of, 26
    debates on, 18–19, 21–22
    literature on, 18
    New Industrial-Organization Theory,
        5–6, 9, 23, 26, 360
    New-Chicago-School Free-Market
        Analysis, 23
    origins and history of, 19–23
    research and scholarship on, 18–19
    time line of, 24–25
    two planes of, 6
Industrial Revolution, 20, 152, 321
Industrial trusts. See Antitrust actions;
    Antitrust policies
Industry
    major sectors of, 11
    new organizational theory of. See New
        Industrial-Organization Theory
    research topics in, 54
    three basic conditions of, 83–84
    topics for research in, 53, 55
Inequity, and competition, 39
Informative advertising, 102
Innovation
    competition's effect on, 113–114, 116
    concepts and relationships of, 109–113
    dominant firms and, 114–115
    dynamic, 34
    economies of scale and, 112
    invention and, 110–120
    monopoly's effect on, 113–115
    optimal technological change and,
        113–116
    patterns of research and development
        in, 116–117
    predatory, 219
    replacement effect of, 111–113
    sources of, 119
Integration
    economies of, 288
    vertical, 255–257
Interdependence
    basic theories of, 227–228

concentration and, 72
    oligopolies and, 81
Interference costs, 325
Internal efficiency. See X-efficiency
International banking, 138
International Harvester Company, 350
Internet, economic effect of, 14–16
Interstate Commerce Commission, 322,
    377, 381
Intrabrand competition, 259
Invention
    defined, 110
    dominant firms and, 115
    economies of scale and, 112
    innovation and, 110–120
    patents and, 118–120
    sources of, 117–118
    types of, 110–111
Invisible hand of competitive market sys-
    tem, 36–38

Japan
    aggregate concentration in, 182
    decline in dominant firms of, 78
    privatization in, 397
    zaibatsu combines in, 182
Jobs
    discrimination in, 123–124
    effect of monopoly on, 44
    good content of, 35
    skills, and technological trends in, 153–
        154
Joint ventures, 248
Joint-maximizing price, 230

Kellogg, 307–308

Lawsuits and legislation, antitrust, 330–
    331, 333–335
Lerner index of monopoly, 41, 238
Life cycles, and market structure, 145
Linux, 274–275
Long-term risk, 180
Loose oligopoly, 13, 79, 82

Management
    agency theory and, 178
    as source of diseconomies, 158
    multiplant economies and, 161

Marginal cost and revenue, 38–40
Market(s)
   for Anheuser-Busch, 283–284
   in antitrust cases, 338
   barriers to entry. *See* Barriers to entry
   of Boeing Aircraft, 296
   of cereal industry, 308
   concentration in, 10
   defining, 62–68, 85–86, 361
   dominance of. *See* Market dominance
   geographic dimensions of, 62–66, 83–84,
     279, 284
   imperfections in, 61, 68–70
   for mainframe computers, 281
   for Microsoft, 274
   performance and, 22
   product dimensions of, 279
   in Section 2 cases, 346
   structural elements of. *See* Market struc-
     ture
   of Ticketmaster, 289–290
   of trash removal industry, 310–311
   vertical patterns in, 253
   for Yellow Pages, 290
Market dominance
   of Anheuser-Busch, 283–285
   competition destroyed by, 17
   concept of, 185
   in electricity industry, 286–289
   first-mover advantages of, 187
   leading cases of, 186
   of local newspapers, 276–278
   of mainframe computers (IBM),
     281–283
   market share and, 84
   mergers and, 188
   monopoly and, 4–5
   perpetuation of, 17
   Section 2 actions toward, 358–359
   slow erosion of, 78–79, 186, 327
   superior performance and, 187
   technical scale economies and, 187
   of telecommunications, 278–281
   trends of, 186
   See also Dominant firms
Market power
   concept of, 4–5
   effect on efficiency, 96–103
   gradations of, 48–50

   imperfections in the market and, 68
   mergers and, 329, 140
   effect on prices and profits, 93–96
   size and, 260–261
   slow erosion of, 327
   social effects of, 127
   vertical, 257–258
   wealth and, 120–121
   See also Monopoly
Market share, 23
   of Boeing Aircraft, 296
   concentration and, 72, 74
   criteria for prosecuting dominance, 338
   defined, 10
   dominance and, 84–86, 189
   excess, 47
   gradations of, 86
   as key element of monopoly, 21
   profitability and, 48–49, 73, 84, 100-102
   rate of decline over time, 49–50
   in Section 2 cases, 346
   as leading structural element, 71
Market structure
   of airline industry, 300
   of Anheuser-Busch, 284
   effect of antitrust on, 146–147
   barriers to entry in. *See* Barriers to entry
   of Boeing Aircraft, 296
   capital markets' roles in, 136–138
   of cereal industry, 308
   composite, and market share, 84
   concentration and, 71–72
   corporate, 173–174
   defining, 62–68
   determinants of. *See* Determinants of
     structure
   econometric studies of, 22
   economies of scope and, 146
   of electricity industry, 287–288
   elements of, 70–75
   Hirschman-Herfindahl Index (HHI),
     72–74, 86, 361
   of IBM, 281
   meaning of, 10
   market share and, 71
   mergers and, 139–145
   of Microsoft, 274
   network industries and, 146
   of newspaper industry, 277

patterns of, 84, 86–87
performance and, 7–8
public policies and, 146–147
of sports industry, 304
of telecommunications industry,
    279–280
of Ticketmaster, 289–290
of trash removal industry, 311
of Yellow Pages, 290–291
Markets
    of airline industry, 299
    categories of, 13
    competitive variation in, 14
    defining by geographic area, 66
    defining by product type, 64, 65
    defining by supply conditions, 67–68
    for electricity industry, 286–287
    estimating, alternative method for, 66–67
    free entry by potential competitors, 9
    imperfections in, 9
    main types of, 13
    major sectors of, 11–12
    for newspaper industry, 276
    potential-competition theory of, 190
    product type and geographic area of, 62
    for sports industry, 303
    structure, behavior and performance of,
        8–9
    subdivided industries and multiple
        market levels, 66
    for telecommunications industry, 279
    varieties of, 83–84
Materials availability, and technological
    trends, 152–153
Matrixes, interpretation of, 229–231
Matsushita, 218–219
Media control, 276
Mergers
    analysis of, and antitrust policies, 329
    Antitrust Division Guidelines for, 66,
        360, 362
    antitrust policies toward, 360–364
    effect on company rankings, 182
    effect on competition, 262
    dominance and, 188
    electric utility, 288
    failed, 143–144
    giantism in, 154
    horizontal, 337–339
    horizontal and vertical, 143
    legislation regarding, 331
    effect on market structure, 145
    motives for, 140–141
    newspaper market structure and, 277
    patterns and waves in, 141–143
    spinoffs, 143–144
    takeover, 143
    topics for research in, 56
    types of, 139
    vertical integration and, 257
MES. *See* Minimum efficient scale
Microsoft, 101
    behavior of, 275
    market dominance of, 274–275
    natural monopoly of, 274
    performance of, 101, 275
    Section 2 case on, 358
    structure of, 274
Military supplies mergers, 363
Minimum efficient scale (MES), 46, 151,
        154–156, 161, 163–164, 197, 212, 284,
        297, 308
Misallocation, 99–100
Monopoly
    adverse effects of, 6
    alternative sources of, 10
    benefits of, 9
    bilateral, 254
    concept of, 4–6
    effect on economic performance, 41–43
    financial rewards of, 44–46
    history of, 19–21
    inelastic demand and, 41
    legislation regarding, 331
    market size and, 62
    effect on price and output, 40–41
    public policies toward, 319–341. *See also*
        Antitrust actions; Antitrust policies
    pure, 13
    See also Market power
Monopsony, 253–255
Multiplant economies, 158, 160–161, 163,
        165

Nash equilibrium, 231
National Broadcasting Company (NBC),
        337, 351
Natural competition, 9, 47, 155, 355, 378

Natural monopoly, 47
  Bell System as, 355
  natural competition and, 155
  of utilities, 286
  regulation of, 376–387
  technical scale economies and, 187
Natural oligopoly, 47, 155
Natural resources, effect of competition on, 102–103
Neoclassical economics, 16, 20, 22, 78
Neoclassical Equilibrium Model, 16
Net entry, 75, 190
Network industries, and market structure, 146
New Industrial-Organization Theory, 5–6, 9, 23, 26, 360. *See also* Game theory
New-Chicago-School Free-Market Analysis, 23
Newspapers, dominance in local markets, 275–278
Noncollusive duopoly, 228
Not-for-profit enterprises, 176

Oligopoly
  advertising in, 102
  evolution of models of, 228
  indeterminacy of, 227
  interdependence of, 227
  joint limiting price strategy in, 198
  natural, 47
  three causes of complexity in, 72
  tight vs. loose, 13, 79–81
OPEC oil cartel, 82, 94
Opportunity, monopoly's effect on, 122–123
Optimal scale, 112, 154, 159, 165
Ownership
  absentee, 263
  chain, 277
  corporate, divorce from control, 177
  private and public, 322

Parallel pricing, 82
Patents, and inventive output, 119–120
Pecuniary economies, 141, 182
Pecuniary gains, 155–156
Perfect competition theory, 14, 16, 36–38
Performance
  in airline industry, 302
  of Anheuser-Busch, 285

  of beer industry, 285
  of Bell System, 280
  of Boeing Aircraft, 297
  in cereal industry, 309–310
  competition and, 36–39
  dominance and, 187
  econometric studies of, 22
  of electricity industry, 289
  of IBM, 283
  market dominance and, 187
  market structure and, 7–8, 22
  of Microsoft, 275
  of newspaper industry, 278
  public enterprises and, 393
  of sports industry, 305–307
  in trash removal industry, 312
Persuasive advertising, 102
Plant-level economies
  sources of diseconomies in, 158
  external but intrafirm costs of, 158
  learning curve in, 159–160
  multiplant costs and learning curves, 158–160
  points of definition, 157
  sources of scale economies in, 157
Political competition, 127
Political power, and size, 261
Potential-competition theory, 190
Power
  firm, non-firm, and spot, 287
  market/monopoly, 4
  purchasing, 206
Predation
  in airline industry, 302
  competition and, 215
  innovation and, 219
  pricing and, 367
Premature deregulation, 378
Price
  caps on, and partial deregulation, 387–388
  discounting, 285, 312–313, 352, 388
  discrimination. *See* Price discrimination
  fair trade and, 260
  joint-maximizing, 230
  leadership, and tacit collusion, 241–243
  level and discriminatory structure of, 76–77
  marginal cost and, 37–38

monopoly's effect on, 93–95
parallel pricing, 82
Ramsey, 213
signaling, 82
structuring, and monopsony, 254
Price discrimination
in airline industry, 219–220, 301–302
analysis of, 207–208
as competitive weapon, 211–212
concept of, 205–210
defending, 214
in drugs and health care, 220–222
effects of, 210–215
efficiency and, 212–213
examples of, 214
in hotel and automobile prices, 220
IBM and, 282
joint costs and, 215
legislation regarding, 331
magazine subscription, 221–222
monopoly power and, 95
price-cost ratios and, 207, 213, 222
promoting or reducing competition
    through, 211–212
Ramsey prices and, 213
sales and, 222
in telephone service, 220–221
in trash removal industry, 312
types of, 209–210
Price fixing
agreements, examples of, 246
antitrust policies toward, 339, 364–368
collusive nature of, 226–227, 244, 246,
    366
punishment for, 334
tacit collusion and, 244, 366
U.S. industry conspiracies, 1961–1970,
    245
vertical, 367
Price-cost margins, industry-wide pat-
    terns in, 95
Price-cost ratios, 93, 282
Price-setting duopolists, 239–241
Privatization
in Britain, 394
in Europe and the U.S., 396
in Japan, 397
leading examples of, 395
public firms and, 393

public services and, 397
response costs and, 325
of utilities, 322
Probability bias, 326
Process innovations, 110
Procter & Gamble, 364
Product
cross-elasticity of demand and, 63
defining markets by, 64–65
differentiation. *See* Product differentia-
    tion
gradation, 64
innovations, 110
substitutability, 299
type, 62–65
Product differentiation
through advertising, 193, 263–266
in Bertrand price-setting analysis, 241
entry and, 197
game theory and, 241
market entry and, 197
Production
flow concept of, 172
three stages of, in electricity, 286–287
Profitability and profits
choices and forms of, 172–174
concept of, 173–176
as goal of firms, 172
market share and, 48–49, 73, 84
mergers and, 140
monopoly's effect on, 95–96
risk and, 180
static maximizing of, 210
stock prices and, 174–176
of Ticketmaster, 290
topics for research on, 56
of Yellow Pages, 291
Public enterprise
coverage and purposes of, 391–392
economic performance of, 393
external impacts of, 392
inadequate private supply and, 391
social and political preferences, 391
sovereignty and, 392
subsidies and efficiency of, 392
Public goods, and competition, 38
Public ownership, 322
Public policies
bias in, 325–327

costs of, 323, 325
   design and amount of, 323–324
   market structure and, 146–147
   standards of efficient, 323–325
Public-utility economics, 22
Pure competition, 14, 36, 264
Pure monopoly, 13, 39, 264

Radio broadcasting, 351
Ramsey prices, 213
Rate of entry, 198–199
Rate of return, 173, 175
Rate-base regulation, 382
Reaction curve, 232, 234, 237, 241
Real markets
   concept of, 61
   degrees of competition in, 83–88
Realist economics, 22
Regulation
   of airlines industry, 298
   benefits and costs of, 329–330
   bias in policies of, 325–326
   concepts of, 379–381
   criteria for, 381, 384
   fitting prices to marginal costs, 384
   of natural monopoly, 319, 376–387
   origins and history of U.S., 320–322
   price level and, 382–383
   price structure and, 383
   process of, 382
   purpose of, 320
   rate-base, 382
   U.S. policies toward, 375–377
   of utility firms, 286
Regulatory commissions, 381
Resale price maintenance (RPM), 260, 367
Research and development
   barriers to market entry, 193
   innovation and technological change,
      116–117
   monopoly's effect on, 117
   optimal technological change and, 113
   patents, statistical analysis of, 118
   technological innovation and, 34
Research papers, topics, methods and
      sources for, 51–58
Residual demand curve, 232
Resistance costs, 326
Revenue, marginal and average, 37, 39

Risk
   as barrier against entry, 194
   competition and, 39
   long-term vs. short-term, 180
   premium, 180
   profit variance and, 95–96
   risk-return relationship, 180
Robust competition, 38

Scale economies. *See* Economies of scale, 46
Scale, minimum efficient, 46, 151, 154–156,
      161, 163–164, 197, 212, 284, 297, 308
Scale-economic theory, 154. *See also* Econo-
      mies of scale
Schumpeter's process of competition, 16,
      77–78
Scope, economies of. *See* Economies of
      scope
Section 2 cases
   Alcoa Aluminum, 351
   AT&T, 354–357
   cereal industry, 353
   IBM, 352–353
   list of major, 348–349
   NBC and radio broadcasting, 351
   Standard Oil Company, 350
   US Steel, 351
   Xerox, 353
Sectors, industrial, 11–12
Securities and Exchange Commission, 176
Security, economic, 35, 39, 44, 126–127
Shareholders/stockholders, 172–173
Sherman Act of 1890, 21, 82, 320, 322, 331,
      336
Short-term risk, 180
Size
   absolute vs. relative, 260
   efficiency and, 261
   market power and, 62, 260–261
   political power and, 261
Small firms, as innovative leaders, 112, 119
Social goals, and regulated monopolies, 391
Socony-Vacuum, 365
Sovereignty, and public enterprise, 392
Specialization, 157–158, 174
Spinoffs, 139, 143–144
Sports industry
   price fixing in, 366–367
   as tight oligopoly, 302–307

Standard Oil Company, 4, 20, 221, 345, 350–351
Standoff advertising, 102, 264
State regulatory commissions, 322
Static efficiency, 32, 34
Stock ownership, prices, and profitability, 172, 176
Structuralist premise of causation, 9
Submarkets, 63
Substitutability, 63–65, 299
Sunk costs, 193
Suppliers, effect of monopoly on, 44
Supply conditions, and market definition, 67–68
Supreme Court, antitrust rulings by, 331, 336–337, 354, 357
Survivor technique, 162–165
Symmetrical matrix, 230

Tacit collusion
    in breakfast cereal industry, 308
    in cigarette and turbine generator industries, 247
    concentration and, 241
    examples of, 247
    price fixing and, 82, 244
    price leadership and, 241–243
    product homogeneity and, 241
    public policy toward, 36
    in tight oligopolies, 366
Takeovers, 143
Taxes, and resistance costs, 326
Technical economies
    mergers and, 140–141
    of scale, 187
Technical efficiency, achieving through vertical integration, 256
Technological change
    appropriability and, 112–113
    measuring net gain against, 111
    normative and positive issues in, 111
    opportunity and, 111
    optimal, 113–114
    replacement effect of, 111–112
Technology
    diversification and, 262
    historical trends in, 152–154
    performance value of progress in, 34
Telecommunications Act, 278, 280, 356

Telecommunications industry
    antitrust actions toward, 354–357
    local telephone-service markets, 278–281
    mergers in, 143
    noncollusive duopoly in, 228
    See also AT&T; Baby Bells, breakup of
Temporary National Economic Committee (TNEC) investigations, 22
Territorial restrictions, 259, 285
Theoretical modeling, pure, 23
Theories
    agency theory, 178–179
    contestability theory, 9, 23, 26, 200–201
    game theory, 228–241
    of interdependence, 227–228
    new IO, 5–6, 9, 23, 26, 360
    perfect competition theory, 36–38
    research topics on, 53
Ticketmaster, 289–290
Tight oligopolies
    airline industry, 298–307
    breakfast cereal industry, 307–310
    case studies of, 295–313
    collusion in, 21
    decline in, 226
    defined, 13
    game theory and, 226
    list of leading, 80
    market structure and, 79, 82
    passenger aircraft industry, 295–297
    sports industry as, 302–307
    trash removal industry, 310–313
Time bias, 326
Trade associations, 247–248, 261
Transportation
    external multiplant costs of, 158
    technological trends in, 153
Trash removal industry, 310–313
Trenton Potteries, 365
Trustbusting. See Antitrust actions

U.S. v. Addyston Pipe and Steel Company, 365
United Shoe Machinery, 351–352
Unstable equilibrium, 230
US Steel Corporation, 346, 350–351
Utilities
    controls on market structure and, 147
    cost structure of, 383, 385–386
    deregulation of, 186

as dominant firms, 76
high entry barriers of, 87
natural competition in, 378
price discrimination and, 211
regulation of, 21, 322, 375
state regulatory commissions and, 322
X-inefficiency of, 98
See also Electricity industry

Values, economic performance. *See* Performance values
Variable-sum symmetrical matrixes, 230
Variance analysis, and market power,
101–102
Vertical economies, and mergers, 140–141
Vertical integration
as barrier to entry, 193
defining, 255–256
measuring, 256
mergers and, 257
monopoly-related incentives for, 257
reasons for, 256
Vertical mergers
Brown Shoe, 363
Du Pont-General Motors, 363
for integration, 257
Yellow Cab, 363

Vertical price fixing, 367
Vertical restrictions, 258–260

Wealth
fairness and, 120–121
market power and, 120–121
Wealth of Nations, 20
Western Electric, 98, 280, 354, 356
WMX (formerly Waste Management, Inc.),
310–312
Worker-owned firms, 177

X-efficiency
concept of, 22
empirical studies on, 56
internal, as performance value, 32
market power's effect on, 96
size and, 261
Xerox, 352–353
X-inefficiency, 32–33, 98
market power's effect on, 98
measuring, 97

Yellow Pages, 290–291
Yield management, in airline industry, 301

Zaibatsu combines, Japanese, 182